Lecture Notes in Artificial Intelligence   11313

Subseries of Lecture Notes in Computer Science

LNAI Series Editors

Randy Goebel
University of Alberta, Edmonton, Canada
Yuzuru Tanaka
Hokkaido University, Sapporo, Japan
Wolfgang Wahlster
DFKI and Saarland University, Saarbrücken, Germany

LNAI Founding Series Editor

Joerg Siekmann
DFKI and Saarland University, Saarbrücken, Germany

More information about this series at http://www.springer.com/series/1244

Catherine Faron Zucker · Chiara Ghidini
Amedeo Napoli · Yannick Toussaint (Eds.)

Knowledge Engineering and Knowledge Management

21st International Conference, EKAW 2018
Nancy, France, November 12–16, 2018
Proceedings

Springer

Editors
Catherine Faron Zucker (iD)
Université Côte d'Azur, CNRS, Inria, I3S
Sophia Antipolis, France

Amedeo Napoli
University of Lorraine, CNRS, Inria, LORIA
Nancy, France

Chiara Ghidini (iD)
Fondazione Bruno Kessler
Trento, Italy

Yannick Toussaint
University of Lorraine, CNRS, Inria, LORIA
Nancy, France

ISSN 0302-9743   ISSN 1611-3349   (electronic)
Lecture Notes in Artificial Intelligence
ISBN 978-3-030-03666-9   ISBN 978-3-030-03667-6   (eBook)
https://doi.org/10.1007/978-3-030-03667-6

Library of Congress Control Number: 2018960674

LNCS Sublibrary: SL7 – Artificial Intelligence

This Springer imprint is published by the registered company Springer Nature Switzerland AG
The registered company address is: Gewerbestrasse 11, 6330 Cham, Switzerland

Preface

This volume contains the proceedings of the 21st International Conference on Knowledge Engineering and Knowledge Management (EKAW 2018), held in Nancy, France, November 12–16, 2018.

The special theme of EKAW 2018 was "Knowledge and AI." We were indeed calling for papers describing algorithms, tools, methodologies, and applications that exploit the interplay between knowledge and artificial intelligence (AI) techniques, with a special emphasis on knowledge discovery.

While the interplay between AI and knowledge engineering and management is not new, recent advances in both disciplines have created new challenges, research efforts, and opportunities. The special topic of this year has therefore given us the chance to emphasize the importance of knowledge engineering and knowledge management with the help of AI, as well as for AI, and to welcome papers about methods, tools, and methodologies relevant to: knowledge and AI, knowledge discovery, knowledge management, knowledge engineering and acquisition, social and cognitive aspects of knowledge representation, and applications in specific domains.

In addition to this specific focus, EKAW covered its traditional topics ranging from all aspects of eliciting, acquiring, modeling, and managing knowledge, to the construction of knowledge-intensive systems and services for the Semantic Web, knowledge management, e-business, natural language processing, intelligent information integration, personal digital assistance systems, and a variety of other related topics.

For the main conference we invited submissions for research papers presenting novel methods, techniques, or analysis supported by appropriate evaluations, as well as in-use papers describing novel applications of knowledge management and engineering in real environments and experience reports. We also invited submissions of position papers describing novel and innovative ideas, or problem analyses that are still in an early stage but may guide future research in the area.

In addition to the regular conference submission, resulting in a Springer conference proceedings paper contained in this book, the authors of the best EKAW papers were invited to submit an extended version of their papers to a *Semantic Web Journal* (IOS Press) special issue to be published in 2019. The extended papers will go through a new review process and it should be noted that the journal follows an open review process, providing for a very transparent evaluation of the submissions.

Overall, we received 142 abstract submissions of which 104 were in the end accompanied by a valid paper submission and included in the review process. The reviewing was performed by a Program Committee of 114 researchers in the field and the two program chairs. Each paper received at least three reviews (often four), and we specifically thank the reviewers for engaging in lively discussions, especially when there were conflicting opinions on papers. In total, 36 submissions were accepted by the Program Committee (34% overall acceptance rate), out of which 31 for a full presentation and five for a shorter presentation. All the 36 accepted papers are included in this volume as full-length papers. There are 31 research papers, four in-use papers and one is a position paper.

To complement the program, we invited four distinguished keynote speakers:

- Jérôme Lang (Université Paris Dauphine, France) gave a talk entitled "Incomplete Knowledge and Collective Decision-Making".
- Marie-Francine Moens (KU Leuven, Belgium) gave a talk entitled "The Discovery of Spatial Knowledge from Images and Language".
- Simone Paolo Ponzetto (University of Mannheim, Germany) gave a talk titled "Entity-Centric Information Access for High-End Semantic Applications".
- Andrea Tettamanzi (Université Côte d'Azur, France) gave a talk titled "Guess What You Don't Know: Towards an Evolutionary Epistemology of Ontology Learning."

The program chairs of EKAW 2018 were Catherine Faron Zucker from Université Côte d'Azur, France, and Chiara Ghidini from Fondazione Bruno Kessler, Italy.

The EKAW 2018 program also included a Doctoral Consortium that gave PhD students an opportunity to present their research ideas and results in a stimulating environment, to get feedback from mentors who are experienced research scientists in the community, to explore issues related to academic and research careers, and to build relationships with other PhD students from around the world. The Doctoral Consortium was intended for students at each stage of their PhD. All accepted presenters had an opportunity to present their work to an international audience, to be paired with a mentor, and to discuss their work with experienced scientists from the research community. The Doctoral Consortium was organized by Francesco Osborne from Open University Milton Keynes, UK, and Laura Hollink from Centrum Wiskunde and Informatica, The Netherlands.

In addition to the main research tracks, EKAW 2018 hosted one satellite workshop and two tutorials.

Workshop:

- Symbolic Methods for Data-Interlinking, organized by Miguel Couceiro from Université de Lorraine, Nancy, France, and Jérôme David from Université Pierre-Mendès-France, Grenoble, France

Tutorials:

- Learning from Knowledge Graphs, organized by Fabrizio Riguzzi, Elena Bellodi, Riccardo Zese and Giuseppe Cota from Università di Ferrara, Italy
- Catching up with Ontological Engineering to Git-commit and Beyond, organized by Alba Fernández-Izquierdo, Ahmad Alobaid and María Poveda-Villalón, Universidad Politécnica de Madrid, Spain

The workshop and tutorial program was chaired by Manuel Atencia, Université Grenoble Alpes, Inria, LIG, France, and Marieke van Erp, KNAW Humanities Cluster, The Netherlands.

Finally, EKAW 2018 also featured a demo and poster session. We encouraged contributions that were likely to stimulate critical or controversial discussions about any of the areas of the EKAW conference series. We also invited developers to showcase their systems and the benefit they can bring to a particular application. The demo and poster program of EKAW 2018 was chaired by Phillipp Cimiano from CITEC/Bielefeld University, Germany, and Olivier Corby from Université Côte d'Azur, Inria, CNRS, I3S, France. The conference organization also included Raphaël Troncy, EURECOM, France, as the sponsorship chair, Anne-Lise Charbonnier, Inria Nancy Grand Est, France, took care of local arrangements, Cassia Trojhan, IRIT, Université de Toulouse, France, acted as Web chair, and together with Jérémie Nevin, LORIA, Inria, Université de Lorraine, France, as proceedings chairs. Amedeo Napoli and Yannick Toussaint, LORIA, Inria, Université de Lorraine, France, were the general chairs of EKAW 2018.

Thanks to everybody, including attendees at the conference, for making EKAW 2018 a successful event.

November 2018

Catherine Faron Zucker
Chiara Ghidini
Amedeo Napoli
Yannick Toussaint

Program Committee

Additional Reviewers

Augusto, Adriano
Balci, Boran Taylan
Bastianelli, Emanuele
Baumgartner, Matthias
Ben Ellefi, Mohamed
Biswas, Russa
Eberhart, Aaron
Ebrahimi, Monireh
Fernández-Izquierdo, Alba
Filtz, Erwin
Gao, Huan
García-Silva, Andrés
Gsponer, Severin

Heist, Nicolas
Hertling, Sven
Kärle, Elias
Leno, Volodymyr
Malaverri, Joana
Panasiuk, Oleksandra
Petersen, Niklas
Safar, Brigitte
Shimizu, Cogan
Şimşek, Umutcan
Teinemaa, Irene
Tietz, Tabea

Contents

Position Papers

Research Papers

An Empirical Evaluation of RDF Graph Partitioning Techniques

Adnan Akhter[1](✉), Axel-Cyrille Ngomo Ngonga[1,2], and Muhammad Saleem[1]

[1] AKSW, Leipzig, Germany
{akhter,ngomo,saleem}@informatik.uni-leipzig.de
[2] University of Paderborn, Paderborn, Germany
axel.ngonga@upb.de

Abstract. With the significant growth of RDF data sources in both numbers and volume comes the need to improve the scalability of RDF storage and querying solutions. Current implementations employ various RDF graph partitioning techniques. However, choosing the most suitable partitioning for a given RDF graph and application is not a trivial task. To the best of our knowledge, no detailed empirical evaluation exists to evaluate the performance of these techniques. In this work, we present an empirical evaluation of RDF graph partitioning techniques applied to real-world RDF data sets and benchmark queries. We evaluate the selected RDF graph partitioning techniques in terms of their partitioning time, partitioning imbalance (in sizes), and query run time performances achieved, based on real-world data sets and queries selected using the *FEASIBLE* benchmark generation framework.

1 Introduction

Data partitioning is the process of logically and/or physically dividing datasets into subsets to facilitate better maintenance and access. Data partitioning is often used for load balancing, improving system availability and query processing times in data management systems. Over recent years, several Big datasets such as Linked TCGA[1] (around 20 billion triples) and UniProt[2] (over 10 billion triples) have been added to the Web of Data. The need to store and query such datasets efficiently has motivated a considerable amount of work on designing clustered triplestores [4,6,8–11,16–18,21,22,27], i.e., solutions where data is partitioned among multiple data nodes. It is noteworthy that current triplestores employ various graph partitioning techniques [22]. It is also well known that the query execution performance of data storage solutions can be greatly affected by the partitioning technique used in the data store [12]. However, no detailed evaluation of the efficiency of the different RDF graph partitioning techniques in terms of scalability, partitioning imbalance, and query run time performances has been undertaken.

---

[1] TCGA: http://tcga.deri.ie/.

[2] UniProt: http://www.uniprot.org/statistics/.

© Springer Nature Switzerland AG 2018
C. Faron Zucker et al. (Eds.): EKAW 2018, LNAI 11313, pp. 3–18, 2018.
https://doi.org/10.1007/978-3-030-03667-6_1

We address this research gap by presenting a detailed empirical evaluation of different RDF graph partitioning techniques. We compare them according to their suitability for balanced load generation, partitioning time, and query runtime performance. Our contributions are as follows:

1. We compared seven RDF graph partitioning techniques in two different evaluation setups.
2. We evaluate the selected RDF partitioning techniques using different performance measures such as partitioning time, variation in the sizes of the generated partitions, number of sources selected in a purely federated environment, and query runtime performance.
3. We perform an evaluation based on two real-world datasets (i.e., DBpedia and Semantic Web Dog Food), and real queries (selected from users' queries log) using the SPARQL benchmark generation framework from queries log FEASIBLE [19].

All of the data, source code, and results presented in this evaluation are available at https://github.com/dice-group/rdf-partitioning.

2   RDF Graph Partitioning

The RDF graph partitioning problem is defined as follows.

Definition 1 (RDF Graph Partitioning Problem). Given an RDF graph $G = (V, E)$, divide G into n sub-graphs $G_1, \ldots G_n$ such that $G = (V, E) = \bigcup_{i=1}^{n} G_i$, where V is the set of all vertices and E is the set of all edges in the graph.

In this section, we explain commonly used [14,15,20,22] graph partitioning techniques by using a sample RDF graph shown in Fig. 1.

Horizontal Partitioning: This partitioning technique is adopted from [20]. Let T be the set of all RDF triples in a dataset and n be the required number of partitions. The technique assigns the first $|T|/n$ triples in partition 1, the next $|T|/n$ triples in partition 2 and so on. In the example given in Fig. 1, the triples 1–4 will be assigned to the first partition (green), triples 5–8 will be assigned to the second partition (red), and triples 9–11 will be assigned to the third partition (blue).

Subject-Based Partitioning: This technique assigns triples to partitions according to a hash value computed on their subjects modulo the total number of required partitions (i.e., hash(subject) modulus total number of partitions) [14]. Thus, all the triples with the same subject are assigned to one partition. However, due to modulo operation this technique may result in high partitioning imbalance. In our motivating example given in Fig. 1, triples (3,10,11) are matched to the red partition, only triple 7 is matched to the blue partition, and the remaining are matched to the blue partition. Thus, a clear partitioning imbalance (3:1:7 triples) results.

```
@prefix hierarchy1: <http://first/r/> . @prefix hierarchy2: <http://second/r/> .
@prefix hierarchy3: <http://third/r/> . @prefix schema: <http://schema/> .
hierarchy1:s1          schema:p1          hierarchy2:s11 .   #Triple 1
hierarchy1:s1          schema:p2          hierarchy2:s2 .    #Triple 2
hierarchy2:s2          schema:p2          hierarchy2:s4 .    #Triple 3
hierarchy1:s1          schema:p3          hierarchy3:s3 .    #Triple 4
hierarchy3:s3          schema:p2          hierarchy1:s5 .    #Triple 5
hierarchy3:s3          schema:p3          hierarchy2:s13 .   #Triple 6
hierarchy2:s13         schema:p1          hierarchy2:s8 .    #Triple 7
hierarchy1:s1          schema:p4          hierarchy3:s9 .    #Triple 8
hierarchy3:s9          schema:p1          hierarchy2:s4 .    #Triple 9
hierarchy2:s4          schema:p4          hierarchy2:s13 .   #Triple 10
hierarchy2:s11         schema:p2          hierarchy1:s10 .   #Triple 11
```

(a) An example RDF triples

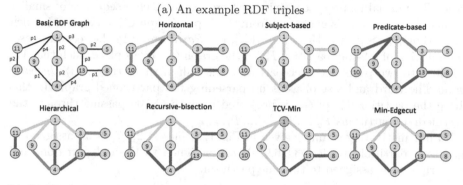

(b) Graph representation and partitioning. Only node numbers are shown for simplicity.

Fig. 1. Partitioning an example RDF into three partitions using different partitioning techniques. Partitions are highlighted in different colors. (Color figure online)

Predicate-Based Partitioning: Similar to Subject-Based, this technique assigns triples to partitions according to a hash value computed on their predicates modulo the number of required partitions. Thus, all triples with the same predicate are assigned to the same partition. In our motivating example given in Fig. 1, all the triples with predicate p1 or p4 are assigned to the red partition, triples with predicate p2 are assigned to the green partition, and all triples with predicate p3 are assigned to the blue partition.

Hierarchical Partitioning: This partitioning is inspired by the assumption that IRIs have path hierarchy and IRIs with a common hierarchy prefix are often queried together [14]. This partitioning is based on extracting path hierarchy from the IRIs and assigning triples having the same hierarchy prefixes into one partition. For instance, the extracted path hierarchy of "http://www.w3.org/1999/02/22-rdf-syntax-ns#type" is "org/w3/www/1999/02/22-rdf-syntax-ns/type". Then, for each level in the path hierarchy (e.g., "org", "org/w3", "org/w3/www", ...) it computes the percentage of triples sharing a hierarchy prefix. If the percentage exceeds an empirically defined threshold and the number of prefixes is equal to or greater than the number of required partitions at any hierarchy level, then these prefixes are used for the hash-based partitioning on prefixes. In comparison to the hash-based subject or predicate partition, this technique requires a higher computational effort to determine the IRI prefixes on which the hash is computed. In our motivating example given in Fig. 1, all the triples having hierarchy1 in subjects are assigned to the green partition, triples having hierarchy2 in subjects are assigned to the red partition, and triples having hierarchy3 in subjects are assigned to the blue partition.

Recursive-Bisection Partitioning: Recursive bisection is a multilevel graph bisection algorithm aiming to solve the k-way graph partitioning problem as described in [15]. This algorithm consists of the following three phases: (1) *Coarsening:* The initial phase is coarsening the graph, in which a sequence of smaller graphs $G_1, G_2, ..., G_m$ is generated from the input Graph $G_0 = (V_0, E_0)$ in such a way that $|V_0| > |V_1| > |V_2| > ... > |V_m|$. (2) *Partitioning* In the second phase, computation of a 2-way partition P_m of the graph G_m takes place, such that V_m is split into two parts and each part contains half of the vertices. (3) *Uncoarsening* The third and last phase is uncoarsening the partitioned graph. In this phase the partition P_m of G_m is projected back to G_0 by passing through the intermediate partitions $P_{m-1}, P_{m-2}, ..., P_1, P_0$.

In our motivating example given in Fig. 1, triples (1,2,4,7,8) are assigned to the green partition, triples (3,5,6,9,10) are assigned to the red partition, and only triple 11 is assigned to the blue partition.

TCV-Min Partitioning: Similar to Recursive-Bisection, the TCV-Min also aims to solve the k-way graph partitioning problem. However, the objective of the partitioning is to minimize the *total communication volume* [2] of the partitioning. Thus, this technique also comprises the three main phases of the k-way graph partitioning. However, the objective of the second phase, i.e. the *Partitioning*, is the minimization of communication costs. In our motivating example given in Fig. 1, triples (1,2,4,5,6,8,9) are assigned to the green partition, triples (3,7,10) are assigned to the red partition, and only triple 11 is assigned to the blue partition.

Min-Edgecut Partitioning: The Min-Edgecut [15] also aims to solve the k-way graph partitioning problem. However, unlike TCV-Min, the objective is to partition the vertices by minimizing the number of edges connected to them. In our motivating example given in Fig. 1, triples (1,2,4,7,8) are assigned to the green partition, triples (3,5,6,9,10) are assigned to the red partition, and only triple 11 is assigned to the blue partition.

3   Evaluation

In this section, we present our evaluation setup followed by evaluation results.

3.1   Evaluation Setup

Partitioning Environments: We used two distinct evaluation environments to compare the selected RDF graph partitioning techniques. **(1) Clustered**

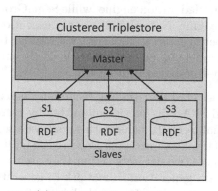

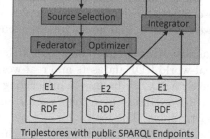

(a) Clustered Architecture   (b) Physically Federated Architecture

Fig. 2. Evaluation environments

RDF Storage Environment In this environment, the given RDF data is distributed among different data nodes within the same machine as part of a single RDF storage solution. Figure 2a shows the very generic master-slave architecture used in our clustered environment. The master assigns the tasks and the slaves perform RDF storage and query processing tasks. There are many RDF storage solutions [4,6,8–11,16–18,21,22,27] that employ this architecture. We chose *Koral* [14] in our evaluation. The reason for choosing this platform was because it allows the data partitioning strategy to be controlled, it is a state-of-the art distributed RDF store, and it is well-integrated with the famous RDF partitioning system *METIS* [15]. **(2) Purely Federated Environment** In this environment, the given RDF data is distributed among several physically separated machines and a federation engine is used to do the query processing task. We chose the well-known SPARQL endpoint federation setup [20] in which data is distributed among several SPARQL endpoints and a SPARQL federation engine is used to do federated query processing over multiple endpoints. Figure 2b shows the two main components (i.e., the federation engine and the SPARQL endpoints) of this architecture. The general steps involved to process a SPARQL query in this evaluation environment are as follows: Given a SPARQL query, the first step is to parse the query and get the individual triple patterns. The next step is source selection, for which the goal is to identify the set of relevant data sources (endpoints in our case) for the query. Using the source selection information, the federator divides the original query into multiple sub-queries. An optimized sub-query execution plan is generated by the optimizer and the sub-queries are forwarded to the corresponding data sources. The results of the sub-queries are then integrated by the integrator. The integrated results are finally returned to the agent that issued the query. Many SPARQL endpoint federation engines [1,3,7,23,25] abide by this architecture. We chose *FedX* [23] and *SemaGrow* [3] in our evaluation. The reason for choosing these two federation engines is their use of different query execution plans. FedX is an index-free heuristic-based SPARQL endpoint federation engine, while SemaGrow is an index-assisted cost-based federation engine. Note that the query execution plan greatly affects the query runtime performances, therefore we wanted to choose federation engines that employ different query planners (FedX is left-deep-trees-based, and SemaGrow is a busy-tree-based solution).

Datasets: We wanted to benchmark the selected partitioning techniques based on real-world RDF datasets and real-world SPARQL queries submitted by users to the SPARQL endpoints of underlying datasets. To achieve this goal, we used two real-word datasets: *DBpedia 3.5.1* and the *Semantic Web Dog Food (SWDF)* for partitioning. The reason for choosing these two datasets is that they are used by the *FEASIBLE* [19] SPARQL benchmark generation framework to generate customized SPARQL benchmarks from the queries log of the underlying datasets. These two datasets vary greatly in their high-level statistics: the DBpedia 3.5.1 contains 232,536,510 triples, 18,425,128 distinct subjects, 39,672 distinct predicates, and 65,184,193 distinct objects while SWDF contains 304,583 triples, 36,879 distinct subjects, 185 distinct predicates, and 95,501 distinct objects.

Queries: We generated the following benchmarks for evaluation using FEA-SIBLE: **(1) SWDF BGP-only** benchmark contains a total of 300 BGP-only SPARQL queries from the queries log of the SWDF data set. These queries only contain single BGP; the other SPARQL features such as OPTIONAL, ORDER BY, DISTINCT, UNION, FILTER, REGEX, aggregate functions, SERVICE, property paths etc. are not used, **(2) SWDF fully-featured** contains a total of 300 queries which are not only single BGPs and may include more features (e.g., the above mentioned) of the SPARQL queries, **(3) DBpedia BGP-only** contains 300 BGP-only, and **(4) DBpedia fully-featured** contains 300 fully-featured SPARQL queries selected from the queries log of DBpedia 3.5.1. Thus, in our evaluation we used a total of 1200 SPARQL queries selected from two different data sets. Note that we only used BGP-only benchmarks with Koral since it does not support many of the SPARQL features used in the fully-featured SPARQL benchmarks.

Number of Partitions: Inspired by [20], we created 10 partitions for each of the selected data sets and the partitioning technique. In Koral, we ran 10 slaves each containing one partition. In the *purely federated environment*, we used 10 Linux-based Virtuoso 7.1 SPARQL endpoints, each containing one partition.

Performance Measures: We used six performance measures to benchmark the selected partitioning techniques – partitions generation time, overall benchmark execution time, average query execution time, number of timeout queries for each benchmark, the ranking score of the partitioning techniques, total number of sources selected for the complete benchmark execution in a purely federated environment, and the partitioning imbalance among the generated partitions. Three minutes was selected as the timeout time for query execution [19]. In addition, we also measured the Spearman's rank correlation coefficients to ascertain the correlation between the sources selected and the query run time in a purely federated environment. The rank score of the partitioning technique is defined as follows:

Definition 2 (Rank Score). Let t be the total number of partitioning techniques and b be the total number of benchmark executions used in the evaluation. Let $1 \leq r \leq t$ denote the rank number and $O_p(r)$ denote the occurrences of a partitioning technique p placed at rank r. The rank score of the partitioning technique p is defined as follows:

$$s := \sum_{r=1}^{t} \frac{O_p(r) \times (t - r)}{b(t - 1)}, 0 \leq s \leq 1$$

In our evaluation, we have a total of seven partitioning techniques (i.e., $t = 7$) and 10 benchmarks executions ($b = 10$, 4 benchmarks by FedX, 4 benchmarks by SemaGrow, and 2 benchmarks by Koral).

The partitioning imbalance in the sizes of the generated partitions is defined as follows:

Definition 3 (Partitioning Imbalance). Let n be the total number of partitions generated by a partitioning technique and $P_1, P_2, \ldots P_n$ be the set of these partitions, ordered according to the increasing size of number of triples. The imbalance in partitions is defined as Gini coefficient:

$$b := \frac{2 \sum_{i=1}^{n} (i \times |P_i|)}{(n - 1) \times \sum_{j=1}^{n} |P_j|} - \frac{n + 1}{n - 1}, 0 \leq b \leq 1$$

Hardware and Software Configuration: All experiments were run on an Ubuntu-based machine with intel Xeon 2.10 GHz, 64 cores and 512GB of RAM. We conducted our experiments on local copies of Virtuoso (version 7.1) SPARQL endpoints. We used METIS 5.1.0.dfsg-2[3] to create TCV-Min, Min-Edgecut and Recursive-Bisection. We used default configurations for FedX, SemaGrow and Koral (except the slaves were changed from 2 to 10 in Koral).

3.2 Evaluation Results

Partition Generation Time: Figure 3 shows a comparison of the time taken by each technique to generate the required 10 partitions, both for DBpedia 3.5.1 and SWDF datasets. As an overall evaluation, the Horizontal partitioning method requires the smallest time followed by the Subject-Based, Predicate-Based, Hierarchical, TCV-Min, Recursive-Bisection, and Min-Edgecut, respectively. The reason for the Horizontal partitioning taking the least time lies in this simplicity: the technique creates the range of triples and assigns them to the

---

[3] http://glaros.dtc.umn.edu/gkhome/metis/metis/download.

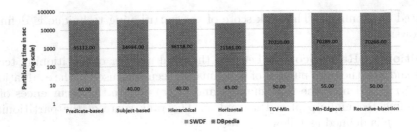

Fig. 3. Time taken for the creation of 10 partitions

desired partitions in the first come first server basis. Both Predicate-Based and Subject-Based partitioning techniques take almost the same time because both techniques simply traverse each triple in the dataset and apply hash functions on the subject or predicate of the triple. Thus, they have the same computational complexity. Hierarchical partitioning takes more time compared with the Subject and Predicate-Based hash partitioning techniques due to the extra time required to compute path hierarchies before hash function is applied. The k-way implementations of graph partitioning, i.e., TCV-Min, Min-Edgecut and Recursive-Bisection consumed even more time (almost double) compared to the other techniques. This is because of their higher complexity in terms of the time required to perform the coarsening, partitioning, and uncoarsening phases.

Query Runtime Performances: One of the most important results is the query runtime performances achieved by using each of the selected partitioning techniques. We used the total benchmark (300 queries) execution time (including timeout queries) and the average query execution time (excluding timeout queries) to encapsulate the runtime performances of the partitioning techniques. To measure the former performance metric, we executed the complete 300 queries from each benchmark over the data partitions created by the selected partitioning techniques and calculated the total time taken to execute the complete benchmark queries. For each timeout query, we add 180 s to the total benchmark execution time. For the latter performance metric, we only considered those queries which were successfully executed within the timeout limit and present the average query execution time for each of the selected partitioning technique. Figure 4 presents the query runtime performances achieved by each of the selected techniques pertaining to the two aforementioned query execution metrics.

Figure 4a shows the total execution time of the complete benchmarks for the selected partitioning techniques based on FedX federation engine. Including all the benchmark execution results (over 4 benchmarks), Horizontal partitioning consumed the least time (26538.7 s), followed by Recursive-Bisection (26962.6 s), Subject-Based (28629.3 s), TCV-Min (28739.9 s), Hierarchical (28867.5 s), Min-Edgecut (30482.8 s) and Predicate-Based (33864.2 s), respectively. The total benchmark execution time of the individual benchmarks (i.e., two from SWDF

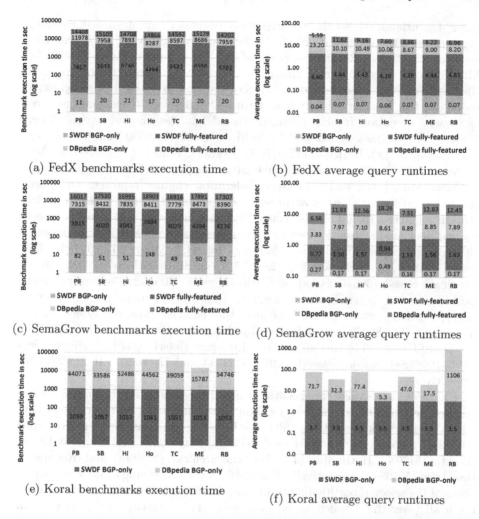

(a) FedX benchmarks execution time

(b) FedX average query runtimes

(c) SemaGrow benchmarks execution time

(d) SemaGrow average query runtimes

(e) Koral benchmarks execution time

(f) Koral average query runtimes

Fig. 4. Benchmarks (300 queries each) total execution time including timeouts and average query runtimes excluding timeouts. (PB = Predicate-Based, SB = Subject-Based, Hi = Hierarchical, Ho = Horizontal, TC = TCV-Min, ME Min-Edgecut, RB = Recursive Bisection)

and two from DBpedia3.51) can be seen from the bar stacked graphs directly. Figure 4b shows the average query execution times of the selected partitioning techniques based on four benchmarks on FedX. The overall (over 4 benchmarks) average query execution results show Recursive-Bisection has the smallest average query runtime (5.020557271 s), followed by Min-Edgecut (5.4330126 s), TCV-Min (5.4456308 s), Horizontal (5.4801338 s), Hierarchical (6.0390115 s), Subject-Based (6.5591146 s) and Predicate-Based (8.3071525 s), respectively.

Figure 4c shows the total execution time of the complete benchmarks for the selected partitioning techniques based on SemaGrow federation engine. From all (over 4 benchmarks) benchmark execution results, Predicate-Based partitioning consumed the least time (27227.9 s) followed by TCV-Min (28772.8 s), Hierarchical (28921.6 s), Recursive-Bisection(29983.9 s), Subject-Based (30012.5 s), Min-Edgecut (30807.5 s) and Horizontal (31145.9 s), respectively. Figure 4d shows the average query execution times of the selected partitioning techniques based on four benchmarks on SemaGrow. Of all (over 4 benchmarks) average query execution results, Predicate-Based has the smallest average query runtime (2.857210203 s) followed by Subject-Based (5.393390726 s), Hierarchical (5.349322361 s), Horizontal (7.077052279 s), TCV-Min (4.024567032 s), Min-Edgecut (5.850084384 s) and Recursive-Bisection (5.535637211 s) respectively.

Since both FedX and SemaGrow federation engines represent the *purely federated environment*, we now present the combined results of the two federation engines. Including all (over FedX+SemaGrow and over 4 benchmarks) benchmark execution results, Recursive-Bisection partitioning consumed the smallest time (28473.233 s), followed by TCV-Min (28756.337 s), Horizontal (28842.264 s), Hierarchical (28894.5275 s), Subject-Based (29320.9305 s), Predicate-Based (30546.0905 s) and Min-Edgecut (30645.1825 s), respectively. Considering all (over FedX+SemaGrow and over 4 benchmarks) average query runtime results, TCV-Min has the smallest average query execution time (5.278097241 s), followed by Recursive-Bisection (5.278097241 s), Predicate-Based (5.582181367 s), Min-Edgecut (5.641548479 s), Hierarchical (5.694166918 s), Subject-Based (5.976252639 s) and Horizontal (6.27859305 s), respectively.

Figure 4e shows the total execution time of the complete benchmarks for the selected partitioning techniques based on Koral. Including all (over two benchmarks) benchmark execution results, the Min-Edgecut consumed the least time (16839 s), followed by Subject-Based (34643 s), TCV-Min (40110 s), Predicate-Based (45170 s), Horizontal (45602 s), Hierarchical (53539 s) and Recursive-Bisection (55798 s), respectively. Figure 4f shows the average query execution times of the selected partitioning techniques based on four benchmarks on Koral. From all (over the 4 benchmarks) average query execution results, Horizontal partitioning has the smallest average query runtime (4.393116824 s), followed by Min-Edgecut (10.48653731 s), Subject-Based (17.91570378 s), TCV-Min (25.26057554 s), Predicate-Based (37.66883389 s), Hierarchical (40.43121192 s) and Recursive-Bisection (554.618705 s), respectively.

The complete benchmark execution results are best summarized in terms of total timeout queries, overall rankings, and the rank scores of the partitioning techniques and are presented in the subsequent sections.

Number of Timeout Queries: Table 1 shows the total number of timeout queries for each of the 4 benchmarks and for each of the partitioning techniques using FedX, SemaGrow and Koral. Overall (i.e., over FedX + SemaGrow + Koral), Min-Edgecut has the smallest timeouts (344 queries), followed by the Subject-Based (422 queries), TCV-Min (455 queries), Predicate-Based (485 queries), Horizontal (498 queries), Hierarchical (544 queries), and Recursive-Bisection (556 queries), respectively.

Table 1. Timeout queries using FedX, SemaGrow and Koral

	FedX				SemaGrow				Koral	
	SWDF		DBpedia		SWDF		DBpedia		SWDF	DBpedia
Partitioning	BGP	FF	BGP	FF	BGP	FF	BGP	FF	BGP	BGP
Predicate-Based	0	35	32	73	0	20	35	81	0	209
Subject-Based	0	24	29	69	0	20	35	83	0	162
Hierarchical	0	28	28	70	0	20	33	79	0	286
Horizontal	0	12	31	73	0	19	34	83	0	246
TCV-Min	0	24	35	70	0	20	33	85	0	188
Min-Edgecut	0	30	35	74	0	22	34	84	0	65
Recursive-Bisection	0	19	32	70	0	21	35	81	0	298

Overall Ranking of Partitioning Techniques: Table 2 shows the results of the overall rank-wise ranking of the selected partitioning techniques based on the total benchmark execution time from a total of 4 benchmarks. Based on FedX, Predicate-Based partitioning ranked 1st and 2nd once each, and 7th twice, suggesting this technique either produces the best or worst query runtime performances among the selected partitioning techniques. Subject-Based partitioning ranked mostly in the middle (once 2nd, twice 4th and once 6th), suggesting this technique produces average runtime performances among the selected partitioning techniques. Hierarchical partitioning ranked in the top, middle, and lower positions, suggesting unpredictable runtime performances. Horizontal partitioning has given the best results twice and on the other two occasions it gave the average results. TCV-Min was very consistent by producing the third best result on three times. Min-Edgecut runtime performance is usually on the lower side. Recursive-Bisection gave three results at the best side of the scale, however it ranked 5th once.

Table 2. Overall rank-wise ranking of partitioning techniques based on two benchmarks from SWDF and DBpedia each. (PB = Predicate-Based, SB = Subject-Based, Hi = Hierarchical, Ho = Horizontal, TC = TCV-Min, ME Min-Edgecut, RB = Recursive Bisection)

	FedX							SemaGrow							Koral						
PT	1st	2nd	3rd	4th	5th	6th	7th	1st	2nd	3rd	4th	5th	6th	7th	1st	2nd	3rd	4th	5th	6th	7th
PB	1	1	0	0	0	0	2	2	1	0	0	0	1	0	0	0	0	1	0	0	1
SB	0	1	0	2	0	1	0	0	0	2	0	1	1	0	0	1	0	0	0	1	0
Hi	1	0	0	1	1	0	1	0	0	2	1	1	0	0	0	0	0	0	1	1	0
Ho	1	1	0	1	1	0	0	1	0	0	0	1	0	2	1	0	0	0	1	0	0
TC	0	0	3	0	1	0	0	1	2	0	1	0	0	0	0	1	1	0	0	0	0
Mi	0	0	0	0	0	3	1	0	1	0	0	0	1	2	1	0	0	1	0	0	0
Re	1	1	1	0	1	0	0	0	0	0	2	1	1	0	0	0	1	0	0	0	1

Based on SemaGrow, Predicate-Based partitioning mostly results to good query runtime performances. The query runtime performances of the Subject-Based and Hierarchical partitioning techniques is on the average or lower sides. Horizontal has given best results once and the rest three times were on the lower ranked side. TCV-Min performance is mostly on the high ranked side. Again, Min-Edgecut runtime performance is usually on the lower side. Recursive-Bisection, however, has stayed on the lower side.

Based on Koral, Predicate-Based partitioning gave below average query runtime performances. Subject-Based ranked 2nd and 6th one time each. Hierarchical ranked on the lower side. Horizontal ranked 1st and 5th one time each. TCV-Min has produced good results by ranking 2nd and 3rd one time each. Similar to TCV-Min, Min-Edgecut also produced better query runtime performances. Recursive-Bisection ranked 3rd and 7th once each. Please note that Koral ranking is based on a total of 2 (BGP-only) benchmarks.

Rank Scores: From Table 2, it is hard to decide which partitioning technique is generally ranked better. We used Table 2 to compute the rank scores (ref., Definition 2) pertaining to each of the partitioning techniques and presented in Fig. 5a. TCV-Min results in the highest rank score, followed by Property-based, Horizontal, Recursive-Bisection, Subject-Based, Hierarchical, and Min-Edgecut respectively.

Partitioning Imbalance: Figure 5b shows the partitioning imbalance (defined in Definition 3) values of the partitions generated by the selected partitioning techniques. As expected, the Horizontal portioning results the smallest partitioning imbalance, followed by Hierarchical, Subject-Based, Min-Edgecut, Recursive-Bisection, TCV-Min and Predicate-Based, respectively.

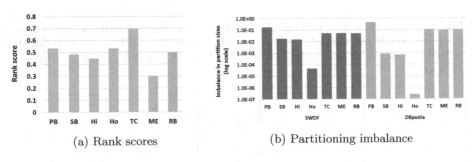

(a) Rank scores   (b) Partitioning imbalance

Fig. 5. Rank scores and partitioning imbalance of the partitioning techniques. (PB = Predicate-Based, SB = Subject-Based, Hi = Hierarchical, Ho = Horizontal, TC = TCV-Min, ME Min-Edgecut, RB = Recursive Bisection)

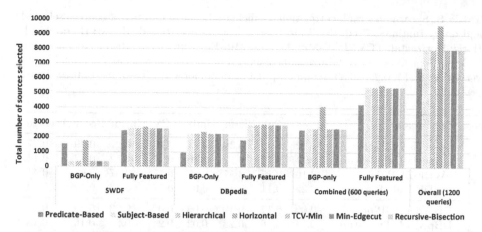

Fig. 6. Total distinct sources selected

Number of Sources Selected: The number of sources selected (SPARQL endpoints in our case) by the federation engine to execute a given SPARQL query is a key performance metric [20]. Figure 6 shows the total distinct sources selected by FedX and SemaGrow. Note that the source selection algorithm of both FedX and SemaGrow select exactly the same sources. Generally (over 4 benchmarks) source selection evaluation, Predicate-Based selects the smallest number of sources, followed by Min-Edgecut, TCV-Min, Recursive-Bisection, Subject-Based, Hierarchical and Horizontal, respectively.

Spearman's Rank Correlation Coefficients: Finally, we want to show how the number of sources selected affects the query execution time. To this end, we computed the Spearman's rank correlation between the number of sources selected and the query execution time. Table 3 shows Spearman's rank correlation coefficients values for the four evaluation benchmarks and the selected partitioning techniques. The results suggest that the number of sources selected, in general, have a positive correlation with the query execution times, i.e. the smaller the sources selected the smaller the execution time and vice versa.

4   Related Work

A plethora of clustered triplestores have been designed in previous works [4,6,8–11,16–18,21,22,27] and mentioned across the paper. Here, we only target the RDF graph partitioning literature. Koral [14] is a distributed RDF triplestore which allows the integration of different RDF graph partitioning techniques. An analysis of three partitioning techniques, i.e., Subject-Based, Hierarchical and Min-Edgecut is presented in [5] based on synthetic data and queries. A brief survey of RDF graph partitioning is provided in [24]. [13] suggests that hash-based partitioning is more scalable as hash values can be computed in parallel. A signature tree-based triple indexing scheme is proposed in [26] to efficiently store the

Table 3. Spearman's rank correlation coefficients between number of sources selected and query runtimes. Pred: Predicate-Based, Sub: Subject-Based, Hierar: Hierarchical, Horiz: Horizontal, TCV: TCV-Min, Mincut: Min-Edgecut, Recur: Recursive-Bisection, S-Grow: SemaGrow. Correlations and colors: $-0.00...-0.19$ very weak (⬤-), $0.00...0.19$ very weak (⬤+), $0.20...0.39$ weak (⬤+), $0.40...0.59$ moderate (⬤+), $0.60...0.79$ strong (⬤+).

	Benchmark	Pred	Sub	Hierar	Horiz	TCV	Mincut	Recur	Average
FedX	DBpedia BGP-only	0.22	0.30	0.30	0.28	0.26	0.27	0.29	0.27
	DBpedia Fully-featured	0.14	0.11	0.11	0.16	0.17	0.12	0.17	0.14
	SWDF BGP-only	−0.10	0.57	0.57	0.10	0.57	0.57	0.57	0.41
	SWDF Fully-featured	0.22	0.11	0.13	0.09	0.11	0.13	0.10	0.12
S-Grow	DBpedia BGP-only	−0.02	0.11	0.10	0.06	0.09	0.30	0.29	0.13
	DBpedia Fully-featured	0.14	0.18	0.23	0.02	0.24	0.26	0.16	0.18
	SWDF BGP-only	0.23	0.64	0.64	0.65	0.66	0.64	0.64	0.59
	SWDF Fully-featured	0.07	−0.02	−0.02	−0.07	−0.02	−0.06	−0.01	−0.02
	Average	0.11	0.25	0.26	0.16	0.26	0.28	0.28	0.23

partitions of the RDF graph. To the best of our knowledge, no detailed empirical evaluation exists to position the different RDF graph partitioning techniques based on real data and real queries in two different evaluation environments.

5   Conclusion and Future Work

We presented an empirical evaluation of seven RDF partitioning techniques. Our overall results of query runtime suggest that TCV-Min leads to smallest query runtimes followed by Property-Based,Horizontal, Recursive-Bisection, Subject-Based, Hierarchical, and Min-Edgecut, respectively. Our T-test[4] analysis shows significant differences in the runtime performances achieved by different partitioning techniques. In addition, the number of sources selected has a direct relation with query runtimes. Thus, partitioning techniques which minimize the total number of sources selected generally lead to better runtime performances. In future, we will add more querying engines into the clustered evaluation environment. We will test the scalability of the partitioning techniques using different sizes of the same datasets and use some more Big RDF datasets. We will also focus on the effects of partitioning pertaining to a given use-case, such as when involving reasoning tasks or data updates etc.

Acknowledgements. This work was supported by the H2020 project HOBBIT (no. 688227).

---

[4] Please see T-Test tab of the excel sheet goo.gl/fxa4cJ.

References

1. Acosta, M., Vidal, M.-E., Lampo, T., Castillo, J., Ruckhaus, E.: ANAPSID: an adaptive query processing engine for SPARQL endpoints. In: Aroyo, L., et al. (eds.) ISWC 2011. LNCS, vol. 7031, pp. 18–34. Springer, Heidelberg (2011). https://doi.org/10.1007/978-3-642-25073-6_2
2. Buluç, A., Meyerhenke, H., Safro, I., Sanders, P., Schulz, C.: Recent advances in graph partitioning. In: Kliemann, L., Sanders, P. (eds.) Algorithm Engineering. LNCS, vol. 9220, pp. 117–158. Springer, Cham (2016). https://doi.org/10.1007/978-3-319-49487-6_4
3. Charalambidis, A., et al.: SemaGrow: optimizing federated SPARQL queries. In: SEMANTICS (2015)
4. Erling, O., Mikhailov, I.: Towards web scale RDF. In: Proceedings of SSWS (2008)
5. Janke, D., et al.: Impact analysis of data placement strategies on query efforts in distributed RDF stores. JWS (2018)
6. Galárraga, L., et al.: Partout: a distributed engine for efficient RDF processing. In: WWW (2014)
7. Görlitz, O., Staab, S.: SPLENDID: SPARQL endpoint federation exploiting void descriptions. In: COLD (2011)
8. Gurajada, S., et al.: Triad: a distributed shared-nothing RDF engine based on asynchronous message passing. In: SIGMOD (2014)
9. Hammoud, M., et al.: DREAM: distributed RDF engine with adaptive query planner and minimal communication. In: VLDB (2015)
10. Harris, S., et al.: 4store: the design and implementation of a clustered RDF store. In: SSWS (2009)
11. Harth, A., Umbrich, J., Hogan, A., Decker, S.: YARS2: a federated repository for querying graph structured data from the web. In: Aberer, K., et al. (eds.) The Semantic Web. ISWC 2007, ASWC 2007. Lecture Notes in Computer Science, vol. 4825, pp. 211–224. Springer, Heidelberg (2007). https://doi.org/10.1007/978-3-540-76298-0_16
12. Herodotou, H., et al.: Query optimization techniques for partitioned tables. In: SIGMOD (2011)
13. Huang, J., et al.: Scalable SPARQL querying of large RDF graphs. In: VLDB (2011)
14. Janke, D., et al.: Koral: a glass box profiling system for individual components of distributed RDF stores. In: BLINK-ISWC (2017)
15. Karypis, G., et al.: A fast and high quality multilevel scheme for partitioning irregular graphs. SIAM JSC 20, 359–392 (1998)
16. Khandelwal, A., et al.: ZipG: a memory-efficient graph store for interactive queries. In: ACM ICMD (2017)
17. Neumann, T., et al.: The RDF-3X engine for scalable management of RDF data. In: VLDB (2010)
18. Owens, A., et al.: Clustered TDB: a clustered triple store for Jena (2008)
19. Saleem, M., Mehmood, Q., Ngonga Ngomo, A.C.: FEASIBLE: a feature-based SPARQL benchmark generation framework. In: Arenas, M., et al. (eds.) The Semantic Web - ISWC 2015. ISWC 2015. Lecture Notes in Computer Science, vol. 9366, pp. 52–69. Springer, Cham (2015). https://doi.org/10.1007/978-3-319-25007-6_4
20. Saleem, M., et al.: A fine-grained evaluation of SPARQL endpoint federation systems. SWJ (2016)

21. Schätzle, A., Przyjaciel-Zablocki, M., Neu, A., Lausen, G.: Sempala: interactive SPARQL query processing on Hadoop. In: Mika, P., et al. (eds.) The Semantic Web - ISWC 2014. ISWC 2014. Lecture Notes in Computer Science, vol. 8796, pp. 164–179. Springer, Cham (2014). https://doi.org/10.1007/978-3-319-11964-9_11

22. Schätzle, A., et al.: S2RDF: RDF querying with SPARQL on spark. In: VLDB (2016)

23. Schwarte, A., Haase, P., Hose, K., Schenkel, R., Schmidt, M.: FedX: optimization techniques for federated query processing on linked data. In: Aroyo, L., et al. (eds.) The Semantic Web - ISWC 2011. ISWC 2011. Lecture Notes in Computer Science, vol. 7031, pp. 601–616. Springer, Heidelberg (2011). https://doi.org/10.1007/978-3-642-25073-6_38

24. Tomaszuk, D., Skonieczny, Ł., Wood, D.: RDF graph partitions: a brief survey. In: Kozielski, S., Mrozek, D., Kasprowski, P., Małysiak-Mrozek, B., Kostrzewa, D. (eds.) BDAS 2015. CCIS, vol. 521, pp. 256–264. Springer, Cham (2015). https://doi.org/10.1007/978-3-319-18422-7_23

25. Wang, X., et al.: LHD: optimising linked data query processing using parallelisation. In: LDOW (2013)

26. Yan, Y., et al.: Efficient indices using graph partitioning in RDF triple stores. In: ICDE (2009)

27. Zeng, K., et al.: A distributed graph engine for web scale RDF data. In: Proceedings of the VLDB Endowment (2013)

Fuzzy Semantic Labeling
of Semi-structured Numerical Datasets

Ahmad Alobaid(✉) and Oscar Corcho

Ontology Engineering Group, Universidad Politécnica de Madrid,
28660 Boadilla del Monte, Madrid, Spain
{aalobaid,ocorcho}@fi.upm.es

Abstract. SPARQL endpoints provide access to rich sources of data
(e.g. knowledge graphs), which can be used to classify other less structured datasets (e.g. CSV files or HTML tables on the Web). We propose
an approach to suggest *types* for the numerical columns of a collection of
input files available as CSVs. Our approach is based on the application
of the *fuzzy c-means* clustering technique to numerical data in the input
files, using existing SPARQL endpoints to generate training datasets.
Our approach has three major advantages: it works directly with live
knowledge graphs, it does not require knowledge-graph profiling beforehand, and it avoids tedious and costly manual training to match values with *types*. We evaluate our approach against manually annotated
datasets. The results show that the proposed approach classifies most of
the types correctly for our test sets.

Keywords: Fuzzy clustering · Semantic labeling · Semantic web

1 Introduction

A massive number of data are stored and made publicly available on the Web
in semi-structured formats, such as spreadsheets. This is especially the case for
open data made available by public administrations, since the publication of
CSV data grants them three stars in the 5-star open data scheme[1].

A major drawback of the publication of data in spreadsheets is the difficulty
for potential data consumers to understand and interpret their content. This is
because the terms used for column headings in these files are commonly not sufficiently informative and lack a data dictionary where their meaning is provided.
Therefore, the automatic classification of such semi-structured dataset may be
useful to improve their usage. For example, such characterization may allow
search engines to improve the relevancy of results [4]. It may also be used to
(partially) automate the generation of mappings (e.g. RML [7] and R2RML [6])
that may be used to generate RDF on the fly without actually transforming the
data.

---

[1] http://5stardata.info/en/.

© Springer Nature Switzerland AG 2018
C. Faron Zucker et al. (Eds.): EKAW 2018, LNAI 11313, pp. 19–33, 2018.
https://doi.org/10.1007/978-3-030-03667-6_2

Meanwhile, data are also exposed on the Web by means of Linked Data principles or via SPARQL endpoints, which can be considered as rich sources of more structured and well-described data. Our hypothesis is that such data can be useful to train models that are able to characterize the numerical semi-structured dataset that we were referring to in the previous paragraph.

In this paper, we describe an approach for the characterization of semi-structured dataset (e.g., CSVs) that uses the content available in SPARQL endpoints for such characterization. Our approach is based on the usage of the *fuzzy c-means* clustering technique. We have identified the following advantages:

- It is domain agnostic. That is, it performs the semantic labeling of semi-structured dataset regardless of their domain, what makes it applicable to a wide range of datasets.
- No manual training is needed. It does not require users to manually type samples of the data beforehand or to use a training dataset that has been constructed before. Instead, it works with existing data available as SPARQL endpoints.
- It does not require exact matches for the numerical values whose columns it classifies. The correct *typing* of dataset is not prevented by having values that are updated over time (e.g. max temperature observed in a city) or entities/values that are not shared between training and testing data (e.g. heights of a local sports team that are not in the knowledge graph).
- Works with live knowledge graphs. It does not require the knowledge graph to be downloaded locally (which is not always feasible).
- No knowledge-graph profiling is required. It works directly with the data and does not need the knowledge graph to be profiled before being able to label the input dataset.

Several approaches have been proposed in the state of the art for the purpose of classifying (a.k.a. semantic labeling) semi-structured data. They use a range of techniques (e.g. graphical probabilistic models [8,9,18,21], linear regression [4, 12], decision trees [17], etc.). These are described in the following section, where we discuss their advantages and disadvantages when compared to the approach presented in this paper.

Section 3 describes our approach, based on fuzzy clustering, to classify numerical dataset, with a running example coming from the domain of Olympic Games. In Sect. 4 we evaluate our approach and discuss the results obtained in our experiments. Finally, Sect. 5 includes a reference to our planned future work.

2   Related Work

Different approaches have been used in the literature to perform semantic labeling. We understand by semantic labeling the process of assigning *types* from knowledge bases to values or a collection of values. In this section, we describe some of the most relevant approaches that have been proposed in the past for tackling semantic labeling of tabular dataset.

Cafarella et al. [4] present an approach for semantic matching of Web tables extracted from Web pages (from the Google crawl). Their approach exploits an attribute correlation statistics database (ACSDb) that contains the frequency of occurrences of schemas and attributes to compute the occurrence probabilities of an attribute given another. For relations retrieval, they use schema ranking which is based on a linear regression estimator with different features such as the number of hits on the table header. They also use a schema coherency score based on Point-wise Mutual Information, which provides a sense on how strongly two items are related.

Limaye et al. [9] use probabilistic graphical models for semantic labeling, entity detection and relation extraction using YAGO. They use three random variables; column type, entity, and the relation between two columns, which are used to construct the features. The features are based on cosine similarity of the cell and column headers, compatibility of the entity and semantic types, and relationship compatibility between different columns types and entity pairs. They weight the features using a weight vector that learns using a generalized Support Vector Machine method.

Syed et al. [17] build an index from Wikipedia pages including the titles, redirects, first sentences, categories, and types. They discover ontology properties from Wikipedia articles and the class hierarchy is inferred from the slots and fillers. Slots are predicted for different entities and compared with the DBpedia infobox ontology and Freebase. Then, Wikitology is used to link entities to the right Wikipedia entities. In addition to that, the relation between pairs of values is discovered by querying DBpedia for pairs of values in each row and selecting the maximum appearing relation.

Ventis et al. [19] semantically label web tables using two databases: isA database and relation database. They start with the isA database to identify the class of each column. After identifying the classes of each column, they inspect the relation between two columns using the relation database, which is in the form of (a, R, b), where a is an instance of class A, b is an instance of class B, and R is the relation between a and b.

Goel et al. [8] semantically label source attributes using probabilistic graphical models, namely Conditional Random Fields, exploiting the latent (hidden) structure within the data. They tokenize the values and apply features depending on the token type. The features for alphabetic tokens are the token length, the starting letter, whether the token is capitalized, all upper case and the token value. For numeric tokens, the length of the number, the number of digits before the decimal points, the number of digits after the decimal points, whether the numeric token is negative, starting digits, the place of the unit and the tenth place unit digit. For the symbol token, the feature is only the value itself. Besides that, they consider the relationship between neighboring labels, tokens and attribute labels.

Zhang et al. [21] match and semantically annotate numeric time-varying attributes in web tables using collective inference based on belief propagation. They take into account tables' headers and context (e.g. surrounding text). They use heuristics to find the subject column and split each table into (n–1) tables, the subject column with each of the other columns. They connect attributes if they have the same year and unit/scale. They also connect attributes if they have the same year and they match after applying any of the conversion rules (e.g. Euro = 1.3 * USD). Possible labels for each table are gathered from the header of the table and its context information and inconsistent labels are eliminated by the use of mutual exclusive labels.

Ritze et al. [15] present T2K, an iterative matching algorithm to match Web Tables to knowledge bases. This algorithm performs entity-level matching and schema-level matching. Entity column is picked by examining columns with the most distinct values and data types are detected using predefined regular expressions. Similarities are computed among values between the Web Tables and DBpedia. Matches between Web Tables and DBpedia properties are aggregated and classes that do not belong are eliminated.

Taheriyan et al. [18] build a semantic model that represents the relationship between fields in dataset rather than only annotating attributes as semantic types. It types the dataset semantically, and then use that semantic labeling with confidence intervals to construct the semantic model. Then, it builds a graph with links that correspond to candidate types inferred by the ontology.

Pham et al. [12] propose a semantic labeling approach based on logistic regression. The features they rely on are similarity measures using Jaccard similarity and TF-IDF besides the attribute name (in the header), Kolmogorov-Smirnov test and Mann-Whitney test. The importance of each feature is computed for each domain, and that importance weight (which depends on the training data) is used afterwards for classifying the dataset.

Neumaier et al. [11] notice that a semantic type can appear in different contexts, so they aim to create a context for the semantic labels instead of mapping properties only. They represent that as a tree with each one of the children being a context. After that, they build a hierarchical background knowledge graph. For constructing the background knowledge graph, they use the *rdfs:subClassOf* and property-object pairs. For predicting the new dataset, they use the Kolmogorov-Smirnov test and nearest neighbors over the background knowledge graph.

From this initial analysis of the state of the art in semantic labeling we obtain the following set of conclusions:

- Some approaches focus only on textual data [9,17] or numerical data [11,21]. Zhang et al. [21] focus on straight numerical matching or numerical matching after applying conversion rules.
- Some approaches use SPARQL endpoints as learning sources, such as YAGO in [9] and DBpedia in [11,15], what makes them applicable to changing learning sets. While others are more focused on learning from scraped web pages which do not provide such ease to focus on a specific domain [4,8,17,19].
- Despite the fact that these approaches may be automatic or semi-automatic[2], some of them require manual actions (e.g., provide predefined conversion rules

---

[2] We are not referring here to the gold standards that are built manually or the semantic models that are constructed by domain experts.

```
SELECT distinct ?property ?class WHERE {
?property rdfs:domain ?class. ?property rdfs:range ?range.
FILTER(?range IN ( xsd:float , xsd:double , xsd:decimal ,
xsd:int , xsd:nonPositiveInteger , xsd:negativeInteger , xsd:long ,
xsd:integer , xsd:short , xsd:byte , xsd:nonNegativeInteger ,
xsd:unsignedLong , xsd:unsignedInt , xsd:unsignedShort ,
xsd:unsignedByte , xsd:positiveInteger ))}
```

Listing 1. Query numerical properties and their corresponding classes using domain and range

[15,21], a blacklist of properties [11] to improve the accuracy and abbreviations resolution [15,21].

3 Approach

Our approach can be divided into three main steps. The first step is *data extraction* for model training, where we extract the data of interest from a chosen SPARQL endpoint. The next step is *training the model* using the extracted data from the previous step. The third step is the *classification (typing) of the input data* using the trained model. The last two steps are explained in Sect. 3.2 as both are closely related to the fuzzy clustering technique.

3.1 Training-Data Extraction

The data extraction step looks for numerical properties and its values. It extracts them from a specified SPARQL endpoint. We explored three ways of getting numerical properties.

Extraction Method 1: the use of *rdfs:domain* and *rdfs:range* to extract classes and properties with numerical objects. We query classes with properties' *range* matching any of the numerical data types [14] (see Listing 1). This approach is fast even with large knowledge bases like DBpedia. The problem is that the obtained class/property pairs cover only a small subset of the actual data, which concurs with the findings reported by Weise et al. [20].

Extraction Method 2: We query the A-Box to get the numerical properties. The query (Listing 2) proposed by Neumaier et al. [11] to get all the numerical properties times out as, reported in their paper. We modified the query to fetch numerical properties for a single class (Listing 3), but that query was timing out as well.

```
SELECT ?p, COUNT(DISTINCT ?o) AS ?cnt
WHERE { ?s ?p ?o. FILTER (isNumeric(?o))} GROUP BY ?p
```

Listing 2. Extract all numerical properties for all classes [11]

```
SELECT ?property WHERE {
?subject a dbo:SoccerPlayer.
?subject ?property ?val FILTER(isNumeric(?val))
} GROUP BY ?property
```

Listing 3. Extract numerical properties for a given class

Extraction Method 3: query all properties for a given class and then filter the numerical properties on the client-side (Listing 4). After getting the list of properties, we query the endpoint to get the list of *objects* for each class/property combination. The added value of filtering numerical properties on the client side, besides overcoming the timeout problem, is distinguishing between numerical properties and properties that are not numerical but happen to have numerical values as a wrong entry (which happen often).

```
SELECT ?property WHERE {
?subject a dbo:SoccerPlayer. ?subject ?property [].
} GROUP BY ?property
```

Listing 4. Extract all properties for a given class

3.2   Fuzzy Clustering

Fuzzy c-means clustering is an unsupervised machine learning technique that generalizes *k-means* clustering [3]. In k-means, each data point belongs to a single cluster, while in fuzzy c-means each data point may belong to multiple clusters. The belonging of each data point is represented as a vector of values between 0 and 1, inclusively. This vector is often referred to as the *membership* vector. The values in each membership vector should sum to 1. The values in the membership vectors reflect how much it belongs to the corresponding cluster; the closer the value to 1 the stronger the belonging is to that cluster.

Notation and Variable Names:[3]

- m: weighting exponent to control fuzziness.
- d_{ik}: the distance between a datapoint k and a cluster center i.
- N: the number of data points.
- y_k: the data point value at index k.
- c: number of clusters.
- v_i: cluster at index i.
- u_{ik}: the membership value of a data point at index k to cluster i

---

[3] We use the same notation and variable names as in [3] (Bezdek et al.) 1984.

Learning: learning from the data extracted from the SPARQL endpoint, clusters are formed. Each cluster represents a class/property pair (e.g. <dbo: SoccerPlayer, dbo:height>). From the data extraction step, the number of clusters and their class/property pairs are fetched, but not the centers of clusters. In the learning step, the cluster centers (centroids) are the values of the computed features.

Features: there are two features used to calculate the centers of the clusters, the mean and the standard deviation. They are calculated for each cluster values (objects of a numerical property of a class) to become the center of it.

Clusters Centroids: computing the cluster centers (centroids) in fuzzy c-means requires the initial values for the membership matrix (which is composed of the membership vectors). We set the initial membership values to zero except for the class/property cluster they belong to, which would be 1. We apply Eq. 1 which uses the initial membership matrix and the computed features to compute the center of each cluster [3].

$$v_i = \left(\sum_{k=1}^{N} (u_{ik})^m y_k \Big/ \sum_{k=1}^{N} (u_{ik})^m \right) ; 1 \leq i \leq c \tag{1}$$

Classification: using the centroids, semantic properties from the SPARQL endpoint are assigned to numerical columns in the input file. This is performed using the *fuzzy c-means* clustering technique. The features of each numerical column in the input file are computed. The set of features are fed to the model (which contains the clusters) and results in a membership matrix. The membership matrix is computed using Eq. 2 by Bezdek et al. [3]. The membership matrix is composed of a list of membership vectors where each numerical column in the input file has a membership vector. Each membership vector contains the belonging to each of the corresponding clusters.

$$u_{ik} = \left(\sum_{j=1}^{c} \left(\frac{d_{ik}}{d_{jk}} \right)^{2/(m-1)} \right)^{-1} ; 1 \leq k \leq N; 1 \leq i \leq c \tag{2}$$

Overall Approach: after extracting numerical properties and their values from the endpoint, the features for each class/property pair is computed for their values. These features will be the centers for their corresponding class/property cluster. A model is then created using the clusters (centers) and their corresponding class/property combinations. The membership matrix is initialized accordingly (with value 1 to the matching cluster and 0 elsewhere). The model is used next to classify each numerical column in the input file(s) using the Eq. 2. The classification of each column will result in a membership vector showing the fuzzy belonging for each column in the input file(s) to clusters computed from the endpoint (see the algorithm in Listing 5).

Looking at the algorithm in Listing 5, the **data extraction** function starts by getting classes and properties (lines 1–2). Then, the values for each class/property combination (lines 4–5) are extracted and stored if the values are numerical (lines 6–7). Then, the values and the class/property pairs are returned (line 10). The variable $list\_of\_values$ (line 3) is a list of columns where a column from the function $getValues$ is appended to the list in each iteration. Next, the **learning** function is called (line 31) with the list of values for each class/property combinations and the list of numerical class/property pairs as arguments. After that, the features for the list of values for each class/property pair is computed (line 15). The features are considered the center of the cluster. The cluster is then created containing the class/property pair and center (line 15) and appended to the list of clusters (line 16). The membership matrix is then calculated from the clusters centers and then returned with the list of clusters (lines 18–19). The last part of the algorithm is to **classify** the input files with computed clusters. It sends the clusters, the membership matrix, and the input files as arguments. The first step in the classify function is getting numerical columns from the input files (line 22). Each of the numeric columns is then classified in the form of membership vector and indexed by the file name and the index of the column (lines 24–27). The classification is returned (line 28).

Differences to Classical Fuzzy C-Means: the above approach is not how classical fuzzy c-means clustering works exactly as in [3], despite the use of the same formulas for computing cluster centers and for classification. The first difference is in setting the initial membership matrix. In our case, we set it to 1's for the corresponding cluster, and 0's everywhere else. This is because we already know the cluster that each of the data points belongs to, which we already extracted from the endpoint. The second difference lies in the flow of the algorithm. In the classical version, the cluster centers adapt and change after the clustering of the data points which in return, affect the membership of the data points. This keeps looping until a threshold is met. In our case, clusters are computed once as we know the cluster each point belongs to (which we extract from the knowledge graph). Hence, the membership for the testing data is computed once. The last difference is that our approach resulted in a classification rather than a mere clustering. In other words, along with the membership result, we obtain the *type/class* for each cluster.

```
                                                          ▷ Data Extraction
 1: function DATAEXTRACTION(classes)
 2:     classes_properties ← getClassesAndProperties(classes)
 3:     list_of_values ← ∅
 4:     for all class, property in classes_properties do
 5:         values ← getValues(class, property)
 6:         if is_numeric(values) then
 7:             list_of_values ← list_of_values + values
 8:         end if
 9:     end for
10:     return list_of_values, classes_properties
11: end function
                                                               ▷ Learning
12: function LEARNING(list_of_values, classes_properties)
13:     clusters ← ∅
14:     for all values, (class, property) in list_of_values, classes_properties do
15:         center ← compute_features(values)
16:         clusters ← clusters + new Cluster(class, property, center)
17:     end for
18:     membership_matrix ← membership_from_clusters(clusters)
19:     return clusters, membership_matrix
20: end function
                                                              ▷ Classifying
21: function CLASSIFY(clusters, membership_matrix, input_files)
22:     input_columns ← getNumericalColumns(input_files)
23:     classifications ← ∅
24:     for all file_name, column_no, column in input_columns do
25:         membership_vector ← predict(clusters, membership_matrix, column)
26:         classifications[file_name][column_no] ← membership_vector
27:     end for
28:     return classifications
29: end function
                                                          ▷ Overall Approach
30: list_of_values, classes_properties ← DATAEXTRACTION(classes)
31: clusters, membership_matrix ← LEARNING(list_of_values, classes_properties)
32: classifications ← CLASSIFY(clusters, membership_matrix, input_files)
```

Listing 5: Algorithm to label semi-structured dataset

4   Evaluation

In this section, we evaluate our approach, checking how accurately it classifies the numerical columns of the input files. We compare the suggested types with our manual annotation and report the scores for the top 1, top 3 and top 5 candidate types for each property. We have the data and the source code publicly available [1,2].

Our evaluation is performed over two sets of data: Olympic Games and Web Data Commons [16]. The first one is collected by us and we report the process in Sect. 4.1. The Web Data Commons contains a set of web tables crawled from the web and annotated manually. In this section, we explain the testing for each used dataset and describe the datasets.

4.1   Olympic Games Dataset

Here we explain the process of collecting the Olympic Games data, describe the data, and report the results.

Data Gathering. After choosing the domain, we went to the Wikipedia page about the Olympics of 2020[4] and collected all the scheduled sports. Using Google search engine, we search for the data found in the SPARQL endpoint. We explore the returned links from the first two pages of results returned by Google. Data gathering is performed in a systematic way to reduce possible bias. In case multiple results are found, we take the first one that we come across. We focus on data that are in tabular forms such as CSV, TSV, Excel or web tables. Since we are using DBpedia for this test, we did not collect any data from Wikipedia (except for getting the list of games) to reduce the amount of possible bias as DBpedia has data extracted from Wikipedia. We show a description of the data set in Table 1.

Classes Lookup. We use Loupe[5] to look for classes from DBpedia. Loupe is an online tool for inspecting datasets [10]. We ignore any property in case it exists in the SPARQL endpoint and doesn't exist (or couldn't be found) on the web or the other way around. Properties co-existing in both are compiled for the tests. It is important to note that our algorithm is not dependant on Loupe, it is only used in data gathering step for the experiment.

Table 1. Information about the Olymic Games dataset

Number of files	12
Number of classes (Concepts)	12
Number of numerical columns	24

Experiment and Results. We perform the test for each class, so we create multiple models, one for each class. Then, for each model, we use the corresponding input files. For example, for the class dbo:Cyclist, we use a CSV file that contains information about cyclists and their weights. We do that for all the gathered classes. The results of each model are validated against the manual annotation. We compute the classification score of each class for k = 1, k = 3,

---

[4] https://en.wikipedia.org/wiki/2020_Summer_Olympics.
[5] http://loupe.linkeddata.es/.

Table 2. Classification score of English DBpedia's test

Top K-Candidates	Score (FCM)	Score (FCM) Merged	Score (MLSL)	Random
1	0.96	0.79	0.07	0.0025
3	0.96	0.92	0.07	0.0075
5	0.96	1.0	0.07	0.0125

and $k = 5$, whether it is in the top k candidates. So for $k = 5$, we check if the correct classification is in the top 5 candidates. After that, we average the scores for each k for each class. The classification scores are reported in Table 2. We refer to our approach as FCM (Fuzzy c-means). The score is the percentage of correct predicted properties in the top k candidates. For example, for $k = 1$ the score is 0.96 while the probability of the correct property to be picked randomly is 0.0025. We compare our approach to the work of Neumaier et al. [11]. We tested it with the same collection of CSV files and report the results in Table 2 (referred to it as "MLSL" which stands for Multi-Level Semantic Labeling). We also explored having a model with all the classes. This would make it generally more challenging to classify as the number of clusters increase. We applied our algorithm and we show the results in Table 2, referred to as "Score (FCM) Merged". We discuss the results in Sect. 4.3.

4.2   Web Data Commons Dataset

The Web Data Commons (T2Dv2) contains a total of 237 annotated tables, with 319 numerical columns in total spanning 41 concepts[6]. In T2Dv2, properties are not annotated, only the entity columns are annotated with DBpedia classes. We utilized this information for building the models.

Experiment and Results. We start by transforming the Web Tables from JSON to CSV. We create a model for each Web Table if it is not created and run the classification algorithm. A model will be created for each file using the class URI that each Web Table is annotated with in T2Dv2. We found that some of the Web Tables do not include numerical columns, so they will not have any classification. For each file, the corresponding model is used for the classification. We found 319 numerical columns in total, 232 of them can be understood while 87 of them were vague. Out of the columns that we understood, 137 of them actually existed in DBpedia. Our application was able to classify 124 out of the 137 columns (Table 3). We report the detailed results for each column (e.g. if it is vague, if it is found in DBpedia, etc.) with the rest of the results on the web [2]. In Table 4, we show the scores. The score is the of number correct annotated columns divided by the total number of columns. We consider the annotation of a column correct if a correct label (property) is in the top k labels. We can see

---

[6] Two files related to the class person is missing from the classification.

Table 3. Description of the classification

# numerical columns	319
# understood columns	232
# found in the knowledge graph	137
# classified columns	124

Table 4. Classification score of web data commons tables

Top K-Candidates	Score (FCM)	Random
1	0.34	0.0004
3	0.55	0.0012
5	0.83	0.002
10	0.91	0.004

that for k = 1, it has the probability of 0.0004 (0.04%) to get the correct label while our application gets it correctly for 0.34 of the input columns. For k = 10, our application gets a correct label 0.91 of the times while getting the correct property randomly is around 0.0004. We discuss the results in Sect. 4.3.

4.3   Discussion

It is obvious that the scoring results of Olympic Games are much higher than the scores of T2Dv2. Looking closely at the data, we can see that numerical data contained in the Olympic Games CSV files tend to be close to normal distribution (e.g. weight of soccer players). Normal distributions are commonly represented by the mean and variance. Looking at the features we used, we use the mean and the standard deviation, which is the square root of the variance. It is intuitive to see that in distributions that are normal (or close to normal) data are concentrated in the middle (close to the mean). For example, looking at the population density of countries, data are concentrated more to the left, looking close to a chi-squared distribution with k = 2. Such numerical properties are harder to classify. It also depends on the distance to other clusters. Some clusters are very close to each other, what results in the points being classified to a nearby but wrong cluster. An example of such cases are the two clusters "areaOfCatchment" and "elevation" of the class dbo:Lake. Sometimes this occurs with unrelevant properties (e.g. wikiPageID or imageSize).

Another thing we noticed is how properties that represent years are akin to understand. Looking at the distribution of values for years, it is hard to guess whether they represent dates of birth of people or dates of football matches. Even with such properties that are easy to mix up, there may be some kind of influence. For example, the birth dates of people are before their death dates. Nonetheless, machine learning techniques often cannot distinguish between birth dates and death dates [18]. The nature of the data used in the model also influences the classification score. For example, if we have two date-related properties, such as birth date (year) of Nobel prize holders, and birth dates (year) of young Internet millionaires, most probably, the classification won't be mixing the two. The first ones are generally older (less) than the birth dates of the young internet millionaires.

It is also important to note that the results we obtained are not comparable to the results we found in the literature without re-examining their data (when publicly available) and test it on all. The main reason is that most of the results reported in the state-of-the-art (except for [11,21]) showed the classification scores for a combination of numeric and non-numeric dataset and did not show the scores of each of them separately. The work by Neumaier et al. [11] is focused on numerical dataset, but the reported results are the scores of the classification of DBpedia's numeric *types* (they divided DBpedia's numeric properties into training and testing sets) and did not perform the test on CSV files. On the other hand, Zhang et al. [21] perform the test on CSV files. They learn from tables rather than from a SPARQL endpoint, and they use context information, such as surrounding text, for matching values and columns. Their approach has a different kind of information to learn from when compared to our approach, which learns from a SPARQL endpoint. To have an accurate comparison between two approaches, both should train on the same training set and test on the same CSV files (test set). This was only feasible in the case of Neumaier et al. [11], which have their software publicly available. We were able to test their approach with our data sets, using the English DBpedia for training. The approach MLSL yields a low classification score, which also concurs with [11] that it is not suitable for classifying CSV files. For Zhang et al. [21] we could not find the software to test it with our data set.

In addition, our approach is domain agnostic in a sense that the endpoint that is queried and the data that is extracted from to create the model is an input, and it does not have to be DBpedia or any specific endpoint. It only has to include data that are of the same *type* that exists in the input CSV files to be classified. Since our approach accepts concepts that are related to the input CSV files, there is no need to explore and include other unrelated concepts in the model. So, only the concepts that matter are included in the model that is used in the classification of the CSV files as shown in the data extraction Sect. 3.1 and the data extraction function Listing 5. Another advantage of our approach is that it does not require numbers to match between the values in the columns and the knowledge graph to label the column with the semantic type. As we focus on how the values reside in the space rather than to which entity these values belong. Moreover, the learning process is semi-automatic (or automatic if the classes are provided, like in the case of Web Tables from Web Data Commons). Despite the fact that concept discovery is not automatic and the user has to provide the concepts as an input to the model creation, the lookup for numerical properties for each concept and the extraction of data for each property is done automatically and included in the model; ergo there is no need to train the model manually by matching columns in CSV files to properties in endpoints.

5   Future Work

There are multiple ways that our work can be extended. One way is to generate R2RML mappings from the annotations that have been obtained. This can be used to generate RDF triples on the fly from the original source files using an application like morph-rdb [13] or ontop [5] while keeping the input files in their original format. Another interesting piece of future work would be to merge duplicate properties due to language differences (e.g. http://es. dbpedia.org/property/peso[7] and http://dbpedia.org/property/weight), different subdomains (e.g. http://dbpedia.org/property/peso and http://es.dbpedia. org/property/peso) or different naming (e.g. http://dbpedia.org/ontology/ elevation and http://dbpedia.org/property/elevationM). Our approach can be also extended to suggest the merge of properties that are similar so that two (or more) properties that represent the same thing can be combined in a single property with objects of both. This can be used to improve the classification and to clean endpoints (e.g. generate code that can be applied to the endpoint if such permission is granted). Furthermore, it can be used in the analysis of endpoints and their evolution (e.g. the change in property names), since our approach can detect similar numerical properties. It would be interesting to see if a property is divided or merged (e.g. max temperature per month vs. per year for a given place) and the effects of such actions. Considering the exact match of numbers as in the work of Zhang et al. [21] and combine it with our approach sounds as promising future work.

Acknowledgment. We would like to thank EIT Digital for their support. This project has been funded by the Spanish Ministry MINECO and FEDER - project TIN2016-78011-C4-4-R.

References

1. Alobaid, A., Corcho, O.: Olympic games 2020 (2018). https://doi.org/10.5281/ zenodo.1408563. https://doi.org/10.5281/zenodo.1408563
2. Alobaid, A., Corcho, O.: TADA-NumCol (2018). https://doi.org/10.5281/zenodo. 1410215. https://doi.org/10.5281/zenodo.1410215
3. Bezdek, J.C., Ehrlich, R., Full, W.: FCM: the fuzzy c-means clustering algorithm. Comput. Geosci. **10**(2–3), 191–203 (1984)
4. Cafarella, M.J., Halevy, A., Wang, D.Z., Wu, E., Zhang, Y.: WebTables: exploring the power of tables on the web. Proc. VLDB Endowment **1**(1), 538–549 (2008)
5. Calvanese, D., et al.: OBDA with the ontop framework. In: SEBD, pp. 296–303. Citeseer (2015)
6. Das, S., Sundara, S., Cyganiak, R.: R2RML: RDB to RDF mapping language (2012). https://www.w3.org/TR/r2rml/. Accessed 26 Oct 2017

---

[7] Which means weight in Spanish.

7. Dimou, A., Vander Sande, M.: RDF mapping language (RML) (2014). http://rml. io/spec.html. Accessed 6 Sept 2018

8. Goel, A., Knoblock, C.A., Lerman, K.: Exploiting structure within data for accurate labeling using conditional random fields. In: Proceedings on the International Conference on Artificial Intelligence (ICAI), The Steering Committee of The World Congress in Computer Science, Computer Engineering and Applied Computing (WorldComp), p. 1 (2012)

9. Limaye, G., Sarawagi, S., Chakrabarti, S.: Annotating and searching web tables using entities, types and relationships. Proc. VLDB Endowment **3**(1–2), 1338–1347 (2010)

10. Mihindukulasooriya, N., Poveda-Villalón, M., García-Castro, R., Gómez-Pérez, A.: Loupe-an online tool for inspecting datasets in the linked data cloud. In: International Semantic Web Conference (Posters and Demos) (2015)

11. Neumaier, S., Umbrich, J., Parreira, J.X., Polleres, A.: Multi-level semantic labelling of numerical values. In: Groth, P., et al. (eds.) The Semantic Web - ISWC 2016. ISWC 2016. Lecture Notes in Computer Science, vol. 9981, pp. 428–445. Springer, Cham (2016). https://doi.org/10.1007/978-3-319-46523-4_26

12. Pham, M., Alse, S., Knoblock, C.A., Szekely, P.: Semantic labeling: a domain-independent approach. In: Groth, P., et al. (eds.) The Semantic Web - ISWC 2016. ISWC 2016. Lecture Notes in Computer Science, vol. 9981, pp. 446–462. Springer, Cham (2016). https://doi.org/10.1007/978-3-319-46523-4_27

13. Priyatna, F., Alonso-Calvo, R., Paraiso-Medina, S., Padron-Sanchez, G., Corcho, O.: R2RML-based access and querying to relational clinical data with morph-RDB. In: SWAT4LS, pp. 142–151 (2015)

14. Prud'hommeaux, E., Seaborne, A.: SPARQL query language for RDF (2008). https://www.w3.org/TR/rdf-sparql-query/. Accessed 11 May 2017

15. Ritze, D., Lehmberg, O., Bizer, C.: Matching html tables to DBpedia. In: Proceedings of the 5th International Conference on Web Intelligence, Mining and Semantics, p. 10. ACM (2015)

16. Ritze, D., Lehmberg, O., Bizer, C.: T2Dv2 Gold Standard for Matching Web Tables to DBpedia (2015). http://webdatacommons.org/webtables/ goldstandardV2.html. Accessed 26 June 2018

17. Syed, Z., Finin, T., Mulwad, V., Joshi, A.: Exploiting a web of semantic data for interpreting tables. In: Proceedings of the Second Web Science Conference, vol. 5 (2010)

18. Taheriyan, M., Knoblock, C.A., Szekely, P., Ambite, J.L.: Learning the semantics of structured data sources. Web Semant. Sci. Serv. Agents World Wide Web **37**, 152–169 (2016)

19. Venetis, P., et al.: Recovering semantics of tables on the web. Proc. VLDB Endowment **4**(9), 528–538 (2011)

20. Weise, M., Lohmann, S., Haag, F.: Extraction and visualization of TBox information from SPARQL endpoints. In: Blomqvist, E., Ciancarini, P., Poggi, F., Vitali, F. (eds.) EKAW 2016. LNCS (LNAI), vol. 10024, pp. 713–728. Springer, Cham (2016). https://doi.org/10.1007/978-3-319-49004-5_46

21. Zhang, M., Chakrabarti, K.: Infogather+: semantic matching and annotation of numeric and time-varying attributes in web tables. In: Proceedings of the 2013 ACM SIGMOD International Conference on Management of Data, pp. 145–156. ACM (2013)

From Georeferenced Data to Socio-Spatial Knowledge. Ontology Design Patterns to Discover Domain-Specific Knowledge from Crowdsourced Data

Alessia Calafiore[1,2](✉), Guido Boella[1], and Leender van der Torre[2]

[1] University of Torino, Turin, Italy
alessia.calafiore@unito.it
[2] University of Luxembourg, Luxembourg City, Luxembourg

Abstract. So far, ontologies developed to support Geographic Information science have been mostly designed from a space-centered rather than a human-centered and social perspective. In the last decades, a wealth of georeferenced data is collected through sensors, mobile and web platforms from the crowd, providing rich information about people's collective experiences and behaviors in cities. As a consequence, these new data sources require models able to make machine-understandable the social meanings and uses people commonly associate with certain places. This contribution proposes a set of reusable Ontology Design Patterns (ODP) to guide a data mining workflow and to semantically enrich the mined results. The ODPs explicitly aim at representing two facets of the geographic knowledge - the built environment and people social behavior in cities - as well as the way they interact. Modelling the interplay between the physical and the human aspects of the urban environment provides an ontology representation of the socio-spatial knowledge which can be used as baseline domain knowledge for analysing and interpreting georeferenced data collected through crowdsourcing. An experimentation using a TripAdvisor data sample to recognize food consumption practices in the city of Turin is presented.

Keywords: Ontology Design Pattern · Socio-spatial knowledge
Data mining · Crowdsourced data · Social behaviour

1 Introduction

Over time, disciplines such as urban planning and design, Geographic Information System (GIS) science as well as urban geography have been concerned with the systematic study of the mutual interaction between people and the built environment. A deep understanding of people behaviour and experiences, describing the human-environment interplay, is pivotal in deciding what to design and why [39]. Scholars have applied several methodologies such as fieldwork through

© Springer Nature Switzerland AG 2018
C. Faron Zucker et al. (Eds.): EKAW 2018, LNAI 11313, pp. 34–49, 2018.
https://doi.org/10.1007/978-3-030-03667-6_3

observations, recording human activities as in the work by Whyte [51] on the *life* of the streets, or collecting surveys [18], as well as more computational techniques specified to urban contexts such as agent-based modeling and cellular automata [24] to simulate urban dynamics and predict the impact of certain urban policies in different scenarios. Through these methodologies the discovery of knowledge about places is almost exclusively on the shoulders of individual planners or geographers [25]. On the contrary, nowadays the spreading of web and mobile georeferenced apps is allowing to collect a wealth of data directly from citizens via crowdsourcing and crowdsensing. An increasing number of studies are relying on these new technologies and geo big data to derive knowledge about the way cities are experienced [8,12,13,32,38,46,47]. The so-called data-driven geography [34] is a research approach to urban studies which is likely to keep growing. However, to transform geographic big *data* into generalizable and sharable *knowledge*, some theoretical and methodological challenges need to be addressed. Thakuriah et al. in [49] have underlined that:

1. the extensive use of data-driven techniques to interpret social dynamics of contemporary cities is posing significant challenges in providing documented and standardized knowledge to integrate and compare different studies;
2. the analysis and interpretation of these new sources of observational big data need adequate cross-fertilization of knowledge with other disciplines (i.e. geography, urban planning) to derive relevant insights.

Regarding the first issue at hand, in information science computational ontologies have been acknowledged to be the core methodology for sharing a standardized and machine readable meta-description of a domain. Therefore, we have explored the state of the art ontologies which specifically apply to the context of GIS, and we have tried to fill the gap in their ability to represent the social and experiential character of the crowdsourced and crowdsensed Geographic Information (GI) taking inspiration from the humanistic notion of place.

In human geography, notions of *space* and *place* have been considered as the opposite extremes of a continuum which goes from the ideal geometrical abstraction of space to the experiential world of place [11]. The former is pivotal to deal with geo-physical phenomena and spatial relations (i.e. distance, mereotopology). The latter describes the environment from the human-centric perspective, and it seems to be the most adequate for representing the real-world semantic behind data coming from a crowd of people, expressing their own worldviews and experiences [48]. Although several ontologies have been developed to support GIS applications, as discussed in [16] and in [15], the geo-spatial domain has been mostly modeled from a space-centered rather than a place-centered perspective [4,20,29,41]. In the last decades, scholars have started discussing how to embed in GIS science thinking the ways human experience and perceive places by mean of ontology engineering [1,26–28,45]. Nevertheless, this research process is still ongoing.

Our work contributes to this wide research area by combining the support of a computational core ontology - decomposed in the form of reusable Content

Ontology Design Patterns (ODP) [2,17] - to represent urban contexts, with data mining techniques.

The paper is structured as follow: (i) background of our study is presented: on the one hand, computational ontology and Ontology Design Patterns; on the other hand, the application of Ontologies to Knowledge Discovery (ii) a set of Ontology Design Patterns to specifically deal with the social facet of the urban environment are described; (iii) an experiment aimed at semantically enrich a real data sample collected from a popular web platform, which of TripAdvisor, is shown; with this experiment we specifically test how the ODP can be used to organize data in the form of a *social* knowledge base about the food consumption practice in the city of Turin; (iv) in conclusion, the analysis results and methods employed are discussed.

2 Background

2.1 Computational Ontologies and Ontology Design Patterns

Computational ontology was originally defined by Gruber at the beginning of the nineties as *an explicit specification of a shared conceptualization* [22]. Ontologies in the context of information systems are designed with the explicit purpose to encode a formal description of knowledge either domain-independent (top-level ontology) or domain-dependent (core ontology and application ontology). They provide a representation of real-world objects and phenomena which is machine-understandable and human-alike. Ontology engineering is an expensive task and promoting the reuse of ontologies is acknowledged to be a valuable approach [2,37]. However, most ontologies, even if well-designed, are generally large and covering more knowledge that what might be needed [17]. Ontology Design Patterns have been introduced to overcome this problem, providing small and documented ontologies which can be seen as ontology's components [2,17]. In this work we present three connected Content ODPs [17] specifically engineered to deal with the social character of the urban environment. They aim at solving common problems in urban domain modelling: from the description of the built environment to the conceptualization of collective behaviour and the dynamic interplay between these two facets. They are presented following a structure consisting in: a motivating scenario, a set of informal competency questions, a diagram representation[1][2].

2.2 Ontology and Knowledge Discovery

In the so-called information age which gave birth to the Smart Cities, the decision-making process in several field, i.e. policies, justice, urban planning, is more and more relying on evidences from big data sources. As a consequence, the

---

[1] Note that: all the object properties depicted in the diagram have their inverse; we reused Dolce Lite Plus (prefix DLP) and a Time pattern (prefix Time).

[2] The owl files are available here: https://gitlab.com/misplaced/urbis.git.

use of data mining techniques in the process of knowledge discovery is becoming significantly relevant to the everyday life of people. In the context of urban areas analysing data to extract knowledge about people behaviour and their social differences is not a new research area. McKenzie and Janowicz [32] mined the geosocial behavior from FourSquare's check-ins to improve the reverse geocoding of locations. Call Detailed Records have been used to human behaviors recognition tasks or land use classification respectively in [13,36]. Social inequality and segregation have been discovered by Shelton et al. [46] using georeferenced social media data, and comparing the daily activity spaces of two different social groups - west end and east end residents in Louisville. These studies have produced interesting results proposing innovative methods and techniques; however, they remain framed into stand-alone case studies which cannot be grounded into a domain knowledge and be managed as knowledge bases.

An ontology-driven approach may overcome such a limitation through a semantic enrichment of the mining results [43].

In our work we provide prior knowledge in the form of ODPs which encode and make machine-understandable the social character of places given by people behavioural patterns. Those ODPs may guide the data mining process towards the exploration of behavioural patterns, concerning ways the city is *used* by targeted population, i.e. teenagers, tourists, elderlies, homeless, and be used to organize a social knowledge base at an urban level.

3   ODPs of the Urban Environment: An Overview

The urban environment is a complex interacting system of humans and human-made objects. From an extensive and interdisciplinary literature review we have identified three key building blocks to represent the urban domain: (1) the built environment; (2) people social behaviour; (3) the dynamic relation between these two facets. On the one hand, the built environment is modelled as composed of artefactual objects, on the other hand, there are people living in cities, whose behaviour strongly influence the social meanings attributed to urban artefacts in terms of the way they are used (i.e. a square as a meeting point place for teenagers). This latent knowledge about places is made explicit through the formalization of behaviour performed by specific social collectives of people. The notion of Social Practice is introduced and modelled to aggregate actions of individual agents into a generalizable behavior which follows a *performing mode* recognized by the carrier of the practice. To bridge these two facets of the urban environment, the physical - built and planned following certain technical principles - and the social - emerging from people collective behavior, we attribute the anti-rigid property of *role-playing* to urban artefacts which models the dynamic and multiple uses people can make of urban artefact. The next subsections describe three ODPs we have designed to model the identified building blocks. Subsections are structured to provide extract of the literature debate on each topic - which of urban artefact, social practice and urban artefact roles - and to document the design choices by mean of a motivating scenario, competency questions and a diagram representation.

3.1   Urban Artefact

As Zalta and Hilpinen in [52] put it "an object is an artefact if and only if it has an author". More recently, Guarino [21] added an other constraint to the identity of what he calls artefactual objects, which of being the result of an intentional act encoded in design specifications. In Borgo et al. [5] a more specific kind of artefact, that of technological artefact, is defined as a physical object which is, firstly, created by the carrying out by an agent (or group of agents) of a make plan for a physical object with a physical description id, and for which, secondly, a use plan exists. Starting from the work of these authors we have extended the notion of artefact into the one of urban artefact. The term urban artefact firstly appeared in Aldo Rossi's 1966 famous book "The architecture of the city" [42]. In his theory, he found the notion of urban artefact as pivotal to express that the elements of the built environment are essentially compliant with an architectural typology, but their realized uses go far beyond those planned by its designer. We argue that urban artefacts normally originate from an act of rational design and intentional construction of its author(s). In its the constitution an urban artefact, indeed, is the result of one or more designers who plan and organize the disposition of several elements to prototype an architectural typology. This is the case, for example, of "residential block", "office block", "hospital", "school". All these are examples of architectural typologies that are encoded in the design[3]. The latter deal with much more detailed information [9]: (i) Urban Design Specifications, which are design constraints concerning the physical structure of the urban artefact and its physical qualities; (ii) Urban Artefact Intended Uses, which are planned usages expressed in terms of modes of deployment, i.e., how an urban artefact is supposed to be used or exploited; (iii) Urban regulations, which are normative constraints concerning forbidden uses or explicit use rights allowed to specific classes of users. For instance, a park may include a playground where children may play, or where only children may play, and a green area where to keep off the grass; (iv) Urban Design Intended values, which are incommensurable values - they may be positive (i.e. sustainability) or negative (i.e. exclusion) - that result from the intentional act of the designer's choices.

Motivating Scenario

Cities generally provide information about buildings or infrastructure mostly focused on their technical characteristics, i.e. construction value, elevation, geometry (see Inspire specifications of building[4]). However, we may have cases where the interests are focused on other, even immaterial, aspects of the built environment such as the incommensurable values attributed to an artefact by the designer's culturally and socially situated intentions (i.e. a member working at

---

[3] Note that the design of an urban artefact may also be informally encoded by members of the community; this is the case of informal settlements or markets which reflect certain typologies of material arrangement but they are not the result of a formal process of construction.

[4] https://inspire.ec.europa.eu/Themes/126/2892.

an environmental council wants to know how many urban artefacts are designed to be sustainable and which architectural typology they mostly are); an urban planner needs to know which urban artefacts in the city are designed to be used for educational uses.

Competency Questions

- Who designed the urban artefacts?
- What urban artefacts were designed by a certain author or are of a certain architectural typology?
- Which are the architectural typologies of urban artefacts?
- What are the uses and the value attributed to urban artefacts by the designer's intentionality?
- Which architectural typologies are designed to fulfill a certain use?
- What are the regulations that rules the design and use of urban artefacts?

A Diagram Representation
This ODP is graphically presented in Fig. 1.

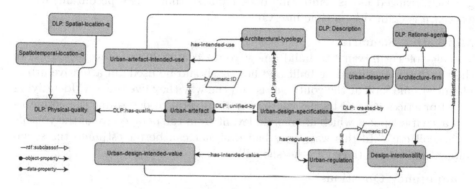

Fig. 1. A content ODP of urban artefacts.

3.2 Social Practice

Social Practice theory (SPT), or, more accurately, theories, are discussed in social science since the seventies by authors such as Bourdieu [6], Giddens [19] and Butler [7], in philosophy by Tuomela [50] and Schatzki [44]. The main objective of these authors is to open the way towards a conceptualization of social reality as lying on the middle ground of a continuum spanning from a purely individualistic view, to the idea of a social totality. Their assumption is that individual behaviour is the result of internalized social structures which vary among different social collectives of people. As a consequence, individual agency should also be considered as part of the wider we-attitude [50] which is carried by the social collective of "practictioners" [40]. Social practice theories have increasingly influenced the study of the city to explain how and why particular forms of human activity have been adopted, made popular, persisted and disappeared, adding a new heuristic to understand how places are socially characterized. From an ontological perspective, modelling social practices is a particularly challenging task, given their dual nature as actions performed by individuals and as the specific way of participating in the action performed by a social collective of people. Guizzardi et al. [23] tackle the issue of a collective entity to ontologically define the notion of powertype. They discuss powertype as proposed in Fine's variable embodiment argumentation: as an entity with two facets, one which is timeless and determines its identity, another which is its manifestation at a certain time. In the ODP we model social practice related to the use of urban artefacts with the following entities: (i) Social Practice - which is modelled as an endurant - is conceptualized as a powertype since on the one hand, it has its own property, it is recognized by a social collective (i.e. the social practice of Muslims praying is recognized by the Muslims collective), and, on the other hand, it is manifested in the actual behaviour of groups of rational agents that make use of urban artefacts with a common performing mode; (ii) the realized uses of an urban artefact, which can be classified as manifestation of a social practice, are collected in the realized use type class. (iii) differently than social practice, realized use is temporally dependent so that it is a perdurant, whose existence is defined by a time interval.

Motivating Scenario
The city of Turin wants to build a new youth center; in order to decide where the youth center should be built and how it should be used, an attentive urban planner would look at the youth needs and the way they live the city. Identifying social practices carried by the youth may be pivotal to determine the activities and activities spaces which are more relevant from the perspective of the youth's social collective. In this way, an urban designer can better estimate the social impact and risk of the choice he/she will make.

Competency Questions

- Who does engage in realized uses that can be classified as social practices?
- Which are the existing social collectives carrying out social practices?
- What are the types of urban artefacts' realized uses?

A Diagram Representation
The diagram of this pattern is depicted in Fig. 2.

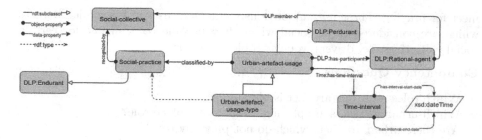

Fig. 2. A content ODP of social practices.

3.3 Urban Artefacts Roles

The final pattern we present has two objectives: on the one hand, it explicitly links the previous two ODBs which describe respectively the artefactual and social facets of the urban environment, allowing the possibility to create a core ontology of the urban domain; on the other hand, it is specifically designed to distinguish and compare between the lived places, realized uses of an urban artefact, and the way urban artefacts are planned to be used. To model the possible mismatch between the uses of an urban artefact attributed by the designer's intentionality and the uses that emerge from people collective behavior we introduce roles as first class citizen in the ontology. In particular, following the distinction made by Masolo in [30] we identified the need ot two kinds of roles: participating and social roles. The former stresses the participation of an entity in an event to play a role, i.e. passenger. This kind of role is temporally dependent on the event. The latter is founded in a relation that does not involve the participation in an event - i.e. citizen, student, teacher: these roles exist on the basis of an event, i.e. having a passport, being enrolled, working in a school, but it is not necessarily the case that the role is being played at the time of the event. Likewise, we have urban artefact participation role which is played by an urban artefact only during the progress of a realized use, and urban artefact social role which is played by an urban artefact when a social practice (an endurant) is related to it by a dependence relation. Actual uses of urban artefacts can be evaluated against the uses intended by design, rendering explicit whether a urban artefact is playing a functional place role - the actual use is compliant with the one intended by design - or not. The choice of introducing the place in terms of role is grounded in the human geography literature which refers to place as a relational concept [31,35], emerging from the interaction between people and the environment.

Motivating Scenario

A real context example which motivates the need of recognizing the possible mismatch between planned uses and collective behaviour has been discussed in [9]. It describes a square in Naples, Piazza del Mercato, which originally was planned to be a market place. Over time, as often happen with public places, several unexpected uses have emerged. Besides being a market place, it has been used as a parking place, as a place for playing football as well as where Muslims meet for praying. These uses are obviously emergent uses of Piazza del Mercato which are considered to be social when they become recognizable for certain social collectives, i.e. drivers, young people, Muslims.

Competency Questions

- Which roles an urban artefact is playing?
- Which urban artefacts are playing a functional place role?
- Are there urban artefacts which do not play any role?

A Diagram Representation
The diagram representation is provided in Fig. 3.

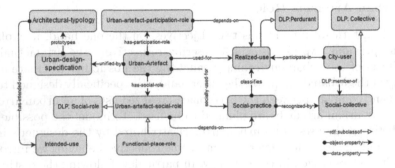

Fig. 3. A content ODP of urban artefacts roles.

4   An Experiment Using a Real-Data Sample

A data sample to experiment the use of the ODPs has been extracted from the TripAdvisor platform. The objective of the experiment was to organize the data and the mining results, following the key building blocks presented above, to provide new socio-spatial knowledge in a sharable and documented form. The datasets retrieved are about restaurants and their reviews in the city of Turin. Given these datasets, the artefactual facet is represented by Turin's restaurants; they prototype the restaurant architectural typology which has intended use the food consumption. Besides the typology of urban artefacts we want to deal with their roles depending on the behavioural and dynamic facet of urban contexts. Therefore, our analysis focuses on the diverse social practices of *dining out* in the city of Turin. We assume that each review corresponds to a realized use of dining out. Through data mining techniques we classify those realized uses which are manifestation of a social practice, so that social collectives of agents share a common performing mode in deciding where to dine out. From the recognition of social practices is possible to characterize restaurants in terms of the roles they are playing when they are socially used for a social practice. Note that, in this experiment, we concentrate on urban artefact social roles only since participation roles need to be temporally defined by a participation relation. Our datasets do not allow to rely on temporal information; it is reasonable to believe that the time associated with the review do not correspond with the actual use of the restaurant. The following sections summarize the workflow of the experiment.

4.1   Data Extraction, Selection, Preprocessing and Transformation

We crawled the TripAdvisor website to extract a sample of data regarding all the restaurants in the city of Turin, their reviews and information about the users' origin, which users may set in their profile's page. From the data collection we selected datasets and data attributes evaluating their relevance with respect to the ODPs models of the socio-spatial domain presented above. The datasets have been cleaned deleting repeated entries due to the extraction process and the user's dataset has been subset by removing unidentifiable users (that which were only known as *Facebook users on TripAdvisor*). The cleaned and preprocessed data have been organized and inserted in the database (see Fig. 5).

4.2   Data Mining

The data mining step mostly aimed at classify users as member of social collectives to partition the realized use of dining out into different type considered as manifestation of social practices. The social collectives which we could classify by our a priori knowledge were related to the users' origin. In particular, we distinguished between: **Italian tourists**, when the user has written reviews in Italian and his/her origin differs from a vector of possible ways to type "Torino" (i.e. "Turin", "Turin, Italy", etc.), else they were classified as **Turin locals**; **Foreign tourists**, when the user writes reviews in a language other than Italian. We also employed a clustering algorithm, the K-means, to identify emergent groups of users with similar preferences in terms of the restaurants' spatial location. Through the geocoding of the restaurants addresses we obtained the position expressed in coordinates. However, as spatial location, instead of directly using coordinates, we aggregated the restaurants and their reviews in neighborhoods since they better refers to what Egenhofer et al. [14] define the "naive geography" of the city. Neighborhoods have been considered as a "key living space [..] which symbolizes aspects of the identity of those living there to themselves and to outsiders" [33]. Given the strong symbolic meaning people associate with neighborhoods, we hypothesized that identifying clusters of users depending on their neighborhood preference structure may render more visible the shared attitude of some city users in dining out in certain areas instead of others as a consequence of the specific meanings that area holds to them.

We applied the K-means algorithm on an $m \times n$ matrix where m is the number of users and n is the number of Turin's neighborhoods. Each a_{mn} corresponds to the number of reviews the m-th user has posted in restaurants located in the n-th neighborhood. The algorithm has been run on five clusters, since running it n times on different k clusters and look at the total within clusters sum of squares, $k = 5$ minimizes the squared error. Figure 4 shows the spatial distribution of reviews in neighborhoods for each cluster of users. Users groups display very similar behaviour regarding the favourite neighborhood - the global maximum corresponds to the city centre in clusters 1, 2, 3 and 5. While the strong preference of dining out in the city centre is rather expected, the distribution of reviews made by users belonging to cluster 4 changes significantly. The latter, comparing to other clusters, has a very low number of reviews in the city centre and a global maximum corresponding to the San Salvario neighborhood. As a consequence of this result, we decided to consider those users as members of an emergent social collective, which we called **San Salvario users**.

4.3   Mapping and Ontology Based Data Access

The classification and clustering of users allow us to distinguish among the *dining out* behaviour of different social collectives - Italian Tourists, Foreign Tourists, Turin Locals and San Salvario users. The database structure is depicted in Fig. 5 using the UML notation. UML classes are represented in two colors to distinguish between those which were the input data and those resulted from the data mining step. The UML classes in the database have been mapped to classes of the ODPs and accessed through an Ontology Based Data Access (OBDA) approach. To manage the mapping we used Ontop, a platform and Protege Plug-in [3,10]. It is an open-source OBDA system that allows for querying relational data sources through a conceptual representation of the domain of interest, provided in terms of an ontology, to which the data sources are mapped. The virtual approach to OBDA of Ontop avoids the need to materialize triples to perform queries over the ontology in SPARQL language. Competency questions, such as *What social practices are performed?* or *What social roles an urban artefact is playing?*, can

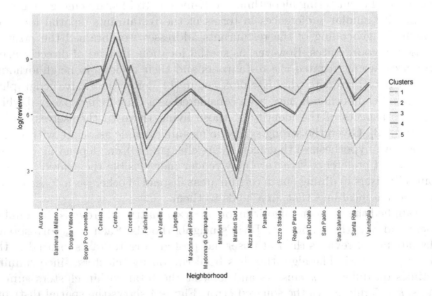

Fig. 4. The city-users neighborhood preference structure grouped in five clusters.

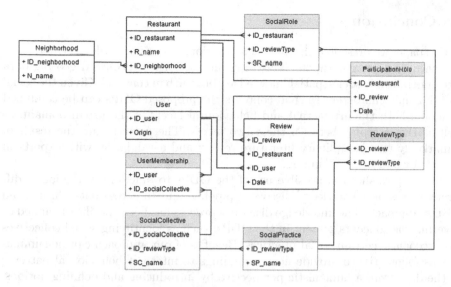

Fig. 5. An UML representation of the TripAdvisor database. Classes in orange resulted from the data analysis phase. (Color figure online)

be answered directly from the Protégé interface. Turin's restaurants are classified not only by their typology (restaurant) but also in their roles of being a dining place for tourists (foreign or Italian), locals or San Salvario users who generally go there. Such classification depends on the uses that are commonly done of those restaurants by certain social collectives, and it is much more dynamic than typological distinctions (Fig. 6).

Fig. 6. Screenshot of the mapping managed with the Ontop plugin in Protégé.

5   Conclusion

In this paper we presented the main contributions of our work, which is motivated by the need to transform the increasing amount of crowdsourced geo big data into generalizable socio-spatial knowledge about urban contexts. Given the social and dynamic character of urban contexts the proposed ODPs can be combined to model both the artefactual and behavioural facets of the urban domain, as well as the interplay between these two facets. The patterns are the result of a markedly interdisciplinary literature review and a validation with experts in geography and urban planning.

Second, we shown a possible use of the ODPs to function as a guide in different stages of a knowledge discovery pipeline and to access data through an OBDA approach. The knowledge discovery process has been specifically aimed at covering the concepts present in the ODPs: such as identifying social collectives that recognize certain social practices. Benefits of our approach can be summarize as follow: (i) we provide new groundings to interpret behavioural patterns in the data from a humanistic perspective by introducing and defining notions, such as social practice, which are inspired by geographical and sociological theories; (ii) the design of linked ODPs which modularize the representation of the urban domain to ease the reuse; (iii) the mapping and interpretation of data sources against each of the reusable ODP or a composition of them would favor the integration and sharing of case studies under a generalized representation.

However, further case studies with richer and diverse data sources are certainly needed. The approach presented here can, in fact, be applied to behaviours other than the dining habits: possible applications include extracting knowledge about the use of public space through the recognition of social practices associated to different demographics (who visits public spaces, e.g., young/old, male/female geographies) or interests (why visiting certain public spaces, e.g., sport, culture, tourism).

References

1. Alazzawi, A.N., Abdelmoty, A.I., Jones, C.B.: What can i do there? towards the automatic discovery of place-related services and activities. Int. J. Geogr. Inf. Sci. **26**(2), 345–364 (2012)
2. de Almeida Falbo, R., Barcellos, M.P., Nardi, J.C., Guizzardi, G.: Organizing ontology design patterns as ontology pattern languages. In: Cimiano, P., Corcho, O., Presutti, V., Hollink, L., Rudolph, S. (eds.) ESWC 2013. LNCS, vol. 7882, pp. 61–75. Springer, Heidelberg (2013). https://doi.org/10.1007/978-3-642-38288-8_5
3. Bagosi, T., et al.: The *Ontop* framework for ontology based data access. In: Zhao, D., Du, J., Wang, H., Wang, P., Ji, D., Pan, J.Z. (eds.) CSWS 2014. CCIS, vol. 480, pp. 67–77. Springer, Heidelberg (2014). https://doi.org/10.1007/978-3-662-45495-4_6
4. Ballatore, A.: Prolegomena for an ontology of place. In: Advancing Geographic Information Science, pp. 91–103 (2016)
5. Borgo, S., Franssen, M., Garbacz, P., Kitamura, Y., Mizoguchi, R., Vermaas, E.P.: Technical artifacts: an integrated perspective. Appl. Ontol. **9**, 217–235 (2014)

6. Bourdieu, P., Nice, R.: Outline of a Theory of Practice, vol. 16. Cambridge University Press Cambridge, London (1977)
7. Butler, J.: Notes Toward a Performative Theory of Assembly. Harvard University Press, Cambridge (2015)
8. Calabrese, F.: WikiCity: real-time location-sensitive tools for the city. In: Handbook of Research on Urban Informatics: The Practice and Promise of the Real-Time City, pp. 390–413. IGI Global (2009)
9. Calafiore, A., Boella, G., Borgo, S., Guarino, N.: Urban artefacts and their social roles: Towards an ontology of social practices. In: LIPIcs-Leibniz International Proceedings in Informatics, vol. 86. Schloss Dagstuhl-Leibniz-Zentrum fuer Informatik (2017)
10. Calvanese, D., et al.: Ontop: Answering sparql queries over relational databases. Semant. Web 8(3), 471–487 (2017)
11. Couclelis, H.: Location, place, region, and space. Geography's Inn. Worlds 2, 15–233 (1992)
12. Crooks, A., et al.: Crowdsourcing urban form and function. Int. J. Geogr. Inf. Sci. 29(5), 720–741 (2015)
13. Dashdorj, Z., Sobolevsky, S., Lee, S., Ratti, C.: Deriving human activity from geo-located data by ontological and statistical reasoning. Knowl.-Based Syst. 143, 225–235 (2017)
14. Egenhofer, M.J., Mark, D.M.: Naive Geography. Springer, Heidelberg (1995)
15. Fonseca, F.T., Egenhofer, M.J., Agouris, P., Câmara, G.: Using ontologies for integrated geographic information systems. Trans. GIS 6(3), 231–257 (2002)
16. Fonseca, F.T., Egenhofer, M.J., Davis Jr., C.A., Borges, K.A.: Ontologies and knowledge sharing in urban GIS. Comput. Environ. Urban Syst. 24(3), 251–272 (2000)
17. Gangemi, A., Presutti, V.: Ontology design patterns. In: Staab, S., Studer, R. (eds.) Handbook on Ontologies. IHIS, pp. 221–243. Springer, Heidelberg (2009). https://doi.org/10.1007/978-3-540-92673-3_10
18. Gehl, J., Svarre, B.: How to Study Public Life. Island Press (2013)
19. Giddens, A.: The Constitution of Society: Outline of the Theory of Structuration, vol. 349. University of California Press (1986)
20. Goodchild, M.F.: Formalizing place in geographic information systems. In: Burton, L., Matthews, S., Leung, M., Kemp, S., Takeuchi, D. (eds.) Communities, Neighborhoods, and Health. Social Disparities in Health and Health Care, vol. 1, pp. 21–33. Springer, New York (2011). https://doi.org/10.1007/978-1-4419-7482-2_2
21. Guarino, N.: Artefactual systems, missing components and replaceability. In: Franssen, M., Kroes, P., Reydon, T., Vermaas, P. (eds) Artefact Kinds. Synthese Library (Studies in Epistemology, Logic, Methodology, and Philosophy of Science), vol. 365, pp. 191–206. Springer, Cham (2014). https://doi.org/10.1007/978-3-319-00801-1_11
22. Guber, T.: A translational approach to portable ontologies. Knowl. Acquis. 5(2), 199–229 (1993)
23. Guizzardi, G., Almeida, J.P.A., Guarino, N., Carvalho, V.A.: Towards an ontological analysis of powertypes. In: International Workshop on Formal Ontologies for Artificial Intelligence, 24th International Joint Conference on Artificial Intelligence, Buenos Aires (2015)
24. Heppenstall, A.J., Crooks, A.T., See, L.M., Batty, M.: Agent-Based Models of Geographical Systems. Springer, Dordrecht (2011)
25. Kahila-Tani, M.: Reshaping the planning process using local experiences: utilising PPGIS in participatory urban planning. Ph.D. thesis (2015)

26. Kuhn, W.: Ontologies in support of activities in geographic space. Int. J. Geogr. Inf. Sci. **15**(7), 1–28 (2001)
27. Kuhn, W.: Semantic reference systems. Int. J. Geogr. Inf. Sci. **17**(5), 405–409 (2003)
28. Kuhn, W.: Geospatial semantics: why, of what, and how? In: Spaccapietra, S., Zimányi, E. (eds.) Journal on Data Semantics III. LNCS, vol. 3534, pp. 1–24. Springer, Heidelberg (2005). https://doi.org/10.1007/11496168_1
29. MacEachren, A.M.: Leveraging big (Geo) data with (Geo) visual analytics: place as the next frontier. In: Zhou, C., Su, F., Harvey, F., Xu, J. (eds.) Spatial Data Handling in Big Data Era. AGIS, pp. 139–155. Springer, Singapore (2017). https://doi.org/10.1007/978-981-10-4424-3_10
30. Masolo, C., Vieu, L., Kitamura, Y., Kozaki, K., Mizoguchi, R.: The counting problem in the light of role kinds. In: AAAI Spring Symposium: Logical Formalizations of Commonsense Reasoning (2011)
31. Massey, D.: A global sense of place. Aughty.org (2010)
32. McKenzie, G., Janowicz, K.: Where is also about time: a location-distortion model to improve reverse geocoding using behavior-driven temporal semantic signatures. Comput. Environ. Urban Syst. **54**, 1–13 (2015)
33. Meegan, R., Mitchell, A.: 'it's not community round here, it's neighbourhood': neighbourhood change and cohesion in urban regeneration policies. Urban Stud. **38**(12), 2167–2194 (2001)
34. Miller, H.J., Goodchild, M.F.: Data-driven geography. GeoJournal **80**(4), 449–461 (2015)
35. Murdoch, J.: Post-structuralist Geography: A Guide to Relational Space. Sage, London (2005)
36. Pei, T., Sobolevsky, S., Ratti, C., Shaw, S., Zhou, C.: A new insight into land use classification based on aggregated mobile phone data. Int. J. Geogr. Inf. Sci., 1–35 (2014)
37. Poveda Villalon, M., Suárez-Figueroa, M.C., Gómez-Pérez, A.: Reusing ontology design patterns in a context ontology network. In: Second Workshop on Ontology Patterns (WOP 2010) co-located at ISWC 2010, 08 de Noviembre 2010, Shangai, China. CEUR-WS (2010)
38. Quattrone, G., Mashhadi, A., Quercia, D., Smith-Clarke, C., Capra, L.: Modelling growth of urban crowd-sourced information. In: Proceedings of the 7th ACM International Conference on Web Search and Data Mining, pp. 563–572. ACM (2014)
39. Rapoport, A.: Human Aspects of Urban Form, vol. 3. Pergamon, Oxford (1977)
40. Reckwitz, A.: Toward a theory of social practices: a development in culturalist theorizing. Eur. J. Soc. Theory **5**(2), 243–263 (2002)
41. Roche, S.: Geographic information science II: less space, more places in smart cities. Prog. Hum. Geogr. **40**(4), 565–573 (2016)
42. Rossi, A.: The Architecture of the City. The MIT Press (1984)
43. Roy, P., Sathya, S.S., Kumar, N.: Ontology assisted data mining and pattern discovery approach: a case study on indian school education system. Adv. Nat. Appl. Sci. **9**(6 SE), 555–561 (2015)
44. Schatzki, T.R.: Social Practices: A Wittgensteinian Approach to Human Activity and the Social. Cambridge University Press, Cambridge (1996)
45. Scheider, S., Janowicz, K.: Place reference systems. Appl. Ontol. **9**(2), 97–127 (2014)
46. Shelton, T., Poorthuis, A., Zook, M.: Social media and the city: rethinking urban socio-spatial inequality using user-generated geographic information. Landsc. Urban Plan. **142**, 198–211 (2015)

47. Steiger, E., Resch, B., Zipf, A.: Exploration of spatiotemporal and semantic clusters of twitter data using unsupervised neural networks. Int. J. Geogr. Inf. Sci. **30**(9), 1694–1716 (2016)
48. Sui, D., Goodchild, M.: The convergence of GIS and social media: challenges for giscience. Int. J. Geogr. Inf. Sci. **25**(11), 1737–1748 (2011)
49. Thakuriah, P.V., Tilahun, N.Y., Zellner, M.: Big data and urban informatics: innovations and challenges to urban planning and knowledge discovery. In: Thakuriah, P.V., Tilahun, N., Zellner, M. (eds.) Seeing Cities Through Big Data. SG, pp. 11–45. Springer, Cham (2017). https://doi.org/10.1007/978-3-319-40902-3_2
50. Tuomela, R.: The Philosophy of Social Practices: A Collective Acceptance View. Cambridge University Press, Cambridge (2002)
51. Whyte, W.H.: City: Rediscovering the Center. University of Pennsylvania Press (1988)
52. Zalta, E.N., Hilpinen, R.: Artifact. In: The Stanford Encyclopedia of Philosophy (2004)

Conceptual Schema Transformation in Ontology-Based Data Access

Diego Calvanese[1(✉)], Tahir Emre Kalayci[1,2], Marco Montali[1], Ario Santoso[1,3], and Wil van der Aalst[4]

[1] KRDB Research Centre for Knowledge and Data, Free University of Bozen-Bolzano, Bolzano, Italy
{calvanese,tkalayci,montali,santoso}@inf.unibz.it
[2] Virtual Vehicle Research Center, Graz, Austria
emre.kalayci@v2c2.at
[3] Department of Computer Science, University of Innsbruck, Innsbruck, Austria
ario.santoso@uibk.ac.at
[4] Process and Data Science (PADS), RWTH Aachen University, Aachen, Germany
wvdaalst@pads.rwth-aachen.de

Abstract. Ontology-based Data Access (OBDA) is a by now well-established paradigm that relies on conceptually representing a domain of interest to provide access to relational data sources. The conceptual representation is given in terms of a *domain schema* (also called an ontology), which is linked to the data sources by means of declarative mapping specifications, and queries posed over the conceptual schema are automatically rewritten into queries over the sources. We consider the interesting setting where users would like to access the same data sources through a new conceptual schema, which we call the *upper schema*. This is particularly relevant when the upper schema is a reference model for the domain, or captures the data format used by data analysis tools. We propose a solution to this problem that is based on using transformation rules to map the upper schema to the domain schema, building upon the knowledge contained therein. We show how this enriched framework can be automatically transformed into a standard OBDA specification, which directly links the original relational data sources to the upper schema. This allows us to access data directly from the data sources while leveraging the domain schema and upper schema as a lens. We have realized the framework in a tool-chain that provides modeling of the conceptual schemas, a concrete annotation-based mechanism to specify transformation rules, and the automated generation of the final OBDA specification.

Keywords: Conceptual schema transformation
Ontology-based data access · Ontology-to-ontology mapping

1 Introduction

During the last two decades, (structural) conceptual schemas have been increasingly adopted not only to understand and document the relevant aspects of

© Springer Nature Switzerland AG 2018
C. Faron Zucker et al. (Eds.): EKAW 2018, LNAI 11313, pp. 50–67, 2018.
https://doi.org/10.1007/978-3-030-03667-6_4

an application domain at a high level of abstraction, but also as live, computational artifacts. In particular, the paradigm of Ontology-Based Data Access (OBDA) exploits conceptual schemas (also called ontologies) as an intermediate layer for accessing and querying data stored inside legacy information systems [23]. In the context of OBDA, the conceptual schema provides end-users with a vocabulary they are familiar with, at the same time masking how data are concretely stored, and enriching those (incomplete) data with domain knowledge. In this light, we call such a conceptual schema *domain schema*. The abstraction mismatch between the domain schema and the underlying data sources is covered by a second conceptual component, namely a mapping specification that declaratively links such two layers, expressing how patterns in the data correspond to domain concepts and relationships. Once an OBDA specification is in place, end-users may inspect the data sources by expressing high-level queries over the domain schema. An OBDA system handles this challenging setting by automatically rewriting such queries into corresponding low-level queries that are directly posed over the data sources, and by automatically reformulating the so-obtained answers into corresponding answers expressed over the domain schema. This supports domain experts in autonomously interacting with legacy data without the manual intervention of IT savvy. Notably, the actual data storage is completely transparent to end-users, who see the data in the form of conceptual objects and relations, *even though no actual materialization takes place*. From the foundational point of view, this is made possible by carefully tuning the expressive power of the conceptual modeling and mapping specification languages, and by exploiting key formal properties of their corresponding logic-based representations [4]. On top of these foundations, several OBDA systems have been engineered, *ontop* being one of the main representatives in this spectrum [3].[1]

OBDA has been subject of extensive research, and its advantages have been concretely shown in a plethora of application domains (see, e.g., [11,15,17]). Surprisingly, though, no research has been carried out on how to suitably extend the OBDA approach to handle the common situation where a higher-level conceptual schema (which we call *upper schema*) is needed to further abstract the knowledge captured by the domain schema. This happens when there is the need of viewing the domain schema and, in turn, the underlying data, according to a predefined structure, described by a reference model or an interchange format. In addition, different users may need to generate different views on the data, possibly using different upper schemas.

There are in particular two situations where the need for such a multi-level approach to data access is apparent. The first is when an OBDA specification is already in place, but certain types of users adopt reference models as an upper schema to understand the organization, create reports, and exchange information with external stakeholders. For example, the manager of an e-commerce company needs to reconstruct the state of contractual relationships and mutual commitments with customers, on top of the domain concepts of orders, pay-

---

[1] http://ontop.inf.unibz.it.

ments, and deliveries. In this setting, which we discuss later on in the paper, the main objective is to reuse the available OBDA specification.

The second is the one where data analysis applications are exploited to extract insights from legacy data. Here, the main problem is that the actual input for such applications consists of specific abstractions that may not be explicitly present in the legacy data, and that have to be represented according to the expected input data format. E.g., the application of process mining techniques to discover, monitor, and improve business processes [1] requires structured event data as input using key notions such as case (process instance), event, timestamp, activity, etc. Only event data that meet these requirements can be mapped onto input formats like XES [14] and used by process mining tools. This is especially challenging in the common case where the organization relies on legacy information systems and/or general-purpose management systems (such as ERP or CRM applications) [1]. Previous approaches [6,8] tackled this problem by hard-coding the XES format inside the log extraction framework. While XES is supported by a wide range of tools (such as *Disco* by Fluxicon, *Celonis Process Mining* by Celonis, *minit* by Gradient ECM, and many more), it does not provide native support for important aspects such as durative and hierarchical events (such as those naturally provided by enterprise systems like SAP, and consequently supported in process mining tools like Celonis Process Mining). Accounting for these aspects would require flexibility in the event log format, that is, the possibility of tuning the upper event schema based on the application context and needs.

To tackle such challenging but common scenarios, we propose to suitably extend the OBDA framework so as to take into account multiple conceptual layers at once. We focus on the case where two conceptual layers are present, accounting for the domain and upper schemas, and call the resulting setting *2-level OBDA* (2OBDA for short). However, all our results seamlessly extend to the case where more layers are present.

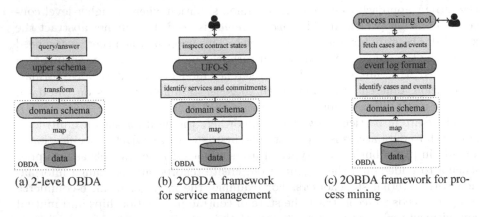

(a) 2-level OBDA   (b) 2OBDA framework   (c) 2OBDA framework for pro-
                          for service management   cess mining

Fig. 1. The 2OBDA framework, and two relevant concrete instantiations

Specifically, our contribution is threefold. First, in Sect. 4, we introduce the 2OBDA model as an elegant extension of OBDA. The core part of the framework is the *conceptual transformation* of concepts and relations in the domain schema into corresponding concepts and relations in the upper schema. This is specified in a declarative way, similarly to OBDA mappings but in this case accounting for ontology-to-ontology correspondences. The resulting framework (sketched in Fig. 1a) is different from well-known approaches for ontology matching [12] and ontology/schema mapping [9], the first being focused on overlapping conceptual schemas that work at the same level of abstraction, the second neglecting the presence of underlying data.

Second, we show how a 2OBDA specification can be automatically compiled into a classical OBDA specification that directly connects the legacy data to the upper schema, fully transparently to the end-users. Consequently, these can query the legacy data through the upper schema, by resorting to standard OBDA systems like *ontop*.

Finally, in Sect. 5, we report on how the approach has been realized in a tool-chain that supports end-users in modeling the domain and upper schema, and in specifying the corresponding transformations as annotations of the domain schema, whose types and features are derived from the concepts present in the upper schema. Notably, the tool-chain fully implements the compilation technique described above.

2   Motivation

In this section, we motivate the need for a multi-level OBDA approach, discussing scenarios in service management. We concentrate on the situation where the upper schema takes the form of a reference model, used by certain users to understand the business relationships existing between an organization and its external stakeholders. This is, e.g., the case of business managers and analysts, who often need to see the organization as an element of a bigger value chain, which consumes and provides services. To illustrate the challenges, we provide a concrete order scenario. In this scenario, the domain schema provides the basis to understand legacy data in terms of key concepts and relationships related to the notion of *order*. At the same time, managers employ the commitment-based core reference ontology for services (UFO-S) [20] as an upper schema, to understand and monitor the state of commitments that contractually relate the company and its customers. While the conceptual modeling community has made major advancements in the creation of reference models for services and commitments (as witnessed by UFO-S itself), no systematic approach to query organizational data through such reference models has been proposed so far. At the same time, recent attempts in formalizing relational, data-aware commitments, have either neglected the presence of legacy data [18] or the role of reference models [10].

2.1   The Order Scenario

In our order scenario, an organization called OHub acts as a hub between companies selling goods and persons interested in buying those goods. In particular,
OHub takes care of an order-to-delivery process that supports a person in placing an order, allows her to pay for the order, and finally deliver the paid goods
where the person desires. We assume that each order contains items that are
all provided by the same company, but different orders may be about goods
offered by different companies. Domain experts operating within OHub understand (some of) the key concepts and relations in this domain as specified by
the UML class diagram of Fig. 2, where the three subclasses of `Order` represent
three distinct order states (for simplicity, we do not consider cancellation).

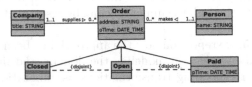

Fig. 2. UML class diagram of the order domain schema

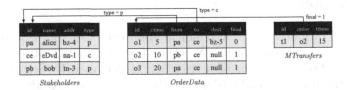

Fig. 3. Legacy schema of the order database, with some sample data. Directed edges
denote foreign keys, contextualized to those tuples that satisfy the filter on the edge

Fig. 4. Fragment of UFO-S used as upper schema extracted from UFO-S

At the same time, the employees of OHub use a legacy management system
to handle orders, and are unaware of how the actual data about orders and their

involved stakeholders are stored. Such a management system relies on a relational database, whose schema is shown in Fig. 3 together with some sample data. The schema consists of three tables, respectively keeping track of the stakeholders of OHub, of the orders managed by OHub, and of the respective money transfers. Specifically, the *Stakeholders* table stores the main information about companies selling and delivering goods, and persons who buy such goods trough OHub. These two kinds of stakeholders are distinguished by the type attribute (which corresponds to string p for persons, and c for companies). The *OrderData* table stores the active and past orders managed by OHub. For each order, the table stores the creation time, the person who made it, the company responsible for the order, the destination address, and a flag indicating whether the order has been finalized by the person, or is still in the creation phase. It is intended that if the destination address is not specified (i.e., it is null), then the address of the person (as specified in the *Stakeholders* table) should be used for delivery. Finally, table *MTransfers* keeps track of monetary transfers related to finalized orders, for simplicity only recalling the transaction id, its time, and the order to which the transaction refers.

Managers of OHub often need to understand orders and their states in contractual terms, that is, as business objects and relationships that contractually bind OHub with its suppliers and customers. This is crucial, in turn, to assess the quality of service of OHub, and to detect whether the mutual commitments induced by order contracts are indeed honored or not. To do so, they adopt UFO-S as a reference model to define which services are offered by OHub, and which commitments relate to those services [20]. A portion of this reference model is shown in Fig. 4. We only included the parts relevant for this small case study. We also incorporated explicit state attributes into the commitment classes, accounting for the different phases in which a commitment can be at a given time (pending, discharged, canceled, etc.) [10,18]. With UFO-S at hand, managers would like to inspect the negotiations and agreements established by companies and persons via OHub. We consider for simplicity only the following two commitments. Contractually, when a person makes an order, she becomes obliged to issuing a corresponding payment. In turn, upon payment the selling company becomes committed towards the actual delivery of the order.

2.2   Challenges

The OHub scenario presents a series of very interesting challenges in conceptual modeling and data access. Let us consider the need of OHub managers to inspect which commitments currently exist, and in which state they are. Obviously, they cannot directly formulate queries of this form on top of the legacy data, due to a vocabulary mismatch. A possible solution would be to create a dedicated OBDA specification that directly connects the legacy data to the UFO-S upper schema. However, this is unrealistic from the conceptual modeling point of view, for a twofold reason. First and foremost, linking data directly to concepts and relations in the upper schema requires to first understand the data in terms of domain notions, and only then to establish suitable connections between the domain and the upper level. For example, to inspect the contractual relationships between OHub's stakeholders, one has to clarify how orders, payments, and deliveries are reflected in the data, before identifying how mutual commitments about payments and deliveries are established and evolved. In addition, an OBDA specification connecting data to the domain schema could already be in place independently on these UFO-S related needs. It is well-known that creating an OBDA specification, especially for what concerns the understanding of the legacy data structures and the construction of corresponding mappings, is a labor-intensive and challenging task, similarly to alternative approaches to data access and integration [8]. If such a specification is already in place, it would be beneficial to build on it so as to gracefully integrate the upper schema into the picture, instead of creating another OBDA specification from scratch.

A second issue is related to the fact that reference models and upper ontologies are typically meant to capture a plethora of concepts and relations spanning over a wide range of application domains, with the purpose of resolving ambiguities and misunderstandings [13,20,22]. In a specific application domain such as that of OHub, only a small portion of the whole reference model is needed to capture the commitments of interest.

To attack these issues, we propose to ground the paradigm shown in Fig. 1a into the concrete framework of Fig. 1b. Here, a standard OBDA approach is adopted to make sense of the legacy data in terms of the domain schema. This can be used, e.g., to declare that each entry in the *OrderData* table corresponds to an order, whose supplying company is obtained from the entry in *Stakeholders* pointed by the to column, and whose making person is obtained from the entry in *Stakeholders* pointed by the from column. The state of the order is, in turn, declared as follows: the order is *open* if the corresponding entry in *OrderData* has final $= 0$; *closed* if the corresponding entry in *OrderData* has final $= 1$, but no monetary transfer exists in *MTransfers* for the order; *paid* if the corresponding entry in *OrderData* has final $= 1$, and there exists an entry in *MTransfers* pointing to the order. Once this OBDA specification is in place, domain experts can forget about the schema of the legacy data, and work directly at the level of the domain schema. The domain schema is then employed to declare which concepts and relations define the UFO-S notions of service provider, target customer, and corresponding offering and customer commitments. This identification step is seen as a declarative specification of how the domain schema of orders can be transformed into (a portion of) the UFO-S upper schema. Here, one could declaratively specify that: *(i)* Each closed order gives rise to a *pending* customer commitment binding its making person (i.e., its target customer) to paying it. *(ii)* Each paid order corresponds to a *discharged* customer commitment related to the order payment, and to a *pending* offering commitment binding its supplying company (i.e., its service provider) to delivering it.

Once the mapping and transformation rules are specified, OHub managers can express queries over UFO-S, and obtain answers automatically computed over the legacy data. For example, upon asking about all the pending commitments existing in the state of affairs captured by the data in Fig. 3, one would get back two answers: one indicating that company eDvd has a pending commitment related to the delivery of order o2, and one telling that person Alice is committed to pay order o3.

This approach favors modularity and separation of concerns, since the mapping and the transformation rules can vary independently from each other. In particular, if the underlying data storage changes, only the mapping to the domain schema needs to be updated, without touching the definition of commitments. If instead the contract is updated, the domain-to-upper schema transformation needs to change accordingly, without touching the OBDA specification. In addition, the approach is driven by the actual querying requirements, that is, only the aspects of the upper schema that are relevant for querying need to be subject of transformation rules. The transformation rules themselves also provide a way to customize the view over the data. Even with the same upper schema, two different sets of transformation rules might provide different views over the data represented by the domain schema. We might even go beyond that, and consider situations where several upper schemas are provided, each with different sets of transformation rules. We do not explicitly consider this latter scenario in the following, since it can be obtained by multiple instantiations of the 2OBDA scenario.

3   Ontology-Based Data Access

We adopt a variant of Description Logics (DLs) [2] as a conceptual modeling language in which to express conceptual schemas. Specifically, we rely on $DL\text{-}Lite_{\mathcal{A}}$ [4], a prominent member of the $DL\text{-}Lite$ family [5] of lightweight DLs, which have been specifically designed for efficiently accessing large amounts of data through an ontology. We introduce now such DL, and recall then the standard formalization of OBDA [4, 21, 23].

$DL\text{-}Lite_{\mathcal{A}}$ [21]. In $DL\text{-}Lite_{\mathcal{A}}$, the domain of interest is modeled through *concepts*, representing sets of (abstract) objects, *roles*, representing binary relations between objects, and *attributes*, representing binary relations between objects and values. Values belong to concrete datatypes, such as strings, integers, etc., but, for simplicity, we do not distinguish between different datatypes, and use a unique datatype instead (e.g., $STRING$) for all values in the system. The syntax of $DL\text{-}Lite_{\mathcal{A}}$ concept expressions B and role expressions R is given by the grammar

$$B \longrightarrow N \mid \exists R \mid \delta(U), \qquad R \longrightarrow P \mid P^-,$$

where N, P, and U (here and in the following) denote a *concept name*, a *role name*, and an *attribute name*, respectively. The role P^- denotes the *inverse of role* P, and the concept $\exists R$, also called *unqualified existential restriction*, denotes the *domain* of a role R, i.e., the set of objects that R relates to some object. Similarly, the concept $\delta(U)$ denotes the *domain* of an attribute U, i.e., the set of objects that U relates to some value. Notice that the domain $\exists P^-$ of the inverse of role P actually represents the *range* of role P. Instead, since we have adopted a unique datatype for all values, there is no need to refer to the range of an attribute (since it is always, e.g., *STRING*).

A *DL-Lite$_A$ Knowledge Base* (KB) $\mathcal{K} = \langle \mathcal{T}, \mathcal{A} \rangle$ consists of a TBox $\mathcal{T}$, modeling intensional information, and an ABox $\mathcal{A}$, modeling extensional information. The *TBox* consists of a finite set of *TBox assertions* of the following forms:

$$
\begin{array}{lll}
B_1 \sqsubseteq B_2, & B_1 \sqsubseteq \neg B_2, & \\
R_1 \sqsubseteq R_2, & R_1 \sqsubseteq \neg R_2, & (\text{funct } R), \\
U_1 \sqsubseteq U_2, & U_1 \sqsubseteq \neg U_2, & (\text{funct } U).
\end{array}
$$

From left to right, assertions of the first column respectively denote *inclusions* between concepts, roles, and attributes; assertions of the second column denote *disjointness* between concepts, roles, and attributes; assertions of the last column denote *functionality* of roles and attributes. In order to ensure the desired computational properties of *DL-Lite$_A$* that make it suitable as an ontology language in the context of OBDA, we impose that in a TBox, the roles and attributes occurring in functionality assertions cannot be specialized (i.e., they cannot occur in the right-hand side of inclusions) [4,5].

Example 1. We give some of the *DL-Lite* TBox assertions that capture the conceptual schema in Fig. 2, where intuitively concepts correspond to classes, roles to binary associations, and DL attributes to UML attributes:

$$
\begin{array}{llll}
Open \sqsubseteq Order, & Paid \sqsubseteq \neg Open, & \exists makes \sqsubseteq Person, & Order \sqsubseteq \exists makes^-, \\
Paid \sqsubseteq Order, & \delta(name) \sqsubseteq Person, & \exists makes^- \sqsubseteq Order, & (\text{funct } makes^-), \quad \ldots
\end{array}
$$

These assertions state that *Open* and *Paid* are sub-concepts of *Order* and that *Paid* and *Open* are disjoint. They further specify the domain of *name* and *makes* and the range of *makes*, that orders are made by someone, and that the inverse of *makes* is functional. ∎

The *Abox* consists of a finite set of *ABox assertions* of the form $N(t_1)$, $P(t_1, t_2)$, or $U(t_1, v)$, where t_1 and t_2 denote *individuals* (representing abstract objects) and v denotes a *value*. A *constant* is an individual or a value. The *domain of an ABox* $\mathcal{A}$, denoted by $\textsc{adom}(\mathcal{A})$, is the (finite) set of constants appearing in $\mathcal{A}$.

For the semantics of *DL-Lite$_A$*, we note that we interpret objects and values over disjoint domains, and that for both we adopt the *Unique Name Assumption*, i.e., different terms denote different objects (or values). The various types of TBox assertions (i.e., inclusion, disjointness, and functionality) are satisfied when the corresponding condition holds for the interpretation of the involved concepts, role(s), or attribute(s). We refer to [4] for details. We also adopt the usual notions of *satisfaction*, *model*, and *entailment* [4].

We point out that *DL-Lite$_R$*, which is the sublanguage of *DL-Lite$_A$* obtained by dropping functionality assertions, is the formal counterpart of the OWL 2 QL language standardized by the W3C [19] as a profile of the Web Ontology Language OWL 2.

Queries. We consider queries that are formulated over the conceptual schema elements, and whose answers are formed by terms of the ABox. A *conjunctive query* (CQ) $q(\vec{x})$ over a TBox $\mathcal{T}$ is a first-order logic (FOL) formula of the form $\exists \vec{y}.conj(\vec{x}, \vec{y})$, whose free variables (a.k.a. *answer variables*) are $\vec{x}$. The formula $conj(\vec{x}, \vec{y})$ is a conjunction of atoms of the form $N(z)$, $P(z, z')$, and $U(z, z')$ where N, P and U respectively denote a concept, a role, and an attribute name of $\mathcal{T}$, and z, z' are constants, or variables in $\vec{x}$ or $\vec{y}$. If q has no answer variables, then it is called *boolean*. A *union of conjunctive queries* (UCQ) $q(\vec{x})$ over $\mathcal{T}$ is a disjunction of CQs with the same answer variables $\vec{x}$, i.e., a FOL formula of the form: $\exists \vec{y}_1.conj_1(\vec{x}, \vec{y}_1) \vee \cdots \vee \exists \vec{y}_n.conj_n(\vec{x}, \vec{y}_n)$.

The *(certain) answers* to a (U)CQ $q(\vec{x})$ over a KB $\mathcal{K} = \langle \mathcal{T}, \mathcal{A} \rangle$ is the set $\mathsf{cert}(q, \mathcal{K})$ of substitutions[2] σ of the answer variables $\vec{x}$ with constants in $\mathrm{ADOM}(\mathcal{A})$, such that the closed FOL formula $q\sigma$ evaluates to true in every model of $\mathcal{K}$. The answer to a boolean query is either true (i.e., the empty substitution) or false (i.e., no substitution). Computing $\mathsf{cert}(q, \mathcal{K})$ of a UCQ q over a *DL-Lite$_{\mathcal{A}}$* KB $\mathcal{K} = \langle \mathcal{T}, \mathcal{A} \rangle$ is polynomial in the size of $\mathcal{T}$ and in AC^0 in the size of $\mathcal{A}$. This is a consequence of the fact that *DL-Lite$_{\mathcal{A}}$* enjoys *FOL rewritability*, which in our setting means that for every UCQ q, one can compute $\mathsf{cert}(q, \mathcal{K})$ by evaluating the UCQ $\mathsf{rew}(q, \mathcal{T})$ over $\mathcal{A}$ considered as a database, where $\mathsf{rew}(q, \mathcal{T})$ is the so-called *perfect rewriting* of q w.r.t. $\mathcal{T}$ [4,5,23].

Ontology-Based Data Access (OBDA). An *OBDA specification* is a triple $\mathcal{S} = \langle \mathcal{R}, \mathcal{M}, \mathcal{T} \rangle$, where: *(i)* $\mathcal{R}$ is relational database schema, consisting of a finite set of relation schemas, possibly with constraints, *(ii)* $\mathcal{T}$ is a *domain schema*, formalized as a *DL-Lite$_{\mathcal{A}}$* TBox; and *(iii)* $\mathcal{M}$ is an *OBDA mapping*, consisting of a set of mapping assertions. These specify how to extract data from the underlying database and how to use them to instantiate the elements of the domain schema. To denote instances of the domain schema, we consider a countably infinite set Λ of (uninterpreted) functions, and apply them to the values retrieved from the database. Specifically, each *mapping assertion* has the form $\varphi(\vec{x}) \rightsquigarrow \psi(\vec{y}, \vec{t})$, where $\varphi(\vec{x})$ is an arbitrary SQL query over $\mathcal{R}$ with $\vec{x}$ as output variables, and $\psi(\vec{y}, \vec{t})$ is a conjunction of atoms over $\mathcal{T}$ using variables $\vec{y} \subseteq \vec{x}$ and terms $\vec{t}$, where each term in $\vec{t}$ has the form $f(\vec{z})$, with $f \in \Lambda$ and $\vec{z} \subseteq \vec{x}$.

Example 2. In our running example, the following mapping assertion is used to populate the concept *Person* and the corresponding attribute *name*, by selecting in the table *Stakeholders* entries for which the value of type equals 'p':

```
SELECT id as pid, name FROM Stakeholders WHERE type = 'p'
```
$$\rightsquigarrow \quad Person(\mathbf{person}(\mathtt{pid})) \wedge name(\mathbf{person}(\mathtt{pid}), \mathtt{name})$$

The following mapping assertion is used to populate the role *makes* with all pairs consisting of an order and the corresponding person who made the order:

```
SELECT OD.id as oid, S.id as pid FROM OrderData OD, Stakeholders S
WHERE OD.from = S.id          ⤳    makes(person(pid), order(oid))
```

■

---

[2] As customary, we view a substitution of $\vec{x}$ as a tuple of constants, one for each variable in $\vec{x}$.

Given an OBDA specification $\mathcal{S} = \langle \mathcal{R}, \mathcal{M}, \mathcal{T} \rangle$ and a database instance $\mathcal{D}$ that conforms to $\mathcal{R}$, the pair $\mathcal{J} = \langle \mathcal{S}, \mathcal{D} \rangle$ is called an *OBDA instance* (for $\mathcal{S}$). Each mapping assertion $m = \varphi(\vec{x}) \rightsquigarrow \psi(\vec{y}, \vec{t})$ in $\mathcal{M}$ generates from $\mathcal{D}$ a set $m(\mathcal{D}) = \bigcup_{\vec{c} \in \mathsf{eval}(\varphi, \mathcal{D})} \psi[\vec{x}/\vec{c}]$ of ABox assertions, where $\mathsf{eval}(\varphi, \mathcal{D})$ denotes the evaluation of $\varphi(\vec{x})$ over $\mathcal{D}$, and where $\psi[\vec{x}/\vec{c}]$ is the set (as opposed to the conjunction) of atoms obtained by substituting in $\psi(\vec{y}, \vec{t})$ each variable $x \in \vec{x}$ with the corresponding constant $c \in \vec{c}$. Then, the *(virtual) ABox*[3] *generated by* $\mathcal{M}$ *from* $\mathcal{D}$ is $\mathcal{M}(\mathcal{D}) = \bigcup_{m \in \mathcal{M}} m(\mathcal{D})$. Given an OBDA instance $\mathcal{J} = \langle \mathcal{S}, \mathcal{D} \rangle$ with $\mathcal{S} = \langle \mathcal{R}, \mathcal{M}, \mathcal{T} \rangle$, a *model* for $\mathcal{J}$ is a model of the KB $\langle \mathcal{T}, \mathcal{M}(\mathcal{D}) \rangle$. We say that $\mathcal{J}$ is *satisfiable* if it admits a model.

A UCQ q over an OBDA specification $\mathcal{S} = \langle \mathcal{R}, \mathcal{M}, \mathcal{T} \rangle$ is simply a UCQ over $\mathcal{T}$, and given an OBDA instance $\mathcal{J} = \langle \mathcal{S}, \mathcal{D} \rangle$, the *certain answers to* q *over* $\mathcal{J}$, denoted $\mathsf{cert}(q, \mathcal{J})$, are defined as $\mathsf{cert}(q, \langle \mathcal{T}, \mathcal{M}(\mathcal{D}) \rangle)$. To compute $\mathsf{cert}(q, \mathcal{J})$, instead of materializing the virtual ABox $\mathcal{M}(\mathcal{D})$, we can apply the following three-step approach [21]: *(i)* rewrite q to compile away $\mathcal{T}$, obtaining $q_r = \mathsf{rew}(q, \mathcal{T})$; *(ii)* use the mapping $\mathcal{M}$ to *unfold* q_r into a query over $\mathcal{R}$, denoted by $q_u = \mathsf{unf}(q_r, \mathcal{M})$, which turns out to be an SQL query; *(iii)* evaluate q_u over $\mathcal{D}$, obtaining $\mathsf{eval}(q_u, \mathcal{D})$. It has been shown in [21] that $\mathsf{cert}(q, \langle \langle \mathcal{R}, \mathcal{M}, \mathcal{T} \rangle, \mathcal{D} \rangle) = \mathsf{eval}(\mathsf{unf}(\mathsf{rew}(q, \mathcal{T}), \mathcal{M}), \mathcal{D})$.

Example 3. Recall our example, and consider the query $q(x) = Person(x)$ that retrieves all persons. Since $\mathcal{T}$ contains $\exists makes \sqsubseteq Person$ and $\exists name \sqsubseteq Person$, the rewriting of $q(x)$ w.r.t. $\mathcal{T}$ gives us the UCQ $q_r(x) = Person(x) \vee \exists y.makes(x, y) \vee \exists z.name(x, z)$, and the unfolding of $q_r(x)$ w.r.t. $\mathcal{M}$ gives us the following SQL query $q_u(x)$:

```
SELECT id as x FROM Stakeholders WHERE type = 'p'     UNION
SELECT S.id as x FROM OrderData OD, Stakeholders S WHERE OD.from = S.id
```

∎

4   2-Level Ontology Based Data Access

Within an OBDA specification $\mathcal{S} = \langle \mathcal{R}, \mathcal{M}, \mathcal{T} \rangle$, the TBox $\mathcal{T}$ provides a specific conceptual view, which we called *domain schema*, of the domain of interest, through which the data sources $\mathcal{R}$ are accessed. However, as illustrated in Sect. 2, users might be interested in accessing the same data sources through a different conceptual schema $\mathcal{T}'$, which we called *upper schema*, without the need to redefine from scratch the relationship between $\mathcal{T}'$ and $\mathcal{R}$. Thus, we need a mechanism to relate the upper schema $\mathcal{T}'$ to the domain schema $\mathcal{T}$, and to exploit this connection, together with the information on $\mathcal{T}$ and $\mathcal{M}$ encoded in $\mathcal{S}$, for answering queries over the upper schema.

---

[3] Such ABox is called *virtual* because in general it is not actually materialized.

Here we introduce a solution based on transformation rules that declaratively map the domain schema $\mathcal{T}$ to the upper schema $\mathcal{T}'$ and that are based on so-called *GAV mappings*. Such form of mappings have been widely used in the data integration setting (cf. [16]) as a natural means to connect a global schema used for querying a data integration system to the schemas of the underlying data sources. Formally, given two TBoxes $\mathcal{T}$ and $\mathcal{T}'$, a *schema transformation* from $\mathcal{T}$ to $\mathcal{T}'$, is a set $\mathcal{N}$ of *transformation rules*, each of the form $\varphi(\vec{x}) \rightsquigarrow \psi(\vec{y}, \vec{t})$, where $\varphi(\vec{x})$ is a UCQ over $\mathcal{T}$ with answer variables $\vec{x}$, and $\psi(\vec{y}, \vec{t})$ is a conjunction of atoms over $\mathcal{T}'$ over variables $\vec{y} \subseteq \vec{x}$ and terms $\vec{t}$.

Similarly to the case of OBDA mappings, the terms in $\vec{t}$ have the form $f(\vec{z})$, with $f \in \Lambda$ and $\vec{z} \subseteq \vec{x}$, and they are used to construct the identifiers of individuals for $\mathcal{T}'$. However, such identifiers might also be returned directly by the query φ. Essentially, such a schema transformation populates the elements of the upper schema $\mathcal{T}'$ with the information obtained from the answers to queries over the domain schema $\mathcal{T}$. Formally, given an ABox $\mathcal{A}$ for $\mathcal{T}$, a transformation rule $r = \varphi(\vec{x}) \rightsquigarrow \psi(\vec{y}, \vec{t})$ in $\mathcal{N}$ generates a set $r(\mathcal{T}, \mathcal{A}) = \bigcup_{\vec{c} \in \mathsf{cert}(\varphi, \langle \mathcal{T}, \mathcal{A} \rangle)} \psi[\vec{x}/\vec{c}]$ of ABox assertions for $\mathcal{T}'$, where $\psi[\vec{x}/\vec{c}]$ is defined as for OBDA mapping assertions. Notice that since a transformation rule is applied to a KB (and not to a database instance), the query in the left-hand side of the rule is interpreted under certain-answer semantics. Then, the ABox generated by $\mathcal{N}$ from $\langle \mathcal{T}, \mathcal{A} \rangle$ is defined as $\mathcal{N}(\mathcal{T}, \mathcal{A}) = \bigcup_{r \in \mathcal{N}} r(\mathcal{T}, \mathcal{A})$.

Example 4. The transformation rule $Person(x) \rightsquigarrow TargetCustomer(\mathbf{tc}(x))$ maps each instance of the domain schema concept *Person* into the upper schema concept *TargetCustomer*.   ∎

We are now ready to formalize the setting of *2-level OBDA*, or *OBDA* for short. A *OBDA specification* is a tuple $\mathcal{S}_{\langle 2 \rangle} = \langle \mathcal{S}, \mathcal{N}, \mathcal{T}' \rangle$, where $\mathcal{S} = \langle \mathcal{R}, \mathcal{M}, \mathcal{T} \rangle$ is an OBDA specification, $\mathcal{T}'$ is an upper schema (expressed as a *DL-Lite$_A$* TBox), and $\mathcal{N}$ is a schema transformation from $\mathcal{T}$ to $\mathcal{T}'$. Given an OBDA instance $\mathcal{J} = \langle \mathcal{S}, \mathcal{D} \rangle$ for $\mathcal{S}$, the tuple $\mathcal{J}_{\langle 2 \rangle} = \langle \mathcal{J}, \mathcal{N}, \mathcal{T}' \rangle$ is called a *OBDA instance* for $\mathcal{S}_{\langle 2 \rangle}$. The notions of virtual ABox and query answering in OBDA can be lifted to 2OBDA as well. Let $\mathcal{J} = \langle \mathcal{S}, \mathcal{D} \rangle$, with $\mathcal{S} = \langle \mathcal{R}, \mathcal{M}, \mathcal{T} \rangle$, be a satisfiable OBDA instance. The (virtual) ABox $\mathcal{N}(\mathcal{J})$ generated by $\mathcal{N}$ from $\mathcal{J}$ is defined as $\mathcal{N}(\mathcal{J}) = \mathcal{N}(\mathcal{T}, \mathcal{M}(\mathcal{D}))$. Moreover, a *model* for $\mathcal{J}_{\langle 2 \rangle}$ is a model of the KB $\langle \mathcal{T}', \mathcal{N}(\mathcal{J}) \rangle$, and $\mathcal{J}_{\langle 2 \rangle}$ is *satisfiable* if it admits a model. A UCQ q over a 2OBDA instance $\mathcal{J}_{\langle 2 \rangle}$ is simply a UCQ over the upper schema $\mathcal{T}'$, and the *certain answers to q over* $\mathcal{J}_{\langle 2 \rangle}$, denoted $\mathsf{cert}(q, \mathcal{J}_{\langle 2 \rangle})$, are defined as $\mathsf{cert}(q, \langle \mathcal{T}', \mathcal{N}(\mathcal{J}) \rangle)$.

To compute $\mathsf{cert}(q, \mathcal{J}_{\langle 2 \rangle})$, instead of materializing the intermediate and final virtual ABoxes, we can use the following 5-step approach: *(i)* rewrite q to compile away the upper schema $\mathcal{T}'$, obtaining $q'_r = \mathsf{rew}(q, \mathcal{T}')$, which is a UCQ over $\mathcal{T}'$; *(ii)* use the schema transformation $\mathcal{N}$ to *unfold* q'_r into a query over the domain schema $\mathcal{T}$, denoted by $q'_u = \mathsf{unf}(q'_r, \mathcal{N})$, which turns out to be a UCQ; *(iii)* rewrite q'_u to compile away the domain schema $\mathcal{T}$, obtaining $q_r = \mathsf{rew}(q'_u, \mathcal{T})$; *(iv)* use the mapping $\mathcal{M}$ to *unfold* q_r into a query over $\mathcal{R}$, denoted $q_u = \mathsf{unf}(q_r, \mathcal{M})$, which turns out to be an SQL query; *(v)* evaluate q_u over $\mathcal{D}$, obtaining $\mathsf{eval}(q_u, \mathcal{D})$. The correctness of this approach for computing the certain answers $\text{cert}(q, \mathcal{J}_{\langle 2 \rangle})$ can be shown by considering that essentially it combines two rewriting and unfolding phases for computing certain answers, and that both combinations are correct since they are based on standard OBDA [21]. We get:

Theorem 1. *Given a 2OBDA instance* $\mathcal{J}_{\langle 2 \rangle} = \langle \mathcal{J}, \mathcal{N}, \mathcal{T}' \rangle$, *where* $\mathcal{J} = \langle \mathcal{S}, \mathcal{D} \rangle$ *and* $\mathcal{S} = \langle \mathcal{R}, \mathcal{M}, \mathcal{T} \rangle$, *and a UCQ* q *over* $\mathcal{T}$, *we have that*

$$\text{cert}(q, \mathcal{J}_{\langle 2 \rangle}) = \text{eval}(\text{unf}(\text{rew}(\text{unf}(\text{rew}(q, \mathcal{T}'), \mathcal{N}), \mathcal{T}), \mathcal{M}), \mathcal{D}).$$

This result provides a way for answering queries in 2OBDA, but at the cost of an ad-hoc solution for query translation. We present now an alternative approach based on deriving from a 2OBDA specification an equivalent standard OBDA specification. Specifically, we show how to compile away from a 2OBDA specification $\mathcal{S}_{\langle 2 \rangle} = \langle \mathcal{S}, \mathcal{N}, \mathcal{T}' \rangle$, where $\mathcal{S} = \langle \mathcal{R}, \mathcal{M}, \mathcal{T} \rangle$, the domain schema $\mathcal{T}$, and synthesize from $\mathcal{S}_{\langle 2 \rangle}$ a standard OBDA specification $\mathcal{S}' = \langle \mathcal{R}, \mathcal{M}', \mathcal{T}' \rangle$ in which the elements of the upper schema $\mathcal{T}'$ are directly mapped to the sources. To construct the OBDA mapping $\mathcal{M}'$ of $\mathcal{S}'$, we first rewrite w.r.t. $\mathcal{T}$ and then unfold w.r.t. $\mathcal{M}$ each query over the domain schema in each transformation rule in $\mathcal{N}$. Formally, for each transformation rule $\varphi(\vec{x}) \rightsquigarrow \psi(\vec{y}, \vec{t})$ in $\mathcal{N}$, the mapping $\mathcal{M}'$ contains a mapping assertion $\varphi'(\vec{x}) \rightsquigarrow \psi(\vec{y}, \vec{t})$, where $\varphi' = \text{unf}(\text{rew}(\varphi, \mathcal{T}), \mathcal{M})$.

Example 5. Continuing Example 4, by applying the steps above, we get the OBDA mapping $q_u(x) \rightsquigarrow TargetCustomer(\textbf{tc}(x))$, where $q_u(x)$ is the SQL query in Example 3. ∎

To show the correctness of this approach, consider a source database $\mathcal{D}$ conforming to $\mathcal{R}$, and the corresponding OBDA instance $\mathcal{J} = \langle \mathcal{S}, \mathcal{D} \rangle$ and 2OBDA instance $\mathcal{J}_{\langle 2 \rangle} = \langle \mathcal{J}, \mathcal{N}, \mathcal{T}' \rangle$. By the correctness of the rewriting and unfolding approach to OBDA (cf. [21]), for each transformation rule $r = \varphi(\vec{x}) \rightsquigarrow \psi(\vec{y}, \vec{t})$ in $\mathcal{N}$, we have that $\text{cert}(\varphi, \mathcal{J}) = \text{cert}(\varphi, \langle \mathcal{T}, \mathcal{M}(\mathcal{D}) \rangle) = \text{eval}(\varphi', \mathcal{D})$, where $\varphi' = \text{unf}(\text{rew}(\varphi, \mathcal{T}), \mathcal{M})$. Hence, $\varphi(\vec{x})$ in r and $\varphi'(\vec{x})$ in the mapping assertion m of $\mathcal{M}'$ derived from r return the same answers, and in both r and m these instantiate the same atoms in $\psi(\vec{y}, \vec{t})$. It follows that $\mathcal{N}$ and $\mathcal{M}'$ populate the elements of the TBox $\mathcal{T}'$ with the same facts. We get:

Theorem 2. *Let* $\mathcal{S}_{\langle 2 \rangle} = \langle \mathcal{S}, \mathcal{N}, \mathcal{T}' \rangle$ *be a 2OBDA specification, where* $\mathcal{S} = \langle \mathcal{R}, \mathcal{M}, \mathcal{T} \rangle$, *and let* $\mathcal{S}' = \langle \mathcal{R}, \mathcal{M}', \mathcal{T}' \rangle$ *be the OBDA specification derived from* $\mathcal{S}_{\langle 2 \rangle}$ *as specified above. Then* $\mathcal{S}_{\langle 2 \rangle}$ *and* $\mathcal{S}'$ *have the same models.*

By relying on this result, query answering over a 2OBDA instance can be delegated to a traditional OBDA system, and we can use for it existing implementations (e.g., [3]).

5   Using Annotations for Specifying Schema Transformations

To specify the schema transformation rules between the domain ontology and the upper ontology, we propose an approach based on annotations, which are then used to actually generate the rules. We employ UML class diagrams as a concrete language for conceptual data modeling, and we rely on their logic-based encoding in terms of OWL 2 QL [4,6]. Therefore, we assume to work with OWL 2 QL compliant ontologies. The available types of annotations are automatically deduced from the upper ontology based on this assumption. In fact, we have developed an editor for annotating the domain ontology with upper ontology concepts that dynamically builds the annotation types accordingly.

Every class/concept in the ontology is considered to be an annotation type. Data properties having this class as domain are considered as fields of this annotation and they will be populated from the fields available in the domain ontology. Object properties are instead populated in their range class. It is possible to select any data property of the domain ontology or enter a static value to the data properties. For object properties, it is necessary to select an annotation instance defined over the domain ontology. For both data and object properties, the user can exploit navigational access, which provides the knowledge of how to access any field or annotation over the UML diagram using relations between classes as paths. After the selection of the corresponding fields, values, or navigational paths for each element in the annotation, queries for the transformation rules are automatically generated and actually used for rule generation (cf. Sect. 4).

The different annotations enrich the domain schema S by indicating which classes/concepts, associations/roles, and attributes in S contribute to the identification of different attributes of the annotations extracted from T'. Towards the automated processing of such annotations, and the consequent automated generation of transformation rules, the first step is to formally represent the annotations using a machine-processable language. To this end, we rely on conjunctive queries encoded in SPARQL, which are used to extract objects/values targeted by the annotations. In this way, we can represent GAV mappings that go well beyond one-to-one correspondences between classes/associations.

We provide a tool-chain that supports the various phases of the 2OBDA design and in particular implements the automated processing technique for annotations. It is available as a stand-alone software, or as a set of plugins running inside the ProM process mining framework[4]. Specifically, it consists of the following components: (i) A *UML Editor*, to model the domain and upper ontologies as UML class diagrams, and to import from and export to OWL 2 QL. (ii) A *Dynamic Annotation Editor*, to enrich the domain ontology with annotations extracted from the upper ontology. The editor supports navigational selections over the diagram via mouse-click operations to simplify the annotation task. The annotations are automatically translated into corresponding SPARQL queries by the editor. (iii) A *Transformation Rule Generator*, which automatically processes the annotations, and generates rules between the domain and upper ontologies. It implements the mapping synthesis technique described in Sect. 4, leveraging the state-of-the-art framework *ontop*[5] [3] for mapping management and query rewriting and unfolding.

---

[4] http://onprom.inf.unibz.it.

[5] http://ontop.inf.unibz.it.

Currently we do not have native tool support for specifying the mapping between the domain ontology and the data sources, and we assume that it is realized manually or by exploiting third-party tools, such as the *mapping editor* in the *ontop* plugin for Protégé (see footnote 5).

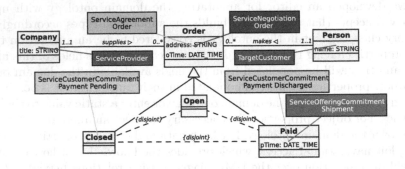

Fig. 5. Annotating the domain ontology using concepts from the upper ontology

(a) Payment pending service customer comm.   (b) Payment discharged service customer comm.

(c) Shipment service offering commitment

Fig. 6. Forms of commitment annotations showing the values

To use the Dynamic Annotation Editor to annotate the domain ontology with the concepts of the upper ontology, a user first defines the upper ontology as the target ontology, and then loads the file with the domain ontology to annotate. For example, if we use the partial UFO-S ontology as our upper ontology, and use it to annotate the order ontology, we can easily extract commitments available in the system. Figure 5 shows example annotations for extracting the commitments required by the company from the order system and Fig. 6 shows the forms of corresponding annotations. Note that Figs. 2 and 4 are image exports taken from the UML Editor, and Fig. 5 is an image export taken from the Dynamic Annotation editor.

According to the annotations defined in Fig. 5, the `TargetCustomers` are extracted from the `Person` concept and `ServiceProviders` from the `Company`. The `Order` concept defines a `ServiceNegotiation` and a `ServiceAgreement` between a `Company` and a `Person`. Two `ServiceCustomerCommitments` for the `Payment` are extracted when a `Person` gives an `Order` over the `Closed` (for pending payment commitment) and `Paid` (for discharged payment commitment) specializations of `Order`. After the `Payment` is successfully discharged, a `ServiceOfferingCommitment` for the `Shipment` will be available in the system. Figure 5 depicts the commitment extraction requirements of the company regarding their order system, and their presentation in the form of a diagram allows users to understand the relations and the requirements in a more intuitive way.

The tool-chain provides an easy annotation mechanism to the users with diagrams, forms, and point-and-click actions, so they don't have to deal with any text processing or ETL kind of approaches. The mapping generator of the tool-chain automatically generates the mapping between the underlying data sources and the upper ontology, using the domain ontology, the mapping specification between data sources and domain ontology, the upper ontology, and the annotations defined over the domain ontology.

6   Conclusions

In this paper, we proposed a framework for accessing data through different conceptual schemas, e.g., a domain schema and an upper schema acting as a reference model for the domain. We have formalized the framework in terms of 2-level OBDA, and have shown how to exploit an existing OBDA specification for the domain schema, together with conceptual mappings between the domain and the upper schema, to automatically derive an new OBDA specification for the upper schema. We have shown how the framework can be realized through schema annotations, and we have implemented a tool-chain supporting such approach. We have illustrated our approach on a use case adopting as upper schema a commitment-based core reference ontology for service (UFO-S).

Another interesting and highly relevant setting that calls for a multi-level approach to data access, is that of *process mining*, sketched in Fig. 1c [1]. In [6–8], a framework for extracting event logs using OBDA has been proposed, considering the XES standard for event logs [14] as a fixed, upper schema that is hard-coded in the framework. The 2OBDA approach presented here allows us to overcome the rigidity of XES and use instead a customized upper schema that can account e.g., for events with start and end time, or for hierarchical process instances. Finally, we observe that the framework of 2-level OBDA and the results in Sect. 4, can be easily generalized to *multiple-levels*, where schema transformations are specified between multiple conceptual schemas.

Acknowledgements. This research is supported by the Euregio IPN12 *KAOS (Knowledge-Aware Operational Support)* project, funded by the "European Region

Tyrol-South Tyrol-Trentino" (EGTC), and by the UNIBZ internal project *OnProm* *(ONtology-driven PROcess Mining)*.

References

1. van der Aalst, W., et al.: Process mining manifesto. In: Daniel, F., Barkaoui, K., Dustdar, S. (eds.) BPM 2011. LNBIP, vol. 99, pp. 169–194. Springer, Heidelberg (2012). https://doi.org/10.1007/978-3-642-28108-2_19
2. Baader, F., Calvanese, D., McGuinness, D., Nardi, D., Patel-Schneider, P.F. (eds.): The Description Logic Handbook: Theory, Implementation and Applications. CUP, New York (2003)
3. Calvanese, D., et al.: Ontop: answering SPARQL queries over relational databases. Semant. Web J. **8**(3), 471–487 (2017)
4. Calvanese, D., et al.: Ontologies and databases: the *DL-Lite* approach. In: Tessaris, S. (ed.) Reasoning Web 2009. LNCS, vol. 5689, pp. 255–356. Springer, Heidelberg (2009). https://doi.org/10.1007/978-3-642-03754-2_7
5. Calvanese, D., De Giacomo, G., Lembo, D., Lenzerini, M., Rosati, R.: Tractable reasoning and efficient query answering in description logics: the DL-Lite family. JAR **39**(3), 385–429 (2007)
6. Calvanese, D., Kalayci, T.E., Montali, M., Santoso, A.: OBDA for log extraction in process mining. In: Ianni, G., et al. (eds.) Reasoning Web 2017. LNCS, vol. 10370, pp. 292–345. Springer, Cham (2017). https://doi.org/10.1007/978-3-319-61033-7_9
7. Calvanese, D., Kalayci, T.E., Montali, M., Santoso, A.: The onprom toolchain for extracting business process logs using ontology-based data access. In: Proceedings of the BPM Demo Track and BPM Dissertation Award, Co-located with BPM 2017, vol. 1920. CEUR (2017)
8. Calvanese, D., Kalayci, T.E., Montali, M., Tinella, S.: Ontology-based data access for extracting event logs from legacy data: the onprom tool and methodology. In: Abramowicz, W. (ed.) BIS 2017. LNBIP, vol. 288, pp. 220–236. Springer, Cham (2017). https://doi.org/10.1007/978-3-319-59336-4_16
9. Catarci, T., Lenzerini, M.: Representing and using interschema knowledge in cooperative information systems. JICIS **2**(4), 375–398 (1993)
10. Chopra, A.K., Singh, M.P.: Custard: computing norm states over information stores. In: Proceedings of AAMAS, pp. 1096–1105 (2016)
11. Daraio, C., et al.: The advantages of an ontology-based data management approach: openness, interoperability and data quality. Scientometrics **108**(1), 441–455 (2016)
12. Euzenat, J., Shvaiko, P.: Ontology Matching, 2nd edn. Springer, Heidelberg (2013). https://doi.org/10.1007/978-3-642-38721-0
13. Guizzardi, G.: On ontology, ontologies, conceptualizations, modeling languages, and (meta)models. In: Proceedings of DB&IS, pp. 18–39. IOS Press (2006)
14. IEEE Computational Intelligence Society: IEEE standard for eXtensible Event Stream (XES) for achieving interoperability in event logs and event streams. Std 1849–2016. IEEE (2016)
15. Kharlamov, E., et al.: Ontology based data access in Statoil. J. Web Semant. **44**, 3–36 (2017)
16. Lenzerini, M.: Data integration: a theoretical perspective. In: Proceedings of PODS (2002)

17. Mehdi, G., et al.: Semantic rule-based equipment diagnostics. In: d'Amato, C., et al. (eds.) ISWC 2017. LNCS, vol. 10588, pp. 314–333. Springer, Cham (2017). https://doi.org/10.1007/978-3-319-68204-4_29
18. Montali, M., Calvanese, D., De Giacomo, G.: Verification of data-aware commitment-based multiagent systems. In: Proceedings of AAMAS, pp. 157–164 (2014)
19. Motik, B., Cuenca Grau, B., Horrocks, I., Wu, Z., Fokoue, A., Lutz, C.: OWL 2 Web Ontology Language Profiles, 2nd edn. W3C Recommendation, W3C (2012)
20. Nardi, J.C., et al.: A commitment-based reference ontology for services. Inf. Syst. **54**, 263–288 (2015)
21. Poggi, A., Lembo, D., Calvanese, D., De Giacomo, G., Lenzerini, M., Rosati, R.: Linking data to ontologies. J. Data Semant. X, 133–173 (2008)
22. Scherp, A., Saathoff, C., Franz, T., Staab, S.: Designing core ontologies. Appl. Ontol. **6**(3), 177–221 (2011)
23. Xiao, G., et al.: Ontology-based data access: a survey. In: Proceedings of IJCAI. AAAI Press (2018)

SWRL Reasoning Using Decision Tables

Maxime Clement[(✉)] and Ryutaro Ichise

National Institute of Informatics,
2-1-2 Hitotsubashi, Chiyoda-ku, Tokyo 101-8430, Japan
{maxime-clement,ichise}@nii.ac.jp
http://ri-www.nii.ac.jp/

Abstract. Ontologies are widely used for representing and sharing knowledge specific to some domain. The Web Ontology Language (OWL) is a popular language for designing ontologies and has been extended with the Semantic Web Rule Language (SWRL) to enable the use of rules in OWL ontologies. However, reasoning with SWRL rules is a computationally complex task, making its use difficult in time-sensitive applications. Such applications usually rely on decision tables, a popular yet simple structure used for fast decision making. Decision tables however are limited to propositional rules, making it impossible to represent SWRL rules using universally quantified variables. In this paper, a technique is proposed to enable reasoning with decision tables for SWRL rules and OWL ontologies by exploiting the classes of the variables and entities. Experimental results show that for many settings, our technique offers faster reasoning speed when compared to a state of the art SWRL reasoner.

Keywords: Ontology reasoning · Propositionalization
Decision table · SWRL

1 Introduction

Ontologies [27] provide the vocabulary necessary to represent knowledge related to a specific domain by formally defining concepts, relationships between these concepts, and instances of these concepts. In recent years, ontologies have been widely used in many fields such as bioinformatics [7] or recommender systems [13, 17], allowing experts to easily exchange knowledge and reason on well-structured data.

The Web Ontology Language (OWL) [18] is the currently recommended language for designing ontologies. It is widely used, with many tools and reasoners available. In order to improve the expressivity of OWL, the Semantic Web Rule Language (SWRL) [12] has been proposed to integrate rules in OWL ontologies. This offers powerful reasoning which is used for the maintenance and query of ontologies, or the matching of different ontologies [22].

The main issue with SWRL rules, is the high computational complexity of reasoning that they incur, even when restricting the rules to be DL-safe [19].

© Springer Nature Switzerland AG 2018
C. Faron Zucker et al. (Eds.): EKAW 2018, LNAI 11313, pp. 68–82, 2018.
https://doi.org/10.1007/978-3-030-03667-6_5

This makes the use of SWRL rules difficult in time-sensitive applications such as automated driving where fast reasoning is critical to avoid accidents [30]. Instead, decision tables [16] can be used to store propositional rules that are typically very fast to evaluate [6]. It is even possible to implement decision tables on a hardware level[1] to further improve the evaluation speed [28]. However, decision tables offer a very limited expressivity, making their combination with ontologies difficult. Compared to SWRL rules which can use universally quantified variables, propositional rules can only use true or false propositions, making it impossible to directly fit SWRL rules into decision tables. Instead, it is possible to transform SWRL rules to propositional form using a process known as propositionalization [15,24]. Using this process naively requires to know the values for the variables (i.e., the entities of our ontology) in advance and will generate a decision table of exponential size, limiting its applications to real-time or embedded applications where entities are constantly changing or where memory is limited.

The advantage of reasoning with ontologies is that we can expect the knowledge base to follow a well-defined structure. Entities will belong to some classes and will be in relation with other entities. In order to fit SWRL rules into decision tables, we thus propose to exploit the classes defined in the ontology to create an intermediate structure between the real entities and the rules. This structure consists of templates of entities with a specific set of classes that can be directly extracted from SWRL rules. For example, if a rule uses a variable which is restricted to belong to classes VEHICLE and STOPPED, we can consider a template for "stopped vehicles" corresponding to these two classes. These templates, which we call *typed placeholders*, can be used as temporary entities to transform SWRL rules to propositional form that can then be fitted into decision tables. During reasoning, we will only need to map the real entities to the typed placeholders to evaluate the decision tables.

In this paper, we propose a technique to enable the use of decision tables for SWRL reasoning. We propose a method called *typed propositionalization* to transform SWRL rules to propositional form using placeholders instead of the real entities, allowing us to prepare the decision table before the reasoning takes place. In our experiments, we use a car ontology designed for automated driving to show that our method can be much faster than a state of the art SWRL reasoner.

The rest of the paper is organized as follows. In Sect. 2, the formalisms for describing ontologies and SWRL rules are presented. In Sect. 3, existing methods to reason with SWRL rules are briefly introduced. In Sect. 4, a naive propositionalization to fit the rules into a decision table is shown. In Sect. 5, our proposed method and its complexity are described. In Sect. 6, experimental results are presented. In Sect. 7 the paper is concluded and ideas for future works are proposed.

---

[1] http://www.zipc.com/product/ZIPC_R&B/index_e.html.

2   Preliminaries

In this section, we present the formalisms used to represent ontologies and SWRL rules and describe the goal of SWRL reasoning.

2.1   Ontologies

An ontology formally defines the vocabulary necessary to describe some specific domain, usually in the form of a set of entities, classes, and properties. Entities are used to represent real-world objects, classes are collections of entities with a common type, and properties are relationships between entities. To describe ontologies, we use a notation similar to first-order logic.

Definition 1 (Ontology). *An ontology $\mathcal{O}$ is a pair (V, A) where $V = CName \cup PName \cup EName$ is the vocabulary of the ontology as a set of symbols and $A = A_C \cup A_P$ is a set of assertions made using the vocabulary V.*

We distinguish three types of symbols with $CName$ the set of class predicate symbols, $PName$ the set of property predicate symbols, and $EName$ the set of entity symbols. We distinguish two types of assertions with A_C the set of class assertions and A_P the set of property assertions. A class assertion is of the form $C(E)$ with $C \in CName$ and $E \in EName$, indicating that entity E belongs to the class C. A property assertion is of the form $P(E, E')$ with $P \in PName$ and $E, E' \in EName$, indicating that E has the property P with E'.

Example 1 (Vocabulary). Let us consider a simple ontology to describe driving situations. We consider the classes CAR, VEHICLE, and SLOWDOWN, the property INFRONTOF, and entities a and b. We have the resulting vocabulary

$$V_{car} = \{\text{CAR}, \text{VEHICLE}, \text{SLOWDOWN}\} \cup \{\text{INFRONTOF}\} \cup \{a, b\}$$

Example 2 (Assertions). The knowledge "vehicle b is in front of car a" and "b is slowing down" using the vocabulary V_{car} is written as the set of assertions

$$A_{car} = \{\text{CAR}(a), \text{VEHICLE}(b), \text{SLOWDOWN}(b)\} \cup \{\text{INFRONTOF}(b, a)\}$$

2.2   SWRL Rules

The Semantic Web Rule Language (SWRL) [12] is a language proposed for expressing rules over OWL ontologies. A SWRL rule is of the form of an implication between an antecedent (called body) and a consequent (called head). Similarly to first-order logic, SWRL rules can use universally quantified variables which requires an additional set of variable symbols $VName$.

Definition 2 (SWRL Rule). *A SWRL rule R is of the form*

$$R = B_1, \ldots, B_n \rightarrow H_1, \ldots, H_m$$

where B_i and H_j, $1 \le i \le n, 1 \le j \le m$, are either axioms of the form $C(V)$
with $C \in CName, V \in EName \cup VName$ or axioms of the form $P(V, V')$ with
$P \in PName$ and $V, V' \in EName \cup VName$. $B_1, \ldots, B_n$ is called the body of the
rule and is denoted by $body(R)$. $H_1, \ldots, H_m$ is called the head of the rule and is
denoted by $head(R)$.

In order to evaluate a rule, the real entities must be mapped to the variables. Considering a mapping $M : VName \to EName$, all occurrences of a variable $V \in VName$ can be replaced by its corresponding entity $M(V)$ in the axioms of a rule. By abusing notation, we write $M(R)$ the rule R where each occurrence of V is replaced by $M(V)$, in which case we say that R is instantiated using M.

For an ontology $\mathcal{O} = (V, A)$, a mapping M and a rule R, if all instantiated axioms in the body of $M(R)$ are true, i.e., $body(M(R)) \subseteq A$, then all instantiated head axioms in $head(M(R))$ must also be true.

Example 3 (SWRL Rule). Using the vocabulary V_{car} of Example 1 and a set of variable symbols $VName = \{?v, ?c\}$, the rule "if a vehicle is slowing down and the vehicle is in front of a car, then the car must slow down" is written as a rule

$$R_{slow} = \text{VEHICLE}(?v), \text{SLOWDOWN}(?v), \text{CAR}(?c), \text{INFRONTOF}(?v, ?c)$$
$$\to \text{SLOWDOWN}(?c)$$

Using the assertions A_{car} of Example 2, let us consider two mappings of the variables $?v$ and $?c$ to the entities a and b:

- $M_1 = \{?v : a, ?c : b\}$.
- $M_2 = \{?v : b, ?c : a\}$.

Using M_1 we obtain the instantiated rule

$$M_1(R) = \text{VEHICLE}(a), \text{SLOWDOWN}(a), \text{CAR}(b), \text{INFRONTOF}(a, b)$$
$$\to \text{SLOWDOWN}(b)$$

and using M_2 we obtain the instantiated rule

$$M_2(R) = \text{VEHICLE}(b), \text{SLOWDOWN}(b), \text{CAR}(a), \text{INFRONTOF}(b, a)$$
$$\to \text{SLOWDOWN}(a)$$

The body of $M_1(R)$ is not true, i.e., it is not part of our knowledge A_{car}. For $M_2(R)$ however, the body is a subset of A_{car} and is thus considered true, meaning that its head $\text{SLOWDOWN}(a)$ must also be true.

2.3 SWRL Reasoning

SWRL rules are commonly used to learn new knowledge about the entities represented in an ontology. Finding all possible assertions that can be inferred from the SWRL rules is a complex task and is the focus of this paper.

Given an ontology $\mathcal{O} = (V, A)$ and a set of rules $\mathcal{R} = \{R_1, \ldots, R_r\}$ using the set of variable symbols $VName$, SWRL reasoning corresponds to finding the set of assertions A^+ corresponding to the head axioms of instantiated rules whose body axioms are part of our knowledge A. We write this set

$$A^+ = \{head(M(R))|R \in \mathcal{R}, body(M(R)) \subseteq A, M \in \mathcal{M}\}$$

where $\mathcal{M}$ is the set of all possible mappings from variables to entities.

3   Related Works

There exists many ontology reasoners that can perform SWRL reasoning.

Many popular reasoners are using the Tableaux [1] algorithm, a widely used method to prove or disprove first-order formulas and which has been adapted for Description Logic. Many popular reasoners based on Tableaux can handle SWRL rules such as Pellet [26], Hermit [25], and Racer [29]. Pellet is the most actively maintained of these reasoners, thanks to its open source implementation Openllet. It provides functionalities to check the consistency of ontologies, compute the classification hierarchy, explain inferences, and perform SWRL reasoning.

Another approach is to convert the rules to a different format that is then used for reasoning. Hoolet [3] is an OWL reasoner based on a first-order logic theorem prover and is able to handle SWRL rules by converting them to first-order logic. SWRLTab [23] is a plugin for Protégé [20], that converts the ontology and its rules into the format used by the rule engines Jess [10], or Drools [4]. SWRL2SPIN [2] is a Prolog program to translate SWRL rules to SPIN [14], a rule format for SPARQL queries.

The reasoning method proposed in this paper converts rules to a propositional format, allowing the use of decision tables for reasoning. As far as we are aware, our approach is the first to consider a conversion to propositional logic and to use decision tables for reasoning.

4   Naive Propositionalization

Propositionalization is the process of converting information from relational form (like in ontologies) to propositional form made exclusively of true or false propositions. For ontologies, it corresponds to transforming axioms such as $C(E)$ to a proposition C_E and $P(E, E')$ to a proposition $P_{E,E'}$, representing the facts that E belongs to class C and that E has the property P with E'. This process is mostly used in Machine Learning applications where it allows the use of propositional learners using relational data [15,24].

In our approach, we use propositionalization to fit ontology rules in a decision table. Once transformed to propositional form, a rule corresponds directly to a row in a decision table where the rule's body is the set of conditions and its head is the set of actions [6].

The naive way to propositionalize a SWRL rule is to consider each possible mapping of entities to the variables. Once a mapping is given, the rules can be converted to a propositional form where each axiom is replaced by a proposition. Similarly, knowledge about entities is also propositionalized, giving us a set of propositions that can be used to determine whether the body of a rule is true or not.

Formally, we consider a function Π which can be applied to assertions and a function Π_M which can be applied to rule axioms given a mapping $M : VName \cup EName \rightarrow EName$ that maps variables to entities while preserving the entity symbols, i.e., $\forall E \in EName, M(E) = E$. We define the propositionalization of assertions as $\Pi(\mathrm{C}(E)) = \mathrm{C}_E$ and $\Pi(\mathrm{P}(E, E')) = \mathrm{P}_{E,E'}$, $E, E' \in EName$, and abuse notation to denote the set of all propositionalized assertions in A as $\Pi(A)$. We define the propositionalization of axioms as $\Pi_M(\mathrm{C}(V)) = \mathrm{C}_{M(V)}$ and $\Pi_M(\mathrm{P}(V, V')) = \mathrm{P}_{M(V),M(V')}$, $V, V' \in VName \cup EName$. We then denote the propositionalization of a rule $R = B_1, \ldots, B_n \rightarrow H_1, \ldots, H_m$ using a mapping M as $\Pi_M(R) = \Pi_M(B_1), \ldots, \Pi_M(B_n) \rightarrow \Pi_M(H_1), \ldots, \Pi_M(H_m)$.

Propositionalization of rules and knowledge allows to directly determine whether the body of a rule is true or not by simply checking if it is part of our propositionalized knowledge, i.e., if $body(\Pi_M(R)) \subseteq \Pi(A)$.

Example 4 (Naive Propositionalization). Given the rule R_{slow} from Example 3 and a mapping $M = \{?v : b, ?c : a\}$, meaning that variable $?v$ maps to the entity b and variable $?c$ maps to the entity a, we generate the propositional rule

$$\Pi_M(R_{slow}) = \mathrm{VEHICLE}_b, \mathrm{SLOWDOWN}_b, \mathrm{CAR}_a, \mathrm{INFRONTOF}_{b,a} \rightarrow \mathrm{SLOWDOWN}_a$$

Assuming the knowledge A_{car} from Example 2, we generate the set of propositions

$$\Pi(A_{car}) = \{\mathrm{CAR}_a, \mathrm{VEHICLE}_b, \mathrm{SLOWDOWN}_b\} \cup \{\mathrm{INFRONTOF}_{b,a}\}$$

We can now evaluate the propositional rule $\Pi_M(R_{slow})$ and determine that its body is true since $\{\mathrm{VEHICLE}_b, \mathrm{SLOWDOWN}_b, \mathrm{CAR}_a, \mathrm{INFRONTOF}_{b,a}\} \subseteq \Pi(A_{car})$. This means that its head $\mathrm{SLOWDOWN}_a$ must also be true.

There exists several limitations with such *naive* propositionalization. Most importantly, the rules generated are for some specific entities, meaning that if the entities change, then new rules need to be generated. Moreover, since each combination of entities to variables needs to be considered, an exponential number of propositional rules are generated and need to be stored. This makes such a naive approach unsuited for the kind of real-time situations we want to handle.

5   Typed Propositionalization

In order to improve the conversion from SWRL rules to decision table, we propose *typed propositionalization* which uses a preprocessing step to perform propositionalization without the need for entities to be defined in advance. The idea of this method is to instantiate the rules using placeholders instead of the real entities. When reasoning, real entities only need to be assigned to these placeholders.

Definition 3 (Typed Placeholder). *A typed placeholder* $T = \{C_0, C_1, \ldots\}$ *is defined as a set of class predicates. where* $C_i \in CName$ *is a class predicate.*

For each rule $R \in \mathcal{R}$, a placeholder is associated to each variable using their corresponding class axioms in the body of the rule. For a variable $V \in VName$, we associate a placeholder $T_V = \{C | C(V) \in body(R)\}$.

For the rule R, using the multiset of generated placeholders T_R, we consider the mapping $M : VName \rightarrow T_R$ such that $M(V) = T_V$. We can now propositionalize our rules without needing any real entity by using the operation Π_M presented in Sect. 4.

Example 5 (Typed Propositionalization). Given the rule R_{slow} from Example 3, we generate the placeholders:

- $T_c = \{\text{CAR}\}$ (placeholder for ?c);
- $T_v = \{\text{VEHICLE}, \text{SLOWDOWN}\}$ (placeholder for ?v).

We then have the mapping $M = \{T_c\ :?c, T_v\ :?v\}$ which we use to generate the propositional rule

$$\Pi_M(R_{slow}) = \text{VEHICLE}_{T_v}, \text{SLOWDOWN}_{T_v}, \text{CAR}_{T_c}, \text{INFRONTOF}_{T_v,T_c}$$
$$\rightarrow \text{SLOWDOWN}_{T_c}$$

After this preprocessing step, we have the set of generated propositional rules, denoted $\Pi(\mathcal{R})$ for simplicity, and for each rule $\Pi_M(R) \in \Pi(\mathcal{R})$, we have the corresponding multiset of placeholders T_R.

In order to make reasoning more efficient, we group together the propositional rules sharing the same multiset of placeholders (ignoring the identifier of the placeholders). Thus, considering a multiset of placeholders $T = \{T_1, T_2, \ldots\}$, we group all corresponding rules into a ruleset $RS_T = \{\Pi_M(R) | T_R = T\}$.

Example 6 (Rule Grouping). Given a set of propositional rules $\Pi(\mathcal{R}) = \{\Pi_M(R_1), \Pi_M(R_2), \Pi_M(R_3)\}$ such that:

- $T_{R_1} = \{\text{CAR}, \text{VEHICLE}\}$; $T_{R_2} = \{\text{TRUCK}, \text{VEHICLE}\}$; $T_{R_3} = \{\text{CAR}, \text{VEHICLE}\}$.

We group the rules into 2 rulesets:

- $RS_{\{\text{CAR}, \text{VEHICLE}\}} = \{\Pi_M(R_1), \Pi_M(R_3)\}$; $RS_{\{\text{TRUCK}, \text{VEHICLE}\}} = \{\Pi_M(R_2)\}$.

Each resulting ruleset RS_T corresponds to a decision table whose conditions are propositions relating to the placeholders in T. During reasoning, this will allow us to evaluate subproblems with only a handful of placeholders whereas having a single decision table containing all rules would require to always look at the problem as a whole, with all its possible placeholders.

5.1   Reasoning with Typed Propositionalization

Once the rules have been propositionalized using placeholders and grouped into the rulesets $\mathcal{RS}$, we are ready to perform reasoning with real entities. To reason using our propositionalized rules, we need to match the real entities to their corresponding placeholders, generate the corresponding propositional knowledge, execute the rules, and translate the newly inferred propositions into ontology axioms. We thus separate the reasoning into 4 phases which needs to be performed for each ruleset $RS_T \in \mathcal{RS}$.

1. Entity matching: match entities with their compatible placeholders in $\mathcal{T}$.
2. Knowledge propositionalization: create propositional facts based on a given mapping of placeholders to entities.
3. Typed Reasoning: evaluate the propositional rules in the ruleset RS_T using the created propositional facts and infer some new propositional knowledge.
4. Translation: translate the new propositional knowledge to ontology axioms expressed on the corresponding entities (instead of the placeholders).

Because several entities can be compatible with a same placeholder, there might be several mappings to consider and steps 2–4 will need to be repeated for each possible mapping.

Entity Matching. Given an ontology $\mathcal{O} = (V, A)$ and a set of placeholders $\mathcal{T}$, entity matching consists in creating mappings from placeholders to entities of the form $M : \mathcal{T} \rightarrow EName$. First, we create for each placeholder $T \in \mathcal{T}$ its set of compatible entities $\mathcal{E}_T = \{E \in EName | T \subseteq classes(E)\}$ where $classes(E)$ is the set of classes for the entity E, i.e., $classes(E) = \{C | C(E) \in A\}$. If for at least one placeholder T there is $|\mathcal{E}_T| > 1$, then we need to consider multiple mappings of entities to the placeholders. The total number of mappings to consider is $\prod_{T \in \mathcal{T}} |\mathcal{E}_T|$.

Example 7 (Entity Matching). Given the placeholders $\mathcal{T} = \{T_c = \{\text{CAR}\}, T_v = \{\text{VEHICLE}\}\}$, and the set of assertions

$$A'_{car} = \{\text{CAR}(a), \text{VEHICLE}(a), \text{VEHICLE}(b)\}$$

we generate the set of matching entities for each placeholder: $\mathcal{E}_{T_c} = \{a\}$; $\mathcal{E}_{T_v} = \{a, b\}$. We can then consider two mappings $M_1 = \{T_c : a, T_v : a\}$ and $M_2 = \{T_c : a, T_v : b\}$.

Knowledge Propositionalization. Given an ontology $\mathcal{O} = (V, A)$ and a mapping $M : \mathcal{T} \rightarrow EName$, we propositionalize all assertions A by replacing references to an entity E by the placeholders mapped to it, i.e., $\{T | M(T) = E\}$.

Formally, we create a propositional knowledge base $A^{prop} = A_C^{prop} \cup A_P^{prop}$ such that

$$A_C^{prop} = \{C_T | C(E) \in A_C, M(T) = E\}$$

and

$$A_P^{prop} = \{P_{T,T'} | P(E, E') \in A_P, M(T) = E, M(T') = E'\}$$

Example 8 (Knowledge Propositionalization). Considering A_{car} from Example 2, and the given mapping $M_1 = \{T_c : a, T_v : a\}$, we obtain the set of propositions

$$A_1^{prop} = \{\text{CAR}_{T_c}, \text{CAR}_{T_v}\}$$

We can notice that in this case, we cannot propositionalize axioms $\text{VEHICLE}(b)$, $\text{INFRONTOF}(b, a)$, and $\text{SLOWDOWN}(b)$ since they reference the entity b which is not part of mapping M_1.

For the given mapping $M_2 = \{T_c : a, T_v : b\}$, we obtain the set of propositions

$$A_2^{prop} = \{\text{CAR}_{T_c}, \text{VEHICLE}_{T_v}, \text{SLOWDOWN}_{T_v}\} \cup \{\text{INFRONTOF}_{T_v, T_c}\}$$

Typed Reasoning. Now that the assertions have been propositionalized into the set A^{prop}, we can evaluate each propositional rule $\Pi_M(R)$ in the ruleset RS_T and obtain a set of new propositional assertions

$$A^{prop+} = \{head(\Pi_M(R)) | body(\Pi_M(R)) \subseteq A^{prop}, \Pi_M(R) \in RS_T\}$$

Example 9 (Typed Reasoning). Given the propositional rule from Example 5,

$\Pi_M(R_{slow}) =$

$\text{VEHICLE}_{T_v}, \text{SLOWDOWN}_{T_v}, \text{CAR}_{T_c}, \text{INFRONTOF}_{T_v, T_c} \rightarrow \text{SLOWDOWN}_{T_c}$

and the set of propositions A_2^{prop} from Example 8, we obtain the new knowledge

$$A^{prop+} = \{\text{SLOWDOWN}_{T_c}\}$$

Translation. Once a ruleset has been evaluated for a given mapping M, we need to convert the new propositions A^{prop+} expressed for the placeholders in T back into axioms expressed for the entities in $EName$. This conversion is the reverse of the knowledge propositionalization where we now replace each placeholder $T \in T$ by its corresponding entity $M(T)$.

Formally, we create the set of inferred axioms A^+ such that:

- for each proposition $C_T \in A^{prop+}, M(T) = E$, we have the class axiom $C(E) \in A^+$;
- for each proposition $P_{T,T'} \in A^{prop+}, M(T) = E, M(T') = E'$, we have the property axiom $P(E, E') \in A^+$.

Example 10 (Translation). Given the inferred propositional knowledge

$$A^{prop+} = \{\text{SLOWDOWN}_{T_c}\}$$

obtained with the mapping $M = \{T_c : a, T_v : b\}$, we obtain the translation

$$A^+ = \{\text{SLOWDOWN}(a)\}$$

Once this translation has been computed for the inferences obtained with each possible mapping and each possible ruleset, then the resulting set of axioms A^+ contains all possible inferences for the current knowledge base.

5.2   Rule Chaining

The method we just described allows to compute axioms that can be inferred from the SWRL rules using the assertions of the ontology. However, it might be possible to infer more axioms if we continue the reasoning using the newly learned axioms in A^+. This is called rule chaining and is a necessary process for the completeness of reasoning.

In order to perform efficient rule chaining, we use a dependency graph whose nodes are the different rulesets in $\mathcal{RS}$. Directed edges indicates that when new axioms are inferred using a ruleset, all its successors in the graph should be evaluated again considering this new knowledge. An edge from ruleset RS_{T_i} to ruleset RS_{T_j} is added if one of the following condition holds:

(i) $\exists \Pi_M(R) \in RS_{T_i}, C_T \in head(\Pi_M(R)), \exists T' \in \mathcal{T}_j, C \in T'$;
(ii) $\exists \Pi_M(R_k) \in RS_{T_i}, \exists \Pi_M(R_l) \in RS_{T_j}, P_{T,T'} \in head(\Pi_M(R_k)), P_{T'',T'''} \in body(\Pi_M(R_l))$.

The first condition indicates that when a class assertion is inferred, we need to reevaluate any ruleset that depends on that class, i.e., at least one of the placeholders used by the ruleset contains that class. The second condition indicates that when a property assertion is inferred, we need to reevaluate rulesets that contains rules whose body makes use of this property.

5.3   Handling OWL Axioms

An important feature of SWRL is its interaction with OWL ontologies which makes use of a number of axioms to express relations between classes and properties, symmetry or transitivity of properties, etc. In order for the inference to be complete, it is important to take into account these axioms during the reasoning process. Previous works [8] have shown that many OWL axioms can be translated to datalog [5], a rule language resembling SWRL. Thus, in order to take into account the OWL axioms of an ontology, we use a similar translation to generate corresponding SWRL rules that we add to the set of rules $\mathcal{R}$ at the start of our method.

5.4   Complexity

We now discuss the worst-case complexity of our method. One of the advantage of decision tables is their linear evaluation complexity. A decision table with n different conditions (corresponding to the different body propositions) and r rules requires at most $n \times r$ checks. With our method, we must evaluate the decision table for each possible mapping of entities in $EName$ to the placeholders $\mathcal{T}$. In the worst case where all rules are grouped into a single ruleset and where all entities can be mapped to all placeholders, there are $|EName|^{|\mathcal{T}|}$ possible mappings, leading to an overall reasoning complexity in $O(|EName|^{|\mathcal{T}|} \times nr)$.

Regarding memory, in addition to the ontology itself, our method only needs to store a set of placeholders $\mathcal{T}$, a set of propositionalized assertions A^{prop}, a set of inferred axioms A^+, the decision table with n conditions and r rules, and the dependency graph with at most $r(r-1)$ edges (if each ruleset is made of a single rule). The size of the set of placeholders is bounded by the number of rules and their size, i.e., $|T| \leq nr$. The number of propositions in A^{prop} is equal to the number of assertions in A and the number of inferred axioms is bounded by the number of rules and the size of their head m, i.e., $|A^+| \leq mr$ leading to an overall memory complexity in $O(|A| + rn + rm + r^2)$.

We can notice that our worst case reasoning complexity is quite high but our memory complexity is very low, which is one of the expected advantages of using decision tables. In practice, the reasoning time will greatly depends on how many rulesets are generated and how many entities are compatible with each placeholder. This means that SWRL rules should be as precise as possible, specifying clearly the types of the variables used, in order to generate less mappings during reasoning.

6   Experiments

6.1   Settings

In order to evaluate the efficiency of the typed propositionalization presented in Sect. 5, we will compare it with Openllet[2], the currently maintained implementation of Pellet [26].

All methods are implemented in Java using the OWLAPI [11] and SWRLAPI [21] to interact with the ontology, using an Intel Core i7-7700K running at 4.20 GHz and with 4 GB of memory dedicated to the JVM.

For experiments, we use the Advanced Driving Assistant System Ontology (ADAS)[3] [30] written in OWL2 [9,18] and expressible in the description logic $\mathcal{ALHI}(D)$. For reasoning, a set of 300 SWRL rules is used, which generates 26 different typed placeholders. Unless otherwise specified, the entities used for reasoning are randomly generated with 1 class assertion and 10 property assertions per entity, with each property having a cardinality of 5, i.e., each entity shares the property with 5 other entities. For each setting considered, we report the average, median, and minimum/maximum reasoning times over 100 runs. Since the preprocessing step of our method can be performed in advance and is always very fast (around 30 ms), we do not include it in our results.

6.2   Results

Varying Number of Entities. First, we compare the typed propositionalization with Openllet when varying the number of entities in the ontology from 10 to 30. Figure 1 uses a logarithmic scale to show the resulting reasoning times. We first notice that the runtime of both methods increases exponentially with the number of entities. Our typed propositionalization averages runtimes from

---

[2] https://github.com/Galigator/openllet.
[3] http://ri-www.nii.ac.jp/ADAS/index.html.

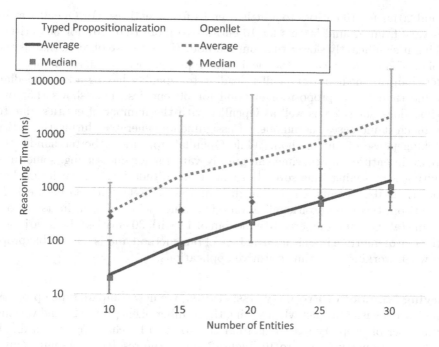

Fig. 1. Reasoning time varying the number of entities.

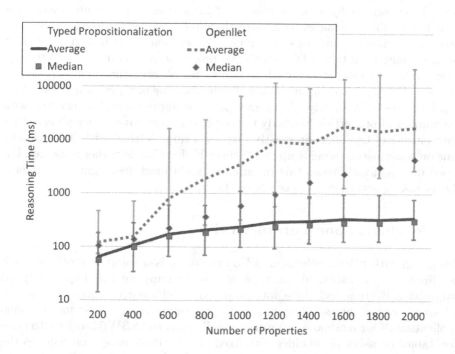

Fig. 2. Reasoning time varying the number of properties.

around 20 ms for 10 entities to a little over 1 s for 30 entities. For Openllet averages vary from around 500 ms for 10 entities to more than 10 s for 30 entities, making it significantly slower than our method. However, we observe that as the number of entities increases, the median for typed propositionalization increases faster than the median for Openllet, leading to Openllet having a lower median runtime than typed propositionalization for 30 entities. This shows that our method does not scale as well as Openllet with the number of entities, due to how much it increases the number of assignments generated during the entity matching phase of our method. While Openllet appears to better handle the increase in entities, its runtime can greatly vary for a same setting, sometimes requiring a reasoning time several orders of magnitude larger than its median (more than 100 s compared to a median of less than 1 s with 30 entities). In comparison, typed propositionalization offers much less variation in its reasoning time (at most 9 s compared to a median of 1 s with 30 entities). Less variation in the reasoning time is a clear advantage of our method and is a desirable property when working with time sensitive applications.

Varying Number of Property Assertions. We now compare typed propositionalization with Openllet when setting the number of entities to 20 and varying the number of property assertions from 200 to 2000 by changing the cardinality of each property from 1 to 10. Figure 2 shows the resulting reasoning times using a logarithmic scale. We first notice that the average runtime of Openllet increases exponentially with the number of properties and ends up taking more than 10 s to solve instances with more than 1600 property assertions. In comparison, the average runtime of the typed propositionalization increases almost linearly, going from taking 66 ms with 200 properties to 414 ms with 2000 properties. When looking at the median values, we observe the same exponential increase of the runtime for Openllet while the runtime of typed propositionalization increases only linearly. This shows that our approach scales very well with the number of properties. Similarly to the previous experiment, we observe that the runtimes of Openllet can greatly vary for a same setting, with the reasoning time on some instances being up to 100 times higher than for other instances. For typed propositionalization, this variation is again much less significant, almost always taking less than 1 s to complete the reasoning.

7   Conclusion and Future Works

Reasoning with SWRL rules and OWL ontologies is a complex problem which can limit its application to real-time decision making. In this paper, a typed propositionalization technique was proposed to efficiently represent ontology rules as decision tables, allowing a faster reasoning more suited for real-time applications. Our method uses propositionalization to fit SWRL rules into decision tables by using placeholder with fixed classes. Reasoning then requires the mapping of the real entities to compatible placeholders and the evaluation of the decision tables. By exploiting the classes of an ontology, typed propositionalization can evaluate rules in a more efficient way. Our experiments showed that our proposed approach can successfully classify OWL ontologies while reasoning with SWRL rules much faster than a state of the art reasoner. By offering reasoning times that are consistently bellow 1 s in some situations in addition to a very small memory complexity, we showed that our typed propositionalization can be useful in time sensitive applications and embedded systems.

In its current version, our approach is still quite sensitive to the number of entities in the ontology and to how much the classes of the ontology can be exploited. In order to make our approach even more scalable, our future works will focus on finding ways to also exploit properties (in addition to classes) to define the placeholders. In addition, we will work towards turning our approach into a full-fledged reasoner by adding support for consistency checking, explanation of results, SWRL built-ins, etc. We also plan to apply our method to other rule languages than SWRL.

Furthermore, we are planning to use our approach in an embedded-system using hardware-implemented decision tables. Since decision tables are at the core of our typed propositionalization, we expect significant speedups allowing real-time reasoning even with larger ontologies.

Acknowledgements. This work was partially supported by the New Energy and Industrial Technology Development Organization (NEDO).

References

1. Baader, F., Sattler, U.: Tableau algorithms for description logics. In: Dyckhoff, R. (ed.) TABLEAUX 2000. LNCS (LNAI), vol. 1847, pp. 1–18. Springer, Heidelberg (2000). https://doi.org/10.1007/10722086_1
2. Bassiliades, N.: SWRL2SPIN: a tool for transforming SWRL rule bases in OWL ontologies to object-oriented SPIN rules. arXiv preprint arXiv:1801.09061 (2018)
3. Bechhofer, S., Horrocks, I.: Hoolet: an OWL reasoner with support for rules (2004). http://owl.man.ac.uk/hoolet
4. Browne, P.: JBoss Drools Business Rules. Packt Publishing Ltd, Birmingham (2009)
5. Ceri, S., Gottlob, G., Tanca, L.: What you always wanted to know about Datalog (and never dared to ask). IEEE Trans. Knowl. Data Eng. **1**(1), 146–166 (1989)
6. Colomb, R.M., Chung, C.: Very fast decision table execution of propositional expert systems. In: Proceedings of the 8th National Conference on Artificial Intelligence, pp. 671–676 (1990)
7. Gene Ontology Consortium: Gene ontology consortium: going forward. Nucleic Acids Res. **43**(D1), D1049–D1056 (2014)
8. Faruqui, R.U., MacCaull, W.: $O_{wl}O_{nt}$DB: a scalable reasoning system for OWL 2 RL ontologies with large ABoxes. In: Weber, J., Perseil, I. (eds.) FHIES 2012. LNCS, vol. 7789, pp. 105–123. Springer, Heidelberg (2013). https://doi.org/10.1007/978-3-642-39088-3_7
9. Grau, B.C., Horrocks, I., Motik, B., Parsia, B., Patel-Schneider, P., Sattler, U.: OWL 2: the next step for OWL. Web Semant. Sci. Serv. Agents World Wide Web **6**(4), 309–322 (2008)

10. Hill, E.F.: Jess in Action: Java Rule-Based Systems. Manning Publications Co., Greenwich (2003)
11. Horridge, M., Bechhofer, S.: The OWL API: a Java API for OWL ontologies. Semant. Web **2**(1), 11–21 (2011)
12. Horrocks, I., Patel-Schneider, P.F., Boley, H., Tabet, S., Grosof, B., Dean, M.: SWRL: a semantic web rule language combining OWL and RuleML. W3C Member Submission 21, 79 (2004)
13. Kang, Y.B., Pan, J.Z., Krishnaswamy, S., Sawangphol, W., Li, Y.F.: How long will it take? Accurate prediction of ontology reasoning performance. In: Proceedings of the 28th AAAI Conference on Artificial Intelligence, pp. 80–86 (2014)
14. Knublauch, H., Hendler, J.A., Idehen, K.: SPIN-overview and motivation. W3C Member Submission 22 (2011)
15. Krogel, M.-A., Rawles, S., Železný, F., Flach, P.A., Lavrač, N., Wrobel, S.: Comparative evaluation of approaches to propositionalization. In: Horváth, T., Yamamoto, A. (eds.) ILP 2003. LNCS (LNAI), vol. 2835, pp. 197–214. Springer, Heidelberg (2003). https://doi.org/10.1007/978-3-540-39917-9_14
16. Metzner, J.R., Barnes, B.H.: Decision Table Languages and Systems. Academic Press, Orlando (1977)
17. Middleton, S.E., Shadbolt, N.R., De Roure, D.C.: Ontological user profiling in recommender systems. ACM Trans. Inf. Syst. (TOIS) **22**(1), 54–88 (2004)
18. Motik, B., et al.: OWL 2 web ontology language: structural specification and functional-style syntax. W3C Recommendation **27**(65), 159 (2009)
19. Motik, B., Sattler, U., Studer, R.: Query answering for OWL-DL with rules. Web Semant. Sci. Serv. Agents World Wide Web **3**(1), 41–60 (2005)
20. Musen, M.A.: The protégé project: a look back and a look forward. AI Matters **1**(4), 4–12 (2015)
21. O'Connor, M.J., Shankar, R.D., Musen, M.A., Das, A.K., Nyulas, C.: The SWRLAPI: a development environment for working with SWRL rules. In: OWLED (2008)
22. Otero-Cerdeira, L., Rodríguez-Martínez, F.J., Gómez-Rodríguez, A.: Ontology matching: a literature review. Expert Syst. Appl. **42**(2), 949–971 (2015)
23. O'Connor, M., Tu, S., Nyulas, C., Das, A., Musen, M.: Querying the semantic web with SWRL. In: Paschke, A., Biletskiy, Y. (eds.) RuleML 2007. LNCS, vol. 4824, pp. 155–159. Springer, Heidelberg (2007). https://doi.org/10.1007/978-3-540-75975-1_13
24. Ristoski, P., Paulheim, H.: A comparison of propositionalization strategies for creating features from linked open data. Linked Data Knowl. Discov. **6** (2014)
25. Shearer, R., Motik, B., Horrocks, I.: Hermit: a highly-efficient OWL reasoner. In: OWLED, vol. 432, p. 91 (2008)
26. Sirin, E., Parsia, B., Grau, B.C., Kalyanpur, A., Katz, Y.: Pellet: a practical OWL-DL reasoner. Web Semant. Sci. Serv. Agents World Wide Web **5**(2), 51–53 (2007)
27. Staab, S., Studer, R.: Handbook on Ontologies. Springer, Heidelberg (2010)
28. Struharik, J.: Implementing decision trees in hardware. In: 2011 IEEE 9th International Symposium on Intelligent Systems and Informatics (SISY), pp. 41–46. IEEE (2011)
29. Ting, S., Wang, W.M., Kwok, S.K., Tsang, A.H., Lee, W.: Racer: rule-associated case-based reasoning for supporting general practitioners in prescription making. Expert Syst. Appl. **37**(12), 8079–8089 (2010)
30. Zhao, L., Ichise, R., Liu, Z., Mita, S., Sasaki, Y.: Ontology-based driving decision making: a feasibility study at uncontrolled intersections. IEICE Trans. Inf. Syst. **E100.D**(7), 1425–1439 (2017). https://doi.org/10.1587/transinf.2016EDP7337

A Framework for Explaining Query Answers in *DL-Lite*

Federico Croce[(✉)] and Maurizio Lenzerini[(✉)]

Dipartimento di Ingegneria Informatica, Automatica e Gestionale "Antonio Ruberti",
Sapienza Università di Roma, Rome, Italy
{croce,lenzerini}@diag.uniroma1.it

Abstract. An Ontology-based Data Access system is constituted by an ontology, namely a description of the concepts and the relations in a domain of interest, a database storing facts about the domain, and a mapping between the data and the ontology. In this paper, we consider ontologies expressed in the popular *DL-Lite* family of Description Logic, and we address the problem of computing explanations for answers to queries in an OBDA system, where queries are either positive, in particular conjunctive queries, or negative, i.e., negation of conjunctive queries. We provide the following contributions: (i) we propose a formal, comprehensive framework of explaining query answers in OBDA systems based on *DL-Lite*; (ii) we present an algorithm that, given a tuple returned as an answer to a positive query, and given a weighting function, examines all the explanations of the answer, and chooses the best explanation according to such function; (iii) we do the same for the answers to negative queries. Notably, on the way to get the latter result, we present what appears to be the first algorithm that computes the answers to negative queries in *DL-Lite*.

1 Introduction

Ontology-based Data Access [10,11] (OBDA) is a relatively new paradigm for accessing data by posing queries over a formal conceptualization of the domain of interest. The intrinsically declarative nature of this approach has several benefits and peculiar features that characterizes both the functionality of the system managing an OBDA application, and the services exposed by it. Indeed, in its most elementary form, the one we refer to in this paper, an OBDA system can be seen as constituted by two components, called the TBox and the ABox, respectively. The TBox is a description of the concepts and the relations that are relevant in the domain of the information system under consideration, and the ABox is the representation of the data about the domain, i.e., the data regarding the instances of the concepts and the relations.

In a traditional database system, the ABox would represent a complete representation of the data (Closed World Assumption), while in the case of an OBDA system, the ABox is a set of data that is valid for the domain, but is not complete (Open World Assumption): more data can be derived by using the axioms in the

© Springer Nature Switzerland AG 2018
C. Faron Zucker et al. (Eds.): EKAW 2018, LNAI 11313, pp. 83–97, 2018.
https://doi.org/10.1007/978-3-030-03667-6_6

TBox. In what follows, we refer to the pair ⟨TBox, ABox⟩ collectively as "the ontology", and, as usual, we assume that such ontology is expressed in terms of a Description Logic of the *DL-Lite* family [4]. Most of the research carried out in the last years on OBDA has concentrated on query answering [4,5,7,13], i.e., on the design of algorithms for computing the answers to queries posed to an ontology, for the case of basic forms of queries, in particular conjunctive queries. Note, however, that even for such simple queries, this problem is more challenging than the classical query answering problem, precisely because of the presence of the TBox axioms. Consequently, the task of explaining why a certain tuple is an answer to a query is far from being trivial. For instance, if b is a student in the ABox, and the TBox sanctions that every student is a person, then explaining the answer "b is a person" involves exhibiting both the fact that b is a student, and the TBox axiom **Student** is-a **Person**.

The usefulness of query explanation spans from helping out knowledge engineers in debugging ontologies to clarifying the automated reasoning of the system to an end user. Moreover, having the query answers explained is valuable for several related applications. First, it helps in improving Data Quality, because explained answers facilitate the understanding of the underlying database. Secondly, explaining query answers is tightly related to tagging the tuples returned by the system with semantic meaningful context, which might be crucial in Open Data publishing. Furthermore, many researches explored other interesting fields in which this topic could be relevant. For example, [8,12] propose a justification-based explanation mechanism, i.e. a form of explanation for inclusion axioms rather than for answers to a query.

The problem of providing explanations for answers in *DL-Lite* has been addressed in two seminal papers [2,6], where a specific technique for this problem is proposed, based on the fundamental assumption that explanations are strictly related to deductions. The main goal of this paper is to present a general framework for explaining conjunctive query answers in an OBDA system, where queries are either positive, or negative, i.e., negation of conjunctive queries. In particular, we provide the following contributions.

- We describe a formal, comprehensive framework for explaining query answers in OBDA systems based on *DL-Lite*. Our framework is inspired by the one described in [2,6], but has important differences. First, our framework aims at defining all possible explanations of a query answer, whereas the approach followed by [2,6] is based on choosing some explanations, and ignoring others. For example, in their approach, an explanation that is longer than another one will never be returned by the proposed algorithm. On the contrary, in our framework, one can decide that an explanation exposing a few facts in the ABox is preferred to an explanation disclosing more ABox axioms, even if the latter is shorter. Secondly, the framework envisions the use of a function that is able to associate to each explanation a weight, so as to compare different explanations of the same answer. Thirdly, we base our notion of explanation on a concept of variant of ABoxes, in such a way that ABoxes that are variant of each other give the same explanations.

- We present a generic algorithm that, given a tuple returned as an answer to a positive query, explores all the explanations of the answer according to the ontology, and is able to choose the best explanation in accordance with a predefined weighting function.
- We do the same for the answers to negative queries. Notably, on the way to get the latter result, we present what appears to be the first algorithm that computes the answers to negative queries in *DL-Lite*.

We believe that the proposed framework brings several advantages both in terms of quality (i.e., completeness) of the derived explanations, and in terms of flexibility with respect to the most preferred explanations. Indeed, the task of choosing the best explanation for the answers of a query is intrinsically subjective, so that the end result should be user-centered and customizable.

The paper is organized as follows. In Sect. 2 we illustrate the background knowledge that we consider essential for a smooth reading of the paper. In Sect. 3 we present the framework for explaining query answers in *DL-Lite*. In Sect. 4 we describe a complete procedure for computing explanations to positive queries, whereas in Sect. 5 we do the same for negative queries. Finally, we conclude the paper in Sect. 6.

2 Background

In this section we provide the background notions and techniques that we refer to in the rest of the paper. In particular, we introduce the *DL-Lite* family [4] of Description Logics which is a well-known set of logic-based ontology languages aiming at an optimal trade-off between expressiveness and computational complexity of the reasoning services. Then, we recall some basic notions about conjunctive queries in the context of OBDA, we introduce the notion of negative conjunctive query, and finally, we discuss the algorithm described in [4], that deals with rewriting a conjunctive query in order to compute its answers.

The* DL-Lite *Family of Description Logics. Description Logics (DLs) [1, 9, 14] represents a domain of interest in terms of *concepts*, denoting sets of objects, *roles*, denoting binary relations between (instances of) concepts, and *attributes*, denoting binary relations between concepts and value sets. In this paper, we refer to the logic $DL\text{-}Lite_{\mathcal{A}}$ [4][1], but our approach is valid for all logics of the *DL-Lite* family.

Concepts and roles in $DL\text{-}Lite_{\mathcal{A}}$ are formed according to the following syntax:

$$B \longrightarrow A \mid \exists R \qquad R \longrightarrow P \mid P^-$$

$$C \longrightarrow B \mid \neg B \qquad E \longrightarrow R \mid \neg R$$

where A, B, and C denote an *atomic concept*, a *basic concept*, and a *general concept*, respectively, whilst P denotes an *atomic role*, and R a *general role*.

---

[1] For the sake of simplicity, we do not deal with attributes in this paper, but they can be added without any problem.

Intuitively, P^- represents the *inverse* of the role P, $\exists P$ (resp. $\exists P^-$) denotes the projection on the first (resp. second) component of the role P (resp. P^-), and $\neg B$ (resp. $\neg R$) denotes the complement of B (resp. of R).

A *DL-Lite$_A$* ontology $\mathcal{O} = \langle \mathcal{T}, \mathcal{A} \rangle$ is a formal description of a domain of interest expressed in *DL-Lite$_A$* constituted of the two sets of axioms $\mathcal{T}$, and $\mathcal{A}$. The TBox $\mathcal{T}$ represents the intensional knowledge regarding the domain, i.e., universally quantified statements about the concepts and the roles used in $\mathcal{O}$, and the ABox $\mathcal{A}$ represents the extensional knowledge, i.e., ground statements about individuals. More precisely, each TBox axiom has one of the following forms: $B \sqsubseteq C$ (concept inclusion), $R \sqsubseteq E$ (role inclusion), and (**funct** R) (global functionality of the role R). More details about the axioms allowed in *DL-Lite$_A$*, and the semantics of the language can be found in [4].

Conjunctive Queries. A *conjunctive query* (CQ) over a *DL-Lite$_A$* ontology has the form:

$$Q(\boldsymbol{x}) \leftarrow \exists \boldsymbol{y} \; conj(\boldsymbol{x}, \boldsymbol{y})$$

where $\boldsymbol{x}$, $\boldsymbol{y}$ are variable vectors, $conj(\boldsymbol{x}, \boldsymbol{y})$ is a conjunction of atoms, each one of the form $A(z)$ or $P(z_1, z_2)$, with A and P atomic concepts and roles of the ontology, respectively, and z, z_1, z_2 are terms, i.e., either individual constants in the ontology or variables in $\boldsymbol{x}$ or $\boldsymbol{y}$. The variables appearing in $\boldsymbol{x}$ are called *distinguished* and represents the output of the query, while those appearing in $\boldsymbol{y}$ are called *non-distinguished*, and are existentially quantified. The cardinality of $\boldsymbol{x}$ is the arity of the query, and, for the sake of simplicity, in what follows we assume it is greater than 0, although all results of the paper still holds for queries of arity 0. When it is irrelevant to indicate which are the non-distinguished variables, we simply write $Q(\boldsymbol{x})$ to refer to the query $Q(\boldsymbol{x})$ instead of $Q(\boldsymbol{x}, \boldsymbol{y})$. An atom with only constants is called *ground*.

The basic reasoning service we are dealing with in this paper is *conjunctive query answering*: given an ontology $\mathcal{O}$ and a conjunctive query $Q(\boldsymbol{x})$ over $\mathcal{O}$, compute the *certain answers* to Q over $\mathcal{O}$, the tuples $\boldsymbol{c}$ of individuals in $\mathcal{O}$ such that $\mathcal{O} \models Q(\boldsymbol{c})$, i.e., $Q(\boldsymbol{c})$ is true in **every** model of $\mathcal{O}$. Here, $Q(\boldsymbol{c})$ denotes the formula obtained from $Q(\boldsymbol{x})$ by substituting every $x_i \in \boldsymbol{x}$ with $c_i \in \boldsymbol{c}$.

In this paper, we will also consider negative conjunctive queries, written in the form $\neg Q(\boldsymbol{x}, \boldsymbol{y})$, where $Q(\boldsymbol{x}) \leftarrow \exists \boldsymbol{y} \; conj(\boldsymbol{x}, \boldsymbol{y})$ is a CQ. The certain answers to $\neg Q(\boldsymbol{x}, \boldsymbol{y})$ over $\mathcal{O}$ is the set of tuples $\boldsymbol{c}$ of individuals in $\mathcal{O}$ such that $\mathcal{O} \models \neg Q(\boldsymbol{c})$, i.e., $\mathcal{O} \models \neg \exists \boldsymbol{y} \; conj(\boldsymbol{c}, \boldsymbol{y})$, which is equivalent to state that $\exists \boldsymbol{y} \; conj(\boldsymbol{c}, \boldsymbol{y})$ is false in **every** model of $\mathcal{O}$. Note, due to the Open World Assumption, the certain answers to $\neg Q(\boldsymbol{x}, \boldsymbol{y})$ over $\mathcal{O}$ are in general different from the complement of the certain answers to $Q(\boldsymbol{x}, \boldsymbol{y})$ over $\mathcal{O}$. Note also that, if $Q(\boldsymbol{x}, \boldsymbol{y})$ is empty w.r.t. $\mathcal{O}$ (i.e., it returns the empty answer in all the models of $\mathcal{O}$), then all tuples of individuals in $\mathcal{O}$ will be a certain answer of $\neg Q(\boldsymbol{x}, \boldsymbol{y})$. For this reason, in the following we will assume to deal with negative queries $\neg Q(\boldsymbol{x}, \boldsymbol{y})$ such that $Q(\boldsymbol{x}, \boldsymbol{y})$ is non-empty.

Computing Certain Answers in DL $-$ Lite$_A$. We refer to [4] for the method we use for computing the certain answers to conjunctive queries in the *DL-Lite* family. The method is based on first rewriting the original query into a set of alternate queries, then by evaluating these queries over the ABox of the ontology treated as a closed database, and finally by returning the union of the results. The rewriting of the query with respect to the ontology is carried out by a combination of applications of the following two fundamental steps:

- *Replacement*: a *replacement step* s w.r.t. a query Q and a *TBox* $\mathcal{T}$ can be applied to an atom α of the query when the corresponding predicate appears on the right hand side of an inclusion axiom in $\mathcal{T}$. It returns a new query (that we say is produced by s from Q) with atom α replaced by another one, using the predicate appearing on the left hand side of the inclusion axiom in $\mathcal{T}$.
- *Unification*: a *unification step* s w.r.t. a query Q and a *TBox* $\mathcal{T}$ produces a query obtained by merging two atoms that have the same predicate and such that the corresponding arguments can be unified, and applying the unification to all atoms of the query.

For the purpose of this paper, we will usually refer to either the *replacement* or the *unification* step by the more general term of *reformulation step*. Once a query is rewritten according to the above rules, all queries resulting from the process are inserted into a set, that constitute the rewriting. All the queries in the rewriting are then evaluated over the ABox, by resorting to the well-known notion of *homomorphisms*.

As for negative queries, we are not aware of any paper illustrating an algorithms for computing the certain answers of such queries. The result presented in Sect. 5 will implicitly provide what appears to be the first algorithm that computes the answers to negative queries in *DL-Lite*.

3   Framework

In this section we describe our framework for explaining query answers in the *DL-Lite* family of Description Logics. We start with a set of definitions that are meant to provide the notions we will use for presenting our proposal.

Definition 1. *Given a TBox $\mathcal{T}$, and a conjunctive query Q, a $(Q, \mathcal{T})$-deductive path is a sequence $\langle Q_0, s_1, Q_1, s_2, \ldots, Q_n \rangle$, where $n \geq 0$, $Q_0 = Q$, and for each $i = 1, \ldots, n$, s_i is a reformulation step that produces Q_i from Q_{i-1}.*

Intuitively, a $(Q, \mathcal{T})$-deductive path $\langle Q_0, s_1, Q_1, s_2, \ldots, Q_n \rangle$ encodes the chain of reasoning justifying the fact that in order to prove that t is a certain answer of Q_0 with respect to $\langle \mathcal{T}, \mathcal{A} \rangle$ is sufficient to prove that t is a certain answer of Q_n with respect to $\langle \mathcal{T}, \mathcal{A} \rangle$.

With the goal of illustrating an example of a deductive path, consider the following ontology.

$\mathcal{T} = \{$ ForeignStud $\sqsubseteq$ Student, AttendedBy $\sqsubseteq$ Attends$^-$,
       Attends$^-$ $\sqsubseteq$ AttendedBy, $\exists$HasCSTopic $\sqsubseteq$ $\exists$HasTopic,

```
                Student ⊑ ¬Professor, AssociateProf ⊑ Professor}
    A = { ForeignStud(Ann), AttendedBy(DB,Ann),
          HasCSTopic(DB,SQL), HasCSTopic(DB,ER)}
```
Now, consider the query:

$$Q(x, y) \leftarrow \text{Student}(x), \text{Attends}(x, y), \text{HasTopic}(y, z)$$

It is easy to see that, for example, $\langle Q, s_1, Q_1, s_2, Q_2, s_3, Q_3 \rangle$ is a $(Q, \mathcal{T})$-deductive path, where

- s_1 is the reformulation step based on ForeignStud ⊑ Student that produces $Q_1(x, y) \leftarrow \text{ForeignStud}(x), \text{Attends}(x, y), \text{HasTopic}(y, z)$ from Q,
- s_2 is the reformulation step based on ∃HasCSTopic ⊑ ∃HasTopic that produces $Q_2(x, y) \leftarrow \text{ForeignStud}(x), \text{Attends}(x, y), \text{HasCSTopic}(y, z)$ from Q_1
- s_3 is the reformulation step based on AttendedBy ⊑ Attends⁻ that produces $Q_3(x, y) \leftarrow \text{ForeignStud}(x), \text{AttendedB}(y, x), \text{HasCSTopic}(y, z)$ from Q_2.

3.1 Explanations for Positive Queries

The most obvious way to define an explanation for $Q(t)$ with respect to the ontology $\langle \mathcal{T}, \mathcal{A} \rangle$ is to see it as a $(Q, \mathcal{T})$-deductive path $\langle Q, s_1, Q_1, s_2, \ldots, Q_n \rangle$ associated to a homomorphism from $Q_n(t)$ to $\mathcal{A}$. Indeed, the presence of the homomorphism proves that $\mathcal{A} \models Q_n(t)$, and the $(Q, \mathcal{T})$-deductive path is a chain of deduction explaining how to conclude $\langle \mathcal{T}, \mathcal{A} \rangle \models Q(t)$ from $\mathcal{A} \models Q_n(t)$.

If we adopt this approach in the above example, one can verify that the $(Q, \mathcal{T})$-deductive path $\langle Q, s_1, Q_1, s_2, Q_2, s_2, Q_3 \rangle$, associated for example to the homomorphism $\{x \mapsto \text{Ann}, y \mapsto \text{DB}, z \mapsto \text{SQL}\}$ from Q_3 to $\mathcal{A}$ is actually an explanation for $Q(\text{Ann}, \text{DB})$.

However, our notion of explanation is more articulated. First, we will rely only on deductive paths that are not redundant, i.e., that do not contain identical subpaths. More precisely, a $(Q, \mathcal{T})$-deductive path $\langle Q, s_1, Q_1, s_2, \ldots, Q_n \rangle$ is said to be non-redundant if for all $i \neq j \in \{1, \ldots, n\}$, we have that $Q_i \neq Q$, and $Q_i \neq Q_j$. Second, in order to explain $Q(t)$ with respect to $\langle \mathcal{T}, \mathcal{A} \rangle$, our approach relies not only on $(Q, \mathcal{T})$-deductive paths $\langle Q, s_1, Q_1, s_2, \ldots, Q_n \rangle$ such that $\mathcal{A} \models Q_n(t)$, but also on $(Q, \mathcal{T})$-deductive paths $\langle Q, s_1, Q_1, s_2, \ldots, Q_n \rangle$ such that $\mathcal{A}' \models Q_n(t)$, where $\mathcal{A}$ and $\mathcal{A}'$ are in a certain mutual relationship, i.e., $\mathcal{A}'$ is a variant of $\mathcal{A}$ with respect to $\mathcal{T}$. Intuitively, by stating that $\mathcal{A}'$ is a variant of $\mathcal{A}$ with respect to $\mathcal{T}$, we sanction that they are indistinguishable from the point of view of a user posing queries to the ontology. The consequence is that, in order to explain a certain answer, we can use $\mathcal{A}$ and $\mathcal{A}'$ interchangeably. For a specific definition of variant, tailored for *DL-Lite* ontologies, we refer the reader to the last part of this section. Here, we want to notice that the notion of variant ABoxes will allow us to consider explanations that are shorter than in the usual approaches. We are now ready to present the definition of $\langle \mathcal{T}, \mathcal{A} \rangle$-explanation for $Q(t)$ in our approach.

Definition 2. *A $(\mathcal{T}, \mathcal{A})$-explanation for $Q(t)$ is a pair $\langle \Pi, \Gamma \rangle$, where*

- Π is a non-redundant $(Q, \mathcal{T})$-deductive path of the form $\langle Q(\boldsymbol{x}), s_1, Q_2(\boldsymbol{x}), s_2, \ldots, Q_n(\boldsymbol{x}) \rangle$, and
- Γ is the image $Q_n(\boldsymbol{t}, \boldsymbol{t'})$ of a homomorphism from $Q_n(\boldsymbol{x}, \boldsymbol{y})$ to any ABox that is a $\mathcal{T}$-variant of $\mathcal{A}$.

In a $(\mathcal{T}, \mathcal{A})$-explanation $\langle \Pi, \Gamma \rangle$, the ground formula constituted by the atoms in Γ is called an explanatory seed *for* Π.

Intuitively, the pattern represented by Γ provides the reason why $\boldsymbol{t}$ satisfies $Q_n(\boldsymbol{x})$ w.r.t. the ABox $\mathcal{A}$, and the $(Q, \mathcal{T})$-deductive path provides explanation why from this pattern we can conclude that $\boldsymbol{t}$ is a certain answer to the query Q. Referring to the example above, it is immediate to verify that both the pair $\langle \Pi_1, \Gamma_1 \rangle$, and the pair $\langle \Pi_1, \Gamma_2 \rangle$ are $(\mathcal{T}, \mathcal{A})$-explanations for $Q(\text{Ann}, \text{DB})$, where

- $\Pi_1 = \langle Q, s_1, Q_1, s_2, Q_2, s_3, Q_3 \rangle$,
- $\Gamma_1 = \{\text{ForeignStud(Ann)}, \text{AttendedBy(DB,Ann)}, \text{HasCSTopic(DB,SQL)}\}$,
- $\Gamma_2 = \{\text{ForeignStud(Ann)}, \text{AttendedBy(DB,Ann)}, \text{HasCSTopic(DB,ER)}\}$.

Indeed, Γ_1 and Γ_2 are the images of two homomorphisms from Q_3 to $\mathcal{A}$. Note, however, that, if the ABox
$$\mathcal{A'} = \{\text{ForeignStud(Ann)}, \text{Attends(Ann,DB)},$$
$$\text{HasCSTopic(DB,SQL)}, \text{HasCSTopic(DB,ER)}\}$$
is a $\mathcal{T}$-variant of $\mathcal{A}$, then another $(\mathcal{T}, \mathcal{A})$-explanation is, for example, $\langle \Pi_2, \Gamma_3 \rangle$, where

- $\Pi_2 = \langle Q, s_1, Q_1, s_2, Q_2 \rangle$,
- $\Gamma_3 = \{\text{ForeignStud(Ann)}, \text{Attends(Ann,DB)}, \text{HasCSTopic(DB,SQL)}\}$

since Γ_3 is the image of a homomorphism from Q_2 to $\mathcal{A'}$.

3.2 Explanations for Negative Queries

In order to define the notion of explanation for negative queries in our approach, we need to introduce a few concepts.

The first one is the concept of disjointness step as a new deduction step when reasoning about a query. Intuitively, a *disjointness step* is applied to a query Q and a disjoint axiom of the form $\beta_1 \sqsubseteq \neg \beta_2$ in $\mathcal{T}$, when β_i $(i \in \{1, 2\})$ unifies with an atom in Q by means of the unification ϕ. The application of such a disjointness step produces the query composed of the atom γ, obtained by applying the unification ϕ to β_j $(j \in \{1, 2\}, \text{ and } j \neq i)$. The second notion is the one of subtuple: a tuple $\boldsymbol{t'}$ is called a subtuple of $\boldsymbol{t}$ if every element of $\boldsymbol{t'}$ appear also in $\boldsymbol{t}$. Finally, the third notion is the one of reverse $\langle Q, \mathcal{T} \rangle$-deductive path, defined as follows.

Definition 3. *Given a TBox $\mathcal{T}$, and a conjunctive query Q, a reverse $(Q, \mathcal{T})$- deductive path is a sequence $\langle \neg Q_n, s_n, \neg Q_{n-1}, \ldots, s_1, \neg Q_0 \rangle$, where $n \geq 0$, $Q_n = Q$, and $\langle Q_0, s_1, Q_1, s_2, \ldots, Q_n \rangle$ is a $(Q_0, \mathcal{T})$-deductive path.*

Analogously to $(Q, \mathcal{T})$-deductive paths, a reverse $(Q, \mathcal{T})$-deductive path $\langle \neg Q_n, s_n, \neg Q_{n-1}, \ldots, s_1, \neg Q_0 \rangle$ encodes the chain of reasoning justifying the fact that in order to prove that t is a certain answer of $\neg Q_n$ with respect to $\langle \mathcal{T}, \mathcal{A} \rangle$ is sufficient to prove that t is a certain answer of $\neg Q_0$ with respect to $\langle \mathcal{T}, \mathcal{A} \rangle$.

Definition 4. *A $(\mathcal{T}, \mathcal{A})$-explanation for $\neg Q(t)$ is a pair $\langle \Sigma, \Gamma \rangle$, where Σ is a sequence of the form $\langle \neg Q, s_1, \neg Q_2, s_2, \ldots, \neg Q_m, s_m, Q_{m+1}, s_{m+2}, \ldots Q_{m+n} \rangle$ such that*

- $m, n \geq 0$,
- $\langle \neg Q, s_1, \neg Q_2, s_2, \ldots, \neg Q_m \rangle$ *is a reverse $(Q, \mathcal{T})$-deductive path,*
- s_m *is a disjointness step that produces Q_{m+1} from $\neg Q_m$, and*
- $\langle \langle Q_{m+1}, s_{m+2}, \ldots, Q_{m+n} \rangle, \Gamma \rangle$ *is a $(\mathcal{T}, \mathcal{A})$-explanation for $Q_{m+1}(t')$, where t' is a subtuple of t.*

Intuitively, $\langle \langle Q_{m+1}, s_{m+2}, \ldots, Q_{m+n} \rangle, \Gamma \rangle$ explains why t' is a certain answer of Q_{m+1}, s_m is the disjointness step proving that t is a certain answer of $\neg Q_m$ by exploiting the fact that t' is a certain answer of Q_{m+1}, and the reverse $(Q, \mathcal{T})$-deductive path $\langle \neg Q, s_1, \neg Q_2, s_2, \ldots, \neg Q_m \rangle$ proves that t is a certain answer of $\neg Q$. Coming back to the example, we can easily verify that, given the query $Q(x) \leftarrow \texttt{AssociateProf}(x), \texttt{Teaches}(x, y)$, a $(\mathcal{T}, \mathcal{A})$-explanation for $\neg Q(\texttt{Ann})$ is $\langle \langle \neg Q, s_1, \neg Q_1, s_0, Q_2, s_2, Q_3 \rangle, \{\texttt{ForeignStud}(\texttt{Ann})\} \rangle$, where Q_1, Q_2 and Q_3 are defined as follows

- $Q_1 \leftarrow \texttt{Professor}(x), \texttt{Teaches}(x, y)$
- $Q_2(x) \leftarrow \texttt{Student}(x)$,
- $Q_3(x) \leftarrow \texttt{ForeignStud}(x)$,

s_1 is the reformulation step that produces Q_1 from Q, s_0 is the disjointness step based on the axiom $\texttt{Student} \sqsubseteq \neg\texttt{Professor}$ to produce Q_2 from $\neg Q_1$, s_2 is the reformulation step that produces Q_3 from Q_2.

3.3   The Notion of Variant in *DL-Lite*

While we left the notion of variant generic in the above considerations, we provide here a specific formalization of the notion of $\mathcal{T}$-variant for the case of *DL-Lite* ontologies. In what follows, we denote with $\mathcal{E}_\mathcal{T}$ the set of *DL-Lite* assertions of the form $E_1 \equiv E_2$ (where E_1, E_2 are either both concepts or both roles) that are logically implied by $\mathcal{T}$. Also, we say that two ground atoms α, β are $\mathcal{T}$-equivalent if $\mathcal{T} \models \alpha \equiv \beta$.

Definition 5. *If $\mathcal{T}$ is a TBox, and $\mathcal{A}, \mathcal{A}'$ are two ABoxes, then $\mathcal{A}$ is a $\mathcal{T}$-variant of $\mathcal{A}'$ if $\mathcal{A}'$ can be obtained from $\mathcal{A}$ by a set of substitutions of atoms with $\mathcal{T}$-equivalent atoms.*

In other words, $\mathcal{A}$ and $\mathcal{A}'$ are $\mathcal{T}$-variant when their logical equivalence can be proved by using only pairwise $\mathcal{T}$-equivalences of atoms.

Coming back to the example, by using the notion of variant just presented, we can verify that another explanation for $Q(\text{Ann}, \text{DB})$ in our approach is based on the $(Q, \mathcal{T})$-deductive path $\langle Q, s_1, Q_2, s_2, Q_3 \rangle$, because, although $\mathcal{A} \not\models Q_3(\text{Ann}, \text{DB})$, the following ABox

$$\mathcal{A}' = \{\texttt{ForeignStud(Ann)}, \texttt{Attends(Ann,DB)}, \texttt{HasCSTopic(DB,SQL)}\}$$

is a $\mathcal{T}$-variant of $\mathcal{A}$, and is such that $\{x \mapsto \text{Ann}, y \mapsto \text{DB}, z \mapsto \text{SQL}\}$ is a homomorphism from Q_3 to $\mathcal{A}'$, thus proving that $\mathcal{A}' \models Q_3(\text{Ann}, \text{DB})$. Notice that ABoxes can be obviously seen as conjunctive queries, in particular, ground conjunctive queries, and therefore the notion of deductive path can be applied to ABoxes as well. This property is exploited in the following theorem, that will be used in the technical development presented in the rest of the paper.

Theorem 1. *The ABox $\mathcal{A}$ is a $\mathcal{T}$-variant of the ABox $\mathcal{A}'$ if and only if there is an $(\mathcal{A}, \mathcal{E}_{\mathcal{T}})$-deductive path of the form $\langle \mathcal{A}, s_1, \mathcal{A}_1, s_2, \ldots, \mathcal{A}' \rangle$.*

Proof. If-part. Suppose that there is an $(\mathcal{A}, \mathcal{E}_{\mathcal{T}})$-*deductive path* that has the form $\langle \mathcal{A}_0, s_1, \mathcal{A}_1, s_2, \ldots, \mathcal{A}_n \rangle$ where $\mathcal{A} = \mathcal{A}_0$, and $\mathcal{A}_n = \mathcal{A}'$. We show by induction on the length n of such path that $\mathcal{A}$ is a $\mathcal{T}$-variant of $\mathcal{A}'$. If n is 0, then the thesis trivially holds. If n is greater than 0, then $\langle \mathcal{A}_1, s_2, \ldots, \mathcal{A}' \rangle$ is an $(\mathcal{A}_1, \mathcal{E}_{\mathcal{T}})$-*deductive path* whose length is $n - 1$. By induction hypothesis, we have that $\mathcal{A}_1$ is a $\mathcal{T}$-variant of $\mathcal{A}'$, i.e., $\mathcal{A}'$ can be obtained from $\mathcal{A}_1$ by a set of substitutions of equivalent atoms. It remains to show that $\mathcal{A} = \mathcal{A}_0$ is a $\mathcal{T}$-variant of $\mathcal{A}_1$, thus showing that $\mathcal{A}'$ can be obtained from $\mathcal{A}$ by a set of substitutions of equivalent atoms. By the definition of $(\mathcal{A}, \mathcal{E}_{\mathcal{T}})$-*deductive path*, we have that $\mathcal{A}_1$ is obtained from $\mathcal{A}$ by means of a reformulation step that substitutes an atom α in $\mathcal{A}$ with an atom β using an axiom of the form $\alpha \equiv \beta$ in $\mathcal{E}_{\mathcal{T}}$. This obviously implies that $\mathcal{A}$ is a $\mathcal{T}$-variant of $\mathcal{A}_1$.

Only-if-part. Suppose that $\mathcal{A}$ is a $\mathcal{T}$-variant of the ABox $\mathcal{A}'$. We proceed by induction on the number n of atoms in $\mathcal{A}$ that we have to substitute in order to obtain $\mathcal{A}'$. If $n = 0$, then the thesis trivially holds. If n is greater than 0, then let $\alpha \in \mathcal{A}$ be one of the atoms to be substituted with $\beta \in \mathcal{A}'$ such that $\mathcal{T} \models \alpha \equiv \beta$, and let $\mathcal{A}_1$ be the ABox obtained from $\mathcal{A}$ by means of such substitution. By induction hypothesis, there is an $(\mathcal{A}, \mathcal{E}_{\mathcal{T}})$-*deductive path* of the form $\langle \mathcal{A}_1, s_2, \mathcal{A}_2, s_3, \ldots, \mathcal{A}' \rangle$, and it is immediate to verify that from $\mathcal{T} \models \alpha \equiv \beta$ we can derive a reformulation step that produces $\mathcal{A}_1$ from $\mathcal{A}$, thus proving that there is an $(\mathcal{A}, \mathcal{E}_{\mathcal{T}})$-*deductive path* of the form $\langle \mathcal{A}, s_1, \mathcal{A}_1, s_2, \ldots, \mathcal{A}' \rangle$. □

3.4 Weighting Explanations

As we said in the introduction, the framework presented in this paper intentionally leaves unspecified the strategy for evaluating the multiple explanations that are computed for the same tuple, query, and ontology. This is reflected by the fact that the framework envisions the existence of a function that is able to associate to each explanation a weight, so as to compare different explanations of the same answer. Although in existing approaches the weighting function is based essentially on the length of the deduction corresponding to the explanation, we argue that such function should reflect the idea that choosing the best explanation for the answers of a query is intrinsically subjective, and can be characterized by different properties in different contexts. For this reason, in the next section we will keep the weighting function completely generic.

4   Computing Explanations for Positive Queries

Given a query Q, a tuple t, and an ontology $\langle \mathcal{T}, \mathcal{A} \rangle$, the algorithm Explain essentially builds a tree τ whose nodes are in one-to-one correspondence with the non-redundant $(Q, \mathcal{T})$-deductive paths, and computes all $(\mathcal{T}, \mathcal{A})$-explanations of $Q(t)$ based on such paths. For each such explanation, it also computes the associated weight, and the final result derives from the one with the maximum weight. The algorithm makes use of the following notions.

- For each node n of the tree τ:
  - father(n) denotes the father of node n in the tree τ; father(n) is assumed to be *null* if n is the root.
  - equivEdge(n, m) is true if n and m are nodes different from *null*, n is the father of m in τ, and the edge from n to m is labeled with a reformulation step based on $\alpha \sqsubseteq \beta$ such that $\mathcal{T} \models \beta \sqsubseteq \alpha$; it is false otherwise.
  - query(n) is set by the algorithm in such a way to denote the query associated to n;
  - images(n) is set by the algorithm in such a way to denote the set of images of all homomorphisms from query(n) that are relevant for computing the explanations; note that every image is a set of ground facts, and that images$(null)$ is assumed to be empty;
- best is a record managed by the algorithm in such a way that it stores information about the best explanation currently found. The record contains three items: best.node stores the node n corresponding to the deductive path representing the explanation; best.image stores the set of facts constituting the image of the homomorphism from query(n) to $\mathcal{A}$ which gives the best explanation, and best.weight is the value of the weight of such explanation.
- transferImages(n, m) denotes the process of transferring the sets of facts stored in images(n) to images(m), in the case where there is an edge e connecting n and m such that equivEdge(n, m) is true. If equivEdge(n, m) is false, then transferImages(n, m) has no effect. Let s be the reformulation step that is the label of e, and let s be based on $\alpha \equiv \beta$, where α is the predicate of an atom in n, and β is the predicate of an atom in m. Then, for each $\gamma_1 \in$ images(n), insert $\gamma_2 \in$ images(m), where γ_2 is obtained from γ_1 by substituting the α-atom with the corresponding β-atom. For example, if images(n) = {{ForeignStud(Ann),AttendedBy(DB,Ann), HasCSTopic(DB,SQL)}, {ForeignStud(Ann),AttendedBy(DB,Ann), HasCS-Topic(DB,ER)}}, and there is an edge e connecting n and m such that equivEdge(n, m) is true, and the reformulation step that is the label of e is based on

AttendedBy $\sqsubseteq$ Attends$^-$ such that $\mathcal{T} \models$ AttendedBy $\equiv$ Attends$^-$, then we have that the execution of transferImages(n, m) results into images(m) = {{ForeignStud(Ann), Attends(Ann,DB), HasCSTopic(DB,SQL)}, {ForeignStud(Ann), Attends(Ann,DB), HasCSTopic(DB,ER)}}.

- If n is a node of τ, and $\gamma \in$ images(n), then ComputeWeight(n, γ) computes the weight associated to the explanation represented by n and γ, and stores it as weight(γ).

We are now ready to present the algorithm, whose main function is Explain. Given query Q, tuple t, and ontology $\langle \mathcal{T}, \mathcal{A} \rangle$ such that $\langle \mathcal{T}, \mathcal{A} \rangle \models Q(t)$, such function returns the record best storing all relevant data used to reconstruct the best $(\mathcal{T}, \mathcal{A})$-explanation of $Q(t)$. As we said before, Explain defines the tree τ initially constituted only by the root r, and then complete the construction of the tree by means of the function BuildTree called on r. The goal of the latter function is indeed to build the tree in such a way that each node n of τ have the associated data described above, namely, query(n), and images(n). On each node, the BuildTree also calls the function EvaluateAndPropagate, whose goal is to compute the weight of each explanation associated to the nodes that it visits, to update the record best, if needed, and to propagate the set images(n) to other nodes of the tree, if needed. In order to compute the weight of the various explanations, it makes use of the function ComputeWeight, that we leave generic: any strategy that associates a positive value to an explanation is valid in our approach. The final result computed by Explain derives from the explanations with the maximum weight.

The following theorems are crucial for proving the correctness of the algorithm.

Theorem 2. *Let τ be the tree built by the execution of Explain$(Q, t, \mathcal{T}, \mathcal{A})$, and let r be the root of τ. From each path from r to a node of τ, it is possible to derive a non redundant $(Q, \mathcal{T})$-deductive path, and, conversely, from each non redundant $(Q, \mathcal{T})$-deductive path, it is possible to derive a path from r to a node of τ.*

Proof. (Sketch) First part. Let n be a node in τ. The proof is based on induction on the length of the path from r to n. If the length is 0, then the thesis trivially holds. If the length is greater than 0, then there is a node m in τ that is the parent of n, and by the induction hypothesis, we can derive a non redundant $(Q, \mathcal{T})$-deductive path Π_i using the path π_1 from r to m. It is easy to see that we can add a subsequence to Π_i in order to obtain a non redundant $(Q, \mathcal{T})$-deductive path associated to n. *Second part.* Let Π a non redundant $(Q, \mathcal{T})$-deductive path. The proof is based on induction on the length of Π. If the length is 0, then it is immediate to verify that the corresponding path in τ is simply constituted by the root r. If the length is greater than 0, then Π can be seen as a $(Q, \mathcal{T})$-deductive path Π', plus an element corresponding to a reformulation step s. By the induction hypothesis there is a node m for which we can single out a path π from r to m corresponding to the $(Q, \mathcal{T})$-deductive path Π'. Now, using s it is

---

Algorithm 1. The algorithm `Explain` for positive query answers.

---

1 **Function** $Explain(Q, t, \mathcal{T}, \mathcal{A}) : record$
2   define τ as a tree with root r
3   query$(r) \leftarrow Q(t)$
4   best $\leftarrow \langle \mathbf{null}, \emptyset, 0 \rangle$
5   BuildTree(r)
6   **return** best

1 **Function** $EvaluateAndPropagate(n)$
2   **foreach** $\gamma \in images(n)$ **do**
3   ComputeWeight(n, γ)
4   **if** $weight(\gamma) \geq best.weight$ **then** update best
5   **if** $images(father(n)) = \emptyset$ and $equivEdge(father(n), n)$ **then**
6   transferImages$(n, father(n))$
7   EvaluateAndPropagate$(father(n))$
8   **foreach** $child$ m of n **do**
9   **if** $images(m) = \emptyset$ and $equivEdge(n, m)$ **then**
10   transferImages(n, m)
11   EvaluateAndPropagate(m)

1 **Function** $BuildTree(n)$
2   **if** $equivEdge(father(n), n)$ and $images(father(n)) \neq \emptyset$ **then**
3   images$(n) \leftarrow$ transferImages$(father(n), n)$
4   **else** images$(n) \leftarrow$ images of homomorphisms from query(n) to $\mathcal{A}$
5   EvaluateAndPropagate(n)
6   **foreach** $reformulation$ $step$ s $that$ $produces$ Q' $from$ $query(n)$ and $such$ $that$ $query(n_i) \neq Q'$ for $every$ $node$ n_i in the $path$ $from$ n to r **do**
7   create child m of n and label the edge from n to m with s
8   BuildTree(m)

---

easy to see that we can add en edge to π', and obtain a new path π from r to a node n corresponding to Π. $\square$

Theorem 3. *Let τ be the tree built by the execution of* Explain$(Q, t, \mathcal{T}, \mathcal{A})$. *Then, for each node n of τ such that $\Gamma \in$ images(n), there is a $(\mathcal{T}, \mathcal{A})$-explanation of $Q(t)$ of the form $\langle \Pi, \Gamma \rangle$, where Π is the $(Q, \mathcal{T})$-deductive path corresponding to the path from the root of τ to n.*

Theorem 4. *Let τ be the tree built by the execution of* Explain$(Q, t, \mathcal{T}, \mathcal{A})$. *Then, for each $(\mathcal{T}, \mathcal{A})$-explanation of $Q(t)$ of the form $\langle \Pi, \Gamma \rangle$, there is a node n of τ such that $\Gamma \in$ images(n), and the path from the root of τ and n is the one corresponding to the $(Q, \mathcal{T})$-deductive path Π.*

Finally, the following theorem shows the correctness of the function Explain with respect to the goal of computing the best explanation for $Q(t)$. The

---

Algorithm 2. The algorithm Explain for negative query answers.

---

1   **Function** *ExplainNegative(Q, T, A, t):* $\langle T, A \rangle$-*explanation for* $\neg Q(t)$

2   Initialize NEP as an empty pair $\langle$sequence,image$\rangle$

3   **foreach** *disjoint axiom* $\Delta \in T$ **do**

4   Let (g_1, g_2) be the two atoms of the violating query associated with Δ

5   **foreach** *atom* α *in* Q **do**

6   Let t' be a subtuple of t

7   Let γ be the predicate associated with α

8   Let η_1, η_2 be the predicates associated with g_1, g_2

9   **if** $T \models \gamma \sqsubseteq \eta_1$ **then**

10   **if** $\langle T, A \rangle \models g_2(t')$ **then**

11              $g' = g_1, g'' = g_2$

12   **else**

13   **if** $T \models \gamma \sqsubseteq \eta_2$ **then**

14   **if** $\langle T, A \rangle \models g_1(t')$ **then**

15                $g' = g_2, g'' = g_1$

16   **if** g' *and* g'' *are defined* **then**

17            $\langle \langle g'', s_n, Q_{n+1}, \ldots, Q_m \rangle, \Gamma \rangle = $ **Explain**(g'', T, A, t')

18   **foreach** *reverse* (Q, T)*-deductive path*
               $\langle \neg Q, s_1, \neg Q_2, s_2, \ldots, \neg g' \rangle$ **do**

19   Let $\Pi =$
               $\langle \langle \neg Q, s_1, \neg Q_2, s_2, \ldots, \neg g', \Delta, g'', s_n, Q_{n+1}, \ldots, Q_m \rangle, \Gamma \rangle$ **if**
               ComputeWeight*(Π)* *is better than* NEP **then**

20   Update NEP with Π

21   **return** NEP

---

proof proceeds by showing that Explain(Q, t, T, A) explores all possible (T, A)-explanations for $Q(t)$, computes the corresponding weight, and then returns the one (or anyone) with the maximum weight.

Theorem 5. *Let* $\langle T, A \rangle$ *be an ontology, Q be a query, and t be a tuple such that* $\langle T, A \rangle \models Q(t)$. *Then* Explain$(Q, t, T, A)$ *computes the best* (T, A)-*explanation for* $Q(t)$, *according to the strategy represented by the function* ComputeWeight.

5   Computing Explanations for Negative Queries

In this section we present the Algorithm 2 that deals with building the negative explanation for a tuple t, with respect to a satisfiable ontology $\langle T, A \rangle$, and a non-empty query Q. For each disjoint axiom in the input ontology, the procedure checks whether the corresponding violating query has a non-empty evaluation over $\langle T, A \cup Q(t) \rangle$ (in *DL-Lite*, if $\langle T, A \rangle \models \neg Q(t)$ this has to be true for some violating query). If this is the case, the algorithm builds a negative explanation, and evaluates it with a predetermined evaluation function that plays the same role as the function `ComputeWeight` in the case of positive explanations. The output will be the explanation with the highest evaluation. Specifically, let ω be an arbitrary violating query, g_1, g_2 be their atoms, and η_1, η_2 their corresponding predicates. For each atom of Q, the algorithm verifies whether its predicate γ is a subset of either η_1 or η_2 in $\mathcal{T}$. Let for instance $\mathcal{T} \models \gamma \sqsubseteq \eta_1$, the algorithm searches for a $\langle \mathcal{T}, \mathcal{A} \rangle$-explanation for the query $g_2(t')$, where t' is a subtuple of t. Then, for all the possible reverse $(\mathcal{Q}, \mathcal{T})$-deductive paths that leads to g_1, the algorithm builds and evaluates a negative explanation by connecting the aforementioned deductive and explanation paths. The correctness of the algorithm is sanctioned by the following theorem.

Theorem 6. *Given a conjunctive query Q, a TBox $\mathcal{T}$, an ABox $\mathcal{A}$ and a tuple t such that $\langle \mathcal{T}, \mathcal{A} \rangle$ is satisfiable, Q is not empty over $\langle \mathcal{T}, \mathcal{A} \rangle$, and $\langle \mathcal{T}, \mathcal{A} \rangle \models \neg Q(t)$, then Algorithm 2 evaluates all and only the $\langle \mathcal{T}, \mathcal{A} \rangle$-explanations for $\neg Q(t)$.*

Proof (sketch). According to a well-known property of the *DL-Lite* language, $\langle \mathcal{T}, \mathcal{A} \rangle \models \neg Q(t)$ if and only if $\langle \mathcal{T}, \mathcal{A} \cup \mathcal{Q}(t) \rangle$ is unsatisfiable. For each disjoint axiom of $\mathcal{T}$, consider the corresponding two atoms violating query. A *DL-Lite* ontology is unsatisfiable if and only if there exists a violating query for which the evaluation over the ontology is not empty. Since by hypothesis $\langle \mathcal{T}, \mathcal{A} \rangle$ is satisfiable, and the input query Q is not empty over $\langle \mathcal{T}, \mathcal{A} \rangle$, for each violating query ω, it has to be that $\langle \mathcal{T}, \mathcal{A} \rangle \not\models \omega$ and $\langle \mathcal{T}, \mathcal{Q}(t) \rangle \not\models \omega$. As a consequence, let ρ_1, ρ_2 be the two atoms of any violating query, and t' a subtuple of t, a negative explanation for $Q(t)$ exists if and only if either $\langle \mathcal{T}, \mathcal{A} \rangle \models \rho_1(t')$ and $\langle \mathcal{T}, \mathcal{Q}(t) \rangle \models \rho_2(t')$, or $\langle \mathcal{T}, \mathcal{A} \rangle \models \rho_2(t')$ and $\langle \mathcal{T}, \mathcal{Q}(t) \rangle \models \rho_1(t')$. The algorithm considers both the above cases and provides explanations for the holding entailments. □

6   Conclusions

In this paper, we addressed the problem of providing explanations both for positive and negative answers to queries over an ontology. In Sect. 3 we introduced a general framework to deal with these issues, and in Sects. 4 and 5 we illustrated techniques for inspecting all possible explanations, both for positive and for negative conjunctive queries.

The issue of multiple explanations is addressed by conceiving the use of a weighting function that assigns a weight to every possible explanation, so that they can be compared according to a set of predefined criteria. We have implemented the procedures described in this paper in the Java tool for Ontology Based Data Access MASTRO [3]. Future works involve dealing with the problem of deriving an effective method for visualizing, and exposing to the users the explanations produced with our techniques, as well as analyzing the effect, on the notions and methodologies introduced in this paper, of extending the ontology to languages that are more expressive than *DL-Lite*.

References

1. Baader, F., Calvanese, D., McGuinness, D.L., Nardi, D., Patel-Schneider, P.F. (eds.): The Description Logic Handbook: Theory, Implementation, and Applications. Cambridge University Press, New York (2003)
2. Borgida, A., Calvanese, D., Rodriguez-Muro, M.: Explanation in the *DL-Lite* family of description logics. In: Meersman, R., Tari, Z. (eds.) OTM 2008. LNCS, vol. 5332, pp. 1440–1457. Springer, Heidelberg (2008). https://doi.org/10.1007/978-3-540-88873-4_35
3. Calvanese, D., et al.: The mastro system for ontology-based data access. Semant. Web **2**(1), 43–53 (2011)
4. Calvanese, D., De Giacomo, G., Lembo, D., Lenzerini, M., Rosati, R.: Tractable reasoning and efficient query answering in description logics: the *DL-Lite* family. J. Autom. Reasoning **39**(3), 385–429 (2007)
5. Calvanese, D., Giacomo, G.D., Lembo, D., Lenzerini, M., Rosati, R.: Data complexity of query answering in description logics. Artif. Intell. **195**, 335–360 (2013)
6. Calvanese, D., Ortiz, M., Simkus, M., Stefanoni, G.: Reasoning about explanations for negative query answers in DL-Lite. J. Artif. Intell. Res. **48**, 635–669 (2013)
7. Eiter, T., Lutz, C., Ortiz, M., Simkus, M.: Answering in description logics with transitive roles. In: IJCAI (2009)
8. Horridge, M.: Justification based explanation in ontologies. Ph.D. thesis, University of Manchester, UK (2011)
9. Levesque, H.J., Brachman, R.J.: Expressiveness and tractability in knowledge representation and reasoning. Comput. Intell. **3**, 78–93 (1987)
10. Lenzerini, M.: Ontology-based data management. In: Proceedings of the 20th ACM International Conference on Information and Knowledge Management, CIKM 2011, pp. 5–6. ACM, New York (2011)
11. Lenzerini, M.: Managing data through the lens of an ontology. AI Mag. **39**(2), 65–74 (2018)
12. Penaloza, R., Sertkaya, B.: Understanding the complexity of axiom pinpointing in lightweight description logics. Artif. Intell. **250**(Supplement C), 80–104 (2017)
13. Straccia, U.: Towards top-k query answering in description logics: the case of DL-Lite. In: Fisher, M., van der Hoek, W., Konev, B., Lisitsa, A. (eds.) JELIA 2006. LNCS (LNAI), vol. 4160, pp. 439–451. Springer, Heidelberg (2006). https://doi.org/10.1007/11853886_36
14. van Harmelen, F., Lifschitz, V., Porter, B.: Handbook of Knowledge Representation. Elsevier Science, San Diego (2007)

DLFoil: Class Expression Learning Revisited

Nicola Fanizzi, Giuseppe Rizzo[✉], Claudia d'Amato, and Floriana Esposito

LACAM – Dipartimento di Informatica, Università degli studi di Bari Aldo Moro,
Via Orabona, 4, 70125 Bari, Italy
{nicola.fanizzi,giuseppe.rizzo1,claudia.damato,
floriana.esposito}@uniba.it

Abstract. The paper presents the ultimate version of a concept learning system which can support typical ontology construction/evolution tasks through the induction of class expressions from groups of individual resources labeled by a domain expert. Stating the target task as a search problem, a FOIL-like algorithm was devised based on the employment of refinement operators to traverse the version-space of candidate definitions for the target class. The algorithm has been further enhanced including a more general definition for the scoring function and better refinement operators. An experimental evaluation of the resulting new release of DL-FOIL, which implements these improvements was carried out to assess its performance also in comparison with other concept learning systems.

1 Introduction

Formal ontologies play a key role in the next generation information systems moving from legacy to linked open data whose semantics is intended to be shared across the *Web of Data* [10]. Differently from former (centralized) knowledge base construction models, a long-term *pay-as-you-go* incremental strategy is generally more appropriate and advisable.

One of the bottlenecks of this process is certainly represented by the definition (and evolution) of the ontologies since different figures play a role in it: *domain experts* contribute data and knowledge that is to be formalized by *knowledge engineers* so that it can be mechanized for the machines.

As the gap between these roles likely makes the process slow and burdensome, this problem may be tackled by resorting to *machine learning* techniques. *Ontology learning* [5] is intended to provide solutions to the problem of (semi-) automated construction of ontologies. Cast as an *information extraction* task, ontology learning has focused on leveraging text corpora. The main drawback of this approach is that the elicited concepts and relations are generally represented with languages of limited expressiveness.

A different approach can be based on *relational learning* [6], which comprises methods that require a limited effort from the domain experts (labeling individual resources as examples or counter-examples of the target concepts) and

© Springer Nature Switzerland AG 2018
C. Faron Zucker et al. (Eds.): EKAW 2018, LNAI 11313, pp. 98–113, 2018.
https://doi.org/10.1007/978-3-030-03667-6_7

leads to the construction of complex concepts even in very expressive languages [14]. Casting the solution to concept learning problems as a search guided by examples of the target concepts through a space of candidate descriptions in the adopted representation, these algorithms can also be extended to solve *ontology evolution* problems. Indeed, while this task has been considered from the deductive point of view of automated logic reasoning, a relevant part of the underlying information in the data that populate the knowledge bases is often overlooked or plays a secondary role.

Solutions to the concept learning problem are revisited, seeking for a trade-off between expressiveness, efficiency and completeness of the resulting method. In our vision, tools based on inductive inference should be employed to help the knowledge engineer construct new concept definitions, that may be further refined by means of other semi-automatic tools. This would save engineer's work aimed at finding regularities in the examples that can be generalized in the induced definition. The paper extends previous works [7,9]. A specific new version of the DL-FOIL algorithm has been devised and implemented to induce class expressions represented in OWL2. The main components of the new version are represented by a custom set of refinement operators inspired by similar algorithms proposed in the literature [11,13] and by a new *information-gain* heuristic defined to better take into account the effects of the open-world semantics on instance checking often leading to having many instances available whose membership to the target concept cannot be deductively ascertained.

This issue requires a different setting, similar to *semi-supervised learning* [4], that does not necessarily treat such individuals as negative examples. Despite the interesting results obtained with the previous version [7], DL-FOIL showed two weak points. The first one concerned the specialization process, that in cases where the residual examples to cover were not positive might lead to the generation of poor specializations from a predictive viewpoint. The second issue is represented by the heuristic function adopted in the previous version, which measures the quality of a refinement in terms of information gain w.r.t. the former partially formed concept. In the definition of this score, the contribution of the unlabeled examples is weighted according to prior distributions computed on the global population disregarding the actual number of unlabeled individuals covered by the specific refinement.

These problems motivate the contribution of this paper, a new release of a concept learning system that extends DL-FOIL with an improved specialization procedure that forces to generate concept descriptions with at least a positive example and a better score function that takes into account the actual number of unlabeled individuals covered by a partial specialization. In an empirical evaluation, we compared the new release against other approaches based on separate-and-conquer strategy whose operator exploits concept constructors similar to those adopted by our algorithm. Thus, we considered CELOE [15], currently implemented in the DL-LEARNER framework and adopted as a subroutine for other learning systems [18,19], and carried out experiments on various artificial learning problems showing promising results in terms of predictiveness of the resulting concept descriptions.

The remainder of the paper is organized as follows. In the next section, the related work concerning concept learning for the Web of Data/Semantic Web representations is given. In Sect. 3 we give a formal definition of the learning problem, while Sect. 4 presents the novel version of DL-FOIL. In Sect. 5 a comparative evaluation on various datasets and related learning problems is reported with a discussion of the outcomes. Finally, further possible developments are reported in Sect. 6.

2   Related Work

In the literature, supervised approaches have been proposed that adopt the idea of *generalization as search* performed through suitable operators that are specifically designed for DL languages [2,11,12,14] on the grounds of the previous experience in the context of *Inductive Logic Programming* (ILP), such as YINYANG [11] and DL-LEARNER [3]. YINYANG is a learning system that produces a concept description resorting to the notion of *counterfactuals* [11] for eliminating the negative examples covered by an overly general concept. DL-LEARNER provides the implementation of various concept learning algorithms based on a covering strategy which essentially differ for the heuristics used to select the best solution. One of the most important algorithms in DL-LEARNER is CELOE [15], which performs an accuracy-driven search of solutions biased towards short intensional concept definitions.

Learning alternative models such as logical decision trees offers another option for concept induction. The introduction of *terminological decision trees* [8, 17], i.e. logical decision trees where test-nodes represented with DL concept descriptions, and algorithms for their conversion into disjunctive descriptions, allows the combination of a *divide-and-conquer* learning strategy together with the standard *separate-and-conquer* strategy followed by most of the algorithms mentioned above. Another approach to concept learning is based on *bisimulation* [20], which adopts a recursive partitioning of a set of individuals (similarly to terminological decision trees). However, instead of using an operator that specializes *on-the-fly* a solution, the bisimulation method exploits a set of precomputed *selectors*, i.e. tests that are used to partition the set of individuals. The bisimulation method has been used also in the perspective of the *roughification* of the target concepts [16] to address the problem of defining *imprecise* concepts (uncertainty as *vagueness*).

Another system called PARCEL [18] adopts a different divide-and-conquer strategy based on the use of a set of workers generating partial solutions, which are subsequently combined in order to generate the complete concept description. Such method has been further extended leading to SPACEL [19]. Unlike DL-FOIL, CELOE and PARCEL, SPACEL is a supervised method that aims at finding *exceptions*, i.e. partial descriptions of negative examples, which can be searched in parallel w.r.t. the intensional definition describing the positive examples. Both PARCEL and SPACEL uses CELOE as a subroutine for building the partial solutions, thus the quality of the global solutions strictly depends on the quality of partial solutions returned by CELOE. Due to the importance of CELOE for the effectiveness of aforementioned systems, in the evaluation we considered only CELOE as a competitor, which is the most similar method to the DL-FOIL both in terms of strategy and adopted operator (that targets a similar expressiveness of the operator exploited by our algorithm).

3 The Concept Learning Problem

In this section, we formalize the concept learning problem applied to knowledge bases modeled through standard representation languages for the Web of Data and we introduce the basics of the refinement operators.

3.1 Notation

In this work we consider knowledge bases modeled through representation languages that can be mapped onto *Description Logics* (DLs) [1], as those adopted for the vocabularies used in the Web of Data. For the sake of explanation, we will consider $\mathcal{ALC}$ language.

In the sequel, we will use the standard notation for DLs:

- $a, b, \ldots$ denote individuals (occurring in the assertions);
- $C, D, \ldots$ denote *concepts* (i.e. classes) and specifically A, B for atomic concepts;
- $R, S, \ldots$ denote *role* names (i.e. properties/relationships);
- N_C and N_R denote, respectively, the sets of *concept* and *role names*;
- the symbols $\sqcap$, $\sqcup$, $\neg$, $\exists$, $\forall$ stand for the standard DL operators for defining complex concept descriptions: *intersection, union, complement, existential* and *universal* role restrictions;
- an *inclusion axiom* of the form $C \sqsubseteq D$ stands for the *subsumption* relation between concept descriptions, with the form $C \equiv D$ representing an *equivalence*: $C \sqsubseteq D$ and $D \sqsubseteq C$ ($C \sqsubset D$ stands for strict subsumption);
- $C(a)$ and $R(a, b)$ denote assertions, ground axioms describing the individuals, their properties and relationships among them;
- $\mathcal{K} = \langle \mathcal{T}, \mathcal{A} \rangle$ indicates a *knowledge base* with a TBox $\mathcal{T}$ containing axioms, and an ABox $\mathcal{A}$ containing assertions about individuals. The set of such individuals is denoted with $\mathsf{Ind}(\mathcal{A})$;
- $\mathcal{K} \models \alpha$ denotes the entailment of an axiom/assertion α
  - besides of inclusion axioms, we will be interested to testing the entailment assertions $\alpha = (\neg)C(a)$, i.e. those regarding the membership of some individual a to some concept C or its complement (*instance check*).

The complete model-theoretic semantics for these notions is given in [1].

3.2 Learning Concepts in DLs

Informally, the goal of concept learning is to build a (new) definition for a target concept name (in the form of a concept description) for which a set of training examples is available: individuals labeled with the correct membership w.r.t. the target concept [7]. We can formally define the learning problem as follows:

Definition 3.1 (learning problem). *Let $\mathcal{K} = \langle \mathcal{T}, \mathcal{A} \rangle$ be a DL knowledge base.*

Given

- *a new concept name $C \in N_C$ (that is not in the signature of $\mathcal{K}$)*
- *a set of individuals $Tr \subseteq \mathsf{Ind}(\mathcal{A})$, whose intended membership w.r.t. C is known, partitioned as follows:*
  - *positive examples $Ps = \{a \in Tr \mid C(a) \in \mathcal{A}_C^+\}$*
  - *negative examples $Ns = \{a \in Tr \mid \neg C(a) \in \mathcal{A}_C^-\}$*
  - *uncertain membership examples $Us = Tr \setminus (Ps \cup Ns)$*

  with $Ns \cap Ps = \emptyset$ and the sets of positive, risp. negative, available assertions for C defined by $\mathcal{A}_C^+ = \{C(a_1), \dots, C(a_P)\}$ and $\mathcal{A}_C^- = \{\neg C(b_1), \dots, \neg C(b_N)\}$

Find *a concept description D, such that, letting $\mathcal{K}' = \langle \mathcal{T} \cup \{C \equiv D\}, \mathcal{A} \rangle$, the following entailments hold:*

- *$\forall a \in Ps$: $\mathcal{K}' \models C(a)$* $\qquad\qquad\qquad$ *C covers the positive ex. a*
- *$\forall b \in Ns$: $\mathcal{K}' \models \neg C(b)$* $\qquad\qquad$ *C does not cover the negative ex. b*

This definition does not favor any specific kind of solution over the others. Further constraints can be introduced to restrain the set of the possible solutions (e.g. syntactic measures of complexity). Note that an induced concept description is mainly intended to be used predictively for determining the membership of new and/or *unseen* individuals, i.e. those that are not included in Tr. Thus, the constraints reported above can be more carefully specified to ensure a good generalization avoiding solutions that overfit the training set remaining poorly predictive [6].

Also, note that the constraints on negative assertions $\mathcal{K}' \models \neg C(b)$ are stronger compared to other settings, yet it seems more coherent with underlying open-world semantics; as KBs are assumed to be inherently incomplete then it is plausible to consider as negative examples only those individuals explicitly indicated as such. Other approaches [12,14,15] tend to assume weaker constraints (especially when the knowledge base is modeled through languages do not support negation), namely $\mathcal{K}' \not\models C(b)$, that leads to problems targeting narrower concepts that should not include both actual counterexamples and individuals whose membership to the target concept cannot be ascertained given the current state of knowledge represented by the KB.

3.3   Refinement Operators

The solution to the learning problem stated above can be sought casting the learning process as a search for a correct concept definition throughout an ordered space. In such a setting, suitable operators can be defined to traverse the search space [6]. Refinement operators can be formally defined as follows.

Definition 3.2 (refinement operators). *Given a quasi-ordered[1] space* $(\Sigma, \preceq)$

- *a* downward refinement operator *is a mapping* $\rho : \Sigma \to 2^{\Sigma}$ *such that*

$$\forall \alpha \in \Sigma \quad \rho(\alpha) \subseteq \{\beta \in \Sigma \mid \beta \preceq \alpha\}$$

- *an* upward refinement operator *is a mapping* $\delta : \Sigma \to 2^{\Sigma}$ *such that*

$$\forall \alpha \in \Sigma \quad \delta(\alpha) \subseteq \{\beta \in \Sigma \mid \alpha \preceq \beta\}$$

In the following, we will consider $(\mathcal{L}, \preceq_{\sqsubseteq})$ space of concept definitions where the quasi-ordering relationship $\preceq_{\sqsubseteq}$ is induced by the concept subsumption $\sqsubseteq$, i.e. $C \preceq_{\sqsubseteq} D$ iff $\mathcal{K} \models C \sqsubseteq D$ [13]. In this case there may be an infinite number of refinements for a concept. The operators are devised to traverse the space in pursuit of the possible solutions for the learning problems guided the provided examples. A downward (resp. upward) refinement operator ρ (resp. δ) may fulfill some important properties (related to its effectiveness), such as:

local finitness for each C, $\rho(C)$ (resp. $\delta(C)$) is finite
completeness for all C, D such that $C \sqsubset D$ (resp. $C \sqsupset D$), an equivalent
   refinement $E \equiv C$ (resp. $E \equiv D$) can be found in $\rho(D)$ (resp. $\delta(C)$)
properness for all C, D, $D \in \rho(C)$ (resp. $D \in \delta(C)$) implies $C \not\equiv D$.

A refinement operator that is endowed with such properties is defined as *ideal*. In particular the completeness is important because allows a concept learning algorithm to find all the possible solutions.

4   The Revised Learning Algorithm

The revised algorithm implemented in DL-FOIL essentially adapts the original sequential covering approach to the specific concept learning problem with DL knowledge bases. The algorithm exploits a (downward) refinement operator to traverse the search space and a heuristic, inspired by the original *information gain*, to select among candidate specialization. A sketch of the main routine of the learning procedure is reported in Algorithm 1.

Given a knowledge base $\mathcal{K}$, the learning procedure requires a training set composed by individuals explicitly deemed as positive or negative for the target concept, possibly including also some with uncertain membership. The INDUCECON-CEPT routine computes a generalization as a disjunct of partial descriptions

---

[1] A space endowed with a *quasi-ordering*, i.e. a reflexive and transitive relationship.

Algorithm 1. Function INDUCECONCEPT

```
 1 {constant values set according to the configuration}
 2 const K: knowledge base
 3 input Ps, Ns, Us: set of Individuals {with positive, negative or uncertain membership}
 4 output Generalization: Concept Description
 5
 6 Generalization ← ⊥
 7 PositivesToCover ← Ps
 8 while (PositivesToCover ≠ ∅) do
 9     PartialDef ← ⊤
10     CoveredPs ← PositivesToCover
11     CoveredNs ← Ns
12     CoveredUs ← Us
13     while (CoveredPs ≠ ∅ and CoveredNs ∪ CoveredUs ≠ ∅) do
14         PartialDef ← GETBESTSPECIALIZATION(PartialDef,CoveredPs,CoveredNs,CoveredUs)
15         CoveredPs ← {p ∈ PositivesToCover | K ⊨ PartialDef(p)}
16         CoveredNs ← {n ∈ Ns | K ⊨ PartialDef(n)}
17         CoveredUs ← {u ∈ Us | K ⊨ PartialDef(u)}
18     Generalization ← Generalization ⊔ PartialDef
19     PositivesToCover ← PositivesToCover \ CoveredPs
20
21 return Generalization
```

---

covering a part of the positive examples (outer loop) and ruling out as many negative examples as possible per inner iteration by refining the current partial concept description. However, the new version of the algorithm the heuristic used to select the (partial) solutions can be configured not to cover uncertain-membership examples.

If either negative-membership or uncertain-membership examples are covered by the current description, the GETBESTSPECIALIZATION routine is invoked for solving these specialization problems. This routine seeks for an optimal specialized description using the (incomplete) refinement operator defined in the next section. The specialization process is iterated until no negative/uncertain membership example is covered. The partial descriptions built on each outer iteration are finally grouped together in a disjunction[2]. A simple modification anticipating the stopping condition of the outer loop may be adopted for avoiding overfitting generalizations.

4.1 Specialization of Partial Definitions

The function GETBESTSPECIALIZATION (reported in Algorithm 2) is called from the inner loop of the generalization procedure to select a good specialization of an overly general (partial) description. Unlike the similar function in the

---

[2] This may be considered a basic upper refinement operator allowed by expressive DL languages (encompassing $\mathcal{ALC}$).

Algorithm 2. Function GETBESTSPECIALIZATION

```
 1  {constant values set according to the configuration}
 2  const ε: real {minimal gain threshold}
 3          n: integer {number of specializations to be generated}
 4  input PartialDef: Concept Description
 5          Ps, Ns, Us: set of Individuals {with positive, negative and uncertain membership}
 6  output bestConcept: Concept Definition
 7
 8  bestGain ← 0
 9  bestConcept ← ⊤
10  while (bestGain < ε) do
11      for i ← 1 to n
12        repeat
13          Specialization ← getRandomRefinement(ρ,PartialDef)
14          CoveredPs ← {p ∈ Ps | 𝒦 ⊨ Specialization(p)}
15          if (CoveredPs ≠ ∅) then
16            CoveredNs ← {n ∈ Ns | 𝒦 ⊨ Specialization(n)}
17            CoveredUs ← {u ∈ Us | 𝒦 ⊨ Specialization(u)}
18            gain ← GAIN(CoveredPs, CoveredNs, CoveredUs, Us, Ps, Ns, Us)
19            {compute the value of the function g}
20            if (gain > bestGain) then
21              bestConcept ← Specialization
22              bestGain ← gain
23        until ( (Ps\CoveredPs) = ∅) {strong constraint that can be relaxed}
24
25  return bestConcept
```

---

previous version of DL-FOIL, the new function searches for proper refinements that satisfy the following conditions:

- a refinement must cover at least a positive example;
- a refinement must yield a minimal gain fixed with a threshold ϵ.

Candidate specializations are generated via a downward operator ρ that, given a concept description C, returns refinements C' in one of the following forms (randomly generated):

ρ_1 $C' = C \sqcap A$

ρ_2 $C' = C \sqcap \neg A$

ρ_3 $C' = C \sqcap \forall R.\top$

ρ_4 $C' = C \sqcap \exists R.\top$

ρ_5 $C' = C_1 \sqcap \cdots \sqcap B \sqcap \cdots \sqcap C_n$ if $C = C_1 \sqcap \cdots \sqcap A \sqcap \cdots \sqcap C_n$ and $\mathcal{K} \models (B \sqsubseteq A)$

ρ_6 $C' = C_1 \sqcap \cdots \sqcap \neg B \sqcap \cdots \sqcap C_n$ if $C = C_1 \sqcap \cdots \sqcap \neg A \sqcap \cdots \sqcap C_n$ and $\mathcal{K} \models (A \sqsupseteq B)$

ρ_7 $C' = C_1 \sqcap \cdots \sqcap \exists R.D \sqcap \cdots \sqcap C_n$ if $C = C_1 \sqcap \cdots \sqcap \exists R.E \sqcap \cdots \sqcap C_n$ and $E \in \rho(D)$

ρ_8 $C' = C_1 \sqcap \cdots \sqcap \forall R.D \sqcap \cdots \sqcap C_n$ if $C = C_1 \sqcap \cdots \sqcap \forall R.E \sqcap \cdots \sqcap C_n$ and $E \in \rho(D)$

The operator described above is recursive – see forms ρ_7 and ρ_8 – while ρ_1–ρ_6 represent the base cases. A first random choice is made between adding an atomic conjunct (cases ρ_1–ρ_4) or refining an existing sub-concepts with (cases ρ_5–ρ_8). In case of an atomic concept is added, the concept name (or the role name for the conjunct in the form $\exists R.\top/\forall R.\top$) is also randomly selected. In the case of refinement of an existing conjunct, the operator picks (randomly) such a candidate and generates a specialization via ρ_5–ρ_8.

Note that this refinement operator is not *ideal*. Particularly, the completeness property is not fulfilled due to the random choices required for building the partial definition.

4.2 Heuristics for Best Specialization Selection

As regards the heuristic employed to guide the search, the gain for selecting the best refinement is computed (by function GAIN) as follows:

$$g(D_0, D_1) = p_1 \cdot \left[\log \frac{p_1}{p_1 + n_1 + u_1} - \log \frac{p_0}{p_0 + n_0 + u_0} \right]$$

where p_1, n_1 and u_1 resp. represent, the numbers of positive, negative and uncertain-membership examples covered by the specialization, say D_0, and p_0, n_0 and u_0 stand for the corresponding numbers of examples covered by the former (partial) definition D_0. To avoid cases of division by 0, a further correction of the ratios is made resorting to Laplace smoothing (m-estimates). The main difference with the formerly adopted gain function [7] is that the examples with an uncertain membership do not contribute to the score according to the prior probabilities (estimated over the distributions of the examples), but according to the actual number of individuals covered by the specific specialization.

4.3 Discussion

Despite its simplicity, the overall complexity of the algorithm is largely determined by the required reasoning services, namely subsumption (satisfiability) and especially instance-checking [1]. whose complexity is never lower than the complexity of the subsumption, and depends on the underlying DL language. For example, if one considers knowledge bases expressed in $\mathcal{ALC}$, the complexity of the instance-check is P-SPACE (in the case of acyclic TBox[3] [1]). However, should the considered knowledge base contain definitions expressed in more expressive languages which, in turn, require more complex reasoning procedures, the inductive algorithm can be thought as a means for building (upper) $\mathcal{ALC}$-approximations of the target concepts. Indeed the specializing routine might diverge (with parameter configurations that lead to strict loop tests) in case the refinement sought cannot be expressed in terms of the language considered. To avoid such cases, the implementation of the algorithm allows for limiting the number of refinement attempts.

5 Empirical Evaluation

This section illustrates the design and the outcomes of a comparative empirical evaluation aimed at assessing the effectiveness of the new release[4] DL-FOIL.

---

[3] An acyclic TBox does not contains multiple definitions for a concept name and such a concept is not used to the right-side of an equivalence axiom.

[4] The source code and the datasets/ontologies are publicly available at: https://bitbucket.org/grizzo001/dl-foil/src/master/.

5.1   Experimental Design and Setup

In order to determine the effectiveness of the compared systems, the quality of the induced concepts was evaluated against a baseline of target concepts. To this purpose, we considered 5 publicly available Web ontologies, which differ in terms of expressiveness, number of individuals and number of concepts/roles. The characteristics of each ontology are reported in Table 1.

Table 1. Facts concerning the ontologies employed in the experiments.

ontology	language	#concepts	obj.properties	data properties	#individuals
BioPAX	$\mathcal{ALCHF}$(**D**)	28	19	30	323
NTN	$\mathcal{SHIF}$(**D**)	47	27	8	724
Hdisease	$\mathcal{SHIF}$(**D**)	1499	10	15	639
Financial	$\mathcal{ALCIF}$	60	17	0	1000
Geoskills	$\mathcal{SHIF}$	596	23	0	2532

Each ontology was used to generate 15 random artificial problems and related datasets as follows:

- For each problem and ontology, a target concept description was generated by randomly picking concepts/roles from the respective signature and combining them through basic concept constructors: union, conjunction, complement, universal or existential restriction.
- All the individuals were labeled as positive/negative/uncertain-membership examples with respect to each target concept (via the instance-checking reasoning service). Table 2 summarizes, for each ontology, the distributions of the examples (averaged over the number of datasets). Note that the generation procedure ensures that individuals that belong to cither to the target concept or to its complement are available.

Table 2. Distributions of the positive, negative, unlabeled instances per ontology

ontology	%pos.exs.	%neg.exs.	%unc.exs.
BioPAX	51.99	45.74	02.27
NTN	15.57	47.31	49.77
Hdisease	08.54	08.46	82.99
Financial	53.78	38.37	7.85
Geoskills	58.00	22.00	20.00

To allow the repetition of the experiments, a seed for the internal pseudo-random generator can be set in the configuration: this value defaulted to 1.

We compared DL-FOIL against CELOE [15], based on a similar sequential covering algorithm available from the latest release of DL-LEARNER. In the experiments with DL-FOIL, the maximum number of specializations to be evaluated per turn is a required parameter. This value was empirically set to 20. In the experiments with CELOE, a proper tuning of the refinement operator was also required. In particular, the operator was configured so that it could return concept descriptions obtained through all the available concept constructors, possibly also using the datatype properties available in the ontologies. Another required parameter is the time-out used to stop the training phase. This value was set to 10 s (larger values were also preliminarily tested but the decreased efficiency of the process led to no significant improvement).

We adopted a .632 bootstrap as the design of the experiments in order to estimate the following indices:

- *match rate* (M%): cases of test individuals that got exactly the same classification[5] w.r.t. the target and the induced concept descriptions;
- *commission error rate* (C%): cases of test individuals that received opposite classifications when checked against the target and the induced definition;
- *omission error rate* (O%): cases of test individuals with a definite membership w.r.t. the target concept that could not be assessed checking the induced definition;
- *induction rate* (I%): cases of test individuals of whose membership w.r.t. the target concept cannot be determined, that a reasoner could classify given the induced definition.

5.2   Results

The experiments showed promising results reported in Table 3. In the experiments with the datasets extracted from BioPAX, NTN, and FINANCIAL, the match rate obtained through DL-FOIL exceeded 90%. For the other datasets extracted from HDISEASE and GEOSKILLS, the rate was substantially lower, yet it was larger than the one obtained in the experiments with CELOE. This was likely due to the large number of concepts that can be found in those knowledge bases (almost 1500 and 600 concepts in the problems on HDISEASE and GEOSKILLS, respectively), resulting in a very large search space to traverse via refinement operator. This might imply that sub-optimal solutions were obtained, also due to the myopic effect of covering methods (that can be regarded as an hill-climbing optimization strategy) and the incompleteness of the refinement operator plugged in the algorithm.

CELOE showed a similar trend. However, the match rate was generally lower than the one observed in the experiments with DL-FOIL (in the problems related to GEOSKILLS, the rate decreased to 30%). Such a worse performance was likely due to the simplicity of the concepts induced by CELOE (see Sect. 5.3 for some examples). Indeed, the algorithm in CELOE is biased towards shorter concept

---

[5] Assessed by JFACT reasoner: http://jfact.sourceforge.net/.

Table 3. Outcomes of the experiments

Dataset	index	DL-Foil	Celoe
Biopax	M%	95.73 + 03.74	94.53 ± 01.17
	C%	00.13 ± 00.20	03.24 ± 00.85
	O%	01.90 ± 03.31	01.62 ± 00.38
	I%	02.23 ± 00.40	00.61 ± 00.18
NTN	M%	97.78 ± 05.05	97.41 ± 00.15
	C%	00.05 ± 00.07	00.00 ± 00.00
	O%	02.17 ± 05.00	00.00 ± 00.00
	I%	00.01 ± 00.01	02.59 ± 00.15
Hdisease	M%	88.75 ± 01.09	88.08 ± 01.09
	C%	00.04 ± 00.10	00.00 ± 00.00
	O%	03.64 ± 01.30	07.69 ± 00.90
	I%	07.57 ± 01.42	04.23 ± 00.24
Financial	M%	93.52 ± 01.02	87.40 ± 04.74
	C%	00.22 ± 00.21	06.33 ± 04.33
	O%	00.00 ± 00.00	00.00 ± 00.01
	I%	06.26 ± 00.88	06.26 ± 00.52
Geoskills	M%	82.60 ± 04.69	50.20 ± 02.31
	C%	00.00 ± 00.00	23.66 ± 02.61
	O%	13.33 ± 04.43	01.34 ± 00.12
	I%	04.07 ± 04.09	24.80 ± 00.89

descriptions to provide a good generalization and improve the readability of the induced concepts. But, as observed in the experiments, this led to induce poorly predictive concepts, often composed by a (negated) concept name. Conversely, in most cases DL-Foil managed to find a definitions whose sets of retrieved instances tended to overlap with the analogous sets for the target concepts: in its algorithm, after having found a good disjunct, the search is started over to cover the remaining positive examples, whereas the search performed by Celoe is sometimes stopped prematurely (because a good solution according to the heuristic was found).

A general consideration, the commission error rate of the concepts induced by DL-Foil was almost null and significantly lower than the ones produced by Celoe. In the experiments with both algorithms, cases of commission were due to the misclassification of test examples whose membership was under-represented in the datasets: there were cases of negative examples were classified as positive in the experiments with Biopax, NTN, Geoskills, while in the experiments with Financial and Hdisease, there were cases of positive examples were misclassified as negative. Similarly to commission errors, omission error cases occurred in the experiments due to the (large) presence of uncertain-membership instances (also considering the availability and the number of disjointness axioms in the ontologies). As a result, DL-FOIL exhibited a more conservative behavior than CELOE, that tended to produce concepts leading to more frequent induction cases.

As regards the efficiency of the approach[6], we noted that, despite the lack of optimizations as those implemented in DL-LEARNER [3], the average training times were quite limited. The overall training time (for all the problems and datasets) elapsed in the specific experiments with DL-FOIL are listed as follows: 22.74 s (BIOPAX), 17.41 s (NTN); 43.75 s (FINANCIAL), 109.21 s (HDISEASE), 669.35 (GEOSKILLS). In the experiments with CELOE, the times were: 12.13 s (BIOPAX), 11.71 s (NTN), 11.54 s (FINANCIAL), 12.41 s (HDISEASE) and 12.98 s (GEOSKILLS). The runtimes were influenced by various aspects: the number of training individuals and the employment of instance checking service to evaluate their membership and determine the score, the number of concepts of the knowledge base needed to generate the candidates.

5.3 Examples of Induced Definitions

For the sake of completeness, for each ontology we report some of the target concepts together with those induced during the experiments. Note that the concepts learned by DL-FOIL are more complex w.r.t. those produced by CELOE (because the former is less biased towards short concept descriptions), yet they are more predictive w.r.t. the instance of the test sets. Of course for a correct qualitative interpretation of the value of these concepts some familiarity with the domains modeled by the ontologies is required.

BIOPAX
DL-Foil :
catalysis ⊔ ∃STEP-INTERACTIONS.⊤
Celoe: ¬ sequence
Target:
(((catalysis ⊔ pathwayStep) ⊓ ¬openControlledVocabulary)
⊓ ¬protein) ⊓ ∀STRUCTURE.sequenceInterval

NTN
DL-Foil : Woman
Celoe: Woman
Target:
Woman ⊓ (Human ⊔ (EvilSupernaturalBeing ⊔ PoliticalBeliefSystem))

HDISEASE
DL-Foil :
NOT_CIE_Disease ⊔ Cough_with_blood_Class ⊔ Diarrhea_Class
⊔ (Eye_redness_Class ⊓ ∃isSymptomOf.Yellow_fever_unspecified_Class)
⊔ (Fontanelle_Class ⊓ ∃isSymptomOf.(∃isSymptomOf.Colic_Class))
⊔ (Vision_problems_Class

---

[6] The experiments were carried out on a 8-core Ubuntu server with 16 GB RAM.

⊓ ∃isSymptomOf.(∃hasLabTest.CT_Scan_unspecified_Class))
⊔ ∃hasSymptom.Dengue_fever_classical_dengue_Class
Celoe: NOT_CIE_Disease
original:
(Strange_and_inexplicable_behaviour_Class
⊔ ¬Other_amnesia_Class
⊔ ¬Plasmodium_falciparum_malaria_with_cerebral_complications) ⊓
¬General_symptoms_and_signs_Class

FINANCIAL
DL-Foil :
Finished ⊔ (DebtRunningLoan ⊓ ∃hasLoanStatusValue.⊤)
⊔ ∃isOwnerOf.⊤
Celoe: DebtRunningLoan
Target:
DebtRunningLoan ⊔ Finished ⊔ ∃isOwnerOf.¬InterestsCredited

GEOSKILLS
DL-Foil :
∀inEducationalRegion.Germany ⊔ ∃requiresCompetency.⊤ ⊔ ∃type.⊤
⊔ Equation
Celoe: ⊤
Target:
Set_up_an_equation
⊔ ∀belongsToEducationalPathway.Germany_Hauptschule_6te

6   Conclusions and Outlook

In this work, we have proposed DL-FOIL for tackling the problem of concept
learning with knowledge bases modeled through standard representations for
the Web of Data, and compared it against other algorithms based on a covering
approach. In particular, the comparison involved CELOE, currently implemented
in a reference framework like DL-LEARNER. The experiments presented in this
paper showed that DL-FOIL is able to better approximate a target concept,
especially when it is particularly complex (i.e. it is made up of many nested
sub-concepts).

We plan to extend the evaluation considering larger knowledge base and further learning problems. However, to this purpose, more attention to efficiency
and scalability aspects is required. In particular, one could consider to design
further refinement operators considering some known patterns to traverse the
DL concept space and new heuristics that can help to speed up the search of a
promising solution. Using approximated inference mechanisms, like those integrated in DL-LEARNER [3], may be an interesting alternative to consider for
improving the efficiency of the method. Further research directions include the
use of parallel computation running, for example, on GPUs, and frameworks for

distributed data processing, such as *Apache Spark*[7] for speeding up the specialization process.

References

1. Baader, F., Calvanese, D., McGuinness, D., Nardi, D., Patel-Schneider, P. (eds.): The Description Logic Handbook. Cambridge University Press, New York (2003)
2. Badea, L., Nienhuys-Cheng, S.-H.: A refinement operator for description logics. In: Cussens, J., Frisch, A. (eds.) ILP 2000. LNCS (LNAI), vol. 1866, pp. 40–59. Springer, Heidelberg (2000). https://doi.org/10.1007/3-540-44960-4_3
3. Bühmann, L., Lehmann, J., Westphal, P.: DL-Learner - a framework for inductive learning on the Semantic Web. J. Web Sem. **39**, 15–24 (2016)
4. Chapelle, O., Schlkopf, B., Zien, A.: Semi-Supervised Learning. MIT Press, Cambridge (2010)
5. Cimiano, P., Mädche, A., Staab, S., Völker, J.: Ontology learning. In: Staab, S., Studer, R. (eds.) Handbook on Ontologies, pp. 245–267. Springer, Heidelberg (2009). https://doi.org/10.1007/978-3-540-24750-0_9
6. De Raedt, L.: Logical and Relational Learning. Springer, Heidelberg (2008). https://doi.org/10.1007/978-3-540-68856-3
7. Fanizzi, N., d'Amato, C., Esposito, F.: DL-FOIL concept learning in description logics. In: Železný, F., Lavrač, N. (eds.) ILP 2008. LNCS (LNAI), vol. 5194, pp. 107–121. Springer, Heidelberg (2008). https://doi.org/10.1007/978-3-540-85928-4_12
8. Fanizzi, N., d'Amato, C., Esposito, F.: Induction of concepts in web ontologies through terminological decision trees. In: Balcázar, J.L., Bonchi, F., Gionis, A., Sebag, M. (eds.) ECML PKDD 2010, part I. LNCS (LNAI), vol. 6321, pp. 442–457. Springer, Heidelberg (2010). https://doi.org/10.1007/978-3-642-15880-3_34
9. Fanizzi, N.: Concept induction in Description Logics using information-theoretic heuristics. Int. J. Semantic Web Inf. Syst. **7**(2), 23–44 (2011)
10. Heath, T., Bizer, C.: Linked Data: Evolving the Web into a Global Data Space. Morgan & Claypool, Palo Alto (2011)
11. Iannone, L., Palmisano, I., Fanizzi, N.: An algorithm based on counterfactuals for concept learning in the Semantic Web. Appl. Intell. **26**(2), 139–159 (2007)
12. Lehmann, J., Hitzler, P.: Foundations of refinement operators for description logics. In: Blockeel, H., Ramon, J., Shavlik, J., Tadepalli, P. (eds.) ILP 2007. LNCS (LNAI), vol. 4894, pp. 161–174. Springer, Heidelberg (2008). https://doi.org/10.1007/978-3-540-78469-2_18
13. Lehmann, J., Hitzler, P.: A refinement operator based learning algorithm for the $\mathcal{ALC}$ description logic. In: Blockeel, H., Ramon, J., Shavlik, J., Tadepalli, P. (eds.) ILP 2007. LNCS, vol. 4894, pp. 147–160. Springer, Heidelberg (2008). https://doi.org/10.1007/978-3-540-78469-2_17
14. Lehmann, J., Hitzler, P.: Concept learning in description logics using refinement operators. Mach. Learn. **78**(1–2), 203–250 (2010)
15. Lehmann, J., Auer, S., Bühmann, L., Tramp, S.: Class expression learning for ontology engineering. J. Web Semant. **9**, 71–81 (2011)
16. Nguyen, L.A., Szalas, A.: Logic-based roughification. In: Skowron, A., Suraj, Z. (eds.) Rough Sets and Intelligent Systems (1). Intelligent Systems Reference Library, vol. 42, pp. 517–543. Springer, Heidelberg (2013). https://doi.org/10.1007/978-3-642-30344-9_19. Chap. 19

---

[7] spark.apache.org.

17. Rizzo, G., Fanizzi, N., Lehmann, J., Bühmann, L.: Integrating new refinement operators in terminological decision trees learning. In: Blomqvist, E., Ciancarini, P., Poggi, F., Vitali, F. (eds.) EKAW 2016. LNCS, vol. 10024, pp. 511–526. Springer, Cham (2016). https://doi.org/10.1007/978-3-319-49004-5_33
18. Tran, A.C., Dietrich, J., Guesgen, H.W., Marsland, S.: An approach to parallel class expression learning. In: Bikakis, A., Giurca, A. (eds.) RuleML 2012. LNCS, vol. 7438, pp. 302–316. Springer, Heidelberg (2012). https://doi.org/10.1007/978-3-642-32689-9_25
19. Tran, A.C., Dietrich, J., Guesgen, H.W., Marsland, S.: Parallel symmetric class expression learning. J. Mach. Learn. Res. **18**, 64:1–64:34 (2017)
20. Tran, T., Ha, Q., Hoang, T., Nguyen, L.A., Nguyen, H.S.: Bisimulation-based concept learning in description logics. Fundam. Inform. **133**(2–3), 287–303 (2014)

Requirements Behaviour Analysis
for Ontology Testing

Alba Fernández-Izquierdo[✉] and Raúl García-Castro

Ontology Engineering Group, Universidad Politécnica de Madrid, Madrid, Spain
{albafernandez,rgarcia}@fi.upm.es

Abstract. In the software engineering field, every software product is delivered with its pertinent associated tests which verify its correct behaviour. Besides, there are several approaches which, integrated in the software development process, deal with software testing, such as unit testing or behaviour-driven development. However, in the ontology engineering field there is a lack of clearly defined testing processes that can be integrated into the ontology development process. In this paper we propose a testing framework composed by a set of activities (i.e., test design, implementation and execution), with the goal of checking whether the requirements identified are satisfied by the formalization and analysis of their expected behaviour. This testing framework can be used in different types of ontology development life-cycles, or concerning other goals such as conformance testing between ontologies. In addition to this, we propose an RDF vocabulary to store, publish and reuse these test cases and their results, in order to allow traceability between the ontology, the test cases and their requirements. We validate our approach by integrating the testing framework into an ontology engineering process where an ontology network has been developed following agile principles.

Keywords: Ontology testing · Ontology requirements
Ontology development

1 Introduction

The increasing uptake of semantic technologies and ontologies has led during the past years to the study of new ontology development methodologies, from agile (e.g., [1,12]) to collaborative approaches (e.g., [15,17]). The majority of these methodologies take into account the importance of functional[1] ontology

---

This work is partially supported by the H2020 project VICINITY: Open virtual neighbourhood network to connect intelligent buildings and smart objects (H2020-688467) and by a Predoctoral grant from the I+D+i program of the Universidad Politécnica de Madrid.

[1] This term is borrowed from the Software Engineering field, in which functional requirements refer to the functionalities the software system should have.

C. Faron Zucker et al. (Eds.): FKAW 2018, LNAI 11313, pp. 114–130, 2018.
https://doi.org/10.1007/978-3-030-03667-6_8

requirements [16] which, written in natural language as competency questions [8], define the knowledge the ontology has to represent.

Nowadays, in software engineering it is inconceivable to deliver a software product without its pertinent tests which guarantee that it fulfils all its requirements. Besides, there are several approaches integrated into the software development process whose aim is to test the software. Unit testing [9], which validates that each unit of the software performs as designed, and behaviour-driven development [19], which focuses on the behaviour the software product is implementing, are examples of these approaches.

However, in ontology engineering there is a lack of clearly defined testing processes in order to be able to ascertain whether an ontology satisfies the requirements. Even though there are approaches to generate tests (e.g., [10,13]), they do not cover the entire testing workflow or are limited to checking for the presence of axioms, which is not enough to validate a requirement.

Inspired by the software engineering evaluation approaches, we propose a testing framework composed by a set of activities (i.e., test design, implementation and execution) with the aim of facilitating the generation and execution of tests associated to functional requirements of OWL ontologies. We propose to extract the behaviour of the requirements and to formalize it into test expressions. These test expressions are implemented into a set of axioms with the aim of validating if the ontology satisfies the intended knowledge produced by the requirements. The goal of this implementation is to solve the limitations of the actual testing approaches by analysing ontology behaviour in different situations to ascertain if the expected knowledge is present, absent or produces a conflict, rather than only checking whether an axiom is entailed by the ontology.

This proposed framework can be integrated into several ontology development life-cycles to support ontology development (e.g., to verify ontologies by users or ontology engineers) and also to carry out conformance analysis. In addition to this, we also propose an RDF vocabulary to represent the tests cases in order to provide traceability between them and the associated requirements.

The paper is organized as follows. Section 2 presents the related work on ontology testing. Section 3 presents the proposed testing activities and Sect. 4 describes the integration of these activities into ontology engineering workflows. Finally, Sect. 5 shows the evaluation of the approach and Sect. 6 presents the conclusions obtained and gives an overview on future work.

2   Related Work

Several approaches which defend the importance of verifying ontologies through their ontology requirements have been developed to the date. Each of these approaches focuses on some testing aspect: methodological background, test implementation, or traceability between the ontology and the tests.

Regarding the methodological background, Vrandevcic and Gangemi [18] introduced the idea of testing ontologies by borrowing ideas from software engineering, proposing techniques such as testing with axioms and negations or formalizing competency questions. Another work presented by Peroni is SAMOD [12], an agile ontology development methodology that uses tests to validate the ontology. These two approaches are focused on methodological aspects but do not mention how to implement the tests or how to maintain traceability.

Concerning test implementation, Keet and Lawrynowicz proposed a test-driven development (TDD) of ontologies [10] in which the competency questions are formalized into axioms and added to the ontology if they are not present. Dealing also with test implementation, the OntologyTest tool [7] allows a user to define and execute a set of tests to check the functional requirements of an ontology; these tests are stored in an XML file for future reuse. Another approach to implement test cases is the one presented by Ren et al. [13]; in this work the authors use natural language processing to analyse competency questions written in controlled natural language from where they create competency question patterns that could be automatically tested in the ontology. Finally, Neuhaus introduced Scone[2], a tool for scenario-based ontology evaluation, which is based on Cucumber[3] and uses controlled natural language to define ontology scenarios which create mock individuals. Even though all these approaches are focused on test implementation, neither of them mention how to maintain traceability between the tests and the ontology nor do they describe the process to integrate ontology testing into ontology engineering methodologies in order to create the tests from the ontological requirements.

To conclude, Blomqvist et al. [2] presented an agile approach which includes a methodological background and introduces in rough outlines several types of tests concerned with the verification of the requirements implementation and the exposure to faults. However, this methodology neither explains how to implement these tests nor when each type of test should be used.

Even if all these works introduce testing through requirements, none of them proposes a complete testing framework which covers all the mentioned testing aspects. Moreover, the majority of these works do not allow the reuse of the tests, limiting the testing process only to a single ontology.

3   Ontology Testing Framework

This paper introduces an ontology testing framework to systematize the generation and execution of tests cases from functional requirements. In the literature, ontology testing approaches are usually divided into two activities, i.e., *test implementation* and *test execution*. In this approach we propose a new one, *test design*. The motivation of this new activity came up due to the ambiguity and assumptions inherent to the natural language [4] and to the fact that different people may be in charge of the design and implementation of tests. As a consequence, in this design activity the knowledge intended to be produced by every requirement is identified, e.g., from the requirement "*A device can have a status*" is expected a relation between two concepts in the ontology. From this

---

[2] https://bitbucket.org/malefort/scone.

[3] https://docs.cucumber.io/.

point on, we are going to call this expected knowledge as the *desired behaviour* of the requirement, which is concrete and unambiguous. In this design activity we provide a collection of test expressions according to the requirements behaviour, and in the test implementation activity we provide possible implementations for each one of the test expressions, which are ready to be executed on an ontology.

In this work we focus on the analysis of the behaviour of the ontology in different situations to verify that certain knowledge is modelled in the ontology, rather than simply checking the presence or absence of particular axioms using semantic reasoners. This is due to the fact that the use of semantic reasoners is not sufficient to validate if a requirement is satisfied. For instance, if we suppose that a requirement asks for a minimum cardinality of 1, the correspondent ontology already has the axiom $A \sqsubseteq B \sqcap \leq 2R.C$, and we check the presence of the axiom $A \sqsubseteq B \sqcap \leq 1R.C$ the reasoner will state that it is entailed, even though that is not what the requirement asks for. In this situation we would like to have a tool to determine that what is entailed in the ontology is not what the requirement claims. Because of this reason, it is needed to go beyond the result provided by the simple execution of reasoners. Another case where the checking for the presence of axioms using semantic reasoners is not sufficient is a situation in which an ontology has a large hierarchy of concepts. In this case, in which it is tedious to manually determine whether a certain concept belongs to that hierarchy, if some classes are not named the reasoner will not detect them in the hierarchy. The analysis of ontology behaviours aims to solve these problems.

In addition to the testing activities, we propose an RDF vocabulary[4] to store the generated test cases and to provide traceability between them and their associated requirements. To improve the readability, we assumed that A and B represent ontology classes, P represents an ontology property, a, $a1$, $b1$ and $b2$ represent individuals and *num* represents a numerical value.

3.1   Test Design

During this activity the desired behaviour of each requirement is extracted. In order to carry out this extraction, we provide a set of possible types of requirements according to their desired behaviour. Besides, each of these types of requirements is associated with a test expression, which represents the desired behaviour in a formal language based on the OWL Manchester Syntax[5]. In order to identify the different types of requirements, we analysed the 248 requirements of the following ontologies[6]: the VICINITY ontologies[7], the Video Game ontology [11] and the SAREF ontology[8]. We extracted the behaviour of each of these requirements and selected the ones that appear more than once or that we expect

---

[4] https://w3id.org/def/vtc.

[5] https://www.w3.org/TR/owl2-manchester-syntax/.

[6] At the time of writing, the authors only had access to the requirements of these ontologies.

[7] http://vicinity.iot.linkeddata.es/vicinity/.

[8] https://w3id.org/saref.

to appear frequently. Table 1 shows the identified types of requirements, their description and their corresponding test expressions. It is worth noting that, even though the greater part of the analysed requirements was categorized with only one type, a requirement could be categorized with more than one and, therefore, could be associated to more than one test expression.

Table 1. Types of requirements according to their behaviour

	ID	Type of requirement	Description	Test expression
Class-related	T1	Equivalence	Equivalence between two classes that have the same intention	A EquivalentTo B
	T2	Subsumption	Definition the relation between the class and the (super)class it belongs to. This subsumption is strict, the two classes cannot be equivalent	A SubClassOf B
	T3	Disjointness	Definition of two disjoint concepts	A disjointWith B
Property-related	T4	Property between two concepts	Definition of a property between two concepts	P Domain A, P Range B, A P B
	T5	Symmetry	A property must be symmetric, this means, the property has itself as an inverse	A Symmetric(P) B
	T6	Maximum cardinality	Definition of the maximum cardinality of a given property between two concepts	A SubClassOf P max [num] B
	T7	Minimum cardinality	Definition of the minimum cardinality of a given property between two concepts	A SubClassOf P min [num] B
	T8	Exact cardinality	Definition of the cardinality between two concepts	A SubClassOf P exactly [num] B
	T9	Intersection	Definition of an intersection between concepts with a cardinality	A SubClassOf P min/max/exactly [num] (B and C)
Individual-related	T10	Definition of an individual	Definition of an individual of a given type	a type A

The output of this activity is an RDF document where the test cases are stored using the proposed testing vocabulary. In this vocabulary, each test case design stores the associated requirement URI, the description of the requirement, and the desired behaviour specified by the test expressions.

Listing 1.1 shows an example of a test case design generated from the requirement which states "*An IoT gateway is a digital entity*". This requirement is categorized with one requirement type: Subsumption (T2). Because of the fact that this test does not have URIs related to the ontology in which the test cases are going to be executed, it can be reused in other ontologies. To improve the readability of the paper, Table 2 shows the prefixes and their associated namespaces that are used through the paper.

Listing 1.1. Example of test case design

```
:testDesignPlatform2 a vtc:TestCaseDesign;
        vtc:isRelatedToRequirement vicinity:platform2;
        dc:description "An IoT gateway is a digital entity";
        vtc:desiredBehaviour "<Gateway> subClassOf <DigitalEntity>".
```

3.2   Test Implementation

In order to implement the tests to verify if a desired behaviour is satisfied, we propose a procedure were each test expression is formalized into a precondition, a set of auxiliary term declarations and a set of assertions to check the behaviour. During this procedure it is also carried out a mapping between the term identified in the test design and the actual term in the ontology where the ontology is going to be executed. The testing framework proposed in this work provides implementation for every test expression identified in Table 1.

Table 2. Summary of the prefixes used through the paper

Prefix	Namespace
core	http://iot.linkeddata.es/def/core
dc	http://purl.org/dc/terms/
vicinity	http://vicinity.iot.linkeddata.es/vicinity/re-quirements/report-core.html
vtc	http://w3id.org/def/vtc

The **precondition** is a SPARQL query which checks whether the terms involved in the ontology requirement are defined in the ontology. In order to execute the tests, these terms need to be declared in the ontology. Otherwise, the test fails and the requirement is not satisfied.

The **axioms to declare auxiliary terms** are a set of temporary axioms added to the ontology to declare the auxiliary terms needed to carry out the assertions. After the addition of these axioms the reasoner is executed and, in order to be able to check the behaviour, the ontology needs to be consistent.

Finally, the **assertions to check the behaviour** are a set of pairs of axioms and expected results that represent different ontology scenarios. For each pair, the axiom is temporary added to the ontology to force a scenario, after which the reasoner is executed. The expected result determines if the ontology status (i.e., inconsistent ontology, unsatisfiable class or consistent ontology) after the addition is the expected one in case the requirement was satisfied. If all the status concur with the expected status, then the requirement is satisfied.

The output of this activity is an RDF document where the test cases are stored using the proposed vocabulary. In this vocabulary, each test case implementation stores the associated test design; the test preparation, which represents auxiliary terms declaration; and the corresponding test assertions. An excerpt of a test case is shown in Listing 1.2. Due to the lack of space the figure only shows the test precondition, which verifies that the classes involved in the test exist in the ontology; the test preparation, which adds the auxiliary terms needed for the execution of the test; and one of the assertions, which adds a class that will be wrong if the ontology satisfies the requirement.

Listing 1.2. Example of test case implementation

```
:testImplPlatform2 a vtc:TestCaseImplementation;
  vtc:isRelatedToDesign :testDesignPlatform2;
  vtc:precondition "ASK{ Class(core:Gateway), Class(core:DigitalEntity)}";
  vtc:hasPreparation :preparation1;
  vtc:hasAssertion [:assertion1; :assertion2; :assertion3].
:preparation1 a vtc:TestPreparation;
  dc:description "Declaration of the auxiliary terms";
  vtc:testAxioms """:NoGateway rdf:type owl:Class;
                        owl:complementOf core:Gateway.
                   :NoDigitalEntity rdf:type owl:Class;
                        owl:complementOf core:DigitalEntity. """.
:assertion1 a vtc:TestAssertion;
  dc:description "Test assertion 1";
  vtc:testAxioms """core:GatewayNoDigitalEntity rdf:type owl:Class;
                        rdfs:subClassOf   core:Gateway;
                        rdfs:subClassOf   :NoDigitalEntity.""";
  vtc:hasAssertionResult vtc:Unsatisfiable .
```

3.2.1 Class-Related Test Expressions

Table 3 shows the implementations to verify equivalence (T1), subsumption (T2), and disjointness (T3) between two concepts.

To check **equivalence** between two concepts, we define a set of auxiliary terms, i.e., the classes that complement A ($\neg A$) and B ($\neg B$). After their definition, we define a set of assertions that force the ontology to present unsatisfiable classes or inconsistencies. The first one, associated to axiom 'E 3' in Table 3, generates a class A' that is defined as a subclass of class B and $\neg A$. If the ontology satisfies the requirement, this addition causes an unsatisfiable class due to the fact that the reasoner would infer that A' is subclass of A and $\neg A$. The second assertion, associated to axiom 'E 4', generates a class A' that is defined as a subclass of class A and $\neg B$. If the ontology satisfies the requirement, this addition causes an unsatisfiable class due to the fact that the reasoner would infer that A' is subclass of B and $\neg B$. The last assertion, associated to axiom 'E 5', generates a class A' that is defined as a subclass of class A and B. If the

Table 3. Test implementation for class-related test expressions

	Preconditions	Axioms to declare auxiliary terms	Assertions to test the ontology behaviour	
			Axiom	Expected status after adding the axiom
T1	Class A and class B exist	(E 1) Declaration of $\neg A$ (E 2) Declaration of $\neg B$	(E 3) A' $\sqsubseteq$ $\neg A \sqcap$ B	Unsatisfiable class
			(E 4) A' $\sqsubseteq$ A $\sqcap \neg B$	Unsatisfiable class
			(E 5) A' $\sqsubseteq$ A $\sqcap$ B	Consistent ontology
T2	Class A and class B exist	(S 1) Declaration of $\neg A$ (S 2) Declaration of $\neg B$	(S 3) A' $\sqsubseteq$ $\neg A \sqcap$ B	Consistent ontology
			(S 4) A' $\sqsubseteq$ A $\sqcap \neg B$	Unsatisfiable class
			(S 5) A' $\sqsubseteq$ A $\sqcap$ B	Consistent ontology
T3	Class A and class B exist	(D 1) Declaration of $\neg A$ (D 2) Declaration of $\neg B$	(D 3) A' $\sqsubseteq$ $\neg A \sqcap$ B	Consistent ontology
			(D 4) A' $\sqsubseteq$ A $\sqcap \neg B$	Consistent ontology
			(D 5) A' $\sqsubseteq$ A $\sqcap$ B	Unsatisfiable class

ontology satisfies the requirement, this assertion causes a consistent ontology due to the fact that there is no problem if A' is subclass of A and B.

We follow the same procedure for each of the test expressions, defining scenarios which cause different behaviours in the ontology.

In the case that the requirement involves **subsumption** between concepts and the ontology meets the requirement, axiom 'S 4' in Table 3 causes an unsatisfiable class. Axioms 'S 3' and 'S 5' are expected to entail consistent ontologies.

Finally, if the requirement involves **disjoint** classes and the ontology satisfies the requirement, axiom 'D 5' in Table 3 causes an unsatisfiable class. Axioms 'D 3' and 'D 4' are expected to entail consistent ontologies.

3.2.2   Property-Related Test Expressions

By the same token, Table 4 shows the implementations related to properties between concepts (T4), symmetry (T5), cardinalities (T6, T7, T8), and intersection (T9).

In order to check a **property between two concepts** A and B, a new individual is added to the ontology. The assertion associated to axiom 'Pst 6' in Table 4 defines a link between two individuals. If the range is defined, this assertion causes an inconsistent ontology due to the fact that the reasoner infers that one individual is of type B and its complement.

In order to check **symmetry**, the assertions add two properties between different individuals. The assertion associated to axiom 'Sy 6' defines a property between individuals that does not cause any inconsistency. However, the assertion associated to axiom 'Sy 7' defines a property between individuals that should not satisfy the constraint and causes an inconsistent ontology.

In order to check cardinality, the assertions define axioms that add new cardinality constraints to the ontology. Depending on the type of cardinality, different axioms cause an unsatisfiable class. If the requirement involves a **maximum cardinality** and the ontology satisfies the requirement, axiom 'Max 3' causes an unsatisfiable class. However, if the requirement involves a **minimum cardinality** and the ontology satisfies the requirement, axiom 'Min 2' causes an unsatisfiable class. Finally, if the requirement involves an **exact cardinality** and the ontology satisfies the requirement, axioms 'Ex 2' and 'Ex 3' cause an unsatisfiable class.

Finally, in order to check **intersection** between B and C, the first assertion follows the same principles than the maximum cardinality tests. In addition, assertions 'I 10' and 'I 11' force an axiom which does not satisfy the cardinality nor does it consider the intersection. These last assertions should lead to an consistent ontology, due to the fact that although they do not satisfy the cardinality constraint they do not satisfy the intersection.

3.2.3   Individual-Related Test Expressions

Regarding the individual-related test expressions, Table 5 defines the implementation for the test related to the **definition of an individual** a of type A (T10).

Table 4. Test implementation for the property-related test expressions

	Preconditions	Axioms to declare auxiliary terms	Assertions to test the ontology behaviour	
			Axioms	Expected status after adding the axiom
T4	Class A, class B and property P exist	(Pst 1) Declaration of ¬B (Pst 2) Assertion A' ⊑ A (Pst 3) Assertion A'(a1) (Pst 4) Assertion ¬B(nob1) (Pst 5) Assertion A' ⊑ ∃P.{nob1}	(Pst 6) Assertion P(a1, nob1)	Inconsistent ontology
T5	Class A, class B and property P exist	(Sy 1) Assertion B(b1) (Sy 2) Declaration A' ⊑ A (Sy 3) Assertion A' ⊑ ∀P.{b1} (Sy 4) Assertion A'(a1) (Sy 5) Assertion B(b2)	(Sy 6) Assertion P(a1, b1)	Consistent ontology
			(Sy 7) Assertion P(b2, a1)	Inconsistent ontology
T6	Class A, class B and property P exist	(Max 1) Declaration of A' ⊑ A	(Max 2) Assertion A' ≤ (num-1)R.B	Consistent ontology
			(Max 3) Assertion A' ≥ (num+1)R.B	Unsatisfiable class
			(Max 4) Assertion A' ≤ (num)R.B	Consistent ontology
			(Max 5) Assertion A' ≥ (num)R.B	Consistent ontology
T7	Class A, class B and property P exist	(Min 1) Declaration of A' ⊑ A	(Min 2) Assertion A' ≤ (num-1)R.B	Unsatisfiable class
			(Min 3) Assertion A' ≥ (num+1)R.B	Consistent ontology
			(Min 4) Assertion A' ≤ (num)R.B	Consistent ontology
			(Min 5) Assertion A' ≥ (num)R.B	Consistent ontology
T8	Class A, class B and property P exist	(Ex 1) Declaration of A' ⊑ A	(Ex 2) Assertion A' ≤ (num-1)R.B	Unsatisfiable class
			(Ex 3) Assertion A' ≥ (num+1)R.B	Unsatisfiable class
			(Ex 4) Assertion A' ≤ (num)R.B	Consistent ontology
			(Ex 5) Assertion A' ≥ (num)R.B	Consistent ontology
T9	Class A, class B and property P exist	(I 1) Declaration of A' ⊑ A (I 2) Declaration of ¬B (I 3) Declaration of ¬C	(I 4) Assertion A' ≤ (num-1).B ⊓ C	Consistent ontology
			(I 5) Assertion A' ≥ (num+1)R.B ⊓ C	Unsatisfiable class
			(I 6) Assertion A' ≤ (num)R.B ⊓ C	Consistent ontology
			(I 7) Assertion A' ≥ (num)R.B ⊓ C	Consistent ontology
			(I 8) Assertion A' ≤ (num)R.B ⊓ C	Consistent ontology
			(I 9) Assertion A' ≥ (num)R.B ⊓ C	Consistent ontology
			(I 10) Assertion A' ≥ (num+1)R.B	Consistent ontology
			(I 11) Assertion A' ≥ (num+1)R. C	Consistent ontology

To check it, axiom 'Id 3' first identifies if there is a problem with the definition of the individual. To conclude, axiom 'Id 4' declares that the individual a is of type complement of A; in this case the assertion causes an inconsistency, due to the fact that an individual cannot be of type A and its complement.

Table 5. Test implementation for the individual-related test expression

Preconditions	Axioms to declare auxiliary terms	Assertions to test the ontology behaviour	
		Axioms	Expected status after adding the axiom
T10 Class A and individual a1 exist	(Id1) Declaration of ¬A (Id2) Declaration of B	(Id3) Assertion B(a1)	Consistent ontology
		(Id4) Assertion ¬A(a1)	Inconsistent ontology

3.3 Test Execution

The test execution activity consists of three parts: the execution of the query which represents the preconditions, the addition of the axioms which declare the auxiliary terms, and the addition of the assertions. After the addition of each axiom, the reasoner is executed to report the status of the ontology. The addition of the auxiliary axioms needs to always lead to a consistent ontology. However, in the case of the assertions, the agreement between the reasoner status after the addition of all the axioms and the status indicated in the test implementation determines whether the ontology satisfies the desired behaviour.

We distinguish three possible results, i.e., *undefined*, if the ontology does not pass the preconditions; *passed*, if the ontology passes the preconditions and the results of the assertions are the expected ones; and *not passed*, if the ontology passes the preconditions but the results of the assertions are not the expected ones. The separation between *not passed* and *undefined* tests distinguishes between an incorrect behaviour of the ontology, where the constraints or characteristics of the tested concepts are not defined, and an absent behaviour, where the tested concepts are not defined. Algorithm 1 summarizes the steps needed to execute each test case. If the test case is passed, then the requirement is satisfied; otherwise, the requirement is not satisfied. Moreover, the *not passed* result implies that the requirement is not correctly implemented, while and *undefined* result implies that the requirement is not taken into account in the ontology implementation.

Algorithm 1. Test case execution

Data: Ontology and test case implementation
Result: Test case result

1 **if** *precondition* = *true* **then**
2   add(ontology, auxiliary terms);
3   **if** *checkOntologyStatus()* = *consistent* **then**
4   **for** *assertion in assertions* **do**
5   add(ontology, assertion.axioms);
6   **if** *checkOntologyStatus()* ≠ *assertion.result*
            then
7   result = not passed;
8   exit loop;
9   **end**
10   remove(ontology, assertion.axioms);
11   result = passed;
12   **end**
13   **else**
14   result = not passed;
15   **end**
16   remove(ontology, auxiliary terms);
17 **else**
18   result = undefined;
19 **end**

The output of this activity is an RDF document where the results of each test case are stored using the proposed vocabulary. In this vocabulary, each test case result stores the URI of the ontology that is tested, the test implementation and the result of the execution on the ontology.

Listing 1.3. Example of test case result

```
:testResultPlatform2 a vtc:TestCaseResult;
    vtc:hasExecution :execution1;
    vtc:testResult vtc:Undefined.
:execution1 a vtc:Execution;
    vtc:executedOn <http://iot.linkeddata.es/def/core/ontology.ttl>;
    vtc:isRelatedToImplementation :testImplPlatform2 .
```

4 Testing process

The proposed testing activities can be used in several *test-last* ontology development life-cycles, such as in waterfall [5] or in agile [12] ones. In the case of waterfall ontology development, the tests are generated and executed at the end of the development process to validate it. On the other hand, in an agile approach the development of the ontology is incremental based on development iterations or sprints and the tests are generated and executed after each iteration.

Moreover, the testing activities can also be integrated into *test-first* approaches, such as Test-Driven Development (TDD), where the tests are generated before the ontology implementation in order to guide the development. Inspired by software engineering, we support another *test-first* approach: Behaviour-Driven Development (BDD). This approach, introduced in the Scone project[9], focuses on the behaviour the ontology needs to implement. In software engineering, BDD is focused on defining specifications of the behaviour of the system, in a way that they can be automated [14]. The main goal of BDD, which is generally regarded as the evolution of TDD, is to get executable specifications of a system that can be used by the users. Figures 1 and 2 depict the workflows of these *test-last* and *test-first* approaches. The application of this approach to ontology engineering may help ontology engineers to be more conscious about the ontology behaviour expected by the users.

In addition to the integration into the ontology development, the proposed testing activities can also be used for other goals, such as to verify the conformance that two ontologies have according to their requirements or to execute regression tests. Because the test design is separated from the test implementation, the test cases design can be reused over different ontologies instead of being generated from scratch.

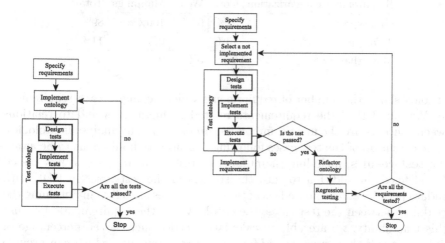

Fig. 1. Test-last approach   **Fig. 2.** Test-first approach

5 Evaluation

To provide an assessment of the validity of the proposed testing framework and its usability in an ontology development project, an empirical analysis has been carried out using three different ontologies, being the VICINITY Core[10]

---

[9] https://bitbucket.org/malefort/scone.
[10] http://iot.linkeddata.es/def/core/.

(Core[11]), the Web of Things[12] (WoT) and the WoT mappings[13] (Mappings) ontologies, which are currently under development in the VICINITY project[14]. To perform such assessment, we have integrated the proposed testing activities into the ontology development process, which was iterative and followed agile principles. Altogether, we gathered 123 ontology requirements, from which 16 were associated to the WoT ontology, 92 to the Core ontology and 15 to the Mappings ontology.

We generated test cases for those ontology requirements that were planned for the different sprints and analysed them to obtain information about their categorization. Table 6 shows the percentage of requirements categorized with one or more of the requirement types identified in Sect. 3. This table gives us information about the complexity of the requirements. We found that most of the requirements are related to only one type of requirement, i.e., relation between concepts.

Table 6. Percentage of requirements whose desired behaviour is categorized with one or more types

Requirement categorization	Core	WoT	Mappings	Total
One type	87%	94%	100%	89%
Two types	13%	6%	0%	11%
More than two types	0%	0%	0%	0%

Table 7 shows the number of requirements which belong to each requirement type. We found that the requirements related to hierarchies and to relations between concepts are the most common requirements in our analysed ontologies.

The execution of the test cases following this approach allows us to be aware of the **test results**, including the number of tests that are passed, not passed and undefined. In addition to this, the storage of the test cases in RDF with metadata permits an automated execution of test cases as well as maintaining the traceability between the test cases, the ontology and the requirements. Because of this traceability, we are able to calculate metrics such as the percentage of tested terms and the percentage of formalized requirements, which can provide us with an outlook about the situation of the testing process. This information is useful for the developers to be aware about which requirements are fulfilled by the ontologies and which ones are not implemented yet, as well as about which ontology terms are present in the tests. To calculate the tested terms we defined a metric called **tested terms coverage** (TTCOV), which is calculated using the expression

$$TTCOV(S, O) = \frac{NTestedT(S)}{NT(O)} \tag{1}$$

---

[11] During the development of this work part of the VICINITY Core ontology was transferred to a new ontology.

[12] http://iot.linkeddata.es/def/wot/.

[13] http://iot.linkeddata.es/def/wot-mappings/.

[14] http://vicinity2020.eu/vicinity/.

Table 7. Number of requirements of each type in the analysed ontologies

Type of requirement	Core	WoT	Mappings	Total
T1 - Equivalence	0	0	0	0
T2 - Subsumption	35	5	1	41
T3 - Disjointness	0	0	0	0
T4 - Relation between two concepts	86	10	9	105
T5 - Symmetry	4	0	0	4
T6 - Maximum cardinality	0	0	1	1
T7 - Minimum cardinality	2	1	0	3
T8 - Exact cardinality	0	0	1	1
T9 - Intersection	1	0	1	1
T10 - Definition of an individual	11	0	0	11

where $NTested(S)$ refers to the number of different terms in the set of tests S and $NT(O)$ refers to the number of terms defined in the ontology O.

To calculate the tested requirements we defined a metric called **formalized requirements coverage** (FRCOV), which is calculated using the expression

$$FRCOV(R, S) = \frac{NR(R)}{NTests(S)} \tag{2}$$

where $NR(R)$ refers to the number of identified requirements and $NTests(S)$ refers to the number of tests cases generated.

Table 8 summarizes the results obtained after the execution of the test cases in the last sprint of each ontology. All the requirements, their test cases and results are published in the VICINITY portal[15]. The results show that, even though the majority of the requirements are passed, there are several *undefined* tests in the Core ontology. This is due to the fact that there are several terms identified in the requirements which are not yet declared in the ontologies because they have not been planned yet for any sprint. Additionally, the results also

Table 8. Metrics extracted from the test cases in their last sprint

Ontology	Test results			Tested terms	Formalized requirements
	Passed	Not passed	Undefined		
Core	59%	17%	24%	41%	100%
WoT	94%	6%	0%	53%	100%
Mappings	100%	0%	0%	83%	100%
Total	68%	14%	18%	49%	100%

---

[15] http://vicinity.iot.linkeddata.es/vicinity/testing.html.

show that both the Core and the WoT ontologies have requirements that are not passed. Table 8 also determines that the tested terms do not exceed the 83%; this result is normal because there are terms that are not defined in the requirements. These terms can be created from the addition of ontology design patterns [6] or from the reuse of terms from other ontologies.

6   Conclusions and Future Work

In this paper we provide a testing framework composed of a set of activities that can be integrated into different ontology development life-cycles. This framework also provides a collection of test expressions to determine the desired behaviour of the requirements. These test expressions were defined after an analysis of 248 requirements from different ontologies. If more requirements with new behaviours are available, the set of test expressions will be extended to support them.

In addition to this, the storage of the tests in an RDF document allows us to extract different metrics, such as the already mentioned TTCOV and FRCOV, with the aim of better monitoring the ontology testing process. We expect that adopting testing activities in the development process will allow ontology engineers and users to be aware about the completeness of ontologies regarding their requirements. Moreover, these testing activities can also be helpful for analysing ontology conformance.

Future work will be directed to a more rigorous analysis of the requirement types. We plan to conduct a lexico-syntactic analysis of the requirements, based on the work presented by Daga et al. [3], in order to be able to identify more enriched test expressions. Furthermore, due to the fact that the test cases analyse the ontology status in different scenarios by adding several axioms, future work will also be directed to support the identification of the reason of why a test is failing. This would make the proposed testing framework helpful not only to verify if all the requirements are satisfied, but also to explain what is left for the ontology to fulfil the requirement.

Finally, we plan to analyse the feasibility and the benefits of the BDD approach applied to ontologies; we consider that this approach may help ontology engineers to provide ontologies more aligned with user expectations. Additionally, in this work we focused on OWL ontologies, and we intend to provide support for ontologies in other languages, e.g., RDF Schema.

References

1. Auer, S.: The RapidOWL Methodology - towards agile knowledge engineering. In: Proceedings of the IEEE International Workshop on Enabling Technologies: Infrastructures for Collaborative Enterprises (WETICE 2006), pp. 352–357 (2006)
2. Blomqvist, E., Seil Sepour, A., Presutti, V.: Ontology testing - methodology and tool. In: ten Teije, A., et al. (eds.) EKAW 2012. LNCS, vol. 7603, pp. 216–226. Springer, Heidelberg (2012). https://doi.org/10.1007/978-3-642-33876-2_20

3. Daga, E., et al.: NeOn D2.5.2 Pattern based ontology design: methodology and software support
4. Dennis, M., van Deemter, K., Dell'Aglio, D., Pan, J.Z.: Computing authoring tests from competency questions: experimental validation. In: d'Amato, C., et al. (eds.) ISWC 2017. LNCS, vol. 10587, pp. 243–259. Springer, Cham (2017). https://doi.org/10.1007/978-3-319-68288-4_15
5. Fernández-López, M., Gómez-Pérez, A., Juristo, N.: Methontology: from ontological art towards ontological engineering. In: Proceedings of the Ontological Engineering AAAI 1997 Spring Symposium Series, pp. 33–40 (1997)
6. Gangemi, A., Presutti, V.: Ontology design patterns. In: Staab, S., Studer, R. (eds.) Handbook on Ontologies, pp. 221–243. Springer, Heidelberg (2009). https://doi.org/10.1007/978-3-540-92673-3
7. García-Ramos, S., Otero, A., Fernández-López, M.: OntologyTest: a tool to evaluate ontologies through tests defined by the user. In: Omatu, S., et al. (eds.) IWANN 2009. LNCS, vol. 5518, pp. 91–98. Springer, Heidelberg (2009). https://doi.org/10.1007/978-3-642-02481-8_13
8. Grüninger, M., Fox, M.S.: Methodology for the Design and Evaluation of Ontologies (1995)
9. Hamill, P.: Unit Test Frameworks: Tools for High-quality Software Development. O'Reilly Media Inc., Sebastopol (2004)
10. Keet, C.M., Ławrynowicz, A.: Test-driven development of ontologies. In: Sack, H., et al. (eds.) ESWC 2016. LNCS, vol. 9678, pp. 642–657. Springer, Cham (2016). https://doi.org/10.1007/978-3-319-34129-3_39
11. Parkkila, J., et al.: An ontology for videogame interoperability. Multimedia Tools Appl. 76(4), 4981–5000 (2017)
12. Peroni, S.: A simplified agile methodology for ontology development. In: Dragoni, M., Poveda-Villalón, M., Jimenez-Ruiz, E. (eds.) OWLED/ORE 2016. LNCS, vol. 10161, pp. 55–69. Springer, Cham (2017). https://doi.org/10.1007/978-3-319-54627-8_5
13. Ren, Y., Parvizi, A., Mellish, C., Pan, J.Z., van Deemter, K., Stevens, R.: Towards competency question-driven ontology authoring. In: Presutti, V. (ed.) ESWC 2014. LNCS, vol. 8465, pp. 752–767. Springer, Cham (2014). https://doi.org/10.1007/978-3-319-07443-6_50
14. Solis, C., Wang, X.: A study of the characteristics of behaviour driven development. In: Proceedings on the EUROMICRO Conference on Software Engineering and Advanced Applications (SEAA 2011), pp. 383–387 (2011)
15. Suárez-Figueroa, M.C., Gómez-Pérez, A., Fernández-López, M.: The NeOn methodology for ontology engineering. In: Suárez-Figueroa, M.C., Gómez-Pérez, A., Motta, E., Gangemi, A. (eds.) Ontology Engineering in a Networked World, pp. 9–34. Springer, Heidelberg (2012). https://doi.org/10.1007/978-3-642-24794-1_2
16. Suárez-Figueroa, M.C., Gómez-Pérez, A., Villazón-Terrazas, B.: How to write and use the ontology requirements specification document. In: Meersman, R., Dillon, T., Herrero, P. (eds.) OTM 2009. LNCS, vol. 5871, pp. 966–982. Springer, Heidelberg (2009). https://doi.org/10.1007/978-3-642-05151-7_16
17. Sure, Y., Erdmann, M., Angele, J., Staab, S., Studer, R., Wenke, D.: OntoEdit: collaborative ontology development for the semantic web. In: Horrocks, I., Hendler, J. (eds.) ISWC 2002. LNCS, vol. 2342, pp. 221–235. Springer, Heidelberg (2002). https://doi.org/10.1007/3-540-48005-6_18

18. Vrandečić, D., Gangemi, A.: Unit tests for ontologies. In: Meersman, R., Tari, Z., Herrero, P. (eds.) OTM 2006. LNCS, vol. 4278, pp. 1012–1020. Springer, Heidelberg (2006). https://doi.org/10.1007/11915072_2
19. Wynne, M., Hellesoy, A., Tooke, S.: The Cucumber Book: Behaviour-Driven Development for Testers and Developers. Pragmatic Bookshelf, Raleigh (2017)

Interactive Interpretation of Serial Episodes: Experiments in Musical Analysis

Béatrice Fuchs[1](✉) and Amélie Cordier[2]

[1] Université de Lyon, UJML3, IAE, LIRIS, 69 008 Lyon, France
`beatrice.fuchs@liris.cnrs.fr`
[2] Université de Lyon, LIRIS, 69 100 Villeurbanne, France
`amelie.cordier@liris.cnrs.fr`

Abstract. We propose an interactive approach for post-processing serial episodes mined from sequential data, *i.e.* time-stamped sequences of events. The strength of the approach rests upon an interactive interpretation that relies on a web interface featuring various tools for observing, sorting and filtering the mined episodes. Features of the approach include interestingness measures, interactive visualization of episode occurrences in the mined event sequence, and an automatic filtering mechanism that remove episodes depending on the analyst's previous actions. We report experiments that show the advantages and limits of this approach in the domain of melodic analysis.

1 Introduction

The aim of knowledge discovery (KD) is to identify pieces of knowledge in large volumes of data through non trivial methods, during an *interactive* and *iterative* process [1]. This process is said to be iterative because several iterations are often needed to understand complex phenomenons captured in data, each one contributing to gradually improve the global understanding of the knowledge hidden in the data. The process is said to be interactive because it is fully guided by the user, an analyst expert in the domain. At each stage, the analyst organizes the tasks to be performed, identifies the relevant knowledge and decides on the next actions to be taken. The role of the analyst is even more important when the domain knowledge is hard to capture and/or when it is not available in the system. In KD, research has long focused on the mining step because it raises a few challenging issues for computer scientists. However, to transform the mining results in actionable knowledge, human expertise is required, and this is a tedious task for the analyst. First, finding good settings for the mining is far from obvious and requires most of the time several trials. Next, the interpretation step is very long and tedious because there may be thousands of results that have to be processed manually. However, all the steps of the KD process should be taken into account when seeking to improve interactivity [2]. The involvement of a human analyst in the KD process is a key challenge, as discussed in [3]. Therefore, the

© Springer Nature Switzerland AG 2018
C. Faron Zucker et al. (Eds.): EKAW 2018, LNAI 11313, pp. 131–146, 2018.
https://doi.org/10.1007/978-3-030-03667-6_9

user is given a central role in the KD process and there is a real need to integrate several features such as visualization techniques, human-computer interactions and knowledge engineering.

In this paper, we focus on the assistance to interpretation during the post-processing stage. Our approach aims to increase the involvement of the analyst by giving him a leading role in order to enhance his cognitive mobilization and by assisting him through different interaction capabilities. The approach is reified in a tool, the TRANSMUTE prototype, a web-based interface supporting interactive interpretation of serial episodes in event sequences that assist the work of the analyst. The approach supports the tracking of the analyst work in an interactive and iterative way. On each iteration, the analyst may visualize, sort and interact with the results of the mining. His actions are taken into account to manage his work and to enable him to focus more quickly on other relevant episodes. The main contributions of the approach rely on the following features:

- a visual and customisable interface to enable user interactions, to navigate into episode occurrences and display them in the sequence,
- the possibility of combining different interestingness measures to rank serial episodes in association to an original and automatic filtering process that discards episode occurrences and episodes depending on previously selected episodes,
- the possibility for the user to express an interpretation of the selected episodes by creating and adding them an annotation in the form of a new type of event,
- and finally to record a new sequence resulting from the interpretation into a data storage.

Thereafter, Sect. 2 presents several related approaches in the literature. Then the main features of TRANSMUTE are presented in Sect. 3 and the underlying principles of the KD process and principles of our approach for interpretation are presented formally in Sect. 4. Section 5 reports on some experiments in the musical domain to verify the efficiency. The paper ends with a discussion on the limits of this approach followed by a conclusion.

2   Related Works

Related works stem from several complementary research areas: data mining, interactive visual analysis and knowledge engineering tend to combine together several complementary features.

In the literature, several methods have been proposed to cope with the surabondance of mining results, such as interestingness measures, concise representations, data compression and post-processing filtering. The exclusive use of objective interestingness measures has proved to be unable to solve the recurring problem of overabundance and redundancy of mining results. An alternative principle has been successfully applied, *minimum description length* (MDL), which is concerned by selecting the best set of patterns based on their ability to compress data [4,5]. Although this approach is well suited for itemsets, its application for serial episodes in event sequences is more delicate because the events composing pattern occurrences are not necessarily contiguous in the sequence and there may be repetitions of the same event types. This makes the coding more complex and decreases the efficiency and finally, the advantage of compression [6]. Moreover, the MDL approach is not always practicable because data may not be suitable for compression. Nevertheless these principles can be useful to develop other methods, without keeping the objective of data compression.

Taking into account the user as a leading actor in the KD process has gradually imposed itself. For a long time the research community recognized that the active involvement of a human expert in the KD process is essential to benefit from his knowledge and expertise [2,7]. In this sense, visualization has been widely explored in order to increase human cognition to better understand the data, through graphical representations into which it is possible to navigate in order to change the point of view on data, according to the mantra *"preview first, zoom/filter, details on request"* [8].

Although apparently close, interactive data exploration using data mining techniques is quite different in its objectives [3] although it benefits from features of interactive data visualization. If it relies on an interface to visualize data and results obtained by mining, it consists more in an assistance to the user looking for significant patterns in the data in order to construct a model explaining the data. Several research works in interactive data exploration have been conducted and workshops dedicated to this field appeared (IDEA, IDA). For example, [9] present an interactive approach to episode mining and analysis that supports visual exploration of episodes mined from health data. [10] specifies precisely outlines of information visualization and visual analysis, recalls that data mining is only one step in the process of KD and shows the different steps of this process related to the visualization facilities. The paper discusses the typical components found in these systems, including a list of interaction techniques reflecting the user's intentions: *select, explore, reconfigure, encode, abstract/elaborate, filter and convert.*

More recent approaches claim that interestingness is subjective in essence and take into account the goals of the user and its knowledge [3] in an interactive way to involve the user in the exploration process. Several works aims to take into account user's actions to learn preferences as for example [11–13]. In this trend, most recent works aim to capture subjective interestingness by learning user's preferences or intentions when interacting with mining results.

To our opinion, these approaches give the user a rather passive role in the KD process. Furthermore, we argue that subjectivity can be expressed in another way: *a priori* knowledge on data or knowledge that, once encoded in the form of interestingness measures or properties can be helpful for choosing mining parameters, choosing a pre-processing strategy or helping ranking and interpreting the results. Our approach aims to integrate several approaches to take full advantage of their combination in an interactive way, where the user is considered a leading actor of the KD process. It does not focus on visualization techniques but aims at providing a simple interface to support interactions and understanding data, where the user has the initiative and leads the KD process with several complementary tools. Interactions aim at assisting the interpretation process and model construction. The main difference of our approach is that interactivity is not focused on the same aspects as most related works: the user drives really the KD process, have an active role, and can bring his expertise to the interpretation. It takes advantage of event-based or temporal-based interestingness measures close to the compactness measure [14] where compactness represents the number of gap events between the events of the episode. Furthermore, the filtering process is closely related to these measures. The results of interpretation are recorded in a persistent data store which can be compared to [5], but with a different objective and in an interactive way. The objective is not to compress data but rather to characterize the potential interestingness of episodes by their relative importance in the sequence explored, and to remove useless episodes after selection, enabling to quicker focus on other candidate episodes. Next, the recording of the chosen episodes associated with their interpretation in a transformed sequence fall rather under a knowledge engineering objective than compression.

We present in the next section the TRANSMUTE system before studying formally its principles.

3   Transmute

The main motivation of this work is to explore *traces*, *i.e.* sequences of actions performed by users during their activity supported by a computer system. Meanwhile, the approach and the tools developed aims at being applied to any sequential data such as a musical score, which serves as an application domain for experiments in this paper.

TRANSMUTE is an interactive tool that implements the KD process from sequential data. The analyst can interact with the elements of the trace, choose mining parameters, launch the miner, and select episodes outputted by the miner to see its occurrences. The interface of TRANSMUTE is shown on Fig. 1, where traces of the serious game TAMAGOCOURS are analyzed. TAMAGOCOURS is a collaborative serious game for learning the rules of diffusion of numerical resources. The main interface of TRANSMUTE has several parts:

On the upper part are the traces: the trace being analysed ① and the trace in which interpreted episodes are stored ②. On top of the trace in ①, new event types are intended to replace occurrences of selected episodes in the trace ②. To facilitate the interpretation of the events in the trace, the trace model is displayed ③: each event type is displayed next to the displayed icon. The lower part of the interface is divided in two sections. On the lower-left ④, the mining parameters chosen by the analyst are displayed. On the lower-right ⑤, the list of episodes found during the mining are displayed, and for each of them, interestingness measures with sorting buttons. At the top we find the episodes chosen by the user, below the remaining episodes to be examined and at the

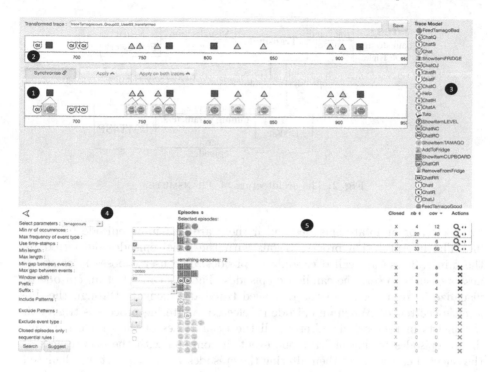

Fig. 1. The interface of TRANSMUTE.

bottom the filtered episodes as a consequence of the previous user's choices. The filtered episodes are faded: they are temporarily discarded and not available for selection. It is possible to undo an episode selection and the remaining episodes are updated consequently.

TRANSMUTE implements the visual interpretation process and is built upon several other components (Fig. 2). The first one is DISKIT which implements the rest of the KD process. DISKIT encapsulates the DMT4SP miner[1] [15], a tool for extracting episodes or sequential rules from one or several sequences of events, in accordance with the minimal occurrence semantic rule [16]. DMT4SP produces a set of frequent serial episodes satisfying the constraints specified in the settings. Next, a visual framework provides basic methods for visualizing and interacting with traces. Finally, a data storage ensures the storage of traces or sequences, and provides basic data management capabilities such as storing sequences associated with an explicit descriptive model, or sequence transformation in order to manipulate them (abstraction, filtering, *etc.*). Sequences and their associated model are stored in a triplestore as RDF triples. The transformations will not be detailed more in this paper.

The main important operations involved in the interpretation process are shown in Fig. 3. The process is repetitive, as many times as the user wants to

---

[1] http://liris.cnrs.fr/~crigotti/dmt4sp.html.

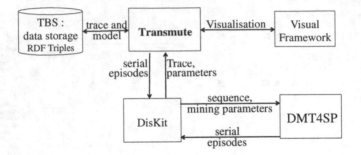

Fig. 2. The architecture of TRANSMUTE.

sort, select or annotate episodes and if there are remaining episode to examine. The interpretation process begins with the serial episodes outputted by the miner. These are called candidate episodes. The user chooses interestingness measures to sort the candidate episodes. Then he can select an episode to visualize its occurrences in the displayed trace and navigate through the different occurrences. When an episode is selected, a filtering process is triggered. It consists in temporarily filtering all the occurrences of the unselected candidate episodes having at least one event in common with the occurrences of the selected episode, and then filtering the episodes whose support, recalculated by taking into account the filtered occurrences, is under the threshold initially set by the user. The episodes thus eliminated remain visible to the user but they are faded in the interface and can not be selected any more. The user can interpret a selected episode by adding an annotation which is displayed with an associated icon in a new trace. The user can record the result of his work in a *transformed* sequence that stores all the annotations resulting from the interpretation. The transformed sequence is built from the original sequence by replacing every occurrence of the selected episode by a new type of event resulting from the annotation. The next section describes formally the main features of TRANSMUTE.

4   Interactive Interpretation of Serial Episodes

Sequences are studied in the context of a classical KD process made up of the main steps: pre-processing (selection of the trace, transformation), mining, and post-processing (visualization and interpretation of candidate episodes). Hereafter, we first describe briefly the basic definitions of the concepts involved in the process and we further develop the post-processing step. The concepts are illustrated in the domain of musical analysis where a typical task consists in analysing a musical score described as a sequence of notes associated with a duration and a time-stamp in order to find recurrent melodic patterns.

candidate serial episodes
mined from event sequence

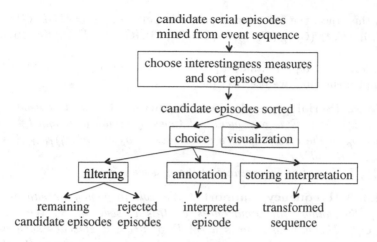

Fig. 3. Overview of the main steps of the interpretation process.

4.1 Definitions

During the pre-processing, a sequence is chosen by the analyst and transformed in the format of the analyser.

Definition 1 (Sequence). *A sequence S is a set of event occurrences – or events for short –, each one having a type and a date. An event is a couple (e_i, t_i) where $e_i \in E$ is a type of event and E is the set of types of events, and $t_i \in \mathbb{N}$ is a time stamp associated with e_i.*

The transformation of the input data into an event sequence is a simple bijective syntactic transformation to conform to the miner's data format[2]. In the musical analysis domain, every music note name and rest of the score corresponds to an event type of the event sequence. The note values (whole notes, quarter note, *etc.*) are used to compute a time stamp associated with each event of the sequence. We can notice that depending on the application domain, the events of a sequence may not always be characterized by a duration. This is the case for numerical traces for example. Let us consider the following extract of a musical score:

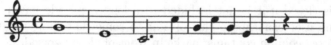

This musical piece can be described by the following input data[3]:

```
Note name G E C C G C G E C
   Duration 4 4 3 1 1 1 1 1 1
 time-stamp 0 4 8 11 12 13 14 15 16
```

---

[2] Event types are represented with integer values.

[3] Here, the notes have 4, 3 and 1 beats, and the corresponding note values are respectively whole note, dotted half note and quarter note.

From this trace, the following sequence is built with $E = \{C, E, G\}$:
$$S = \{(G, 0), (E, 4), (C, 8), (C, 11), (G, 12), (C, 13), (G, 14), (E, 15), (C, 16)\}$$

In the following step, the analyst provides the parameters to guide the mining. In our implementation, we use DMT4SP.

Definition 2 (Serial episode, occurrence). *A serial episode* $p = (e_1, e_2, \ldots, e_n)$, $e_i \in E$ *is a sequence of types of events of length* $l_p = n$. *An occurrence* o_p *of the episode* p *is a set of events* $o_p = \{(e'_i, t'_i)\}_{i=1,n}\}$ *such as* $(e'_i, t'_i)_{i=1,n} \in S$ *and* $\forall\, i, e_i = e'_i$.
$O_p = \{o_p^j\}_j$ *is the set of occurrences of the episode* p *in* S.

Definition 3 (Frequency, support). *We call frequency or support of an episode* p *the number of occurrences of this episode in* S. *We denote it* $\sigma(p) = |O_p|$. *The mining returns a set* P *of frequent episodes such as* $P = \{p_i\}, \forall\, i,\ \sigma(p_i) \geqslant \sigma_{min}$, *where* σ_{min} *is the minimal support chosen by the analyst.*

In the example, if $\sigma_{min} = 2$, the occurrences of the episode (G, E, C) are:
$op_1 = \{(G, 0), (E, 4), (C, 8)\}$ and $op_2 = \{(G, 14), (E, 15), (C, 16)\}$.
$\sigma((G, E, C)) = 2 \geqslant \sigma_{min}$.

Additional constraints may be specified but outside the scope of this article and will not be detailed: time constraints (gap min, window size, and in a limited way a constraint similar to gap max), syntactic constraints (min/max size, prefix, last element), episode closure, sub-episode inclusion/exclusion, event type filtering.

4.2   Post-processing and Interactive Interpretation

The serial episodes outputted by the miner are displayed in the Transmute application with appropriate chosen icons (Fig. 1).

Interestingness Measures

To help the user sort and choose episodes, some interestingness measures are computed. First, the closure property of episodes is important because it leads to a more compact representation and limits the number of episodes generated. An episode is closed if it is not included in a longer episode having the same support[4]. The user can choose this option to somewhat limit the results. In Fig. 1, the *closed* column contains marks in front of closed episodes.

In addition to the closed episodes, we propose some interestingness measures below in order to measure the combinatorial redundancy and the *compactness* of episodes. The first measure is *event coverage* and takes into account the number of event of the sequence. The second measure is the *temporal coverage* and takes into account the event durations.

---

[4] The computation of the closure property in TRANSMUTE is based on the number of occurrences of a serial episode. It is not detailed in this paper.

Definition 4 (Event coverage). *The event coverage EC_p is the set of distinct events of the occurrences of an episode p. $EC_p = \bigcup_{i=1}^{\sigma(p)} o_p^i$. The event coverage indicator ECI_p of an episode is the number of distinct events: $ECI_p = |EC_p|$.*

Definition 5 (Event spreading). *The time interval $Int(s)$ of a sequence s is the time interval between the first and the last event of the sequence. $Int(s) = [t_{min}, t_{max}], t_{min} = min(t_i), t_{max} = max(t_i), \forall (e_i, t_i) \in s$. The spreading ES_p of an episode p of length n is the set of events of S having a time-stamp included in the time intervals $Int(o_p^i)$ of the occurrences of p. $ES_p = |\{(e_k, t_k) \in S, \forall \, Int(o_p^i) = [t_{min}^i, t_{max}^i], t_{min}^i \leqslant t_k \leqslant t_{max}^i\}|$. The event spreading indicator is the number of events whose time-stamp is included in the time intervals of the occurrences of p: $ESI = |ES_p|$.*

Definition 6 (Noise). *The noise N_p of an episode is the number of events not belonging to the occurrences of a given episode and inserted in the temporal interval of a episode: $N_p = ES_p \backslash EC_p$.*
The noise indicator NI_p is the number of events not belonging to the occurrences of a given episode and inserted in the temporal interval of a episode: $NI_p = ESI_p - ECI_p$.

As explained before, in some situations when the events are associated with a duration, it is possible to compute temporal indicators of the same nature than the previous event indicators but that focus on the duration of the events. This is the case in the domain of musical analysis where each note has a duration.

Definition 7 (Temporal coverage). *Temporal coverage TC_p of an episode $p \in P$ is the total duration of the events of the event coverage. We note $d(o)$ the duration associated with the event o. Let p an episode of event coverage $EC_p, \forall o_i \in EC_m, TC_p = \Sigma_i d(o_i)$.*

In the previous example, let consider the episodes $p_1 = (G, C)$ and $p_2 = (G, E, C)$.
$EC_{p_1} = \{(G, 0), (C, 8), (C, 12), (C, 13), (G, 14), (C, 16)\}, ECI_{p_1} = 6$,
$ES_{p_1} = \{(G, 0), (E, 4), (C, 8), (G, 12), (C, 13), (G, 14), (E, 15), (C, 16)\}$,
$ESI_{p_1} = 8$,
$N = \{(E, 4), (E, 15)\}, NI_{p_1} = 2$ and $TC_{p_1} = 11$,
$EC_{p_2} = \{(G, 0), (E, 4), (C, 8), (G, 14), (E, 15), (C, 16)\}, ECI_{p_2} = 6$,
$ES_{p_2} = \{(G, 0), (E, 4), (C, 8), (G, 14), (E, 15), (C, 16)\}, ESI_{p_2} = 6$,
$N_{p_2} = \emptyset, NI_{p_2} = 0$ and $TC_{p_2} = 14$.

The event coverage indicator aims at giving an estimate of the importance of an episode in the sequence. When many episodes differ only with a very few number of events, this indicator helps decide which episode seems to be the best to choose. The event coverage aims at finding all the episode occurrences the events own to and consequently the episodes in competition with a given chosen episode. These definitions enable us to describe the principles of interactive filtering.

Interactive Filtering

Once episodes are sorted and displayed in the interface of TRANSMUTE, the analyst can select them to highlight their occurrences in the trace, and choose the most relevant ones. When an episode is selected by the expert, all the occurrences of the episode are framed in the interface and all the occurrences of the other episodes whose occurrences have at least one event in common with the occurrences of selected episode are eliminated, the support is re-calculated consequently, and the episodes having an insufficient support are temporarily discarded from the available selection. This process constitutes the *filtering* operation. As a consequence of the filtering process, there is a progressive decrease of the number of results that the analyst has to investigate, which facilitates the next choices because there are less episodes to consider. In the previous example, if the episode (G, E, C) is chosen, it may become obsolete to consider other episodes such as (G, E) or (E, C) because some of their occurrences may include events appearing in (G, E, C). The filtering operation addresses this observation: all the redundant episodes given the chosen episode are discarded which enables the analyst to focus more quickly on other episodes. As the interpretation step is iterative, during each iteration, the selection of an episode is followed by a filtering step which as a consequence filters the remaining episodes and the list of remaining episodes progressively decreases. Filtering plays an important role when providing assistance to the analyst during the interpretation phase. This step relies on the notion of event coverage for searching episodes to delete.

Definition 8 (Filtering). *Let p_s an episode selected by the expert, having an event coverage defined as EC_s. Let $p_i \in P, p_i \neq p_s$ an episode, the set of occurrences of p_i invalidated by the selection of p_s is: $O(p_i|p_s) = \{\forall o_i \in O(p_i), o_i \cap EC_c \neq \emptyset\}$. We denote $P_{p_s} \subset P$ the set of episodes of P invalidated by the choice of p_s by the analyst: $P_{p_s} = \{p_i \in P, p_i \neq p_s,$ such as $\sigma(O(p_i|p_s)) < \sigma_{min}\}$. When the episode p_s has been selected, the set of remaining episodes to consider during the next iteration is: $P \setminus P_{p_s}$.*

In the example, let's consider the following episodes:
$p_1 = (G, E, C)$, $p_2 = (G, E)$ and $p_3 = (G, C)$,
$CE_{p_1} = \{(G, 0), (E, 4), (C, 8), (G, 14), (E, 15), (C, 16)\}$,
The occurrences of p_2 and p_3 are:
$o_{p_2}^1 = \{(G, 0), (E, 4)\}$, $o_{p_2}^2 = \{(G, 14), (E, 15)\}$,
$o_{p_3}^1 = \{(G, 0), (C, 8)\}$, $o_{p_3}^2 = \{(G, 12), (C, 13)\}$, $o_{p_3}^3 = \{(G, 14), (C, 16)\}$.

If the expert chooses the episode p_1, $o_{p_2}^1$ and $o_{p_2}^2$ are deleted, as well as $o_{p_3}^1$ and $o_{p_3}^3$. The supports of p_2 and p_3 respectively become 0 and $1 < \sigma_{min}$. The filtering after the selection of p_1 therefore eliminates p_2 and p_3. In this example, the event types of the episodes p_2 and p_3 are included in the event types of p_1, but it does not mean that all the events of the occurrences of p_2 and p_3 are included in the events of the occurrences of p_1 (for example $o_{p_3}^2 = \{(G, 12), (C, 13)\}$). In other domains, for example TAMAGOCOURS previously mentioned, there are two important episodes: (S, A, F) and (A, F), and the deletion of (S, A, F) do not remove the (A, F) episode because there are a lot of (A, F) occurrences without the S event before.

The filtering initially starts with the set P of all the episodes that have been mined. In each iteration, the set P is progressively cleaned around a selected episode as if it eliminates the neighbouring episodes in the search space, often redundant episodes.

5 Experiments

In order to verify the effectiveness of the interpretation strategy, we propose to apply it on real musical pieces in the field of melodic analysis. We have studied three music pieces. For each of them, a music expert gave before the experiment a list of relevant episodes. In the following, we call these episodes the *expert episodes*. We launched the miner with parameters chosen in order to guarantee that all the expert episodes were recalled in the mining results ($\sigma_{min} = 2$). The results are listed in the table below:

Title of the music piece	Number of mined episodes	Number of expert episodes
1. Reichert, Tarentelle	3 853	29
2. Ibert, Entr'acte	12 947	20
3. Debussy, Syrinx	59 786	11

Then we propose to assess the efficiency of the process by measuring the effort it takes the analyst to find all the expert episodes according to different strategies. The effort is defined as the total number of episodes the expert has to examine before finding every expert episode. The effort of the expert is estimated with the rank of each expert episode in the candidate episodes, if we assume that episodes are examined in sequence by the expert from the beginning of the mining results. The lower the rank, the lower the number of episodes to examine before reaching an expert episode and consequently the effort, showing the efficiency of the strategy. The effort is measured in several circumstances where the episodes are sorted using different criteria: natural order of the mining (no sorting), frequency, event coverage and temporal coverage. A second experiment uses the noise as a first sorting criteria, and the four previous criteria as second sorting criteria.

Once episodes are sorted, we note the rank of the expert episodes for each sorting criteria, which, as explained before, indicates the effort required by the expert to find each episode. We report the results in the two tables below. In the first table, the effort is first measured without filtering. In the second table, the effort is measured with filtering applied each time an expert episode is found and considered as selected. Intuitively, it is clear that the deletion of episodes each time an expert episode is selected should lead to a decrease of the number of episodes and should have an immediate effect on the new ranks of remaining expert episodes. Nevertheless, experts episodes may be wrongly eliminated because of the filtering process. We measure this bias through the recall measure.

With no filtering, the effort of the expert is measured with the rank of the last expert episode and is given in Table 1 for the three pieces, according to the used criteria ($\nearrow$ indicates and ascending sorting, and $\searrow$ a descending sorting). With no filtering, the best results are obtained with a sorting by ascending noise and descending temporal coverage for piece 1, by descending temporal coverage for pieces 2 and 3. The recall is 100% as no episode is deleted in this experiment. Compared to no sorting at all, the reduction of the expert's effort is respectively 94%, 26%, and 43%. For all the criteria, the use of measures has enabled an improvement as it always enables to reduce the effort of the expert. Meanwhile, this result is not completely satisfactory because the effort required from the expert remains too important.

Table 1. Effort of the expert without filtering.

Piece	Mining episodes	Expert episodes	Without sorting	$\sigma\searrow$	$ECI\searrow$	$TC\searrow$	Noise $\nearrow$ and		
							$\sigma\searrow$	$ECI\searrow$	$TC\searrow$
1	3 853	29	3 838	3 838	3 797	2 735	240	369	**233**
2	12 947	20	12 818	12 829	12 591	**9 516**	12 667	12 672	12 668
3	59 786	11	57 424	57 935	34 886	**32 847**	52 928	52 906	52 906

When filtering is introduced, the effort of the expert is computed differently. As the candidate episodes are sorted after each selection of an expert episode, the expert must resume the episode review from the beginning. Therefore, the effort of the expert equals the sum of the ranks of the different expert episodes after each filtering. The results are reported in Table 2. The best results are obtained with a sorting with ascending noise and descending temporal coverage for piece 1, descending temporal coverage for piece 2 and event coverage for piece 3. We can note that, without sorting, review of episodes with revision requires a much higher number of interactions than the initial number of episodes, which is possible because after each choice review starts again from the beginning. We can note that the variations obtained between the different pieces do not make it possible to definitively conclude on the utility of the interestingness measures. This implies that it is important to propose a range of measures to the user. However, the filtering process associated with a measurement always leads to a significant gain.

The diminution of the effort obtained with the filtering strategy with regard to a processing without sorting and without filtering (Table 3) is significant and shows the efficiency of the filtering strategy combined with the interestingness measures. Nevertheless, the recall for the expert episodes is 82% for piece 1, 100% for piece 3 and 33% for piece 2 when the sorting does not use the noise

Table 2. Effort of the expert with filtering.

Music piece	Mined episodes	Experts episodes	Without sorting	$\sigma\searrow$	$ECI\searrow$	$TC\searrow$	Noise $\nearrow$ and		
							$\sigma\searrow$	$ECI\searrow$	$TC\searrow$
1	3 853	29	1442	175	138	66	60	68	**45**
2	12 947	20	3056	638	317	**231**	619	481	481
3	59 786	11	204 851	55 956	**9274**	9 772	12 792	11 482	11 531

and 62% when noise is introduced. The introduction of the noise favoured the episodes composed of closer notes and has improved the recall, which remains however perfectible.

Table 3. Recall rate of expert episodes and diminution of the effort for the strategy with filtering vs without filtering and without sorting.

Piece		$\sigma\searrow$	$ECI\searrow$	$TC\searrow$	Noise $\nearrow$ and		
					$\sigma\searrow$	$ECI\searrow$	$TC\searrow$
1	Diminution	95%	96%	98%	98%	98%	98%
	Recall	82%			82%		
2	Diminution	95%	98%	98%	95%	96%	
	Recall	33%			62%		
3	Diminution	3%	84%	83%	78%	80%	
	Recall	100%			100%		

The order in which the episodes are chosen has an impact on the episodes eliminated by the filtering, hence the importance of the choice of the sorting criteria and the possibility for the user to undo episode selection. These results show that it is important to have several measures to take into account the various characteristics of the data. For example, in the musical domain, it is important to observe the pieces before the analysis, to take into account their specificities and then, to choose the appropriate measures. Subjective measures have not been introduced in this work but would be probably helpful to complete these objective measures.

6 Discussion

In the literature, interactive approaches to knowledge discovery rely most of the time on visualizing data and mining results along different perspectives, and interactions with the user aim at changing the point of view on the data and filtering the results in order to focus on a subset of the data, according to the mantra *"preview first, zoom/filter, details on request"* [8].

Our approach differs in the particular way the interactions with the user are taken into account. It is based on the notion of coverage reflecting the relative importance of an episode in the analyzed trace. Coverage is exploited in two very closely related ways to assist interpretation: It is used firstly as a interestingness measure to rank mining results, and secondly to filter episode as a result of a selection, acting a bit like a filter in the pattern space "around" a selected episode. The coverage is expressed in several ways: in number of events and in total duration, which makes it possible to characterize events associated or not with a duration. The noise measurement is also based on this principle because it derives from the coverage and can be compared with the compactness measure in [14]. Meanwhile, the choice of an interestingness measure and the filtering process are independent. Currently the measures proposed in TRANSMUTE are predefined, and a perspective is to enable the user to choose them among a set.

Our approach can also be compared with to *minimum description length* principle [4] but with a rather different goal. In the MDL approach, the aim is to select a set of patterns that best compress the data. This principle is found in an underlying way with the use of coverage in our approach, that expresses the relative importance of an episode in a sequence, and thus serves to order and filter them. However, the aim of our approach is not to compress data, but rather to explicit significant episodes and to record the interpretation of the expert with the analyzed trace. In addition, the MDL approach has limitations on the one hand in computing complexity and, on the other hand, difficulties when applied to sequential data [6]. From this perspective, an *interactive* MDL approach is promising because it gives the initiative to the user in order to fully take advantage of his knowledge, and together with the exploitation of computational capabilities to assist him with useful filtering mechanisms to eliminate results that have become obsolete as a result of previous choices. Finally, the MDL approach is only applicable if the analyzed data is suitable for compression. This may often not be the case, for example for traces collected from technology enhanced learning environments, where further experimentation are still needed to evaluate the effectiveness of the approach. TRANSMUTE has been used to analyze the traces of the serious game TAMAGOCOURS and the first results are encouraging, but a comprehensive evaluation remains to be conducted to conclude the effectiveness of the interpretation strategy.

Experiments showed that the effectiveness of the coverage to focus quickly on interesting episodes vary a lot between the various musical pieces. It is therefore essential to propose several measures to allow the user making several trials. Currently, the measures implemented in the TRANSMUTE tool are predefined, and a perspective to this work is to allow the user to choose other objective or subjective interestingness measures, but also measures that express domain knowledge. We previously experimented a domain-dependent interestingness measure, such as the beginning musical sentence boundary. Most of the time in music, all the pieces start at the same moment in a measure (first beat or last half of the last beat, *etc.*). Once implemented, this property can be taken into account in the form of a domain-specific constraint which makes it possible to filter a very large number of redundant and irrelevant patterns.

The proposed evaluation is based on episodes provided by a domain expert, the expert episodes, but the experiment consisted in automatically simulating the selection of expert episodes. It gives a first idea of the gain in ranking episodes, and consequently in expert effort that can hypothetically be expected from this approach. A first qualitative evaluation was carried out with a group of five non-specialist users. They were asked to retrieve a set of given expert patterns from a score extract and then to complete a questionnaire to assess the usability of the prototype. They were provided a user guide and the mining parameters, and the evaluation focused exclusively on the interpretation. Users have all been able to easily identify the expert patterns and found TRANSMUTE easy to use. Nevertheless, this evaluation was carried out on a small sequence with a reduced number of expert patterns and there still needs to confront a user with much larger data in order to evaluate the time saved and the help provided by the assistance to interpretation.

The TRANSMUTE prototype that implements this approach has limitations due to its interface, and to a lack of optimisation. TRANSMUTE is limited since it is able to process a single small trace at a time, and does not allow to process too many episodes (a few thousands of events and episodes) and work still remain to be done for leveraging this issue. Meanwhile a separate optimized version of the filtering process has been implemented and shows reasonable execution time for a few million episodes. The KD process implemented in the DISKIT module is however able to process large traces and huge numbers of episodes (a few millions episodes). Moreover, a recent version allows processing several traces, the filtering operation can process a few millions episodes and enables to undo user's episode selections. The next step is to develop a new interface to display and analyze multiple traces.

7   Conclusion and Future Work

We have presented an approach for interactive and iterative interpretation of serial episodes. This approach rests upon interestingness measures to sort episodes, an interactive visualization tool where the expert can immediately see the impact of his actions on the sequence and a dynamic filtering process following an episode selection. This approach is reified in the TRANSMUTE web-based prototype where the user can annotate the selected episode by creating new labeled events and storing a transformed trace into the data store to save the interpretation work. The experiments show a significant improvement in the ranking of episodes, which augurs an easier identification of interesting episodes.

References

1. Frawley, W.J., Piatetsky-Shapiro, G., Matheus, C.J.: Knowledge discovery in databases: an overview. AI Mag. **13**(3), 57–70 (1992)

2. Holzinger, A.: Human-computer interaction and knowledge discovery (HCI-KDD): what is the benefit of bringing those two fields to work together? In: Cuzzocrea, A., Kittl, C., Simos, D.E., Weippl, E., Xu, L. (eds.) CD-ARES 2013. LNCS, vol. 8127, pp. 319–328. Springer, Heidelberg (2013). https://doi.org/10.1007/978-3-642-40511-2_22

3. van Leeuwen, M.: Interactive data exploration using pattern mining. In: Holzinger, A., Jurisica, I. (eds.) Interactive Knowledge Discovery and Data Mining in Biomedical Informatics. LNCS, vol. 8401, pp. 169–182. Springer, Heidelberg (2014). https://doi.org/10.1007/978-3-662-43968-5_9

4. Rissanen, J.: Modeling by shortest data description. Automatica **14**(5), 465–471 (1978)

5. Vreeken, J., Leeuwen, M., Siebes, A.: KRIMP: mining itemsets that compress. Data Mining Knowl. Disc. **23**(1), 169–214 (2011)

6. Lam, H.T., Mörchen, F., Fradkin, D., Calders, T.: Mining compressing sequential patterns. Stat. Anal. Data Mining **7**(1), 34–52 (2014)

7. Bertini, E., Lalanne, D.: Surveying the complementary role of automatic data analysis and visualization in knowledge discovery. In: Proceedings of the ACM SIGKDD Workshop on Visual Analytics and Knowledge Discovery: Integrating Automated Analysis with Interactive Exploration, pp. 12–20. ACM (2009)

8. Shneiderman, B.: The eyes have it: a task by data type taxonomy for information visualizations. In: IEEE Symposium on Visual Languages. Proceedings, pp. 336–343. IEEE (1996)

9. Gotz, D., Wang, F., Perer, A.: A methodology for interactive mining and visual analysis of clinical event patterns using electronic health record data. J. Biomed. Inform. **48**, 148–159 (2014)

10. Stahl, F., Gabrys, B., Gaber, M.M., Berendsen, M.: An overview of interactive visual data mining techniques for knowledge discovery. Wiley Interdiscip. Rev. Data Min. Knowl. Discov. **3**(4), 239–256 (2013)

11. Dzyuba, V., Van Leeuwen, M., Nijssen, S., De Raedt, L.: Active preference learning for ranking patterns. In: 2013 IEEE 25th International Conference on Tools with Artificial Intelligence (ICTAI), pp. 532–539. IEEE (2013)

12. Bie, T.: Subjective interestingness in exploratory data mining. In: Tucker, A., Höppner, F., Siebes, A., Swift, S. (eds.) IDA 2013. LNCS, vol. 8207, pp. 19–31. Springer, Heidelberg (2013). https://doi.org/10.1007/978-3-642-41398-8_3

13. Boley, M., Mampaey, M., Kang, B., Tokmakov, P., Wrobel, S.: One click mining: interactive local pattern discovery through implicit preference and performance learning. In: Proceedings of the ACM SIGKDD Workshop on Interactive Data Exploration and Analytics, pp. 27–35. ACM (2013)

14. Tatti, N.: Discovering episodes with compact minimal windows. Data Min. Knowl. Discov. **28**(4), 1046–1077 (2014)

15. Nanni, M., Rigotti, C.: Extracting trees of quantitative serial episodes. In: Džeroski, S., Struyf, J. (eds.) KDID 2006. LNCS, vol. 4747, pp. 170–188. Springer, Heidelberg (2007). https://doi.org/10.1007/978-3-540-75549-4_11

16. Mannila, H., Toivonen, H., Verkamo, A.I.: Discovery of frequent episodes in event sequences. Data Min. Knowl. Discov. **1**, 259–289 (1997)

Network Metrics for Assessing the Quality of Entity Resolution Between Multiple Datasets

Al Koudous Idrissou[1,2]([✉]), Frank van Harmelen[1], and Peter van den Besselaar[2]

[1] Department of Computer Science, Vrije Universiteit Amsterdam, Amsterdam,
Netherlands
{o.a.k.idrissou,frank.van.harmelen,p.a.a.vanden.besselaar}@vu.nl
[2] Department of Organization Sciences, Vrije Universiteit Amsterdam, Amsterdam,
Netherlands

Abstract. Matching entities between datasets is a crucial step for combining multiple datasets on the semantic web. A rich literature exists on different approaches to this entity resolution problem. However, much less work has been done on how to *assess* the quality of such entity links once they have been generated. Evaluation methods for link quality are typically limited to either comparison with a *ground truth dataset* (which is often not available), *manual work* (which is cumbersome and prone to error), or *crowd sourcing* (which is not always feasible, especially if expert knowledge is required). Furthermore, the problem of link evaluation is greatly exacerbated for links between more than two datasets, because the number of possible links grows rapidly with the number of datasets. In this paper, we propose a method to estimate the quality of entity links between multiple datasets. We exploit the fact that the links between entities from multiple datasets form a network, and we show how simple metrics on this network can reliably predict their quality. We verify our results in a large experimental study using six datasets from the domain of science, technology and innovation studies, for which we created a gold standard. This gold standard, available online, is an additional contribution of this paper. In addition, we evaluate our metric on a recently published gold standard to confirm our findings.

Keywords: Entity resolution · Data integration · Network metrics

1 Introduction

Matching entities between datasets (known as entity resolution) is a crucial step for the use of multiple datasets on the semantic web. There exists a fair amount of entity resolution tools for *generating* links between pairs of resources: AGDIS-TIS [15], LIMES [12] Linkage Query Writer [7,8], SILK [16], etc. However, much fewer methods exist for *validating* the links produced by these methods. Currently, only three validation options are available for such validation: (1) *ground truth*, which is often not available; (2) *manual work*, which is a cumbersome

© Springer Nature Switzerland AG 2018
C. Faron Zucker et al. (Eds.): EKAW 2018, LNAI 11313, pp. 147–162, 2018.
https://doi.org/10.1007/978-3-030-03667-6_10

task prone to error; (3) *crowd sourcing*, which is not always feasible especially if specialist knowledge is required. Furthermore, the problem of link evaluation is greatly exacerbated for entity resolution between more than two datasets, because the number of possible links grows rapidly with the number of datasets. Therefore, it is important to investigate *the accurate automated evaluation of discovered links*. Any answer to this question should generalise beyond the setting of just two datasets, and be applicable to the general setting of links between multiple datasets. In such a multi-dataset scenario, linked resources cluster in small groups that we call *Identity Link Networks (ILNs)*. The goal of this paper is not to propose any new method for entity resolution but instead to provide a method to estimate the quality of an identity link network, and consequently validate a set of discovered links. To do so, *we hypothesize that the structure of an identity link network correlates with its quality*. We test our hypothesis in two experiments where we show that the proposed metrics indeed reliably estimates the quality of an identity network. We also test our hypothesis on recently published experimental data from ESWC 2018 (see Sect. 8). Here too, the results confirm that our quality metric reliably predicts human assessment of entity links.

In summary, our contributions is a method that estimates the quality of an identity network. It is tested against human judgement in three large experiments and correctly classifies large amount of ILNs available online.[1]

This paper begins with a short motivation in Sect. 2. Section 3 discusses the related work and Sect. 4 describes the proposed metric. In Sect. 5 we describe the datasets involved in our experiments. Sections 6, 7 and 8 describe our three experiments, and Sect. 9 concludes.

2   Identity Link Networks

We assume the well known setting of a real-world entity that has one or more digital representations in multiple datasets. The task of entity resolution is to discover which entity (or entities) in each dataset denotes the same real world entity. An Identity Link Network (ILN) is a network of links between entities from a number of datasets that are found by one or more entity resolution algorithms to represent the same real world entity. An ILN can be derived directly from entity resolution results (Sects. 6 and 7), or it may be generated by sophisticated clustering methods as in our experiment in Sect. 8. In this work we do *not* propose any new entity resolution algorithm. Instead, we propose a method to automatically *evaluate* discovered links, particularly when they involve more than two datasets. Unfortunately, gold standards in initiatives such as OAEI do not go beyond two datasets.

Figure 1 shows two examples of such ILNs that have been generated by an entity resolution algorithm between entities from six datasets taken from the field of Science, Technology and Innovation studies (STI) (more details in Sect. 5). Figure 1a shows the ILN for the real world entity University of Trier, Fig. 1b shows

---

[1] https://github.com/alkoudouss/Identity-Link-Network-Metric.

the same for the National Chung Cheng University. *In this paper, we hypothesise that the structure of these ILNs is a reliable indicator for the correctness of the links in the network they form.*

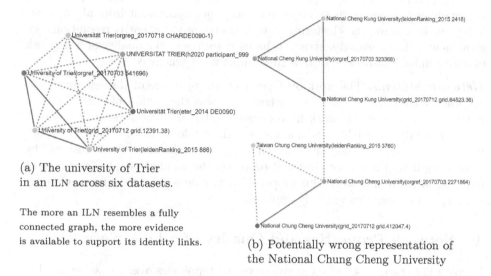

(a) The university of Trier
in an ILN across six datasets.

The more an ILN resembles a fully
connected graph, the more evidence
is available to support its identity links.

(b) Potentially wrong representation of
the National Chung Cheng University

Fig. 1. Two real life examples of Identity Link Networks (ILNs); dotted lines indicate links with a low confidence.

3   Related Work

We briefly discuss a number of related areas from the literature, and indicate how our work differs from these in aim and scope.

Schema Matching. Much work in the literature focuses on ontology matching, especially schema matching [5]. Some rely on concept distance or an extended version of it [3,10,17]. Some rely on alignment similarities [4], others relies on formal logical conflicts between ontologies to detect and possibly repair mappings at a schema-level [9]. The current paper does not aim to match ontologies, nor does it critically rely on using ontological or schema information. We only assume the existence of external entity resolution algorithms for suggesting links between entities. Such algorithms may or may not exploit ontological information, but this does not affect our central hypothesis.

Information Gain. The work in [14] also uses network structure to evaluate link quality, but in a very different way. The main intuition there is that an individual link in an ILN is more reliable when it leads to a greater information gain. The paper does not consider the structure of the ILN as a whole, as we do in this paper.

Entity Clustering. Part of the literature also uses clustering of the digital representations of the same real world entity in one or multiple sources. While their data sources are mainly unstructured [1,2], our interest lies in clusters derived from the mappings of entities exclusively across knowledge-bases. In addition, they also do not consider the structure of the ILN as a whole. Another part of the literature specifically focuses on clustering algorithms. The FAMER [13] framework for example provides and compares seven different link-based entity clustering approaches. The aim of our work is different from all of these. Whereas these works use clustering algorithms to *construct* entity resolutions, we show how a cluster-based metric can be used to *assess* the quality of a network of entity links, irrespective of how these links were generated.

Network Metrics. The work by Guéret et al. [6] is one of the few papers to our knowledge that uses network metrics to assess the quality of links. The key point that separates this work from ours is that it uses *local* network features, i.e. only the direct neighbours of a single node, while we employ *global* network features. [11] also addresses the same challenge. It evaluates a given cluster G by comparing it to a reference cluster R based on the number of splits and merges required to go from G to R. Our proposed metric does not need such a reference cluster, and is hence more easily applicable.

4   Network Properties and Quality of a Link-Network

Figure 2 illustrates a set of six simple network topologies over the same number of nodes. Our proposed metric is based on the intuition that multiple links provide corroborating evidence for each other, suggesting that in the case of an ILN, the ideal topology is a ***fully connected*** network. It illustrates a total agreement between all resources (not the case for any other topology), and it does not require any intermediate resource to establish an identity-link between two resources (again, not the case for any other topology). Hence, intuitively, the amount of redundancy between paths in an ILN is an indicator for the quality of the links in the ILN. We will capture these and similar intuitions using three different global graph features over ILNs: *Bridge*, *Diameter* and *Closure*.

We will now first define and explain the rationale behind each metric, then normalise each metric to values[2] between 0 and 1, and finally average the sum of all metrics to obtain the metric which we will use for estimating the quality of the ILN.

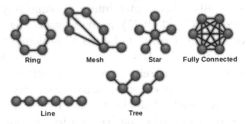

Fig. 2. Example of network topologies. Source: https://en.wikipedia.org/wiki/Network_topology

Bridge Metric. A bridge (also known as an isthmus or a cut-edge) in a graph is an edge whose removal increases the number of connected components of the graph, or equivalently, an edge that does not belong to any cycle. The intuition for this measure is that a bridge in an ILN suggests a potentially problematic link which is not corroborated by any other links. As a

---

[2] The metric value indicates the negative impact of one or more missing links in an ILN.

graph with n nodes contains at most $n - 1$ bridges (e.g. in a **Line** network), the bridge value is normalised as $n_b = \frac{B}{n-1}$, where B is the number of bridges. An ideal link network would have no bridge ($n_b = 0$). As n_b is sensitive to the total number of nodes in the graph (it decreases for large graphs, even when the number of bridges is constant), we "soften" the value of n_b with a sigmoid function: $n'_b = max(n_b, sigmoid(B))$, where the function $sigmoid(x) = \frac{x}{|x|+1.6}$ helps stabilising the impact of the size of the graph by providing a minimal value for n'_b. The value 1.6 is a hyper-parameter that has been determined empirically.

Diameter Metric. The diameter D of a graph with n nodes is the maximum number of edges (distance) in a shortest path between any pair of vertices (i.e. the longest shortest path). In an ideal scenario, if three resources A, B and C are representations of the same real world object, there would be no need for an intermediate resource for confirming the identity of any of the resource in the network. In a fully connected graph of n nodes, the diameter $D = 1$. The longest diameter is observed in a **Line** network structure, with $D = n - 1$ for a line network of n nodes. To scale to the [0,1] interval, the diameter is normalised as $n_d = \frac{D-1}{(n-1)-1}$. Like the bridge, because the diameter is also sensitive to the number of nodes, the normalised diameter is calculated as $n'_d = max(n_d, sigmoid(D - 1))$.

Closure Metric. In a connected graph of n nodes, the closure is the ratio of the number of arcs A in the graph over the total number of possible arcs $\frac{1}{2}n(n - 1)$. In a complete graph, this ratio has value 1. Hence, to evaluate how far the observed graph is from the ideal (complete) one, we normalise the closure metric as $n_c = 1 - \frac{A}{\frac{1}{2}n(n-1)}$. The minimum number of connections is $n - 1$, as observed in **Line** and **Star** network structures.

Estimated Quality Metric. All of these metrics capture the same intuition: the more an ILN resembles a fully connected graph, the higher the quality of the links in the ILN. Of course, these three metrics are not independent: $n_c = 0$ or $n'_d = 0$ implies $n'_b = 0$. However, using only n_c or n'_d would be too uninformative since the converse of the implication does not hold. Table 1 shows that each of n_c, n'_d and n'_b capture different (though related) amounts of redundancy in the ILN and that each metric by itself fails to properly discriminate between the seven ILNs depicted in Fig. 2. For example, n_c and n'_c treat a *Tree*, *Star* and *Line* as qualitatively equal but disagree on whether a *Full Mesh* is as good as a *Ring*. Consequently, to compute an overall estimated quality e_Q of an identity link network, we combine the three separate metrics by taking their average, and invert them so that the value 1 indicates the highest quality: (We apply e_Q to ILNs of size ≥ 3 as it is the smallest network where redundancy can be observed.)

$$e_Q = 1 - \frac{n'_b + n'_d + n_c}{3}.$$

Discrete Intervals. The e_Q metric scores all ILNs on a continuous value in the [0,1] interval. To automatically discriminate potentially good networks from bad ones, we divide this interval into three segments: ILNs with values $0.9 \leq e_Q \leq 1$

will be rated as **good**, with values $0.75 < e_Q < 0.9$ as **undecided**, and with values $0 \leq e_Q \leq 0.75$ as **bad**. These boundaries are empirically determined, and can be adjusted depending on the use-case. The specific values of these boundaries does not affect the essence of our hypothesis.

Hypothesis. We can now state our hypothesis more formally: *"The e_Q intervals defined above are predictive of the quality of the links in an entity link network between multiple datasets"*.

Example. By way of illustration, Table 1 gives the value of our e_Q metric for the six networks from Fig. 2, and shows that the metric does indeed capture redundancy in a network.

In the following sections, we will test this hypothesis against human evaluation on hundreds of ILNs containing thousands of links in three experiments using between three to six datasets.

Table 1. Metrics values for each of the topologies from Fig. 2.

Link-Network Quality Estimation						
ILN	Bridge		Diameter		Closure		Est. Quality
Ring	$B = 0$	$n_b = 0.00$	$D = 3$	$n_d = 0.56$	$C = 0.40$	$n_c = 0.60$	$e_Q = 0.61$
Mesh	$B = 1$	$n_b = 0.38$	$D = 3$	$n_d = 0.56$	$C = 0.47$	$n_c = 0.53$	$e_Q = 0.51$
Star	$B = 5$	$n_b = 1.00$	$D = 2$	$n_d = 0.38$	$C = 0.33$	$n_c = 0.67$	$e_Q = 0.32$
Full Mesh	$B = 0$	$n_b = 0.00$	$D = 3$	$n_d = 0.00$	$C = 1.00$	$n_c = 0.00$	$e_Q = 1.00$
Line	$B = 5$	$n_b = 1.00$	$D = 1$	$n_d = 1.00$	$C = 0.33$	$n_c = 0.67$	$e_Q = 0.11$
Tree	$B = 5$	$n_b = 1.00$	$D = 4$	$n_d = 0.38$	$C = 0.33$	$n_c = 0.67$	$e_Q = 0.34$

5   Datasets

We considered using datasets and gold standards from the OAEI[3] initiative, but none of these go beyond links between two datasets. We therefore created our own gold standard on realistic datasets taken from the domain of social science, more specifically from the field of Science, Technology and Innovation studies. We consider this to be an important contribution of this paper. All datasets and our gold standard are available online at the locations given in later paragraphs.

Entities of interest to the STI domain of study are (among others) universities and other research-related organisations, such as R&D companies and funding agencies. Our six datasets are widely used in the field, and describe organisations and their properties such as name, location, type, size and other features.[4]

---

[3] http://oaei.ontologymatching.org/.

[4] The information provided here about the datasets was collected in January 2018. The datasets themselves are of earlier dates: Grid: 2017.07.12; Orgref: 2017.07.03; OpenAire: 2018.08.16; OrgReg: 2017.07.18; Eter: 2014; Leiden Ranking 2015: 2017.6.16; and Cordis-H2020: 2016.12.22. All these datasets are available on the RISIS platform at http://datasets.risis.eu/.

Grid[5] describes 80248 organisations across 221 countries using 12308 relationships. All organisations are assigned an address, while 96% of them have an organisation type, and only 78% have geographic coordinates.

OrgRef[6] collates data about the most important worldwide academic and research organisations (31000) from two main sources: Wikipedia and ISNI.

The Leiden Ranking dataset[7] offers scientific performance indicators of more than 900 major universities. These universities are only included when they are above the threshold of 1000 fractionally counted Web of Science indexed core publications. This explains its coverage across only 54 worldwide countries.

Eter[8] is a database on European Higher Education Institutions that not only includes research universities, but also colleges and a large number of specialized schools. The dataset covered 35 countries in 2015.

OrgReg[9] is based on Eter but adds to the about 2700 HE institutions some 500 public research organizations and university hospitals. Collected between 2000 and 2016, its organisations are distributed across 36 countries.

The European Organisations' Projects H2020 database[10] documents the Horizon 2020 participating organisations.

6 e_Q Put to the Test

We test our hypothesis on a real life case study that revolves around the six datasets described in Sect. 5, with as goal to investigate the coverage of OrgReg (coverage analysis of datasets is a typical question asked by social scientists before including a dataset in their studies). This is done by comparing the entities in OrgReg to those in the other five datasets (Fig. 3).

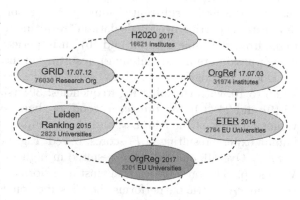

Fig. 3. Disambiguating OrgReg. To evaluate e_Q, all possible links are evaluated. So, the lack of one or more links is considered a potential evidence for suggesting the corresponding entities being different.

---

[5] https://www.grid.ac.

[6] http://www.orgref.org.

[7] http://www.leidenranking.com/.

[8] https://www.eter-project.com/.

[9] http://risis.eu/orgreg/.

[10] http://www.gaeu.com/sv/item/horizon-2020.

6.1 Experiment Design

Organizations are linked across or within datasets using an approximate string matching on their names with minimal similarity threshold 0.8. Based on this, we generate links between each pair of datasets, resulting in 21 sets of links (including linking a dataset to itself in order to detect duplicate entities in the dataset). We then take the union of all 21 sets of links, resulting in a collection of ILN's of varying size (see Fig. 4).

Now that we have constructed a large collection of multi-dataset ILNs, we will compute the e_Q value for all of them. Then, the machine-predicted good/bad categories (using e_Q) will be checked against the ground truth by a non-domain expert (the first author of this paper) and further verified by a domain expert (the third author). This ground truth is available online.[11]

Notice that we have deliberately used a very weak entity resolution algorithm in this experiment (approximate string matching). This produces links of both very high and rather low quality, providing a genuine test for our e_Q metric to distinguish between them.

6.2 Results of First Evaluation

Ideally, we would find only ILNs of size 6 if each OrgReg entity were linked with one and only one entity in each of the five other datasets. With less than 100% coverage of OrgReg, we also expect to find ILNs of size < 6. Figure 4 shows that we also find a substantial number of ILNs of size > 6. This is due to (a) duplicates occurring in a single dataset, resulting in links in the ILN between two items from the same dataset, and (b) an imperfect matching algorithm (in our case approximate name matching), resulting in incorrect links in the ILN.

Due to the high number of ILNs generated[12], we evaluate only the 846 ILNs of size 5 to 10, with the following frequencies: 391 (size 5), 224 (6), 96 (7), 66 (8), 45 (9) and 24 (10). We predict a 'good' or 'bad' score based on the e_Q interval values for each of the 846 ILNs, and then compare the scores against those of a human expert, resulting in F_1 scores. In red, Fig. 4 displays the F_1 value for each ILN size. Overall, our e_Q metric resulted in high F_1 values ($0.806 \leq F_1 \leq 0.933$). We also pitched our e_Q metric against a Majority Class Classifier. Table 2 shows that our e_Q metric outperforms the Classifier on F_1 measure, Accuracy (ACC) and Negative Predicted Value (NPC) for ILNs of all sizes.

All of these findings show the very strong predictive power of our e_Q metric for the quality of ILNs when compared to human judgement.

---

[11] https://github.com/alkoudouss/Identity-Link-Network-Metric.

[12] On a 6th Gen Intel®Core™i7 notebook with 8 GB RAM, it takes about 1:40 min to automatically evaluate all 4398 clusters of size three and above (see Fig. 4).

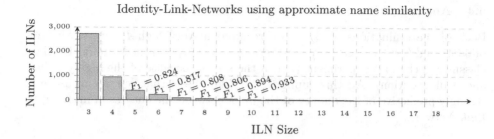

Fig. 4. Overview of the generated Identity Link Networks.

6.3   Results of Second Evaluation

For a further evaluation by a Dutch domain expert from the field of STI (the third author of this paper), we selected 148 ILNs (ranging from size 3 to 10 as depicted in Table 2) in which at least one entity is located in the Netherlands. The expert deviated from the first evaluation in only 12 out of 148 cases. Although the changes slightly affect the ground truth for each ILN size, the F_1 values computed here are even higher ($0.848 \leq F_1 \leq 1$) as compared to the previous experiment. This shows that the non-expert nature of the first human judgement was not detrimental to our results.[13] This second experiment confirms our finding in the first experiment that e_Q is a reliable predictor of ILN quality.

Table 2. Network-metric (e_Q) results compared to the MCC baseline using non expert Ground Truth (left), and Expert sampled Ground Truth (right).

Majority Class Classifier (Baseline) vs Network Metric (e_Q)								
		$\frac{MajorityClassClassifier}{NetworkMetrics}$						
		GT_P = Ground Truth Positive GT_N = Ground Truth Negative						
Size	$GT_P\|GT_N$	F_1	ACC	NPV	$GT_P\|GT_N$	F_1	ACC	NPV
3					56 | 8	$\frac{0.933}{0.931}$	$\frac{0.875}{0.875}$	$\frac{-}{0.5}$
4					19 | 5	$\frac{0.884}{0.878}$	$\frac{0.792}{0.792}$	$\frac{-}{0.5}$
5	272 | 119	$\frac{0.821}{0.824}$	$\frac{0.696}{0.747}$	$\frac{-}{0.598}$	14 | 1	$\frac{0.966}{0.929}$	$\frac{0.933}{0.867}$	$\frac{-}{0}$
6	139 | 85	$\frac{0.766}{0.817}$	$\frac{0.621}{0.768}$	$\frac{-}{0.709}$	14 | 5	$\frac{0.848}{0.848}$	$\frac{0.737}{0.737}$	$\frac{-}{-}$
7	50 | 56	$\frac{0.685}{0.808}$	$\frac{0.521}{0.792}$	$\frac{-}{0.810}$	10 | 2	$\frac{0.909}{1.0}$	$\frac{0.833}{1.0}$	$\frac{-}{1.0}$
8	35 | 31	$\frac{0.693}{0.806}$	$\frac{0.530}{0.803}$	$\frac{-}{0.765}$	4 | 0	$\frac{1.0}{1.0}$	$\frac{1.0}{1.0}$	$\frac{-}{-}$
9	21 | 24	$\frac{-}{0.894}$	$\frac{0.533}{0.889}$	$\frac{0.533}{1}$	8 | 1	$\frac{0.941}{1.0}$	$\frac{0.889}{1.0}$	$\frac{-}{1.0}$
10	8 | 16	$\frac{-}{0.933}$	$\frac{0.007}{0.958}$	$\frac{0.007}{0.941}$	1 | 0	$\frac{1.0}{1.0}$	$\frac{1.0}{1.0}$	$\frac{-}{-}$

---

[13] However, the very imbalanced character of the ground truth makes it hard to always outperform the baseline as illustrated in Table 2.

6.4   Analysis

Both of the evaluations of e_Q above resulted in very high F_1 average values of 0.847 and 0.961 respectively. Furthermore, e_Q outperformed a majority-class classifier in the first experiment (not in the second because of the highly imbalanced distribution). All this supports our hypothesis that our e_Q measure is strongly predictive of the quality of the links between the entities in an Identity Link Network.

7 e_Q Estimations in Noisy Settings

The previous experiment created links between entities using a rather weak entity resolution heuristic. This was an interesting setting because such weak matching strategies are a fact of daily life on the semantic web (and in data integration in general). In the next experiment, we will use e_Q to evaluate ILN's that have been constructed using a more sophisticated matching heuristic, where we can control the amount of incorrect links in the ILNs. We will see that also in this case, e_Q is strongly predictive of human judged link quality.

The stronger matching heuristic that we use in this second experiment combines organisation names with the geo-location of the organisation. The experiment is run over Eter, Grid and OrgReg as they are the only datasets at our disposal that contain such geo-coordinates for organisations. To test the performance of the e_Q metric at various levels of noise, we implement three subexperiments where noise (the number of false positive links) is introduced by decreasing the name similarity threshold from 0.8 (experiment 1) to 0.7 and by increasing the geographic proximity distance threshold as described in the next sub-section.

7.1   Experiment Design

This subsection describes in three phases how the experiment is conducted.

Phase-1: Create Links. The first phase links organizations across the three datasets whenever they are located within a radius of 50 m, 500 m and 2 km. This creates nine sets of links (three for each radius).

Phase-2: Refine Links. Each set of links is then refined by applying an approximate name comparison over the linked resources with a threshold of 0.7.

By now, we have **geo-only** (without name comparison) and **geo+names** sets of links, organised in three subgroups (50 m, 500 m and 2 km) each.

Phase-3: Combine Links. To generate the final ILNs, the sets of links within each subgroup are combined using the union operator. The goal of this is to compare, within a specified distance, ILNs that where generated without name matching to those generated with name matching.

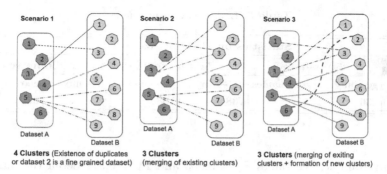

Fig. 5. Decrease/Increase of ILNs

7.2 Strict vs. Liberal Clustering

To understand how link-networks are formed as we increase the geo-similarity distance, Fig. 5 illustrates how ILNs may evolve as we move from strict constraints (scenario 1) to liberal constraints (scenario 3). First, in **scenario 1**, four ILNs are derived from the six links: $c_1 = \{\{a_1\}, \{b_3\}\}$, $c_2 = \{\{a_3\}, \{b_1\}\}$, $c_3 = \{\{a_4\}, \{b_4\}\}$ and $c_4 = \{\{a_5\}, \{b_6, b_8, b_9\}\}$. Then, the new link between a_3 and b_3 in **scenario 2** forces c_1 and c_2 to **merge**. We now have a total of three ILNs: $c_1 = \{\{a_1, a_3\}, \{b_1, b_3\}\}$, $c_3 = \{\{a_4\}, \{b_4\}\}$ and $c_4 = \{\{a_5\}, \{b_6, b_8, b_9\}\}$. Finally, in **scenario 3**, two new links appear. The first link between a_4 and b_8 causes the merging of c_3 and c_4 while the second link connecting a_6 to b_2 causes the creation of a new ILN. Thereby, the total number of ILNs remains 3. These scenarios show that, as the ILN constraints become more liberal, the number of links discovered increases while the number of ILNs may increase, remain equal, or even decrease. In other words, when the matching conditions become liberal or less strict, two types of event may happen: (1) formation of new ILNs and/or (2) merging of ILNs. Table 3, shows that, in experiment 2, phenomenon (1) overtakes (2), which explains the increase in the number of ILNs as the near-by distance increases.

7.3 Result and Analysis

Overall, as illustrated in Table 3, the number of ILNs generated in this experiment increases with the increase of the geo-similarity radius. Within a radius of 50 m, a total of 230 ILNs are generated based on geo-distance only. This number reached 841 ILNs at a 2 km radius. After performing name matching, many links are pruned. Depending on the matching radius, the number of ILNs then varies from 36 to 371.

Due to manpower limitations we restrict our evaluation efforts to networks of size 3. These ILNs cover 86% of the overall ILNs within 50 m radius and 92% within 500 m and 2k radius. Table 4 shows the results of pitching our e_Q metric against the human evaluation of the ILNs under both the geo-only and the geo+names conditions.

Table 3. Link-network overview.

Statistics on ILNs of size > 2					
	50 meters		**500 meters**		**2 kilometres**	
Size	geo-only	geo+names	geo-only	geo+names	geo-only	geo+names
≥ 3	230	36	738	168	841	371

As an example, the values $F_1 = 0.803$ and $F_1 = 0.912$ detail the machine quality judgements versus human evaluations of the networks generated within 2 km radius under respectively geo-only and geo+names conditions.[14]

Table 4. Automated flagging versus human evaluation.

	50 meters		**500 meters**		**2 kilometres**	
Size	geo-only	geo+names	geo-only	geo+names	geo-only	geo+names
= 3	92	31	249	155	198	342
Machine statistics on ILN's of size 3						
Machine	M_{good}: 45 M_{maybe}: 0 M_{bad}: 47	M_{good}: 19 M_{maybe}: 12 M_{bad}: 0	M_{good}: 115 M_{maybe}: 0 M_{bad}: 134	M_{good}: 127 M_{maybe}: 0 M_{bad}: 28	M_{good}: 81 M_{maybe}: 0 M_{bad}: 117	M_{good}: 279 M_{maybe}: 0 M_{bad}: 63
Human evaluation on ILN's of size 3						
Human	H_{good}: 31 H_{maybe}:4 H_{bad}: 57	H_{good}: 27 H_{maybe}:1 H_{bad}: 3	H_{good}: 64 H_{maybe}:7 H_{bad}: 176	H_{good}: 148 H_{maybe}:1 H_{bad}: 6	H_{good}: 61 H_{maybe}:3 H_{bad}: 134	H_{good}: 322 H_{maybe}:8 H_{bad}: 12
F_1 measures						
	$F_1 = 0.693$	$F_1 = 0.826$	$F_1 = 0.682$	$F_1 = 0.909$	$F_1 = 0.803$	$F_1 = 0.912$

Analysis. In this experiment, we test the behaviour of the proposed e_Q metric in both noisy (*proximity only*) and noise-less (*proximity plus name*) scenarios. The proposed e_Q metric is in general able to exclude poor networks in noisy environments and to include good networks in noise-less environments. In addition, on the one hand, the relatively low F_1 measures displayed in Table 5 in noisy scenarios, highlight that for the data at hand, proximity alone is not a good enough criterion for identity. On the other hand, the relatively high F_1 measures in noise-less scenarios is an indication of stability and consistency that is in line with results outlined in experiment 1.

The results depicted in Table 5 show an uneven distribution of the candidate-sets. In a relatively balanced candidate-set scenario, our approach works well as can be seen in the first experiment and in the *proximity only* scenario. However,

---

[14] All confusion matrices supporting the analysis can be found on the RISIS project website at http://sms.risis.eu/assets/pdf/metrics-link-network.pdf.

even though in extreme cases (*proximity plus name*) the Majority Class Classifier takes the lead, the network metric does not fall far behind.

Table 5. Network-metric (e_Q) result versus the MCC baseline.

Majority Class Classifier (Baseline) vs Network Metrics (e_Q)					
$\frac{MajorityClassClassifier}{NetworkMetrics}$					
GT = Ground Truth	GT_P = Ground Truth Positive		GT_N = Ground Truth Negative		
50m geo-only	GT=92	GT_P=30 GT_N=62	$F_1 : \frac{-}{0.693}$	ACC:$\frac{0.674}{0.75}$	NPV:$\frac{0.674}{0.915}$
500m geo-only	GT=249	GT_P=66 GT_N=183	$F_1 : \frac{-}{0.682}$	ACC:$\frac{0.735}{0.779}$	NPV:$\frac{0.735}{0.978}$
2km geo-only	GT=198	GT_P=61 GT_N=137	$F_1 : \frac{-}{0.803}$	ACC:$\frac{0.692}{0.859}$	NPV:$\frac{0.692}{0.966}$
50m geo+names	GT=31	GT_P=27 GT_N=4	$F_1 : \frac{0.931}{0.826}$	ACC:$\frac{0.871}{0.742}$	NPV:$\frac{-}{0.333}$
500m geo+names	GT=155	GT_P=148 GT_N=7	$F_1 : \frac{0.977}{0.909}$	ACC:$\frac{0.955}{0.839}$	NPV:$\frac{-}{0.179}$
2km geo+names	GT=342	GT_P=322 GT_N=20	$F_1 : \frac{0.97}{0.912}$	ACC:$\frac{0.942}{0.845}$	NPV:$\frac{-}{0.238}$

As in the first experiment, for further evaluation, we extracted a sample based on ILNs in which at least one organisation originates from the Netherlands. Out of the **107** sampled ILNs, the domain expert deviated from the first evaluation in only 1 case.

8 e_Q Put to a Ranking Test

The authors of the recently published paper [13] compared seven algorithms for clustering entities from multiple sources at different string similarity thresholds. They evaluated the quality of the clusters that these algorithms generated on three gold standard datasets[15], one manually built (referred here as GT1), and two syntactically generated. We take the evaluation results from [13] on GT1, and then test if our e_Q score is able to correctly predict the ranking of the algorithms as found in the reported evaluation. In contrast to the earlier experiments (where we use e_Q to assess the quality of clusters), we are now testing if e_Q can be used to correctly rank different clustering algorithms across datasets.

A slightly complicating factor is that the evaluation in [13] relies on F_1 values computed on *true pairs of entities found*. Since e_Q evaluates entire clusters (i.e. *sets* of pairs of entities) of size greater than 2 ($S > 2$), we recompute the F_1 values based on *true clusters found*($S > 2$) and plot these performance measures for each algorithm in Fig. 6 as *Baseline*. The resulting plot is comparable to the original one in [13]. We then ran the e_Q metric over the outputs of each algorithm at the same thresholds, displayed in Fig. 6 as e_Q *Evaluation*.

---

[15] https://dbs.uni-leipzig.de/de/research/projects/object_matching/famer.

The results show that the ranking of the algorithms by e_Q (**e$_Q$** *Evaluation*) does not significantly deviate from the recomputed ranking (***Baseline***). This illustrates the usefulness of the e_Q metric as it demonstrates its potential to rank algorithms whenever they show *significant performance differences*.

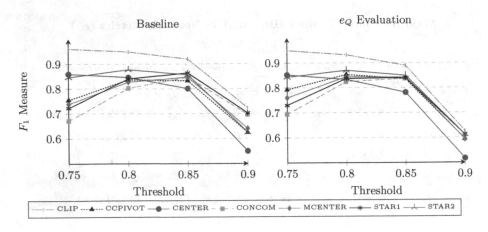

Fig. 6. Evaluation of e_Q on the ranking from [13]

9   Conclusions and Future Work

9.1   Conclusion

Entity resolution is an essential step in the use of multiple datasets on the semantic web. Since entity resolution algorithms are far from being perfect, the links they discover must often be human validated. Since this is both a costly and an error-prone process, it is desirable to have computer support that can accurately estimate the quality of links between entities. In this paper, we have proposed a metric for precisely this purpose: it estimates the quality of links between entities from multiple datasets, using a combination of graph metrics over the network (>2) formed by these links. Our metric captures the intuition that high redundancy in such a linking-network correlates with high quality.

We have tested our metric in three different scenarios. Using a collection of six widely used social science datasets in the first two experimental settings, we compared the predictions of link quality by our metric against human judgements on hundreds of networks involving thousands of links. In both evaluations, our metric correlated strongly with human judgement ($0.806 \leq F_1 \leq 1$), and it consistently beats the Majority Class Classifier baseline (except in cases where this is numerically near impossible because of a highly skewed class distribution). In the experimental condition where we deliberately constructed noisy and non-noisy link-networks, we showed that our metric is in general able to exclude poor networks in noisy environments and to include good networks in noise-less environments. With the last experiment, we also show that our metric is able to rank entity resolution algorithms on their quality, using an externally produced dataset and corresponding ground truth. All this amounts to testing the e_Q metric on a dozen different algorithms and parameter settings. Across these different experimental conditions, our quality metric consistently agrees with human judgement.

To encourage replication studies and extensions to our work, all the datasets used in these experiments are available online.

9.2 Future Work

Including Link Strength. The metric e_Q is based on the presence and absence of links, but does not consider any strength associated with these links. We are currently working on refinements of e_Q that use link confidence scores produced by entity resolution algorithms.

Dynamic Link Adjustment. The current work simply takes the output of an entity resolution algorithm as given, and tries to estimate the quality of that output. A closer coupling between our metric and an entity resolution algorithm would allow the algorithm to dynamically adjust its output based on the e_Q quality estimates. Similarly, embedded in a user-interface, the score of our metric could help the user to give the final judgement to accept or reject an ILN.

Parameter Tuning. In this work, we empirically determined the 1.6 sigmoid hyper-parameter, the discrete e_Q intervals and the string similarity thresholds. Experimenting on fine-tuning these parameters using the current ground truths and data from other domains would help understanding how and when different choices could lead to an increase or a decrease of the metrics' predictive power.

Acknowledgement. We kindly thank *Paul Groth* for his constructive comments and proofreading, *Alieh Saeedi* for sharing her experiments data and supporting the reproducibility of their experiments, and the *EKAW reviewers* for constructive comments. This work was supported by the European Union's 7th Framework Programme under the project RISIS (GA no. 313082).

References

1. Baron, A., Freedman, M.: Who is who and what is what: experiments in cross-document co-reference. In: Proceedings of the Conference on Empirical Methods in Natural Language Processing, pp. 274–283. Association for Computational Linguistics (2008)
2. Cucerzan, S.: Large-scale named entity disambiguation based on Wikipedia data. In: Proceedings of the 2007 Joint Conference on EMNLP-CoNLL (2007)
3. David, J., Euzenat, J.: Comparison between ontology distances (Preliminary Results). In: Sheth, A., et al. (eds.) ISWC 2008. LNCS, vol. 5318, pp. 245–260. Springer, Heidelberg (2008). https://doi.org/10.1007/978-3-540-88564-1_16

4. David, J., Euzenat, J., Šváb-Zamazal, O.: Ontology similarity in the alignment space. In: Patel-Schneider, P.F., et al. (eds.) ISWC 2010. LNCS, vol. 6496, pp. 129–144. Springer, Heidelberg (2010). https://doi.org/10.1007/978-3-642-17746-0_9
5. Euzenat, J., Shvaiko, P.: Ontology Matching, 2nd edn. Springer, Heidelberg (2013)
6. Guéret, C., Groth, P., Stadler, C., Lehmann, J.: Assessing linked data mappings using network measures. In: Simperl, E., Cimiano, P., Polleres, A., Corcho, O., Presutti, V. (eds.) ESWC 2012. LNCS, vol. 7295, pp. 87–102. Springer, Heidelberg (2012). https://doi.org/10.1007/978-3-642-30284-8_13
7. Hassanzadeh, O., Kementsietsidis, A., Lim, L., Miller, R.J., Wang, M.: A framework for semantic link discovery over relational data. In: 18th ACM Conference on Information and Knowledge Management, pp. 1027–1036. ACM (2009)
8. Hassanzadeh, O., Xin, R., Miller, R.J., Kementsietsidis, A., Lim, L., Wang, M.: Linkage query writer. Proc. VLDB Endow. 2(2), 1590–1593 (2009)
9. Li, W., Zhang, S., Qi, G.: A graph-based approach for resolving incoherent ontology mappings. In: Web Intelligence, vol. 16, pp. 15–35. IOS Press (2018)
10. Maedche, A., Staab, S.: Measuring similarity between ontologies. In: Gómez-Pérez, A., Benjamins, V.R. (eds.) EKAW 2002. LNCS (LNAI), vol. 2473, pp. 251–263. Springer, Heidelberg (2002). https://doi.org/10.1007/3-540-45810-7_24
11. Menestrina, D., Whang, S.E., Garcia-Molina, H.: Evaluating entity resolution results. Proc. VLDB Endow. 3(1–2), 208–219 (2010)
12. Ngomo, A.-C.N., Auer, S.: Limes-a time-efficient approach for large-scale link discovery on the web of data. In: IJCAI, pp. 2312–2317 (2011)
13. Saeedi, A., Peukert, E., Rahm, E.: Using link features for entity clustering in knowledge graphs. In: Gangemi, A., et al. (eds.) ESWC 2018. LNCS, vol. 10843, pp. 576–592. Springer, Cham (2018). https://doi.org/10.1007/978-3-319-93417-4_37
14. Sarasua, C., Staab, S., Thimm, M.: Methods for intrinsic evaluation of links in the web of data. In: Blomqvist, E., Maynard, D., Gangemi, A., Hoekstra, R., Hitzler, P., Hartig, O. (eds.) ESWC 2017. LNCS, vol. 10249, pp. 68–84. Springer, Cham (2017). https://doi.org/10.1007/978-3-319-58068-5_5
15. Usbeck, R., et al.: AGDISTIS - graph-based disambiguation of named entities using linked data. In: Mika, P., et al. (eds.) ISWC 2014. LNCS, vol. 8796, pp. 457–471. Springer, Cham (2014). https://doi.org/10.1007/978-3-319-11964-9_29
16. Volz, J., Bizer, C., Gaedke, M., Kobilarov, G.: Discovering and maintaining links on the web of data. In: Bernstein, A., et al. (eds.) ISWC 2009. LNCS, vol. 5823, pp. 650–665. Springer, Heidelberg (2009). https://doi.org/10.1007/978-3-642-04930-9_41
17. Vrandečić, D., Sure, Y.: How to design better ontology metrics. In: Franconi, E., Kifer, M., May, W. (eds.) ESWC 2007. LNCS, vol. 4519, pp. 311–325. Springer, Heidelberg (2007). https://doi.org/10.1007/978-3-540-72667-8_23

Making Sense of Numerical Data - Semantic Labelling of Web Tables

Emilia Kacprzak[1,2]([⊠]), José M. Giménez-García[3], Alessandro Piscopo[1,2], Laura Koesten[1,2], Luis-Daniel Ibáñez[1], Jeni Tennison[2], and Elena Simperl[1]

[1] Electronics and Computer Science, University of Southampton, Southampton, UK
{l.d.ibanez,e.simperl}@soton.ac.uk
[2] The Open Data Institute, London, UK
{e.kacprzak,alessandro.piscopo,laura.koesten,jeni}@theodi.org
[3] Laboratoire Hubert Curien, University of Lyon, UJM-Saint-Étienne, CNRS, Lyon, France
jose.gimenez.garcia@univ-st-etienne.fr

Abstract. With the increasing amount of structured data on the web the need to understand and support search over this emerging data space is growing. Adding semantics to structured data can help address existing challenges in data discovery, as it facilitates understanding the values in their context. While there are approaches on how to lift structured data to semantic web formats to enrich it and facilitate discovery, most work to date focuses on textual fields rather than numerical data. In this paper, we propose a two level (row and column based) approach to add semantic meaning to numerical values in tables, called NUMER. We evaluate our approach using a benchmark (NumDB) generated for the purpose of this work. We show the influence of the different levels of analysis on the success of assigning semantic labels to numerical values in tables. Our approach outperforms the state of the art and is less affected by data structure and quality issues such as a small number of entities or deviations in the data.

Keywords: Semantic labelling · Numerical values · Linked data

1 Introduction

Data is being generated on the web at an ever-increasing speed. Yet, most of this data is published in formats that are not machine-processable, hampering our ability to gain value from it. Whereas the Semantic Web has gained traction as a way to provide semantics and interoperability to data, its coverage is still limited: looking at Open Government Data, in 2016 only ~2% of datasets were published as linked data in the UK [1]. Most data is still published in non-semantic formats, especially in tables. In Open Data portals the majority of datasets are collected and published as CSV or Excel files, accompanied by metadata from

© Springer Nature Switzerland AG 2018
C. Faron Zucker et al. (Eds.): EKAW 2018, LNAI 11313, pp. 163–178, 2018.
https://doi.org/10.1007/978-3-030-03667-6_11

vocabularies such as DCAT[1] or Schema.org[2]. Integrating tables in the Web of Data is useful for enriching structured knowledge bases (KB), improving search over data, or to enable question-answering systems to use larger corpora of information. Motivated by this, solutions to lift tabular data into the Semantic Web have been proposed. These solutions aim at solving the following scientific problem: given a table and a target knowledge base *KB*, return a mapping of columns to classes or properties in *KB*. However, in spite of numerical columns being the most popular column type in open governmental datasets [2], existing approaches focus mostly on mapping textual data [3–8]. This is also reflected in the benchmarks available for the problem. For instance, one of the most commonly used benchmarks, T2D [9,10], contains only 12 of 1748 tables with numerical columns disambiguated to DBpedia properties. Previous efforts [11,12] compare distributions of numerical values in columns with the distribution of literal values in a KB, matching (within a given certainty) columns to the numerical properties with the most similar distribution. However, these approaches use information surrounding the numerical column to assign a semantic label.

Inspired by Venetis *et al.* [6], who reported increased accuracy if a main (subject) column was identified, we introduce NUMER—an approach which uses the context of numerical columns to assign semantic labels to them. We leverage existing approaches for identifying the subject column of a table by matching textual columns to entities in a knowledge base. We propose using the subject column of the table to pick potential labels which are then matched against the numerical column. Each cell in a subject column is disambiguated to a concept (entity) in the target KB. The numerical values associated with the subject columns are subsequently examined following a composite approach: (i.) a *column level analysis*, which looks at their distribution in a column; (ii.) a *row level analysis*, which compares each of them to the values associated to the disambiguated entities in the target KB. As a result, we generate a ranked list of properties for each numerical column. By selecting a table-specific set of possible semantic labels based on the subject column we were able to narrow down the possible values in a KB to those that are likely related to the context of the table. The preselected semantic labels are than ranked according to their fit to data in a column. This reduces memory requirements (as only data related to those values needs to be processed), and may make it more suitable in cases where KB are large, diverse, or rapidly changing such as DBpedia or Wikidata.

To evaluate our approach, we created the benchmark NumDB [13]. This consists of tables with numerical values constructed from types and numerical properties from DBpedia. NumDB introduces two dimensions of benchmarking: first, it includes deviations in the values drawn from DBpedia to test the sensitivity of approaches to values that are not exactly the same as the ones in the target KB. Second, it considers versions of the same table with different number of entities, to test the accuracy of approaches when facing smaller versus larger tables. Our evaluation suggests that our approach, which includes both row and

---

[1] https://www.w3.org/TR/vocab-dcat/, consulted on 1 May 2018.
[2] http://schema.org/, consulted on 1 May 2018.

column levels of analysis, outperforms the state of the art in terms of sensitivity to value deviation and effectiveness on smaller tables. NUMER shows itself more adaptable for use in a real world scenario in terms of time and memory consumption, as it does not require to generate the background knowledge necessary for approach proposed by Neumaier *et al.* [11].

The paper is structured as follows: Sect. 2 introduces the semantic labelling problem. Section 3 presents related work in assigning semantic labels to tables. Section 4 presents our approach. In Sect. 5 we provide details about the experiment, specifically about benchmark, set-up, and evaluation. Finally, Sects. 6 and 7 discuss our findings and outline future work.

2   Problem Statement

In this section, we introduce definitions of the concepts used, define the problem statement of assigning semantic labels to numerical columns in tables, and introduce a running example.

Definitions: We define a **table** T as a collection of related data on a specific topic. A table consists of m rows and n columns represented by a $m \times n$ matrix. Each row in a table has the same structure and can be seen as a single record of related data. Columns in a table are of specific type depending on their content; possible column types are **Numerical and Textual Columns.** A numerical column is a column where more than 50% of cells contain at least one digit. We chose this definition to not rule out cells that contain units of measure (*e.g.*, 2 km) or dates. A column that is not numerical is considered textual. One column per table is a **Subject Column**. That is, a textual column which represents the main subject of the table and connects the other columns semantically through binary relations [6,7,10]. Those connections are represented through properties from a KB. The process of determination of subject columns is detailed in Sect. 3.

Problem Statement: Given a table T and a target knowledge base KB, for each numerical column in T, return the list of properties in KB that most likely correspond to the numerical columns, ordered by likelihood score.

Running Example: Figure 1 shows an excerpt of a table from the T2D benchmark [14] with four columns: two textual (Country and City), and two numerical (Population and Population Density). The goal of the process is to produce a ranked list of labels for each numerical column based on the information generated from the subject column.

In this work we aim to disambiguate columns with numerical vales with use of the information from subject column in the table. We distinguish a list of scenarios that can be encountered when solving this problem. We look at the scenarios when the subject column is known and if the selection of subject column was not successful with existing approaches:

1. When the information on which textual column in the table is a subject column is known:

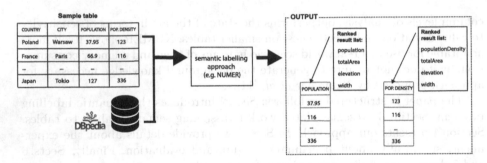

Fig. 1. Running example. A table with two textual and two numerical columns, with DBpedia as target KB.

(a) *Full match of numerical properties values* in the KB with numerical values in a table. This scenario is the most trivial and could be solved with basic matching techniques.

(b) *Numerical values in the numerical column could deviate from the values in the KB.* Some values could be more distinct than others, some could be missing in the KB entirely. Our approach includes mechanisms to make the influence of the following problems negligible: the *Column Level Analysis* (presented in Sect. 4) compares the distribution of values in the numerical column against that of values from numerical properties, which helps when values are missing. We also take into account numerical properties connected to entities of each type that were recognised in the subject column, which helps minimise the influence of partially correct disambiguation of the cells in the subject column.

(c) *Subject column cells can be disambiguated to a range of types* which could indicate a lack of consistency within the table or incorrect disambiguation of the cell value. Analysing tables per row allows us to compensate for the latter and detect the property the values of which are the closest to the values in the KB (Sect. 4 *Row Level Analysis*).

(d) *Numerical columns can be properties of types different from the types of entities found in the subject column.* They can be properties of other textual columns (that are not the subject column) or not connected to any other column (their meaning could be identified from the context). This scenario is out of the scope of this work and for such cases alternative approaches could be used (e.g. Neumaier *et al.* [11]) which do not rely on additional information provided with the numerical column.

(e) A property describing a numerical column could not be represented in the KB, in which case the approach will fail as the correct result of the disambiguation process is impossible to achieve.

2. Approaches for the detection of a subject column could fail, in which case the scenario is similar to the one described in 1(d).

From these scenarios we can see that the knowledge of the subject column can be used as a basis for improving the accuracy and efficiency of labelling of numerical columns. We present the details of our approach in Sect. 4.

3 Related Work

Several approaches have been proposed to assign semantic labels to structured data. Some of them focus on tables embedded in web pages (in HTML <table> elements [7,9]; others analyse any type of structured data with a specific focus on tabular or comma-separated data [4,5,8,15]. Humans can be involved in the process to achieve better results [16]. Many approaches make use of content descriptions associated with the table (e.g., information in an HTML page [6, 17,18], headers within tables [7,17]) or rely on data in textual columns within the table to assign semantic labels [10]. Others match table rows to KB entities, leaving out of the scope matching the table columns to KB properties [19,20]. It is important to point out that only a few of the existing approaches propose solutions specifically targeted towards numerical values in structured data.

Numerical Values present different challenges than textual information when assigning semantic labels to columns in tables. An approach targeting specifically the problem of labelling numerical values in structured data was first shown by Ramnandan *et al.* [21]. They propose an algorithm that learns a semantic labelling function. The authors introduce a list of features, differentiated between those targeted at numerical and at textual values in structured data. They propose testing the distributions of numerical values corresponding to semantic labels based on the idea that the distributions of values for each semantic label are expected to be different (e.g., the distribution of population of cities will be different from the distribution of population density). They used three different tests: the Welch's t-test, the Mann-Whitney U test, and the Kolmogorov-Smirnov test (KS test). Their results show that the latter achieved the best results. Neumaier *et al.* [11] and Pham *et al.* [12] used similar metrics. The solution proposed by Neumaier *et al.* [11] focuses exclusively on numerical values, and it is based on building a background knowledge graph from properties in DBpedia. They use DBpedia types and property-value pairs to structure their background knowledge with bags of numerical values which are later compared to numerical values from a data source using the KS test. However, creating and keeping the background knowledge is memory intensive. Pham *et al.* [12] introduce a number of additional features for different column types in their semantic labelling function. In addition to the KS test, they propose using metrics such as a modified Jaccard similarity for numeric data where the ranges of values are compared and measures which affect both textual and numerical values in a data source.

Our approach builds upon these by analysing numerical columns in two ways: first, in terms of the similarity (measured in terms of the KS test) of distribution of values with respect to those of properties in a target KB; second, by calculating the relative difference between numerical values in a column and numerical values of properties associated to entities of the type identified from the column that holds the main entities of the table. The main observation is that tables often include a column that identifies the entities described by the table (called the *subject column*), while the rest of the columns hold values of properties linked to those entities (or *objects*). Venetis *et al.* [6] reported 75% of the tables in their corpus of web tables had a single main subject column, and that the accuracy of semantic labelling increases when first determining a subject column.

Subject Column Identification. To determine which of the columns in a table is a subject column, Venetis *et al.* [6] suggest two methods: taking the left-most column that is not a number or date column, or treating it as a binary classification problem. They propose learning a classifier for subject columns with features that are dependent on the name and type of the column and the values in different cells of the column. Wang *et al.* [7] and Ermilov *et al.* [10] proposed similar characteristics of the column: (1) the *connectivity* of a column (*i.e.*, how it is connected with other columns of the table by means of properties mapped to the KB) and (2) *support* of the column (*i.e.*, ratio of cells disambiguated to KB entities in the column). A combination of both connectivity and support is then used to determine which of textual column is the most likely the subject column. In this work we focus on labelling columns with numerical data, assuming a subject column has been previously identified.

Semantic Labelling Benchmarks. The benchmark dataset created by Limaye *et al.* [3] comprises 400 tables mapped to DBpedia and YAGO at instance– and schema-level. Efthymiou *et al.* [19] introduce a benchmark including 485 K tables from Wikipedia, which were mapped to DBpedia by leveraging the links in their label column. Neither of these two benchmarks was suitable for our experiment, which aims to map columns to properties. Instead, the dataset in [3] contains cell-to-entity mappings, while that in [19] row-to-entity. T2D [9] is a set of 1,748 tables[3] with schema and instance-level mappings to DBpedia. However, it does not contain a sufficient number of numeric columns to be suitable for our case (the large majority of disambiguated column were textual columns). Therefore, we decided to create a new benchmark, that we detail in Sect. 5.1.

4   Approach

Our approach comprises four stages, described below. We assume the availability of a tool that enables the match of textual cells to entities in the target KB, and of a tool that allows the identification of a subject column.

Preprocessing. We preprocess the input table as follows: (1) Partition columns into *numerical* and *textual* columns. Following the definition in Sect. 2, we define a numerical column as a column that has $\geq 50\%$ numerical values. (2) From the subset of textual columns, select one subject column. This may be done following any the approaches described in Sect. 3. (3) Match each cell in the

---

[3] http://webdatacommons.org/webtables/goldstandard.html#toc0.

subject column to an entity in the target KB. (4) In numerical columns, we strip out cells containing non-numerical characters (*e.g.*, "2 km"), leaving only numerical values (*e.g.*, "2").

<table>
<tr><td></td><td colspan="2">subject column</td><td></td><td></td></tr>
<tr><td></td><td>COUNTRY</td><td>CITY</td><td>POPULATION</td><td>POP. DENSITY</td></tr>
<tr><td>dbr:Poland ◄—</td><td>Poland</td><td>Warsaw</td><td>37.95</td><td>123</td></tr>
<tr><td>dbr:France ◄—</td><td>France</td><td>Paris</td><td>66.9</td><td>116</td></tr>
<tr><td></td><td>...</td><td>...</td><td>...</td><td>...</td></tr>
<tr><td>dbr:Japan ◄—</td><td>Japan</td><td>Tokio</td><td>127</td><td>336</td></tr>
<tr><td></td><td colspan="2">textual columns</td><td colspan="2">numerical columns</td></tr>
</table>

Fig. 2. Information resulting from performing preprocessing steps a table.

Figure 2 shows the output of preprocessing our running example. Columns *Country* and *City* were classified as textual, *Country* was identified as the subject column. All values in the subject column were disambiguated to a DBpedia entity. Columns *Population* and *Population Density* were classified as numerical.

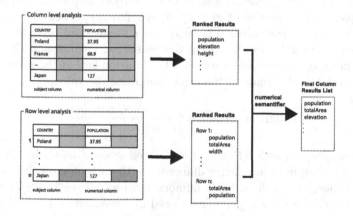

Fig. 3. An overview of the analysis stages in the semantification process.

Column Level Analysis. Similarly to [11,12], we compare the distribution of values in numerical columns with bags of values from the target KB. However, instead of comparing to all bags of values in the target KB, we consider only the properties that have a semantic relation with the types of the entities identified by the subject column, hence reducing both number of comparisons and memory requirements. From the entities identified in the subject column in the preprocessing stage, we query the target KB for the list of all types associated to them. In our running example, a sample list of types could be: [dbo:CapitalCity, dbo:Country, dbo:PopulatedPlace]. Next, for each type, we generate a list of all its instances in the target KB. Then, for each entity, we select properties of rdf:type owl:DatatypeProperty associated to it. In our example, Poland, dbo:PopulatedPlace has the properties population, area, existsFrom, and dbo:Country has population, area, populationDensity. For each property, we select its associated values and compare them to those in the numerical columns using the two-sample Kolmogorov-Smirnov test [21], as shown in Eq. 1.

$$D_{n,m} = \sup_x |F_{1,n}(x) - F_{2,m}(x)| \tag{1}$$

The output of the comparison is a list of properties for each numerical column, ordered by the probability given by the KS test. The output for the population column in our running example is [(populationTotal, 0.98), (populationDensity, 0.44), (elevation, 0.14), (area, 0.08)].

Row Level Analysis. Comparing value distributions does not necessarily result in meaningful matches. The size of a numerical column in a dataset and popularity of a specific property in the KB influences the accuracy of the results when comparing the distributions. To improve accuracy, we also analyse numerical values based on the context provided by the row they are in.

In this level of analysis, we perform the following steps for each row in the table: (1) From the entity disambiguated in the subject column at preprocessing stage, we query all properties of rdf:type owl:DatatypeProperty associated to it, together with their values. (2) Next, we compute the relative difference (Eq. 2) between the value of the cell in the numerical column and the value of each of the properties collected in step 1. The intuition is that the property with the smallest relative difference is the right match for the value.

$$\text{Rel diff}(val_1, val_2) = \left| \frac{val_1 - val_2}{max(|val_1|, |val_2|)} \right| \tag{2}$$

In our running example (Fig. 3), for the cell Poland 37.95 in the column Population we compute the relative difference with each of the values of the 33 numerical properties and the value in numerical column (here 37.95). Producing a ranking of candidate labels per row ordered by decreasing relative difference.

(3) Finally, we generate a final ranking of candidate labels from the rankings generated in step 2. This is done by selecting all properties that appear in any of the lists. For each unique property we also assign its best relative difference value, intuitively giving more importance to a property that was able to exactly match one row. In case of a tie, we break it by computing the average position between all intermediate lists.

Numerical Semantifier. In the last step, we create the final ranking by combining the outputs from the row level analysis (relative distance and average position) and the column level analysis (probability). Concerning the column level results list, a higher score represents a higher rank. As regards the row level analysis, a lower score means a higher rank. In order to merge the two analyses we order all outputs based on the closeness of the predictions to the highest ranking, independently of whether these represent outputs of row or column analysis (distance and probability). In case of a tie we prioritize the row level analysis labels over the column level analysis, as we identified in our evaluation row level analysis performs better than column level analysis on average.

Our final results list consists from predictions of semantic labels for a numerical column with their confidence score. We call the overall approach *NUMerical SemantifiER* (NUMER).

5   Evaluation

We evaluated our approach under two aspects: resource consumption (**Ev1.**) and accuracy in matching the correct property (**Ev2.**). For both, we compared against the approach developed by Neumaier *et al.* [11] as a baseline—which we refer to as *MultiLevelLabelling* (MLL). We generated a new benchmark for the purpose of our evaluation, which is described in the following section. All code used and results of the evaluation are available in a Github repository[4].

5.1   Benchmark

To evaluate our approach we needed a set of tables containing at least one textual subject column (*i.e.*, the column to which the values in the other columns refer) and one numerical column. We generated a benchmark by extracting tables from DBpedia. Each table has three columns: the first is the subject textual column; the second contains the DBpedia URIs corresponding to the entities listed in the first column (ignored by our algorithm); and the third numerical column.

We extracted the tables according to the following process: first, we took a set of properties that could be mapped to numerical columns, namely those identified in [11]. These included the 46 most popular numerical DBpedia properties[5]. Second, we extracted the type of information (*i.e.*, the classes) of all subject entities for each property p_i in the property set and the number of entities of each type. For each property, we left out all classes whose entities comprised less than 0.1% of all the property subjects, in order to exclude possible erroneous triples, and selected a number of random classes above this threshold, 10 when available, less otherwise. Subsequently, for each subset of classes we took all triples $p_i(i, o)$ for the corresponding property, where $type(i, C_j)$ for C_j in the class subset. Labels were collected for all entities and properties. All these steps were performed by querying the live DBpedia endpoint[6]. We transposed all the resulting triples into tables (see Fig. 4). This produced a total of 389 tables, which we used to generate our benchmark. We created tables with different levels of sampling and introduced varying degrees of errors, with respect to the data subsequently used to disambiguate them, to also allow conclusions around the

---

[4] https://github.com/chabrowa/semantification.

[5] 50 most popular properties excluding those linking to DBpedia internal ids.

[6] https://dbpedia.org/sparql.

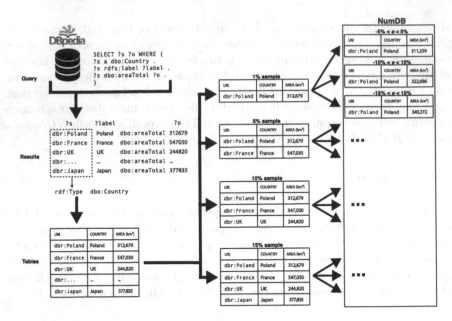

Fig. 4. Tables in the benchmark were created by extracting data from DBpedia and transposing it into tables. The figure represents the whole pipeline.

robustness of our approach in respect to inaccuracies in the data. We used four different sample sizes (*Very Small*:1% of all entities; *Small*:5%; *Medium*:10%; *Large*:15%). A statistical description of each sample can be seen in Table 1. For each sample size we generated three additional tables, to which a degree of error e of $-5\% < e < 5\%$, $-10\% < e < 10\%$, or $-15\% < e < 15\%$ to each value v was introduced. The total number of tables created was 3952, 247 for each combination of sample size and error degree. The dataset is available at [13].

5.2   Evaluation Results

For both resource consumption and accuracy we compared the performance of NUMER and MLL for each table size and degree of error in the NumDB benchmark. The resource consumption evaluation (**Ev1.**) included processing time and memory consumption. The accuracy evaluation (**Ev2.**) examined the percentage of correctly disambiguated columns, examining both the top 1 and the top 3 semantic labels on the ranked results list. Moreover, we generated scores for each level of analysis (*i.e.*, row and column) separately and compared it against the overall score, in order to gain a better overview of the influence of different levels of analysis on the results. Finally, we applied ANOVA to test for statistical significance between table sizes and between various degrees of error. We believe that this range of experiments was able to provide a better picture of the performance of our approach and to detect directions for further research.

Experiment Setup. We deployed a SPARQL endpoint for DBpedia v.2016-4 using Virtuoso and AWS services[7]. We run the evaluation on a virtual machine with 6 cores and 66 GB of memory running Ubuntu Linux. MLL was evaluated using code provided by authors on an associated Github account[8].

Resource Consumption. We tested the overall performance of NUMER and MLL by measuring the **processing time** and **RAM** consumption to assign semantic labels to NumDB datasets without deviation. It is important to notice that both approaches differ significantly in their implementation. MLL requires to build a background knowledge, which in our experiment environment took 01:02:22 and 16.48 GB of memory. Keeping a large amount of data in the memory allowed the MLL approach to analyse the tables with an average of 3 s per file. However, in the current set-up we used, following [11]'s evaluation, only 46 DBpedia properties. The resources required to build the background knowledge will grow with the number of properties used. As all the necessary information is selected based on the subject column, NUMER does not require prior set-up, resulting in a significantly lower memory consumption. However, requesting all of the information from the DBpedia endpoint at run time resulted in an average processing time of 13 s per table. Table 1 the processing times per set.

Table 1. Set statistics and processing time for NUMER and MLL (V.S - very small, S - small; M - medium; L - large set; Avg - average; S.dev - standard deviation).

Set	Statistics					MLL			NUMER		
	#rows	Median	Avg	S.dev.	Δ	Total	Avg	Δ	Total	Avg	Δ
V.S	11,456	79.5	137.69	127.76	-	555	2.256	-	2168	8.815	-
S	56,604	390	682.75	633.08	3.94	630	2.561	0.45	3147	12.793	0.14
M	113,054	808.5	1366.58	1265.55	1.00	816	3.317	0.14	3564	14.486	0.30
L	169,484	1255.5	2069.16	1899.65	0.50	936	3.915	0.11	3973	16.152	0.18

NUMER – Levels of Analysis. The row level analysis achieved better scores compared to the column level (Table 2). On the other hand, the combination of both levels was often more accurate of to the best performing scores of each level of analysis alone. We found varying levels of accuracy, the **row level analysis** performed consistently well compared to the column level analysis. The difference between accuracy scores by table size was not statistically significant, in contrast to a comparison by error deviation. The performance of the **column level analysis** differed significantly by table size but not by error deviation. The column level analysis used the KS test to assign semantic labels to bags of numerical values. The lower levels of accuracy of the column level analysis suggest a higher dependency on the deviation of the numerical values in a specific

---

[7] https://aws.amazon.com/marketplace/pp/B012DSCFEK.
[8] https://github.com/sebneu/number_labelling.

column than the row level analysis. Concerning NUMER, which integrated row and column level analysis, it was able to assign semantic labels with a higher degree of precision than the two approaches it is based on, selecting the correct semantic label in over 80% of cases regardless of sampling size or error rate.

Comparative Evaluation. We compared the performance of NUMER and MLL for all tables sizes and error degrees within the NumDB benchmark. NUMER consistently outperforms the latter, across all the dimensions in which the datasets change (Table 3). NUMER was not affected by variations in table sizes, whereas it was sensible to different degrees of error in the data. Accuracy for top 1 results drops 10.5% on average when introducing any error in the original data from DBpedia. On the other hand, MLL's performance significantly decreased according to both table size and error degree. Overall, the behaviour of MLL appears to be similar to that of our column level analysis, to which it had similar, yet higher, scores. Nevertheless, whereas MLL's performance rises as table size increase, column level analysis' scores are roughly constant for *small*, *medium*, and *large* table sizes, dropping only for *very small* tables.

Table 2. Percentage of correctly assigned labels within top 1 and top 3 results in a results list for NUMER approach split by level of analysis (V.S - very small set, S - small set; M - medium set; L- large set).

Set	Top k	Row level				Column level				NUMER			
		V.S	S	M	L	V.S	S	M	L	V.S	S	M	L
0% dev	1	75.61	77.24	73.98	77.64	28.46	34.96	36.18	34.15	90.65	93.50	91.87	93.09
	3	93.50	95.93	93.50	95.53	40.65	55.28	56.10	54.88	93.50	96.34	93.90	95.93
5% dev	1	75.20	77.24	76.83	78.46	23.58	30.89	30.89	28.05	80.49	84.15	78.86	81.30
	3	93.50	95.53	92.68	95.53	35.77	50.00	52.03	48.78	93.50	95.53	93.09	95.93
10% dev	1	75.61	73.98	71.14	77.64	22.76	28.05	28.05	28.86	78.05	78.86	75.61	80.89
	3	93.09	95.12	93.09	93.90	37.40	48.37	48.78	47.56	93.09	98.37	93.50	94.31
15% dev	1	75.20	73.58	69.11	76.83	23.58	26.02	26.83	26.02	78.46	76.02	73.98	78.05
	3	93.09	93.90	92.28	94.31	36.59	46.75	47.15	45.12	93.09	94.72	93.90	94.72

Table 3. Percentage of correctly assigned labels within top 1 and top 3 results in a results list for NUMER and MLL. For MLL, we show results generated with average distance and majority vote (in brackets) (V.S - very small set, S - small set; M - medium set; L - large set).

Set	Top k	NUMER				MLL			
		V.S	S	M	L	V.S	S	M	L
0%	1	90.65	93.50	91.87	93.09	40.65(34.96)	53.66(40.24)	55.28(40.24)	58.13(40.65)
	3	93.50	96.34	93.90	95.93	60.16(62.20)	73.98(73.98)	78.86(76.42)	77.24(75.20)
5%	1	80.49	84.15	78.86	81.30	39.43(30.89)	48.37(33.74)	50.41(34.15)	49.59(32.52)
	3	93.50	95.53	93.09	95.93	53.25(52.44)	64.63(63.01)	66.67(66.26)	65.45(64.23)
10%	1	78.05	78.86	75.61	80.89	39.02(30.89)	47.56(30.08)	47.15(31.30)	48.78(30.49)
	3	93.09	98.37	93.50	94.31	52.85(52.44)	62.20(59.35)	63.01(60.57)	62.60(60.98)
15%	1	78.46	76.02	73.98	78.05	38.21(30.89)	42.28(28.86)	45.12(27.64)	43.90(28.86)
	3	93.09	94.72	93.90	94.72	52.85(52.85)	58.94(56.91)	59.76(57.32)	59.76(59.35)

6   Discussion and Limitations

The experiments used to evaluate NUMER enabled us to gain a number of insights about its performance, which indicate directions for future research. NUMER was highly accurate in predicting semantic labels for numerical columns, outperforming the state of the art. MLL, the approach used as a baseline, achieves better scores over the column level analysis aspect of NUMER; however, comparing the combination or row and column level analysis, NUMER outperforms MLL consistently. In most cases, the row level analysis is responsible for most of the accuracy of the whole approach. Only when there is no deviation the integration of the column level analysis yields a significant increase in accuracy.

The results in Table 3 show a large difference in terms of performance between top 1 and the top 3 results. Additional scoring factors could be introduced based on other columns or additional textual information available together with the table besides the subject column, in order to improve the top 1 result. The correct semantic labels could be listed after the top 3 (e.g., as a 4th semantic label in a result list), to provide users with a set of potentially valid semantic properties from which they could choose the correct one. This type of interaction may be applied to several contexts, e.g., when generating a summary, or to create dataset to train a more sophisticated machine learning model to assign properties.

When comparing both approaches according to their time and memory consumption, NUMER requires longer time (13 s) to analyse a single NumDB table than MLL (~3 s). However, it does not need to generate the background knowledge which, in the case of MLL, carries a cost in memory consumption and initialization time. We believe that this makes NUMER more suitable for use in a real-world scenario, dealing better with memory limitations and KB evolution.

Neumaier et al. [11] deliberately excluded any additional textual information in MLL. Conversely, NUMER requires textual information in the table to detect potential correct semantic properties. This makes our approach more dependent on textual content in the data: the lack of a subject column or multiple subject columns would likely have a negative impact on the results. A possible solution to that could be to combine NUMER and MLL depending on the presence of the subject column in the table. Moreover, we used textual information in the tables only to disambiguate subject columns to DBpedia entity types. In the future, methods to extract further semantic information from text should be explored, e.g., finding relations between the extracted entities, in order to better understand how different elements in a table relate to each other which could further inform the task of assigning semantic labels to numerical values.

Limitations. As with most approaches there are some limitations connected to this approach. First, a subject column might not be present, or several columns may be considered as subjects. Those scenarios present an additional layer of complexity which would require approaches that are independent of a subject column or other, more tailored solutions. Second, we evaluated our approach by using a set of synthetic tables extracted from DBpedia. Although we processed our tables to test our approach under different conditions, an evaluation in a real world scenario, *i.e.*, with tables found on web pages, should be carried out in the future to provide more solid indications about the applicability of NUMER.

7   Conclusion and Future Work

We presented NUMER—an approach to derive semantic representations of numerical values in tables. Approaches to add semantic meaning to numerical values are particularly valuable, as these represent the most popular column type in open governmental datasets [2]. We applied a column level analysis—based on the types of entities found in the subject column of the table and the related values in a KB—matched to the column values in the table. We further applied a row level analysis in which we matched the individual values in a row to the corresponding entity in the KB and approximate the closest numerical values linked to this specific entity. This enabled us to create a table-specific ranked list of potential semantic labels for numerical columns. Automatically inferring the meaning of numerical values found in tables has the potential to significantly improve the discovery of structured data as it can add context to otherwise obscure values. We evaluated our approach using a benchmark (NumDB), created by us, and investigate the influence of the number of rows (percentage of entities of specific type in the KB) and the influence of (intentionally introduced) deviation in the data. We can see that both levels of analysis have a positive influence on the final score in our approach, outperforming the state of the art under the given conditions.

Existing benchmarks have shown not to be useful when the focus of evaluation in the task of assigning semantic labels is mainly on numerical columns. For instance, in T2D [9,10], only 11 of 1748 tables contain numerical columns disambiguated to DBpedia properties. This indicates a need for new reliable benchmarks to test approaches such as MLL and NUMER, preferably in a real world scenario, without the bias of automatically generated tables. NumDB, although automatically generated, can be seen as a step in that direction. We believe NUMER can provide important context to numerical values in tables. This can, for instance, support search over tables on the web and make numerical columns discoverable even if their meaning is not explicitly available in a textual format [22]. We further see the potential of our approach to be used in recommendation systems for datasets by finding similar or semantically connected tables [23].

In future work we plan to extend this work by integrating multiple knowledge bases. We aim to further improve this approach by using additional information from the numerical columns such as currencies or units of measurements (*e.g.*, kilometre, million, percentage) that might be attached to the values for disambiguation. Correlating numerical columns to other, non-numerical columns, or column headers could further improve the results. This strategy would take advantage of instances in which, for example, one column is the percentage value of another column, or witch longitude and latitude in two separate columns.

Acknowledgements. This project is supported by the European Union Horizon 2020 program under the Marie Skłodowska-Curie grant agreement No. 642795.

References

1. Kacprzak, E., Koesten, L., Heath, T., Tennison, J.: Position paper: Dataset profiling for un-linked data. In: Proceedings of the 3rd International Workshop (PRO-FILES), The 13th ESWC Conference (2016)
2. Mitlöhner, J., Neumaier, S., Umbrich, J., Polleres, A.: Characteristics of open data CSV files. In: 2nd International Conference on Open and Big Data, OBD 2016, Vienna, Austria, 22–24 August 2016, pp. 72–79 (2016). https://doi.org/10.1109/OBD.2016.18
3. Limaye, G., Sarawagi, S., Chakrabarti, S.: Annotating and searching web tables using entities, types and relationships. PVLDB **3**(1), 1338–1347 (2010)
4. Mulwad, V., Finin, T., Syed, Z., Joshi, A.: Using linked data to interpret tables. In: Proceedings of the First International Workshop on Consuming Linked Data. CEUR Workshop Proceedings, vol. 665 (2010)
5. Syed, Z., Finin, T., Mulwad, V., Joshi, A.: Exploiting a web of semantic data for interpreting tables. In: Proceedings of the 2nd Web Science Conference (2010)
6. Venetis, P., et al.: Recovering semantics of tables on the web. Proc. VLDB Endow. **4**(9), 528–538 (2011). https://doi.org/10.14778/2002938.2002939
7. Wang, J., Wang, H., Wang, Z., Zhu, K.Q.: Understanding tables on the web. In: Atzeni, P., Cheung, D., Ram, S. (eds.) ER 2012. LNCS, vol. 7532, pp. 141–155. Springer, Heidelberg (2012). https://doi.org/10.1007/978-3-642-34002-4_11
8. Taheriyan, M., Knoblock, C.A., Szekely, P., Ambite, J.L.: A scalable approach to learn semantic models of structured sources. In: Proceedings of the International Conference on Semantic Computing (2014)
9. Ritze, D., Lehmberg, O., Bizer, C.: Matching HTML tables to DBpedia. In: Proceedings of the International Conference on Web Intelligence, Mining and Semantics, pp. 10:1–10:6 (2015)
10. Ermilov, I., Ngomo, A.-C.N.: TAIPAN: automatic property mapping for tabular data. In: Blomqvist, E., Ciancarini, P., Poggi, F., Vitali, F. (eds.) EKAW 2016. LNCS (LNAI), vol. 10024, pp. 163–179. Springer, Cham (2016). https://doi.org/10.1007/978-3-319-49004-5_11
11. Neumaier, S., Umbrich, J., Parreira, J.X., Polleres, A.: Multi-level semantic labelling of numerical values. In: Groth, P., et al. (eds.) ISWC 2016. LNCS, vol. 9981, pp. 428–445. Springer, Cham (2016). https://doi.org/10.1007/978-3-319-46523-4_26
12. Pham, M., Alse, S., Knoblock, C.A., Szekely, P.: Semantic labeling: a domain-independent approach. In: Groth, P., et al. (eds.) ISWC 2016. LNCS, vol. 9981, pp. 446–462. Springer, Cham (2016). https://doi.org/10.1007/978-3-319-46523-4_27
13. Piscopo, A., Kacprzak, E.: Numdb (2018). https://doi.org/10.6084/m9.figshare.6205814.v4. https://figshare.com/articles/numdb_0105_zip/6205814/4
14. Ritze, D., Lehmberg, O., Oulabi, Y., Bizer, C.: Profiling the potential of web tables for augmenting cross-domain knowledge bases. In: WWW, pp. 251–261. ACM (2016)
15. Knoblock, C.A., et al.: Semi-automatically mapping structured sources into the semantic web. In: Simperl, E., Cimiano, P., Polleres, A., Corcho, O., Presutti, V. (eds.) ESWC 2012. LNCS, vol. 7295, pp. 375–390. Springer, Heidelberg (2012). https://doi.org/10.1007/978-3-642-30284-8_32

16. Ermilov, I., Auer, S., Stadler, C.: User-driven semantic mapping of tabular data. In: Proceedings of the 9th International Conference on Semantic Systems, New York, NY, USA, pp. 105–112. ACM (2013). https://doi.org/10.1145/2506182.2506196

17. Adelfio, M.D., Samet, H.: Schema extraction for tabular data on the web. Proc. VLDB Endow. **6**(6), 421–432 (2013). https://doi.org/10.14778/2536336.2536343

18. Wienand, D., Paulheim, H.: Detecting incorrect numerical data in DBpedia. In: Presutti, V., d'Amato, C., Gandon, F., d'Aquin, M., Staab, S., Tordai, A. (eds.) ESWC 2014. LNCS, vol. 8465, pp. 504–518. Springer, Cham (2014). https://doi.org/10.1007/978-3-319-07443-6_34

19. Efthymiou, V., Hassanzadeh, O., Rodriguez-Muro, M., Christophides, V.: Matching web tables with knowledge base entities: from entity lookups to entity embeddings. In: d'Amato, C., et al. (eds.) ISWC 2017. LNCS, vol. 10587, pp. 260–277. Springer, Cham (2017). https://doi.org/10.1007/978-3-319-68288-4_16

20. Bhagavatula, C.S., Noraset, T., Downey, D.: TabEL: entity linking in web tables. In: Arenas, M., et al. (eds.) ISWC 2015. LNCS, vol. 9366, pp. 425–441. Springer, Cham (2015). https://doi.org/10.1007/978-3-319-25007-6_25

21. Ramnandan, S.K., Mittal, A., Knoblock, C.A., Szekely, P.: Assigning semantic labels to data sources. In: Gandon, F., Sabou, M., Sack, H., d'Amato, C., Cudré-Mauroux, P., Zimmermann, A. (eds.) ESWC 2015. LNCS, vol. 9088, pp. 403–417. Springer, Cham (2015). https://doi.org/10.1007/978-3-319-18818-8_25

22. Koesten, L.M., Kacprzak, E., Tennison, J.F.A., Simperl, E.: The trials and tribulations of working with structured data:-a study on information seeking behaviour. In: Proceedings of the CHI Conference on Human Factors in Computing Systems, pp. 1277–1289 (2017). https://doi.org/10.1145/3025453.3025838

23. Goel, A., Knoblock, C.A., Lerman, K.: Exploiting structure within data for accurate labeling using conditional random fields. In: Proceedings of the 14th International Conference on Artificial Intelligence (ICAI) (2012)

Towards Enriching DBpedia from Vertical Enumerative Structures Using a Distant Learning Approach

Mouna Kamel and Cassia Trojahn[✉]

Institut de Recherche en Informatique de Toulouse, Toulouse, France
{prenom.nom,cassia.trojahn}@irit.fr

Abstract. Automatic construction of semantic resources at large scale usually relies on general purpose corpora as Wikipedia. This resource, by nature rich in encyclopedic knowledge, exposes part of this knowledge with strongly structured elements (infoboxes, categories, etc.). Several extractors have targeted these structures in order to enrich or to populate semantic resources as DBpedia, YAGO or BabelNet. The remain semi-structured textual structures, such as vertical enumerative structures (those using typographic and dispositional layout) have been however under-exploited. However, frequent in corpora, they are rich sources of specific semantic relations, such as hypernyms. This paper presents a distant learning approach for extracting hypernym relations from vertical enumerative structures of Wikipedia, with the aim of enriching DBpedia. Our relation extraction approach achieves an overall precision of 62%, and 99% of the extracted relations can enrich DBpedia, with respect to a reference corpus.

1 Introduction

In many fields such as artificial intelligence, semantic web or question answering, applications require a reasoning ability, based on semantic resources that describe concepts and relations between. Manually constructing this kind of resource is cost-intensive and results in domain-specific resources of low coverage. However, more than ever automated support for large scale construction of such resources becomes essential. This involves automatically extracting relations from text for building, enriching or populating them. This task usually relies on general purpose corpora as Wikipedia or WordNet and on knowledge extractors mainly exploiting their specific structural elements [22] or sub-corpora [15]. Several of these extractors have targeted these structures in order to enrich or to populate resources as DBpedia [2], YAGO or BabelNet [23].

Enriching DBpedia means identifying new semantic relations from Wikipedia pages. A Wikipedia page is composed of different textual structures which can be divided into three main categories: strongly structured elements, paragraphs which contain plain text, and semi-structured textual units. Strongly structured elements such as infoboxes or User Generated Categories (UGCs) benefit from

© Springer Nature Switzerland AG 2018
C. Faron Zucker et al. (Eds.): EKAW 2018, LNAI 11313, pp. 179–194, 2018.
https://doi.org/10.1007/978-3-030-03667-6_12

a strong layout, convey a well defined semantics and contain poor written text. Extractors exploiting these elements usually focus on relations (*birthPlace*, *birthDate*, *win-prize*, etc.) which are mostly limited to named entities such as cities, persons, species, etc. With respect to plain text, it has been exploited by numerous relation extraction systems, more often abstracts (whose first sentence is a definition) for identifying hypernym relations[1], other paragraphs for identifying relations in a context of Open Information Extraction. Wikipedia pages are also composed of textual structures, such as titles, subtitles, vertical enumerative structures (i.e. enumerations using typographical and dispositional markers (Fig. 1)). We consider these textual structures as semi-structured ones, as they have the particularity to combine well-written text and layout. Although they express relations which are more often hierarchical relations, these types of structures remain under-exploited as they can not be correctly processed by most classical NLP tools.

The aim of this paper is to show to what extent DBpedia may be enriched with hypernym relations extracted from vertical enumerative structures (VES) present in Wikipedia pages. This kind of relation is central to the construction and enrichment of resources, providing the hierarchical backbone structure of knowledge bases and allows for assigning types to entities. Taking the example in Fig. 1, while several hypernym relations can be identified, e.g., (*Oxfords,Men's shoes*) or (*Derby, Men's shoes*), few of them are present in BabelNet and none in DBpedia.

We first propose a knowledge extraction approach for identifying hypernym relations carried out by VES. We implement a learning approach for the following reasons (1) the corpus has many regularities that can emerge with this kind of approach and (2) features of different nature (syntactic, lexical, typographical, dispositional, semantic or distributional) can be combined together. In particular, the choice of a distant learning is motivated by the fact that it is free of manual annotation and that the learning knowledge base (here BabelNet) and the learning text (Wikipedia) are aligned, as recommended by the method. We then evaluate the enrichment rate from an experiment we led on a corpus made of VES extracted from French Wikipedia pages.

This work is part of the SemPedia[2] project aiming at enriching DBpedia for French, by specifying and implementing a set of new Wikipedia extractors dedicated to the hypernym relation. We focus on French because semantic resources targeting this language are scarce. We have already proposed a distant supervised approach and implemented a tool for identifying hypernym relations from disambiguation Wikipedia pages [15]. We propose to adapt this approach in this new context, i.e. identifying hypernym relations from vertical enumerative structure of Wikipedia pages, ensuring that the approach is:

– free of manual annotation;

---

[1] A hypernym relation link two entities E_1 and E_2 when E_2 (hyponym) is subordinate to E_1 (hypernym). From a lexical point of view, this relation is called "isa".
[2] http://www.irit.fr/Sempedia.

Men's shoes can be categorized by how they are closed:
- Oxfords (also referred as "Balmorals"): the vamp has a V-shaped slit to which the laces are attached; also known as "closed lacing". The word "Oxford" is sometimes used by American clothing companies to market shoes that are not Balmorals, such as Blüchers.
- Derby shoe: the laces are tied to two pieces of leather independently attached to the vamp; also known as "open lacing" and is a step down in dressiness. If the laces are not independently attached to the vamp, the shoe is known as a blucher shoe. This name is, in American English, often used about derbys.
- Monk-straps: a buckle and strap instead of lacing.
- Slip-ons: There are no lacings or fastenings. The popular loafers are part of this category, as well as less popular styles, such as elastic-sided shoes.

Fig. 1. Example of VES (https://en.wikipedia.org/wiki/Shoe)

- language independent, thus may be reused for enriching DBpedia in several languages;
- reproducible on any corpus which contains VES having same discourse properties that those of Wikipedia pages.

The rest of this paper is structured as follows. Section 2 presents the background on enumerative structures and on distant learning. We present then our learning model in Sect. 3. Section 4 describes the experimentation and the evaluation. Section 5 discusses the main related work. Finally, Sect. 6 concludes the paper and discusses future work.

2 Background

In this section, we first describe the main principles of distant learning. We then introduce the discursive properties of enumerative structures we lean on to implement our approach.

2.1 Distant Learning

The distant learning method follows the same principles as the supervised learning ones, except that the annotation for constructing the learning examples is carried out using an external semantic resource. In the context of relation extraction from text, it consists in aligning an external knowledge base to a corpus and in using this alignment to learn relations [6,21]. The learning ground is based on the hypothesis that "if two entities participate in a relation, all sentences that mention these two entities express that relation". Although this hypothesis seems too strong, Riedel *et al.* [26] show that it makes sense when the knowledge base used to annotate the corpus is derived from the corpus itself. Thus, for a pair of entities appearing together within a sentence, a set of features are extracted from the sentence and added to a feature vector for that entity pair.

If the entities are linked in the knowledge base, that entity pair constitutes a positive example, a negative example otherwise.

This approach has been exploited for identifying relations expressed in sentences which are syntactically and semantically correct. Our contribution relies on adapting this approach to different textual structures, especially for those where a part of semantics is carried out by layout. For each type of textual structure, it is then necessary to define a process for building learning examples and to define discriminant features.

2.2 Vertical Enumerative Structures

An enumerative structure (ES) is a textual structure which expresses hierarchical knowledge through different components. According the definition of Ho-Dac *et al.* [12], "it encompasses an *enumerative theme* justifying the union of several elements according to an identity of statut". Different types of enumerative structures exist and different typologies have been proposed.

From a visual point of view, a vertical ES (VES) is expressed using typographic and dispositional markers. More specifically, a VES is composed of (1) a primer (corresponding to a sentence or a phrase) which contains the "enumerative theme" and which introduces (2) a list of items (at least two items) which belong to the same conceptual domain, and (3) possibly of a conclusion. If we consider the example of Fig. 1, "Men's shoes can be categorized by how they are closed:" is the primer, "Oxfords ... such as Blüchers." is an item, *Men's shoes* is the "enumerative theme" and *Oxfords, Derby shoes, Monk-straps* and *Slip-ons* are entities of the same conceptual domain. This VES has no conclusion.

From a discursive point of view, VES may be classified according to the discourse relations between their components. Before introducing VES properties our approach relies on, we first briefly remind the major principles of the Segmented Discourse Representation Theory (SDRT) [1] which is the discourse theory we used for analyzing VES. A discourse analysis in that context consists in breaking down the text into segments (called discourse units or DU) and in linking adjacent segments with *coordinating* or *subordinating* relations. *Coordinating* relations link entities of the same importance, whereas *subordinating* relations link an entity to an entity of lower importance. Thus, if we consider the primer and items of a VES as DUs (resp. DU_{Primer} and DU_{Item_j} $(j = 1, ..., N)$ if VES is composed of N items), a manual discourse analysis of such a VES allows to state that the primer is linked to the first item with a *subordinating* relation. When all items are linked with *coordinating* relations, we qualify such VES as *paradigmatic* [9] and refer to it as P-VES (Fig. 2(a)).

According again to the SDRT, if DU_{Item_1} is subordinated to DU_{Primer}, hence each DU_{Item_j} coordinated to $DU_{Item_{(j-1)}}$ $(j = 2, ..., N)$, is subordinated to DU_{Primer}. Thereby, N subordinating relations between DU_{Primer} and DU_{Item_j}, $(j = 1,...,N)$, can be inferred (Fig. 2 (b)). In that context and as the *elaboration* relation is a sub-relation of the *subordinating* one, we can also say that each DU_{Item_j} *elaborates* DU_{Primer}. When DU_{Primer} and DU_{Item_j} are broken down into more fine-grained DUs as terms, these discourse relations are kept between

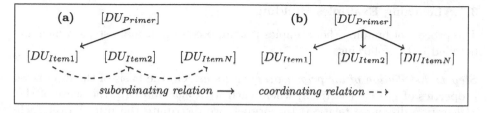

Fig. 2. Discursive representations of P-VES according to the SDRT.

at least one term H in the primer and one term h in the item. From a lexical point of view, these N relations may be specialized in at least N lexical relations $R(H, h_i)_{i=1,...,N}$.

We are interested with P-VES as Wikipedia pages contain many P-VES often expressing definitions and properties of entities. These pages are written according to the guide "The Manual Of Style"[3] which recommends the same grammatical form for all items. An analysis of 100 Wikipedia pages randomly chosen shows that more than 80% of VES respect those instructions and thus are paradigmatic.

We are aware that a P-VES can, however, bear more relations (hierarchical or no hierarchical). The example in Fig. 3 shows that more than one hierarchical relations exist between the primer and the first item which is itself composed of a list (*act of worship* and *sacrifice, act of worship* and *libation*, etc.), as well as one no hierarchical (syntagmatic) relation expressed in the last item (*preaching* and *Abrahamic religions*).

The main acts of worship are:

- sacrifice, libation, the offering and education;
- pray (invocation, praise, etc.);
- preaching which plays an important role in Abrahamic religions;

Fig. 3. P-VES containing hierarchical relations and one no hierarchical relation.

3 Proposed Approach

We describe here how the distant learning approach has been adapted for learning hypernym relations from P-VES. We describe in particular the process of building learning examples and the learning model.

---

[3] http://en.wikipedia.org/wiki/Wikipedia:Manual_of_Style.

3.1   Learning Examples Building

The process of building the examples is composed of four main steps, which are detailed in the following.

Step 1: distribution of the primer over the items. On the basis of the discursive properties of P-VES (Sect. 2.2) where each item *elaborates* (in the sense of the *elaboration* discourse relation) the primer, we distribute the primer over each item, giving rise to new textual units called TU. Each *TU* corresponds to the concatenation of the primer and of one item. N *TU* are thus generated if the P-VES is composed of N items. For illustrating this step, we consider the P-VES depicted in Fig. 1. Four TU are thus generated:

1. [Men's shoes ... are closed: Oxfords ... such as Blüchers.]
2. [Men's shoes ... are closed: Derby shoe... often used about derbys.]
3. [Men's shoes ... are closed: Monk-straps: ... instead of lacing]
4. [Men's shoes ... are closed: Slip-ons... such as elastic-sided shoes.]

Distributing the primer over the different items does not make us fall back on the classic extraction of relations because we are still confronted with the presence of some typographic markers that replace lexical markers.

Step 2: annotation of terms. In this step, we firstly extract the terms from the external semantic resource (i.e. the terminology provided by the resource, such as synset terms or concept labels). Then, this list is used to annotate the set of generated TUs.

Step 3: building the couples of terms. Several terms may be present in the primer or in an item. Learning examples are then built from couples of terms $(Term_1, Term_2)$ which respectively belong to the primer and to one of the items. Relying on the *elaboration* relation between the primer and an item, we empirically define the following heuristics for selecting couples of terms:

- $Term_2$ should belong to the first part of the item, i.e. the string starting at index 0 and ending at the next final punctuation (point, line return, etc.) of the item. As Fig. 1, an item may be composed of several sentences.
- Items for which no terms are linked to at least one term of the primer by a hypernym relation, according to the external semantic resource, are left aside. Indeed, this case contradicts our underlying assumption about P-VES that states that each item *elaborates* the primer. This case may nevertheless be explained by a possible incompleteness of the external resource.

For constructing the set of examples, we have generated all the combinations of terms $(Term_1, Term_2)$ from the primer and retained items. Thus a couple of terms will correspond to a positive example if a hypernym relation between $Term_1$ and $Term_2$ exists in the external semantic resource, to a negative example otherwise. We are aware however that, depending on the coverage of the external semantic resource adopted, negative examples may be false negative ones given the fact that the relation is simply missing in the resource.

Step 4: associating a set of features to couple of terms. Each couple of terms $Term_1$ and $Term_2$ is associated with a set of features coming from the textual units from which they have been extracted. Currently, we focus on lexical features, grammatical features, layout features, and some heuristics inspired by [18], such as the context of $Term_1$ and $Term_2$ (text window). Furthermore, features impact different levels of P-VES: those involving the whole enumerative structure, those involving the example, those involving the primer and those involving the item. Table 1 introduces the set of selected features as used in the experiments described in Sect. 4.

Table 1. Set of learning features (*an enumerative theme is used for organizing the concepts involved into an enumerative structure and is one of the following expressions *list of, types of, kind of*, etc.).

Scope	Features	Description	Datatype
ES	itemsNumber	number of items present in the VES	integer
Example	lexicalInclusion	lexical inclusion between the terms	boolean
Primer	nbTokens_P	number of tokens in the primer	integer
	lemmaPOSWindow_P	sequence of POS of the window corresponding to 3 tokens preceding $Term_1$, 3 tokens following $Term_1$	string
	lemmaPosTerm1	sequence of POS of all tokens included into $Term_1$	string
	NbTokensBeforeTerm1	number of tokens before $Term_1$	int
	NbTokensAfterTerm1	number of tokens after $Term_1$	int
	capitalizedInitialTerm1	initial of $Term_1$ is capitalized	boolean
	capitalizedTerm1	$Term_1$ is capitalized	boolean
	endsWithColon	primer ends with a colon	boolean
	verbPresence	the primer contains a verbal form	boolean
	theme*	the primer contains an enumerative theme	boolean
	nbTokensTerm1Org	number of tokens between $Term_1$ and the theme	integer
	ordinal	the primer contains a numeral	boolean
	nbTokensTerm1Ord	number of tokens between $Term_1$ and the numeral	integer
Item	nbTokens_I	number of tokens in the item	integer
	nbSentences_I	number of sentences in the item	integer
	lemmaPOSWindow_I	sequence of POS of the window including 3 tokens preceding $Term_2$, 3 tokens following $Term_2$	string
	lemmaPosTerm2	sequence of POS of all tokens included into $Term_2$	string
	NbTokensBeforeTerm2	number of tokens before $Term_2$	int
	NbTokensAfterTerm2	number of tokens after $Term_2$	int
	capitalizedInitialTerm2	initial of $Term_2$ is capitalized	boolean
	capitalizedTerm2	$Term_2$ is capitalized	boolean

3.2 Learning Model

In order to perform a binary classification task (*isA* or *not-isA* classes), we chose the Maximum Entropy classifier (MaxEnt) [3] which is relevant when the conditional independence of the features cannot be assured. This is particularly true in NLP where features are usually words which obviously are not independent in their use (they are bound by syntactic and semantic rules). Furthermore, MaxEnt allows the management of a high number of features. It relies on the maximum entropy principle. Hence, it requires to define a set of constraints for each observation and to choose the distribution which maximizes the entropy while remaining consistent with the whole set of constraints [14]. In this context of optimisation under constraints, it is mathematically proved that a unique solution exists and that an iterative algorithm converges towards this solution [25]. The classical formula of MaxEnt is the following:

$$P(y|x) = \frac{1}{Z} \exp\left(\sum_i w_i f_i(x,y) \right)$$

where $P(y|x)$ gives the probability that the individual x (here a relation) belongs to the class y (here *isA* or *not-isA* classes). Each individual is encoded as a feature vector. The function f_i is a function called *feature* which determines the constraints of the model. The weights w_i associated to each feature account for the probability to belong to a class. Z is a normalization constant which ensures that the sum of probabilities of one individual is equal to 1.

To estimate the parameter values $\hat{w}$, we use the likelihood function that aims at determining the best estimators:

$$\hat{w} = argmax \sum_j log(P(y_j|x_j))$$

where the (x_j, y_j) belongs to the set of training data. We used the OpenNLP (version 1.5.0) implementation of the MaxEnt algorithm[4].

4   Experiments

Our experiments were carried out on the French Wikipedia corpus aiming at enriching French DBpedia, using BabelNet as external semantic resource. These choices are motivated by the fact that (1) semantic resources targeting French language are scarce (French DBpedia is about 20,000 times poorer than DBpedia in English); (2) BabelNet [23] is a multilingual network of concepts and named entities that results from the automatic integration of various background knowledge resources (WordNet, Open Multilingual WordNet, Wikipedia, GeoNames, WoNef, etc.); and the learning knowledge base (BabelNet) and the learning text (Wikipedia) are aligned, as recommended by the method. While in BabelNet some mappings (Wikipedia-WordNet) have been manually checked, YAGO [29] assures a better accuracy of the whole knowledge base. However, we choose BabelNet due to its better coverage of French. It consists of about 14 million entries, including concepts and named entities. Using BabelNet publicly available resource allows for a reproducible approach. We used BabelNet 3.7 version.

4.1   Corpus

We built a corpus from a set of enumerative structures extracted from the 2016 dump of French Wikipedia pages. We have used the WikiExtractor tool[5] for

---

[4] http://opennlp.apache.org/.
[5] https://github.com/attardi/wikiextractor.

extracting plain text of vertical lists based on HTML tags of lists. We then pre-processed the extracted structures by (1) removing the (multiple) malformed lists; (2) reducing the primer to its last sentence, when the WikiExtractor has extracted a whole paragraph as a primer; (3) reformatting each enumerative structure according to the XML schema we defined; and (5) annotating the corpus with BabelNet label concepts and processing the corpus using Tokenizer, SentenceSplitter, TreeTagger, Gazetteer tools available in the GATE system[6]. This resulted in a corpus of 75446 annotated enumerative structures.

4.2   Learning Examples

From the corpus, 134170 examples were built (2766 positive examples and 131404 negative examples), as the method described in Sect. 3.1:

- an example is positive if $Term_1$ (present in the primer) and $Term_2$ (present in an item) are linked by a direct hypernym relation in BabelNet. We could observe that, given the polysemous nature of terms, considering a high path in the network between them introduce noise. We have then restricted to length 1 the path for classifying the example as positive;
- an example is negative if no path of length lower than 3 exists between $Term_1$ and $Term_2$ in BabelNet. This relaxes the assumption in Sect. 3.1, where examples are assumed to be negative if the relation is simply missing in the resource. From an empirical analysis, we fix to 3 the path length. We could observe that, even if two terms are linked in the resource (with a path length higher than 3), this link may not reflect a hierarchical relation given the polysemous nature of the terms (terms loosely related).

We thus built a training set of 3688 examples (1844 positive and 1844 negative examples) and a test set made of 1844 examples (922 positive and 922 negative examples). Examples have been randomly chosen among the initial sets of positive and negative examples.

4.3   Evaluation Setting

We evaluated our approach on the test set and on 2 reference corpora. These reference corpora have been used by [8] for evaluating their supervised learning approach intended to also identify hypernym relations from enumerative structures. To the best of our knowledge, this is the only corpus of same nature available for comparison. Each reference corpus concerns a set of Wikipedia pages having the same topic, respectively *Computer science* and *Transport*. They have been annotated with terms obtained from both YaTeA and Acabit term extractors. In that work, the results have been reported only in terms of precision on the top 500 hypernym relations extracted. Here, we have used these reference corpora and the reported results as baseline.

---

[6] https://gate.ac.uk/sale/tao/splitch6.html#chap:annie.

The reference sets correspond to examples built from these annotated reference corpora. We have produced several learning models, varying the different features, and with different sizes of sentence. A linear regression analysis of features gives features listed in Table 1 as discriminant. We keep the model (we named DLM for Distant Learning Model) taking into account these features.

4.4 Results and Discussion

Table 2 presents the results of our approach considering the test set, in terms of precision, recall, F-measure and accuracy. Table 3 presents those considering the reference corpus, in terms of precision. We can observe good values of precision and recall on the test set, while observing varying results in terms of precision on the two reference sets. The low performance of our approach on the *Transport* corpus can be explained by two main reasons. First, this corpus contains several contextual spatial relations, which are expressed using nested VES, where the context is expressed in the primer of one of these nested VES. However, our approach takes the VES independently of each other and hence can not correctly deal with this contextual parameter. Second, these VES are generally composed of numerous items. For the *Computer* corpus our approach outperforms the baseline. Overall, we obtain a precision up to 0.62.

Table 2. Results for the test set for all features of Table 1.

	Precision	Recall	F-measure	Accuracy
DLM on the test set	0.73	0.83	0.78	0.76

Table 3. Results for the reference set for all features of Table 1.

	Precision
DLM on Computer reference set	0.73
DLM on Transport reference set	0.51
Baseline on Computer reference set	0.6
Baseline on Transport reference set	0.6

We could identify some sources of noise in the learning process. First, we could observe that the external resource used here is not exhaustive, which may lead to the generation of false negative examples. That goes against the hypothesis of distant learning approach. Second, false positive examples are introduced due to the fact that the term ambiguity is propagated when exploring the network. Third, the knowledge may be expressed in a different way according to the language. In fact, we can observe cycles in the French network. For instance, the cycle "microprocessor" is a "microprocessor" in the French network does not exist in the English one.

Besides that, our approach is able to correctly identify the hypernym relations between textual entities (primer, item) that are not contiguous in the text, such as the set of hypernym relations in Fig. 1. These kinds of relations can not be in fact correctly treated by the classical NLP parsers. Furthermore, we can observe that the model is able to correctly identify the cases of head modifiers, and identifies hypernym relations such as (*Ministères, Ministère de la Sécurité publique*), (*Ministères, Ministère de la Supervision*), (*Ministères, Ministère de la Justice*), as from the VES in Fig. 4.

Ministres et Commissions

- Ministre de la Scurit publique
- Ministre de la Supervision
- Ministre de la Justice

Fig. 4. Hypernym relations identified from head modifiers.

4.5 DBpedia Enrichment

We have evaluated how much our approach could enrich DBpedia with the extracted hypernym relations. These relations contribute to enrich DBpedia in two ways: terms participating in the relations and relations themselves. To do so, we checked the presence/absence in DBpedia of them. The list of checked relations comes from the set of 307 true positive (TP) relations classified by our training model (with a confidence ≥ 0.5) on the reference corpus (168 TP from the *Computer* corpus and 139 TP from the *Transport* corpus).

First of all, we checked how many of the annotated terms are present in DBpedia. For that, we followed two strategies: (i) using a SPARQL query with an exact match between the relation terms and labels of DBpedia resources and (ii) using the DBpedia Spotlight service[7], a tool for automatically annotating mentions of DBpedia resources in texts [7]. We have used the Docker available for French[8]. With the first strategy, for the *Computer* corpus, we found 20 (out of 192) terms in DBpedia, against 9 (out of 168) terms from the *Transport* corpus. Using DBpedia Spotlight, with a confidence of 1 and a support of 20, we found only 3 out of 192 terms from the *Computer* corpus against 6 out of 168 terms from the *Transport* corpus. All of these terms referring to named entities. With a confidence of 0.6, we found 40 terms from the *Computer* corpus and 49 from the *Transport* corpus. However, wrong correspondences have been

---

[7] https://www.DBpedia-spotlight.org/.

[8] https://github.com/DBpedia-spotlight/spotlight-docker/tree/master/nightly-build/french.

identified lowering the confidence, as somehow expected. This shows that most of the annotated terms from the reference corpus can in fact enrich the resource.

With respect to the 307 TP relations annotated by our model, Table 4 shows the number of relations existing in DBpedia with respect to the presence of their terms in the resource. We can observe that, although some terms participating in the identified relations are present in the resource, only 4 of them participate in the same relation (Spotlight conf = 0.6 in Table 4). Looking at the number of TP relations present in DBpedia, 99% of them are not present in DBpedia. These results confirm that the Wikipedia pages, which are under-exploited by Wikipedia extractors, provide rich hypernym relations other than those found in structured elements (infoboxes, categories, etc.).

Table 4. Presence of relations and their corresponding terms in DBpedia.

	2 terms in DBpedia	Only $Term_1$	Only $Term_2$	None them	Number of present relations
Computer (exact match)	0	17	2	149	0
Transport (exact match)	0	5	3	131	0
Computer (Spotlight conf = 1)	0	6	0	162	0
Transport (Spotlight conf = 1)	0	3	0	136	0
Computer (Spotlight conf = 0.6)	1	35	3	129	0
Transport (Spotlight conf = 0.6)	3	41	2	93	2

5 Related Work

Our approach is related to three main fields of study, whose main related works are discussed in the following.

Enumerative Structures. Firstly, concerning the works on ES, we can mention typologies such as the one proposed by Vergez *et al.* [31], where the items can be present or not in the primer (one-step vs. two-step), or that of Ho-Dac *et al.* [12] where ESs have been classified according to their level of granularity (intra-paragraphic vs. multi-paragraphic). Concerning VES (particularly studied in the context of text generation), Hovy and Arens [13] distinguish the list of items (set of elements of same level) from the enumerated list (for which the order of items is important), while Luc [19] proposes a typology that opposes parallel ES (paradigmatic, visually homogeneous and isolated) to non-parallel ES. This latter is based on the composition of the rhetorical model of Rhetorical Structure Theory (RST) [20] and Textual Architecture Model (TAM) [32]. Drawing inspiration from these works, we also proposed a typology of ES in [9] (we refer to this topology in Sect. 2.2) relying on its discursive properties. These are the discursive properties of paradigmatic VES we exploit in this work.

Hypernym Relation Extraction. Numerous studies have been done in this field and a relevant short overview of them can be found in [33]. The pioneering work of the linguistic methods is that of Hearst [11] which defined a set of lexico-syntactic patterns specific to the hypernym relation for English. This work has been adapted and extended to improve recall for instance with the concept of "star-pattern" [24], or by progressively integrating learning techniques. Snow *et al.* [28] and Bunescu *et al.* [5] apply supervised learning methods to a set of manually annotated examples. While the cost of manual annotation is the main limit of supervised learning, distant learning method consists in building the set of examples using an external resource to automatically annotate the learning examples. For instance, Mintz *et al.* [21] use Freebase as external resource in their distant approach for identifying around 102 different relations. They implement a multi-class optimized logistic classifier using L-BFGS with Gaussian regularization. Another way to avoid manual annotation is the bootstrapping which uses a selection of patterns to construct the set of examples [4]. Some of these works are based on distributional analyses [17].

Enriching Semantic Resources. With respect to the exploitation of Wikipedia for the construction and enrichment of semantic resources, several extractors have been developed to analyze each type of structured data in Wikipedia. Morsey *et al.* [22] developed 19 of such extractors that produce a formal representation of entities and relations identified within various structural elements from Wikipedia: abstracts, images, infoboxes, etc. Other works have targeted specific relations, mainly hypernym relations. For example, Suchanek *et al.* [29] used the User Generated Categories (UGCs) hierarchy of Wikipedia to build hypernym relations in the Yago knowledge base. Kazama and Torisawa [16] exploited the abstract part of the pages, whereas Sumida and Torisawa [30] extracted knowledge from the menu items. Recent works proposed the automatic creation of MultiWiBi [10], an integrated bitaxonomy of Wikipedia pages and categories in multiple languages. Still, extracted relations from the text in Wikipedia pages have been little used to feed DBpedia [27]. Hence, most of the knowledge from these pages remains unexploited.

Here, we target the extraction of hypernym relations from paradigmatic VES (P-VES), which are under-exploited in the literature aiming at enriching existing semantic resources. A previous approach with the same objectives, based on supervised learning and which exploit semantic properties of a P-VES when considering it as a whole semantic unit, have been proposed by [8]. In that context, a precision of about 60% has been obtained. Given the cost-intensive manual annotation of examples, the expertise required for this task, and in order to improve these results, we adopt a different approach based on a distant supervised learning algorithm, and for which P-VES are no longer semantically considered as a whole unit, but are split into N independent textual units (a textual unit is then composed of the primer and one item) if N is the number of items which compose the P-VES. This approach can be carried out on any corpus presenting structural and/or linguistic regularities, such as web documents, and it is language-independent. Indeed, the proposed approach relies on a multilingual resource that can be used for annotating a corpus and on shallow learning features whose extraction does not depend on deep language analyzers.

6   Conclusion and Future Work

This paper has proposed a knowledge extraction approach that exploits vertical enumerative structure, which are frequent in corpora and are rich sources of hypernym relations. They are however under-exploited by knowledge approaches aiming at enriching semantic resources. We applied a distant learning approach for extracting hypernym relations from vertical enumerative structures expressed in French Wikipedia pages, aiming at enriching the French DBpedia. The aim was at evaluating how hypernym relation extraction can take advantage of enumerative structures for enriching existing resources that have been constructed from the same basis. In that sense, we observed that 99% of the extracted relations could be used for enriching the French DBpedia.

As perspectives, we plan to extend our learning features with additional features such as semantic and distributional features and to deal with the disambiguation of terms, as well as to combine different external resources. We intend as well to apply term extractors in order to identify terms before identifying potential relations that can be used for enriching an existing semantic resource. Finally, we plan to exploit different ontology matching methods in order to integrate the extracted relations into the French DBpedia.

References

1. Asher, N.: Reference to Abstract Objects in Discourse: A Philosophical Semantics for Natural Language Metaphysics. SLAP, vol. 50. Kluwer, Dordrecht (1993)
2. Auer, S., Bizer, C., Kobilarov, G., Lehmann, J., Cyganiak, R., Ives, Z.: dbpedia
3. Berger, A.L., Pietra, V.J.D., Pietra, S.A.D.: A maximum entropy approach to natural language processing. Comput. Linguist. **22**(1), 39–71 (1996)
4. Brin, S.: Extracting patterns and relations from the World Wide Web. In: Atzeni, P., Mendelzon, A., Mecca, G. (eds.) WebDB 1998. LNCS, vol. 1590, pp. 172–183. Springer, Heidelberg (1999). https://doi.org/10.1007/10704656_11
5. Bunescu, R.C., Mooney, R.J.: A shortest path dependency kernel for relation extraction. In: Proceedings of the Conference on Human Language Technology and Empirical Methods in Natural Language Processing, pp. 724–731 (2005)
6. Bunescu, R.C., Mooney, R.J.: Learning to extract relations from the web using minimal supervision. In: Proceedings of the 45th Annual Meeting of the Association for Computational Linguistics (ACL 2007), Prague, Czech Republic, June 2007
7. Daiber, J., Jakob, M., Hokamp, C., Mendes, P.N.: Improving efficiency and accuracy in multilingual entity extraction. In: Proceedings of the 9th International Conference on Semantic Systems (I-Semantics) (2013)
8. Fauconnier, J.P., Kamel, M.: Discovering hypernymy relations using text layout. In: Joint Conference on Lexical and Computational Semantics, Denver, Colorado, pp. 249–258. ACL (2015)
9. Fauconnier, J.-P., Kamel, M., Rothenburger, B.: Une typologie multidimensionnelle des structures énumératives pour l'identification des relations termino-ontologiques. In: Conférence Internationale sur la Terminologie et l'Intelligence Artificielle - TIA 2013, pp. 137–144, Paris, France, October 2013
10. Flati, T., Vannella, D., Pasini, T., Navigli, R.: MultiWiBi: the multilingual Wikipedia bitaxonomy project. Artif. Intell. **241**, 66–102 (2016). (Complete)

11. Hearst, M.A.: Automatic acquisition of hyponyms from large text corpora. In: Proceedings of the 14th Conference on Computational Linguistics, pp. 539–545. Association for Computational Linguistics (1992)
12. Ho-Dac, L.-M., Péry-Woodley, M.-P., Tanguy, L.: Anatomie des Structures Énumératives. In: Traitement Automatique des Langues Naturelles, Montréal, Canada (2010)
13. Hovy, E., Arens, Y.: Readings in intelligent user interfaces. In: Automatic Generation of Formatted Text, pp. 256–262. Morgan Kaufmann Publishers (1998)
14. Jaynes, E.: Information theory and statistical mechanics. Phys. Rev. **106**(4), 620 (1957)
15. Kamel, M., Trojahn, C., Ghamnia, A., Aussenac-Gilles, N., Fabre, C.: A distant learning approach for extracting hypernym relations from Wikipedia disambiguation pages. In: International Conference on Knowledge Based and Intelligent Information and Engineering Systems, 6–8 September 2017, France (2017)
16. Kazama, J., Torisawa, K.: Exploiting Wikipedia as external knowledge for named entity recognition. In: Proceedings of the 2007 Joint Conference on Empirical Methods in Natural Language Processing and Computational Natural Language Learning, pp. 698–707 (2007)
17. Lenci, A., Benotto, G.: Identifying hypernyms in distributional semantic spaces. In: Proceedings of the First Joint Conference on Lexical and Computational Semantics, pp. 75–79. Association for Computational Linguistics (2012)
18. Lin, Y., Shen, S., Liu, Z., Luan, H., Sun, M.: Neural relation extraction with selective attention over instances. In: ACL (2016)
19. Luc, C.: Représentation et composition des structures visuelles et rhétoriques du textes. Approche pour la génération de textes formatés. Ph.D. thesis (2000)
20. Mann, W.C., Thompson, S.A.: Rhetorical structure theory: toward a functional theory of text organization. Text **8**(3), 243–281 (1988)
21. Mintz, M., Bills, S., Snow, R., Jurafsky, D.: Distant supervision for relation extraction without labeled data. In: Proceedings of the Joint Conference of the 47th Annual Meeting of the ACL and the 4th International Joint Conference on Natural Language Processing of the AFNLP, pp. 1003–1011 (2009)
22. Morsey, M., Lehmann, J., Auer, S., Stadler, C., Hellmann, S.: DBpedia and the live extraction of structured data from Wikipedia. Program Electron. Libr. Inf. Syst. **46**, 27 (2012)
23. Navigli, R., Ponzetto, S.P.: BabelNet: the automatic construction, evaluation and application of a wide-coverage multilingual semantic network. Artif. Intell. **193**, 217–250 (2012)
24. Navigli, R., Velardi, P.: Learning word-class lattices for definition and hypernym extraction. In: Proceedings of the 48th Annual Meeting of the Association for Computational Linguistics, ACL 2010, Stroudsburg, PA, USA, pp. 1318–1327. Association for Computational Linguistics (2010)
25. Ratnaparkhi, A.: Maximum entropy models for natural language ambiguity resolution. Ph.D. thesis, University of Pennsylvania (1998)
26. Riedel, S., Yao, L., McCallum, A.: Modeling relations and their mentions without labeled text. In: Balcázar, J.L., Bonchi, F., Gionis, A., Sebag, M. (eds.) ECML PKDD 2010. LNCS (LNAI), vol. 6323, pp. 148–163. Springer, Heidelberg (2010). https://doi.org/10.1007/978-3-642-15939-8_10
27. Rodriguez-Ferreira, T., Rabadan, A., Hervas, R., Diaz, A.: Improving information extraction from Wikipedia texts using basic English. In: Proceedings of the 10th International Conference on Language Resources and Evaluation (LREC) (2016)

28. Snow, R., Jurafsky, D., Ng, A.Y.: Learning syntactic patterns for automatic hypernym discovery. In: Advances in Neural Information Processing Systems 17 (2004)
29. Suchanek, F.M., Kasneci, G., Weikum, G.: Yago: a core of semantic knowledge unifying WordNet and Wikipedia. In: Proceedings of the 16th International Conference on World Wide Web, WWW 2007, pp. 697–706 (2007)
30. Sumida, A., Torisawa, K.: Hacking wikipedia for hyponymy relation acquisition. IJCNLP **8**, 883–888 (2008)
31. Vergez-Couret, M., Prevot, L., Bras, M.: Interleaved discourse, the case of two-step enumerative structures. In: Proceedings of Contraints In Discourse III, Postdam, pp. 85–94 (2008)
32. Virbel, J.: Structured Documents, pp. 161–180. Cambridge University Press, New York (1989)
33. Wang, C., He, X., Zhou, A.: A short survey on taxonomy learning from text corpora: issues, resources and recent advances. In: Proceedings of the Conference on Empirical Methods in Natural Language Processing, pp. 1190–1203 (2017)

The Utility of the Abstract Relational Model and Attribute Paths in SQL

Weicong Ma[1], C. Maria Keet[2], Wayne Oldford[1], David Toman[1(✉)], and Grant Weddell[1(✉)]

[1] Cheriton School of Computer Science, University of Waterloo, Waterloo, Canada
{w34ma,rwoldford,david,gweddell}@uwaterloo.ca
[2] Department of Computer Science, University of Cape Town, Cape Town, South Africa
mkeet@cs.uct.ac.za

Abstract. It is well-known that querying information is difficult for domain experts, for they are not familiar with querying actual relational schemata due to the notions of primary and foreign keys and the various ways of representing and storing information in a relational database. To overcome these problems, the Abstract Relational Model and the query language, SQLP, have been proposed. They are the theoretical foundations and ensure that explicit primary and foreign keys are hidden from the user's view and that queries can be expressed more compactly. In this paper we evaluate these theoretical advantages with user studies that compare SQLP to plain SQL as the baseline. The experiments show significant statistical evidence that SQLP indeed requires less time for understanding and authoring queries, with no loss in accuracy. Considering the positive results, we develop a method to reverse engineer legacy relational schemata into abstract relational ones.

1 Introduction

Writing and understanding queries, especially by domain experts, is well-known to have a steep learning curve. Therefore, four strategies have been proposed to alleviate this problem: either SQL is hidden behind a controlled natural language or a visual query language, or the relational or conceptual model is also shown as convenient overview of the database whilst querying in SQL. They have been shown to result in improvements over plain SQL at the database schema layer, demonstrating equal or fewer errors always in less time, and that a "good match of query language and database structure leads to better performance" [10] (see [3, 10] and references therein). A conceptual view (cf. SQL only) also enabled domain experts to invent new queries [4].

The major drawback of conceptual query languages is that most of them support only a subset of the full SQL and therefore have little uptake in industry. Querying with SQL and the relational model (RM) is one step up from the baseline of SQL on the SQL schema, but it still entails the drawback of premature resolution of identification issues (e.g., primary keys). In order to abstract away

© Springer Nature Switzerland AG 2018
C. Faron Zucker et al. (Eds.): EKAW 2018, LNAI 11313, pp. 195–211, 2018.
https://doi.org/10.1007/978-3-030-03667-6_13

from that, the notion of *referring expression types* has been proposed [1,2], which are object identifiers taken from a separate domain, D_{oid}, and included in each table in a schema as a `self` attribute. Each `self` is a single column with a functional dependency to an n-attribute ($n \geq 1$) identifier meaningful to the modeler. With this extension, the RM can be pushed up toward the conceptual layer into an *Abstract Relational Model* (ARM), which makes orthogonal those issues of identification [1,2], and approaches a conceptual data model through lossless projections (vertical partitioning). Yet, SQL can be retained fully for data manipulation. Moreover, since each `self` is a single column, foreign key joins can always be expressed more compactly as *attribute paths*.

Attribute paths enable seamless path queries that do not require declaring multiple SQL joins manually. *SQL with paths*, SQLP (an extension of full SQL), is such a path query language (extending SQL^{path} [2]) where the foreign key joins are expressed with sequences of dot-separated attributes, which is a longstanding feature of class-based conceptual models [9]. This results in shorter queries and thus fewer chances of making mistakes, and it affords explicit navigation across the ARM to the desired elements. These are advantages in theory. It is not known whether this holds also in practice, especially regarding path query languages. In fact, while multiple path query languages have been proposed, to the best of our knowledge, only PathSQL that collapses left outer joins has been evaluated [7], claiming shorter writing time and fewer errors cf. plain SQL.

We seek to shed light on this issue with, first, a user evaluation that compares SQLP+ARM against the baseline of SQL+RM, testing for both time to write and to comprehend a query and correctness of the written queries. The main outcome of the evaluation is that working with SQLP has been shown to be statistically significantly faster, with the same level of correctness. Therefore, we have devised a novel method that transforms a legacy RM into the richer ARM. This method resolves the issues of identification automatically thanks to the referring expression type assignment inferred during the construction of the ARM, which is identity resolving, and therewith is also capable of making certain implicit constraints of the RM explicit in the ARM, such as disjointness and class subsumption (backward compatibility from SQLP→SQL and ARM→RM is already possible and ARM may be reconstructed in a Description Logic [2]). We also show that the space of SQLP queries remains invariant with respect to vertical partitioning, so that domain experts can use SQLP over a conceptual-like view of an ARM schema while database administrators can view the same schema as tables with many attributes.

In the remainder of the paper, we present the background and the novel method first in Sects. 2 and 3 and subsequently the user evaluation in Sect. 4. We discuss related work in Sect. 5 and conclude in Sect. 6.

2   Background

We begin by introducing the *abstract relational model* (ARM), which is based largely on an earlier version presented in [2], and extended where indicated below. An ARM augments the underlying domain of concrete values assumed in the *relational model* (RM) with an additional abstract domain of entities.

Definition 1 (Tables and Constraints). Let TAB, AT, and CD be sets of table names, attribute names that includes `self`, and *concrete domains* (data types), respectively, and let `OID` be an *abstract domain* of *entities (surrogates)*, disjoint from all concrete domains. A *general relational model schema* Σ is a set of *table declarations* of the form[1] `table` T $(A_1\ D_1,\ \ldots,\ A_k\ D_k,\ \varphi_1,\ \ldots,\ \varphi_\ell)$, where $T \in$ TAB, $A_i \in$ AT, $D_i \in$ (CD $\cup$ {OID}), and φ_j are *constraints* attached to table T. We write $\text{ATTRS}(T)$ to denote $\{A_1,\ldots,A_k\}$ and $\text{TABLES}(\Sigma)$ to denote all table names declared in Σ. A_i is *abstract* if D_i is OID, and *concrete* otherwise, and `self` must always be abstract. In addition to attribute declarations "$(A_i\ D_i)$", a variety of constraints φ_j can occur in a table declaration of T, e.g.,

1. (*primary keys*) `primary key` $(A_1,\ldots,A_k)$
2. (*foreign keys*) `constraint` N `foreign key` $(A_1,\ldots,A_k)$ `references` T
3. (*inheritance*) `isa` T_1
4. (*disjointness constraints*) `disjoint with` $(T_1,\ldots,T_k)$
5. (*path functional dependencies*) `pathfd` $(\text{Pf}_1,\ldots,\text{Pf}_k) \to \text{Pf}$ $\qquad\qquad\square$

Primary keys and named foreign keys ("N" in item 2, above) are supported by standard SQL. Inheritance and disjointness constraints are only meaningful when `self` occurs as one of the attributes of T and each T_i, and are satisfied when all (resp. no) `self`-value occurring in T occurs as a `self`-value in some (resp. all) T_i in the inheritance (resp. disjointness) cases. Path functional dependencies are a generalization of functional dependencies introduced in [13] that allow *attribute paths* in place of attributes. An attribute path Pf is either `self` or a dot-separated sequence of attribute names excluding `self`, as defined in [2]. A path functional dependency is satisfied when any pair of T-tuples that agree on the value of each Pf_i also agree on the value of Pf. Finally, RM and ARM are obtained by restricting how tables and constraints can be declared:

Definition 2 (RM and ARM). In RM: attributes A_i can only be declared to be *concrete*, and only primary and foreign key constraints are allowed. In ARM, every table has the attribute `self` declared to be its primary key. Consequently, every foreign key constraint must use a single abstract attribute. $\qquad\square$

Example 3. A commonly used visualization of RM schemata for a hypothetical course enrollment application is given in Fig. 1: each rectangle is a table, labelled by name, containing the attributes defined on that table. Attributes above the line in a rectangle give the primary key and directed edges between tables show foreign keys. The same visualization approach is used for a counterpart ARM schema in Fig. 2, where abstract attributes are indicated with an '*'. The respective definitions for, e.g., the `CLASS` table are as follows:

---

[1] This is essentially the syntax for SQL's `create table` commands.

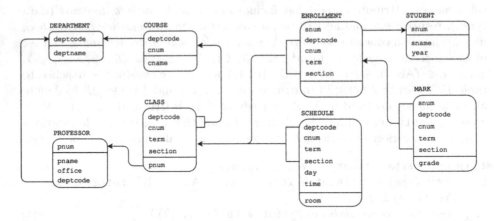

Fig. 1. Course Enrollment as an RM Schema.

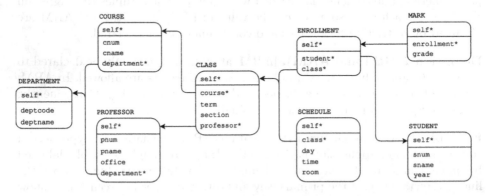

Fig. 2. Course Enrollment as an ARM Schema.

```
table CLASS ( deptcode INT, cnum INT, term STR, section INT, pnum INT,
    primary key ( deptcode, cnum, term, section ),
    constraint course foreign key ( deptcode, cnum ) references COURSE,
    constraint professor foreign key ( pnum ) references PROFESSOR )
table CLASS ( self OID, course OID, term STR, section INT, professor OID,
    constraint course foreign key ( course ) references COURSE,
    constraint professor foreign key ( professor ) references PROFESSOR,
    pathfd ( course, term, section ) → self,
    disjoint with ( COURSE, DEPARTMENT, PROFESSOR, STUDENT ),
    disjoint with ( ENROLLMENT, SCHEDULE, MARK ) )
```

Logical Implication in Schemas. Given $T \in \mathsf{TAB}(\Sigma)$ and constraint $\varphi \in T$ (possibly not occurring in Σ), we write $\Sigma \models (\varphi \in T)$ to say that φ always holds for T in *any* database over Σ. For example, the requirement of foreign key constraints to be unary in ARM yields the following deduction:

$$\{(\texttt{foreign key } (A) \texttt{ references } T_2) \in T_1, (B\ D) \in T_2\} \models (A.B\ D) \in T_1$$

in which the deduced constraint "$(A.B\ D) \in T_1$" states (with slight abuse of notation) that the attribute path "$A.B$" originating in T_1 always ends in D. It is easy to see that the deduction above can be generalized to yield longer paths.

ARM can be formalized in a Description Logic (DL), e.g., the PTIME decidable $\mathcal{CFDI}_{nc}^{\forall -}$ [11], where the problem of deciding when $\Sigma \models (\varphi \in T)$ holds in ARM schemata can be reduced to reasoning about logical consequence [2].

SQLP Queries. Since ARM schemata resemble RM schemata, simple revisions to the SQL standard yield SQLP: Fig. 3 shows a relationally complete fragment of the SQL query language grammar modified to allow attribute paths (definition for full SQL is analogous but beyond the limits of this paper). Example 4 illustrates the potential advantages of SQLP.

$\langle query \rangle ::=$ **select distinct** $x_1.\mathsf{Pf}_1\,[\textbf{as}\,A_1]$, $\ldots$, $x_m.\mathsf{Pf}_m\,[\textbf{as}\,A_m]$ $\langle body \rangle$
$\quad\quad\quad |\ \langle query \rangle$ **union** $\langle query \rangle$
$\langle body \rangle ::=$ **from** $T_1\ x_1$, $\ldots$, $T_n\ x_n$ $[\textbf{where}\ \langle pred \rangle]$
$\langle pred \rangle ::= x_1.\mathsf{Pf}_1\ op\ x_2.\mathsf{Pf}_2$ $\quad |\quad x.\mathsf{Pf}_1\ op\ c$ $\quad |\quad \langle pred \rangle$ **and** $\langle pred \rangle$
$\quad\quad\quad |\ \langle pred \rangle$ **or** $\langle pred \rangle$ $\quad |\quad$ **not** $\langle pred \rangle$ $\quad |\quad$ **exists (** **select** * $\langle body \rangle$)

Fig. 3. SQLP (fragment), extended from [2].

Example 4. Consider a query over the RM schema of Fig. 1, computing the *names of students who have experienced being taught by professor Alan John.*

```
select distinct s.sname as name
from STUDENT s, ENROLLMENT e, CLASS c, PROFESSOR p
where e.snum = s.snum and e.deptcode = c.deptcode
and e.cnum = c.cnum and e.term = c.term and e.section = c.section
and c.pnum = p.pnum and p.pname = 'Alan John'
```

The same query in SQLP over the corresponding ARM schema (Fig. 2) is:

```
select distinct e.student.sname as name from ENROLLMENT e
where e.class.professor.pname = 'Alan John'
```

Invariance of SQLP Under Vertical Partitioning. A hitherto unnoticed implicit benefit of ARM and SQLP, is SQLP's invariance under vertical partitioning, which we specify explicitly and precisely here.

Definition 5 (Vertical Partition). Let Σ an ARM schema and $T(\texttt{self OID}, A_1\ D_1, \ldots, A_k\ D_k, \varphi) \in \Sigma$. We say that an ARM schema Σ' is a *partition of Σ (with respect to T)* if

$$\Sigma' = \Sigma - \{T(\texttt{self OID}, A_1\ D_1, \ldots, A_k\ D_k, \varphi)\}$$
$$\cup \{T(\texttt{self OID}, A_1\ D_1, \ldots, A_i\ D_i, \varphi, \texttt{isa } T'),$$
$$T'(\texttt{self OID}, A_{i+1}\ D_{i+1}, \ldots, A_k\ D_k, \varphi, \texttt{isa } T)\}$$

where $T' \notin \mathsf{TAB}(\Sigma)$. □

Observe that vertical partitioning constitutes a lossless-join decomposition, and that every instance DB of Σ can be transformed to an instance DB' of Σ' with no loss of information. A repeated application of vertical partitioning ultimately leads to an ARM schema in which all tables are at most binary. This obtains a schema that comes very close to matching class and attribute-based conceptual models: a unary "self" table that may be viewed as a class, and binary tables that may in turn be viewed as attributes of the class. Our first result is that, for SQLP queries, answers are invariant with respect to such vertical partitioning:

Proposition 6. Let φ be a SQLP query over an ARM schema Σ, DB an instance of Σ and DB' a corresponding instance of Σ' a partition of Σ. Then $\varphi(DB) = \varphi(DB')$.

This feature allows users the freedom of formulating SQLP queries equivalently over a wide range of ARM schemata, as long as they are related by the "partition of" relation introduced in Definition 5. In particular, domain experts can now use SQLP over a conceptual-like view of a particular ARM schema while SQL programmers can think about the same schema in terms of tables with many attributes (this follows from the bi-directionality of Definition 5).

3   On Deriving ARM Schemata from RM Schemata

To present our second contribution, we need to introduce the notion of *referring types* and *referring type assignments* to tables in ARM that will be constructed by our algorithm together with the ARM schema. They enable one to execute SQLP queries formulated over the created ARM schema translations in [2].

Referring Expression Types and Assignments. To connect ARM and RM schemata, we use the notion of referring expression types from [2]: descriptions of how abstract OID values used to identify entities in an ARM schema are represented in a corresponding RM schema. In particular, this entails a *referring expression type assignment* for each T in the ARM schema, denoted RET(T), with the general form given by

$$T_1 \to (\mathsf{Pf}_{1,1} = ?, \ldots, \mathsf{Pf}_{1,n_1} = ?) ; \cdots ; T_k \to (\mathsf{Pf}_{k,1} = ?, \ldots, \mathsf{Pf}_{k,n_k} = ?)$$

where $k > 0$, and each attribute path $\mathsf{Pf}_{i,j}$ is defined on table T_i. Each subexpression separated by *preference indicators* ";" is called a *component* of the RET, and the "$T_i \to$" part its *guard*. The last component of the RET may not have its guard, which is then inferred to be "$T \to$". Assigning a RET of this form to each table in the ARM schema, is *identity resolving* if naming issues are sufficiently resolved to enable translating *any* SQLP query over the ARM schema to an equivalent SQL query over its corresponding RM schema [2].

Example 7. The RET for the table CLASS in Example 3 is given by

(course.department.deptcode $=?$, course.cnum $=?$, term $=?$, section $=?$)

stating that a class can be identified by a combination of the four values defined by the indicated paths. This yields the definition of the corresponding CLASS table in RM (see Fig. 1).

Observe that this simple kind of RET is still a strict generalization of traditional primary keys due to the possible use of the attribute paths, and that this example relies on this expressiveness. To see why more than one component might be needed, consider where self-values in the PROFESSOR and STUDENT tables could overlap (i.e., if professors could also be students). Were this possible, naming issues could still be resolved by choosing the RET STUDENT $\to$ (snum $=?$); (pnum $=?$) for PROFESSOR. A professor who is also a student would then be identified by their snum-value in preference to her pnum-value. (This would also require additional attributes to be added to an RM counterpart to the PROFESSOR table declaration, attribute snum for example; see [1,2] for details.)

From RM to ARM. In [2], a GENRM procedure is defined that computes an RM schema given an ARM schema and RET assignment as input. We now introduce a complementary GENARM procedure for reverse engineering RM schemata: given a RM schema Σ_1 as input, GENARM modifies Σ_1 to a corresponding ARM schema Σ_2 and computes an RET for Σ_2, for which GENRM(Σ_2, RET) re-obtains Σ_1 (up to names of re-introduced concrete attributes), and for which RET is *identity resolving*, which is a condition defined in [2] ensuring that any SQLP query over Σ_2 can be mapped to an equivalent SQL query over Σ_1.

GENARM modifies Σ and computes RET with the use of a stack S of tables in TABLES(Σ), and a *pending assignment* set PA. The latter consists of 4-tuples (T, Pf, T', A) that are used to incrementally compute RET as each table in S is processed. A 4-tuple asserts: *the primary key of T has component* $\mathsf{Pf} \circ A$, *and depends via foreign key join path* Pf, *on table T' having attribute A.* Here, "$\circ$" composes attribute paths, in particular: $\mathsf{Pf}_1 \circ \mathsf{Pf}_2$ denotes Pf_1 (resp. Pf_2) if Pf_2 (resp. Pf_1) is self, and $\mathsf{Pf}_1 . \mathsf{Pf}_2$ otherwise. GENARM is defined as follows:

(*initialize S, PA and RET*)

1. $S \leftarrow []$, $\mathsf{PA} \leftarrow \emptyset$.
2. For each $T \in$ TABLES(Σ) with primary key $(A_1, \ldots, A_m)$:
   2.1 $\mathsf{RET}(T) \leftarrow "T \rightarrow (A_1 = ?, \ldots, A_m = ?)"$.
   2.2 Add $(T, \mathsf{self}, T, A_i)$ to PA for $1 \leq i \leq m$.
3. Construct a directed graph $G(\text{TABLES}(\Sigma), E)$, where E is obtained as follows: for each $T_1 \in$ TABLES(Σ) with primary key $(A_1, \ldots, A_m)$, and each foreign key constraint "$\mathsf{foreign\ key}\ (B_1, \ldots, B_n)\ \mathsf{references}\ T_2$" from T_1: when $\{A_1, \ldots, A_m\} \cap \{B_1, \ldots, B_n\}$ is not empty and T_1 is not reachable from T_2 in G, add $T_1 \rightarrow T_2$ to E.
4. While there exists $T \in V_G$ where T's *outdegree* is 0:
   4.1 Push T on S.
   4.2 Remove T from G together with incident edges.

(*conversion to an ARM schema, and refinement of RET*)

5. While S is not empty, do the following:
   5.1 Pop T from S, where the primary key of T is $(A_1, \ldots, A_m)$.
   5.2 Add "($\mathsf{self\ OID}$)" to the definition of T.
   5.3 Let L consist of all tables $T_i \in$ TABLES(Σ), where $(A_{i,1}, \ldots, A_{i,k})$ is the primary key of T_i, for which $\{A_{i,1}, \ldots, A_{i,k}\} \neq \{A_1, \ldots, A_m\}$. Add disjointness constraint "$\mathsf{disjoint\ with}\ L$" to T if L is nonempty.
   5.4 For each $\varphi = $ "$\mathsf{foreign\ key}\ (B_1, \ldots, B_k)\ \mathsf{references}\ T_1$" from T, where the primary key of T_1 is $(C_1, \ldots, C_k)$, do the following:
      5.4.1 If $\{B_1, \ldots, B_k\} = \{A_1, \ldots, A_m\}$, then replace φ by specialization constraint "$\mathsf{isa}\ T_1$", assign self to NA, and proceed to 5.4.3.
      5.4.2 Assign the constraint name of φ to NA, and replace φ by foreign key constraint "$\mathsf{foreign\ key}\ (\mathsf{NA})\ \mathsf{references}\ T_1$".
      5.4.3 For each B_i, $1 \leq i \leq k$, if $C_i \in$ ATTRS(T_1) and if all remaining foreign key constraints φ' for T are free of B_i, then do the following:
         – Remove B_i from ATTRS(T).
         – If $B_i \in \{A_1, \ldots, A_m\}$, then for every tuple $t = (T_2, \mathsf{Pf}, T, B_i)$ in PA, for some T_2 and Pf: Replace "$\mathsf{Pf} \circ B_i = ?$" in $\mathsf{RET}(T_2)$ by "$(\mathsf{Pf} \circ \mathsf{NA}) \circ C_i = ?$", and replace t itself by $(T_2, (\mathsf{Pf} \circ \mathsf{NA}), T_1, C_i)$.
6. For each $T \in$ TABLES(Σ), replace the primary key constraint in T by path functional dependency "$\mathsf{pathfd}\ \mathsf{Pf}_1, \ldots, \mathsf{Pf}_m \rightarrow \mathsf{self}$", where $\mathsf{RET}(T) = $ "$T \rightarrow (\mathsf{Pf}_1 = ?, \ldots, \mathsf{Pf}_m = ?)$".

Computation of S in the initialization phase of GENARM encodes a total order that ensures RETs are free of cycles. RETs not free of cycles might happen otherwise, e.g., where two RM tables had complementary foreign keys to each other from their primary keys. Regarding the conversion to an ARM schema, note the replacement of foreign key constraints with unary counterparts or with specialization constraints (lines 5.4.1, 5.4.2), the addition of disjointness constraints (line 5.3), path functional dependencies (line 6). Both are necessary to ensure RET is ultimately identity resolving in the sense outlined above.

The addition of disjointness constraints between any pair of tables with primary keys that differ in any way are justified by virtue of the fact that an input RM schema has no way of detecting when respective primary key values could co-refer otherwise. For example, if students can also be professors, then it becomes impossible to compile a SQLP query for *department names of professors who are not students*.

The GENARM procedure achieves the first of our main goals:

Proposition 8. Let Σ_1 be a RM schema and Σ_2 and R the ARM schema and referring type assignment generated by GENARM(Σ_1), respectively. Then for every SQLP query φ and database instance DB over Σ_2 we have

$$\text{SQLPTOSQL}(\varphi)(\text{CONCRETE}(DB, R)) = \text{CONCRETE}(\varphi(DB))$$

where the functions CONCRETE and SQLPTOSQL map ARM instances and SQLP queries to their corresponding relational counterparts using the referring type assignment R.

Note that, for the above proposition to hold, it is essential that the referring type assignment R produced in Step 6 of GENARM is *identity resolving* in order to map equalities between OID attributes in Σ_2 to equalities over attributes in Σ_1. Case analysis of the procedure shows that indeed R is identity resolving.

4 User Evaluation

The aim of the user evaluation is to ascertain whether querying with the ARM and SQLP has advantages over querying with the RM and SQL. We expect that it will take less time to construct the SQLP queries and they may also have fewer errors, for one does not have to painstakingly declare all the joins individually (recall also Example 4), which reduces the cognitive load as well as the size of the query, which may affect comprehension and authoring of queries. Two variables measure the potential difference: time taken and correctness, which lead to the following null (H) and alternative (A) statistical hypotheses:

H_t : there is no difference between SQL and SQLP in the mean time taken;
A_t : reading and writing in SQLP is faster than in SQL in the mean time taken;
H_c : there no difference between SQL and SQLP in the mean correctness;
A_c : SQLP queries have a higher level of correctness than SQL queries.

Because we assume SQLP will show an advantage over SQL, they will be assessed against the one sided alternatives, rather than the weaker two-sided option.

4.1   Experimental Design

Methods. Participants were recruited from undergraduate Computer Science major students at the University of Waterloo (UW)'s third year database class (CS348) and graduate students in Computer Science from UW's Data Systems Lab. (The experimental design was reviewed and approved by the Human Research Ethics Committee of UW before recruitment of subjects.) The set-up of the experiment uses a cross-over design for the graduate students, and a simple comparison for the undergraduate students. Undergraduate students were treated differently, because only one-third of them turned out to have had SQL experience, whereas all graduate students had. Half of the undergraduates were randomly assigned to answer the six questions using SQLP (group U_p, $n = 5$) and the other half to answer the SQL questions (group U_s, $n = 4$). The graduate students answered all six questions using the cross-cover approach; they were randomly assigned to answer either first the SQL questions and then SQLP (group G_s, $n = 8$) and the other in reverse order (group G_p, $n = 7$). Of the undergraduates, only 2 were native English speakers (both had been randomly assigned to U_p); of the graduate students, 5 were native English speakers (4 of these had been randomly assigned to G_p).

The experimental protocol is as follows. All subjects were given five minutes to read instructions about the protocol and then 10 min to read instructions and examples on the use of SQL or SQLP, or both in case of the cross-over design. The subjects were not allowed to ask questions. Subsequently, each subject received each question sealed in its own envelope, noting that no student knew which query language would be required until their session began. Subjects recorded (to the nearest second) their start time on an envelope when they opened it as well as their completion time when their answer to that question was returned in the envelope. Questions Q1-Q6 (see below) were answered by all subjects in that order and no previous question could be consulted. The questions in a question set used only one of SQL or SQLP. All answers were given in hand-written form and subjects had no access to any other electronic device or information source. There was no time limit. Given the international nature of our students, the subjects also answered the question whether their first language was English or not. Upon completion of the experiment, each subject received a gift voucher.

Performance is measured on the time taken to complete each question and the correctness of each answer. Time taken is based on the self-reported time (see procedure). To measure correctness, answers for each question are independently scored by three assessors (authors WM, DT, and GW) and the scores averaged; the assessors are blinded to all aspects about the subject and the experimental conditions. The assessors agreed to score on a 4 point scale with half points allowed, where 0 meant to them completely wrong; 1: meant 'does not solve the question but the subject has grasped the basic concepts' (of SQL or SQLP); 2: meant 'the answer contains mistakes, but is on the right track and joined most of the required tables correctly'; 3: meant 'mostly correct, may only contain minor mistakes'; and 4: meant 'solves the question completely and correctly'.

Regarding the statistical analysis, different methods can be applied depending upon whether the results of all students are combined, or separated by graduate/undergraduate. We will analyze both, as both have advantages (more data points and the cross-over insights, respectively).

Materials. Six questions were devised to cover both query comprehension and authoring: Q1-Q3 present code in SQL or SQLP and subjects have to provide a written summary of the query in English (comprehension); Q4-Q6 present a query in English and subjects have to code the query in SQL or SQLP (authoring), alike depicted in Example 4. The comprehension and authoring tasks focus on conjunctive cases involving no more than six table variables, except for Q2 that includes a not exists predicate. Authoring tasks were designed to be progressively more difficult (requiring more joins), as were comprehension questions Q1 and Q3. Figures 1 and 2, without marking abstract attributes with '*', are the RM and ARM schemata used in the experiment. Details can be found in [8].

4.2   Results and Discussion

We will first present the combined results, and then the cross-over results.

Performance: all subjects combined. There are a total of 39 answers (20 for SQLP, 19 for SQL) for each performance measure with $30 = 2 \times 15$ from the graduate students ($|G_p|+|G_s|$) and $9 = |U_p|+|U_s|$ from the undergraduates. The fact that each graduate student provides values for both SQLP and SQL is of little concern since the experimental design randomly assigned half of them to using SQLP first and half to using SQL first, thus balancing any order effect. Figure 4 shows the estimated values and 95% confidence intervals for the expected (or mean) performance for the correctness (left), and time taken (right). In both plots, SQL results are solid colored red, SQLP dashed blue.

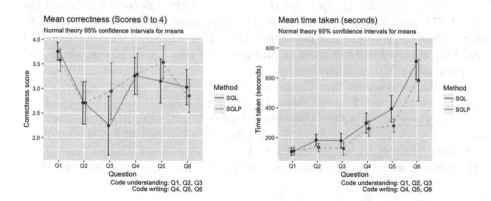

Fig. 4. Mean performance for all subjects: SQL solid; SQLP dashed.

Consider only the results for the comprehension questions Q1-Q3 for correctness. Looking at the SQL curve, we see increasing difficulty of these questions (as by design) in the decreasing mean values and increasing variability (interval length). The same pattern holds when performance on Q1-Q3 is measured by the expected time taken, though Q2 and Q3 are essentially indistinguishable.

Similarly, following the SQL curve for the authoring tasks given by Q4-Q6, we see increasing difficulty as measured by correctness and by time taken. For correctness, the difficulty shows as decreasing mean performance; for time taken, it shows dramatically as increasing mean time taken and as increased variability. A comparison of the SQL curves in both plots shows students taking less time and scoring more poorly on code reading (comprehension) questions and much more time but generally better scores on the code writing (authoring) questions.

More interesting are the results for the SQLP curve: except for Q1, *the expected time to complete each question using SQLP is consistently lower, and typically has smaller variability than, when using SQL!*

These estimates and intervals were based on standard normal theory (t-based confidence intervals), so to be conservative we also performed non-parametric two-sample Wilcoxon (or Mann-Whitney) tests comparing the sample times taken for SQL to those for SQLP for each question. The one sided test (H_t versus A_t) was performed giving the following p-values for each question: Q1 ($p = 0.63$), Q2 ($p = 0.021$), Q3 ($p = 0.018$), Q4 ($p = 0.27$), Q5 ($p = 0.009$), and Q6 ($p = 0.03$). Each p-value is the probability (assuming SQL and SQLP have the same distribution) of observing at least as large a difference as we did observe as measured by this test. The smaller the p-value is, the stronger the evidence against the null hypothesis (H_t) and in favor of the alternative (A_t). All but Q1 and Q4 would be judged to be highly statistically significant; *SQLP outperforms SQL in time taken.*

In contrast, *no statistically significant difference between SQLP and SQL in correctness was found* when the same tests were applied to the correctness scores. For correctness, the test yielded p-values for each question of Q1 ($p = 0.90$), Q2 ($p = 0.63$), Q3 ($p = 0.097$), Q4 ($p = 0.41$), Q5 ($p = 0.07$), and Q6 ($p = 0.77$). Such high probabilities mean that, as measured by this test, the data were consistent with the null hypothesis (H_c). If anything, in the two cases (Q3 and Q5) approaching statistical significance, the (left hand) plot shows SQLP outperforming SQL in correctness.

Finally, we consider how the performance fares with respect to English as first language or not. Figure 5 shows the confidence intervals for the mean time taken in these cases. Again, the expected time taken using SQLP is often the same or lower than when using SQL and often with less variability. Most striking are those cases where the student's first language was not English; except for Q1, they appear to perform more quickly using SQLP than they do using SQL.

Performance: Graduate students only. The randomized cross-over design allows us to work with the difference between performance results for each student on each question and performance measure. The differencing should reduce varia-

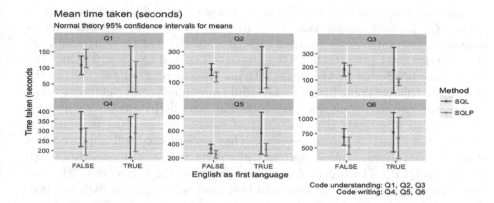

Fig. 5. Mean time taken estimates and confidence intervals by question separating the results of subjects based on whether their first language was English or not.

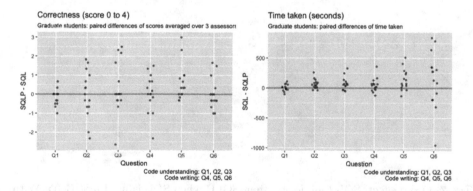

Fig. 6. Performance differences. Values above the horizontal line favor SQLP over SQL in both plots; random horizontal jittering separate points by question.

tion between students. Figure 6 shows the differences plotted by question for each performance measure. As before, with the possible exception of Q5 ($p = 0.00813$ for a one-sided test) where SQLP clearly outperforms SQL, *there is no statistically significant difference between SQLP and SQL observed for correctness* of the answers. Also as before, with the exception of Q1 *SQLP significantly outperforms SQL for both comprehension and authoring in time taken* with p-values (one-sided alternatives) by question: Q1 ($p = 0.500$), Q2 ($p = 0.00269$), Q3 ($p = 0.00488$), Q4 ($p = 0.0661$), Q5 ($p = 0.00413$), and Q6 ($p = 0.0820$). The last p-value is affected by the single outlying student near -1000 (Q6); as the plot shows, the remaining points for Q6 would have produced a significant value.

Because graduate students used both SQL and SQLP on the same questions, we can investigate the effect on performance of the order in which the methods were used. A priori, we expect that performance will improve when students faced the same questions again, albeit via a different model (RM+SQL or ARM+SQLP). The order effect was as expected for correctness, with the exception of Q5 where SQLP produced better answers than did SQL independently of the order. The results for time taken are shown in Fig. 7: as expected, when SQL is used first, students took longer to answer than when they subsequently used SQLP (points being above the horizontal line in the left hand plot) on the same questions. In contrast, when students used SQLP first, again with Q1 as an exception, their performance with SQL was surprisingly *not* a marked improvement on SQLP (points were *not* below the horizontal line in the right hand plot). That is, SQL still took longer than SQLP even though it was used *after* SQLP on the *same* questions.

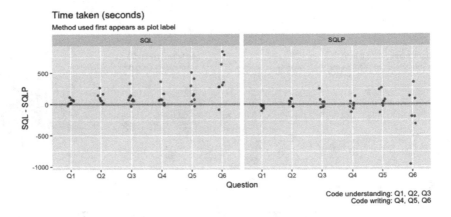

Fig. 7. Order effect: SQL took longer than SQLP when SQL is used first (left); With the possible exception of Q1, SQL takes about the same length of time when SQLP is used first (right). Random horizontal jittering used to separate points for each question.

Discussion of the Results of the Experiment. The results of the experiments demonstrated that noted theoretical advantages of SQLP over SQL translated to SQLP outperforming SQL in time to completion (being consistently lower and having less variation), i.e., A_t was accepted. H_c could not be rejected, although wherever observed differences approached statistical significance, they also favoured SQLP over SQL. Also, the learning curve for SQLP appeared to be low, given that no participant knew about SQLP or ARM before they began the experiment and were given only 10 min to learn about it.

There was no statistically significant difference in performance for Q1. It was the easiest question, and as difficulty increased, the differences between SQLP and SQL often increased (recall Fig. 4, right). Therefore, examining in further detail the effects of query difficulty levels and different types of queries is a promising direction for future experimental work, as it may refine insights into the practical advantages of using SQLP over SQL.

In other experiments that vary the model (or notation thereof) or the query language, a difference in either semantic or syntactic accuracy and in time take is observed when notation is the variable [3,6], or both when the query language abstracts away from plain SQL [7], and both when both are variables [10]. Our results on different query languages show a similar trend. The look-and-feel of the ARM diagram was made to look alike an RM one, in order to minimize the possibility that any difference observed could be attributable to the representation of the information rather than the query language. A future HCI experiment may be to devise more notations for ARM that have more or less vertical partitioning so as to examine those effects, which may then benefit also the accuracy.

5   Related Work

While many path query languages have been proposed, to the best of our knowledge, there has been only one experimental evaluation to compare it to a 'non-path' version. Junkkari and co-authors used PathSQL, which in their experiment showed that it reduces query writing time and have fewer errors cf. SQL [7][2]. PathSQL [12] constructs paths for queries over aggregation hierarchies as a way to represent a series of left outer joins more compactly. In contrast, SQLP's paths can be constructed over joins in the direction of the functional dependencies.

Due to lack of other related work, we broadened the scope on conceptual queries that still relate to relational models. It has been shown that models at a higher level of abstraction have either equal or higher accuracy (fewer semantic errors) in the queries and are always formulated in less time when querying with the aid of a relational or conceptual model [6,10]. Fewer syntax errors were observed when the aid was a textual relational model, but it was slower cf. a graphical depiction of the relational model, with no difference in accuracy of the queries [6]. It is not clear where the border lies between how detailed the graphically depicted relational model has to be to be optimal, but some parsimony seems to be favored especially for more complex SQL queries [3]. Thus, the results obtained in our experiment is in line with related, albeit different,

---

[2] as stated in their abstract; despite efforts, we were not able to obtain the full paper.

experiments. Examining Bowen et al's parsimonious and detailed diagrams [3], the ARM depicted in Fig. 2 may strike a good balance, but this deserves further assessment by HCI experts.

Querying at the conceptual layer has recently gained interest because of the relative popularity of Ontology-Based Data Access (OBDA). However, since SQLP is much more expressive than the queries one can use in a typical OBDA setting due to the *open world assumption*, OBDA techniques do not directly apply in our setting. However, note that many of the advantages of querying at the conceptual level are retained here. In particular, the ARM schema can be presented equivalently in an alternative graphical notation based on classes and features that resembles object diagrams [5] and can be formalized, e.g., in the description logic $\mathcal{CFDI}_{nc}^{\forall -}$.

6   Conclusions

Querying for information with the SQLP path query language and the Abstract Relational Model has been shown to be significantly faster than the baseline of SQL with the Relational Model, whilst maintaining accuracy. Thanks to the referring expression types and the lossless vertical partitioning it permits, an Abstract Relational Model can be made look like either a conceptual data model or function as a relational model. Therewith it can take advantage of both the benefit of conceptual queries and the full SQL support with the relational model within one formalism, whilst keeping an actual SQLP queries invariant in the face of such partitioning decisions. We have proposed a novel method to reverse engineer legacy relational models up to abstract relational models to facilitate its uptake, which, thanks to the automated analysis of the keys, also uncovers implicit constraints in the model, such as subsumption and disjointness.

References

1. Borgida, A., Toman, D., Weddell, G.: On referring expressions in query answering over first order knowledge bases. In: Proceedings of KR 2016, pp. 319–328. ACM (2016)
2. Borgida, A., Toman, D., Weddell, G.: On referring expressions in information systems derived from conceptual modelling. In: Comyn-Wattiau, I., Tanaka, K., Song, I.-Y., Yamamoto, S., Saeki, M. (eds.) ER 2016. LNCS, vol. 9974, pp. 183–197. Springer, Cham (2016). https://doi.org/10.1007/978-3-319-46397-1_14
3. Bowen, P.L., O'Farrell, R.A., Rohde, F.H.: An empirical investigation of end-user query development: the effects of improved model expressiveness vs. complexity. Info. Syst. Res. **20**(4), 565–584 (2009)
4. Calvanese, D., Keet, C.M., Nutt, W., Rodríguez-Muro, M., Stefanoni, G.: Web-based graphical querying of databases through an ontology: the WONDER system. In: Proceedings of ACM SAC 2010, pp. 1389–1396. ACM (2010)
5. Jacques, J.S., Toman, D., Weddell, G.E.: Object-relational queries over $\mathcal{CFDI}nc$ knowledge bases: OBDA for the SQL-Literate. In: IJCAI 2016, pp. 1258–1264 (2016)

6. Jih, W.J., Bradbard, D.A., Snyder, C.A., Thompson, N.G.A.: The effects of relational and entity-relationship data models on query performance of end-users. Int. J. Man-Mach. Stu. **31**(3), 257–267 (1989)
7. Junkkari, M., Vainio, J., Iltanenan, K., Arvola, P., Kari, H., Kekäläinen, J.: Path expressions in SQL: a user study on query formulation. J. DB Mgmt. **22**(3), 22p (2016)
8. Ma, W.: On the Utility of Adding an Abstract Domain and Attribute Paths to SQL. Master's thesis, University of Waterloo (2018)
9. Mylopoulos, J., Bernstein, P.A., Wong, H.K.T.: A language facility for designing database-intensive applications. ACM TODS **5**(2), 185–207 (1980)
10. Siau, K.L., Chan, H.C., Wei, K.K.: Effects of query complexity and learning on novice user query performance with conceptual and logical database interfaces. IEEE Trans. Sys., Man Cybern. **34**(2), 276–281 (2004)
11. Toman, D., Weddell, G.E.: On adding inverse features to the description logic $\mathcal{CFD}_{nc}^{\forall}$. In: Proceedings of PRICAI 2014, pp. 587–599 (2014)
12. Vainio, J., Junkkari, M.: SQL-based semantics for path expressions over hierarchical data in relational databases. J. Info. Sci. **40**(3), 293–312 (2014)
13. Weddell, G.: Reasoning about functional dependencies generalized for semantic data models. TODS **17**(1), 32–64 (1992)

Support and Centrality: Learning Weights for Knowledge Graph Embedding Models

Gengchen Mai[(✉)], Krzysztof Janowicz, and Bo Yan

STKO Lab, University of California Santa Barbara, Santa Barbara, CA, USA
`gengchen_mai@geog.ucsb.edu`

Abstract. Computing knowledge graph (KG) embeddings is a technique to learn distributional representations for components of a knowledge graph while preserving structural information. The learned embeddings can be used in multiple downstream tasks such as question answering, information extraction, query expansion, semantic similarity, and information retrieval. Over the past years, multiple embedding techniques have been proposed based on different underlying assumptions. The most actively researched models are translation-based which treat relations as translation operations in a shared (or relation-specific) space. Interestingly, almost all KG embedding models treat each triple equally, regardless of the fact that the contribution of each triple to the global information content differs substantially. Many triples can be inferred from others, while some triples are the foundational (basis) statements that constitute a knowledge graph, thereby *supporting* other triples. Hence, in order to learn a suitable embedding model, each triple should be treated differently with respect to its information content. Here, we propose a data-driven approach to measure the information content of each triple with respect to the whole knowledge graph by using rule mining and PageRank. We show how to compute triple-specific weights to improve the performance of three KG embedding models (TransE, TransR and HolE). Link prediction tasks on two standard datasets, FB15K and WN18, show the effectiveness of our weighted KG embedding model over other more complex models. In fact, for FB15K our TransE-RW embeddings model outperforms models such as TransE, TransM, TransH, and TransR by at least 12.98% for measuring the *Mean Rank* and at least 1.45% for *HIT@10*. Our HolE-RW model also outperforms HolE and ComplEx by at least 14.3% for *MRR* and about 30.4% for *HIT@1* on FB15K. Finally, TransR-RW show an improvement over TransR by 3.90% for *Mean Rank* and 0.87% for *HIT@10*.

Keywords: Knowledge graph embedding · Rule mining · PageRank

1 Introduction

A knowledge graph (KG) is a data repository that describes entities and their relationships across domains according to some schema, e.g., an ontology, and

C. Faron Zucker et al. (Eds.): EKAW 2018, LNAI 11313, pp. 212–227, 2018.
https://doi.org/10.1007/978-3-030-03667-6_14

is typically organized in the form of a graph, e.g., a directed multi-relational graph [11], such that the nodes represent (real-world) entities and edges represent their relations. As argued by Paulheim [9] there is no commonly agreed upon formal definition of the term nor a common technology stack. Examples range from the Google Knowledge Graph, Microsoft's Satori, and Freebase to KGs based on W3C technologies such as DBpedia, YAGO, and Wikidata. In fact, one can consider the entire Linked Data cloud as a global, densely interlinked knowledge graph. A statement in such KG is represented in the form of a triple. In the Linked Data community, these triples are often referred to as *subject-predicate-object* triple, while the knowledge graph embeddings community has settled on the term *head-relation-tail*; which we will use throughout this work to ease comparison to previous research. To give a concrete example, such triples may encode the statement that Santa Barbara is part of California (dbr: Santa_Barbara,_California, dbo:isPartOf, dbr:California) or that Santa Barbara has a certain population count (dbr:Santa_Barbara,_California, dbo:populationTotal, 88410^^xsd:integer). In the first case, the relation is a so-called object property, while the second case shows a datatype property.

Similar to word embedding which encodes each word as a dense continuous vector, knowledge graph embedding [1,8,12] aims at representing components of a knowledge graph including entities and relations into continuous vectors or matrices while preserving the structural information of the KG. Those learned entities and relations embeddings can be used in multiple downstream tasks such as KG completion [5], relation inference, relation extraction, knowledge fusion, question answering, query expansion, information extraction, information retrieval [7], and recommender system. Over the past years, multiple embedding techniques have been proposed based on different assumptions. The most actively researched category are translation-based models including models such as *TransE* [1], *TransH* [12], *TransM* [3] and *TransR* [5] which treat relations as translation operations in a shared (or relation specific) space. Recently, methods that measure the plausibility of triples by matching the latent semantics of entities and relations have been proposed such as *HolE* [7] and *ComplEx* [10]. [2]. Interestingly, most work on learning knowledge graph embeddings focuses entirely on object properties, and, therefore, we will restrict our examples and model to those as well[1]. Furthermore, most KG embedding models treat all triple equally, despite the fact that their information content, i.e., their contribution to the overall graph, differers substantially. Some triples act as foundational (basis) statements that cannot be reconstructed from others, while most other triples can be inferred. Put differently, the first kind of triples offer *support* for the second kind. Consequently, in order to emphasize the information content contribution of each triple to the knowledge graph and to learn a suitable embedding model, each triple should be weighted differently.

The research contributions of our work are as follows: we proposed a data-driven approach to measure the information content of each triple with

---

[1] Counter-examples include KG embedding techniques such as RESCAL which also includes literals [8].

respect to the entire knowledge graph. We apply rule mining and PageRank to estimate the *inference structure* of the current KG and derive the information content of each triple. Rule mining, here AMIE+ [4], enables us to measure the *support* between triples, while PageRank is used to determine the centrality of triples within a secondary graph created from the left-hand side and right-hand sides of the mined rules. The PageRank scores of this secondary graph are then used to compute triple weights which are then used in the loss function of the KG embedding model. In order to demonstrate the effectiveness of the proposed measure, we modify the translation-based KG embedding model TransE, TransR and the semantic matching model HolE by introducing a triple-specific weighting schema. We use two commonly used datasets, FB15K and WN18, and a link prediction task to show the effectiveness of our weighted model over other models. In fact, for FB15K our TransE-RW[2] embeddings model outperforms models such as TransE, TransM, TransH, and TransR by at least 12.98% for measuring the *Mean Rank* and at least 1.45% for *HIT@10*. Our HolE-RW model also outperforms HolE and ComplEx by at least 14.3% for *MRR* and about 30.4% for *HIT@1* on FB15K. In addition, our TransR-RW model also show an improvement over TransR by 3.90% for *Mean Rank* and 0.87% for *HIT@10*. The smaller improvement of our method over TransR may be caused by the higher complexity (larger number of parameters) of TransR.

The remainder of this paper is structured as follows. First, we discuss work related to our proposed method in Sect. 2. Then, in Sect. 3, we present the methods to measure the information content of triples and describe a weighted KG embedding model. Next, experiment results are presented and discussed in Sect. 4. Finally, in Sect. 5, we summarize our work.

2 Related Work

Here, we review existing work on knowledge graph embeddings, point out their advantages and disadvantages, and compare them with our proposed models.

KG embedding aims at learning distributional representations for components of a knowledge graph. Entities are usually represented as continuous vectors while relations, i.e., object properties, are typically represented as vectors [1,12], matrices [5], or tensors. More complex representation methods are more expressive while at the same time suffer from their higher complexity. In order to set up a learning problem, a scoring function $f_r(h, t)$ is defined on each triple/statement (h, r, t) which measures the accuracy of translation or the probability of the correctness of the current triple.[3] Finally, a loss function is defined to set up an optimization problem. In order to learn meaningful representations of entities and relations, we aim at minimize the loss while maximize the total plausibility of the observed triples.

---

[2] **R**ule-supported **W**eights.
[3] Recall that r stands for a given relation, h for head, i.e., a triple's subject, and t for tail, i.e., an entity in the object position.

Most KG embedding models treat a knowledge base as a collection of triples $S^+ = \{(h, r, t)\}$ and take each triple as one training sample. According to [11], KG embedding models can be classified into two groups: (1) *translation-based models* (e.g. *TransE, TransH, TransR, and TransD*) and (2) *semantic matching models* (e.g. *RESCAL, HolE* [7], and *ComplEx* [10]). We will focus on three models from these two groups: *TransE, TransR* and *HolE*.

Translation-based models treat relations as translation operations on the entity space or a relation specific space. The first and most well-known translation-based model is *TransE* [1]. The idea is inspired by the linguistic regularities discovered among the learned word embeddings. For example, the relationship between Angola and Kwanza is similar to the relationship between Iran and Rial which can be expressed by an equation of their corresponding word vectors: $w_{Rial} \approx w_{Kwanza} - w_{Angola} + w_{Iran}$ or $w_{Angola} - w_{Kwanza} \approx w_{Iran} - w_{Rial}$. A hidden translation vector is assumed to operate between Angola and Kwanza which represent the currency relation between a country and the currency it uses. As an analogy, given a triple (h, r, t), *TransE* assumes that relation r is an explicit translation operation which translates the head entity h to the tail entity t. In other words, it assumes $\mathbf{h} + \mathbf{r} \approx \mathbf{t}$ when (h, r, t) holds. Scoring is defined as the distance between $\mathbf{h} + \mathbf{r}$ and $\mathbf{t}$. In Eq. 1, $\| \cdot \|$ can be L_1- or L_2-norm.

$$f_r(h, t) = \| \mathbf{h} + \mathbf{r} - \mathbf{t} \| \tag{1}$$

Although *TransE* is effective at modeling one-to-one relations, the assumption that $\mathbf{h} + \mathbf{r} \approx \mathbf{t}$ when (h, r, t) holds is less suitable when dealing with one-to-many, many-to-one, and many-to-many relations. It also has difficulty handling reflexive and transitive relations. Based on the observation of these limitations of *TransE*, many translation-based models have been proposed to address these issues. *TransH* projects head entity h and tail entity t into the relation specified hyperplane which is defined by the norm vector $\mathbf{u_r}$ of the current relation r. Then the score function is defined as the distance between $(\mathbf{h} - \mathbf{u_r}^\top \mathbf{h} \mathbf{u_r}) + \mathbf{r}$ and $(\mathbf{t} - \mathbf{u_r}^\top \mathbf{t} \mathbf{u_r})$ in this hyperplane. In Eq. 2, $\| \cdot \|_2^2$ represents the square of L_2-norm.

$$f_r(h, t) = \| (\mathbf{h} - \mathbf{u_r}^\top \mathbf{h} \mathbf{u_r}) + \mathbf{r} - (\mathbf{t} - \mathbf{u_r}^\top \mathbf{t} \mathbf{u_r}) \|_2^2 \tag{2}$$

TransR and *TransD* share a similar idea as *TransH*; however, rather than project entities into hyperplanes, they introduce relation-specific spaces.

Besides allowing different relation-specific embeddings for each entity, another line of research is relaxing the overly restrictive requirement of $\mathbf{h} + \mathbf{r} \approx \mathbf{t}$. *TransM* associates each training triple (h, r, t) with a weight w_r which represents the degree of mapping of the corresponding relation r (See Eq. 3). The weight w_r is calculated by using (1) the average number of head entities per tail entity, denoted by $h_r pt_r$ (head per tail) and (2) the average number of tail entities per head entity, denoted by $t_r ph_r$ (tail per head). This means that a triple will receive lower weight if its relation r has more complex mapping properties. Our proposed method is similar to *TransM* in the sense that both of them give a weight to each triple. However, *TransM* uses the same weight for all triples with the same relation, while our method given each triple a different weight according to its information content wrt. the KG. We will show that this substantially improves over the results reported for *TransM*. It also addresses the issue that *TransM* essentially simply puts more weight on those triples that are more in line with *TransE's* underlying $\mathbf{h} + \mathbf{r} \approx \mathbf{t}$ assumption.

$$f_r(h, t) = w_r \parallel \mathbf{h} + \mathbf{r} - \mathbf{t} \parallel = \frac{1}{log(h_r pt_r + t_r ph_r)} \parallel \mathbf{h} + \mathbf{r} - \mathbf{t} \parallel \tag{3}$$

Another groups of KG embeddings models, so-called semantic matching models, measure the plausibility of triples by matching the latent semantics of entities and relations. Different models capture the interactions between latent factors of entity and relation embeddings in different ways. Here we discuss *HolE* as an example. The scoring function of Holographic Embeddings (*HolE*) is shown in Eq. 4. By using circular correlation operation $\star$ to compose entity representations, *HolE* is able to capture rich interactions between entity embeddings while maintaining its efficiency and simplicity. The non commutativeness of $\star$ also make it keep the asymmetry of the relations. σ is the logistic function and $-$ is used to align the interpretation of the scoring function with other models which implies that smaller score indicates a higher plausibility of the triple.

$$f_r(h, t) = -\sigma\left(\mathbf{r}^\mathsf{T}(\mathbf{h} \star \mathbf{t})\right) = -\sigma\left(\sum_{i=0}^{d-1} [\mathbf{r}]_i \sum_{k=0}^{d-1} [\mathbf{h}]_k \cdot [\mathbf{t}]_{(k+i) \bmod d} \right) \tag{4}$$

3   Methodology

Consider the problem of measuring the information content contribution of each triple to a KG; intuitively a triple $T_i = (h_i, r_i, t_i)$ will have a higher contribution if other triples can be inferred from it. These inferred triples can be derived either purely based on T_i or based on a conjunction condition including T_i and other triples. Hence, one way to interpret the information content contribution of a triple T_i is that if T_i is excluded from the current KG, a certain number of triples cannot be inferred from it any longer. For example, as for DBpedia, if the triple T_i (dbr:Santa_Barbara,_California, dbo:isPartOf, dbr:California) is excluded from DBpedia, hundreds of triples which can be inferred from it based on the transitive property of parthood, e.g., that University of California, Santa Barbara is part of California given that we know that it is located in Santa Barbara, will no longer be reachable. Put differently, number of inferred triples of triple T_i is a measure of the information content contribution of T_i to the KG. However, there are some shortcomings to such measure.

First, enumerating each triple and executing inferences on the entire KG may be computationally complex given a large graph and ontology (particularly using an expressive description logic). Second, this type of reasoning also requires a formal ontology in the first place and thus only applies to Semantic Web style knowledge graphs that use ontologies that explicitly make use of language features such as subclassing. In addition, *isolated triples* become a substantial problem. Isolated triples are triples in a KG which can neither be used to infer any another triples nor can be inferred by any triples. By using the method above, these triples will have a very low information content because they cannot infer any triples and excluding them from the KG will not affect the number of inferred triples. However, information theory tells us that those *isolated triples* should have a high information content as they cannot be compressed. Consequently, we need to go beyond the intuitive notion of information content for triples introduced above. At the same time, and to appeal to the broader KG community, we want to work buttom-up first, i.e. not rely on the existence of a strong formal ontology. In order to provide an automatic and general method for measuring the information content of triples, and as will be detailed below, we will use rule mining to estimate the *support* between triples and then measure the centrality of triples within a secondary graph formed by these support relations using PageRank. The result will be individual weights per triple that we will use in the loss function to learn embeddings.

Given a KG (the training dataset) represented as a set of triples $S^+ = \{(h_i, r_i, t_i)\}$. For each triple (h_i, r_i, t_i), its head and tail entity are $h_i, t_i \in E$ (the set of entities) and its relation is $r_i \in L$ (the set of relations). Our model measures the contribution of each triple to the global information content of the KG by investigating the inference relationships among these triples and use this measure to learn a suitable KG embedding model for the current KG. Our method can be divided into four steps: (1) rule mining; (2) rule instantiation; (3) triple inference graph construction and triple weights calculation; and (4) learning a weighted KG embedding model. Fig. 1 illustrates the first three steps of our workflow and each of these four steps will be described in detail below.

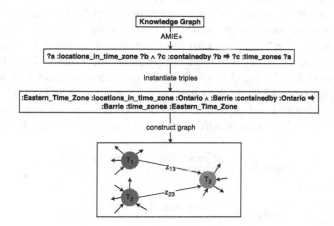

Fig. 1. The workflow of computing the information content of each triple in a KG

3.1   Rule Mining

Generally speaking, logical rule mining is a machine learning method to find rules in a KG that describe the common correlations between triples. Modern rule mining systems like AMIE and AMIE+ [4] aim at mining logical rules efficiently from large RDF-based knowledge bases. An atom in a Horn rule R_i is a triple whose subject or/and object is replaced by variables. A Horn rule R_i is composed of a head $r(x, y)$ and a body $\{B_1, B_2, ..., B_n\}$, where the head $r(x, y)$ is a single atom and the body is the conjunction of multiple atoms or just one atom [4]. Eq. 5 shows the general form of a Horn rule R_i where both $r(x, y)$ and B_i are atoms. Note that in $r(x, y)$, r represents a specific relation where x and y are subject and object who can be either real entities or variables. R_i can be abbreviated as $\overrightarrow{B} \Rightarrow r(x, y)$. We utilize AMIE+ for rule mining. The rule in the second box from Fig. 1 is an example of a mined rules from AMIE+.

$$R_i: \ B_1 \ \wedge \ B_2 \ \wedge ... \ \wedge \ B_n \ \Rightarrow \ r(x, y) \tag{5}$$

AMIE+ requires three parameters: a threshold $minHC$ of the head coverage of the mined rules, a maximum rule length $maxLen$, and a threshold $minConf$ for the PCA confidence score. We will describe each of them in detail below.

Given a rule $R_i: \overrightarrow{B} \Rightarrow r(x, y)$, the *support* of R_i is the number of correct predictions of rule R_i in the current KG, or, in other words, the number of distinct pairs of head and tail entities $\#(x, y)$ in the rule head among all the instantiations of the current rule. *Rule instantiation* is the process to substitute the variables in a rule with entities (constants) in the KG such that all instantiated atoms/triples in the rule head and rule body are in the KG. The result rules are called *grounded rules*.

Based on the definition of *rule instantiation*, a naive way to define how good a mined rule is can be computed as the number of instantiation of the current rule over the size of the current KG (See Eq. 6). In Eq. 6, $\#(S^+)$ represents the number of triples in S^+. We refer to it as *frequency* in the following. Instead of using *frequency*, AMIE+ uses *head coverage* which is defined as the *support* of a rule divided by the number of statements with rule head relation r (See Eq. 7). Each rule from AMIE+ has a head coverage value. The parameter $minHC$ controls the minimum head coverage value of the mined rules such that all rules with head coverage less than $minHC$ will be excluded. The default is 0.01.

$$freq(R_i) = \frac{\#(instatiate(\overrightarrow{B} \Rightarrow r(x, y)))}{\#(S^+)} \tag{6}$$

$$hc(R_i) = \frac{support(\overrightarrow{B} \Rightarrow r(x, y))}{\#(r)} \tag{7}$$

Second, $maxLen$ restricts the maximum length of the mined rules. The length of rules is defined as the number of atoms in the rule including head and body. For example, the rule in the second box in Fig. 1 has length 3. A longer rule length means a larger rule search space for AMIE+. The default $maxLen$ is 3.

Third, *minConf* controls the minimum PCA confidence scores of mined rules. Head coverage does not take into consideration false predictions of the mined rule, while the confidence scores provide a way to obtain counterexamples for the rule mining. The mined rules are associated with two confidence scores - *standard confidence score* (Closed-World Assumption) and *PCA confidence score* (Partial Completeness Assumption) - which describe how confident AMIE+ is about the currently mined rules based on the observed triples in the KG. The higher the confidence scores is, the more likely the rule will make correct predictions. Further detail for these two confidence scores, are described in [4]. AMIE+ utilizes the PCA confidence scores and excludes rules whose confidence scores are less than *minConf*, with a default of 0.1.

Head coverage, standard confidence score, and PCA confidence score are three ways to represent the inference power of a rule. Although these three parameters can take other values than the default values, [4] does not suggest to do so. Hence, our model utilizes the default parameter setting of AMIE+.

3.2 Rule Instantiation

After rule mining is applied to get the inference relationship between triples, the mined rules are instantiated to get grounded rules. As per the definition of *rule instantiation* above, variables in each atom need to be instantiated by entities in the KG such that these entities satisfy both the rule head and rule body. As for rule R_k in the second box from Fig. 1, the instantiating process can be understood as sending a SPARQL SELECT query to the original KG in which atoms in both the rule head and rule body are the graph patterns in this query.

The third box in Fig. 1 shows one example of the grounded rule for R_k. Note that each mined rule is associated with four rule predication quality/correctness measures: *frequency, head coverage, standard confidence score*, and *PCA confidence score*. These measures can also be used in their grounded rules to indicate the likelihood of correct predication.

3.3 Triple Inference Graph Construction and Weights Calculation

Given a rule $R_h : B_1 \wedge B_2 \Rightarrow B_3$, one of its grounded rules is $R_{hj} : T_1 \wedge T_2 \Rightarrow T_3$ with *frequency* f_{freq}, *head coverage* f_{hc}, *standard confidence score* f_{cwa}, and *PCA confidence score* f_{pca}. After applying rule mining and rule instantiation, we are able to obtain the inferencing relationships between different triples. In order to provide a holistic view of these rules and the relationships between triples, we construct a triple inference graph based on these grounded rules from different rules. Each triple (statement) is represented as a node and each directed edge e_{ij} from node T_i to node T_j indicates that statement T_i infers statement T_j. As for $R_{hj} : T_1 \wedge T_2 \Rightarrow T_3$, two edges can be obtained: e_{13} from nodes T_1 to T_3 and e_{23} from nodes T_2 to T_3. The weights of each edges are derived from the four rule predication correctness measures f_{freq}, f_{hc}, f_{cwa}, and f_{pca}. Note that one triple T_j can be the rule heads of many grounded rules which may or may not instantiated from the same rules. As for those grounded rules, another triple T_i can appear in the rule bodies of some of them. Let GR_1, GR_2, ..., GR_k, ..., GR_r be all grounded rules which are instantiated from the mined rules from AMIE+. Let f_1, f_2, ..., f_k, ..., f_r be one rule predication correctness measure from those four measures. All grounded rules should use the same type of measures. Let L_1, L_2, ..., L_k, ..., L_r be the rule lengths of those grounded rules. α_{ik} is an indicator function to indicate whether triple T_i appear in the rule body of grounded rule GR_k ($\alpha_{ik} = 1$ when T_i is in the rule body of GR_k; 0 otherwise). β_{jk} is an indicator function to indicate whether triple T_j is the rule head of grounded rule GR_k ($\beta_{jk} = 1$ when T_j is the rule head of GR_k; 0 otherwise). Then the equation to calculate edge weight z_{ij} of e_{ij} from triple T_i to triple T_j is shown in Eq. 8.

$$z_{ij} = \sum_{i=1}^{r} \alpha_{ik}\beta_{jk}\frac{f_k}{L_k - 1} \tag{8}$$

Following the method above, we construct a secondary triple inference graph based on those grounded rules. The third and fourth boxes of Fig. 1 illustrate the graph construction process. In this triple inference graph, the more incoming links a triple has, the more likely this statement is able to be inferred by other statements which implies that this triple has less information, at least from an information theoretic compression perspective. Information content is calculated as the negative logarithm of the probability. The probability in this context is the probability of inferencing a triple (statement) in our triple inference graph. In order to obtain the inferencing probability of each triple in the graph, we model it as a stochastic process and more specifically a Markov Chain. Each state in the Markov Chain corresponds to a node in our graph and the transition probability between states are determined by the number of links/edges and edge weights between nodes. E.g., if there are 5 outgoing links/edges from node T_i and one of them connects to node T_j, then the transition probability from node T_i to T_j is 0.2 if those 5 edges have equal weights. The stationary distribution of this Markov Chain gives us the inferencing probability of each triple in the graph.

However, this method only works when the graph (Markov Chain) is strongly connected, meaning every node can be reach from any other node in the graph, otherwise the stationary distribution may not be unique. This requirement translated into our case would imply that every statement can be inferred by any other statement, which is less likely to be true. Disconnected components, dangling links and loops are common in our inferencing graph. To deal with these cases, we use the PageRank algorithm which solves these issues by providing a teleport probability which allows the random walker to jump to a random node in the graph with a certain probability at each time step. In this case, the stationary distribution of the Markov Chain with the teleport probability becomes unique again. We use this stationary distribution as our inferencing probability to calculate the information content. Disconnected or isolated triples will have a lower inferencing probability, thus possessing richer information content.

In this work, an edge weighted PageRank is applied to the constructed triple inference graph. The final weight of each triple is calculated based on the

PageRank value PR_i of each node/triple (See Eq. 9). Here $\frac{\#(S^+)}{\sum -log_2(PR_i)}$ is a normalization factor to make the mean value of result triple weights to be 1.0.

$$w_i = -log_2(PR_i) \times \frac{\#(S^+)}{\sum -log_2(PR_i)} \tag{9}$$

3.4   Learning a Weighted Knowledge Graph Embedding Model

After obtaining the triple weights, we deploy a weighted KG embedding model based on multiple existing models (*TransE*, *TransR*, and *HolE*). The training dataset is the observed triples in S^+. The plausibility scoring function of a triple $T_i = (h_i, r_i, t_i) \in S^+$ with weight w_i can be any scoring function of any translation-based models (*TransE*, *TransH*, *TransR*, and *TransD*) or semantic matching models (*TATEC*, *DistMult*, and *HolE*) as long as these models use pairwise ranking loss functions to set up the learning task. The plausibility scoring functions of *TransE* and *HolE* are shown in Eqs. 1 and 4. We will denote the weighted version of *TransE*, *TransR* and *HolE* as *TransE-RW*, *TransR-RW* and *HolE-RW*.

To learn the KG embedding, we use the pairwise ranking loss function as other models do. However, in the loss function, we multiply w_i with the subtraction value between the plausibility score of triple $T_i = (h_i, r_i, t_i)$ and the score of one of T_i's corrupted triples $T_i' = (h_i', r_i, t_i')$ (See Eq. 10). The intuition is that as in the margin idea in support vector machine, the pairwise ranking function aims to make the observed triples well separated from the corrupted triples in the plausibility score space and $f_r(h_i, t_i) - f_r(h_i', t_i')$ is a measure of the distinction degree or distance for triple T_i. Since different triples have different contribution to the global information content of the KG, the loss function should consider T_i more if it has larger information content.

$$\mathcal{L} = \sum_{(h_i, r_i, t_i) \in S^+} \sum_{(h_i', r_i, t_i') \in S^-_{(h_i, r_i, t_i)}} \left[\gamma + w_i \big(f_r(h_i, t_i) - f_r(h_i', t_i') \big) \right]_+ \tag{10}$$

The set of corrupted triples for triples $T_i' = (h_i', r_i, t_i')$ is constructed according to Eq. 11. Two negative sampling methods are used: (1) replacing either the triple's head or tail entity with a random entity (denoted as *unif.*) and (2) the negative sampling method proposed by [12] which uses head per tail $h_r pt_r$ and tail per head $t_r ph_r$ (denoted as *bern.*). The second method will corrupt a triple by replacing the head with probability $\frac{t_r ph_r}{t_r ph_r + h_r pt_r}$ and corrupt a triple by replacing the tail with probability $\frac{h_r pt_r}{t_r ph_r + h_r pt_r}$.

$$S^-_{(h_i, r_i, t_i)} = \left\{ (h_i', r_i, t_i) \mid h_i' \in E \right\} \cup \left\{ (h_i, r_i, t_i') \mid t_i' \in E \right\} \tag{11}$$

As for *TransE-RW*, the same constraint as *TransE* has been applied during embedding model training which restricts the L_2-norm of the embeddings of entities to be 1. It prevents the loss from being trivially minimized by enlarging the norms of the embeddings of entities. We follow the same training process of

TransE. First, the entity embedding matrix $\mathbf{E}$ and relation embedding matrix $\mathbf{L}$ are initialized by using uniform distribution $uniform(-\frac{6}{\sqrt{K}}, \frac{6}{\sqrt{K}})$ where K is the embedding dimension. Then, the relation embeddings are normalized before the training process begins. In each iteration, L_2 normalization has been applied to entity embeddings before gradient decent. The *adam* optimizer is used for the optimization. The same process is also utilized for *HolE-RW*.

4   Experiment

Two standard datasets - FB15K and WN18 - are used to evaluate all models. FB15K and WN18 are standard datasets which have been used to evaluate KG embedding models [1,5,12]. WN18 is extracted from WordNet in which entities are word senses and relations correspond to the lexical relationships between word senses. FB15K is a subset extracted from Freebase in which entities have at least 100 mentions in Freebase and also appear in Wikilinks dataset. Given the richer relational structure of FB15K, we expect a larger rule set, and, thus, a more visible difference to the baseline due to the learned weights.

First, we calculate the weights for each triple in the training datasets of those two datasets as described above. As for the rule mining step, we use AMIE+[4] as the rule mining system. Next, we construct the triple inference graphs based on these mined rules and apply edge weighted PageRank. As expected AMIE+ was able to identify substantially more rules for the Freebase dataset (41195) than for WordNet (140). The triple weights for each triple from the training datasets of FB15K and WN18 are calculated based on the PageRank values. Since there are four types of rule predication correctness measures (*frequency* f_{freq}, *head coverage* f_{hc}, *standard confidence score* f_{cwa}, and *PCA confidence score* f_{pca}), four different triple inference graphs can be constructed for each dataset based on different measures. This results in four different types of triple weights for each dataset which are indicated by *freq*, *hc*, *cwa*, and *pca*. For each dataset, we compute Spearman's correlation coefficients between each pair of triples weights. Tables 1 and 2 show the Spearman's correlation coefficients matrix of triples weights on WN18 and FB15K. As can be seen from Tables 1 and 2, the calculated triple weights from different methods are highly correlated (at least 0.704 for WN18 and 0.788 for FB15K).

The computed triple weights are used in *TransE-RW*, *TransR-RW* and *HolE-RW* models as shown in Eq. 10. To show the effectiveness of our weighted model, we empirically evaluate *TransE-RW*, *TransR-RW* and *HolE-RW* together with related models by using a common link prediction task on these standard datasets by following the evaluation protocol of [1]. Given a correct triple $T_k = (h_k, r_k, t_k)$ from the testing dataset of FB15K (or WN18), we replace the head entity h_k (or tail t_k) with all other entities from the dictionary of FB15K (or WN18). If there are n entities in the current dataset, this triple corruption operation will result in n triples in which $n - 1$ triples are corrupted triples together

---

[4] https://www.mpi-inf.mpg.de/departments/databases-and-information-systems/
   research/yago-naga/amie/.

Table 1. Spearman's correlation coefficients between weights calculated by different rule predication correctness measures on WN18

ρ	freq	hc	cwa	pca
freq	1	0.704	0.899	0.879
hc	-	1	0.790	0.779
cwa	-	-	1	0.889
pca	-	-	-	1

Table 2. Spearman's correlation coefficients between weights calculated by different rule predication correctness measures on FB15K

ρ	freq	hc	cwa	pca
freq	1	0.788	0.877	0.855
hc	-	1	0.805	0.848
cwa	-	-	1	0.972
pca	-	-	-	1

with the correct triple T_k. The plausibility scores for each of those n triples can be computed based on the plausibility score functions of *TransE, HolE* (See Eqs. 1 and 4) and *TransR-RW* by using the trained entity and relation embeddings. By ranking the scores in the ascending order, we can get the rank of the original correct triple T_k. Note that some of the corrupted triples may also appear in the KG. For example, as for triple (dbr:Santa_Barbara,_California, dbo:isPartOf, dbr:California), if we replace the head dbr:Santa_Barbara,_California with dbr:San_Francisco, the result corrupted triple (dbr:San_Francisco, dbo:isPartOf, dbr:California) is still in the DBpedia KG. These false negative samples need to be filtered out. We report both the original rank and the rank after filtering out those false negatives (denote as *Raw* and *Filter*). Aggregated over all triples in the testing dataset of FB15K (or WN18), multiple metrics are reported: (1) the *Mean Rank*; (2) the mean reciprocal rank *MRR*; (3) the proportion of ranks not larger than K (denoted as *HIT@K where K can be 1, 3, 10*). A KG embedding model with lower *Mean Rank*, higher MRR, and higher *HIT@K* is better. Note that different papers report different metrics. So we use different metrics for *TransE-RW, TransR-RW* (*Mean Rank, MRR*[5], and *HIT@10*) and *HolE-RW* (*MRR, HIT@1, HIT@3*, and *HIT@10*) to make our results comparable to the related models. RDF2VecGlove [2] also utilizes PageRank to facilitate RDF graph embedding learning. However, it applies PageRank on the original KG while we apply PageRank on the triple inference graph. RDF2VecGlove does not define a plausibility scoring function for each triple which make it difficult to directly apply RDF2VecGlove to the KG completion task.

We implemented the *TransE-RW, TransR-RW* and *HolE-RW* models using TensorFlow. Hyperparameters are selected using grid search. The hyperparameters we use for FB15K are: the embedding dimension $K = 50$, the margin $\gamma = 1.0$, distance norm $d = L_1$, and learning rate $\alpha = 0.0001$ for *TransE-RW* ($K = 80$, $\gamma = 1.0$, $d = L_1$, and $\alpha = 0.0001$ for *TransR-RW*; $K = 200$, $\gamma = 1.0$, and $\alpha = 0.002$ for *HolE-RW*). The hyperparameters we use for WN18 are: the

---

[5] [7] points out that *MRR* is less sensitive to outliers than *Mean Rank*. So we also report *MRR* in *TransE-RW* and *TransR-RW*.

Table 3. Link Prediction Result of *TransE-RW* and *TransR-RW* (*unif* indicates using random negative sampling method; *bern* indicates using the method proposed by [12])

DataSet	WN18						FB15K					
Metric	Mean Rank		MRR		HIT@10		Mean Rank		MRR		HIT@10	
	Raw	Filter	Raw	Filter	Raw	Filter	Raw	Filter	Raw	Filter	Raw	Filter
TransE [1]	263	251	-	-	75.4	89.2	243	125	-	-	34.9	47.1
TransM [3]	293	281	-	-	75.7	85.4	197	94	-	-	44.6	55.2
TransH (unif.) [12]	318	303	-	-	75.4	86.7	211	84	-	-	42.5	58.5
TransH (bern.) [12]	401	388	-	-	73.0	82.3	212	87	-	-	45.7	64.4
TransR (unif.) [5]	232	**219**	-	-	78.3	91.7	226	78	-	-	43.8	65.5
TransR (bern.) [5]	238	225	-	-	**79.8**	92.0	198	77	-	-	48.2	68.7
TransE-RW$_{freq}$ (unif.)	298	286	0.361	0.487	77.8	91.4	216	69	0.225	0.422	46.8	69.4
TransE-RW$_{freq}$ (bern.)	**231**	**219**	**0.391**	**0.516**	78.1	91.0	243	144	0.252	0.424	49.4	67.8
TransE-RW$_{hc}$ (unif.)	266	253	0.371	0.496	77.1	90.7	212	**67**	0.226	0.420	46.8	68.8
TransE-RW$_{hc}$ (bern.)	272	260	0.377	0.495	77.3	89.8	235	134	**0.258**	0.444	**50.2**	69.6
TransE-RW$_{cwa}$ (unif.)	281	269	0.359	0.483	77.0	90.8	213	**67**	0.225	0.418	47.0	69.0
TransE-RW$_{cwa}$ (bern.)	277	265	0.378	0.486	75.4	86.8	245	149	0.241	0.386	47.2	63.4
TransE-RW$_{pca}$ (unif.)	292	279	0.353	0.472	76.2	89.6	217	71	0.227	0.423	47.1	**69.7**
TransE-RW$_{pca}$ (bern.)	318	305	0.375	0.484	75.4	86.9	232	132	0.256	**0.445**	50.1	**69.7**
TransR-RW$_{freq}$ (unif.)	351	336	0.319	0.448	77.8	**93.4**	230	76	0.173	0.356	44.2	67.1
TransR-RW$_{freq}$ (bren.)	320	306	0.326	0.442	78.0	92.0	**196**	74	0.230	0.426	48.3	69.3

embedding dimension $K = 20$, the margin $\gamma = 2.0$, distance norm $d = L_1$, and learning rate $\alpha = 0.0005$ for *TransE-RW* ($K = 30$, $\gamma = 2.0$, $d = L_1$, and $\alpha = 0.001$ for *TransR-RW*; $K = 150$, $\gamma = 1.5$, and $\alpha = 0.00005$ for *HolE-RW*).

Table 3 shows the link prediction results of *TransE-RW* and *TransR*[6] on both *Raw* and *Filter* settings by comparing with other models. *TransE-RW* outperforms other translation-based models on both *Mean Rank* and *HIT@10* on both datasets, i.e., FB15K and WN18. As for FB15K, all of TransE-RW models except *TransE-RW*$_{cwa}$ (bern) outperform *TransE*, *TransM*, and *TransH* on *HIT@10* with an improvement ranging from **8.23% to 47.98%**. Even for *TransR*, Most TransE-RW models shows a imporove over *TransR* on *HIT@10* for FB15K. All *TransE-RW* models with *unif* negative sampling setting produce lower *Mean Rank* than the baseline models like TransE, TransM, TransH, even TransR with improvement ranging from **7.79% to 12.99**. As for WN18, all of our models except *TransE-RW*$_{cwa}$ (bern) out perform *TransE*, *TransM*, and *TransH* on *HIT@10* with improvement ranging from **2.46% to 11.06%** while have a slightly lower *HIT@10* than TransR. *TransE-RW*$_{freq}$ (bern) produces the lowest *Mean Rank* than all other models, while other *TransE-RW* produce comparable results on *Mean Rank* compared to TransE, TransM, and TransH. The results for WN18 are dominated by the very small set of inferred rules. In general, KG are expected to be similar to Freebase, DBpedia, Wikidata, and so forth, for which *TransE-RW* yields substantial improvements over all baselines. We report WordNet results here to stay in line with the literature. Note that TransR has much higher time complexity ($\mathcal{O}(n_e K + n_r K + n_r K^2)$) compared to TransE

---

[6] Note that we only implement *TransR-RW* on *freq* weight as an example.

$(\mathcal{O}(n_e K + n_r K))$. We demonstrate that by including the weighted strategy, even the most simple model such as TransE can outperform a much more complex model such as TransR. To demonstrate the generalization of our weight method, we also implemented $TransR\text{-}RW_{freq}$ (unif.)/(bern.). Compared to the original TransR, $TransR\text{-}RW_{freq}$ (bern.) provide lower *Mean Rank* and higher *HIT@10* for FB15K and higher *HIT@10* for WN18. The only metric TransR-RW does worse than TransR is *Mean Rank* for WN18 while $TransE\text{-}RW_{freq}$ (bern) can beat TransR on this metric. Compared to TransE-RW, TransR-RW does not show a substantial improvement.

Table 4. Link prediction results of *TransE-RW* on FB15K by relation categories

Task	Predicting head (HITS@10)				Predicting tail (HITS@10)			
Relation category	1-to-1	1-to-n	n-to-1	n-to-n	1-to-1	1-to-n	n-to-1	n-to-n
TransE [1]	43.7	65.7	18.2	47.2	43.7	19.7	66.7	50
TransM [3]	76.8	86.3	23.1	52.3	76.3	29	85.9	56.7
TransH (unif.) [12]	66.7	81.7	30.2	57.4	63.7	30.1	83.2	60.8
TransH (bern.) [12]	66.8	87.6	28.7	64.5	65.5	39.8	83.3	67.2
$TransE\text{-}RW_{freq}$ (unif.)	75.5	88.5	37.5	**70.3**	74	41.6	86.5	72.7
$TransE\text{-}RW_{freq}$ (bern.)	81.1	92.6	27.5	68.2	78.8	34.4	92	71.3
$TransE\text{-}RW_{hc}$ (unif.)	74.1	88.9	**39.1**	69	73.7	42	86.6	71.8
$TransE\text{-}RW_{hc}$ (bern.)	**81.9**	**93.8**	30	70.1	78	36.5	**93.1**	**73.4**
$TransE\text{-}RW_{cwa}$ (unif.)	75	89.2	38.1	69.4	74.9	42	87.6	71.9
$TransE\text{-}RW_{cwa}$ (bern.)	77.7	90.2	23.9	63.2	74.8	29.3	90.5	66.6
$TransE\text{-}RW_{pca}$ (unif.)	75.2	89.2	38.5	70.2	74.5	**43.0**	87.2	72.8

Similar to [1,12], we classify the relations into 1-to-1, 1-to-n, n-to-1, and n-to-n categories according to the head per tail $h_r pt_r$ and tail per head $t_r ph_r$ values of each relation. We classify the left side or right side to 1 or n according to the fact whether $h_r pt_r$ (left side) and $t_r ph_r$ (right side) is less than 1.5. For example, a given relation is classified as 1-to-n if its $h_r pt_r$ value is less than 1.5, while its $t_r ph_r$ value is larger than or equal to 1.5. After classifying the relations into these four categories, we aggregate the *HIT@10* by each category for head prediction and tail prediction of *TransE-RW* on FB15K. Table 4 shows the results of *TransE-RW* and compare them with the results from other models. We can see that our *TransE-RW* models outperform other models on *HIT@10* for every relation category in both head and tail prediction (Table 5).

We also report *HolE-RW* performance on the link prediction tasks and compare it with HolE and ComplEx. $HolE\text{-}RW_{cwa}$ (bern.) outperforms HolE and ComplEx by at least 14.3% for *MRR*, about 4.1% for *HIT@3*, and about 30.4% for *HIT@1* on FB15K. $HolE\text{-}RW_{cwa}$ (bern.) and $HolE\text{-}RW_{pca}$ (bern.) can outperform HolE for *HIT@10* on FB15K while ComplEx has the best performance. As for WN18, $HolE\text{-}RW_{cwa}$ (unif.) can outperform both HolE and ComplEx on

Table 5. Link prediction results of *HolE-RW*

DataSet	WN18					FB15K				
Metric	MRR		HIT			MRR		HIT		
	Filter	Raw	1	3	10	Filter	Raw	1	3	10
HolE	0.938	0.616	93	**94.5**	94.9	0.524	0.232	40.2	61.3	73.9
ComplEx	0.941	0.587	**93.6**	**94.5**	94.7	0.692	0.242	59.9	75.9	**84**
HolE-RW$_{freq}$ (unif.)	0.91	0.624	89.5	92.1	93.4	0.702	0.699	69.0	70.0	72.1
HolE-RW$_{freq}$ (bern.)	0.913	0.645	89.5	92.7	94.0	0.675	0.671	65.8	67.5	70.6
HolE-RW$_{hc}$ (unif.)	0.932	0.688	92.3	93.6	94.5	0.646	0.64	62.5	64.4	68.2
HolE-RW$_{hc}$ (bern.)	0.922	0.686	90.8	93.2	94.1	0.705	0.699	69.2	70.4	72.6
HolE-RW$_{cwa}$ (unif.)	**0.942**	**0.693**	93.5	**94.5**	**95.5**	0.695	0.692	68.3	69.3	71.6
HolE-RW$_{cwa}$ (bern.)	0.922	0.684	91.0	93.2	93.9	**0.791**	**0.788**	**78.1**	**79.0**	81.1
HolE-RW$_{pca}$ (unif.)	0.931	0.686	92.3	93.7	94.5	0.635	0.63	61.5	63.4	67.1
HolE-RW$_{pca}$ (bern.)	0.926	0.688	91.4	93.5	94.4	0.756	0.754	74.6	75.4	77.3

almost all the metrics while ComplEx outperform it by 0.1% on *HIT@1*. As discussed above, few rules can be derived from WN18 and HolE and ComplEx already achieve 90%+ performance. Hence, we do not see a large change on WN18.

5   Conclusion

In this work, we proposed a bottom-up method to measure the information content of each triple with respect to the whole knowledge graph and implement weighted knowledge graph embedding models based on the idea that not all triples should be weighted equally. Instead, triples that can be used to infer other triples offer support for those, thereby also decreasing their information content. We applied rule mining to derive the inference structures of a knowledge graph and to construct a secondary, directed, weighted graph based on these support relations and their confidence. Next, we apply an edge-weighted PageRank (PR) to this secondary graph to get a centrality score of each triple and then compute its information content as $-log(PR_i)$. To demonstrate the effectiveness of the weighting, we modifed three popular models from different KG embedding model groups and performed link prediction on two standard datasets. The results show that our TransE-RW models outperform other models including TransE, TransM, TransH, and TransR by at least 12.98% for *Mean Rank* and 1.45% for *HIT@10* on FB15K. HolE-RW outperforms HolE and ComplEx by at least 14.3% for *MRR* and about 30.4% for *HIT@1* on FB15K.

References

1. Bordes, A., Usunier, N., Garcia-Duran, A., Weston, J., Yakhnenko, O.: Translating embeddings for modeling multi-relational data. In: Advances in Neural Information Processing Systems, pp. 2787–2795 (2013)

2. Cochez, M., Ristoski, P., Ponzetto, S.P., Paulheim, H.: Global RDF vector space embeddings. In: dAmato, C., et al. (eds.) ISWC 2017. LNCS, vol. 10587, pp. 190–207. Springer, Cham (2017). https://doi.org/10.1007/978-3-319-68288-4_12

3. Fan, M., Zhou, Q., Chang, E., Zheng, T.F.: Transition-based knowledge graph embedding with relational mapping properties. In: Proceedings of the 28th Pacific Asia Conference on Language, Information and Computing (2014)

4. Galárraga, L., Teflioudi, C., Hose, K., Suchanek, F.M.: Fast rule mining in ontological knowledge bases with amie + +. VLDB J. **24**(6), 707–730 (2015)

5. Lin, Y., Liu, Z., Sun, M., Liu, Y., Zhu, X.: Learning entity and relation embeddings for knowledge graph completion. In: AAAI, vol. 15, pp. 2181–2187 (2015)

6. Mai, G., Janowicz, K., Yan, B.: Combining text embedding and knowledge graph embedding techniques for academic search engines. In: SemDeep-4 (2018)

7. Nickel, M., Rosasco, L., Poggio, T.A., et al.: Holographic embeddings of knowledge graphs. In: AAAI, pp. 1955–1961 (2016)

8. Nickel, M., Tresp, V., Kriegel, H.P.: A three-way model for collective learning on multi-relational data. In: ICML, vol. 11, pp. 809–816 (2011)

9. Paulheim, H.: Knowledge graph refinement: a survey of approaches and evaluation methods. Semantic Web **8**(3), 489–508 (2017)

10. Trouillon, T., Dance, C.R., Gaussier, É., Welbl, J., Riedel, S., Bouchard, G.: Knowledge graph completion via complex tensor factorization. J. Mach. Learn. Res. **18**(1), 4735–4772 (2017)

11. Wang, Q., Mao, Z., Wang, B., Guo, L.: Knowledge graph embedding: a survey of approaches and applications. IEEE Trans. Knowl. Data Eng. **29**(12), 2724–2743 (2017)

12. Wang, Z., Zhang, J., Feng, J., Chen, Z.: Knowledge graph embedding by translating on hyperplanes. In: AAAI, vol. 14, pp. 1112–1119 (2014)

OmniScience and Extensions – Lessons Learned from Designing a Multi-domain, Multi-use Case Knowledge Representation System

Véronique Malaisé[(✉)], Anke Otten, and Pascal Coupet

Elsevier BV, 1043 NX Amsterdam, Netherlands
{v.malaise,a.otten,p.coupet}@elsevier.com

Abstract. With growing research across scientific domains and increasing daily publications volumes, it is essential to provide our users, at Elsevier, with up to date, comprehensive and to the point data. One of the key aspects of that offer is to have a global Knowledge Organization System (KOS) overarching scientific branches but also going deep enough into each domain to provide rich annotation or classification capacities. Knowing that the endeavor of creating one global "ontology of everything" is an utopia, we designed a dual/multi-vocabulary model where domain-specific extensions can be used in junction with a high-to-mid-level KOS covering the broad spectrum of scientific research. In this paper, we present our design model along with our updating procedure and our lessons learned in different use cases: the Evise submission system, the Topic Pages project and a Semantic Annotation Proof of Concept experiment in the field of Engineering.

Keywords: Multi-ontology design · Multi-ontology annotation
Use-case fitness of knowledge organization system

1 Introduction

Research crosses classic scientific domains [1–4] and new topics emerge daily. At Elsevier, we help users access and publish research papers and data in a variety of (cross) fields. Underlying our services lies a set of Knowledge Organization Systems (KOS) used in automated processes such as: automatic display of the domain hierarchy that a paper belongs to for Reference Modules[1], annotation of large content sets, classification of data for improved navigation or recommendation in online tools, Topic Pages[2] linked to articles content on Science Direct[3], etc.

---

[1] For example: https://www.sciencedirect.com/science/referenceworks/9780124095489.

[2] https://www.elsevier.com/about/press-releases/science-and-technology/elsevier-launches-sciencedirect-topics-to-help-researchers-quickly-build-their-knowledge-and-save-valuable-time-searching.

[3] http://sciencedirect.com/.

© Springer Nature Switzerland AG 2018
C. Faron Zucker et al. (Eds.): EKAW 2018, LNAI 11313, pp. 228–242, 2018.
https://doi.org/10.1007/978-3-030-03667-6_15

In order to synchronize the different legacy systems linked to existing products (ScienceDirect, Mendeley[4], internal classification systems, to name a few) and to enable annotation or publication services that range from Medicine to Aquaculture, we needed a Knowledge Organization System (KOS) covering all fields of science. We needed a KOS with full ownership, fit to serve different use cases: annotation, submission time support, classification, crosswalks of metadata generated by different systems. We were then faced with the classic problem of building a "vocabulary of everything", knowing that it is not possible to build a vocabulary of everything.

The approach we went for was to design a dual or multiple entity structure: a highly curated, validated high-to-medium level KOS called OmniScience, associated with one or more extension(s) that allow to cater for fast-growing detailed fields of science. The main modeling question that underpins our design is fitness: how do we make sure that we propose a set of Concepts as close as possible to the ideal one required for a given use case or product? How do we make sure that we cover enough of the domain(s), but do not propose too much? How can we design a single high-to-mid-level structure that can be sliced and diced in relevant ways to fit multiple purposes and products? How do we make sure that we are as much compliant as possible with the current standards in terms of KOS publication, but also in terms of consensual vocabulary used by established research communities?

Section 2 describes our main use cases in more detail, from which we draw one set of requirements on OmniScience design. Section 3 focuses on the diversity of points of view that we consider to build a representative structure, including state of the art classification ontologies, to make sure we cover the proper set of high level concepts. In Sect. 4, we describe the dual/multi model itself, along with statistics on size and growth rate. Section 5 is dedicated to the methods used to build out the parallel sets of structures in the shape of a walk-through of one of our projects, in the Engineering domain. We conclude in Sect. 6 by a recapitulation of the lessons learned and future research points we are investigating.

2   Use Cases for a Multi-KOS Model

Our users range from researchers in Chemistry to engineers in Geology, to Medical Doctors. What they are looking for is very different, but the way to access it is through metadata. OmniScience was designed with the following use cases in mind:

- Linking different products together; one of the implications of this goal is to enable crosswalks between metadata derived from different systems, on different domains
- Enabling the browsing of a given branch of science (including paths to highly related branches of science)
- Enabling the annotation of content or data to facilitate (semantic) search, classification, recommendation

---

[4] https://www.mendeley.com/.

We were expecting from the start a roll-out of products, coming with their own specific requirements around the above use-cases. This had the following high-level design implications:

- Strong guidelines for the taxonomy design: atomicity of Concepts, Explicit labels (independently from their placement in the hierarchy), tracing of Provenance information
- Continuous improvement to the core to keep it consistent when significant updates are made across domains: we do regular redesign of (middle-level of) scientific branches when a new product or project brings newly added content
- Extension mechanism to allow fast evolution of our coverage to support new use cases

New adopters arrive and are integrated on a regular basis, which has also an influence on the release cycle: we need to have frequent releases so the KOS can be adapted to a new use case or extended when needed. We choose a monthly cycle.

In this paper, we present two concrete application examples that focus on the use cases around browsing and annotation[5]: the requirements as design choices that were derived from the Evise[6] system (Elsevier's journal submission and reviewing system) and the Topic Pages project.

Evise covers more than 20 fields of science and serves around 1000 journals, a good proportion of which use a controlled vocabulary for author profile, reviewer profile and submission-time controlled keywords selection. OmniScience is the global KOS used for these operations; Fig. 1 shows the main topics it covers.

For interdisciplinary journals, such as Heliyon[7] or iScience[8], browsing across fields of science in one single structure is a must have, but even journals or books focusing mostly on "one" topic often require the inclusion of sub-branches in different areas: a journal on Neuroscience might require the inclusion of concepts around Proteins, although Proteins would not be classified as part of the Neuroscience domain per se (they are biochemicals, by nature). [1, 4] also mentions that different ontologies in a given domain cover different aspects of this domains, stressing the added value of a combined use.

The metadata in Evise has to not only cover these different fields of science, but also reach a level of depth that is relevant for authors to select their topics from when submitting an article and for reviewers to select their domains of expertise. The metadata organization also needs to be compatible with standards that research communities are familiar with, to make sure we have the appropriate breadth of coverage and a terminology that specialists are used to.

Each journal also wants to be somewhat independent of other journals' choices in terms of metadata selection, even if they are in the same field of science: some journals opt for flat list of controlled terms, while others are interested in giving a whole branch

---

[5] We chose to focus on these two use cases as these are the most visible for the international community and cover the requirements that are derived from the crosswalk use case.

[6] https://www.elsevier.com/en-gb/editors/evise.

[7] https://www.journals.elsevier.com/heliyon.

[8] https://www.journals.elsevier.com/iscience.

as options for submitting keywords; some prefer high-level terms, some prefer more specialized terms. In any case, no journal wants their users to start browsing at the very root of the hierarchical classification of *all* scientific domains to drill down to the individual topics of interest that their communities are specialized on. The resulting requirements for OmniScience design to support Evise are the following:

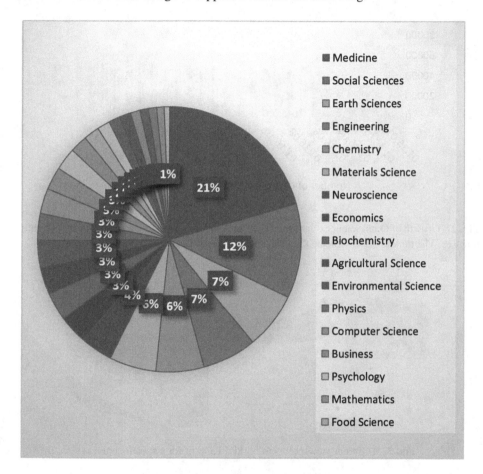

Fig. 1. OmniScience concepts distribution in terms of scientific fields

- Breadth of fields: a broad coverage of the main scientific domains
- Depth per domain that corresponds to authors submission, profile and reviewer profile level (high-to-mid level of specialization in the domain)
- SME-validated, solid organization of the branches and terminology that is familiar to specialists in the domain

- Coverage of (at least the high levels of) the concepts from community-recognized standard KOS, such as ACM or JEL; we are also considering new vocabularies that are likely to aggregate communities in the future such as the Computer Science Ontology[9].
- Concept-level means of selecting fields of science or sub-branches thereof

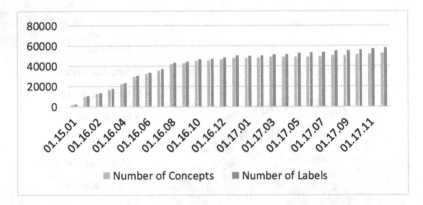

Fig. 2. Growth of OmniScience over time. The time axis shows version numbers of the monthly releases. The middle digits indicate the year, the last digits the month.

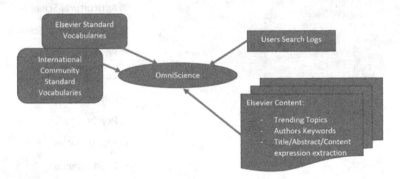

Fig. 3. Different view-points to build a KOS fit for a specific context

The requirements regarding the Science Direct Topic Pages[10] are centered around automatic annotation within one domain of science, at a high level of specialization. Highlighted terms in Science Direct articles link to a Topic Page that gives the user more information about that term: a definition, related concepts and carefully selected book snippets. The definitions, snippets and related terms are extracted by combined strategies of machine learning, ranked, and the most reliable candidates are validated by Subject Matter Experts.

---

[9] https://cso.kmi.open.ac.uk.
[10] https://www.elsevier.com/solutions/sciencedirect/topics.

The highlight in Science Direct is based on articles and books annotations: the concepts identified in articles are used in turn for extracting definitions from reference book content. There are currently over 112 000 published Topic Pages, across 17 domains as varied as: Medicine and Dentistry, Neuroscience, Chemistry, Chemical Engineering, Earth and Planetary Sciences, Agriculture and Biological Sciences; more domains are in the pipeline for future releases.

Each Topic Page is built within a given field of science, and brings information about mid-to-specialized concepts: items that a new person in the field might not know too much about, or would like to get related data around. Moreover, very specific topics can be present in research articles, including brand new research topics; each topic can be expressed in several ways (including highly ambiguous acronyms); the scope of Topic Pages covers more than a dozen different domains (so far). For this application, it is not possible to use only Subject Matter Expert (SME) curated metadata sets in a reasonable delivery time frame (at least not without employing an army of SMEs): the required set of concepts is too vast, the set of synonyms even larger. Very specialized metadata is out of the scope of OmniScience: as mentioned in the introduction, our aim is not to design one global KOS of everything. For this project, we worked in the divide and conquer approach of a satellite set of vocabularies, around the core of OmniScience, much like the suggested architecture of [1, 2]: [1] gives access to multiple ontologies to a manual annotator, while [2] uses a corpus to build out modules that are complementary to a core vocabulary, also for manual annotation. In our case, we provide an automatic annotation system with different KOS (OmniScience and Extensions), some of which are built based on domain-specific corpora. This type of modularization follows the Partitioning method defined in the typology from [5]. The requirements for OmniScience to support this project are:

- Identification of scientific domains
- Identification of generic terms, not suitable for a Topic Page
- Identification of acronyms and ambiguous terms, for the annotation mechanism
- Compatible with one or more large KOS per domain
    - Built within a short time frame,
    - With a reasonable quality (structure is not required),
    - Covering the set of terms at the level of the Science Direct article content, including trending topics

The next two sections describe in more details how we built OmniScience, to make it versatile enough to support the two use cases mentioned here, but also fit to other purposes, multiple content type and users (as fitness is at the heart of our design process), and also compatible with rapidly growing domain-specific Extensions.

3 We Are One

Our design for versatility was to identify as many aspects of concepts and labels as relevant across domains, projects and use cases. In order to be compatible with international standards, external vocabularies and to be able to attach information at the Label level, we opted for the SKOS-XL [6] standard of the W3C[11] extending SKOS [7], aimed at publishing and exchanging KOS on the Web. The identification of scientific branches is done by attaching a "type" property from the W3C RDF set[12] property at the concept level. We add source information using the Dublin Core Terms[13] property "source" both at the concept and label level. At the concept level, we add information about the level of genericity of a term: is a concept a generic notion or a specialized term (Core-Domain or Core-Concept in Fig. 4). This information is derived from corpus-specific Document Frequency information, correlated with general lists of top 1000 most common English words and validated by SMEs. Our first approach was to define product or project-specific blacklisting properties but this was neither reusable across project, neither meaningful within a project, so we went for more explicit "flags" with a globally valid value such as "Generic Term". At the time of our first release, the Lemon model[14] was not yet published and we did not find a suitable international standard to represent this piece of information so we opted for an Elsevier-local property to represent this notion; we will do an impact analysis and evaluate whether we could migrate it to the now-standard "Lexical Form" Lemon construct. Using the same Elsevier-local property, we also markup acronyms, chemical symbols (often single letter terms) and term identified upfront as ambiguous: terms that we know at editing time are polysemic, either within one single field of science, such as CAT (standing for both Computer Aided Transcription and Computer Aided Teaching), or across fields of science, such as Hybridization, a different process in Chemistry or Plant Science. The same term can have multiple properties: Optimization is at the same time a Generic Term and Ambiguous. Using these different properties, it is possible to select subsets for a given application: only high-level concepts of all branches of science for general browsing or high-level classification; only one specific branch of science, excluding its generic terms for indexing, to generate topic pages. As the latter set identifies concepts at different places in the hierarchy, it is not possible to export a valid SKOS-XL file that contains only the relevant concepts, but we export a full branch with the properties at the concept and label level that the application can use as filters. Some applications will only accept to use concepts from given sources, or will want to get any expanded branch of OmniScience from a seed of ASJC codes (see the following section for a description of ASJC codes). We have mapped the full set of ASJC codes into OmniScience, therefore it is straightforward to deliver that specific set. This concept and label level properties set has served all our use cases to date, to define the most relevant subsets for given projects, products and use-cases, while keeping the vocabulary whole.

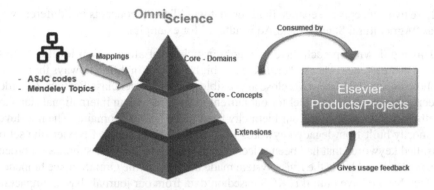

Fig. 4. OmniScience and Extensions workflow

To make sure that OmniScience is adapted to our needs in terms of conceptual coverage, but also representative of the current state of the art in research classification, we looked at both Elsevier and external standards describing a global set of scientific domains to define its generic coverage target. Among Elsevier classifications, the "All Sciences Journal Classification" (ASJC) is used to characterize submissions at the journal level on Science Direct: any article gets the code or set of codes that is assigned to the journal it was accepted in. ASJC has around 300 concepts, covering any field of science; its top nodes are accessible in the expert search functionality of Science Direct[15]. This breadth of fields was our first target, and was covered in the early stages of development. We completed this high-level set by identifying the gaps that we then had with the high levels (one to three levels of hierarchy) of the following vocabularies, and closing these gaps with our own content-based extraction: the Library of Congress Subject Headings[16], Plos One[17], Web of Science's general organization, Wikipedia Branches of Science[18], WordNet Domains[19] (also incorporated in YAGO[20]). To be compatible with KOS that use composite scientific domains, we decided to make sure we were creating "atomic" domains wherever possible:

- "Arts and Humanities": this was kept as a single field of science, to avoid the duplication of most children across the "would be independent branches" of "Arts" and "Humanities"; we also used a majority vote for that choice, across the reference vocabularies mentioned above.
- "Agricultural and Biological Sciences": this single concept from ASJC was incorporated in OmniScience as the *two concepts* of "Agricultural Sciences" and "Biological Sciences", to be able to link out to other vocabularies that would either have

---

[15] https://www.sciencedirect.com/science?_ob=MiamiSearchURL&_method=request-Form&_temp=all_boolSearch.tmpl&md5=052b06d957a9d8c82e07acf1d7eef1b7.

[16] http://id.loc.gov/authorities/subjects.html.

[17] https://github.com/PLOS/plos-thesaurus/blob/develop/README.md.

[18] https://en.wikipedia.org/wiki/Branches_of_science.

[19] http://wndomains.fbk.eu/.

[20] https://www.mpi-inf.mpg.de/departments/databases-and-information-systems/research/yago-naga/yago/.

these two concepts as separate fields or that would group concepts in a different way (as "Agricultural Sciences and Aquaculture" for example).

This top-down approach gave us a consensual set of atomic high-level concepts. Most of the references checked organize this high-level set in different ways though, so we chose one model that was as close as possible to our Elsevier classifications (in order to keep a familiar look and feel for our current users) but was an international standard nonetheless and mostly drew our hierarchy from the WordNet Domains. The mid-level was mostly built from legacy keywords lists from journals across Elsevier: the set of controlled keywords that had been selected by the journals for their submission procedure, now accessible via the Evise system made the meat of the OmniScience branches. The fact that we have built this KOS based on data from our journals has an impact on the balance of topics shown in Fig. 1, but also gives us an indication of fitness with respect to our content. The high level conceptual coverage of OmniScience is shown in Fig. 1.

To make sure that we were taking the right perspectives into account when building our vocabulary, besides the vocabularies mentioned above, and its link to the domains covered in our content, we also took other view-points in consideration: the user's needs perspective and the direct document-based view (Fig. 3).

While the global users' perspective is captured in the community standard vocabularies, standards are built over time and are "averaging" over topics. To get immediate and individual user's needs into account, we have two strategies: we consider search logs for evaluating the coverage of OmniScience and we have a direct feedback form on our intranet. The document-based view is done by regular intake of candidate terms extracted from domain-specific corpora, for strengthening a given branch of science. The extraction from the title and abstract sections of articles (or book sections) is done using the Rake algorithm, enriched with Part of Speech tagging[21] and complemented with a TF.iDF-based extraction (Python implementation using the Gensim package[22], retrieving single-word terms only). These two sets are combined with author keywords extracted from articles, which can come from a controlled vocabulary or be freely chosen by the authors. The latest influential and trending topics are also extracted from the latest literature, using an approach based on information decay, developed within Elsevier [8].

OmniScience is continuously evolving based on these different sources; in the course of the two years since Evise started using OmniScience, we only got as direct feedback request to add only around 400 terms, showing a rather good fitness in the highest levels. The following processes are applied either on a monthly basis or on a specific need-basis to add new candidates: we analyze the overlap between the different sources (keeping their provenance information) after normalization, using the AnAGram [9] set of normalization steps. AnAGram was chosen over other off-the-shelf mapping algorithms for its versatility, its extensible and configurable model, besides the comparison with the state of the art that was run and is presented in [9]. We get Document Frequency information for the global list against our content and define a threshold of interest per use case and per project. Once the relevant set is defined, we run some classification to

---

[21] https://gist.github.com/soeffing/b0e026fd597015826d1a389ac739212f.

[22] https://pypi.org/project/gensim/.

regroup similar candidates (k-nearest neighbors, also a Python Gensim package) and mapping using AnAGram to identify where the candidates fit best into the existing OmniScience structure: we use the hierarchical information of the concepts that new candidates map to in order to infer possible placements in OmniScience. The validation and actual placement is mostly a manual work. We then define a time-period for the integration of the selected candidates (typically within the calendar of a monthly release) or decide that the set to be integrated for the use case at hand is too big to be included in a finely curated (poly)hierarchical vocabulary within the time frame that the project or product requires; we then add it to a non-structured, minimally reviewed set of Extensions. One question we are then faced with is: how do we deal with (possible) duplication? How do we use the global set of KOS in an automated process, such as an annotation service?

4   And We Are Multiple

OmniScience is the core of a system of vocabularies. It is multi-disciplinary, displays a deep structure, is manually curated and subject to regular quality checks. In contrast to this, the OmniScience Extensions are domain-specific vocabularies which aim at the annotation use cases. The requirements for hierarchy structure and Label style are relaxed, and the focus lies on gathering a high number of fine-grained concepts which are currently relevant to the scientific community.

The extensions follow the same data model as the OmniScience core and can be used in any combination a product requires. Concept identifiers are unique across all vocabularies to avoid any confusion for the consuming product. However, the usage of multiple vocabularies introduces duplicates in the total vocabulary set. Duplications occur between OmniScience core and each extension, but also between extensions. Even though the extensions are limited to specific domains, there is an inevitable topical overlap. In practice, the duplication between core and extensions is the most problematic for the products, as most annotations select one deep dive Extension vocabulary in combination with OmniScience.

We added mappings between overlapping concepts in extensions and core to help products deal with them. For example, a product may prefer to use only the OmniScience core concept, or to use the combined set of labels of the mapped concepts for annotation. We used the AnAGram matcher [9] to identify potential overlaps, combined with few manual corrections. The global model works as shown in Fig. 4.

The expansion of OmniScience and its Extensions is driven by the needs of our products. The first phase was devoted to a rapid building of the OmniScience core (see Fig. 2), in order to serve our journals. When all subject areas were sufficiently covered, the number of concepts reached a plateau of ca. 50000. Since then, the number of labels continued to grow slowly as synonyms were added. The number of concepts shows small fluctuations, as concepts are both added based on user feedback and removed in the course of a continuous optimization of the structure.

In the second phase of the project we expanded the extensions (Fig. 5). The number of concepts grows much quicker than in OmniScience, reflecting the lower amount of manual curation and the reliance on bulk processes. The sharp increase around release 01.17.06 marks the launch of Topic Pages for multiple domains at a time. Further growth is expected when new domain extensions are ready.

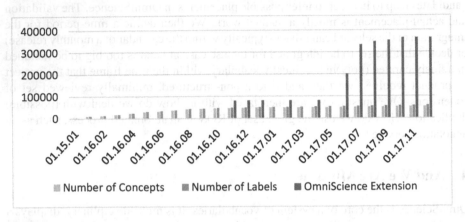

Fig. 5. Growth of OmniScience and its Extensions over time. The time axis shows version numbers of the monthly releases. The middle digits indicate the year.

5 Semantic Search in the Engineering Domain Proof of Concept

For an experiment in Semantic Annotation of books in the Engineering domain, we used OmniScience as a baseline and built ad-hoc Extensions to reach the project's goals. We had around 600 books in the Chemical Engineering domain, the OmniScience KOS (including an Engineering branch with around 6000 concepts built based on the coverage needs of the Evise system), and a set of 170 000 candidate terms: uni, bi- and trigrams automatically extracted from these 600 books, without any kind of Part-of-Speech based filtering (moving window-based extraction on the full set of words, including stop-words).

We did a first round of indexing with the full set of OmniScience concepts, to identify which branches would be relevant for the project, in the aim of providing the most suitable subset of OmniScience rather than its full 50 000 concepts. We assumed that the books would contain concepts from more domains than in Engineering alone (starting by chemical concepts, classified in Chemistry), but it turned out that no branch could be pruned from the global KOS, as even concepts in Philosophy and Environmental Sciences had matches. Figure 6 shows a distribution of the top domains found in the first round of annotation.

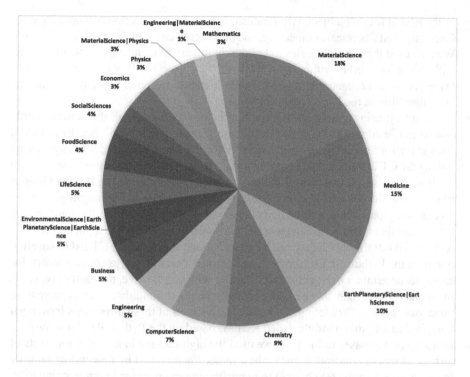

Fig. 6. Distribution of the top concepts found in the annotation of Engineering books

We decided to keep all of OmniScience as a source for the annotation and use the concepts from branches other than engineering in the conceptual vectors describing the different documents. The application (a set of rules built on top of a Lucene SOLR[23] index) could also filter out the annotation results based on the OmniScience branch(es) it belonged to, if necessary.

Only OmniScience is not enough for a complete, in-depth annotation of the books and the 170 000 candidates are too noisy to represent conceptual entities without filtering. We worked towards a middle-ground of using OmniScience together with a set of minimally organized terms for this project. We used our set of existing vocabularies, our content, rule based filtering and Subject Matter Experts (SME) feedback to build the proper KOS set. Indeed, we had three indexing rounds assessed by SMEs to get our baseline set of vocabularies up to speed, showing areas of least coverage and maximal ambiguity. The different build out steps are described below.

- Existing vocabularies: we compiled a set of vocabularies owned by Elsevier on the Chemical Engineering domain and checked their overlap to get the best candidate Extension(s) for OmniScience, but also checked their overlap with the candidate terms (CT) set: whatever CT belonged to an existing vocabulary was a proper term and had already some context in our KOS set. Three of our vocabularies were selected

---

23 http://lucene.apache.org/solr/.

as the best fit for this project: two Extensions built for the creation of Topic Pages in Chemistry and Chemical engineering, and one vocabulary built by the Knovel[24] team. We also used these vocabularies to build a dictionary to identify possible synonyms with substring overlap within the CT set, such as "Hoechst-Wacker oxidation" and "Hoechst-Wacker reaction" (using a simple implementation of the K-nearest neighbors algorithm in the Python Gensim library).

- Our Content: using simple DF information helped us rule out all the generic words that would be common to most scientific publications but not conceptually relevant, such as Fig for figure. We also built word vectors for attempting to identify synonyms among the CT list that would not share a sub-string. This approach works so far only for unigrams, as we took out of the box methods (available in the Python Gensim library) and did not lead very good results yet. Some fine-tuning might give more means to regroup terms, but the first clusters of similar terms showed homogeneous sets of members, that were however not particularly related to the input word.

- Rule-based filtering of CT: we ran a Part of Speech tagger on the CT list (a baseline one from the Python NLTK library[25]) and defined a set of patterns for non-terms, for example: determiner only, candidates starting with an adjective, numeral only, verbs in another form than the gerund (gerund are good candidates for representing processes, such as "Soldering"). The implementation of these three steps have been compiled in a Python module called Koalas, based on the Python Pandas library[26].

- Indexing output based refinement: we used the high-ranking indexing output (sets of terms and sets of concepts in the highest ranks when ranked by descending number of occurrences, in the 600 books) to identify ambiguous terms in our vocabularies. Some terms were nouns but their verb form got annotated in the text (examples: Lead, Bear), which was corrected on the annotation engine side; some of our terms were ambiguous across domains: a Drone is either a stingless male bee or an unmanned aerial vehicle. These were temporarily disambiguated by adding a qualifier that refers to the domain of science they should be considered in. In the future, more solid techniques should be used (such as word, phrase or sense vectors). These options are currently being investigated, in collaboration with the team developing the annotation engine. Working hand in hand with the tool using the KOS in an application is a very privileged situation. The Quality Assessment of the annotations also showed some coverage problems: some chemical elements and alloys were missing, which we corrected. Methods were also missing and could not be extracted or found in simple closed lists. For that we did a targeted extraction of terms starting with an Eponym and followed by one "suffix" such as the following: method, reaction, law, effect. We built a list of 47 of these suffixes based on a local corpus analysis, and expanded our set of methods by a couple of 100 concepts using this process. We added these items directly to OmniScience, as they are likely to serve multiple purposes and could easily be validated with high confidence.

---

[24] https://www.elsevier.com/en-gb/solutions/knovel-engineering-information.

[25] https://www.nltk.org/.

[26] https://pandas.pydata.org/.

- SME evaluation: the final set of CT was sent out to suppliers for an evaluation of the relevancy of the last candidates with respect to the domain of Chemical Engineering, to regroups synonyms under the same concept and to add more synonyms than the set present in the CT list. The original set of 60 000 CT sent to the suppliers led to around 40 000 concepts, directly used as a second Chemical Engineering Extension.

One tricky situation that we were faced with was the conceptual overlap of content between OmniScience and the different Extensions. The annotation mechanism that we are using (the Finger Printing Engine -FPE-, acquired by Elsevier) allows for the annotation of a given corpus with multiple ontologies at the same time (which was still a challenge at the time of [4]). The FPE lets us identify a preferred vocabulary, or a ranked list of vocabulary preferences for the annotation: use a vocabulary of rank n + 1 only if no concept was identified for that chunk of text in the vocabulary with rank n. This could take care of overlapping conceptual coverage, but works only partially so: if a set of synonyms is linked to a concept in one vocabulary, while another set of synonyms is linked to its equivalent concept in another vocabulary, the annotation of text containing synonyms from the two sets will use the unique identifier of the two different concepts while the annotation should refer to only a single concept. Therefore, a mapping of equivalent concepts has to be performed, as mentioned in Sect. 4, but the only operation that is required for the FPE to efficiently process a corpus with a set of KOS input is to add to the vocabulary of highest rank the global set of synonyms for the overlapping concept.

6 Conclusion

In this paper, we have presented the rationale, constructs and use cases for which OmniScience was built, as a high-to-mid-level vocabulary covering the main branches of science. We showed how it can be used in combination with large and mostly non-structured Extensions that provide the breadth of conceptual coverage needed for a good level of annotation recall in research articles and books. The past years' experience showed us that we should build it not only following the classic bottom up and top down approaches, but also to include direct users feedback (in the form of feedback forms and search logs) to make it fit to our use cases, our documents but also to our community of users. The automatic annotation experiment described above also shows that the development of a KOS can benefit from close interactions with the development of the automatic processes that use it, such as the FPE, to find out where and how some problems should be solved: resolving all the ambiguity between OmniScience and the Extensions used or having a selection mechanism built in the annotation tool?

Our lessons learned (besides confirming that even in a domain-specific use case different scientific domains should be considered in the automatic processes) showed that the main advantage of our dual model is the versatility of OmniScience and its ease of use in combination with Extensions; its main drawback is the need for a good curation pipeline for Extensions and a good matching algorithm to identify redundancy and incompatibilities between vocabularies when creating an Extension or between OmniScience and an Extension. Therefore, we are constantly doing investigative research in the domains of similarity or duplicate identification (for example using word vectors or sense vectors to overcome the limitations of string-based duplicate identification) and in the steps to perform an efficient candidate terms workflow, as drafted in Sect. 5. This part includes automatic ontology learning and machine learning to learn possible placements for our candidates.

Acknowledgements. Our thanks go our colleagues Anique van Berne, Subhradeep Kayal and Till Bey for AnAGram, the Trending and Influential Topics extraction and the Koalas Python module; the teams we interact with on a daily basis: Akileshwari Chandrasekhar, Olga Fedorova, Marleen Rodenburg, Anda Grigorescu, Marcela Haldan, Monica Paravidino, Jenny Truong and Georgios Tsatsaronis.

References

1. Corrêa e Castro Gomes, P., de Carvalho Moura, A.M., Cavalcanti, M.C.: A multi-ontology approach to annotate scientific documents based on a modularization technique. J. Biomed. Inform. **58**, 208–219 (2015)
2. Gennaria, J.H., Neal, M.L., Galdzicki, M., Cook, D.L.: Multiple ontologies in action: composite annotations for biosimulation models. J. Biomed. Inform. **44**(1), 146–154 (2011)
3. Gómez-Berbís, J.M., Colomo-Palacios, R., López-Cuadrado, J.L., González-Carrasco, I., García-Crespo, Á.: SEAN: multi-ontology semantic annotation for highly accurate closed domains. Int. J. Phys. Sci. **6**(6), 1440–1451 (2011)
4. Belloze, K.T., Monteiro, D.I.S.B., Lima, T.F., Silva-Jr, F.P., Cavalcanti, M.C.: Analyzing tools for biomedical text annotation with multiple ontologies. In: International Conference on Biomedical Ontology (ICBO) (2012)
5. d'Aquin, M., Schlicht, A., Stuckenschmidt, H., Sabou, M.: Criteria and evaluation for ontology modularization techniques. In: Stuckenschmidt, H., Parent, C., Spaccapietra, S. (eds.) Modular Ontologies. LNCS, vol. 5445, pp. 67–89. Springer, Heidelberg (2009). https://doi.org/10.1007/978-3-642-01907-4_4
6. SKOS-XL. https://www.w3.org/TR/skos-reference/skos-xl.html. Accessed 10 July 2018
7. SKOS. https://www.w3.org/2004/02/skos/. Accessed 10 July 2018
8. Kayal, S., Groth, P., Tsatsaronis, G., Gregory, M.: Scientific topic attentionality: influential and trending topics in science. In: The Fourth International Conference on Machine Learning, Optimization, and Data Science (LOD) (2018)
9. Van Berne, A., Malaise, V.: Evaluation of string normalisation modules for string-based biomedical vocabularies alignment with AnAGram. In: Poster of the Thirteenth International Semantic Web Conference (ISWC) (2014)

A Semantic Use Case Simulation Framework for Training Machine Learning Algorithms

Nicole Merkle[1]([✉]), Stefan Zander[2], and Viliam Simko[1]

[1] Information Process Engineering, FZI Forschungszentrum Informatik am KIT,
Haid-und-Neu-Str. 10-14, 76131 Karlsruhe, Germany
{merkle,simko}@fzi.de
[2] Institute for Computer Science, University of Applied Sciences Darmstadt,
Schöfferstrasse 8B, 64295 Darmstadt, Germany
stefan.zander@h-da.de

Abstract. To train autonomous agents, large training data sets are required to provide the necessary support in solving real-world problems. In domains such as healthcare or ambient assisted living, such training sets are often incomplete or do not cover the unique requirements and constraints of specific use cases, leading to the cold-start problem. This work describes a semantic simulation framework that generates qualitative use case specific data for Machine-Learning (ML) driven agents, thus solving the cold-start problem. By combing simulated data with axiomatically formalized use case requirements, we are able to train ML algorithms without real-world data at hand. We integrate domain specific guidelines and their semantic representation by using SHACL/RDF(S) and SPARQL CONSTRUCT queries. The main benefits of this approach are (1) portability to other domains, (2) applicability to various ML algorithms, and (3) mitigation of the cold-start problem or sparse data.

1 Introduction

Real-world problems and domain-specific use cases are often so diverse and complex, that a thorough formalization of all requirements and interdependencies at design time is difficult, if not impossible. Moreover, use cases are often not generalizable because their performance depend on individual and varying parameters (e.g. user-preferences, goal-oriented requirements, context-dependent requirements etc). In order to provide sufficient support in such situations, agents usually require formal specifications (e.g. in the form of rules) or large datasets that cover domain and problem characteristics. However, problem-specific datasets are neither always available nor—in most of the cases sufficiently—representative for a given problem. Especially not in situations, where agents have to deal with personalization and context-dependent use cases in indeterministic and heterogeneous environments. Privacy policies as well as regulative, governmental, and

© Springer Nature Switzerland AG 2018
C. Faron Zucker et al. (Eds.): EKAW 2018, LNAI 11313, pp. 243–257, 2018.
https://doi.org/10.1007/978-3-030-03667-6_16

technical restrictions further contribute to the lack of sufficient data. Moreover, as starting, virtual agents have neither an appropriate trained model nor an individual knowledge representation that enables them to train a specific and individualized prediction model on-the-fly. In most of the cases, the only thing available are guidelines or domain expert knowledge, which need to be represented in a machine-processable way. Furthermore, teaching a machine learning-based system needs time, especially when the data have to be gathered and preprocessed first during its runtime. This leads to the undesirable situation that an agent acts in a random and uncertain way (cold-start problem) at the beginning of its lifecycle, resulting in an unwanted and inappropriate behaviour for a given situation or context [5]. Especially, in critical situations (e.g. user interactions) this can be problematic. Moreover, almost every performed agent activity generates new data, since every activity has an impact to the states, conditions and actors in an environment. The presented approach aims at providing use case specific and personalized synthetic data in order to overcome the outlined cold-start problem. The assumption underlying our approach is that semantically created synthetic simulation data serve as substitute of missing real-world data, thus enabling machine learning based agents to immediately perform appropriate activities although the required data are not available at the beginning of an agent's life cycle.

In order to accomplish this objective, our approach provides a simulation framework that utilizes ontological semantics for defining and processing general meta-model specifications for use cases of different domains. Under consideration of the discussed problems and challenges, our approach addresses the following research questions:

RQ1 Does the presented simulation framework generate data of sufficient quality to solve the cold-start problem in uncontrolled environments?

RQ2 Is the simulation framework capable of adapting its data-generation process to different problem domains sufficiently?

In order to evaluate the proposed simulation framework, we (a) apply our approach in two heterogeneous domains—healthcare and smart home environment—in order to show the universal validity of our approach and (b) test if it sufficiently solves the cold-start problem.

The remainder of this work is structured as follows: Sect. 2 discusses related work. Section 3 presents the fundamental concepts of the semantic simulation framework. Section 4 demonstrates through two example applications from the health-care and smart home domain, that the approach is sufficiently generic for its application in different problem domains. Section 5 evaluates the approach by applying it to the two example use cases. Therefore, we consider appropriate guidelines from the Chronic Kidney Disease Pathway (CKDPathway)[1] and rules for controlling devices in an smart home environment in order to compare our results with the results of some trained and applied ML algorithms. Section 6

---

[1] http://ckdpathway.ca.

concludes the work by deriving *lessons learned* and provides an outlook to future activities.

2   Related Work

The cold-start problem has been extensively researched in the domain of recommender systems (e.g. [5,7,15,17]). Several solutions have been proposed to tackling both *item* and *user cold start* problems: Active learning, which is a special field of semi-supervised machine learning (cf. [2,14,16]), aims at evaluating the usefulness of data points in order to improve recommender system performance and data quantity. Collaboration and data exchange strategies are often deployed in agent-based system environments to help agents in providing appropriate assistance in new and unanticipated situations by learning from the experiences of other agents [4,12]. Hybrid approaches, e.g. combining content-based matching approaches and collaborative filtering [15] or association rules and clustering techniques [1] revealed to be helpful in mitigating the cold-start problem by deducing similarity indicators from content-based characteristics. In order to address the sparsity of user profiles, Yahoo! research developed a collective learning representation framework to tackle both the item cold start and the user cold start by using matrix factorization techniques (cf. [7]) such as alternating least squares and multiplicative updates [6].

Although several solutions have been proposed to tackle cold-start problems, the deployment of semantic technologies, ontology-based description frameworks, and semantic simulation frameworks have received only marginal attention. The synergies between recommender systems and semantic knowledge structures such as ontologies have first been studied by Middleton et al. [8]. Nouali et al. [11] demonstrated that a semantically enhanced description of user and resource information increases precision, coverage and quality of recommendation systems. A review about general semantic recommender systems has been published by [13] whereas DiNoia and Ostuni [3], Musto et al. [10], and Tomeo et al. [20] (among others) specifically focus on systems that have been extended with data from the Linked Open Data (LOD) initiative. Although the positive effects of semantic technologies on recommender systems, in particular for content-based filtering, are broadly acknowledged (cf. [21]), many recent approaches (e.g. [3,10,20]) started to analyze the extent to which recommender systems can be enhanced using LOD (cf. [10]). However, a semantic simulation framework comparable to one in this work was not specifically addressed. A very similar approach to the one proposed here that addresses the sparsity and scarcity problem was developed by Thanh-Tai et al. [19]. In contrast to generating new data via simulation, their approach uses a semantic model to generate similarity data for a given original dataset.

3   Approach

The presented simulation framework can be considered as part of a bigger system architecture that acts as a recommendation- and task-execution- framework for given use cases. Thereby, a use case constitutes an aggregate representation of evident states and possible activities that are performed by virtual agents in order to solve given problems. Domain knowledge is necessary and provided by human experts in a formal representation. This domain knowledge is used by the simulator component in order to generate numerical state representations and compute reward or punishment values that are relevant for making decisions and executing activities in the appropriate use case. The transformation into a numerical state representation is required because in neural networks as well as in many other ML algorithms, only numerical representations are processed. Therefore, nominal values are encoded by applying one-hot-encoding to generated feature values. Moreover, all values are normalized before they are sent to the appropriate agent. The machine learning (ML) algorithms that the targeted agents apply, are either reinforcement learning (RL) (e.g. Deep-Q-Networks) or (un-) supervised (e.g. deep neural networks, collaborative filtering, K-Means, latent semantic analysis) ML algorithms. Therefore, the simulator generates during the online-training of the RL agent the appropriate CSV[2] files as a side-product. While the RL agent is trained online in several thousand episodes by means of rewards and punishments, the generated CSV files serve as datasets for the (un-) supervised algorithms.

The application of the entire system architecture is divided in two phases, a *learning phase* and an *adaption phase*. The learning phase addresses the training of machine learning (ML) models based on generated guideline-rules and domain knowledge data, represented as RDF(S) instances. The learning phase is conducted in order to avoid the cold-start of the ML components. However, before the learning phase can start, the simulator component requires a formal representation of use cases that require to be simulated. The general architecture and step-by-step process are represented in Fig. 1. First, the domain expert specifies by means of an arbitrary RDF editor (e.g. Topbraid, Protge, Semantic MediaWiki) the use cases' A-Box representation, comprising states, activities and guideline-rules following the use case meta-model constraints. The simulator

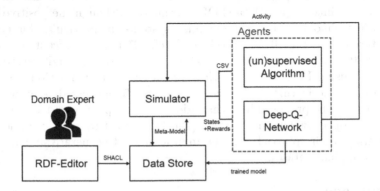

Fig. 1. Overview of the system architecture

---

[2] Comma separated values.

utilizes this A-Box representation for generating the numerical state representations (numerical state vector + reward and CSV) for the appropriate ML algorithms. Our approach utilizes different semantic web technologies, such as the *Shape Constraint Language (SHACL)*[3] and *SPARQL*[4] in order to represent and request simulation use cases, so that the simulator can process this representation. We use SHACL as a vocabulary because it allows to define validation constraints for RDF(S) graphs. Moreover, its application assures a closed-world assumption that is necessary in order to avoid inconsistency and undefined states within the simulation framework. Since the different states are defined by conditions and guideline-rules, the simulator transforms these rules into SPARQL CONSTRUCT queries in order to derive the appropriate state in that the simulation currently resides. This step is necessary because the simulator generates or adjusts during the training phase just single values of a state vector representation. Therefore, it needs to derive the new state after the values are updated. According to the constructed and derived state, the simulator reasons the appropriate reward value of a state. This reward value represents the acceptability of a state and is in particular required in reinforcement learning algorithms. According to the reinforcement learning paradigm [18], reward values are utilized in order to train strategies for a given task by rewards and punishments of the environment.

Later in the *adaption phase*, the ML algorithms adjust their model representation by collected real-world data that have been gathered during the system runtime. *Adaption* means in this context that individualized data is used in order to personalize general ML models that initially were only trained based on guideline-rules.

3.1   The Framework Architecture

The architecture of the framework consists of different components that interact with each other via event-driven Web protocols.

As soon as the simulation starts, the appropriate ML agent sends an initial message to the simulator. This message includes information about the requested use case and in how many iterations or episodes the training has to be performed. An episode starts on a random start state and finishes first, as soon as a goal state of the use case is achieved by the agent. Usually several thousand episodes are required in order to train an agent.

The use case information is necessary for the simulator in order to request from the graph store the appropriate meta-information regarding the specific use case that shall be simulated. The use case simulation meta-model (SHACL shape definitions) together with use case instances are stored in a graph database. The simulator and other components can request the entire meta-model graph representation via a SPARQL endpoint. Internally, the simulator generates an in-memory RDF store that is created and utilized using the RDF4J[5] API.

---

[3] https://www.w3.org/TR/shacl/.
[4] https://www.w3.org/TR/rdf-sparql-query/.
[5] http://rdf4j.org/.

Based on semantically represented use case guidelines or use case pathways (e.g. clinical pathway), the simulator generates a numeric vector representation of the current use case state. This vector representation is sent as event message to the corresponding ML algorithm. The algorithm is capable, by means of the graph store, to send *activity* URIs to the simulator. Subsequently, the simulator looks up what *effects* the received activity might have. Considering for instance the healthcare domain, an *effect* can be the increase of the patient's *heartrate* value, after the patient has made some kind of sports activity. The simulator looks then up the last stored heartrate value in the state vector and increases this value, in order to send the updated state representation to the ML algorithm. The change of single values in the state vector ensures that the states are adapted according to the performed activity effects. This interaction between simulator and agent happens iteratively in thousands of episodes, depending on the agents iteration request or until it has finished its training.

During the training, the simulator stores all generated vector states as data samples in a CSV file, so that this CSV file can be utilized by additional ML algorithms for training a use case specific model.

3.2   The Simulation Meta-model

Often, use cases and domain guidelines are described by domain experts, in a human-readable documentation. In order to allow the simulator to process use case- as well as guideline-representations and generate realistic data for the algorithms, we propose a RDF(S)-based simulation meta-model that we discuss here. The appropriate shape definitions are described in the next sections. Figure 2 provides an overview of the simulation meta-model elements. The SHACL definition of the simulation meta-model can be found at this URL[6]. It is planned to enhance our devised meta-model by classes of already existing ontologies such as the universAAL[7] and QUDT[8] ontology in order to follow the Linked Open Data principles of the semantic web.

Simulation Tasks

A simulation task encapsulates all information, required by the simulator. It is linked to the use case that shall be simulated.

Use Cases

The use case node shape comprises the related *states-of-interest* and *activities* that an agent can perform or recommend. Moreover, it is linked to all required *observation features*, that are monitored by the agent in order to make decisions.

---

[6] https://raw.githubusercontent.com/vcare-project/vcare-models/master/simulation.shapes.ttl.

[7] http://ontology.universaal.org/.

[8] http://qudt.org/.

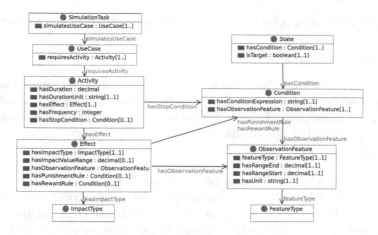

Fig. 2. UML representation of the simulation meta-model

States

The state shape is represented and derived by conditions that hold for the state. A state can be either a target state or an intermediate state, indicated by a boolean value. If a target state is achieved, the task is fulfilled by the agent and the next training episode can start.

State Conditions

State conditions reflect the guidelines for a use case. More concretely, they define whether all gathered observations apply to a single state. These conditions are specified in the form of mathematical expressions as illustrated below: The following expression types are allowed.

1. Ordinal expression — (e.g. Heart rate < 100)
2. Nominal expression — (e.g. Eye-color: brown, blue, green)
3. Logical expression — (e.g. Heart rate < 100 AND Heart rate >= 40)

The simulator takes these condition expressions for utilizing them within SPARQL query FILTER expressions. Moreover, the condition expressions provide the range boundaries in which the simulator can generate values in order to simulate a certain state. Therefore, the simulator parses the condition expressions and preprocesses the generated values by feature scaling into a normalized numerical feature vector representation, sorts and keeps them in-memory in order to select the appropriate values in a context-dependent manner. Nominal values are transformed by *one-hot-encoding* into a numerical vector representation consisting of ones and zeros. Thereby, every nominal value has a fixed position inside the vector. The value one at the appropriate position indicates that the nominal feature is present while the value zero indicates that it is absent. As logical operators are *AND*, *OR* and *XOR* allowed, since they are sufficient for specifying logical conditions. Furthermore, a state condition is linked to one or multiple *observation features*, since the conditions are build up by observation values.

Observation Features

An observation feature defines the feature type (e.g. nominal, numerical), the feature's value unit (e.g. kg, cm), and the value range containing a starting point number and ending point number. Within this range definition, the observation values are generated by the simulator.

Activities

Activities reflect what an agent or user can perform in order to achieve a goal and solve a task. The most important property of an activity in this approach, is its effect to the environment, since activity effects are changing the state of the environment. Therefore, activities lead to new observable states. Moreover, an activity can have a duration (e.g. 10 min) and can be performed in a certain frequency. Every activity has a stop condition that indicates whether it can be finished by the agent.

Effects

Since states are represented to the RL agent as numerical vectors, an effect can either *increase, decrease* a value by a certain amount or *convert* an one-hot-encoded nominal value to its opposite (e.g. true (1) to false (0) or vice versa). For this reason, the effect has an *impact* that indicates, whether a value shall be increased, decreased or converted. Moreover, an effect is linked to the appropriate observation feature to which it has an impact. Every activity is related at least to one effect, since activities cause state changes by their effects. The simulator is enabled by the effect representations to update state representations. Thereby, the *impact value range* property specifies how much the effect impacts an observation feature. Furthermore, the effects's reward- and punishment-rules are utilized by the simulator in order to reason rewards and punishments for certain performed activities in a given state because the effects of an activity are either desired or not desired effects depending on the observed state.

3.3   The Generation of Numerical State Representations

In this section, we comment on how single state vector values are adapted in order to generate new states according to performed activity effects. Since the state conditions are mathematical expressions, the simulator queries these conditions from a given state representation and parses them in order to create, based on their operators, appropriate expressions. These expressions provide an instruction for the simulator to create values within certain ranges. Subsequently, every observation feature value is sorted and stored in an in-memory data structure together with the generated values. The sorting of the values allows to update the state vector with higher or lower values depending on the current activity effects. Let us assume, we have a mathematical expression that expresses that the body mass index (BMI) requires to be in between a range of 18.5 and 25, as the depicted condition in Eq. 1.

$$(\text{BMI} \geq 18.5) \wedge (\text{BMI} \leq 25.0) \tag{1}$$

This condition holds for instance for the state *TargetBMI*. The simulator parses this expression and selects the start and end value of the BMI range as well as the operators (e.g. >=, <=). Based on these expression tokens, values are generated for the state *TargetBMI* inside the given range.

Every observation feature is stored with a list of generated values, restricted by the given guideline conditions. As soon as the simulator receives an activity, it looks up its effect to the observation features from the meta-model and compares the previous observation feature values in order to increase, decrease or convert them. This is easy to handle, since the values are sorted. Therefore, the simulator is able to select values from the lists that are higher or lower or the opposite (0 versus 1) than the last stored value.

3.4   State Reasoning Using SPARQL Queries

In every state-update-loop, the simulator needs to be aware of the currently generated state. Since only single observation values in the state vector are adapted, the state in which the simulation resides is not evident. Therefore, the simulator generates a statement for every updated observation, such as the following assertion:

```
:BMI :hasValue "22.4"^^xsd:double .
```

The simulator adds this assertion to the in-memory RDF(S) representation and infers the states in which an ML agent might be. This is done by using automatically generated SPARQL CONSTRUCT queries. Every generated query has the same structure:

```
CONSTRUCT {?agent :isInState ?state.}
WHERE {
  ?agent rdf:type :Agent.
  :BMI :hasValue ?bmi.
  FILTER(?bmi >= 18.5 && ?bmi <= 25.0)}
```

The CONSTRUCT queries are generated during the parsing of the condition expressions. Therefore, the simulator retrieves the states and their conditions and maps them to SPARQL FILTER expressions. The simulator generates by the CONSTRUCT query a new graph statement that expresses that the agent is in a certain state. The state conditions are listed in the WHERE clause within FILTER functions. In this way structured queries are universally applicable since they allow to reason the current state of an agent according to the given observations.

Considering the previous BMI example, the simulator would infer the *TargetBMI* state, provided that the given FILTER conditions hold.

3.5   The Reasoning of Rewards

The simulator has also the task to assign rewards to the agent according to the performed activity of the agent in a given state. This requires that the simulator determines the reasoned state of the agent and the appropriate effect of the performed activity. After the current state is reasoned as discussed in Sect. 3.4, the simulator reasons by means of CONSTRUCT queries the appropriate reward value for a state and the performed activity. The SPARQL query looks as follows:

```
CONSTRUCT {:DecreaseBMI :hasReward "-1.0"^^xsd:double.}
WHERE {
?agent :performsActivity ?activity.
?activity :hasEffect :DecreaseBMI.
{?agent :isInState :Underweight.} UNION {?agent :isInState :NormalBMI.}}
```

In the given example, the simulator reasons a punishment of minus one for the *DecreaseBMI* effect, if the agent is in the state *Underweight* or in the state *NormalBMI*. Therefore, rewards and punishments are assigned based on states and activity effects, since an effect can be desired or not, depending on the given states.

4   Proof-of-Concept

We selected two use cases from different domains, in order to demonstrate the generalizability of the presented approach. The first use case (*CKDPathway*) stems from the healthcare domain. The objective of this use case is to allow a virtual coach to make activity recommendations based on the given clinical pathway and by made vital sign observations. The second use case is about the intelligent control of IoT devices in a smart home environment depending on user activities and environmental states. In the next subsections, we describe the use cases and their relevant entities.

4.1   The Chronic Kidney Disease Pathway

The CKDPathway provides guidelines for the diagnosis and treatment of Chronic Kidney Disease (CKD). The pathway recommends lifestyle management activities, such as e.g. low sodium diet, physical exercises and medication. Nineteen different states can be identified (CKDWithDiabetes, CKDWithoutDiabetes, NoCKDRisk, CKDRisk, TargetA1C etc.) and thirty-seven possible activities (FluidIntakeRegulation, FruitVegetableConsumption, Walking, TestACR, TesteGFR, etc.). Moreover, the CKDPathway contains target states (TargetBMI, TargetA1C, TargetBloodpressure, etc.) that represent the long-term objectives of the CKDPathway. Every state in our setting is represented by a numerical vector, consisting of twenty-one observation values. The sensed observation features are: eGFR, ACR, Hematuria, Diabetes, BMI, systolic value, diastolic value etc. The diagnosis of CKD requires different rules (e.g. eGFR < 60ml/min/1.73^2, ACR $>= 3$ mg/mmol) that are also provided by the *CKD-Pathway*. For more details regarding the pathway, we refer to the appropriate online source (see footnote 1) and our shape definition[9].

4.2 Intelligent Smart Home Control Systems

The *intelligent smart home control* (SHC) use case has the objective to control or regulate context-dependent devices in the environment. The state space consists of different states, such as e.g. (1) *UserInFrontOfTV*, (2) *TVOn*, (3) *TVOff*, (4) *RoomTemperatureCold*, (5) *RoomTemperatureWarm*, (6) *RoomBrightnessDark*, (7) *RoomBrightnessBright*. The concrete objectives of this use case are:

– Autonomously switch the TV on or off, depending on the user location.
– Autonomously regulate the brightness in the rooms according to the user location, states of the installed lamps and brightness sensors.
– Autonomously regulate the temperature in the rooms according to the preferences of the user and the room temperature.

Considering these objectives, we determined the following observation features that are related to the previous mentioned states:

– BrightnessInLUX - Numerical value
– TemperatureInCelsiusDegree - Numerical value
– DistanceToTVInCentimeters - Numerical value
– UserLocatedRoom - Nominal value (Name of the room)

The according activities of the smart home system are: (1) *TurningLightOn*, (2) *DimLight*, (3) *TurningLightOff*, (4) *IncreaseTemperature*, (5) *DecreaseTemperature*, (6) *TurnTVOn*, (7) *TurnTVOff*. An excerpt of the appropriate rules are defined in Eq. 2. The appropriate states are determined by the given rule conditions.

$$\text{BrightnessInLUX} \leq 100 \rightarrow \text{RoomBrightnessDark}$$
$$\text{TemperatureInCelsiusDegree} \geq 25 \rightarrow \text{RoomTemperatureWarm}$$
$$\text{UserLocatedRoom} : XY \rightarrow \text{UserInRoomXY} \tag{2}$$

5 Evaluation

In this section, we aim at answering posed research questions RQ1 and RQ2. The goal is to explore if the generated simulation data can be used to avoid the cold-start problem. Moreover, we want to prove that our approach is applicable to

---

[9] https://github.com/vcare-project/vcare-models/blob/master/vcare.shapes.ttl.

multiple domains. Therefore, we evaluate if (a) the trained algorithms enable a RL agent to maximize its collected rewards by learning to recommend activities, yielding in the highest expected rewards and (b) the generated state vectors allow ML algorithms to predict, for unseen feature vectors, the correct states. Thereby, the clinical pathway guidelines as well as the given smart home rules provide the ground-truth of our evaluation. Based on the simulation meta-model, we created RDF(S) instances of the previously discussed use cases. Then, based on their representation, we trained a Deep-Q-Network RL algorithm[10], which was proposed by DeepMind in their paper [9]. We adopted for our evaluation, Karpathy's reinforcejs library because it implements different RL algorithms and is usable in browser as well as server environments. In order to prove the quality of the generated data, we counted the absolute rewards over time that the ML agent received during the evaluation phase. The diagram in Fig. 3a represents the execution steps (x-axis) with a window size of 70, while the y-axis represents the collected relative absolute rewards. We shows the positive rewards and received punishments using differently colored lines, comprising 4000 data samples. Figure 3a shows that the *CKDPathway* use case provided a good separation between the negative and positive rewards. As the learning phase starts, the lines start to diverge in opposite directions. However, neither the blue line increases nor the red line decreases significantly. This indicates that the RL algorithm does not improve after some training time. In the ideal case the blue line would increase steadily, while the red line would decrease, so that the agent achieves the maximum expected reward. Figure 3b, representing the agent improvement for the *SHC* use case is even worse. It seems that the agent learns nothing and that it even collects more punishments than rewards. Considering this result, the agent learns nothing from the generated simulation data. In order to explore the separation of the generated states, we plotted every feature of the SHC case as multiple 2D-projections in Fig. 4. Every state in the plot is represented by a specific color. The better the separation of states, the better is the generated data for training ML algorithms. Here, the 4000-samples data set (b) provides an apparent advantage over the 1000-samples data set (a). This insight indicates: the more data is generated the more are the states separable. A feature vector representing several states in the same time leads to an insignificant separation of states. Therefore, the approach can be improved if the simulator generates sparse feature vectors representing only one state in a single training step. Moreover, states, represented by the same features, require significant guideline-rules. This observation can be later used to improve the quality of the models prepared by the domain experts.

Our evaluation has the following limitations. (1) We did not compare our approach against a baseline due to the cold-start problem – no data sets are available that can act as a baseline. For this reason, the domain expert's guideine-rules and the proposed clinical pathway provide already a baseline against that we can evaluate our approach. However, it is planned to implement additionally a rule-based agent in order to compare its performance against the trained RL

---

[10] Implementation from Karpathy under https://github.com/karpathy/reinforcejs.

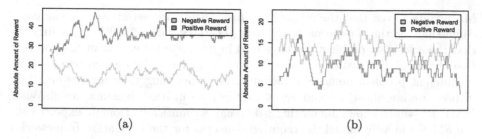

Fig. 3. (a) CKD: Absolute Reward over time. (roll sum, win = 70) and (b) SHC: Absolute Reward over time. (roll sum, win = 70)

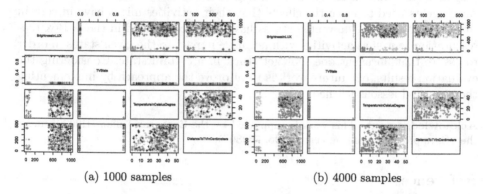

(a) 1000 samples   (b) 4000 samples

Fig. 4. Distribution of states projected to two dimensions (pairs of observations).

agent's performance. (2) Another limitation is that we did not evaluate the training of a ML agent with and without the simulator. Therefore, it is required to show in a future evaluation that the simulator allows a faster convergence of the ML algorithm than a training without a simulator. In a later stage, we would like to prove that the trained RL agent generalizes better than a rule-based agent does due to the limitations of rules.

6 Conclusion and Outlook

We proposed and evaluated a semantic simulation framework that utilizes a general meta-model for use cases and their guideline rules. In the framework's evaluation, we showed for RQ1 and RQ2 its limitations when it comes to solving the cold-start problem and its application to multiple domains. We demonstrated what a crucial role the domain experts play in the process. The approach is rather sensitive to the quality of rules and rewards modeled. Model validation (we used SHACL) is essential for keeping the quality of the A-Box representation at a usable level. We also showed that the approach can be improved by modeling the state representations using sparse numerical vectors (for better separation) or by providing more samples (which is usually the case in the

ML world). Given that the proposed improvements are performed, we can conclude that (a) the simulation framework generates data of sufficient quality so
that the cold-start problem can be solved in uncontrolled environments and (b)
that the simulation framework is capable of adapting its data-generation process
to different problem domains sufficiently. As supporting tools for the creation
of use case specifications and agent profiles, we utilized Semantic MediaWiki
(SMW)[11], which allows annotating wiki pages semantically. Domain experts can
use SMW to easily model the required concepts for the simulation framework.
For the implementation of the RL-agent, we adopted the library reinforcejs[12],
which implements different RL algorithms. We demonstrated that rewards and
punishments should be assigned depending on the given state and activity effects,
since agents need to learn the effects that their activities might have in certain
situations. Moreover, unwanted states have to be considered in the A-Box representation as well as activities with negative impact to the given states in order
to assure that an agent does not get stuck in a certain state. Considering the
evaluation results, our future work is to improve the approach by implementing
the discussed lessons learned.

Acknowledgement. This work is supported by the European Union (H2020) under
the vCare project (grant agreement No. 769807).

References

1. Mariappan, A.K., Sobhanam, H.: A hybrid approach to solve cold start problem
   in recommender systems using association rules and clustering technique. Int. J.
   Comput. Appl. **74**(4), 17–23 (2013)
2. Carlson, A., et al.: Toward an architecture for never-ending language learning. In:
   AAAI. vol. 5, p. 3. Atlanta (2010)
3. Di Noia, T., Ostuni, V.C.: Recommender systems and linked open data. In: Faber,
   W., Paschke, A. (eds.) Reasoning Web 2015. LNCS, vol. 9203, pp. 88–113. Springer,
   Cham (2015). https://doi.org/10.1007/978-3-319-21768-0_4
4. Godoy, D., Amandi, A.: An agent-based recommender system to support collaborative web search based on shared user interests. In: Haake, J.M., Ochoa, S.F.,
   Cechich, A. (eds.) CRIWG 2007. LNCS, vol. 4715, pp. 303–318. Springer, Heidelberg (2007). https://doi.org/10.1007/978-3-540-74812-0_24
5. Lika, B., Kolomvatsos, K., Hadjiefthymiades, S.: Facing the cold start problem
   in recommender systems. Expert. Syst. Appl. **41**(4, Part 2), 2065–2073 (2014).
   https://doi.org/10.1016/j.eswa.2013.09.005
6. Mantrach, A.: Cold start solutions for recommender systems. https://research.
   yahoo.com/_c/uploads/SeminarUCSD.pdf
7. Mehta, R., Rana, K.: A review on matrix factorization techniques in recommender
   systems. In: 2017 2nd International Conference on Communication Systems, Computing and IT Applications (CSCITA), pp. 269–274, April 2017
8. Middleton, S.E., Alani, H., Roure, D.D.: Exploiting synergy between ontologies
   and recommender systems. CoRR arXiv:cs/0204012 (2002)

---

[11] https://www.semantic-mediawiki.org/wiki/Semantic_MediaWiki.
[12] https://github.com/karpathy/reinforcejs.

9. Mnih, V., et al.: Playing atari with deep reinforcement learning. CoRR arXiv:cs/0204012 (2013)
10. Musto, C.: Introducing linked open data in graph-based recommender systems. Inf. Process. Manag. **53**(2), 405–435 (2017). https://doi.org/10.1016/j.ipm.2016.12.003
11. Nouali, O., Belloui, A.: Using semantic web to reduce the cold-start problems in recommendation systems. In: 2009 Second International Conference on the Applications of Digital Information and Web Technologies, pp. 525–530, August 2009
12. Palau, J., Montaner, M., López, B., de la Rosa, J.L.: Collaboration analysis in recommender systems using social networks. In: Klusch, M., Ossowski, S., Kashyap, V., Unland, R. (eds.) CIA 2004. LNCS (LNAI), vol. 3191, pp. 137–151. Springer, Heidelberg (2004). https://doi.org/10.1007/978-3-540-30104-2_11
13. Peis, E., et al.: Semantic recommender systems. Analysis of the state of the topic. Hipertext.net 6 (2008). http://hipertext.net/english/pag1031.htm
14. Rubens, N., Elahi, M., Sugiyama, M., Kaplan, D.: Active learning in recommender systems. In: Ricci, F., Rokach, L., Shapira, B. (eds.) Recommender Systems Handbook, pp. 809–846. Springer, Boston, MA (2015). https://doi.org/10.1007/978-1-4899-7637-6_24
15. Schein, A.I., Popescul, A., Unger, L.H., Pennock, D.M.: Methods and metrics for cold-start recommendations. In: Proceedings of SIGIR 2002, pp. 253–260. Tampere, Finland (2002). https://doi.org/10.1145/564376.564421
16. Settles, B.: Active learning literature survey. Computer Sciences Technical Report 1648, University of Wisconsin-Madison (2010). http://axon.cs.byu.edu/~martinez/classes/778/Papers/settles.activelearning.pdf
17. Son, L.H.: Dealing with the new user cold-start problem in recommender systems: a comparative review. Inf. Syst. **58**, 87–104 (2016). http://www.sciencedirect.com/science/article/pii/S0306437914001525
18. Sutton, R.S., Barto, A.G.: Introduction to Reinforcement Learning, 1st edn. MIT Press, Cambridge, MA, USA (1998)
19. Thanh-Tai, H., Nguyen, H.-H., Thai-Nghe, N.: A semantic approach in recommender systems. In: Dang, T.K., Wagner, R., Küng, J., Thoai, N., Takizawa, M., Neuhold, E. (eds.) FDSE 2016. LNCS, vol. 10018, pp. 331–343. Springer, Cham (2016). https://doi.org/10.1007/978-3-319-48057-2_23
20. Tomeo, P., et al.: Exploiting linked open data in cold-start recommendations with positive-only feedback. In: Proceedings of the 4th Spanish Conference on Information Retrieval. pp. 11:1–11:8. CERI 2016. ACM, New York (2016). https://doi.org/10.1145/2934732.2934745
21. Yang, R.: Using semantic technology to improve recommender systems based on slope one. In: Li, J., Qi, G., Zhao, D., Nejdl, W., Zheng, H.T. (eds.) Semantic Web and Web Science, pp. 11–23. Springer, New York (2012). https://doi.org/10.1007/978-1-4614-6880-6_2

KnIGHT: Mapping Privacy Policies to GDPR

Najmeh Mousavi Nejad[1,2]($\boxtimes$), Simon Scerri[1,2], and Jens Lehmann[1,2]

[1] Smart Data Analytics (SDA), University of Bonn, Bonn, Germany
{nejad,scerri,jens.lehmann}@cs.uni-bonn.de
[2] Fraunhofer Intelligent Analysis and Information Systems (IAIS), Sankt Augustin, Germany
http://sda.cs.uni-bonn.de
https://www.iais.fraunhofer.de

Abstract. Although the use of apps and online services comes with accompanying privacy policies, a majority of end-users ignore them due to their length, complexity and unappealing presentation.pite the potential risks. In light of the, now enforced EU-wide, General Data Protection Regulation (GDPR) we present an automatic technique for mapping privacy policies excerpts to relevant GDPR articles so as to support average users in understanding their usage risks and rights as a data subject. *KnIGHT* (Know your rIGHTs), is a tool that finds candidate sentences in a privacy policy that are potentially related to specific articles in the GDPR. The approach employs semantic text matching in order to find the most appropriate GDPR paragraph, and to the best of our knowledge is one of the first automatic attempts of its kind applied to a company's policy. Our evaluation shows that on average between 70–90% of the tool's automatic mappings are at least partially correct, meaning that the tool can be used to significantly guide human comprehension. Following this result, in the future we will utilize domain-specific vocabularies to perform a deeper semantic analysis and improve the results further.

Keywords: Privacy policy · General data protection regulation
Semantic text matching

1 Introduction

As technologies for analysis of Web data have grown, data privacy concerns (e.g., fraud, identity theft, etc.) among end-users have become a major issue. Enterprises try to employ automated techniques to analyze customer's personal data in order to achieve their business goals, but unsurprisingly they do not always adhere to the law. In 2015, the Belgian privacy commission reported that Facebook's privacy policy breaches European law[1]. Moreover, in 2017 the

---

[1] https://www.theguardian.com/technology/2015/feb/23/facebooks-privacy-policy-breaches-european-law-report-finds.

© Springer Nature Switzerland AG 2018
C. Faron Zucker et al. (Eds.): EKAW 2018, LNAI 11313, pp. 258–272, 2018.
https://doi.org/10.1007/978-3-030-03667-6_17

Dutch data protection authority (DPA) announced that Microsoft's Windows 10 breaches data protection law, since it is not clear which personal data it collects and why[2]. As a result, people apply self protection methods to ensure that their personal information are not being misused. According to a study, the users attempt to protect their data either by installing a privacy protection software or by providing false information to the websites [2]. In addition to the public's distrust, the majority also tend to skip the privacy policies when signing up for products and services. A survey claims that only 26% of participants in a lab study read privacy policies and this percentage is expected to be much lower outside of laboratory conditions [15]. Furthermore, these findings were verified by another recent experiment in which 543 university students were asked to agree to a fictitious social network's privacy policy and terms of service in order to join the network [17]. The study shows only 26% did not select the 'quick join' and unsurprisingly the average reading time of those who read privacy policy was 73 s.

The supervisory authorities worldwide enact strict regulations regarding data protection of a natural person. The European Union as well, have recently upgraded the current data protection directive to harmonize data privacy laws across Europe. The (GDPR)[3] legislation came into force on May 25th, 2018. It is 88 pages long and has 99 articles, grouped into 11 chapters and an extra 171 recitals with explanatory remarks. All EU members must now comply with GDPR.

The novel approach behind *KnIGHT* exploits semantic similarity between words to associate the privacy policy sentences to the corresponding paragraphs in GDPR. We investigate semantic text matching techniques that map privacy policy segments with relevant GDPR articles. The targeted beneficiaries of our tool are regular users who would like to become more aware of the contents of a privacy policy. *KnIGHT* offers them shortcuts to the underlying legislation so that they can learn more about their risks and rights; empowering them with the possibility to stop using a specific service if its privacy policy includes suspicious clauses, or to report it to an authority. Nevertheless, more advanced users (e.g. lawyers, legal experts and compliance officers) would also benefit from future improved versions of *KnIGHT*.

KnIGHT takes a privacy policy and GDPR articles and finds the correlations between the two documents at sentence and paragraph level. Since not all sentences in a privacy policy are related to data usage and analysis, first the candidate sentences will be identified using a *GATE* pipeline [9]. This step will significantly reduce the number of processed excerpts in the policy text. After that, for each candidate the most related article will be found. Finally, the best paragraph match from the identified article will be detected for that candidate sentence. It is worth to mention that *KnIGHT* is independent of policy type or the regulatory documents. Whenever a policy must comply with some laws, this technique can be applied. However, since the recently enforced GDPR has become of crucial importance it is the focus of this study.

---

[2] https://www.bbc.com/news/technology-41634617.
[3] https://gdpr-info.eu/.

To the best of our knowledge, in spite of the importance of this issue, there is no automated approach to match a company's policy to regulatory documents in order to assist regular end-users to check the lawfulness of a company's activities and to familiarize themselves with their rights as a consumer. As explained in Sect. 2, although there have been numerous efforts addressing regulatory compliance, the objectives were somehow different. In Sect. 3, we describe *KnIGHT*'s workflow and its architecture. In Sect. 4 the experiments are explained and finally Sect. 5 concludes this paper with a list of possible directions for future work.

2   Related Work

We compare and contrast our approach with efforts in three main categories: (1) regulatory compliance (2) semantic text matching and (3) privacy policy studies.

GaiusT is a tool which semi-automatically extracts rights and obligation from a regulatory document [20]. According to the paper, these obligations should be considered in the requirement model of a system software design. For extracting rights, duties and actors from a regulatory text, a semantic annotation framework is applied and extended. Finally, the approach is verified by presenting the result of two case studies: the U.S. Health Insurance Portability and Accountability Act (HIPPA) and the Italian accessibility law for information technology instruments. In a similar study, a process called "Semantic Parameterization" has been applied to privacy rules from HIPAA [5]. First, rights and obligations are reformulated into Restricted Natural Language Statements (RNLS) and then RNLSs are mapped into semantic models to clarify ambiguities. At the end, the authors listed some limitation which arose from their incomplete set of phrase heuristics. Last but not least, a prominent group in regulatory compliance is GRTCT[4]. The group has recently developed *Ganesha* platform which uses semantic technologies and assists the industry professionals to track and compare legislations, leading to better financial compliance. It employs OMG Standards[5] (SBVR[6], FIBO[7], etc.) to semantically enrich the regulatory texts.

As opposed to our approach, none of the above efforts prioritize the regular end-users needs and concerns. Our goal is to design a policy reading system to assist consumers to familiarize themselves with a specific policy and the relevant regulation. We strive to motivate them to make themselves aware of what they are agreeing to by using a service and encourage them to know their rights as a citizen according to their regional laws. Furthermore, since the previous methods have dealt with a single target regulatory document, they are not suitable to be applied in our approach. Our identified problem tackles the overlap of a company's policy and the relevant legislations and therefore is addressing two sources of legal texts.

---

[4] http://www.grctc.com/.
[5] http://www.omg.org/.
[6] https://www.omg.org/spec/SBVR.
[7] https://www.omg.org/spec/EDMC-FIBO/FND/.

In the context of semantic text matching, the closest field to our approach is intelligent plagiarism. Intelligent plagiarism techniques find semantically similar matches in different documents (e.g., finding similar paragraphs in two papers). An extensive study of state-of-the-art has been conducted in [3]. The paper focuses on two main steps for plagiarism detection: first the latest techniques for retrieval of candidate documents are explained; then the exhaustive analysis of suspicious candidates for plagiarism detection is presented. For the first step two main approaches are usually used: information retrieval models (fingerprints, hash-based models, vector space models, etc.) and clustering techniques. For the second step, depending on the plagiarism type (literal or intelligent), different methods can be applied. In the case of intelligent plagiarism, semantic and fuzzy based method are used. Semantic features include word synonyms, antonyms, hypernyms and hyponyms. Furthermore, the use of thesaurus dictionaries and lexical databases gives more insights into the semantic meaning of the text. In addition, POS tagging and semantic dependencies will enrich semantic based methods. Regarding fuzzy based methods, word embeddings are similar to the "fuzzy" concept, since both implement a spectrum of similarity values for each word, e.g., there is a degree of similarity for each word and the associated fuzzy set. Finally, the authors recommend that semantic and fuzzy methods are the most proper approaches for intelligent plagiarism detection.

In contrast to our problem, intelligent plagiarism performs the information retrieval step only once to find the candidate documents, whereas in our case, the retrieval process for finding the related GDPR article(s) should be applied for each candidate sentence in the privacy policy. Therefore, we need a better solution to decrease the computation cost. However, we learned from the state-of-the-art that the most appropriate approach for finding similar matches is the semantic methods and hence we exploit semantic techniques in *KnIGHT*.

Some studies dealt specifically with privacy policies. Costante et al. and Guntamukkala et al. developed a system which evaluates the completeness of privacy policies [7,11]. To achieve this goal, first some categories are defined following privacy regulations and guidelines. Then, employing text categorization and machine learning techniques, the corresponding categories of privacy policy paragraphs are determined. In this case, the user can examine the policy in a structured format and study those parts that she is interested in. Although both papers propose promising approaches, most of current privacy policies are already in a structured format and use rich HTML representation (for example *ReseachGate*[8] & *Unilever* [9]). In addition, both approaches have used supervised machine learning and complied a training data set manually whereas our method is independent of the subject material.

The Usable Privacy Policy Project initiated in 2013, aims to extract information from privacy policies and make it available for consumers, developers and regulators[10]. The team has compiled a dataset called, *Online Privacy Policies*

---

[8] https://www.researchgate.net/privacy-policy.
[9] http://www.unileverprivacypolicy.com/en_gb/policy.aspx.
[10] https://usableprivacy.org/.

(OPP-115) which was annotated by 3 experts into 10 categories [19]. Polisis[11], an online service for privacy policy analysis, leverages OPP-115, NLP and deep learning techniques to extract segments from a privacy policy [12]. Each segment has a set of labels which describe its data practices. The authors claim that they reach 88.4% accuracy for the automatic generation of labels. Despite the encouraging work done by the whole team, we believe that the missing part is relating the privacy policies to the data protection laws in the favor of both end-users and regulators. Nevertheless, analyzing the OPP-115 dataset and utilizing the segment's labels for improving our mapping approach is one of our future direction.

3   Approach

In this section we explain the architecture and implementation of *KnIGHT* which builds on *GATE* embedded and *Deeplearning4j* [1] open source APIs. *Deeplearning4j* or *DL4J* implements deep learning algorithms with a specific focus on neural network techniques. The library offers word2vec and paragraph2vec as well, with a default word2vec model trained on Google News Corpus[12]. Figure 1 shows the architecture and workflow of *KnIGHT* that consists of two main steps: preparation phase which is independent of input; and the main semantic matching phase. Each of the following subsections presents how each phase fits within the architecture.

3.1   Preparation

Our approach deals specifically with GDPR legislation, therefore the preprocessing procedure can be done independently from the input (which is a privacy policy in the natural language). The preparation phase exploits a ready-made application called *GATE TermRaider*[13]. *TermRaider* is an English term extraction tool that runs over a text corpus and produces noun phrase term candidates together with a score which shows the salience of each term candidate in a domain specific corpus. Benefiting from this plugin, the preparation phase includes the following steps:

1. Twenty privacy policies from European Union companies were collected to build a privacy policy corpus.
2. Having this corpus, *TermRaider* was executed on top of it to find the most important terms in privacy policies which carry essential information. This step creates an annotation set called *Term Candidate*.

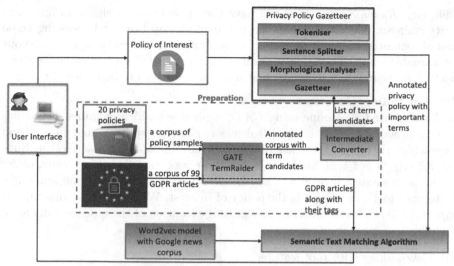

Fig. 1. Architecture and workflow of *KnIGHT*

3. The annotation set produced in the previous step is converted to a text file to be used in the semantic text matching phase. Therefore, an intermediate converter processes all *Term Candidate* annotations and generates a list of terms with their corresponding roots (root is only meaningful when the term is a single token).

4. Another corpus was built with all 99 GDPR articles and *TermRaider* was executed on this corpus separately to generate a set of tags (also known as fingerprints) for each GDPR article. These tags are used in the related article retrieval phase (explained in the next subsection).

Since the preparation phase happens only once, the final response time will be reduced significantly. Furthermore, this layer architecture enables us to add more data privacy legislations in future with a small effort.

3.2 Semantic Text Matching

Once the initial processing has been done, the system will be ready to accept a privacy policy. As mentioned before, *KnIGHT* relates a sentence in a policy to (a) paragraph(s) in GDPR. The rational behind choosing the sentence level in the privacy policy is the existence of different layouts in writing those policies, e.g., it is complicated to determine the size and boundaries of a paragraph in an arbitrary policy. On the other hand, specifying the boundaries of a sentence is much easier in any form of a page style. However, processing all sentences in a privacy policy and relating them to GDPR is not logical, since some sentences carry service specific information and do not have a direct connection to

GDPR, e.g., *Ryanair* says: "You will have the option to stay signed-in into your myRyanair account by checking the **remember me** box".[14] Processing these kind of sentences will only impose extra computation cost on the system without any valuable result. Therefore, a simple pipeline called *Privacy Policy Gazetteer* will first find candidate sentences that have the potential to be matched to GDPR.

Privacy Policy Gazetteer

We have created a pipeline using *GATE* embedded which contains some common preprocessing steps in NLP (tokeniser, sentence splitter, root finder) and a gazetteer that includes a list of all *Term Candidate*. As described in Subsect. 3.1, the input text file for this gazetteer was compiled using *TermRaider* and an intermediate converter. The gazetteer parses the text file and annotates the terms which are present in the policy of interest. We called these annotations *Important Term*. To summarize, a successful execution of the pipeline will create the following annotation types:

(i) *Token* along with root feature;
(ii) *Sentence*; and
(iii) *Important Term*.

Based on our repeated observation, almost every sentence in a policy has at least one *Important Term*. Around 75–85% of sentences have two, 65–75% have three and 50–70% have four *Important Terms*. Since two seems too broad and four is too narrow, we set our threshold to three. Thus, if a *Sentence* includes at least three *Important Terms*, it will be considered as a candidate.

Semantic Text Matching Algorithm

This component is the main element of *KnIGHT* and has three inputs: the annotated privacy policy with *Important Term* annotations, GDPR articles along with their tags (tags are the generated *Term Candidate* by *TermRaider*) and a word2vec model. Algorithm 1 shows the sketch of our semantic matching approach and has two main steps for each candidate sentence:

(i) Retrieval of the most related GDPR article (lines 3 to 14).
(ii) Finding the best paragraph match in the identified article (lines 15 to 25).

In the first step, the most related GDPR article is found for each candidate sentence. To achieve this goal, we compare the semantic similarity between two sets: Set_1 which contains *Important Terms* in the current candidate sentence and Set_2 that loops over all GDPR articles and in each loop, it contains the corresponding article tags.

Assuming sets S_1 and S_2 consist of n and m terms corresponding to T_{11}, ..., T_{n1} and T_{12}, ..., T_{m2}, the similarity between the two sets is calculated as shown in Eq. 1. In this equation $compositionalSim(Term1, Term2)$ is an extension of word2vec similarity function. Word2vec represents every word as an n-dimensional vector and then computes the semantic similarity between two words

---

[14] https://www.ryanair.com/gb/en/corporate/privacy-policy.

Algorithm 1. Sketch of Text Matching Algorithm

Require: privacy policy candidate sentences, GDPR fingerprints, word2vec model
```
 1: for all candidate sentences in the privacy policy do
 2:     candidateSentence ← current sentence
 3:     Set1 ← all important terms in candidateSentence
 4:     MatchesList ← an empty list
 5:     for all GDPR articles do
 6:         ArticleNum ← article number
 7:         Set2 ← article tags
 8:         Sim ← similarity between Set1 & Set2
 9:         if Sim1 > threshold then
10:             add Sim1 & ArticleNum to MatchesList
11:         end if
12:     end for
13:     SortedList ← Sort MatchesList acc. to sim
14:     BestArticleMatch ← SortedList[0]
15:     MaxSim ← 0
16:     Vec1 ← word2vec vector of candidateSentence
17:     for all paragraphs in BestArticleMatch do
18:         currPar ← current paragraph
19:         Vec2 ← word2vec vector of currPar
20:         Sim2 ← similarity between Vec1 & Vec2
21:         if Sim2 > MaxSim then
22:             MaxSim ← Sim2
23:             bestParMatch ← current paragraph
24:         end if
25:     end for
26: end for
```
Ensure: Policy excerpts & their relevant GDPR paragraphs

using *Cosine* similarity of two vectors. However, the default library does not provide a function for computing the similarity between multi-words terms. To solve this issue, we have defined a formula (Eq. 2) which composes all individual words vectors in a multi-words term by summation and creates a single vector for that term. Having two composed vectors for each multi-words term, the *Cosine* function is again applied to calculate the similarity between two terms. Finally, if the similarity between two sets is greater than a fixed threshold (line 9 in Algorithm 1), it will be added to a list along with the similarity score. In the presence of a gold standard, the threshold can be determined by changing its value and finding the best one which produces the highest F-measure. Due to lack of such gold standard in our case, the threshold is calculated by considering the average of all the similarity scores. Last but not least, our approach is able to find the TOP-n matches of GDPR. However for simplicity, only the best match is shown in the algorithm sketch.

$$Sim(S_1, S_2) = \frac{\sum_{i=1}^{n} \max_{1 \le j \le m}[CompositionalSim(T_{i1}, T_{j2})]}{\frac{n+m}{2}} \qquad (1)$$

$$CompositionalSim(T_1, T_2) =$$
$$cosineSim(\sum_{i=1}^{n} wordVector(T_{i1}), \sum_{j=1}^{m} wordVector(T_{j2})) \qquad (2)$$

Having retrieved the best GDPR article for the current candidate sentence, the most related paragraph in the identified article should be found (second step). Lacking a large domain specific corpus, we have modified word2vec model to be able to generate a vector for a sentence and paragraph. According to the literature, a simple yet an efficient way to represent a sentence or a paragraph as a vector is computing the average of all word vectors [16]. In the preparation phase, all GDPR paragraph vectors are calculated and stored, whereas the candidate sentence vector is computed in real time. Employing *Cosine* similarity between the candidate sentence vector and all paragraph vectors of the retrieved article, the paragraph with the highest similarity will be identified as the best match.

It is worth to mention that *KnIGHT* is policy and legislation independent. As an example it can be applied to cookie policy which is sometimes embedded into the privacy policy itself. Cookies should comply with the ePrivacy directive[15] that will be soon replaced by proposed ePrivacy regulation[16]. In this case, a corpus of cookies policy in their natural text should be collected to be ingested to *TermRaider*.

4   Evaluation and Discussion

Semantic text mapping is a non-trivial task and its evaluation is just as complex. The ideal assessment method would be to create a gold standard with the help of domain experts; legal experts in this case. For a number of reasons, pursuing this method was not feasible. It was not possible to procure legal experts to perform extremely lengthy tasks (legal policies are lengthy and dense in terms of terminology and implications). Pro bono or voluntary participation from a sufficient amount of experts was also not an option. In addition, legal terms are still rather subjective (and it appears to be markedly more difficult to resolve differences in ideas between legal professionals), and therefore achieving a satisfactory Inter Annotator Agreement (IAA) to generate a gold standard based on which to run the experiment was not possible. For the above reasons, after the first expert concluded (dedicating a total of almost 3 h) that manual annotation of 4 policies is a time-consuming and subjective task, we changed our strategy and decided to go for a posteriori assessment as our primary experiment. The objective here

---

[15] http://eur-lex.europa.eu/legal-content/EN/TXT/?qid=1525876803065&uri=CELEX:32002L0058.

[16] https://eur-lex.europa.eu/legal-content/EN/TXT/?uri=COM:2017:0010:FIN.

was to obtain an expert-rated F-measure of the results produced by *KnIGHT*, for the same 4 policies. That said, the primary targeted end-users of the tool are non-experts. Therefore to contextualize these results we conducted the second experiment: 2 lay users were also asked to do what *KnIGHT* does. In this case, to have a realistic yardstick they were instructed to spend between at least 1 and at most 2 h to go through all 4 policies and identify GDPR sections which helped them better understand the makeup of each policy. This exercise, being directly comparable to the first expert's manual annotation, shows the expected success rate of non-expert vs expert GDPR mapping.

4.1 Posteriori Assessment

In order to perform a posteriori assessment, 4 privacy policies from European Union companies were selected and the approach was applied to these policies in their natural language text. Posteriori assessment means running *KnIGHT* over privacy policy texts, finding the matches in GDPR and then validating them by legal experts. A successful execution of our pipeline generates some links between privacy policy sentences and GDPR paragraphs. Afterwards, in order to reach a semi-conclusive result, 4 legal experts (lawyers or senior law students) were asked to go through the detected links and categorize them into three classes: **related; partially related; or unrelated**[17]. Although *KnIGHT* can generate TOP-n matches of GDPR paragraphs for a single candidate sentence, only the best match was considered in the current assessment to reduce the examination time required by experts. In total, 77 annotations were sent to each assessor. Table 1 shows the results per each expert and privacy policy. The *Avg* column denotes the average number for 4 experts per each class, e.g., for *Booking.com* privacy policy, on average 6 out of 23 detected matches were assessed as **related**. However, since privacy and data protection regulations are general in nature and subject to interpretation, there is always a part of subjectivity in legal text assessment. This means that the average column may not necessarily refer to the same annotations for all assessors, e.g., for *Booking.com*, we can not claim that the 6 annotations for **related** class in *Avg* column is the same annotations for all observers.

Table 1. Posteriori assessment by 4 experts (E1-E4) for four privacy policies

Privacy policy	#Matches	Related					Partially Related					Unrelated				
		E1	E2	E3	E4	**Avg**	E1	E2	E3	E4	**Avg**	E1	E2	E3	E4	**Avg**
Booking.com	23	7	6	5	6	**6**	12	8	10	9	**9.75**	4	9	8	8	**7.25**
ResearchGate	29	11	14	8	14	**11.75**	8	9	12	4	**8.25**	10	6	9	11	**9**
Ryanair	10	2	3	2	3	**2.5**	4	4	4	3	**3.75**	4	3	4	4	**3.75**
Unilever	15	7	7	2	6	**5.5**	4	4	8	4	**5**	4	4	5	5	**4.5**

---

[17] Although we strived to increase the number of evaluators, it was notably hard to find legal experts that agreed to participate in this voluntary task.

IAA is an agreement measure which can be calculated in Kappa or F-meaure. When the observers have the choice to determine the span of the text for annotation, F-measure is recommended [14]. On the other hand, Kappa is appropriate when observers have the same number of classes but with different labels and ranges between -1 and 1 (1:complete disagreement, 0:random agreement, 1:full agreement). Kappa and observed agreements are conventionally computed for two annotators [13]. The extension to more than two annotators is usually taken as the mean of the pair-wise agreements [10]. Furthermore, if the categories (A, B, C, ...) are ordered, weighted Kappa is considered [6]. Our three classes can be treated as an ordered list, because if one expert classifies a match into group **related** and the other into group **partially related**, this is closer than if one classifies into **related** and the other into **unrelated**.

Tables 2 and 3 show observed agreement and weighted kappa with linear weights. E1 to E4 represent experts and the scores are calculated for all four privacy policies. The results prove that even with a strict number of classes, there is still a part of subjectivity in the assessment and reconfirms the complexity of legal texts. We have provided some examples of agreement and disagreement in Table 4. The first sentence from *Booking.com* informs the user that their personal data will only be used with their consent. *KnIGHT* maps this sentence to one of GDPR articles about "conditions for consent" and specifically to the paragraph related to the conditions for withdrawing a consent by the data subject. Two experts assessed this match as **partially related**, one as **related** and the other as **unrelated**. Those who annotated this mapping as a partial or perfect match believe that although the sentence is not about withdrawing a consent, the detected GDPR paragraph helps end-users to be aware of their rights. Apart from subjectivity issue, we have realized that the experts tend to have less agreement for short sentences because a short sentence does not say much and it is more controversial. Increasing the window size and considering neighbor sentences will solve this problem. Another issue identified, was generation of incomplete set of tags for some GDPR articles. The second sentence in Table 4 is mapped to article 77 about "right to lodge a complaint with a supervisory authority" and was labeled as **unrelated** by all experts. This article is a short one with two paragraphs and the generated set of tags contains only three terms: {*supervisory authority, personal data, complaint*}. Therefore the best article retrieval phase detects this article as the best match. This problem can be resolved by narrowing down the domain of the approach, since *KnIGHT* currently uses a general approach without any human involvement. Choosing a specific legislation makes it possible to get help from the domain experts, e.g., in our case we can ask legal experts to manually create some tags for each GDPR article. Finally, our evaluations proved that when the similarity score between the candidate sentence and detected paragraph is high, the degree of agreement increases. As an example, the third sentence in Table 4 is the best match detected by *KnIGHT* with the similarity equals to 0.75 (max $= 1$) and it shows complete agreement.

Table 2. Pair-wise agreement between experts

Experts	Booking.com	ResearchGate	Ryanair	Unilever
E1 & E2	47.8	79.3	80	66.7
E1 & E3	56.5	62.1	40	53.3
E1 & E4	47.8	82.8	70	73.3
E2 & E3	47.8	62.1	40	60
E2 & E4	52.2	75.9	60	40
E3 & E4	47.8	72.4	50	53.3
Average	**50**	**72.4**	**56.7**	**57.8**

Table 3. Pair-wise weighted kappa between experts

Experts	Booking.com	ResearchGate	Ryanair	Unilever
E1 & E2	30.9	73	76.2	63.4
E1 & E3	38.1	56.5	25	40.6
E1 & E4	34.6	82	63.4	63.4
E2 & E3	33.7	56.8	28.6	43.2
E2 & E4	37.1	66.8	43.2	25
E3 & E4	26.1	70.9	39	43.2
Average	**33.4**	**67.7**	**46**	**46.4**

4.2 Potential End-Users Impact

According to the literature, end-users tend to skip privacy policies and time plays a serious barrier in this case [8]. In order to estimate the time and effort required by end-users for privacy policy comprehension, we asked two non-experts to find the obvious links between four privacy policies of Subsect. 4.1 and GDPR. Here we have used the first expert (E1) annotations (in total 204 links) as a loose gold standard. Table 5 shows the comparison of non-experts annotations and *KnIGHT*'s mapping against E1 gold standard. Since in some cases, the non-experts mapped a single excerpt of a policy to multiple articles, we computed an OR conjunction, e.g., if one of the articles was correct according to E1 gold standard, it was considered as a true positive. As expected, precision and recall are low compared to E1 gold standard and this is inevitable, because experts have a high understanding of privacy policies and in some cases the created links do not have any similar vocabularies but represent an expert inference. On the other hand, the results proves that *KnIGHT* can be a valuable tool for non-experts. Lay end-users spend a lot of time and effort but achieved almost the same F-measure, as opposed to zero effort and instant results of *KnIGHT*.

Table 4. Example of detected links & experts (E1–E4) assessments (R: related, P: partially related, U: unrelated)

Policy sentence	Detected GDPR Paragraph	E1	E2	E3	E4
Any additional personal details that you give us as a part of the market research will be used only with your consent	Article 7(3): *The data subject shall have the right to withdraw his or her consent at any time. The withdrawal of consent shall not affect the lawfulness of processing based on consent before its withdrawal. Prior to giving consent, the data subject shall be informed thereof. It shall be as easy to withdraw as to give consent*	R	P	U	P
We will comply with all applicable data protection laws and regulations and we will co-operate with data protection authorities	Article 77(1): *Without prejudice to any other administrative or judicial remedy, every data subject shall have the right to lodge a complaint with a supervisory authority, in particular in the Member State of his or her habitual residence, place of work or place of the alleged infringement if the data subject considers that the processing of personal data relating to him or her infringes this Regulation*	U	U	U	U
Where a Unilever Site is intended for use by a younger audience, we will obtain consent from a parent or guardian before we collect personal information	Article 8(1): *Where point (a) of Article 6(1) applies, in relation to the offer of information society services directly to a child, the processing of the personal data of a child shall be lawful where the child is at least 16 years old. Where the child is below the age of 16 years, such processing shall be lawful only if and to the extent that consent is given or authorised by the holder of parental responsibility over the child. Member States may provide by law for a lower age for those purposes provided that such lower age is not below 13 years*	R	R	R	R

Table 5. Average F-measure & total time of 2 regular end-users annotations for 4 privacy policies

	Precision	Recall	F1	Time (min)
User1	0.2	0.11	0.14	120
User2	0.46	0.08	0.14	30
KnIGHT	0.3	0.1	0.15	3

4.3   Discussion

The F-scores obtained in Subsect. 4.2 indicates that there is value in the extraction and mapping method behind *KnIGHT*. On average, based on the experts' ratings between 70–90% of the tool's automatic mappings are at least partially correct (observed agreement with consideration of two classes: partial or perfect match; incorrect match). Of course, the posteriori assessment has its limitations, most notably the lack of consideration for false negatives (missing links). Nevertheless, the results are encouraging more so when considering they are generated instantly whereas typical end-users who performed the annotation task manually - when restricted to 2 h - only demonstrated an agreement with the expert of just 14%.

Based on the above results, we can conclude that although *KnIGHT* is incomparable to an experts' review of a privacy policy, it does facilitate the mapping of text to relevant articles. As such, it can also be used as a shortcut for both kinds of users alike. For non-experts, it offers a new opportunity for wider awareness of their rights. Furthermore, it should be stressed out that the number of selected privacy policies and participants in the experiment was a bare minimum. However, we believe that our experimental settings were sufficient to return positive indicative results, ahead of a broader experiment that is in consideration pending sufficient funding.

5   Conclusion and Future Work

In this article, we presented *KnIGHT*, a tool for automatic mapping of privacy policies to GDPR. To the best of our knowledge, this is the first comprehensive approach for privacy policies interpretation and helps regular end-users to familiarize themselves with respective data protection law and be aware of their rights as a citizen. *KnIGHT* employs semantic text matching for mapping privacy policy sentences to GDPR paragraphs. Our evaluation showed that interpretation of legal text is a challenging task due to its subjectivity. A comparison of *KnIGHT*'s automatic mapping with two lay end-user annotations proved that *KnIGHT* is able to produce a satisfactory result within a short response time. We deem this work to be a significant step forward to make the regular end-users aware of the their rights as a data subject.

Regarding future work, we aim to make *KnIGHT* a domain specific tool and tailor its workflow for better interpretation of GDPR. Due to the increasing interest in GDPR, there have been initial efforts to represent its article in the form of vocabularies and ontologies [4, 18]. Exploiting the domain specific ontologies enables us to perform a deeper analysis of the texts and extract more knowledge from respective regulations. Furthermore, benefiting from available labeled data set (OPP-115), we seek to improve the candidate sentence detection phase and our matching algorithm.

References

1. Deeplearning4j: Open-source distributed deep learning for the JVM Apache Software Foundation License 2.0 (2015). http://deeplearning4j.org/word2vec.html
2. Acquisti, A., Grossklags, J.: Privacy and rationality in individual decision making. IEEE Secur. Priv. **3**(1), 26–33 (2005). https://doi.org/10.1109/MSP.2005.22
3. Alzahrani, S., Salim, N., Abraham, A.: Understanding plagiarism linguistic patterns, textual features, and detection methods. IEEE Trans. Syst. Man Cybern. Part C (Appl. Rev.) **42**, 133–149 (2012)
4. Bartolini, C., Muthuri, R.: Reconciling data protection rights and obligations: an ontology of the forthcoming EU regulation. In: Proceedings of the Workshop on Language and Semantic Technology for Legal Domain (LST4LD) (2015)

5. Breaux, T.D., Vail, M.W., Anton, A.I.: Towards regulatory compliance: Extracting rights and obligations to align requirements with regulations. In: Proceedings of the 14th IEEE International Requirements Engineering Conference, pp. 46–55. RE 2006. IEEE Computer Society, Washington, DC (2006). https://doi.org/10.1109/RE.2006.68

6. Cohen, J.M.: Weighted kappa: nominal scale agreement with provision for scaled disagreement or partial credit. Psychol. Bull. **70**(4), 213–20 (1968)

7. Costante, E., Sun, Y., Petković, M., den Hartog, J.: A machine learning solution to assess privacy policy completeness: (short paper). In: Proceedings of the 2012 ACM Workshop on Privacy in the Electronic Society, pp. 91–96. WPES 2012. ACM, New York (2012). https://doi.org/10.1145/2381966.2381979

8. Cranor, L.F., Guduru, P., Arjula, M.: User interfaces for privacy agents. ACM Trans. Comput.-Hum. Interact. **13**(2), 135–178 (2006). https://doi.org/10.1145/1165734.1165735

9. Cunningham, H., Maynard, D., Tablan, V.: JAPE: a Java Annotation Patterns Engine (Second Edition). Research Memorandum CS-00-10, Department of Computer Science, University of Sheffield (November 2000). http://www.dcs.shef.ac.uk/~diana/Papers/jape.ps

10. Fleiss, J.L.: Measuring agreement between two judges on the presence or absence of a trait. Biometrics **31**(3), 651–659 (1975). http://www.jstor.org/stable/2529549

11. Guntamukkala, N., Dara, R., Grewal, G.W.: A machine-learning based approach for measuring the completeness of online privacy policies. In: 2015 IEEE 14th International Conference on Machine Learning and Applications (ICMLA), pp. 289–294 (2015)

12. Harkous, H., Fawaz, K., Lebret, R., Schaub, F., Shin, K.G., Aberer, K.: Polisis: automated analysis and presentation of privacy policies using deep learning. CoRR abs/1802.02561 (2018)

13. Hripcsak, G., Heitjan, D.: Measuring agreement in medical informatics reliability studies. J. Biomed. Inform. **35**(2), 99–110 (2002). https://doi.org/10.1016/S1532-0464(02)00500-2

14. Hripcsak, G., Rothschild, A.S.: Agreement, the F-Measure, and Reliability in Information Retrieval. JAMIA 12(3), 296–298 (2005). https://doi.org/10.1197/jamia.M1733

15. Jensen, C., Potts, C., Jensen, C.: Privacy practices of internet users: self-reports versus observed behavior. Int. J. Hum.-Comput. Stud. **63**(1–2), 203–227 (2005). https://doi.org/10.1016/j.ijhcs.2005.04.019

16. Kenter, T., Borisov, A., de Rijke, M.: Siamese CBOW: optimizing word embeddings for sentence representations. CoRR abs/1606.04640 (2016). http://arxiv.org/abs/1606.04640

17. Obar, J.A., Oeldorf-Hirsch, A.: The biggest lie on the internet: Ignoring the privacy policies and terms of service policies of social networking services. Inf. Commun. Soc. (2018). https://doi.org/10.1080/1369118X.2018.1486870

18. Pandit, H.J., Lewis, D., O'Sullivan, D.: Gdprtext - gdpr as a linked data resource, January 2018. https://doi.org/10.5281/zenodo.1146351

19. Wilson, S., et al.: The creation and analysis of a website privacy policy corpus. In: ACL (2016)

20. Zeni, N., Kiyavitskaya, N., Mich, L., Cordy, J.R., Mylopoulos, J.: Gaiust: supporting the extraction of rights and obligations for regulatory compliance. Requir. Eng. **20**(1), 1–22 (2015). https://doi.org/10.1007/s00766-013-0181-8

Automating Class/Instance Representational Choices in Knowledge Bases

Ankur Padia[1], David Martin[2], and Peter F. Patel-Schneider[2(✉)]

[1] University of Maryland, Baltimore County, Baltimore, USA
pankur1@umbc.edu
[2] Nuance Communications, Sunnyvale, USA
David.Martin@nuance.com, pfpschneider@gmail.com

Abstract. We present a method for making decisions as to whether an entity in a knowledge base should be a class or an instance based on external evidence in the form of corresponding textual corpora such as Wikipedia articles. The approach, based on machine classification of the text, avoids the need for feature engineering and provides valuable guidance when building or refining large knowledge bases. The approach works well over different domains and outperforms a variety of other state-of-the-art approaches.

1 Introduction

One of the many tasks in building a knowledge base (KB) is determining whether an entity is a class or an instance (or more generally, determining the level of the entity in the class hierarchy) in the KB. Correct class/instance determination is a critical step in building an error free class hierarchy (Mirylenka, Passerini, and Serafini 2015; Spitz et al. 2016). Mistakes in this task negatively impact use of the KB—such as for Named Entity Recognition, semantic search, question answering, or reasoning—substantially limiting its utility.

Careful ontologists will not make such mistakes in most cases, i.e., they are very unlikely to make *baker* an instance of *person* or *Ronald Reagan* a subclass of *person*. However, in crowd-sourced KBs or very large KBs, as exemplified by Wikidata, mistakes can be made even in these very simple situations, particularly when only limited information as to the meanings of related entities is available in the KB. In even slightly more complicated situations mistakes are much more common, such as making *battleship* an instance of a *ship* class that is supposed to have actual ships as instances. When metaclasses (classes of classes) are permitted, such as *grape tomato* being an instance of the class *tomato variety* but itself having instances, the situation becomes even more complex and more mistakes can be made. When a KB framework permits an item to be both an instance and a class, the situation becomes even more complex and more mistakes are made. For example, in Wikidata currently, each variety of *tomato*

© Springer Nature Switzerland AG 2018
C. Faron Zucker et al. (Eds.): EKAW 2018, LNAI 11313, pp. 273–288, 2018.
https://doi.org/10.1007/978-3-030-03667-6_18

(*Heirloom tomato, grape tomato*, etc.) is modeled as both an *instance* of *vegetable* and a *subclass* of *tomato*, which in turn is a subclass of *vegetable*. Thus, each of the tomato varieties (but not tomato itself) is both an instance and a subclass of *vegetable*.

In our work we are exploring the value of external evidence, primarily textual evidence, in guiding the construction and evolution of KBs, and identifying and rectifying problems in existing ontologies. We view class/instance determination (or, more generally, class level determination) as a crucial activity within the larger process of constructing an ontology, and one that would benefit from better tool support. We hypothesize that textual corpora can provide an excellent source of guidance regarding challenges like this one and can thus help in KB construction activities and avoid many of the modeling mistakes and inconsistencies that are prevalent in large and crowd-sourced KBs. Encyclopedic articles, such as those of Wikipedia, which aim to comprehensively describe one or more domains in a consistent style, provide the most suitable type of corpus for this purpose. Additionally, we hypothesize that a class/instance determination system can effectively capture the expertise of a human ontology engineer. Such expertise may include both general experience with ontology construction and best practices, as well as knowledge of the applications for which the ontology will be used. This paper substantiates both of these hypotheses, and describes an approach and system that build on them to save work for ontology engineers in making these determinations.

More concretely, our system[1] learns from a human ontology engineer to classify (label) entities as instances or classes, for use in a given KB. The approach assumes that (1) a set of entities belonging to a single domain (subject area) has been selected; (2) a textual description is available for each of the entities; and (3) the correspondence between each entity and its textual description is given. For purposes of this paper, we also assume that the representational paradigm of the KB requires that each entity be either a class or an instance, but not both. Given those things, the approach requires only that the ontology engineer annotates, as class or instance, an appropriately-sized subset of the selected entity descriptions. Given those "gold standard" annotations, we train our system to mimic the performance of the engineer, so that the system can then be used to label each of the remaining descriptions as class or instance. Our experiments show very high accuracy in this task, and the system outperforms a variety of baseline approaches.

This system can be exploited in several different ontology engineering activities. In the task of new KB construction, or the task of KB expansion (in which a new set of entities is added into a KB), the system can perform a large part of the effort of class/instance labeling of new entities. (In these activities, selecting the set of entities to be labeled—assumption (1) above—could be the same as selecting a set of textual descriptions—assumption (2) above. In such cases, assumption (3) would hold vacuously.) In the task of KB validation (in which one wishes to check existing class/instance labels in a KB), the system can help

---

[1] The code for our system and the data used will be made available before publication.

to assemble a set of labels that reflect an expert's judgments, which can then be compared to the existing labels.

Class/instance determination, of course, is only one task within the larger activities of KB construction, KB expansion, and (in some cases) KB validation. In this paper we focus on this particular task for several reasons. First, in many approaches to KB construction, it is an essential prerequisite for subsequent steps. Second, in our experience, class/instance determination can consume substantial effort by ontology engineers, in all but the simplest KB development efforts. Third, it's not hard to find class/instance inconsistencies in open source general knowledge KBs. Fourth, class/instance determination, as a distinct task, has received relatively little attention in the literature. For all of these reasons, additional research on class/instance determination is warranted. For the first 3 reasons, automating it, in the form of an independent system, can have significant benefits.

In closing this subsection, we emphasize that an optimal class/instance labeling for a set of entities depends in large measure on the intended uses of the ontology and data in the KB. Accordingly, we do not claim that an optimal labeling can be determined solely from the analysis of textual descriptions of the entities. On the contrary, our approach relies upon the informed judgments of an ontology engineer, which reflect domain knowledge and knowledge of the intended uses of the KB. In our approach, we ask the ontology engineer to apply this expertise by annotating natural language descriptions (e.g., Wikipedia articles) with class/instance labels, and we show that these annotated descriptions provide a basis for training a system to exhibit expert performance in making additional class/instance judgments.

1.1 Contributions

The work reported here explores the use of textually-encoded knowledge to lessen the time, effort, and number of mistakes that are involved in making class/instance choices in KB construction (and other KB development activities). To that end, we investigate the following hypotheses:

- Within a domain (subject area), linguistic patterns recur frequently within groups of articles that call for the same label (class or instance), and typify those groups.
- These patterns appear in a consistent manner - consistent enough to support machine-learning approaches to the task of distinguishing instances from classes. An appropriate approach can effectively learn to make this distinction, for a given modeling context (domain and application), from examples provided by an ontology engineer.
- These patterns do not require part of speech tagging to be used effectively.

  This paper makes the following contributions:

- We present a novel automated approach to making class/instance representational choices, based on external evidence in the form of textual corpora. The approach employs both word-based and character-based embedded representations, which have not previously been applied to this problem.

– Whereas the prior approaches to class/instance discrimination require feature engineering, our approach employs a neural network model that avoids the need for feature engineering.
– We evaluate the effectiveness of our model and demonstrate that our approach outperforms several other state-of-the-art machine learning-based approaches, and all other tested baseline approaches.
– We demonstrate that our approach works well across domains having varied characteristics.

In the following sections, after discussing related work, we present our approach and then describe its experimental evaluation. Following that, we discuss the results and the applicability of the approach. We employ Wikipedia articles to ground the discussions, examples, and experiments.

2   Related Work

There has been considerable work done to support the construction of KBs, creation of ontologies, acquisition of content for KBs, etc. [1–4]. However, the problem of discriminating instances from classes has received less attention [5].

An approach to class/instance discrimination was developed in [6]. Their approach served as the first phase of the task of bootstrapping an ontology from Wikipedia. The authors solved the problem using titles of Wikipedia pages and shallow features, but did not investigate the use of neural network-based approaches or embeddings as explored here. Our approach does not require the presence of titles, however, as demonstrated here, their use improves the overall performance of our system.

[6] is the only work, of which we are aware, that embodies our class/instance task as a separate, testable component. For that reason, we turn now to efforts in document classification, which involve similar tasks, and which provide baseline systems that can perform our task in a comparable manner.

The Deep Average Network (**DAN**) [7] involves a similar architecture and philosophy to ours used for sentence and document classification. However, the model was employed for different tasks—sentiment analysis and factoid question answering. Moreover, it was proposed to understand the usefulness of ordering in compositionality of the inputs to a neural network. Contrary to our approach, it does not explore the connection of sentences within documents for document classification.

To fill the need for combining sentences for document classification, [8] proposes a gated recurrent neural network (GRNN) architecture. It learns the sentence representation for each of the sentences mentioned in the document and creates a sequence of such representations, feeding them to the GRNN to obtain a document representation. Finally, the document representation is fed to a Softmax layer to obtain a probability distribution. Such an approach works well when the word order or sentence sequence matter. However, for our task we found it performs poorly.

There are other related approaches which perform either sentence classification or document classification using Convolutional Neural Networks (CNN) [9,10] or Recursive Convolutional Neural Networks [11]. [9] explores the use of CNN for sentence classification. Although not included in Section "Experiments", for our task [9] was found to perform less well than our approach. We also experimented with character-based CNN [10] for document classification and found it to perform less well than our approach. [11] uses a combination of recursive network with CNN network to learn features for document classification.

3 Approach

The objective of our approach is to train a system to make expert judgments about whether an entity should be represented as a class or an instance, in a way that is applicable for a given set of applications (i.e., anticipated uses of the ontology under construction). These judgments are modeled by a human ontologist, who is knowledgeable about the domain of the ontology (e.g., People, Music, Computer Science) and the anticipated uses of the ontology.

Our approach assumes the existence of textual descriptions for a large number of entities in the given domain. In our experiments, each of these textual descriptions is given by a Wikipedia article. The human ontologist models their own expertise by labeling a subset of these articles (i.e., the entities described by the articles) as classes or instances. This set of labeled articles is used as a gold standard for training a classifier. The classifier can then label the remaining articles in a way that reflects the expert choices of the ontologist.

We chose Wikipedia as the source of our titles and textual descriptions partly because Wikipedia has been used for similar tasks before and partly because Wikipedia has a large number of titled articles for both instances and classes. The general-purpose nature of Wikipedia is not an issue here both because we select only those articles that are in the domain and because the gold standard labeling gives evidence for the desired class/instance distinction.

In the following subsections, we present the representational and algorithmic details of the approach.

3.1 Word Representation Learning

Word embedding is a distributed representation where each word is represented as a dense vector. Word embedding-based methods have been shown to perform better than more conventional techniques [12]. One of the reasons for this better performance is the capability of word embeddings to capture syntactic and semantic information. Moreover, dense representations are better than one-hot encodings as they do not suffer from the "curse of dimensionality" [13]. To obtain dense word embeddings we use the Continuous Bag-of-Words model (CBoW) from Word2Vec [14]. CBoW learns the embedding of a word by maximizing the log probability of the word given the surrounding words. Formally, for a sequence of words (italicized) $w_1, w_2, \ldots, w_t, \ldots, w_n$, CBoW tries to maximize the likelihood of the word w_t given $w_{cntx} = [w_{t-c}, \ldots, w_{t-1}, w_{t+1}, \ldots, w_{t+c}]$, as shown in Eq. 1.

$$max \quad \frac{1}{n} \sum_{t=1}^{n} \sum_{-c \leq j \leq c, j \neq 0} log \quad p(w_t | w_{t+j}) \tag{1}$$

$$p(w_t | w_{t+j}) = \frac{1}{1 + e^{\mathbf{w}_{w_t}^T \cdot \mathbf{w}_{w_{t+j}}}} \tag{2}$$

The (bold-faced) word vector $\mathbf{w}_{w_t}$ represents the embedding of the corresponding word w_t. The training of the model finds optimal values of $\mathbf{w}_{w_t}$. Here we use CBoW but other models like Skip-gram can also be used to learn word embeddings. Further details on the models can be found in [14].

3.2   Bag-of-Embeddings

We use the average of the word embeddings to capture the textual description of an entity as it does not consider order and performs better than vector sum [15,16]. Formally,

$$d_j = \underset{w \in D_j}{average} \ \mathbf{E}(w) \tag{3}$$

where D_j is the document containing the textual description, d_j is the encoded representation of the document as a vector, and $\mathbf{E}(w)$ is the function to obtain an embedding of word w.

3.3   Sub-syntactic Representation Learning

In addition to the representations of entity descriptions (from Wikipedia articles), we also learn sub-syntactic representations of article titles such as "Barack Obama", etc., which also frequently serve as KB entity labels. We call such representations "sub-syntactic" because titles sometimes adhere to a set of guidelines or conventions, which can be detected at the level of characters. (For example, if an entity is a class its title is more likely to be a plural form [6]). Of course, such conventions do not hold uniformly, but as we demonstrate in the "Experiments" Section, the addition of these representations significantly boosts performance.

In order to capture sub-syntactic representations, we model the titles as sequences of characters. Sequences are effectively learned using Recurrent Neural Networks (RNNs). Recurrent neural network models, like Elman's Simple RNN (SRNN) [17], Long-Short Term Memory (LSTM) [18], and Gated Recurrent Unit (GRU) [19] have been shown to learn subtle patterns that can support high performance in text classification tasks. Any of the RNN models can be used for our task; however we have found SRNN to perform consistently best across the domains, and also to be faster to train. In the following we formally define the SRNN model and describe its use in our approach.

SRNN takes sequences (or, in our case, matrices) and learns to recognize patterns by looking at t time steps of input. At each time step, it learns internal state vectors, considering the current input $\mathbf{x}_i$ and the previous internal state vector, $\mathbf{s}_{t-1}$. Each of the internal state vectors is further processed to produce an output vector and a final vector, $\mathbf{y}_i$, representing an entire sequence. Equation 4 formally defines our use of SRNN, treating a title as a sequence of n characters, $c_1, c_2,..., c_n$, and encoding the title as a one-hot representation matrix $\mathbf{X}$.

$$\mathbf{X} = [v(c_1), v(c_2), v(c_3), \ldots, v(c_n)] \tag{4}$$

$$\mathbf{s}_t^{(i)} = g\left(\mathbf{W}_R^{(i)}\mathbf{x}_t + \mathbf{U}_R^{(i)}\mathbf{s}_{t-1} + \mathbf{b}_R^{(i)}\right) \tag{5}$$

$$\mathbf{y}_t^{(i)} = \mathbf{s}_t^{(i)}; 1 \le i \le 3 \tag{6}$$

where $\mathbf{x}_t = v(c_t)$, $v(\cdot) \in \mathbb{R}^c$ is a one-hot encoding function, and c is the cardinality of the alphabet used in Wikipedia article titles (similar to the alphabet of [10]). Here g is the activation function; in our case ReLu. Superscript i denotes the ith layer, $\mathbf{s}_t^{(i)}$ denotes the internal state of layer i at time t, and $\mathbf{y}_t^{(i)}$ denotes the output sequence representation from layer i, which is input to the next layer. y_{title} is the output of the final layer at final time stamp.

3.4   Document Representation and Classification

Input to our classifier is the concatenation of (i) the average of a document's word embeddings obtained using Eq. 3 and (ii) the sub-syntactic representation of its title obtained from Eq. 6. Figure 1 shows the architecture of our system. For a given title string, e.g. "Punched Tape", each character is converted into one-hot encoding and given as input to an RNN to obtain the title's sub-syntactic representation, which is concatenated with the average of the document's word embeddings. The concatenated representation is input to a Multilayer Perceptron (MLP) of three fully connected layers and classified either as class or instance.

Formally, for each document representation $\mathbf{r}_j$, each layer learns a more abstract representation from the previous layer as shown in the following equations:

$$\mathbf{r}_j = [d_j; \mathbf{y}_{title}] \tag{7}$$

$$\mathbf{h}^{(i)} = g^{(i)}\left(\mathbf{h}^{(i-1)}\mathbf{W}^{(i)} + \mathbf{b}^{(i)}\right); 1 \le i \le 3 \tag{8}$$

$$\hat{\mathbf{y}} = softmax(\mathbf{W}^{(4)}\mathbf{h}^{(3)}) \tag{9}$$

The final representation, $\mathbf{h}^{(3)}$, is projected on to a lower dimension, equal to the number of classification labels, and normalized with softmax to obtain a probability distribution over the labels. Here g represents an activation function to introduce non-linearity. We used ReLu [20] as the activation function. We used dropout [21] and L2 regularization to avoid overfitting.

Despite its relative simplicity we have found our approach to be effective at learning document characteristics relevant to making the class/instance distinction.

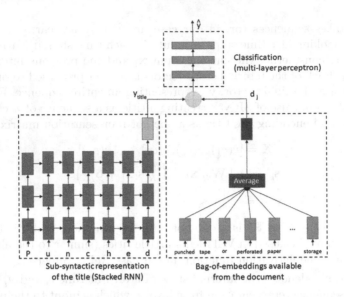

Fig. 1. Neural network architecture for the class/instance classification task, showing part of the Wikipedia article title "Punched Tape", and article content beginning with "Punched tape or perforated tape is a form of data storage". All three components of the network are described in the text. The yellow circle represents vector concatenation. (Color figure online)

3.5   Training

As discussed above, our approach employs two neural network models: (i) a feed-forward Multilayer Perceptron (MLP) for the classification task, and (ii) an SRNN model to learn sub-syntactic characteristics of titles. We use θ_{MLP} to denote the parameters for (i) and θ_{SRNN} to denote the parameters for (ii). Formally,

$$\theta = \theta_{MLP} \cup \theta_{SRNN} \tag{10}$$

$$\theta_{MLP} = \left\{ \mathbf{E}, \mathbf{W}^{(4)}, \mathbf{W}^{(i)}, \mathbf{b}^{(i)} \right\}; 1 \leq i \leq 3 \tag{11}$$

$$\theta_{SRNN} = \left\{ \mathbf{W}_R^{(i)}, \mathbf{U}_R^{(i)}, \mathbf{b}_R^{(i)} \right\}; 1 \leq i \leq 3 \tag{12}$$

The parameters for our approach include the word embeddings matrix and transformation matrices for the SRNN and MLP. We pre-train word embeddings, $\mathbf{E} \in \mathbb{R}^{|v|+e}$, using CBoW with window size of 5. Here, $\mathbf{W}_R^{(i)} \in \mathbb{R}^{c \times p}$, $\mathbf{U}_R^{(i)} \in \mathbb{R}^{p \times p}$ are the transformation matrices for SRNN and $\mathbf{W}^{(i)} \in \mathbb{R}^{(e+p) \times (e+p)}$ are the transformation matrices for MLP. Biases for the model are denoted by $\mathbf{b}^{(i)} \in \mathbb{R}^{e+p}$ and $\mathbf{b}_R^{(i)} \in \mathbb{R}^p$ respectively. Here e is the dimension of word embeddings, c is the cardinality of the character set, and p is the dimension of sequence representation obtained from the last state of the SRNN. (If LSTM is substituted for SRNN, as in one of our experiments, the same parameters apply.)

Table 1. Dataset statistics: annotated documents; avg. sentences per document; avg. words per document; vocabulary size; number of documents allocated to training/development/testing; avg. sentence length

Dataset	#docs	#s/d	| V |	#w/d	train/dev/test	avg. sent. length
Person - class	904	58.28	69770	854.7	732/86/86	14.67
Person - instance	3623	14.91	75590	201.73	2935/344/344	13.53
Computing - class	410	40.80	25830	573.72	334/38/38	14.06
Computing - instance	2319	22.03	53854	307.84	1879/220/220	13.97

To learn the remaining parameters we use back-propagation with AdaDelta [22] as a momentum-based gradient descent algorithm and fine tune the parameters as described in the experiments.

$$\mathcal{L}(\mathbf{y}, \hat{\mathbf{y}}) = -\sum_k y_k log(\hat{y}_k) \tag{13}$$

We use cross entropy (Eq. 13) as the loss function and initialize all the parameters using Xavier Initialization [23].

4   Experiments

We evaluated the performance of our approach, guided by the following questions:

1. How well does our approach perform relative to state-of-the-art systems that addressed the class/instance problem [6]? (Subsection "Baselines From Ontology Construction Efforts")
2. How well does it perform compared to conventional and embedding-based document classification methods? (Subsections "Conventional Document Classification" and "Embedding-based Document Classification")
3. What is the impact of 2 different sub-syntactic representations of article titles? (Section "Analysis of Sub-syntactic Representations")

Before discussing the details of the evaluation, we describe the datasets and experimental settings.

4.1   Datasets

We chose one relatively straightforward, generic domain and one relatively complex, specialized domain with which to evaluate our approach: the domains of Persons and Computing. Each of the two datasets (textual corpora) consists of the text of a number of Wikipedia articles, with their associated titles. All markup, links, info boxes, and other meta-information were removed from the text.

Each article was manually annotated as a class or instance. The annotator was instructed to make representational choices guided by typical tasks of a large, general knowledge graph (e.g., generation of info boxes to accompany search results). The annotator knew that a gold standard was being generated and thus spent adequate time to make high-quality determinations. None of the determinations were particularly difficult.

For the person dataset the presence of a person-type infobox is a strong indication that the article is for a person instance. We did not retain this information as we want our approach to work for any encyclopedic source, not just Wikipedia. In the computing dataset there is no good structural source for class/instance determination.

To select the articles of the **Person** dataset, we leveraged prior work on YAGO [24], which itself was derived (primarily) from Wikipedia and WordNet [25]. We selected articles corresponding to the descendants of the Person class in YAGO. We skipped pages like 'List of Athletes' which contain no descriptive text.

Dataset statistics are shown in Table 1.

To the best of our knowledge, there are no publicly available datasets that meet the needs of our experiments. We considered using Wikipedia categories but found them to contain an inconsistent mix of instances and classes. Similarly, we considered using PetScan[2] to perform breath-first search on Wikipedia categories to create the gold standard but we found it to list instances far more frequently than classes, making it difficult to go through thousands of examples to annotate. We also considered the datasets for SemEval-2016 Task 13[3], which is concerned with taxonomy construction, but found them to be unsuitable because the class/instance distinction isn't a requirement of the task, because the datasets are too small and, most important, because the data predominantly contains items that clearly ought to be categorized as classes.

To construct the **Computing** dataset, we found nearly 3000 entities (articles) listed under Wikipedia's Computing category. The articles were manually annotated by a Knowledge Representation researcher, in consultation with experienced ontology engineers. Wikipedia lists (e.g., "List of Artificial Intelligence Projects") and outlines (e.g.,"Outline of Computing") were excluded, resulting in 2729 documents.

4.2   Baseline Approaches

We compared the performance of our approach with a broad range of methods that are applicable to class/instance determination or to similar problems. Here, we describe the competing approaches in four groups: (i) two state-of-the-art methods based upon an approach that has previously been applied to the class/instance task in a larger context of ontology construction from Wikipedia

---

[2] https://petscan.wmflabs.org/.
[3] http://alt.qcri.org/semeval2016/task13/.

Table 2. Performance comparison on the class/instance discrimination task, showing accuracy (acc) and area under curve (auc) metrics

Model	Person		Computing	
	acc	auc	acc	auc
Simple baselines				
Random Choice	50	–	50	–
ZeroR (always instance)	80	50	85.27	50
Baselines from ontology construction efforts				
[6] + SVM	91.28	90.13	85.08	50
[6] + LR	91.28	84.92	85.08	50
Conventional document classification				
BoW+LR	97.67	94.62	85.27	61.97
BoW+SVM	96.97	94.62	86.05	65.69
BoBigrams+LR	80	50	85.27	50
BoBigrams+SVM	80	50	85.27	50
Embedding-based document classification				
Avg Embedding + LR	98.13	97.52	86.43	53.95
Avg Embedding + SVM	97.90	96.51	86.05	52.63
Neural network-based document classification				
Char-level CNN [10]	80	50	85.27	50
Recurrent CNN [11]	95.08	95.61	85.06	50
Our Approach				
Avg-Embedding(Text) + MLP	99.30	99.13	96.90	94.91
Avg-Embedding(text) + Simple-RNN(title) + MLP	**100**	**100**	**97.67**	**97.55**

content, (ii) conventional document classification methods, (iii) embedding-based document classification methods, and (iv) neural network based document classification methods. We implement each of these approaches with logistic regression (LR) and also with Support Vector Machine (SVM). These approaches are characterized in the following subsections, and listed in Table 2. We also include ZeroR[4] and random-choice baselines. ZeroR classifies *all* articles according to the majority category, which for each of our datasets is *instance*.

As described above, our approach (Avg-Emb(text) + SRNN(title) + MLP) concatenates the text representation and title representation and uses a deep network to perform the classification task. The document classification approaches are just given the text without the title. As the title almost always appears in the text, adding the title would not make much of a change to their behavior.

---

[4] http://chem-eng.utoronto.ca/~datamining/dmc/zeror.htm.

Baselines from Ontology Construction Efforts

1. [6] + SVM, as discussed in Related Work, is a feature-based approach to class/instance choice, which focuses on Wikipedia article titles.
2. [6] + LR is a variant of the above, replacing SVM with Logistic Regression, created by us to provide both SVM and LR versions of all the baseline models.

Conventional Document Classification. There are several strong baselines recommended for text classification in [26] using unigrams and bigrams as features.

1. **BoW + LR/SVM**: Pre-process the document to tokenize, remove punctuations and remove stopwords to create a bag-of-words representation. For a document, each feature is equal to its frequency count classified using either Logistic Regression (LR) or SVM with linear kernel.
2. **BoBigram + LR/SVM**: Similar to the above, except with a bag-of-bigrams representation.

Embedding-Based Document Classification

1. **Avg. Emb + LR/SVM**: We learn 400-dimensional word vectors using word2vec [14], average a document's word vectors to get document representation for the entity, and train a classifier.

Neural Network-Based Document Classification. We also compare our approach with the recent and strong state-of-the-art systems of [10,11]. Systems such as [10] have frequently been used due to their generic applicability to different tasks.

1. Character CNN [10] uses character level representation on a fixed set of 70 characters (one-hot encoding) and classifies text documents with a deep network of 7 layers (convolutional neural network) operating on the initial 1460 characters of each document.
2. Recurrent CNN [11] combines bi-directional recurrent and convolution neural networks for document classification. It combines left and right context word representation with embedded word representation followed by a max-pooling, feed-forward neural network for classification.

We considered comparing our system with those of [16,27,28], but found these comparisons to be infeasible because of their idiosyncratic annotated tree structures designed for specific sentiment classification tasks.

Hyper-parameters. Uni/Bigram/Avg Emb + LR/SVM: We applied L2 regularization [29] for Logistic Regression (LR) and Support Vector Machine (SVM) with linear kernel for unigrams, bigrams and average embedding. For the L2 penalty, we chose the value from the set $\{10, 0.1, 0.01, 0.001\}$ that gave best performance on the development set. For LR we set 0.1 as penalty for all datasets for unigram and bigram, and 0.001 and 0.1 for average embedding on Person and Computing respectively. For SVM we set penalty to 10 for unigram and bigram, and 0.1 and 0.01 for average embedding on Person and Computing. **Neural Networks**: To tune the parameters for all the models we used co-ordinate descent [30] in which we changed only one hyper-parameter at a time, always making a change from the best configuration of hyper-parameters found up to now. During co-ordinate descent, we tested with multiple values of learning rate, α, to be $\{0.1, 0.01, 0.001\}$ and chose $\alpha = 0.1$ as it gave better performance on the development dataset. We used AdaDelta as optimizer with momentum of 0.9, dropout of 0.5, and L2 penalty term of 10. We used 300 epochs for all models. We set the SRNN latent representation, p, to 100 and word embedding dimension, e, to 400.

5   Discussion

Table 2 summarizes the performance results for all approaches above, in terms of accuracy (acc) and area under curve (auc). As shown by the last line, our full approach with SRNN showed the best performance under both measures, for both domains. As expected, performance on the Person domain was higher than Computing. We attribute this primarily to the relative simplicity and familiarity of the domain, which allows for a greater consistency of style in writing about persons and classes of persons.

Overall, the results clearly indicate that title and text taken together yield better results than either in isolation. Both variants of [6] operate on titles only, whereas our full approach, which scores markedly higher, makes use of both titles and text, indicating a significant gain by the inclusion of article text. The next to last row is the same as our full approach, except with the exclusion of the title representation. The comparison of these 2 rows shows that the title representation adds to the performance, albeit a very modest gain, especially for the Person domain.

The 3rd group of approaches, Conventional Document Classification, shows that there is no gain with the use of bigrams; indeed, there are losses in several measures.

Although not reflected in the results shown, we found that adding the 2nd and 3rd MLP layers each improved our performance.

6   Analysis of Sub-syntactic Representations

In order to understand the effect of sub-syntactic title representations on performance, we tested our approach with two sequential RNN models, SRNN and LSTM, and we also tested these sequential models in isolation. As shown in Table 3, LSTM performs extremely well using only titles for the Person category while it performs poorly for the Computing category. We believe that the reason for this is that the Person category is simple and well understood by Wikipedians and hence they create very consistent entity titles making it easy to distinguish between instances and classes. On the other hand, the Computing category is more complex and does not end up with simple title patterns that can be learned by a simple model.

Table 3. Performance of sub-syntactic representations

Model	Person		Computing	
	acc	auc	acc	auc
SRNN(title)	80	50	97.67	97.55
Our approach + SRNN	**100**	**100**	**97.67**	**97.55**
LSTM(title)	100	100	81.01	84.51
Our approach + LSTM	99.53	99.71	95.35	97.27

7 Conclusion and Future Work

We have presented an approach for automatic classification of entities described by textual resources (such as Wikipedia articles) as instances or classes and demonstrated its effectiveness. Our approach is simple and efficient but nevertheless outperforms previous systems on this task. We have also investigated the relative contributions of document title and document body to the success of our approach, and the relative effectiveness of a variety of well-understood baseline approaches.

Due to the fundamental nature of this choice and its pervasiveness in KB development, high performance on this task can increase ontology engineering productivity and provide significant benefit to a range of KB engineering tools and processes. Effective automated class/instance discrimination can provide guidance not only for new KB construction, but also for diagnosis and correction of problems in existing KBs. It can serve as a building block in larger tasks, such as the bootstrapping of entire ontologies from textual corpora.

The need to manually annotate a substantial training set is a weakness of our approach, and sometimes will present a significant deterrent to using it. To help address this challenge, our top priority for future work is to explore the effectiveness of domain adaptation; i.e., transfer learning across domains. (In other words, training the system on annotated documents from a single domain, and subsequently applying the system to other domains, without needing additional training.)

As part of a larger roadmap to support ontology construction, refinement, and rectification, we also plan to build on this approach and extend its capabilities to the identification of entity types (classes to which instances belong), and the identification of class relationships. We also plan to investigate the suitability of other types of corpora for class/instance discrimination, explore the effectiveness of other corpora characteristics with our approach, and match up different types of corpora with different types of KBs (e.g., corpora and KBs with varying degrees of specialization, intended for different applications). Finally, because some representational schemes allow for multi-level class hierarchies, we plan to extend our approach to distinguish between individuals, classes, and metaclasses, and to diagnose when entities have been placed at the wrong level in existing KBs.

References

1. Nickel, M., Tresp, V., Kriegel, H.P.: Factorizing yago: scalable machine learning for linked data. In: Proceedings of the 21st International Conference on World Wide Web, pp. 271–280. ACM (2012)
2. Padia, A., Kalpakis, K., Finin, T.: Inferring relations in knowledge graphs with tensor decompositions. In: 2016 IEEE International Conference on Big Data (Big Data), pp. 4020–4022. IEEE (2016)
3. Lin, Y., Liu, Z., Sun, M., Liu, Y., Zhu, X.: Learning entity and relation embeddings for knowledge graph completion. In: AAA, vol. I, pp. 2181–2187 (2015)
4. Wang, Z., Zhang, J., Feng, J., Chen, Z.: Knowledge graph and text jointly embedding. In: EMNLP, vol. 14, pp. 1591–1601 (2014)
5. Ponzetto, S.P., Strube, M.: Deriving a large scale taxonomy from wikipedia. In: AAAI, vol. 7, pp. 1440–1445 (2007)
6. Mirylenka, D., Passerini, A., Serafini, L.: Bootstrapping domain ontologies from wikipedia: a uniform approach. In: IJCA, vol. I, pp. 1464–1470 (2015)
7. Iyyer, M., Manjunatha, V., Boyd-Graber, J.L., Daumé III, H.: Deep unordered composition rivals syntactic methods for text classification. In: ACL, vol. 1, pp. 1681–1691 (2015)
8. Tang, D., Qin, B., Liu, T.: Document modeling with gated recurrent neural network for sentiment classification. In: EMNLP, pp. 1422–1432 (2015)
9. Kim, Y.: Convolutional neural networks for sentence classification. arXiv preprint arXiv:1408.5882 (2014)
10. Zhang, X., Zhao, J., LeCun, Y.: Character-level convolutional networks for text classification. In: Advances in Neural Information Processing Systems, pp. 649–657. (2015)
11. Lai, S., Xu, L., Liu, K., Zhao, J.: Recurrent convolutional neural networks for text classification. In: AAAI, vol. 333, pp. 2267–2273 (2015)
12. Collobert, R., Weston, J., Bottou, L., Karlen, M., Kavukcuoglu, K., Kuksa, P.: Natural language processing (almost) from scratch. J. Mach. Learn. Res. 12(Aug), 2493–2537 (2011)
13. Bengio, Y., Ducharme, R., Vincent, P., Jauvin, C.: A neural probabilistic language model. J. Mach. Learn. Res. 3(Feb), 1137–1155 (2003)
14. Mikolov, T., Sutskever, I., Chen, K., Corrado, G.S., Dean, J.: Distributed representations of words and phrases and their compositionality. In: Advances in Neural Information Processing Systems, pp. 3111–3119 (2013)
15. Kalchbrenner, N., Grefenstette, E., Blunsom, P.: A convolutional neural network for modelling sentences. arXiv preprint arXiv:1404.2188 (2014)
16. Irsoy, O., Cardie, C.: Deep recursive neural networks for compositionality in language. In: Advances in Neural Information Processing Systems, pp. 2096–2104 (2014)
17. Elman, J.L.: Finding structure in time. Cogn. Sci. 14(2), 179–211 (1990)

18. Hochreiter, S., Schmidhuber, J.: Long short-term memory. Neural Comput. **9**(8), 1735–1780 (1997)
19. Chung, J., Gulcehre, C., Cho, K., Bengio, Y.: Empirical evaluation of gated recurrent neural networks on sequence modeling. arXiv preprint arXiv:1412.3555 (2014)
20. Glorot, X., Bordes, A., Bengio, Y.: Deep sparse rectifier neural networks. In: Proceedings of the Fourteenth International Conference on Artificial Intelligence and Statistics, pp. 315–323 (2011)
21. Srivastava, N., Hinton, G.E., Krizhevsky, A., Sutskever, I., Salakhutdinov, R.: Dropout: a simple way to prevent neural networks from overfitting. J. Mach. Learn. Res. **15**(1), 1929–1958 (2014)
22. Zeiler, M.D.: Adadelta: an adaptive learning rate method. arXiv preprint arXiv:1212.5701 (2012)
23. Glorot, X., Bengio, Y.: Understanding the difficulty of training deep feedforward neural networks. In: Proceedings of the Thirteenth International Conference on Artificial Intelligence and Statistics, pp. 249–256 (2010)
24. Suchanek, F.M., Kasneci, G., Weikum, G.: Yago: a core of semantic knowledge. In: Proceedings of the 16th International Conference on World Wide Web, pp. 697–706. ACM (2007)
25. Fellbaum, C.: WordNet. Wiley Online Library (1998)
26. Wang, S., Manning, C.D.: Baselines and bigrams: simple, good sentiment and topic classification. In: Proceedings of the 50th Annual Meeting of the Association for Computational Linguistics: Short Papers vol. 2, pp. 90–94. Association for Computational Linguistics (2012)
27. Socher, R., Pennington, J., Huang, E.H., Ng, A.Y., Manning, C.D.: Semi-supervised recursive autoencoders for predicting sentiment distributions. In: Proceedings of the Conference on Empirical Methods in Natural Language Processing. EMNLP 2011, Stroudsburg, PA, USA, pp. 151–161. Association for Computational Linguistics (2011)
28. Tai, K.S., Socher, R., Manning, C.D.: Improved semantic representations from tree-structured long short-term memory networks. arXiv preprint arXiv:1503.00075 (2015)
29. Hoerl, A.E., Kennard, R.W.: Ridge regression: Biased estimation for nonorthogonal problems. Technometrics **12**(1), 55–67 (1970)
30. Bengio, Y.: Practical recommendations for gradient-based training of deep architectures. In: Montavon, G., Orr, G.B., Müller, K.-R. (eds.) Neural Networks: Tricks of the Trade. LNCS, vol. 7700, pp. 437–478. Springer, Heidelberg (2012). https://doi.org/10.1007/978-3-642-35289-8_26

Comparative Preferences in SPARQL

Peter F. Patel-Schneider[1]([✉]), Axel Polleres[2,3], and David Martin[1]

[1] NAIL Laboratory, Nuance Communications, Sunnyvale, CA, USA
pfpschneider@gmail.com
[2] Vienna University of Economics and Business/Complexity Science Hub Vienna,
Wien, Austria
[3] Stanford University, Stanford, CA, USA

Abstract. Sometimes one does not want all the solutions to a query but instead only those that are most desirable according to user-specified preferences. If a user-specified preference relation is acyclic then its specification and meaning are straightforward. In many settings, however, it is valuable to support preference relations that are not acyclic and that might not even be transitive, in which case though their handling involves some open questions. We discuss a definition of desired solutions for arbitrary preference relations and show its desirable properties. We modify a previous extension to SPARQL for simple preferences to correctly handle any preference relation and provide translations of this extension back into SPARQL that can compute the desired solutions for all preference relations that are acyclic or transitive. We also propose an additional extension that returns solutions at multiple levels of desirability, which adds additional expressiveness over prior work. However, for the latter we conjecture that an effective translation to a single (non-recursive) SPARQL query is not possible.

1 Introduction

Preferences and the notion of the Semantic Web are tightly interwoven: the seminal vision article often cited as coining the term "Semantic Web" already mentions preferences in several places [1], for instance: *"Pete [...] set his own agent to [...] search with [...] preferences about location and time."*. The same article also already mentions standardization in terms of languages defining such preferences, such as the Composite Capability/Preference Profile (CC/PP) [2], which allows a user agent (typically a client application) to declare its preferences, e.g., in terms of device capabilities.

Interestingly this early interest in expressing preferences and retrieving Semantic Web data compliant with these preferences has not found its way

---

A poster of part of this paper is being presented at ISWC 2018. An extended technical report version of this paper, including proofs and the main algorithm, is available at http://polleres.net/publications/patel-schneider-etal-2018TR.pdf
Axel Polleres' work was supported under the Distinguished Visiting Austrian Chair Professors program hosted by The Europe Center of Stanford University.

C. Faron Zucker et al. (Eds.): EKAW 2018, LNAI 11313, pp. 289–305, 2018.
https://doi.org/10.1007/978-3-030-03667-6_19

into later Semantic Web Standards, such as SPARQL. There is no built-in way to express and evaluate queries with preferences in SPARQL, but there have been several proposals [3–5] for adding preferences to SPARQL and defining a meaning for such preferential queries.

We argue that preferences in their full generality are not correctly handled in the proposals so far, and show how this can be addressed with a modified semantics. Additionally, we show that certain kinds of preferences can be expressed in a single SPARQL 1.1 query, although the most recent proposal that translates preferences into standard SPARQL queries fails to work on relatively simple examples due to problems in the SPARQL 1.1 query standard [6].

Example 1 (Running Example). As a running example, let us assume data in a navigation scenario, where a user would be looking for gas stations with preferences among features such as *brand*, *distance* to the user's location, and different *shops* that sell various *antifreeze* products, given as an RDF Graph G_1:

```
:p123 a :GasStation; :brand :Mobil;   :dist 1.1;
      :shop :TigerMart; :antifreeze :Prestone .
:p456 a :GasStation; :brand :Chevron; :dist 0.5;
      :shop :KwikieMart; :antifreeze :StarBrite .
:p789 a :GasStation; :brand :Shell; :dist 0.8;
      :shop :711; :antifreeze :Zerex .
:p012 a :GasStation; :brand :Citgo; :dist 6 .
```

User preferences could be of different forms, such as:

> **P1** "I prefer gas stations within 1 mile distance" (simple boolean)
> **P2** "I prefer the closest gas station" (quantitative)
> **P3** "I prefer Mobil over Chevron" (comparative)
> **P4** "I prefer solutions within 1 mile (**P1**) and among those I prefer Mobil over Chevron gas (**P3**), and Kwikie Mart over 7-11, and otherwise just the closest (**P2**)" (combinations)

So atomic preferences can be *simple boolean*, i.e. stating preferences for solutions fulfilling a certain boolean condition, *quantitative*, i.e., where each solution is given a score from a totally ordered set, or *comparative*, i.e., preferences expressed as a binary relation *between solutions*. Such atomic preferences can be combined in various ways.

A preference query takes the results of a non-preferential subquery (in this case, a subquery that returns gas stations), and selects most preferred ones. (The precise definition of "most preferred" is part of what we are examining in this paper.) The preferences we wish to handle call for a generalization of the skyline operator [7] in databases so we will talk about obtaining the skyline of a preference relation, i.e., the most preferred results based on a preference.[1] Subsidiary preference results can be defined, such as the nth skyline, i.e., the

---

[1] In databases, skyline involves a multiway combination of totally ordered comparisons between the values in tuples; qualitative preferences here instead allow an arbitrary comparison relation.

skyline after the first $n - 1$ skylines have been removed, or returning solutions along with their skyline number (which gives a rank for each solution).

We focus on comparative preferences, partly because (i) comparative preferences are more general than simple boolean or quantitative preferences, (ii) comparative preferences can capture combined preferences as part of their preference relation representation, (iii) user preferences are often comparative [8,9].

As for (i), we note that quantitative preferences generalize simple boolean preferences, and comparative preferences generalize quantitative preferences, by preferring solutions with a better score to solutions with a worse score.

2   Foundations and Motivation

We adapt our formal definition of comparative preferences from that of Chomicki [10] as also used by other work in the area such as Troumpoukis et al. [5].

Definition 1. *Given a set of potential solutions P, a preference relation $\succ$ is any relation over $P \times P$. A solution s_1 is* dominated *by a solution s_2 if $s_2 \succ s_1$.*

Although a preference relation is defined over a universe of *potential* solutions, it is applied to finite sets of *candidate* solutions. Typically, potential solutions are all solutions that are representable under the schema of some information source. Candidate solutions are then solutions returned from the ordinary (non-preferential) part of a query.

Example 2. Referring back to Example 1, the four gas stations shown could be the *candidate* solutions returned by the ordinary SPARQL query, Q_1:

Q_1: `SELECT * {?X a :GasStation; :brand ?B; :dist ?D. FILTER(?D<=10)}`

The *potential* solutions would be a much larger set (i.e., all gas stations that could be represented in an information source). The preference relation for **P3** would include all pairs (m, c) where m is a Mobil station and c a Chevron station. After applying this preference relation, for reasons discussed below, one would be left with the Mobil, Shell, and Citgo stations.

In this paper, we ground candidate solutions in results of SPARQL 1.1 queries [6] (that is, multisets of variable bindings). We also allow for solutions from SPARQL extended with external services.[2] The examples in this paper will not use such service extensions; for simplicity we will just use preferences over solutions of SPARQL queries over a RDF graph, such as G_1 in Example 1.

We do not require any other properties of preference relations. In particular, a preference relation here need not be irreflexive, asymmetric, acyclic, or transitive.[3] It may seem that these should be required aspects of a preference relation but we want to study what happens with arbitrary preference relations, such as those likely to be obtained directly from users.

---

[2] SPARQL 1.1 provides a basic mechanism for such external services (e.g., to look up or compute current prices or exchange rates), using the SERVICE keyword [11].

[3] To review the basic properties of binary preference relations see Chomicki [10].

Example 3. We allow a combination of comparative preferences on different aspects of gas stations. For example **P6a**: a preference for Mobil brand gas stations over Chevron; **P6b**: a preference for gas stations with KwickieMart stores over those with 7-11's; and **P6c**: a preference for gas stations selling Zerex antifreeze over those selling Prestone. (What is important here is that the preferences on the aspects are only *partial* orders, not total orders.)

Example 4. We also allow the obviously cyclic preference relation consisting only of **P3a**: a preference for Mobil brand gas stations over Chevron brand; **P3b**: a preference for Chevron over Citgo; and **P3c**: a preference for Citgo over Mobil.

The implementation of our preference relations in SPARQL will be arbitrary SPARQL expressions. If solutions contain objects from some sort of knowledge repository the relation can depend on anything accessible in the repository. (Troumpoukis et al. [5] call preferences that do not use external information intrinsic preferences.) In SPARQL this means that an expression defining a preference relation can access properties of a solution object from the underlying graph (such as the brand of fuel sold at a gas station, its current distance, or whether it has a roof over its pumps), and other information in the graph (such as whether it is currently raining, etc.), without having this information in the solution itself.

Our preference relations are not examinable in general, and the set of *potential* solutions will generally be very large, or even infinite.

Example 5. For instance, the preference **P5**: "I prefer between two solutions the one closer in distance", could apply to infinitely many *potential* solutions (not knowing the underlying graph G). Note also that there could be other gasoline brands in G that are not named explicitly in the preferences at hand.

It can thus be practically infeasible to compute the transitive closure of a preference relation, or indeed determine whether a preference relation is irreflexive, asymmetric, acyclic, or transitive.

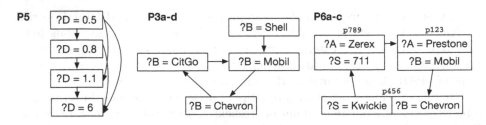

Fig. 1. Preference relations **P5**, **P3a-d**, and **P6a-c** for the solutions of query Q_1 over graph G_1.

Example 6. For instance, **P5** is transitive on all sets of candidate solutions. However, if we view **P3a-c** as a single preference relation, transitivity does not hold. As well, additional preferences such as **P3d** "I prefer Shell over Mobil" could make the preference relation lose completeness[4] (every element comparable with every other). See Fig. 1 for a graphical illustration. Similarly, **P6a-c** produces a preference cycle on our example gas stations.

The basic operation in comparative preferences is the winnow operator [10]. The intuitive notion is that given an candidate set of solutions and a preference relation, the winnow operator returns those solutions that have no solution dominating them. Based on its similarity to skylines in databases, we call the result of the winnow operator the skyline of a preference relation. Formally this is (again adapted from Chomicki [10]):

Definition 2. *If S is a finite set of (candidate) solutions and $\succ$ a preference relation over some (potentially infinite) superset of S then the* skyline *of S with respect to $\succ$ is*

$$\omega_\succ(S) = \{s \in S | \neg \exists s' \in S.s' \succ s\}$$

We loosely refer to the definition of skyline as the "semantics" of preference relations. Note here that $\succ$ has access to extrinsic information about objects in solutions in S. In the SPARQL setting this means that $\succ$ has access to the graph being queried.

We can also define the second skyline as the skyline after the initial skyline has been removed from the solution set, and so on, thus defining "levels" of skyline solutions:

Definition 3. *If S is a finite set of (candidate) solutions and $\succ$ a preference relation over some superset of S then the nth* skyline *of S with $\succ$ is defined as*

$$\omega_\succ^n(S) = \{s \in S \setminus \bigcup_{i=1}^{n-1} \omega_\succ^i(S) \mid \neg \exists s' \in S \setminus \bigcup_{i=1}^{n-1} \omega_\succ^i(S) . s' \succ s\}$$

The rank *of a solution, s, in S with respect to $\succ$ is the number of the skyline that it is in, i.e., $rank_\succ^S(s) = n$ for $s \in \omega_\succ^n(S)$. If a solution is not in any skyline, then its rank is undefined.*

Returning multiple skylines is valuable if all elements of the top skyline might be deemed unsuitable by later processing, or if a minimum number of solutions is required, which could exceed the size of the top skyline.

Example 7. Looking at Fig. 1 let us assume for the moment a slight reformulation of **P5** to be "I prefer between two solutions the one closer or equal in distance". This obviously is not very intuitive as it makes the preference relation reflexive, and thereby makes *each solution dominate itself* – resulting in an empty skyline. However, as we will see current proposals for encoding preferences in SPARQL allow such preferences.

---

[4] Chomicky calls this *connectivity* [10, Definition 2.1].

Example 8. Cyclic preferences can appear in practice by collecting single user preferences, expressed on separate occasions, and with the definitions above can lead to unexpected results. We take here the example of **P3a-d** from Fig. 1. Intuitively, among *all four* candidate solutions the solution with brand `Shell` is most preferred, but then under Definition 3 the second skyline is *empty*, since *each remaining solution is dominated by another candidate solution.* Our intuition is that in such a case all of these three solutions should be equally preferred, and in the second skyline. Note that **P6a-c** also produce a cycle in the 4 candidate solutions, even though their expression does not look obviously cyclic.

Assuming, on the other hand, that `Citgo` was *not* within the candidate solutions, say by changing Q_1 to Q_2 as follows:

Q_2: SELECT * {?X a :GasStation; :brand ?B; :dist ?D. FILTER(?D<=5)}

That would reduce the number of candidate solutions to just `Shell`, `Mobil`, and `Chevron`, which would be in the first, second and third skyline, respectively (this time in accord with our intuitions). So, we see that removing (and likewise adding) candidate solutions can change the rank and ordering of solutions.

To complicate things further, if we consider **P3a-d** or **P6a-c** in combination with **P1** the handling of the combined preference relation becomes even less clear, depending on the semantics of combinations and their respective consideration of candidate solutions.

Given examples such as these, we aim to shed more light on the semantics for preferences in queries, and provide definitions that handle these situations more intuitively and satisfy basic desiderata, such as that each level of skyline should contain at least one solution, even in cases where preferences are not necessarily coherent.

Our primary contributions in the present work are

- an analysis of what goes wrong with a widely used definition of the skyline operator when a preference relation fails to be acyclic and/or transitive,
- a definition that works for arbitrary preference relations,
- a slightly simpler definition that can be used with transitive preference relations, with performance benefits,
- translations to SPARQL 1.1 (based on translations proposed in prior work [5,12]) to implement these new definitions, and
- a further extension that allows a query to request *multiple levels* of skylines.

In the next section, we will review some earlier approaches to the formulation of preferences in SPARQL, in the light of whether they can express comparative semantics at all and how they would handle the cases above. We will then approach the analysis of preference relations and variations of the definition of the skyline operator more formally in Sects. 4 and 5, by discussing what we call simple (i.e., acyclic and/or transitive) preferences and non-simple preferences separately. Along the way we will refine the notion of skyline operators and provide two more variations thereof. Finally, in Sects. 6 and 7 we will discuss which of these proposed variations can be implemented in SPARQL 1.1, and which require extensions in terms of bespoke evaluation algorithms. In this topic, we will identify problems in existing approaches to translating preference handling to SPARQL, and propose repairs, where possible.

3   Previous Work

The notion of preference has a central role in many disciplines, including economics, psychology and other social sciences, some areas of philosophy, decision theory and game theory (themselves interdisciplinary topics), and computer science. The formalization of comparative preferences as binary preference relations runs throughout much of this work, although the definitional details vary. Much work on preference relations assumes, mandates, or arranges for them to be acyclic and/or transitive (or constrained in other ways), for a variety of reasons. Nonetheless, there is a large literature showing that cyclic and/or intransitive preference relations do arise naturally in the real world of human judgments [8,9].

Turning to preferences used with query languages, Rosati et al. [13] show how a set of preferences modeled as a CP-net can be represented in RDF, and how generated SPARQL queries can use the RDF representation to rank the results of an ordinary (non-preferential) SPARQL query. Whereas the preferences semantics discussed here are determined primarily by the definition of skyline, in their approach the semantics are determined by the CP-net formalism. Whereas we are concerned with preferences expressed directly in a SPARQL query, along with non-preferential query clauses, their preferences are acquired and represented independently of the non-preferential SPARQL queries to which they apply[5].

Chomicki [10] analyzes intrinsic comparative preferences in a relational database setting. He considers preferences as multidimensional combinations of atomic preferences where each atomic preference is a built-in SQL function (such as numeric ordering). A preference function could be to consider distance and fuel brand separately, which ends up with the closest gas station for each brand, or to first consider distance and then some ordering of brands, which ends up with the closest gas station but if there is a tie for closest then chooses by brand. He analyzes the properties of his winnow operator with an eye to how it can be optimized in SQL queries.

Siberski et al. [3] transform a subset of these preferences into an early version of SPARQL, producing a SPARQL query extension for conjunctive (combine preferences over two different values) cascaded (consider preference over one value before preference over another) intrinsic preferences. They implement these preferences as an extension to ARQ[6], with a syntax inspired by an early version of the Preference SQL language [14].

---

[5] In a later version of [13], available on semanticscholar.org, the approach is extended to handle CP-theories.

[6] https://jena.apache.org/documentation/query/.

Gueroussova et al. [4,12] transform a version of Chomicki's preferences (which they call conditional preferences) to SPARQL, extending the work of Siberski et al. by adding more combination operators. They define an extension to SPARQL, which they call PrefSPARQL (after the later version of Preference SQL [15] which incorporates these features) and provide a mapping from Pref-SPARQL to both SPARQL 1.0 queries [16] and SPARQL 1.1 queries.

Unfortunately their mapping to SPARQL 1.1 uses the SPARQL EXISTS operator. SPARQL EXISTS has many known problems [17], and their solution falls prey to one them, namely that the SPARQL BOUND operator does not work correctly inside EXISTS. Their mapping to SPARQL 1.0 is not affected by this problem, as shown by the next example.

Both the approaches by Siberski et al. and Gueroussova et al. focus on combined preferences over boolean preferences, that is, while they allow the combination of different preferences, these preferences do not give the full flexibility of comparing arbitrary solutions pairwise, but only by declaring boolean "preferred conditions" C, that divide the solution space into preferred and non-preferred solutions according to the preference, according to the schema in Eq. (1).

$$\text{SELECT } V \text{ WHERE } \{ \ P \text{ PREFERRING } \quad C \ \} \tag{1}$$

Example 9. In both the approaches above preferences like **P1** can be written by extending queries like Q_1. In PrefSPARQL this is:

```
Q3: SELECT * { ?X a :GasStation; :brand ?B; :dist ?D .
              PREFERRING (?D <= 1) }
```

Combined preferences can be expressed (so long as they do not involve comparisons between different attributes of solutions), such as this variant of **P4**:

P4' "I prefer solutions within 1 mile and among those I prefer Mobil, and otherwise just the closest."

which in PrefSPARQL could be written as the following query:

```
Q4: SELECT * { ?X a :GasStation; :brand ?B; :dist ?D .
              PREFERRING ((?D <= 1) AND ?B="Mobil") PRIOR TO LOWEST ?D) }
```

While referring for details to [12], we illustrate PrefSPARQL's translation back to "vanilla" SPARQL by the example of Q_3 which in SPARQL 1.1 yields $Q_3^{1.1}$:

```
Q3^{1.1}: 1  SELECT * { {?X a :GasStation; :brand ?B; :dist ?D .}
          2    FILTER NOT EXISTS { ?X' a :GasStation; :brand ?B'; :dist ?D' .
          3                       FILTER ((?D' <= 1) > (?D <= 1)) } }
```

That is, the translation relies in principle on creating a copy of the query pattern within a SPARQL 1.1 NOT EXISTS clause (line 2) and then encoding dominance of the solutions to this copy in an inner FILTER expression (line 3).

As shown in [12], this principle can be easily extended to combined preference relations (through encoding AND and PRIOR TO, and adding conditional IF-THEN-ELSE preferences from Preference SQL to more complex inner

FILTER expressions). Specific quantitative comparative preference relations are also expressible with the keyword HIGHEST or LOWEST, but not general comparative preferences.

Example 10. The quantitative preference **P2** would be expressible in PrefS-PARQL as query

```
Q₄: SELECT ?X ?B ?D { ?X a :GasStation; :brand ?B; :dist ?D.
                      PREFERRING LOWEST ?D }
```

However, there exists as mentioned above a problem with this translation due to the semantics of NOT EXISTS, as illustrated with the following example:

Example 11. Let us assume **P7** saying "I prefer gas stations with a shop", which in PrefSPARQL could be expressed as

```
Q₅: SELECT * { ?X a :GasStation. OPTIONAL { ?X :shop ?S. }
              PREFERRING ( BOUND(?S) ) }
```

in which case the translation from [12] no longer works, as shown in $Q_5^{1.1}$:

```
Q₅¹·¹: 1   SELECT * { { ?X a :GasStation. OPTIONAL { ?X :shop ?S. } }
       2     FILTER NOT EXISTS { ?X' a :GasStation. OPTIONAL { ?X' :shop ?S'. }
       3                         FILTER(BOUND(?S') > BOUND(?S)) } }
```

This fails because the substitution semantics of EXISTS here produces algebra expressions like BOUND (:TigerMart) that are undefined in SPARQL 1.1; we refer to details in [17]. We note though, that Gueroussova et al.'s [12] SPARQL 1.0-based way of encoding non-existence through a combination of OPTIONAL and !BOUND(), as illustrated in the following query $Q_5^{1.0}$, works as intended:

```
Q₅¹·⁰: 1   SELECT * { { ?X a :GasStation. OPTIONAL { ?X :shop ?S. } }
       2             OPTIONAL { ?X' a :GasStation. OPTIONAL { ?X' :shop ?S'. }
       3                        FILTER ( BOUND(?S') > BOUND(?S) ) }
       4             FILTER ( !BOUND(?X') } }
```

Troumpoukis et al. [5] expand on this work to allow arbitrary SPARQL expressions as the ≻ operator; that is, they define an extension to SPARQL 1.1 that can express full comparative preferences called SPREFQL, and also provide a mapping from SPREFQL into SPARQL 1.1 queries. They implemented SPREFQL and compared its performance to the performance of their mapping.

As opposed to PrefSPARQL, in SPREFQL one can express comparative preferences by explicitly referring to variables in the "copy" of the query pattern over which preferences are defined using a clause PREFER-TO-IF which creates two explicit copies V_1, V_2 of the variables V in the SELECT clause that can be referenced in a comparative condition C:

$$\text{SELECT } V \text{ WHERE } \{ P \} \text{ PREFER } V_1 \text{ TO } V_2 \text{ IF } C \qquad (2)$$

Example 12. The quantitative preference **P2** would be expressible in SPREFQL as a comparative preference in query Q_6:

```
Q₆: SELECT ?X ?B ?D { ?X a :GasStation; :brand ?B; :dist ?D. }
    PREFER ?X1 ?B1 ?D1 TO ?X2 ?B2 ?D2 IF (?D1 < ?D2)
```

More general comparative preferences such as **P3** can also be expressed in SPREFQL, as in query Q_7:

```
Q7: SELECT ?X ?B ?D { ?X a :GasStation; :brand ?B; :dist ?D . }
    PREFER ?X1 ?B1 ?D1 TO ?X2 ?B2 ?D2
         IF (?B1 = :mobil && ?B2 = :chevron)
```

Combined preferences are also supported, through AND and PRIOR TO clauses. Unfortunately, however, with the syntactic expansion over PrefSPARQL, it is quite possible for the preference relation to be non-transitive or to have loops.

Example 13. For instance, imagine Q_6 modified by replacing $<$ with $\leq$ (which we will refer to as Q_6' below), so that each solution dominates itself. Another example involves expressing **P6a-c** as:

```
Q8: SELECT ?X ?B ?S ?T {?X a :GasStation; :brand ?B; :shop ?S; :antifreeze ?A.}
    PREFER ?X1 ?B1 ?S1 ?A1 TO ?X2 ?B2 ?S2 ?A2
    IF ( (?B1 = :Mobil && ?B2 = :Chevron) ||
         (?S1 = :KwikieMart && ?S2 = :711) ||
         (?A1 = :Zerex && ?A2 = :Prestone) )
```

This is problematic, as Troumpoukis et al. only use the simple definition of winnowing above. If there is a preference loop in the candidate solutions, as for Q_8 on the example data, then none of the solutions in the loop will ever be returned, because each of them is dominated by another solution. The preference combination operators do not help: AND will just produce the same cyclic preference and PRIOR TO does not have a suitable meaning. This problem also occurs for reflexive loops, as for Q_6' where each solution dominates itself. We provide a simple but general solution for these problems below. As we will see, the absence of transitivity does not cause a problem by itself, but does complicate the problem of loops.

Also, note that Troumpoukis et al. provide a mapping to SPARQL 1.1 where the schema of Eq. (2) is replaced by (again, we refer for details to [5]):

$$\text{SELECT } V \text{ WHERE} \{ P \text{ FILTER NOT EXISTS} \{ P_{(V/V_1)} \text{ FILTER } C_{(V_2/V)} \}\} \tag{3}$$

This is a straightforward extension of the PrefSPARQL translation, which however depends again on SPARQL EXISTS and also falls prey to the problem with BOUND, as in Example 11.

4   Simple Comparative Preferences

We first establish that acyclic preference relations are non-problematic: they are guaranteed to determine a nonempty skyline over any finite, non-empty set of solutions and ranks behave well. In addition, as we discuss in detail in Sect. 6, a skyline query over an acyclic preference relation is specifiable in SPARQL 1.1. As every transitive and irreflexive relation is acyclic, handling acyclic preference relations also handles this common requirement imposed on preference relations.

Theorem 1. *If the preference relation $\succ$ is acyclic over a finite, non-empty set of candidate solutions S, i.e., there is no candidate solution s for which there is a sequence of candidate solutions starting and ending with s such that each dominates the next, then $\omega_\succ(S)$ is non-empty.*

Because each skyline is non-empty for a finite, non-empty set of solutions if the preference relation is acyclic, each solution has a uniquely defined rank.

Corollary 1. *If the preference relation $\succ$ is acyclic over a finite, non-empty set of candidate solutions S then $rank_\succ^S(s)$ is defined for each $s \in S$.*

Dominance between solutions is reflected in their relative ranks.

Theorem 2. *If the preference relation $\succ$ is acyclic over a finite, non-empty set of candidate solutions S then $s_1 \succ s_2$ implies $rank_\succ^S(s_1) < rank_\succ^S(s_2)$.*

As Troumpoukis et al. [5] use $\omega_\succ$ as their winnow operator, their solution performs correctly on acyclic preference relations. However, if the preference relation has loops, then none of the solutions in the loop will be in any skyline (and thus none of them will have a rank), even if there is no other solution dominating any solution in the loop. Even a simple reflexive loop, such as accidentially writing $\leq$ instead of $<$ as in Example 13, query Q_6' above, causes problems for Definition 2. A preference written like this seems unintuitive, but it is not forbidden in SPREFQL. As arbitrarily complex SPARQL expressions can occur in the IF clause it might not be obvious or even possible beforehand to determine whether a preference is irreflexive.

5   Non-Simple Comparative Preferences

To address such cases, we begin by addressing the empty-skyline problem mentioned above, which can be done by modifying the definition of skyline.

What makes intuitive sense in the presence of preference loops *in the candidate solutions* is to consider all the solutions in the loop as if they were equally preferred, i.e., they don't count as dominating each other or themselves. This regains the desirable property that a finite, non-empty set of candidate solutions has a non-empty skyline.

Formally, we modify the definition of skyline (Definition 2) as follows:

Definition 4. *If S is a finite set of solutions and $\succ$ a preference relation over some superset of S then the skyline of S with $\succ$ is*

$$\omega_\succ^l(s) = \{s \in S \mid \neg \exists s' \in S.(s' \succ^* s \wedge \neg(s \succ^* s'))\}$$

where $\succ^*$ is the transitive closure of $\succ$ over candidate solutions, i.e., there is a sequence of candidate solutions, each dominating the next.

In English, this says that a solution is in the skyline if there is no solution that transitively dominates it and that it does not transitively dominate.

This definition regains the desirable properties from above, slightly modified.

Theorem 3. $\omega^l_\succ(S)$ *is non-empty for* S *any finite, non-empty set of candidate solutions.*

Corollary 2. $rank^S_\succ(s)$ *is defined for each* $s \in S$ *for* S *any finite, non-empty set of candidate solutions.*

Loops cause the rank of solutions in the loop to be the same, so dominance only produces a rank at least as large.

Theorem 4. *For any preference relation* $\succ$ *over a finite, non-empty set of candidate solutions* S, $s_1 \succ s_2$ *implies* $rank^S_\succ(s_1) \le rank^S_\succ(s_2)$.

Note that, in Definition 4, transitive closure is needed for both the ancestor and the descendant of s. Consider a solution s that dominates only a single element s_1 of a minimal domination cycle[7] $s_1, \ldots, s_n, s_1$, with $n > 2$. Now s should knock each s_i out of a skyline but no s_j should. To get to *only* s requires looking at the transitive dominators of s_i, not just its direct dominators.

Example 14. Getting back to the preference relation from the right-hand-side of Fig. 1, the solution s_{Shell} dominates s_{Mobil} directly, but $s_{Chevron}$ and s_{Citgo} are dominated only indirectly. Thus, if in Definition 4 $s' \succ^* s$ were replaced by $s' \succ s$, then $s_{Chevron}$ and s_{Citgo} – counter to our intuition – would end up in the first skyline. On the other hand, if we replaced $\neg(s \succ^* s')$ with $\neg(s \succ s')$, it is easy to see that the second skyline would be empty, again going counter to our intuition.

As a special case (specifically considered here because of its relationship to SPARQL), if the preference relation is known to be transitive then there is no need to compute its transitive closure; that is, the following simpler definition suffices to deal such known transitive (including reflexive) preferences, even if they are cyclic. Here, in English, a solution is in the skyline if there is no solution that *directly* dominates it and that it does not *directly* dominate.

Definition 5. *If* S *is a finite set of (candidate) solutions and* $\succ$ *a transitive preference relation over some superset of* S *then the skyline of* S *with* $\succ$ *is*

$$\omega^t_\succ(S) = \{s \in S | \neg \exists s' \in S.(s' \succ s \wedge \neg(s \succ s'))\}$$

This definition maintains the desirable properties from Theorems 2, 3, and 4, for transitive preference relations. They all come from the simple observation that the transitive closure of a transitive relation is itself, so Definitions 4 and 5 coincide for transitive preference relations. Note that transitivity is not actually required in general for Definition 5 to suffice, but only transitivity into loops, i.e., a direct dominator of any solution in a loop is a direct dominator of every solution in the loop. We call the preference relation $\succ$ *clique-cyclic* in this case.

Theorem 5. *Let* S *be any finite set of (candidate) solutions. Let* $\succ$ *be clique-cyclic, i.e., for any solutions* s_1 *and* s_2, *if* $s_1 \succ^* s_2$ *and* $s_2 \succ^* s_1$ *then for any solution* s *if* $s \succ s_1$ *then* $s \succ s_2$. *Then* $\omega^t_\succ(S) = \omega^l_\succ(S)$.

---

[7] A domination cycle is minimal if the only domination relationships between elements of the cycle are those from one element of the cycle to the next.

6   Comparative Preferences in SPARQL

As discussed in Sect. 3 above, languages like PrefSPARQL and SPREFQL have suggested translations to native SPARQL, thus showing a – not necessarily very efficient – implementation path in terms of off-the-shelf engines, and proving that the respective languages do not add expressivity on top of SPARQL. However, since both these translations only implement the simple winnow operator from Definition 2, we now turn to the question whether $\omega_{\succ}^t(S)$ and $\omega_{\succ}^l(S)$ can likewise be expressed in SPARQL 1.1.

As we want to allow for general comparative preferences, we adopt the SPREFQL syntax [5] as opposed to the syntax of earlier work such as PrefSPARQL [4].

We recall the mapping from SPREFQL to SPARQL 1.1 by the schema given in Eq. (3). While Troumpoukis et al. already suggest that evaluating this translation is potentially more expensive than directly implementing PREFER, for now we are only concerned with the expressibility of the different variations of skyline operators we introduced in SPARQL.

We recall there are two problems in the original translation: first, the use of NOT EXISTS in the translation into SPARQL, and second, that the reliance on the skyline operator of Definition 2 only works for the simple case of acyclic preference relations.

The first problem can be overcome using the translation that uses OPTIONAL and !BOUND() instead of NOT EXISTS from Gueroussova et al. [12], cf. Example 11. This idea can be generalized to SPREFQL with the following mapping for Eq. (2).

Mapping 1 (Simple Mapping to SPARQL)

```
SELECT  V  WHERE {  P
        OPTIONAL {  P(V/V₁)  FILTER (  C(V₂/V)  ) BIND (1 TO ?exists) }
        FILTER (!BOUND(?exists)) }
```

Theorem 6. *Mapping 1 correctly implements $\omega_{\succ}$.*

Proof. (Sketch) The OPTIONAL part only binds a value to ?exists when a dominator exists so the final filter only lets through solutions that are not dominated.

Handling the second problem however requires changing the semantics of PREFER. When we view the intuitive meaning of Eq. (2) decoupled from the mapping to SPARQL it conceptually reduces to first constructing the solution set S for

$$\text{SELECT } V \text{ WHERE} \{ P \}$$

and then eliminating non-dominated solutions of this query according to the chosen winnow operator. So we need to repair the semantics to use our winnow operator ω^l, which as we showed above produces desirable results for any preference relation, instead of the original ω. Of course this is quite a significant change. On the plus side, it doesn't have problems with loops. On the negative side, it may require computing (a part of) the transitive closure of $\succ$. We will discuss next whether and how this computation can also be realized within SPARQL itself, or by means of bespoke algorithms.

7   Implementing SPARQL Preferences

This repaired version of comparative preferences semantics can be efficiently implemented. Instead of just checking whether a solution has a direct dominator we have to check its transitive dominators and see whether they are in a loop. This sounds expensive, going around the loops repeatedly, but can actually be done relatively efficiently.

The basic idea[8] behind the algorithm is to check $\succ$ between each pair of candidate solutions. The algorithm keeps track of a representative for each solution which represents all the solutions that are in loops involving the solution. When a new loop is found, the solutions in the loop are given the same representative. This operation has to be done efficiently over the entire exploration. Fortunately, the union-find algorithm [18] does precisely this in time $O(n\log^*(n))$, where n is the number of candidate solutions. After the representatives are found, all that is needed is to check whether a solution has a direct dominator with a different representative.

The algorithm checks $\succ$ between each pair of solutions so its running time is dominated by the n^2 computations of $\succ$; the union-find algorithm only adds $O(n\log^*(n))$. The most significant change in actual running time between the computation of $\omega_\succ$ and $\omega_\succ^l$ will be due to not being able to quit checking for dominators of a solution when the first one is found.

If the preference relation is known to belong to either of the special cases discussed in the context of Definition 5, i.e., if either the preference relation is acyclic, transitive or clique-cyclic, then it is possible to translate preferences back into SPARQL itself. For an *acyclic* preference relation the translation is the one in Mapping 1. For transitive preference relations (or, likewise, if $\succ$ is clique-cyclic) a slightly more complex translation is needed.

Mapping 2 (Mapping to SPARQL for transitive Preferences)

```
SELECT  V  WHERE {  P
        OPTIONAL {  P_(V/V_1) FILTER ( C_(V_2/V) && ! C_(V_1/V,V_2/V_1) )
                    BIND (1 TO ?exists) }
        FILTER (!BOUND(?exists)) }
```

Theorem 7. *Mapping 2 correctly implements the winnow operator* $\omega_\succ^t$.

The general case is much tougher to translate back to a single SPARQL query as it has to compute (part of) the transitive closure of $\succ$ over the solutions. If, however, we allow for multiple queries we can first construct a graph that reifies

---

[8] The full algorithm is in the extended technical report version of the paper.

the solutions and asserts $\succ$ between them and then determine the skyline with a subsequent query against the union of that constructed graph and the original graph.

8 Multiple Skylines

There are situations where more solutions than the top skyline are desired, and it is inconvenient to submit multiple different queries to get those additional solutions, manually eliminating prior solutions. Thus, a SPARQL extension that returns multiple levels of skylines, possibly including an indicator of each solution's rank, seems natural.

Siberski et al. [3] propose that a use of SPARQL's existing keyword pattern "LIMIT k", in combination with their proposed keyword PREFERRING, can inform the query evaluator to retrieve enough levels of skyline to produce solutions numbering at least k. However, this approach has 3 weaknesses: it gives the LIMIT modifier a counterintuitive special meaning when it is used in that combination; it precludes the use of LIMIT with its usual meaning; and it does not support the specification of an explicit number of complete skylines to be returned.

To address these issues, we propose the addition of the keyword SKYLINE, to be used in conjunction with LIMIT, in either of the following patterns:

- LIMIT SKYLINE n [TO m] [AS v_{rank}] ... return complete skyline(s) with rank n (or with ranks n to m, with $1 \leq n \leq m$).
- LIMIT SKYLINE ALL AS v_{rank} ...   return all skylines.

The AS v_{rank} is optional if explicit limits are given. If present it adds a new binding to the solution bindings of the query assigning to variable v_{rank} the rank of the solution. Ranks are counted starting at 1, and the absence of a LIMIT SKYLINE clause is equivalent to LIMIT SKYLINE 1.

Our implementation of ω_l can be simply extended to compute which skyline a solution is in. Each solution is initially given a tentative skyline of 1. When a non-looping dominator of a solution is found the solution's representative is assigned to the tentative skyline that is the maximum of its previous tentative skyline and one plus the tentative skyline of the dominator's representative. As non-looping dominators are only found when their dominators have been completely processed their tentative skyline is their final one. This way each solution representative is assigned to their skyline number so the algorithm can produce the first (top) skyline, solutions in skyline(s) ranked between n and m along with their skyline number, or all solutions with their skyline number.

9 Conclusions

We have considered the semantics of queries that rely on user preferences, extensions of SPARQL that would allow for handling such queries, and their possible implementation by translation into SPARQL. We identified several categories of preference relations with different characteristics that are significant in terms of specifying preference query semantics and specifying translations to SPARQL.

We summarize our conclusions, in order of increasing generality of the allowed preference relations: The semantics of *acyclic* preference relations are as (implicitly) indicated by Troumpoukis et al. [5]. However, we identified a problem with their translation to SPARQL, and showed how it can be repaired. *Transitive, irreflexive* preference relations, which occur in many applied settings, as a special case of acyclic preference relations, are subject to the same observations. For *transitive* preference relations in general, a modified semantics is needed, as well as a slightly more complex translation into SPARQL. This semantics allows for more efficient processing than the most general semantics mentioned below. We defined a category of *clique-cyclic* preference relations (a superset of transitive preference relations, cf. Theorem 5), which can be handled with the same semantics as transitive preference relations. Finally, for *arbitrary* preference relations, we gave a semantics that is slightly more complex than for transitive preference relations, and showed that preference queries can be implemented by translation to multiple (sequentially executed) SPARQL queries.

In addition, we showed that our proposed semantics and implementation for each of these categories satisfies basic desiderata for the results of queries with preferences, and we discussed an algorithm that would be more efficient than the implementation by multiple, nested SPARQL queries. Finally, we proposed an additional SPARQL extension that provides a

References

1. Berners-Lee, T., Hendler, J., Lassila, O.: The semantic web. Sci. Am. **284**(5), 28–37 (2001)
2. Klyne, G., et al.: Composite Capability/Preference Profiles (CC/PP): Structure and Vocabularies 1.0. W3C Recommendation, January 2004
3. Siberski, W., Pan, J.Z., Thaden, U.: Querying the semantic web with preferences. In: Cruz, I., Decker, S., Allemang, D., Preist, C., Schwabe, D., Mika, P., Uschold, M., Aroyo, L.M. (eds.) ISWC 2006. LNCS, vol. 4273, pp. 612–624. Springer, Heidelberg (2006). https://doi.org/10.1007/11926078_44
4. Gueroussova, M., Polleres, A., McIlraith, S.A.: SPARQL with qualitative and quantitative preferences. In: 2nd International Workshop on Ordering and Reasoning (OrdRing 2013), at ISWC 2013. CEUR Workshop Proceedings, vol. 1059 (2013)
5. Troumpoukis, A., Konstantopoulos, S., Charalambidis, A.: An extension of SPARQL for expressing qualitative preferences. In: d'Amato, C., et al. (eds.) ISWC 2017. LNCS, vol. 10587, pp. 711–727. Springer, Cham (2017). https://doi.org/10.1007/978-3-319-68288-4_42
6. Harris, S., Seaborne, A.: SPARQL 1.1 Query Language. W3C Recommendation, March 2013. http://www.w3.org/TR/sparql11-query/
7. Borzsonyi, S., Kossmann, D., Stocker, K.: The skyline operator. In: Proceedings 17th International Conference on Data Engineering, pp. 421–430 (2001)
8. Tversky, A.: Intransitivity of preferences. Psychol. Rev. **76**(1), 31–48 (1969)

9. Nurmi, H.: Making sense of intransitivity, incompleteness and discontinuity of preferences. In: Zaraté, P., Kersten, G.E., Hernández, J.E. (eds.) GDN 2014. LNBIP, vol. 180, pp. 184–192. Springer, Cham (2014). https://doi.org/10.1007/978-3-319-07179-4_21

10. Chomicki, J.: Preference formulas in relational queries. ACM Trans. Database Syst. **28**(4), 427–466 (2003)

11. Buil-Aranda, C., Arenas, M., Corcho, O., Polleres, A.: Federating queries in SPARQL 1.1: Syntax, semantics and evaluation. J. Web Semant. **18**(1), 1–17 (2013)

12. Gueroussova, M., Polleres, A., McIlraith, S.A.: SPARQL with qualitative and quantitative preferences (extended report). University of Toronto CSRG Report 619 (2013)

13. Rosati, J., Di Noia, T., Lukasiewicz, T., De Leone, R., Maurino, A.: Preference queries with ceteris paribus semantics for linked data. In: Debruyne, C., et al. (eds.) On the Move to Meaningful Internet Systems: OTM 2015 Conferences. OTM 2015. Lecture Notes in Computer Science, vol. 9415. Springer, Cham (2015). https://doi.org/10.1007/978-3-319-26148-5_28

14. Kießling, W., Köstler, G.: Preference SQL - design, implementation, experiences. In: 28th International Conference on Very Large Data Bases, pp. 990–1001 (2002)

15. Kießling, W., Endres, M., Wenzel, F.: The preference SQL system - an overview. IEEE Data Eng. Bull. **34**(2), 11–18 (2011)

16. Prud'hommeaux, E., Seaborne, A.: SPARQL query language for RDF. W3C Recommendation (2008). https://www.w3.org/TR/rdf-sparql-query/

17. Patel-Schneider, P.F., Martin, D.: EXISTStential aspects of SPARQL. In: The 15th International Semantic Web Conference (ISWC 2016), October 2016

18. Tarjan, R.E.: Efficiency of a good but not linear set union algorithm. J. ACM **22**(2), 215–225 (1975)

Interplay of Game Incentives, Player Profiles and Task Difficulty in Games with a Purpose

Gloria Re Calegari and Irene Celino[✉]

Cefriel – Politecnico of Milano, Viale Sarca 226, 20126 Milan, Italy
{gloria.re,irene.celino}@cefriel.com

Abstract. How to take multiple factors into account when evaluating a Game with a Purpose? How is player behaviour or participation influenced by different incentives? How does player engagement impact their accuracy in solving tasks? In this paper, we present a detailed investigation of multiple factors affecting the evaluation of a GWAP and we show how they impact on the achieved results. We inform our study with the experimental assessment of a GWAP designed to solve a multinomial classification task.

1 Introduction

Games with a Purpose [1] are a well-known Human Computation approach [2] to encourage users to execute tasks with an entertaining reward. While several metrics are proposed in literature to evaluate the ability of GWAPs to achieve their intended purpose, there is a large number of factors that influences their success and effectiveness.

In order to fully understand the strengths as well as the weaknesses of a GWAP, we propose an approach that takes into account *player characteristics* (reliability, participation, behaviour and accuracy), *game aspects* (playing incentive, playing style and game nature) and *features of the task* to be solved (level of difficulty and variety). Our goal is to investigate the interplay between those different factors, by proposing a multi-faceted analysis framework that allows for a deep assessment and understanding of the efficacy of a GWAP to achieve its purpose. We apply the proposed framework to a specific GWAP to show the empirical results and the insights that can be drawn through our approach.

The original contributions of this paper are: (1) an extension of traditional GWAP metrics to take temporal evolution and incentive effects into account; (2) a comparison of engagement metrics and engagement profiles with non-gaming citizen science; and (3) the definition of GWAP-specific engagement profiles and their interplay with different factors (incentive, task difficulty and task variety).

The remainder of the paper is organized as follows: Sect. 2 illustrates the main related work; Sect. 3 gives details about the GWAP that we use to exemplify our approach; in the following sections, we propose different evaluation methods,

© Springer Nature Switzerland AG 2018
C. Faron Zucker et al. (Eds.): EKAW 2018, LNAI 11313, pp. 306–321, 2018.
https://doi.org/10.1007/978-3-030-03667-6_20

by extending state-of-the-art metrics: global GWAP metrics and interplay with incentive are adopted in Sect. 4, Sect. 5 offers a comparison with citizen science user engagement profiles and Sect. 6 proposes new GWAP player profiling driven by measures of participation and accuracy; finally, Sect. 7 concludes the paper.

2   Related Work

The basic metrics to evaluate GWAPs [1–3] are global indicators computed as means over the entire data; while effective in summarizing the behaviour of GWAP players, those are very simple measures that do not tell the entire story: an analysis of data distribution and temporal evolution is usually required to get a deeper understanding of a GWAP.

Some work exists on cross-feature analysis of GWAPs [4] and similarly on citizen science [5] and crowdsourcing [6]; our goal is to contribute to making such evaluation easier to replicate and reproduce.

Participation incentives are usually classified as intrinsic or extrinsic motivation [7]. Some comparative analysis of incentives exists for GWAPs [8], especially in contrast to different methods like micro-working [9–11] or machine learning [12]. The effect of competition and tangible rewards on participation and quality of results has also been explored, both in the context of GWAPs [13] and online citizen science campaigns [14], revealing the pros and cons of designing different motivation mechanisms.

Other metrics to evaluate GWAPs can be borrowed from studies of social community [15] and citizen science evolution [16]; in those cases, however, user participation's "success" is measured through simple indicators like number of participants and contributions, while a deeper investigation is needed to assess the effectiveness of participation. Behavioural studies in HCI research have investigated volunteer characterization in citizen science, defining engagement metrics and profiles [17,18], which may or may not apply to GWAP players.

In the context of (paid) crowdsourcing, assessment is usually conducted in relation to micro-work platforms [19], in which important features are related to cost minimization [20,21] which is out of scope with respect to our work.

While Games with a Purpose are a well-known and widely adopted human computation method to involve users in task solution, a comprehensive assessment of their ability to address their "purpose" needs to take into account multiple factors affecting the game and the players. We therefore propose a multi-faceted analysis framework for GWAPs that includes game aspects, player characteristics and task features, with specific focus on the effect of game incentives on the overall GWAP efficacy.

3   Use Case: The Night Knights GWAP

The GWAP that we will use as running example is Night Knights, an online game for the multinomial classification of images[1]. Pictures come from a massive

---
[1] Cf. https://www.nightknights.eu/.

public-domain dataset provided by NASA and they can be classified according to six different categories depending on their visual content. The classified images – in particular those labeled with three of the six categories – are then used in a subsequent scientific workflow in the field of astronomy and environmental sciences to measure light pollution effects (cf. [12]).

The GWAP is inspired by the ESP game [3], because users play in random pairs according to an output-agreement mechanism [1]. The game adopts a repeated labeling approach [22] by asking different players to classify the same image; conversely, the same image is never given twice to the same player. Night Knights is built on top of our open source software framework for GWAPs [23].

The players visualize a picture and six buttons reporting the six possible categories (cf. Fig. 1); the labeling task is therefore executed by clicking on the category that better fits the picture content. Each game round lasts one minute, during which players can classify as many images as they can (as detailed in the following, on average 15 pictures are played per round); each time the two players agree, they gain points and level up in the game leaderboard; some badges are also assigned in special conditions as additional game intrinsic incentives.

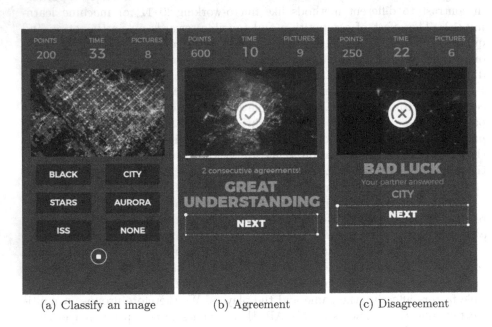

(a) Classify an image   (b) Agreement   (c) Disagreement

Fig. 1. Night Knights: the gameplay

Players' contributions are aggregated through an incremental truth inference algorithm [24] that (1) processes inputs as soon as they are provided, (2) weights players' answer with a round-specific reliability measure [25] taking into account players' answers on control tasks (for which the "true" solution is known), and (3) dynamically adjusts the number of required contributions. Our truth inference approach accounts for the very nature of GWAPs, in which usually there is no "deadline" for contributing, players' varying attention can impact answer quality and task difficulty needs a dynamic estimation of the required number of repeated labeling.

In this paper, we use the data collected through Night Knights. The game was released in February 2017 and then it was more extensively advertised for a related competition whose winner joined the 2017 Summer Expedition to observe the Solar Eclipse in USA. The competition lasted about one month, from mid June to mid July 2017, and was addressed to all EU University students. After the end of the competition, the game has still been available online, but without any additional advertising. Overall, the data we analyse was collected in 9 months, one month of competition and 4 months before and after it[2].

In the following experimental sections, we apply a set of assessment methods on this game data. On the one hand, we exemplify the analyses we propose for a thorough multi-faceted assessment of GWAPs; on the other hand, we provide concrete results from the evaluation of Night Knights, which are – at least partially – typical of GWAPs.

4   Extending GWAP Metrics

The main metrics adopted in literature [2] to evaluate GWAPs are: **throughput**, computed as the average number of solved task per unit of time, **average life play** or ALP, i.e. the average time spent by each user playing the game, and **expected contribution** or EC, measured as average number of tasks solved by each player. A task is solved when player contributions, aggregated by the truth inference algorithm [26], output a "true" solution. Those indicators are global measures, as they are computed as mean values over the entire GWAP use. Hereafter, we extend this analysis by assessing the *influence of different game incentives* and the *evolution over time* of game-play and engagement.

In particular, we investigate how player participation and GWAP results change with and without an extrinsic motivation such as a tangible reward [7]. We analyse incentive effect in terms of both general statistics and specific metrics adopted in GWAP evaluation. We show that users participation can be highly influenced by the presence of an extrinsic motivation.

4.1   [Q1] How Do User Participation and GWAP Results Change with Different Incentives?

In 9 months, Night Knights managed to engage about 650 users that played a substantial amount of time and classified almost 28,000 photos (cf. Table 1).

Measuring the main metrics in the three periods (*before*, *during* and *after* the competition), we notice a significant increase of player participation during the competition, both in terms of given contributions and classified images (one order

---

[2] Data is available with a CC-BY license at http://ckan.stars4all.eu/.

Table 1. Experimental results in the three periods (before, during and after the introduction of the extrinsic motivation)

	Before	During	After
Time span (months)	4	1	4
Classified images	1,830	24,600	1,300
Contributions	13,000	187,600	3,600
Users	285	174	174
Total play time (hours)	65	471	29
Throughput (tasks/hour)	69	212	113
ALP (mins/user)	5.5	65	4
EC (tasks/user)	6.4	141	7.5

of magnitude higher with the additional incentive in both cases). This difference is clearly highlighted in Fig. 2, which shows the temporal evolution of the number of images classified per day. The difference between throughput, ALP and EC in the competition and non-competition periods is statistically significant (t-test or Wilcoxon rank sum test at the 0.01 significance level). Also the play time significantly increases *during* the competition period, as demonstrated by the ALP metrics which reaches values over 65 min/player (cf. Table 1).

Those results prove that providing a tangible reward to players can make them contribute more efficiently, speeding up the classification process (higher throughput), engaging them for a longer time (higher ALP), and ensuring a larger contribution rate to the human computation task (higher EC). As a global result, more tasks get solved.

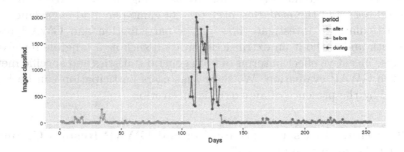

Fig. 2. Number of images classified per day in the three periods

4.2   [Q2] Do the Extrinsic Reward Effects Last over Time?

Adding a tangible prize to a game does not seem to ensure lasting effects. In Night Knights, looking deeper in the *before* and *after* periods in Table 1, we do not notice substantial differences in terms of classification and participation rate. The metrics of the *before* period are slightly higher, probably due to the fact that more users tried the game, attracted by advertising campaigns (small peaks in Fig. 2) and by the novelty of the game.

Given this similarity, in our analysis we think it worth distinguishing only between *intrinsic motivation* periods (e.g., Night Knights *before* and *after* periods together, when users play only to have fun) and *extrinsic motivation* periods (e.g., the *during* phase of Night Knights, with the tangible and valuable reward).

4.3 [Q3] Does Playing Style Change with the Incentive?

Defining *contribution speed* the number of images played in each round, we check if also this metrics is influenced by a tangible reward.

As explained in Sect. 3, each round in Night Knights lasts one minute and each user is asked to classify one image at a time, so users have to be quick and classify as many images as possible to increase their score and being successful in the game. Given the image loading time, connection delays and waiting time for the other player's answer, we estimate that in this case classifying each image takes at least 3–5 s, which means 12–20 photos per round.

As Fig. 3 shows, in the *extrinsic motivation* period, the contribution speed follows a normal distribution centered around 15 photos/round, while, in the *intrinsic motivation* phase, the distribution is flat and most players played less than 10 images/round. This indicates that, during the competition, all players did their best to classify as many images as possible, reaching a median value of 15 that coincides with the estimated image classification time. On the other hand, in the *intrinsic motivation* period, people play the game in a more "relaxed" way, just to try and explore it, taking more time to answer.

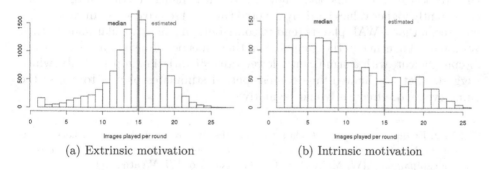

(a) Extrinsic motivation   (b) Intrinsic motivation

Fig. 3. Distribution of the number of images played in each round

5 Applying Citizen Science Engagement Profiles

As a first step to the assessment of player behaviour, we adopt the *engagement metrics* proposed by [17]: **activity ratio**, number of days a user plays a game divided by the total number of days the user remains linked to the game; **daily**

devoted time, average time (e.g. in hours) a user plays the game in each active day; **relative active duration**, ratio of days during which a player remains linked to the game and the total number of days since the player joined the game until the day the game is over (this metric can be computed only if a "game end" is envisaged, which is not always the case in GWAPs); and **variation in periodicity**, standard deviation of the intervals between each pair of non-consecutive active days. Computing those metrics for each player and then applying clustering techniques leads to the identification of *engagement profiles*. Our goal is to assess if the profiles recognized in citizen science literature with respect to volunteer behaviour are also detected in GWAP player behaviour and if player profiles are affected by game incentives. Indeed, we expect player behaviour to differ from volunteer engagement.

5.1 [Q4] How Does GWAP Behaviour Compare to Traditional Citizen Science Engagement?

The mean values (and in brackets standard deviation) of the four main *engagement metrics* defined by [17] are shown in Table 2. For Night Knights, we distinguish the global values and those measured during the competition only (extrinsic motivation period); for comparison, we also report the values for the citizen science initiatives illustrated in [17,18]. Daily devoted time for Night Knights is measured by approximation, multiplying the number of game rounds per 1-min duration (the actual time is higher, because players also browse leaderboards, badges, played pictures, etc.); relative active duration is computed only during the competition time, where a "project finish time" is defined with the contest deadline.

We observe that Night Knights players display quite a different behaviour with respect to volunteers: they show a 2–3 times higher activity ratio, and also consistently higher values for daily devoted time and relative active duration; this may mean that GWAP players tend to contribute in a more regular manner than volunteers. Focusing on the competition, those metrics also show a clear increase in engagement, with a significantly lower value of variation in periodicity, which suggests that the limited-time contest period stimulates players to access the game even more frequently and regularly.

Table 2. Engagement metrics (mean values and standard deviation in brackets): comparison of Night Knights (global values and competition-only metrics) with citizen science campaigns (MW: Milky Way, GZ: Galaxy Zoo, WI: Weather-it).

	Night Knights		MW	GZ	WI
	Global	Compet.	[17]	[17]	[18]
Activity ratio	**0.96** (0.17)	**0.95** (0.16)	0.40 (0.40)	0.33 (0.38)	0.32 (0.35)
Daily devoted time	0.68 (1.94)	**1.80** (3.30)	0.44 (0.54)	0.32 (0.40)	–
Rel. active duration	–	**0.54** (0.35)	0.20 (0.30)	0.23 (0.29)	0.43 (0.44)
Var. in periodicity	14.53 (17.9)	**2.53** (2.12)	18.27 (43.3)	25.23 (49.2)	5.11 (5.36)

Clustering players to identify engagement profiles does not give the same results as in the cited citizen science analyses [17,18]. Cross-validation between different methods (within groups sum of squares and Silhouette statistics) suggests an optimal clustering with 3 groups. Applying both agglomerative hierarchical clustering and K-means clustering yields to similar and very unbalanced grouping, with one big cluster (around 90% of players) roughly corresponding to the *hardworker* profile (high activity ratio and low variation in periodicity); the remaining players are grouped in a small cluster that we can name *"focused" hardworkers* (similar to hardworkers but with higher daily devoted time) and another small cluster that does not clearly correspond to known profiles (low values of all metrics, but higher variation in periodicity). The spasmodic, persistent, lasting and moderate profiles defined in [17] are not observed. This can be interpreted as another difference between players and volunteers engagement, with game users either heavily playing and contributing, or simply trying out the game without being actually engaged.

5.2 [Q5] What Does Player Behaviour Tell About the Game Nature?

If we also evaluate user engagement in terms of when players participated, i.e. for how long they played the game, from the first to the last played round, we discover that only few users played the game both in the intrinsic motivation and extrinsic motivation periods; in particular, only 13 users played both *before* and *during* the competition and only 17 users became aware of the existence of the game during the competition and went on playing it *after* its end.

In addition, by analysing the users' total active time (difference between the last and the first time a user played the game), we discover that most of the users played for a very short amount of time; 75% of players used the game for less than 5 min and only the 10% played for more than a day.

These statistics are not surprising, because they are strong indicators of the game nature, which is a so-called *casual game*. Casual games are usually designed to be played in short bursts of a few minutes and then set aside. By their very nature, casual games target the short free/leisure time between the myriad of everyday tasks, such as between work and domestic obligations or between attention and distraction [27]. Regarding the overall time spent playing mobile games, the literature shows that an average gamer spends every day approximately 24 min playing games on mobile devices, with *heavy gamers* spending about 1 h/day and *light gamers* about 2 min/day [28].

6   Defining GWAP Engagement Profiles

Given that volunteer profiles in citizen science do not seem to suitably describe GWAP players, we focus our investigation on two additional main metrics, player accuracy and player participation, more closely related to human computation, and analyse their interplay with different factors, like game incentive, task difficulty and task variety. The goal is to uncover GWAP-specific user behaviours and to identify *GWAP-specific player profiles*.

Player accuracy is measured ex-post by counting how many tasks each user correctly solved over the total number of tasks he/she played with; in this context, "correct" refers to the final task solution computed by the truth inference algorithm. Accuracy takes values between 0 and 1 and corresponds to the worker precision or labeling quality metrics used in crowdsourcing literature (e.g. [26]). **Player participation** is measured as the total number of contributions given by each user in the game rounds he/she played. While there are of course alternative ways to measure participation (e.g., number of game rounds, total played time), we prefer to consider the number of contributions, since this indicator is more closely related to the "task" execution and the game purpose.

6.1 [Q6] What Kind of GWAP Player Profiles Can Be Identified?

Referring again to Night Knights data, we plot each user as a data point along participation and accuracy axes (cf. Fig. 4). To divide players into groups, we applied clustering as in Sect. 5, but – at least in the case of Night Knights – the results put 98–99% of players in the same cluster, placing only "outliers" in the other clusters. Therefore, to define GWAP-specific profiles, we propose to simply set separation thresholds on the two axes dividing the space into quadrants; more specifically, we adopt the *median* as separation value, which is a commonly used measure and robust statistic. While this definition is arbitrary, it is also data-independent, thus the proposed approach can be adopted to analyse and compare different GWAPs without loss of generality.

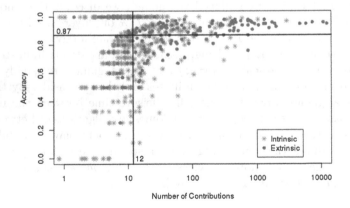

Fig. 4. Players' participation vs. accuracy and median values

The thresholds calculated on the Night Knights dataset are 12 contributions for the x-axis and 0.87 accuracy for the y-axis. The median value for participation roughly corresponds to the separation between those who played just a couple of game rounds from those who were more deeply engaged (cf. Sect. 4). The median accuracy value is quite high and this is a good sign about the GWAP efficacy to achieve its purpose; in other cases, when a specific minimum value of accuracy is required, the threshold choice could be driven by domain-specific consideration instead of being identified by the median.

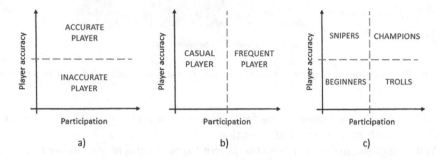

Fig. 5. Definition of GWAP-specific player profiles

By using this approach, the investigation space is divided into areas that represent different "behavioral" profiles as follows. Along the accuracy axis, we obtain two profiles: *accurate players*, i.e. players with an accuracy higher than the median, and the remaining *inaccurate players* (cf. Fig. 5-a). Along the participation axis (cf. Fig. 5-b), we define *casual players* those who contribute less than the median, and *frequent players* the most addicted and loyal contributors. Considering both dimensions, we define four profiles (cf. Fig. 5-c):

- *Beginners* (bottom-left): this is the set of users that play the game for a short period of time, just for curiosity; this kind of players gives only few contributions with low accuracy.
- *Snipers* (top-left): users that are very accurate in their contributions but they contribute only a little. Ideally, they should be motivated to become champions, since their contributions are valuable.
- *Champions* (top-right): this is the most desirable category of players, since they have high level of participation with very high accuracy.
- *Trolls* (bottom-right): this is the category of less desirable users, since they give a lot of inaccurate contributions; having a lot of *Trolls* in the game either makes the classification process longer, since it is harder to reach an agreement, or even leads to undesired results.

Observing again Night Knights data, we can also quantitatively analyse the effect of game incentive on the profile composition (cf. Fig. 6). With extrinsic motivation, most users (53%) acted as champions, and this share is much higher than in the total (32%). On the other hand, with the intrinsic motivation only, the presence of champions was lower, only 25%. This difference may indicate that the different incentives lead to different user behaviour; the presence of

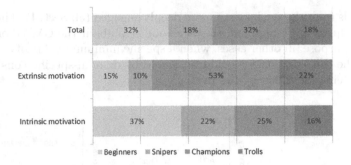

Fig. 6. Distribution of players between profiles, in total and with different incentives

tangible rewards can engage users for a longer time and can motivates them to contribute with more effort and attention.

With intrinsic motivation, also the percentages of snipers was higher than the average. The largest group of users in the intrinsic motivation period, however, was beginners (37%): probably this happened because they tried the game just for curiosity or to understand how the game works, without paying too much attention to the answers they gave. As expected, the number of beginners was very low with the extrinsic motivation, since they had a clear goal to play the game. Fortunately, the percentages of trolls were low in both periods. This means that the Night Knights game succeeded in avoiding too many spammers that could have made the classification process longer or more inaccurate.

While the above results are specific to Night Knights, the profile analysis can be applied to any other GWAP; indeed, examining the composition of a GWAP player population can reveal different behaviour and inform game re-design.

Finally, we would like to point out an insight that is not immediately evident in Fig. 4: since the players on the right part of the plot are those who contributed more, if we sum the contributions from the four profiles, we obtain the figures in Table 3. In the case of our GWAP, therefore, the large majority of contributions comes from the most active and accurate players, which is reassuring with respect to the achievement of the game purpose.

Table 3. Distribution of contributions across players profiles

	Beginners	Snipers	Champions	Trolls
Task contributions	0.7%	0.4%	95.9%	3.0%

In the following, we analyse the interplay between player accuracy and player participation by taking into account additional factors. More specifically, we check if there is a statistically significant difference between the mean accuracy of *casual* and *frequent players* with respect to some control variables, namely the incentive type, the task difficulty and the task variety.

6.2   [Q7] Does Player Behaviour Change with Different Incentives?

To answer this question, we check for mean difference in accuracy for casual and frequent players in the intrinsic and extrinsic motivation periods.

In Night Knights, the average accuracy of the *frequent players* is higher than the one of *casual players* in both periods, as shown in the first two boxplots of Fig. 7; this difference is also significant from a statistically point of view (p-value of the t-test less than 0.05). We also notice a mean accuracy increase of about 10% when a tangible rewards is present (from 0.74 to 0.81 for casual and from 0.83 to 0.90 for frequent): since during the competition users were encouraged to play to win the prize, they paid more attention to the image classification, raising also the answers' quality.

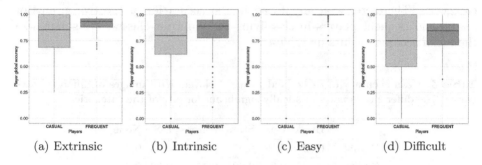

| (a) Extrinsic | (b) Intrinsic | (c) Easy | (d) Difficult |

Fig. 7. Accuracy distribution of *casual* and *frequent* players with different incentives (*a* and *b*) and with different task difficulty (*c* and *d*). The difference between players' profiles is statistically significant in all cases except for easy tasks.

This may indicate that in GWAPs *frequent players* contribute in a more accurate way than *casual* ones, and that extrinsic motivation has a positive impact on accuracy.

6.3   [Q8] Does Player Behaviour Change with Task Difficulty?

We define *task difficulty* as the number of different users needed to solve it (the higher the number, the harder the task); this is because our incremental truth inference algorithm (cf. Sect. 3) dynamically estimates the number of contributions required to solve a task. We split the images in two sets based on their difficulty and we check if this impacts player behaviour.

For Night Knights, we marked as "easy" the images that requires only 4 contributions (the minimum number to reach an agreement according to our domain experts), and as "difficult" those that required more contributions. "Easy" images are 58% of all classified images, while the number of contributions required to classify "difficult" images ranges from 5 to 17.

As shown in the (c) and (d) boxplots in Fig. 7, accuracy on "easy" images is almost the same between *casual* and *frequent players* (indeed, the difference in mean accuracies is not statistically significant). On the contrary, this difference is statistically significant for "difficult" images (mean accuracy is 0.84 for *frequent players* and 0.68 for *casual players*).

Those results suggest a *learning effect* in GWAPs: the more a user plays the game, the more he/she understands the task to be solved, thus increasing his/her accuracy and consequently also result quality.

6.4 [Q9] Does Player Behaviour Change with Task Variety?

Since Night Knights aims to solve a multinomial classification task, we investigate whether there is any evident phenomenon related to the different image categories. Therefore, we compute again the accuracies of the two groups of casual and frequent players in classifying the 6 output classes. We summarize the mean accuracy values in Table 4.

Table 4. Mean accuracy of *casual* and *frequent* players with images of different categories. The difference is not statistically significant for any of the categories.

	Black	City	Stars	Aurora	ISS	None
Casual	0.69	0.88	0.57	0.74	0.63	0.70
Frequent	0.79	0.91	0.68	0.77	0.77	0.77

Applying the t-test to check if the mean accuracy is different for the two players' profiles, we cannot reject the null hypothesis. This may mean that any player is equally able/unable to distinguish the different categories, independently of his/her level of participation; indeed, in our GWAP, there is no need for background- or domain-specific knowledge to play the game. This analysis can help in identifying the need for training or expert knowledge of GWAP players.

On the other hand, the mean accuracy values change a lot across different categories, spanning between 0.57 and 0.91. This is also explained by the different distribution of easy/difficult tasks across the variety of classes, as shown in Fig. 8. Indeed, some categories are intrinsically more difficult to classify than others, but Table 4 shows that this complexity related to task variety is equally perceived by players with low and high levels of participation.

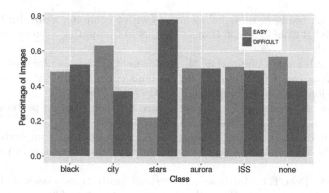

Fig. 8. Distribution of easy/difficult tasks across different image categories.

7   Conclusions

In this paper, we presented an investigation of the interplay of different factors in the evaluation of GWAP results. More specifically, we focused on the profiling of players according to different user metrics and we studied the influence of game incentive and task characteristics.

To inform our discussion, we described the results of such multi-dimensional analysis over the data collected by a GWAP for multinomial classification of images. While some of our considerations result from the quantitative analysis of a single game, and are not *per se* generalizable, we believe that the proposed approach is replicable to evaluate any other GWAP. We believe that such deeper analysis is an important (and sometimes neglected) investigation to understand players' behaviour, to evaluate the impact of various factors on reliability and quality, and finally to assess the ability of GWAPs to achieve their intended purpose and its sustainability over time.

Finally, we would like to point out that, even when player participation is limited in time, a classification GWAP can be used to build a reasonably large training set to be used in traditional machine learning settings to train classifiers for larger-scale labeling. In our previous work, we showed that humans and machines indeed agree on image classification for the Night Knights dataset [12].

Acknowledgments. This work is partially supported by the STARS4ALL project (H2020-688135), co-funded by the European Commission. We thank all the Night Knights players who contributed to the classification task solution and allowed us to perform this work.

References

1. Von Ahn, L., Dabbish, L.: Designing games with a purpose. Commun. ACM **51**(8), 58–67 (2008)
2. Law, E., Ahn, L.v.: Human Computation. Synthesis Lectures on Artificial Intelligence and Machine Learning, vol. 5, no. 3, pp. 1–121 (2011)

3. Von Ahn, L., Dabbish, L.: Labeling images with a computer game. In: Proceedings of the SIGCHI Conference on Human Factors in Computing Systems, pp. 319–326. ACM (2004)
4. Singh, A., Ahsan, F., Blanchette, M., Waldispuhl, J.: Lessons from an online massive genomics computer game. In: Proceedings of the Fifth Conference on Human Computation and Crowdsourcing (HCOMP 2017) (2017)
5. Sauermann, H., Franzoni, C.: Crowd science user contribution patterns and their implications. Proc. Natl. Acad. Sci. **112**(3), 679–684 (2015)
6. Yang, J., Redi, J., Demartini, G., Bozzon, A.: Modeling task complexity in crowdsourcing. In: Fourth AAAI Conference on Human Computation and Crowdsourcing (2016)
7. Ryan, R.M., Deci, E.L.: Intrinsic and extrinsic motivations: classic definitions and new directions. Contemp. Educ. Psychol. **25**(1), 54–67 (2000)
8. Prestopnik, N., Crowston, K., Wang, J.: Gamers, citizen scientists, and data: exploring participant contributions in two games with a purpose. Comput. Hum. Behav. **68**, 254–268 (2017)
9. Thaler, S., Simperl, E., Wolger, S.: An experiment in comparing human-computation techniques. IEEE Internet Comput. **16**, 52–58 (2012)
10. Feyisetan, O., Simperl, E., Van Kleek, M., Shadbolt, N.: Improving paid microtasks through gamification and adaptive furtherance incentives. In: Proceedings of the 24th International Conference on World Wide Web, WWW 2015, pp. 333–343, Republic and Canton of Geneva, Switzerland, International World Wide Web Conferences Steering Committee (2015)
11. Feyisetan, O., Simperl, E.: Social incentives in paid collaborative crowdsourcing. ACM Trans. Intell. Syst. Technol. **8**(6), 73:1–73:31 (2017)
12. Re Calegari, G., Nasi, G., Celino, I.: Human computation vs. machine learning: an experimental comparison for image classification. Hum. Comput. J. **5**(1), 13–30 (2018)
13. Siu, K., Zook, A., Riedl, M.O.: Collaboration versus competition: design and evaluation of mechanics for games with a purpose. In: Proceedings of Foundations of Digital Games Conference (2014)
14. Reeves, N., West, P., Simperl, E.: "A game without competition is hardly a game": the impact of competitions on player activity in a human computation game. In: Proceedings of Human Computation Conference (2018)
15. Reeves, N., Tinati, R., Zerr, S., Van Kleek, M., Simperl, E.: From crowd to community: a survey of online community features in citizen science projects. In: Proceedings of the 2017 ACM Conference on Computer Supported Cooperative Work and Social Computing, CSCW 2017, pp. 2137–2152 (2017)
16. Celino, I., Corcho, Ó., Hölker, F., Simperl, E.: Citizen science: design and engagement (dagstuhl seminar 17272). Dagstuhl Reports 7(7), 22–43 (2017)
17. Ponciano, L., Brasileiro, F.: Finding volunteers' engagement profiles in human computation for citizen science projects. Hum. Comput. J. **1**(2), 247–266 (2015)
18. Aristeidou, M., Scanlon, E., Sharples, M.: Profiles of engagement in online communities of citizen science participation. Comput. Hum. Behav. **74**, 246–256 (2017)
19. Allahbakhsh, M., Benatallah, B., Ignjatovic, A., Motahari-Nezhad, H.R., Bertino, E., Dustdar, S.: Quality control in crowdsourcing systems: issues and directions. IEEE Internet Comput. **17**(2), 76–81 (2013)
20. Karger, D.R., Oh, S., Shah, D.: Budget-optimal task allocation for reliable crowdsourcing systems. Oper. Res. **62**(1), 1–24 (2014)

21. Han, T., Sun, H., Song, Y., Wang, Z., Liu, X.: Budgeted task scheduling for crowd-sourced knowledge acquisition. In: Proceedings of the 2017 ACM on Conference on Information and Knowledge Management, pp. 1059–1068. ACM (2017)
22. Sheng, V.S., Provost, F., Ipeirotis, P.G.: Get another label? Improving data quality and data mining using multiple, noisy labelers. In: Proceedings of the 14th ACM SIGKDD International Conference on Knowledge Discovery and Data Mining, pp. 614–622. ACM (2008)
23. Re Calegari, G., Fiano, A., Celino, I.: A framework to build games with a purpose for linked data refinement. In: The Semantic Web - ISWC 2018 - 17th International Semantic Web Conference, Part II. pp. 154–169. Monterey, CA, USA (2018). https://doi.org/10.1007/978-3-030-00668-6_10
24. Celino, I., Re Calegari, G.: An Incremental Truth Inference Approach to Aggregate Crowdsourcing Contributions in GWAPs. In: currently under revision (2018)
25. Celino, I., et al.: Linking smart cities datasets with human computation – the case of UrbanMatch. In: Cudré-Mauroux, P., et al. (eds.) ISWC 2012. LNCS, vol. 7650, pp. 34–49. Springer, Heidelberg (2012). https://doi.org/10.1007/978-3-642-35173-0_3
26. Zheng, Y., Li, G., Li, Y., Shan, C., Cheng, R.: Truth inference in crowdsourcing: is the problem solved? Proc. VLDB Endow. **10**(5), 541–552 (2017)
27. Anable, A.: Casual games, time management, and the work of affect (2013)
28. Hwong, C.: Leveling up your mobile game: using audience measurement data to boost user acquisition and engagement (2016)

Inferring Types on Large Datasets Applying Ontology Class Hierarchy Classifiers: The DBpedia Case

Mariano Rico[✉], Idafen Santana-Pérez, Pedro Pozo-Jiménez,
and Asunción Gómez-Pérez

Ontology Engineering Group, Universidad Politécnica de Madrid, Madrid, Spain
{mariano.rico,isantana,ppozo,asun}@fi.upm.es

Abstract. Adding type information to resources belonging to large knowledge graphs is a challenging task, specially when considering those that are generated collaboratively, such as DBpedia, which usually contain errors and noise produced during the transformation process from different data sources. It is important to assign the correct type(s) to resources in order to efficiently exploit the information provided by the dataset. In this work we explore how machine learning classification models can be applied to solve this issue, relying on the information defined by the ontology class hierarchy. We have applied our approaches to DBpedia and compared to the state of the art, using a per-level analysis. We also define metrics to measure the quality of the results. Our results show that this approach is able to assign 56% more new types with higher precision and recall than the current DBpedia state of the art.

Keywords: DBpedia · Machine learning · Type prediction
Data quality · Linked data · Semantic web

1 Introduction

DBpedia is one of the largest and most relevant knowledge bases available nowadays, which contains structured information about millions of entities extracted from Wikipedia. These resources have different types, from different ontologies, including the DBpedia ontology, as well as from other well-known vocabularies such as FOAF or schema.org. Even when considering only classes from the DBpedia ontology, as we do in this work, each resource usually has more than one type. For example, the resource Cervantes has types Agent, Person and Artist, because the DBpedia ontology defines a hierarchy of classes.

According to our study, a large amount of DBpedia resources, around 16%, do not have any type. Having correct types is important when working with

This work was partially funded by grant CAS18/00333 (Castillejo), and projects RTC-2016-4952-7 (esTA) and TIN2016-78011-C4-4-R (Datos 4.0), from the Spanish State Investigation Agency of the MINECO and FEDER Funds.

© Springer Nature Switzerland AG 2018
C. Faron Zucker et al. (Eds.): EKAW 2018, LNAI 11313, pp. 322–337, 2018.
https://doi.org/10.1007/978-3-030-03667-6_21

semantic information, as it allows for a better data queryability and discoverability. Thus, the more types we have and the more precise they are, the better data quality. DBpedia, in its 3.9 (English) version, has more than four million resources, but only around 50% of them have a type beyond level 1 (we consider Thing as level 0). In this work we aim at improving the overall quality of the DBpedia dataset by (1) providing type(s) to those resources lacking of it, and (2) adding more specialized types to already typed resources. Following the previous example about Cervantes, this would mean inferring that it also has type Writer, a more specific one, although this fact is not in the dataset.

We use machine learning methods to create a predictive model from the dataset and the class hierarchy of the ontology. In this paper we use the DBpedia dataset and its ontology. This model is used to predict the types for resources with no type, and to predict new types for already typed resources. In this paper we show the results of two different approaches and the comparison to relevant previous approaches.

Our study starts with a naive approach based on multi-class classifiers. We compare the results of this approach (approach 1) with the state of the art, achieving worse results in general. Our second approach considers the ontology class hierarchy and achieves better results than the state of the art. We also evaluate our approach with a well-known gold standard of curated types, and our best approach achieves higher results in terms of precision and recall.

This work also measures the quality of the results using different metrics. Our approach obtains better results than existing approaches, up to 39% higher value for F-measure, depending on the system being compared and the metric used.

For sake of reproductibility, the training datasets used in the experiments, as well as the source code of the approaches, are available at http://es-ta. linkeddata.es.

2   Related Work

Resource typing over large datasets is a problem that has been widely addressed during the last decade. One of the most prominent approaches in the area is the SDType [11] system, which has been applied to DBpedia both for its evaluation as well as for the dataset itself when being published. SDType exploits the information about the statistical distribution of properties over types to infer new ones. Based on their empirical evaluation, authors conclude that properties targeting a resource (i.e. ingoing properties) are more useful for inferring types than those with the resource as subject (i.e. outgoing properties). It also shows that the more properties a resource has (i.e. ingoing degree) the more precise the results are. Based on these conclusions to define our experimental setup, so as to provide a valid framework for comparing our results.

Our approach differs from SDType in that we do not rely on the statistical distribution of the properties, but rather use them as features for training our models by using machine learning techniques. We have used these techniques successfully in previous works [14].

When evaluating our system, following the aforementioned statements, we select each training set using only ingoing properties and their degree.

In this same way, recent studies have proposed the use of machine learning techniques, as we do, in order to improve resources with types in a datasets

Different contributions have been explored in this context, using multilabel approaches [16,18], varying on the algorithms applied and how the training data is selected. In general, all of them define the process of assigning types as a multilabel classification problem, as several types are expected for each resource. Approaches that do not rely on ontologies can be defined as domain-agnostic, having the advantage of being able to work without any context information, but not guaranteeing that the results are consistent with the expected data hierarchy. They also provide worse results than those including the taxonomy information. Many of these approaches are modelled as binary classifiers [5], trained either at the class level or at a general level.

Taxonomy-based classification approaches use the ontology to divide the training data into different subsets according to different criteria [15]. According to [7], which provides a comprehensive discussion on the state of the art, four main types of hierarchical multilabel approaches can be defined.

- **Global approach:** in which the system is trained with one single set, including the taxonomy, guaranteeing that for each type assigned, all its parent types in the hierarchy are also included, ensuring taxonomy consistency.
- **Local Classifier Per Node** (*LCN*): in which binary classifiers are created for each type. These classifiers are similar to general multilabel classifiers, which is used in the SLCN system [7], providing an scalable manner of generating types.
- **Local Classifier Per Parent Node** (*LCPN*): in which for each type a classifier is generated to classify its direct sub-types, thus only applied to non-terminal nodes. That is, each trained model is able to disambiguate and add more specific knowledge from the next level in the hierarchy.
- **Local Classifier Per Level** (*LCL*): in which a multilabel model is generated for each level of the hierarchy. LCL approaches have not been fully explored, as they do not guarantee taxonomy-consistent results. LCL models generate one type per level, but not necessarily following the class hierarchy.

As we will introduce in Sect. 3, our system explores the use of an LCL classifier applied to DBpedia, using its taxonomy, to provide an efficient and more precise solution for inferring types. We argue that using the level context information, combined with a set of complementary binary models for each level, we are able to increase the effectiveness of the predictions. Our system provides better results in terms of precision and recall for the empirical studies we have conducted, as we discuss in Sect. 5.

The main potential problem faced when defining a multilabel classifier is the partial depth problem, that is, when to stop assigning more concrete types to a resource. In order to solve this problem, our system includes a set of binary decision models, which define the maximum level to which the system should assign types. Even when our system provides types for all the levels in the hierarchy, we discard those for which the binary level classifier returns false. As we discuss in Sect. 5 our solution does not fully guarantee taxonomy consistency, which would still require a post-processing stage.

Finally, it is worth to consider other contributions that provide means for measuring the effectiveness of type prediction systems. Several gold standards are available, containing a list of resources and their types, curated by humans experts. Through the OKE challenge series several systems have been proposed [2,3], as part of their types inference tasks, being evaluated against the gold standards provided by organizers[1,2]. These tasks are intended to generate new classes and align them to existing ones, based on the textual description of resources. The related gold standards provide links to such classes and alignments. Another relevant gold standard available, which fits better our problem, is the LHD dataset[3], which provides a list of DBpedia resources and a curated list of types from the DBpedia ontology for each one of them. This data is generated using crowdsourcing, reaching sufficient consensus for each type list. The gold standards provided are used to evaluate the performance of the LHD system [4] itself, which uses text mining techniques for class inductions, as well as to evaluate how it compares to the aforementioned SDType. Thus, we will use the LHD gold standard to evaluate our system.

3 Methodology

In this section we introduce our approaches and how they take advantage of the DBpedia class hierarchy. Before going into the details of the approaches it is important to analyze the types of the resources in the dataset.

3.1 Type Paths in DBpedia Resources

We work under the assumption that the types of the typed resources follow a unique path of types, from level 0 (Thing) to the most specific one, having only one type per level. For example, for the 3.9 version of DBpedia, the resource Shakespeare has types Thing, Agent, Person, Artist and Writer. These types are in different levels of the class hierarchy but, for each level, there is only one type. If the types of a given resource follow our assumption, we say that these types form a 'coherent' path.

However, some resources have types that do not follow this assumption, which are due to two main reasons: (1) two parent classes for a type, which occurs when a class is a subclass of two different classes, and (2) broken paths, which occurs when a class does not have a parent class. That is, the path do not reach the top-level class of the ontology class hierarchy.

---

[1] https://github.com/anuzzolese/oke-challenge.
[2] https://github.com/anuzzolese/oke-challenge-2016.
[3] http://ner.vse.cz/datasets/linkedhypernyms/evaluation/.

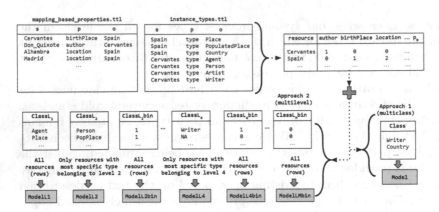

Fig. 1. Preparation process for training sets from DBpedia files. There is a common set of features for each resource but, each approach has additional features.

To test the validity of our assumption, we have conducted an empirical study for the resources in DBpedia 3.9, exploring their type paths. The results show a tree with 7 levels, from level 0 for class `Thing` to level 6 for the most specific types found in DBpedia (e.g. `SubMunicipality`, `RoadTunnel`). Only 0.95% of the resources in DBpedia do not follow our assumption. This is due to two main reasons: (1) the class `SportSeason` is not subclass of any other class, generating incomplete paths for 22,072 resources; (2) the classes `Mountain` and `Library` are, each of them, subclasses of two classes, resulting in 13,245 resources with more than one path.

As shown by this study, most DBpedia resources follow a single and complete type path, supporting our assumption and allowing us to define a set of models based on the levels of the ontology, in which each resource has up to one type per level.

3.2   Features Description

For selecting the features of our models we have used different DBpedia files. The DBpedia dataset comprises 20 files, from which we have used the two files containing the type information, namely `mapping_based_properties_en.ttl` and `instance_types_en.ttl`, as shown in the upper side of Fig. 1. These files contain RDF triples obtained from Wikipedia infoboxes. The first one has information about the attribute-value pairs extracted from the infoboxes tables. The second contains the information about the types of the resources, as established by each infobox type. Most types in DBpedia come from these two files.

We look into `instance_types_en.ttl` for resources with some valid DBpedia type, that is, we exclude resources without type (as they do not provide information for our training) or with type `SportSeason` (as it does not have any parent class) and its subclasses. Then, we look into the `mapping_based_properties_en.ttl` file for triples with any of these resources in the object. That is, we look for typed resources with ingoing properties. In this way, we obtain around

1,439K resources with type(s) that are links (URIs) in the "value side" of the infobox attribute-value pair.

The content of these two files is merged in a features file, containing as many rows as resources and as many columns as features (ingoing properties). Top right side of Fig. 1 shows this features file, with features `author`, `birthPlace` and `location` for resources `Cervantes` and `Spain`. For each resource we compute the number of triples with that property and that resource in the object. For instance, for resource `Spain`, we have two triples with `Spain` as object and property `location`, and one triple with `Spain` as object for property `birthPlace`. In the case of resource `Cervantes`, we have one triple with `Cervantes` as object of the `author` property.

In addition to this features file, each of our approaches add more features (lower side of Fig. 1). Approach 1 includes one more feature entitled `Class`, and Approach 2 includes 11 features. In the next sections we introduce the approaches and their features.

3.3 Approach 1: Naive Approach for Type Prediction

This approach uses a multi-class classifier in order to predict the most specific type for each resource. From this most specific type, we can compute the parent types from the ontology class hierarchy.

Our study started with a simple approximation ('Approach 1 (multi-class)' in Fig. 1). As we know that most typed resources have a 'coherent' path, by knowing the most specific (detailed/deeper) type we can compute the complete type path. Therefore, this approach tries to predict this most specific class. For this approach, as shown in Fig. 1, we add only one column to the common training set: the column entitled `Class` in the figure. In the figure, for resource `Cervantes` we have type `Writer`, and resource `Spain` has type `Country`, because these are their most specific types.

For this approach we have used three different training methods: Naïve Bayes [10], Random Forest [1] and Deep Learning (multi-layer feedforward) [6].

3.4 Approach 2: Ontology Class Hierarchy for Type Prediction

This approach is a Local Classifiers Per Level (LCL), as described in Sect. 2, although it is was modified to include extra binary models. These binary models are aimed at solving the 'partial depth problem' explained in the related work section. Solving this problem we can know, for each resource, which levels do not 'produce' types. There are 11 models, 6 of them are multi-class, and the remaining 5 are binary models (as shown in Fig. 2). The multi-class models are intended for predicting the type for that level. The binary models decide if the type should be assigned to the resource.

This approach was named 'Approach 2 (multilevel)' because we have models for each ontology class level. For this approach we used Random Forest and Deep Learning, as well as C5.0 [17], an improved version of C4.5 [13], belonging to the well known Weka J48 method family of decision trees.

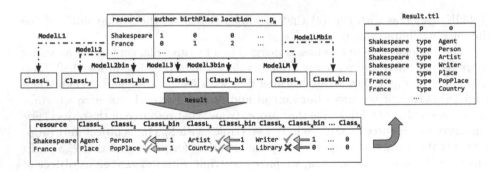

Fig. 2. Predicting with Approach 2.

In Fig. 1 we can see how these 11 models are built. In Approach 2, each model is built using only one additional feature. For instance, feature $ClassL_1$ for model $ModelL1$, feature $ClassL_2$ for model $ModelL2$, etc.

Following the example, for resource `Spain`, the feature $ClassL_1$ should have `Place` in the second row because type `Place` belongs to level 1. The feature $ClassL_2bin$ is 1 because the type `PopulatedPlace` belongs to level 2. However, for feature $ClassL_4bin$ is 0 because the resource `Spain` has no type belonging to level 4.

Figure 2 shows the prediction process. For an input file with the same structure as the one used for training (a 'features file'), we apply $ModelL1$ to get $ClassL_1$ as a new feature. From the input file and the $ClassL_1$ feature we apply $ModelL2$ to create $ClassL_2$ as a new feature and a binary feature $ClassL_2bin$ from the input file. We repeat the process for level 3 and the remaining levels in the data.

Notice that for low populated levels we have omitted the model for that level. In our case, for level 6, the training set would have only 304 resources and the prediction model is not reliable. Therefore, for our tests we have removed models $ClassL_6$ and $ClassL_6bin$. Instead of the theoretical 11 models, indeed we have used 9 models. As a comparison, for level 5 we have 21.1K resources and for level 4 around 257.9K resources.

4   Evaluation

In this section we describe the different evaluations processes we have carried out and the metrics used to evaluate the results.

4.1   SDType Evaluation

We started our study trying to reproduce the experiments carried out by Paulheim et al. [12] by using the dataset and source code referenced in that paper. However, our results differed from the ones published. Table 1 shows the results achieved in our reproduction (CRA) and the result of our better approach (approach 2 with C5.0). The column 'CRA only dbo' focuses only in DBpedia properties. This table also shows the four most frequent types predicted (and the percentage of the whole set of predicted types) ordered by frequency.

Table 1. Comparison of the SDType approach and our Approach 2.

Versions	Original paper	DBpedia site[a]	CRA[b]	CRA only dbo	Approach 2 (C5.0)
Newly typed instances	626,662	630,346	476,661	473,050	786,876
Total type statements	3,402,539	3,402,114	2,694,729	1,373,404	2,151,900
Distinct classes	159	159	165	133	256
Most frequent types					
Person	292,398 (46.7%)	292,830 (46.4%)	273,552 (57.4%)	273,552 (57.8%)	342,313 (43.5%)
Organization	119,123 (19.0%)	120,029 (19.0%)	81,335 (17,1%)	81,335 (17,2%)	117,866 (15.0%)
Place	114,093 (18.2%)	114,965 (18.2%)	75,830 (15,9%)	75,830 (16,0%)	85,572 (10.9%)
Work	37,176 (5.9%)	37,368 (5.9%)	16,838 (3,5%)	16,838 (3,6%)	47,294 (6.0%)

[a]Datasets available at https://wiki.dbpedia.org/data-set-39
[b]CRA: Current Replication Attempt

Following the experimentation process proposed in [12], for each experiment we have computed precision and recall in 3 different connectivity contexts: (1) resources with at least one 'ingoing' property (the so name test 1), (2) resources with at least 10 'ingoing' properties (test 10), and (3) resources with at least 25 'ingoing' properties (test 25). In this way we get a measure of the dependence of results on the connectivity of resources. The evaluation set is obtained by randomly selecting 10K typed resources, according to the aforementioned criteria. From the total of approximately 1,439K typed resources available we have selected 10K with 1, 10 and 25 'ingoing' properties respectively. These 'reserved' resources are removed from the training set.

Notice that, as resources are randomly selected, a given resource can be in test1, but also in test 10, as it has at least 10 'ingoing' properties. Therefore, for each approach, we have 3 training sets, each of them with 1,429 resources (i.e. 1,439 - 10K).

Once the system is trained, we apply the model to the 10K 'reserved' resources and compare the predicted types to the original types. That is, following the methodology used in [12], we use the original set of types as reference. Using this approach, and depending on the metrics used to measure precision and recall, we can obtain different results. In Sect. 4.4 we introduce the set of metrics used.

4.2 K-Fold Evaluation

We have also carried out a 5-fold evaluation, in order to compare our method to the SLCN system defined in [7], following the same experimental setup, using the DBpedia 2014 dataset. We split the dataset into five parts, removing one in each test and training with the remaining four. We have then tested the performance using the reserved part. Each fold contains 287,783 resources, with a homogeneous type distribution. Around 47% of the types are of level 1, 39% of level 2, and 17% of level 3. The contribution of the remaining types is lower than 1.5%.

4.3 Gold Standard

As introduced in the related work section, we have selected the LHD dataset for testing the performance of our system. For that, we have trained a model using all the resources from DBpedia, except those included in the gold standard. Afterwards we used the trained system over the resources from the gold standard, which do not have any type associated to them. We use only Approach 2 for this gold standard evaluation, as it is the one showing best results overall, as we will discuss in Sect. 5.

From the three gold standards provided in LHD, we have selected GS 2. It contains the set of resources and types from DBpedia 3.9, used for evaluating LHD and SDType. We did not include GS 1 and GS 3 because many of the resources they contain (around 1K) have no ingoing properties (only 227 and 243 resources respectively have ingoing properties), which is a requirement in our model.

4.4 A Novel Set of Measure Criteria

Following the example, let us assume that the resource Cervantes, with types Agent, Person and Writer has been 'reserved' and we predict its types. Let us assume that the model predicts the types Agent, Writer and Athlete. We consider the following statements when deciding whether the predicted type of a resource is correctly predicted or not. **True positive (TP):** the type predicted was in the original list of types (e.g. For Cervantes, Agent and Writer are TP). **False positive (FP):** the type predicted was not in the original list of types (e.g. For Cervantes, Athlete is a FP). **False negative (FN):** the non-predicted types that should be predicted (e.g. for Cervantes, Person is a FN).

As shown in Table 2, the distribution of types across resources and levels is unbalanced. Therefore, a different kind of analysis was conducted to measure the performance of the compared approaches, according to different measure criteria:

- **General:** we measure precision by summing up all the TP of all resources, and dividing by the sum of TP and FP for all resources. For recall we divide by the sum of TP and FN for all resources.
- **Average per resource:** we calculate for each resource its precision and recall, and compute the average over all the resources.
- **Leaves:** only the most specific types are considered. That is, only those types that are the deepest in the class hierarchy.

– **Level** N: only types belonging to level N of the taxonomy are considered, level 0 being `Thing`.

In our case, we have studied types from level 1 to 5 for the DBpedia ontology (version 3.9). We have excluded level 0 because `Thing` is a trivial case, as well as level 6, due to the lack of typed resources belonging to this level, as depicted in Table 2.

Table 2. Relation between object resources with type level scope and tests distribution.

Levels and sets	Test 1	Ingoing ≥ 1 (Total)	Test 10	Ingoing ≥ 10 (Total)	Test 25	Ingoing ≥ 25 (Total)
Level 1	9,965	1,438,911	9,997	89,511	9,999	39,272
Level 2	5,500	688,409	9,893	88,701	9,904	38,878
Level 3	4,574	571,764	8,440	73,665	9,021	33,822
Level 4	2,106	257,916	5,302	45,237	5,929	21,588
Level 5	162	21,117	140	1,459	90	477
Level 6	3	304	1	14	0	0

The following example illustrates how different the results can be, depending on the measure criteria. That is, how different ways of measuring precision and recall affect the results. Supposing that the resource `Picasso` was originally typed as `Agent` (level 1), `Person` (level 2), and `Artist` (level 3), we consider the next three possible situations: (a) we generate types `Agent`, `Person`, `Artist` and `Painter` (level 4), (b) we generate types `Agent`, `Person`, and (c) We generate types `Agent`, `Organization` (level 2).

In the first situation a new type is discovered and, although it could be a correct prediction, it is a FP in the general analysis because it was not in the original list of types. For this reason, we have included the level analysis, in order to evaluate how types are predicted at each level. As depicted in Table 2, around 10K resources are evaluated for test 25 for the general analysis, but only 5,929 of them can be evaluated for level 4 analysis. In this example, this result in a 75% general precision (3 TP/(3 TP + 1FP)), 100% general recall (3 TP/(3 TP + 0FN)), but obtains an undetermined precision and recall for level 4 because `Picasso` had no level 4 types.

For the second situation, all predicted types are correct, but the `Artist` type is missing from the prediction. Thus, 100% precision and 66.67% recall are obtained as general analysis. At level 3, precision and recall obtain 0% because `Picasso` had type `Artist` in level 3. For the third situation, where `Agent` is correctly predicted, `Organization` was wrongly predicted, and `Person` and `Artist` are missing, we assign 50% precision and 33.33% recall as general analysis, 100% precision and recall for level 1, and 0% for levels 2 and 3.

This variability between measures and type level distribution is the main reason for considering an analysis based on **leaves**, as it measures how the most specific type is predicted. Our approaches produce good results for the analysis based in leaves, as shown in Sect. 5.

5   Results

Based on the experimental setup defined in Sect. 4 we have obtained a set of results that show how our approaches behave under different measure criteria and machine learning algorithms, and how they can be compared to previous systems (SDType, K-fold and Gold standard).

5.1   Comparison with SDType Results

These results are summarized in Table 3. In this table we show precision (p), recall (r) and F-measure (F_1) for our approaches (1, 2), using different machine learning methods, as well as the results for related studies (SDType and SDType-DBO). Notice the detailed results for different measure criteria (general, leaves, etc.) and resource connectivity (test 1, test 10 and test 25). The difference between SDType and SDTypeDBO is that the second excludes all the types that do not belong to the DBpedia ontology.

Our approach 2 C5.0 produces better results than previous approaches for the **leaves** measure criteria, in terms of precision and recall, for the three connectivity tests considered (row of bold numbers). For test 1, our results almost double the best previous values, moving from $\{p = 43.43, r = 44.04\}$ to $\{p = 83.03, r = 83.11\}$. For test 10, our results are also remarkably higher, moving from $\{p = 63.78, r = 64.01\}$ to $\{p = 76.99, r = 77.04\}$. For test 25 (highest connectivity), our results move from $\{p = 59.83, r = 57.25\}$ to $\{p = 79.86, r = 79.86\}$.

These results show that our solution has lower dependency on the connectivity of the resource, with precision values in the range $[76.99\text{--}83.03]\%$ for the connectivity ranges considered and recall values in the range $[77.04\text{--}83.11]\%$, while previous approaches had a wider range for precision, $[44.43\text{--}63.78]\%$, and recall, $[44.04\text{--}64.01]\%$.

Concerning the number of triples that can be generated, as shown in Table 1, our system is able to generate around 2.15 million type statements, whereas our reproduction of SDType generates around 1.38 million (only considering types from the DBpedia ontology, in both cases). We generate more triples covering more types (256 distinct classes), compared to those from SDType DBO (133 distinct classes).

Also we have studied how our predicted types overlap with the types predicted by the SDTypes approach. Figure 3 shows graphically this overlap. The small circle represents the number of types predicted by the SDType approach (1.38M). The big circle represents our approach, which produces 56.7% more types (2.15M). Our approach predicts most of the types predicted by the SDTypes approach, specifically 96.5% of them. Therefore we conclude that our approach predicts most of the types predicted by the SDTypes approach.

Table 3. Results for previous approaches (SDType and SDTypeDBO) and for our approach 1 (global) and approach 2 (multilevel) and their respective learning methods: Naïve Bayes (NB) for approach 1, C5.0 for approach 2, and Deep Learning (DL) and Random Forest (RF) for both approach 1 and approach 2.

Measure criteria	Approach	Test 1 (*ingoing* > 0)			Test 10 (*ingoing* ≥ 10)			Test 25 (*ingoing* ≥ 25)		
		p	r	F_1	p	r	F_1	p	r	F_1
General	SDType	64.69	**90.86**	75.58	**94.33**	88.81	**91.49**	**97.54**	82.75	89.54
	SDTypeDBO	60.94	87.99	72.01	92.37	85.35	88.72	96.27	80.22	87.52
	Approach 1 NB	48.66	27.24	34.93	15.09	6.20	8.78	21.06	9.68	13.26
	Approach 1 DL	87.24	85.86	86.54	84.02	83.52	83.77	82.34	81.87	82.11
	Approach 1 RF	87.16	74.93	80.58	88.51	77.75	82.78	90.00	79.99	84.70
	Approach 2 C50	**90.40**	89.74	**90.07**	90.88	**91.31**	91.10	91.39	**91.66**	**91.53**
	Approach 2 DL	89.32	88.67	89.00	89.71	89.73	89.72	91.08	90.66	90.87
	Approach 2 RF	89.22	86.89	88.04	88.98	**89.90**	89.44	91.65	90.15	90.89
Average per resource	SDType	69.28	89.93	78.27	**95.36**	89.11	**92.13**	97.87	81.92	89.19
	SDTypeDBO	67.19	88.37	76.34	94.47	86.26	90.18	**97.26**	80.22	87.82
	Approach 1 NB	91.97	49.52	64.38	47.99	5.73	10.23	48.00	8.83	14.91
	Approach 1 DL	94.06	90.24	92.11	90.71	83.56	86.99	91.93	80.94	86.08
	Approach 1 RF	**95.91**	83.02	89.00	94.43	78.41	85.68	95.33	79.80	86.88
	Approach 2 C50	94.25	**93.04**	**93.64**	92.12	**91.60**	91.86	92.29	**91.63**	**91.96**
	Approach 2 DL	93.72	92.16	92.93	90.94	90.03	90.48	91.46	90.68	91.07
	Approach 2 RF	93.50	90.64	92.05	90.31	89.49	89.90	92.62	89.76	91.17
Leaves	SDType	44.15	43.64	43.89	63.63	63.54	63.59	59.16	55.40	57.22
	SDTypeDBO	43.43	44.04	44.23	63.78	64.01	63.89	59.83	57.25	58.51
	Approach 1 NB	44.5	44.50	44.50	0.04	0.04	0.04	0.04	0.04	0.04
	Approach 1 DL	80.75	80.75	80.75	69.26	69.26	69.26	69.32	69.32	69.32
	Approach 1 RF	76.42	76.42	76.42	69.44	69.44	69.44	71.69	71.69	71.69
	Approach 2 C50	**83.03**	**83.11**	**83.07**	**76.99**	**77.04**	**77.02**	**77.86**	**77.86**	**77.86**
	Approach 2 DL	81.54	81.71	81.62	73.81	73.93	73.87	74.86	74.88	74.87
	Approach 2 RF	80.37	80.45	80.41	74.68	74.73	74.71	74.39	74.40	74.40
Level 1	SDType	71.61	93.94	81.27	**98.42**	97.82	97.82	**99.34**	92.50	95.80
	SDTypeDBO	71.50	93.99	81.22	98.31	98.30	98.30	99.24	94.42	96.77
	Approach 1 NB	52.82	52.82	52.82	11.07	11.07	11.07	17.75	17.75	17.75
	Approach 1 DL	96.95	96.95	96.95	91.82	91.82	91.82	87.38	87.38	87.38
	Approach 1 RF	88.22	88.22	88.22	84.57	84.57	84.57	85.08	85.08	85.08
	Approach 2 C50	**98.88**	**98.98**	**98.93**	98.33	**98.40**	**98.36**	97.96	97.97	97.96
	Approach 2 DL	98.32	98.42	98.37	98.32	98.39	98.35	**99.06**	**99.07**	**99.06**
	Approach 2 RF	96.49	96.58	96.53	94.00	94.06	94.03	94.49	94.50	94.49
Level 2	SDType	89.26	**95.76**	92.39	94.55	95.47	95.01	**97.92**	88.39	92.91
	SDTypeDBO	89.04	95.84	92.31	94.45	**95.67**	95.06	97.74	90.36	93.90
	Approach 1 NB	85.39	14.98	25.49	68.05	9.62	16.86	70.28	15.71	25.68
	Approach 1 DL	88.36	88.07	88.21	88.37	87.50	87.93	85.15	83.86	84.5
	Approach 1 RF	92.60	74.80	82.75	94.73	81.50	87.62	95.56	82.6	88.61
	Approach 2 C50	**92.86**	92.91	**92.88**	95.47	95.26	95.36	95.46	95.04	**95.25**
	Approach 2 DL	92.08	92.22	92.15	94.16	94.26	94.21	94.05	94.08	94.06
	Approach 2 RF	91.95	91.96	91.95	**95.57**	95.46	**95.51**	95.23	**95.16**	95.19
Level 3	SDType	**82.02**	80.98	81.49	87.70	78.99	83.12	**93.83**	69.49	79.84
	SDTypeDBO	81.95	**81.90**	**81.92**	87.43	79.46	83.26	93.55	72.51	81.70
	Approach 1 NB	2.83	0.48	0.82	2.85	0.38	0.67	2.65	0.54	0.9
	Approach 1 DL	76.36	73.57	74.94	80.34	77.69	78.99	79.35	77.4	78.36
	Approach 1 RF	80.44	61.01	69.39	**89.59**	74.09	81.11	90.92	77.43	83.63
	Approach 2 C50	81.10	79.01	80.04	**88.95**	**86.59**	**87.75**	89.71	87.53	88.61
	Approach 2 DL	78.98	77.34	78.15	85.98	84.66	85.31	86.78	85.72	86.25
	Approach 2 RF	79.92	72.93	76.27	88.03	86.87	87.45	90.66	**89.77**	**90.21**
Level 4	SDType	92.08	55.74	69.45	93.01	50.90	65.80	**96.44**	50.33	66.14
	SDTypeDBO	92.05	56.08	69.70	92.70	51.49	66.21	95.91	51.51	66.94
	Approach 1 NB	3.66	0.14	0.27	0.32	0.06	0.10	0.25	0.07	0.11
	Approach 1 DL	84.76	61.54	71.31	85.67	70.78	77.52	89.21	76.96	82.63
	Approach 1 RF	**94.69**	49.10	64.67	**94.83**	65.09	77.19	96.81	71.75	82.42
	Approach 2 C50	84.07	**68.19**	**75.30**	88.19	**79.03**	**83.36**	90.04	**82.02**	**85.84**
	Approach 2 DL	82.64	65.34	72.98	87.20	74.14	80.14	90.16	78.63	84.00
	Approach 2 RF	83.90	64.81	73.13	87.67	77.35	82.19	94.28	75.61	83.92
Level 5	SDType	95.27	87.04	90.97	88.33	75.71	81.54	91.07	56.67	69.86
	SDTypeDBO	95.30	**87.65**	**91.32**	87.10	77.14	81.82	88.14	57.78	69.80
	Approach 1 NB	-	-	-	-	-	-	-	-	-
	Approach 1 DL	98.17	66.05	78.97	98.89	63.57	77.39	90.62	32.22	47.54
	Approach 1 RF	**100.00**	53.09	69.36	**100.00**	46.43	63.42	**100.00**	34.44	51.23
	Approach 2 C50	98.47	79.63	88.05	98.35	**85.00**	**91.19**	97.22	77.78	86.42
	Approach 2 DL	98.46	79.01	87.67	98.26	80.71	88.62	95.95	**78.89**	86.59
	Approach 2 RF	98.46	79.01	87.67	99.15	83.57	90.70	96.43	60.00	73.97

Table 4. Comparison of our approach to Melo et al. approach for three machine learning methods (C5.0, Deep Learning (DL), Random Forest (RF)) for the English DBpedia 2014 version.

Criteria	C5.0			DL			RF		
	p	r	f	p	r	f	p	r	f
General	89.75±0.04	88.91±0.04	**89.33±0.04**	89.00±0.25	87.87±0.04	88.43±0.14	87.54±0.72	86.48±1.49	86.99±0.47
Mean	94.58±0.02	92.96±0.03	**93.76±0.02**	94.24±0.23	92.24±0.07	93.23±0.13	93.54±0.65	91.02±0.98	92.25±0.23
Leaves	82.33±0.06	82.33±0.07	**82.33±0.06**	81.18±0.39	81.18±0.39	81.18±0.39	79.58±0.34	79.58±0.34	79.58±0.34
Level1	98.43±0.03	98.44±0.03	**98.44±0.03**	98.10±0.08	98.10±0.08	98.10±0.08	96.23±0.25	96.23±0.25	96.23±0.25
Level2	91.45±0.05	91.19±0.06	**91.31±0.06**	90.28±0.22	89.99±0.17	90.13±0.19	90.60±0.52	88.25±4.29	89.35±2.06
Level3	80.45±0.13	75.08±0.12	**77.67±0.12**	78.79±0.40	73.13±0.16	75.85±0.23	78.07±0.96	72.27±2.72	75.02±1.12
Level4	82.71±0.20	59.63±0.18	**69.30±0.17**	81.69±0.23	57.03±0.44	67.17±0.33	81.99±0.27	58.15±1.23	68.03±0.79
Level5	99.16±0.01	75.95±1.42	**86.01±0.89**	99.33±0.12	74.65±1.72	85.23±1.13	99.33±0.07	73.91±1.62	84.75±1.05

An analysis per levels shows that for any level, our approach predicts most of the types predicted by SDTypes (between 95% for level 3 to 98% for level 1). However, SDtypes only predicts between 45% (for level 3) and 76% (for level 1) of the types predicted by our approach.

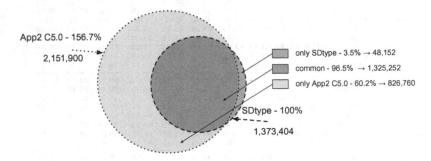

Fig. 3. Overlapping between the types predicted by our best approach and the ones predicted by the SDTypes approach.

5.2   Comparison with K-Fold Results

Here we compare our best approach (approach 2) to the results provided by Melo et al. [7]. The results of applying the 5-fold evaluation over DBpedia 2014 are shown in Table 4, which includes the results for the three methods used (Random Forest, Deep Learning, and C5.0). The SLCN system reports an overall F-measure of 84.7%, when using ingoing properties over typed objects, as we do in our system. This table shows that our system provides a general F-measure (f in table) of 86.99% for Random Forest, 88.43% for Deep Learning, and 89.33% for C5.0. That is, our systems provides 3–4.6% better results than Melo's et al. approach.

5.3   Comparison with Gold Standard Results

As shown in Table 5, we have evaluated our approach 2, including its 3 main methods, and SDType, using the GS 2 gold standard, as described in Sect. 4.

Results show that whereas we obtain slightly lower results for precision under the general criteria, we improve SDType in terms of recall and F-measure. For the leaves criteria our method achieves better results for precision, recall and F-measure (highlighted in bold in Table 5). In [4], the LHD system reports an overall result of $\{p = 80.9, r = 64.1, f = 71.5\}$, which also provides better precision, but worse recall and F-measure than our system. Under the leaves criteria, LHD reports a 33.8 precision and recall, which is slightly worst than the 36.48 achieved by our system (for C5.0 method).

This is consistent with the results obtained in Table 3, for resources with medium and high connectivity (tests 10 and 25), where precision is lower but recall provides better results. We must also consider that GS 2 contains only 160 resources, which is a small sample compared to the size of the dataset being evaluated.

Table 5. LHD GS 2 results for SDType and approach 2 (C5.0, DL, RF).

Criteria	SDType			C5.0			DL			RF		
	p	r	f	p	r	f	p	r	f	p	r	f
General	**79.19**	67.00	72.59	74.12	**72.47**	**73.29**	43.42	38.06	40.56	75.71	59.31	66.52
Mean	87.22	69.31	77.24	81.15	74.86	77.88	63.70	40.78	49.72	86.39	61.81	72.06
Leaves	33.76	33.33	33.54	**36.48**	**36.48**	**36.48**	20.75	20.75	20.75	33.33	33.33	33.33
Level1	91.61	89.31	90.45	91.19	91.19	91.19	64.78	64.78	64.78	82.39	82.39	82.39
Level2	86.49	84.77	85.62	86.00	85.43	85.71	40.00	33.11	36.23	89.47	67.55	76.98
Level3	69.49	38.32	49.40	64.77	53.27	58.46	26.19	20.56	23.04	63.16	33.64	43.90
Level4	74.07	29.85	42.55	77.14	40.30	52.94	46.43	19.40	27.37	72.73	35.82	48.00

6   Conclusions and Future Work

In this paper we have introduced our approaches for type prediction in large semantic datasets, exploiting the ontology class hierarchy information to provide more accurate results, tackling successfully the partial depth problem. We have applied it to DBpedia, one of most relevant datasets in the Linked Data cloud. We have provided a comprehensive comparison of our approach and the existing approaches, as well as using curated datasets.

As shown by the empirical results, our approach is highly accurate predicting the complete list of types for a given resource, not adding extra types. Even when these extra types could be potentially valuable and correct, in this paper we have focused only in matching the existing list of types (the so named leaves measure criteria). We achieve precision and recall values that enhance the F-measure achieved by SDType between 12% and 39% (by using our approach 2 with C5.0). We are also able to generate more type statements (up to 54% more), with more diversity and accuracy. Our system also provides better results than those by the SLCN system, providing an improvement between 3% and 4.6% (F-measure) under the general criteria.

For future work we are going to validate our approach with other datasets. We will start with the Spanish DBpedia [8], the second biggest DBpedia after the English one, as well as other datasets not related to DBpedia. We are interested in the connectivity of the DBpedia graph [9], but we are still far from ranking the relevance of the resources in order to know which resources and properties are most important to solve a set of queries. Using this sort of ranking we could provide a better measure (a new measure criteria) for the quality of the predictions.

References

1. Breiman, L.: Random forests. Mach. Learn. **45**(1), 5–32 (2001)
2. Faralli, S., Ponzetto, S.P.: DWS at the 2016 open knowledge extraction challenge: a hearst-like pattern-based approach to hypernym extraction and class induction. In: Sack, H., Dietze, S., Tordai, A., Lange, C. (eds.) SemWebEval 2016. CCIS, vol. 641, pp. 48–60. Springer, Cham (2016). https://doi.org/10.1007/978-3-319-46565-4_4
3. Gangemi, A., Nuzzolese, A.G., Presutti, V., Draicchio, F., Musetti, A., Ciancarini, P.: Automatic typing of DBpedia entities. In: Cudré-Mauroux, P., et al. (eds.) ISWC 2012. LNCS, vol. 7649, pp. 65–81. Springer, Heidelberg (2012). https://doi.org/10.1007/978-3-642-35176-1_5
4. Kliegr, T., Zamazal, O.: LHD 2.0: a text mining approach to typing entities in knowledge graphs. Web Semant. **39**, 47–61 (2016)
5. Luaces, O., Díez, J.: Binary relevance efficacy for multilabel classification. Prog. Artif. Intell. **1**(4), 303–313 (2012)
6. Marini, F., Magrì, A., Bucci, R.: Multilayer feed-forward artificial neural networks for class modeling. Chemom. Intell. Lab. Syst. **88**, 118–124 (2007)
7. Melo, A., et al.: Type prediction in noisy RDF knowledge bases using hierarchical multilabel classification with graph and latent features. IJAIT **26**(02) (2017)
8. Mihindukulasooriya, N., Rico, M., García-Castro, R., Gómez-Pérez, A.: An analysis of the quality issues of the properties available in the Spanish DBpedia. In: Puerta, J.M., Gámez, J.A., Dorronsoro, B., Barrenechea, E., Troncoso, A., Baruque, B., Galar, M. (eds.) CAEPIA 2015. LNCS (LNAI), vol. 9422, pp. 198–209. Springer, Cham (2015). https://doi.org/10.1007/978-3-319-24598-0_18
9. Mihindukulasooriya, N., Rico, M., et al.: Repairing hidden links in linked data: enhancing the quality of RDF knowledge graphs. In: K-CAP Proceedings (2017)
10. Murphy, K.P.: Naive Bayes classifiers. University of British Columbia (2006)
11. Paulheim, H., Bizer, C.: Type inference on noisy RDF data. In: Alani, H., et al. (eds.) ISWC 2013. LNCS, vol. 8218, pp. 510–525. Springer, Heidelberg (2013). https://doi.org/10.1007/978-3-642-41335-3_32
12. Paulheim, H., Bizer, C.: Improving the quality of linked data using statistical distributions. IJSWIS **10**(2), 63–86 (2014)
13. Quinlan, J.R.: C4.5: Programs for Machine Learning. Morgan Kaufmann Publishers Inc., San Francisco (1993)
14. Rico, M., Mihindukulasooriya, N., et al.: Predicting incorrect mappings: a data-driven approach applied to DBpedia. In: Proceedings of SAC, pp. 323–330. ACM (2018)

15. Ristoski, P., Paulheim, H.: Feature selection in hierarchical feature spaces. In: Džeroski, S., Panov, P., Kocev, D., Todorovski, L. (eds.) DS 2014. LNCS (LNAI), vol. 8777, pp. 288–300. Springer, Cham (2014). https://doi.org/10.1007/978-3-319-11812-3_25

16. Tsoumakas, G., Vlahavas, I.: Random k-labelsets: an ensemble method for multilabel classification. In: Kok, J.N., Koronacki, J., Mantaras, R.L., Matwin, S., Mladenič, D., Skowron, A. (eds.) ECML 2007. LNCS (LNAI), vol. 4701, pp. 406–417. Springer, Heidelberg (2007). https://doi.org/10.1007/978-3-540-74958-5_38

17. Wu, X., et al.: Top 10 algorithms in data mining. Knowl. Inf. Syst. 14(1), 1–37 (2008)

18. Zhang, M.-L., Zhou, Z.-H.: Multilabel neural networks with applications to functional genomics and text categorization. IEEE TKDE 18(10), 1338–1351 (2006)

A Framework for Tackling Myopia
in Concept Learning on the Web of Data

Giuseppe Rizzo[⊠], Nicola Fanizzi, Claudia d'Amato, and Floriana Esposito

Università degli Studi di Bari "Aldo Moro",
Via Orabona 4, 70125 Bari, Italy
{giuseppe.rizzo1,nicola.fanizzi,
claudia.damato,floriana.esposito}@uniba.it

Abstract. A prominent class of supervised methods for the representations adopted in the context of the *Web of Data* are designed to solve *concept learning* problems. Such methods aim at approximating an intensional definition for a target concept from a set of individuals of a target knowledge base. In this scenario, most of the well-known solutions exploit a *separate-and-conquer* approach: intuitively, the learning algorithm builds an intensional definition by repeatedly specializing a partial solution with the aim of covering the largest number of positive examples as possible. Essentially such a strategy can be regarded as a form of *hill-climbing search* that can produce sub-optimal solutions. To cope with this problem, we propose a novel framework for the concept learning problem called DL-FOCL. Three versions of this algorithmic solution, built upon DL-FOIL, have been designed to tackle the inherent myopia of the separate-and-conquer strategies. Their implementation has been empirically tested against methods available in the DL-Learner suite showing interesting results.

1 Introduction

In the last years, datasets and their vocabularies in the context of the *Web of Data* [8] have come to represent important sources of structured knowledge that can be accessed through several query services that may exploit the power of automatic reasoning. However, the impossibility of a total knowledge assumption in a such large-scale distributed scenario (where an open-world semantics is naturally adopted) and often also the quality of the vocabularies does not ensure a proper model of the domain, yielding severe problem of incompleteness that become especially evident when deductive inference is coupled with querying services.

To tackle this problem, a growing interest developed in the design of solutions based on machine learning methods to support the knowledge base *completion* task. Particularly, specific symbolic methods have been devised for multi-relational representations for *Linked Data* and related vocabularies – languages based on *Description Logics*, henceforth DLs. In particular, we are interested in solutions devised for solving the *concept learning* problem [10]. The general

© Springer Nature Switzerland AG 2018
C. Faron Zucker et al. (Eds.): EKAW 2018, LNAI 11313, pp. 338–354, 2018.
https://doi.org/10.1007/978-3-030-03667-6_22

goal is to induce new concept descriptions that are consistent w.r.t. a limited set of pre-classified individuals, i.e. whose intended membership is assumed to be available, and meant to be used to predict the membership of (new) unseen individuals. The induced definitions in the form of new axioms provide a twofold advantage w.r.t. other solutions based on machine learning techniques: they can be exploited for both the enrichment of its vocabulary, i.e. completing the intensional part of a knowledge base, and for classifying individuals thus giving the chance of discovering new assertions for the completion of the assertional part of the knowledge base.

In the related literature various approaches have been proposed, which are often based on *separate-and-conquer* (*sequential covering*) strategy: these methods attempt to build a new concept description by specializing a partial solution to correctly cover (i.e. decide a consistent classification for) as many training instances as possible. For example, DL-FOIL [5] and various methods in the DL-Learner suite, such as CELOE [12], are based on such a strategy. These methods can be regarded as adopting a sort of *hill-climbing* optimization strategy: similarly to the case of propositional/numerical representations, the quality of the complete solution depends on a sequence of local changes applied to the current solution (in our case, the working partial definition to be refined for approximating the target concept) resulting in a possible sub-optimal solution. Hence, such methods perform only a myopic search in the space of the solutions [15].

To mitigate this problem, various enhancements may be devised. A first type of approach involves the use of a refinement operator with a *lookahead* to extend the search space: at each step the learner assesses the quality of a concept description looking at the refinements will be enabled afterwards in the search process. An alternative strategy is based on the integration of *meta-heuristics*, as in *repeated-hill climbing* and *tabu-search* [7], that proved their effectiveness in a number of real-world applications.

Thus, the contribution of this paper consists in the design and integration of the aforementioned techniques with a base greedy covering learner for the induction of concepts in the standard representation languages for Web ontologies. Specifically, the resulting framework, DL-FOCL, extends the latest release of DL-FOIL. To assess their performance, it has been empirically compared also against other concept learning systems, showing that the predictiveness of concepts induced through DL-FOIL can be further improved.

The remainder of the paper is organized as follows: the next section gives an brief overview on the concept learning problem and its solutions in the literature; Sect. 3 provides the basics about the representation language and the formalization of the problem; Sect. 4 describes DL-FOCL as a new concept learning framework; Sect. 5 reports the empirical evaluation and discusses the outcomes; Sect. 6 concludes the paper delineating further ongoing extensions.

2   Related Work

Learning concepts in Description Logics stemmed from the induction of Horn clauses from examples [4]. However inducing concepts through the operators usually adopted in *Inductive Logic Programming* cannot be straightforwardly made because they represent a remarkable source of complexity [2]. This motivated the need for ad-hoc solutions targeting the specific representation language.

One of the first approaches, YINYANG [9], built a complete solution using both specializations and generalization steps. Specifically when a wrong definition is learned, the algorithm finds a sub-description covering the negative examples and negates this sub-concept, dubbed as *counterfactual*. The counterfactual is then generalized to rule out the instances wrongly covered. This approach was extended by adapting FOIL learning system [5]. The resulting system, dubbed DL-FOIL outputs a concept description using a covering approach based on an heuristic similar to the information gain. More recent solutions for solving the problem are CELOE [12], OCEL [14] and $\mathcal{EL}$ [13] TREE LEARNER. The implementation of such algorithms is currently available in DL-LEARNER, a reference framework that adopts several optimizations in order to ensure simple concept descriptions and the scalability also on large knowledge bases [3]. All the methods described above share the same strategy for learning concepts in Description Logics but differ for either the heuristics or the specialization operator. The separate-and-conquer strategies adopted by the methods reported above performs a myopic search of the best solution. In this perspective, DL-FOCL (introduced in this paper) attempts to overcome such limits using a similar strategy employed by FOCL in the context of clausal learning [15]. Indeed, FOCL uses *non-operational predicates* (predicates defined in terms of other predicates) that allows the hill-climber to takes larger steps finding solutions that cannot be obtained without using such predicates.

Concepts definitions in DLs can be elicited from the paths of a *Terminological Decision Trees* (TDTs) [6,16], a decision tree whose inner nodes contains concepts and each edges correspond to a result of the instance-check. The model can be induced by recursively partitioning of the set of examples according to concept description generated on-the-fly via a specialization operator. Learning TDTs is also strictly related to the bisimulation approach [19], that is based on the employment of a set of pre-computed selectors, i.e. tests, to partition the set of individuals, instead of concepts generated via specialization operators. The last algorithm to be mentioned is PARCEL, a learning algorithm that combines top-down and bottom-up refinements in the search space [17]. The learning problem is split into various sub-problems according to a divide-and-conquer strategy that are solved by running CELOE as a subroutine. Once these partial solutions are obtained, they are combined in a bottom-up fashion. PARCEL has been extended in [18]. The resulting system, SPACEL, performs a symmetrical specialization of a concept description for the positive and negative examples.

3 Concept Learning Problem and Hill-Climbing Optimization

In this section, we formalize the concept learning problem applied to knowledge bases modeled through standard representation language for the Web of Data and we introduce the basics of the refinement operators.

3.1 Notation

In this work we consider knowledge bases modeled through representation languages that can be mapped onto *Description Logics* (DLs) [1] In the sequel, we will use the standard notation for DLs:

- $a, b, \ldots$ denote individuals (occurring in the assertions);
- $C, D, \ldots$ denote *concepts* (i.e. classes) and specifically A, B for atomic concepts;
- $R, S, \ldots$ denote *role* names (i.e. properties/relationships);
- N_C and N_R denote, respectively, the sets of *concept* and *role names*;
- the symbols $\sqcap$, $\sqcup$, $\neg$, $\exists$, $\forall$ stand for the standard DL operators for defining complex concept descriptions: *intersection, union, complement, existential* and *universal* role restrictions;
- an *inclusion axiom* of the form $C \sqsubseteq D$ stands for the *subsumption* relation between concept descriptions, with $C \equiv D$ representing an *equivalence* axiom: $C \sqsubseteq D$ and $D \sqsubseteq C$ ($C \sqsubset D$ stands for strict subsumption);
- $C(a)$ and $R(a, b)$ denote assertions, ground axioms describing the individuals, their properties and relationships among them;
- $\mathcal{K} = \langle \mathcal{T}, \mathcal{A} \rangle$ indicates a *knowledge base* with a TBox $\mathcal{T}$ containing axioms, and an ABox $\mathcal{A}$ containing assertions about a set of individual resources, denoted with $\mathsf{Ind}(\mathcal{A})$;
- $\mathcal{K} \models \alpha$ denotes the entailment of an axiom α or the *instance check* when $\alpha = (\neg)C(a)$.

The complete model-theoretic semantics for these notions is given in [1].

3.2 Learning Concepts in DLs

Informally, the goal of concept learning is to build a (new) definition for a target concept name (in the form of a concept description) for which a set of training examples is available: individuals labeled with the correct membership w.r.t. the target concept. We can formally define the learning problem as follows:

Definition 3.1 (learning problem). *Let $\mathcal{K} = \langle \mathcal{T}, \mathcal{A} \rangle$ be a DL knowledge base.*

Given

- *a new concept name $C \in N_C$ (that is not in the signature of $\mathcal{K}$)*

– a set of individuals $Tr \subseteq Ind(\mathcal{A})$, whose intended membership w.r.t. C is known, partitioned as follows:
- positive examples $Ps = \{a \in Tr \mid C(a) \in \mathcal{A}_C^+\}$
- negative examples $Ns = \{a \in Tr \mid \neg C(a) \in \mathcal{A}_C^-\}$
- uncertain membership examples $Us = Tr \setminus (Ps \cup Ns)$

with $Ns \cap Ps = \emptyset$ and the sets of positive, risp. negative, available assertions for C defined by $\mathcal{A}_C^+ = \{C(a_1), \ldots, C(a_P)\}$ and $\mathcal{A}_C^- = \{\neg C(b_1), \ldots, \neg C(b_N)\}$

Find a concept description D, such that, letting $\mathcal{K}' = \langle \mathcal{T} \cup \{C \equiv D\}, \mathcal{A} \rangle$, the following entailments hold:

- $\forall a \in Ps$: $\mathcal{K}' \models C(a)$ C covers the positive ex. a
- $\forall b \in Ns$: $\mathcal{K}' \models \neg C(b)$ C does not cover the negative ex. b

Note that an induced concept description is mainly intended to be used predictively for determining the membership of new and/or *unseen* individuals, i.e. those that are not included in Tr. Thus, the constraints reported above can be more relaxed in order to ensure a good generalization avoiding solutions that overfit the training set remaining poorly predictive [4].

A further remarks concerns the constraints on negative assertions $\mathcal{K}' \models \neg C(b)$ are stronger compared to other settings, yet it seems more coherent with underlying open-world semantics; as KBs are assumed to be inherently incomplete then it is plausible to consider as negative examples only those individuals explicitly indicated as such. Other approaches [11,12] tend to assume weaker constraints, namely $\mathcal{K}' \not\models C(b)$, that leads to problems targeting narrower concepts that should not include both actual counterexamples and individuals whose membership to the target concept cannot be ascertained given the current state of knowledge represented by the KB.

3.3   Refinement Operators

Solving the concept learning problem stated above can be cast as a search for a correct concept definition throughout a quasi-ordered space, i.e. a space endowed with a reflexive and transitive relationship. To our purposes, we will consider a space of concept definitions $\mathcal{L}$ ordered by the subsumption relationship $\sqsubseteq$ [4]. The search space can be traversed through a set of suitable operators, called refinement operators, which can be formally defined as follows.

Definition 3.2 (refinement operators). Given a quasi-ordered space $(\mathcal{L}, \preceq)$

– a downward refinement operator is a mapping $\rho : \mathcal{L} \to 2^{\mathcal{L}}$ such that

$$\forall \alpha \in \mathcal{L} \quad \rho(\alpha) \subseteq \{\beta \in \mathcal{L} \mid \beta \sqsubseteq \alpha\}$$

– an upward refinement operator is a mapping $\delta : \mathcal{L} \to 2^{\mathcal{L}}$ such that

$$\forall \alpha \in \mathcal{L} \quad \delta(\alpha) \subseteq \{\beta \in \mathcal{L} \mid \alpha \sqsubseteq \beta\}$$

In the sequel, we will be interested to the downward refinement operators. A downward (resp. upward) refinement operator ρ (resp. δ) may fulfill some important properties (related to its effectiveness), such as: (1) *local finitness* – for each C, $\rho(C)$ (resp. $\delta(C)$) is finite; (2) *completeness* – for all C, D such that $C \sqsubseteq D$ (resp. $C \sqsupseteq D$), an equivalent refinement $E \equiv C$ (resp. $E \equiv D$) can be found in $\rho(D)$ (resp. $\delta(C)$); (3) *properness* – for all C, D, $D \in \rho(C)$ (resp. $D \in \delta(C)$) implies $C \not\equiv D$ A refinement operator that is endowed with such properties is defined as *ideal* [12,13]. In particular the completeness is important because allows a concept learning algorithm to find all the possible solutions.

3.4   The Hill-Climbing Optimization Strategy

In numerical analysis, the *hill climbing strategy* is an optimization technique that, starting from an arbitrary solution, iteratively attempts to find a better solution, applying a sequence of changes.

Thus, given a target function $f(x)$ to be maximized/minimized, the hill-climbing algorithm starts with an arbitrarily initialized vector x, which represents the candidate solution; the algorithm, also called *hill-climber*, adjusts a single element in x at a time. Any change improving $f(x)$ is accepted and further considered for the next steps. The hill-climber will iterate until further changes are not possible. In this case, the resulting vector x will be the local optimal solution for the problem. If the problem is *convex* the local optimal solution will be also a *global* one. Note that the resulting x depends on the sequence of the local choices made to build the solution.

Despite the myopia of the hill-climber, there are several advantages deriving from its use: for instance, it is an *any-time algorithm*, thus hill-climbing can be stopped after a certain amount of time returning a complete (yet potentially sub-optimal) solution. Also, the general strategy can be straightforwardly applied to symbolic representations, resulting in the sequential covering methods typically employed for tackling concept learning problems in the targeted representations. In this case, the hill-climber considers concepts instead of numerical vectors and each change is meant to be performed by means of a refinement operator.

4   The DL-FOCL Framework

In this section, we illustrate the DL-FOCL framework for solving the concept learning problem. Specifically, three strategies built upon DL-FOIL, are described. For the sake of explanation we will firstly describe the latest version of DL-FOIL adopted as the basic hill-climber and then we will describe the basic features of each version. We will refer to DL-FOCL endowed with the repeated hill-climbing strategy as DL-FOCL I and the versions implementing the *looka-head* and the *tabu-search* as DL-FOCL II and III.

4.1   The DL-Foil Algorithm

The algorithm implemented in DL-Foil is a sequential covering method exploiting a (downward) refinement operator to traverse the search space of DL concept definitions and a heuristic, inspired by the original *information gain*, to select among candidate specialization. A sketch of the main routine of the learning procedure is reported in Algorithm 1.

Algorithm 1. Function INDUCECONCEPT

```
1  input Ps, Ns, Us: set of Individuals {with positive,          12   PartialDef ← GETBESTSPECIALIZATION
       negative or uncertain membership}                                (PartialDef,CoveredPs,CoveredNs,CoveredUs)
2  output Generalization: Concept Description                     13   CoveredPs
3                                                                         ← {p ∈ PsToCover | 𝒦 ⊨ PartialDef(p)}
4  Generalization ← ⊥                                             14   CoveredNs ← {n ∈ Ns | 𝒦 ⊨ PartialDef(n)}
5  PsToCover ← Ps                                                 15   CoveredUs ← {u ∈ Us | 𝒦 ⊨ PartialDef(u)}
6  while (PsToCover ≠ ∅) do                                       16   end while
7    PartialDef ← ⊤                                               17   Generalization ← Generalization ⊔ PartialDef
8    CoveredPs ← PsToCover                                        18   PsToCover ← PsToCover \ CoveredPs
9    CoveredNs ← Ns                                               19   end while
10   CoveredUs ← Us                                               20
11   while (CoveredPs ≠ ∅ and CoveredNs ∪ CoveredUs               21   return Generalization
        ≠ ∅) do
```

The learning procedure requires a training set composed by individuals explicitly deemed as positive or negative for the target concept, possibly including also some with uncertain membership. The INDUCECONCEPT routine computes a generalization as a disjunct of partial descriptions covering a part of the positive examples (outer loop) and ruling out as many negative examples as possible per inner iteration by refining the current partial concept description. However, to give a chance of tuning the compliance to with the open-world semantics, the heuristic used to select the (partial) solutions can be configured not to cover uncertain-membership examples.

If either negative-membership or uncertain-membership examples are covered by the current description, the GETBESTSPECIALIZATION routine is invoked for solving these specialization problems. This routine seeks for an optimal specialized description using the (incomplete) refinement operator defined in the next section. The specialization process is iterated until no negative/uncertain membership example is covered.

The partial descriptions built on each outer iteration are finally grouped together in a disjunction[1]. A simple modification anticipating the stopping condition of the outer loop may be adopted for avoiding overfitting generalizations.

Specialization of Partial Definitions. The function GETBESTSPECIALIZATION (reported in Algorithm 2) is called from the inner loop of the generalization procedure to select a good specialization of an overly general (partial) description. Unlike the similar function in the previous version of DL-Foil, the new function searches for proper refinements that satisfy the following conditions:

---

[1] This may be considered a basic upper refinement operator allowed by expressive DL languages (encompassing $\mathcal{ALC}$).

– *a refinement must cover at least a positive example;*
– *a refinement must yield a minimal gain fixed with a threshold ϵ.*

Algorithm 2. Function GETBESTSPECIALIZATION

```
1   {constant values set according to the configuration}
2   const ε: real {minimal gain threshold}
3   n: integer {number of specializations to be generated}
4   input PartialDef: Concept Description
5   Ps, Ns, Us: set of Individuals {with positive, negative and
              uncertain membership}
6   output bestConcept: Concept Definition
7   bestGain ← 0
8   while (bestGain < ε) do
9     for i ← 1 to n
10    repeat
11      Specialization ← GETRANDOMREF(ρ,PartialDef)
12      CoveredPs ← {p ∈ Ps | K ⊨ Specialization(p)}
13      if (CoveredPs ≠ ∅) then
```
```
14      CoveredNs ← {n ∈ Ns | K ⊨ Specialization(n)}
15      CoveredUs ← {u ∈ Us | K ⊨ Specialization(u)}
16      gain
          ← GAIN(CoveredPos, CoveredNs, CoveredUs, Ps, Ns, Us)

17      if (gain > bestGain) then
18        bestConcept ← Specialization
19        bestGain ← gain
20    until (CoveredPs = ∅) {relaxable strong constraint}
21    end for
22   end while
23
24   return bestConcept
```

Candidate specializations are randomly generated via a downward operator ρ that, given a concept description C, returns refinements C' in one of the following forms:

$$\rho_1 \quad C' = C \sqcap A$$
$$\rho_2 \quad C' = C \sqcap \neg A$$
$$\rho_3 \quad C' = C \sqcap \forall R.\top$$
$$\rho_4 \quad C' = C \sqcap \exists R.\top$$
$$\rho_5 \quad C' = C_1 \sqcap \cdots \sqcap B \sqcap \cdots \sqcap C_n \qquad \text{if } C = C_1 \sqcap \cdots \sqcap A \sqcap \cdots \sqcap C_n \text{ and } B \sqsubseteq A$$
$$\rho_6 \quad C' = C_1 \sqcap \cdots \sqcap \neg B \sqcap \cdots \sqcap C_n \qquad \text{if } C = C_1 \sqcap \cdots \sqcap \neg A \sqcap \cdots \sqcap C_n \text{ and } A \sqsupseteq B$$
$$\rho_7 \quad C' = C_1 \sqcap \cdots \sqcap \exists R.D \sqcap \cdots \sqcap C_n \text{ if } C = C_1 \sqcap \cdots \sqcap \exists R.E \sqcap \cdots \sqcap C_n \text{ and } E \in \rho(D)$$
$$\rho_8 \quad C' = C_1 \sqcap \cdots \sqcap \forall R.D \sqcap \cdots \sqcap C_n \text{ if } C = C_1 \sqcap \cdots \sqcap \forall R.E \sqcap \cdots \sqcap C_n \text{ and } E \in \rho(D)$$

The operator described above is recursive – see forms ρ_7 and ρ_8 – while ρ_1–ρ_6 represent the base cases. A first random choice is made between adding an atomic conjunct (cases ρ_1–ρ_4) or refining an existing sub-concepts with (cases ρ_5–ρ_8). In case of an atomic concept is added, the concept name (or the role name for the conjunct in the form $\exists R.\top/\forall R.\top$) is also randomly selected. In the case of refinement of an existing conjunct, the operator picks (randomly) such a candidate and generates a specialization via ρ_5–ρ_8. Note that this refinement operator returns specialization using $\mathcal{ALC}$ concepts. However, different languages can be considered extending or limiting the constructs described above. From a theoretical viewpoint, it is straightforward to note the refinement operator is not *ideal*. Particularly, the completeness property is not fulfilled due to the random choices required for building the partial definition.

Heuristics. Concerning the heuristic for selecting the best refinement, DL-FOIL computes the score for each refinement using a sort of *weighted information gain*: the score represents the difference of the information conveyed by two partial definitions. Such a gain, denoted by g, is computed (through the function GAIN) as follows:

$$g(D_0, D_1) = p_1 \cdot \left[\log \frac{p_1}{p_1 + n_1 + u_1} - \log \frac{p_0}{p_0 + n_0 + u_0} \right]$$

where p_1, n_1 and u_1 resp. represent, the numbers of positive, negative and uncertain-membership examples covered by the specialization, say D_0, and p_0, n_0 and u_0 stand for the corresponding numbers of examples covered by the former (partial) definition D_0[2]. The main difference with the formerly adopted gain function [5] is that the examples with an uncertain membership do not contribute to the score according to the prior probabilities (estimated over the distributions of the examples), but according to the actual number of individuals covered by the specific specialization.

4.2   DL-FOCL I: Repeated Sequential Covering

The first solution to cope with the myopia problem of the sequential covering methods is the use of a *repeated hill-climbing* approach built upon the specific algorithm. The underlying idea for such strategy is to search a solution again and again until the returned solution satisfies a criterion. DL-FOCL I implements such a strategy (the algorithm is sketched in Algorithm 3): it induces a concept description invoking the DL-FOIL algorithm described above (INDUCECONCEPT) that may return a potentially poor predictive definition. If the current solution cannot satisfy a desired criterion, DL-FOCL I starts a new search in order to find a better solution than the current one. Such a process is repeated until the criterion is satisfied.

In order to check if further iterations are required, DL-FOCL I compares the score of the current concept definition with the score of the best concept obtained so far.

Various scores can be plugged into the algorithm according to the desired qualities of the learned concept. However, in order to mitigate the incompleteness due to the open-world semantics, the score concept employed in DL-FOCL I is computed as the *omission rate*, i.e. cases of individuals with a positive/negative membership w.r.t. the target concept with an uncertain membership w.r.t. the induced concept description, evaluated on the same training set. Such cases are estimated invoking the auxiliary function EVALUATE. If the omission rate obtained by classifying individuals w.r.t the current concept description is lower than the rate obtained from the previous step and it does not exceed a given threshold ν, the iteration stopped returning the concept description induced so far. Alternatively, the repeated sequential covering ends after a user-defined number of iterations (chosen accordingly the size –in terms of concepts and individuals – of the knowledge base).

---

[2] A further correction of the ratios is made resorting to Laplace smoothing (m-estimates) to avoid divisions by 0.

Algorithm 3. Function DL-FOCL I

---

1 **const** maxValue: **real**
2 **input** Ps, Ns, Us: set of Individuals {with positive,
       negative or uncertain membership}
3   m: **integer** {maximum number of trials}
4 **output** bestGeneralization: Concept Description
5
6 i ← 0
7 bestGeneralization ← ⊤
8 bestScore ← maxValue

9 **repeat**
10   i ← i +1
11   generalization ← INDUCECONCEPT(Ps, Ns, Us)
12   score ← EVALUATE(bestGeneralization, Ps ∪ Ns)
13   **if** (score ≤ bestScore) **then**
14   bestScore ← score
15   bestGeneralization ← generalization
16 **until** (bestScore ≤ ν) **or** i ≥ m
17 **return** bestGeneralization

4.3 DL-FOCL II: Sequential Covering with Lookahead

The second version of DL-FOCL, dubbed DL-FOCL II implements a similar solution to the one proposed in the context of the Inductive Logic Programming [15]. The original learning algorithm uses *non-operational* predicates, i.e. predicates being defined in terms of other predicates. In principle, using such predicates should allow the algorithm, to find a solution in a larger space considering candidates that could be ignored otherwise. Thus, exploiting non-operational predicates can be regarded as a kind of *lookahead* that is necessary to make larger steps in the search process. This idea can be adapted in the context of Web of Data knowledge bases as follows: DL-FOCL II learning algorithm exploits a modified specialization procedure GETRANDOMREF of DL-FOIL (Algorithm 2), which invokes the refinement operator ρ more than once: each specialization returned by ρ is given again to the same operator as an input in order to further specialize the partial definition. This process can be controlled via a parameter, say l, that indicates the maximum number of calls of ρ before a specialization is returned to be evaluated. Note that, DL-FOCL II may return, at each step, longer specializations than DL-FOIL because it is affected by the value of l and the number of recursive calls of ρ. To overcome the problem, further constraints can be considered to stop the refinement process, e.g limiting the depth of the recursive calls.

4.4 DL-FOCL III: Sequential Covering with Tabu Search

The last version of DL-FOCL, dubbed DL-FOCL III implements another strategy to cope with the problem of sub-optimal solutions: the *tabu search* [7]. The tabu search is a modified hill-climbing strategy that is able to prevent the myopic choice of partial solutions thank to the use of a *local memory*, i.e. the *tabu list* used to prevent to re-consider sub-optimal choices and/or to guide the search towards particular subspaces. To our purposes, we are interested to prevent the repeated generation of poor refinements. Thus, the specialization procedure is modified as follows: the specialization function (Algorithm 4) initializes the tabu list and, at each step, the algorithm adds the poor refinements to the tabu list. In the next iterations, the algorithm checks if a refinement has been already generated. If this is not the case, the algorithm evaluates the best refinement according to the heuristic of DL-FOIL. After specializations that are not in the tabu list have been generated, the specialization procedure returns the best one.

Algorithm 4. Function GETBESTSPECIALIZATION in DL-FOCL III

```
 1  {constant values set according to the configuration}
 2  const ε: real {minimal gain threshold}
 3    n: integer {number of specializations to be generated}
 4  input PartialDef: Concept Description
 5    Ps, Ns, Us: set of Individuals {with pos., neg. and unc.
         membership}
 6  output bestConcept: Concept Definition
 7
 8  tabuList ← ∅
 9  bestConcept ← ⊤
10  bestGain ← 0
11  while (bestGain < ε) do
12    for i ← 1 to n
13    repeat
14      Specialization ← GETRANDOMREF(ρ,PartialDef)
15      if (Specialization ∉ TabuList) then
16        CoveredPs ← {p ∈ Ps | 𝒦 ⊨ Specialization(p)}
17        if (CoveredPs ≠ ∅) then
18          CoveredNs ← {n ∈ Ns | 𝒦 ⊨ Specialization(n)}
19          CoveredUs ← {u ∈ Us | 𝒦 ⊨ Specialization(u)}
20          gain
               ← GAIN(CoveredPs, CoveredNs, CoveredUs, Ps, Ns, Us)
21          if (gain > bestGain) then
22            bestConcept ← Specialization
23            bestGain ← gain
24          else TabuList ← TabuList ∪ Specialization
25        until ((Ps \ CoveredPs) = ∅)
26    end for
27  end while
28
29  return bestConcept
```

---

5   Empirical Evaluation

This section illustrates the design and the outcomes of a comparative empirical evaluation aimed at assessing the effectiveness of the DL-FOCL^3.

5.1   Experimental Design and Setup

In order to determine the effectiveness of the compared systems, the quality of the induced concepts was evaluated against a baseline of target concepts. To this purpose, we considered 5 publicly available Web ontologies, which differ in terms of expressiveness, number of individuals and number of concepts/roles. The characteristics of each ontology are reported in Table 1.

Table 1. Facts concerning the ontologies employed in the experiments.

ontology	language	#concepts	obj.properties	data properties	#individuals
BioPAX	$\mathcal{ALCHF}(\mathbf{D})$	28	19	30	323
NTN	$\mathcal{SHIF}(\mathbf{D})$	47	27	8	724
Hdisease	$\mathcal{SHIF}(\mathbf{D})$	1499	10	15	639
Financial	$\mathcal{ALCIF}$	60	17	0	1000
Geoskills	$\mathcal{SHIF}$	596	23	0	2532

---

[3] The source code and the datasets and ontologies are publicly available at: https://bitbucket.org/grizzo001/dlfocl/src/master/.

Learning Problems. Each ontology was used to generate 15 random artificial problems and related datasets. For each problem and ontology, a target concept description was generated by randomly picking concepts/roles from the respective signature and combining them through basic concept constructors: union, conjunction, complement, universal or existential restriction. All the individuals were labeled as positive/negative/uncertain-membership examples with respect to each target concept (via the instance-checking reasoning service). Table 2 summarizes, for each ontology, the distributions of the examples (averaged over the number of datasets). Note that the generation procedure ensures that individuals that belong to either to the target concept or to its complement are available. To allow the repetition of the experiments, a seed for the internal pseudo-random generator can be set in the configuration: this value defaulted to 1.

Table 2. Distributions of the positive, negative, unlabeled instances per ontology

ontology	%pos.exs.	%neg.exs.	%unc.exs.
BioPAX	51.99	45.74	02.27
NTN	15.57	47.31	49.77
HDisease	08.54	08.46	82.99
Financial	53.78	38.37	7.85
Geoskills	58.00	20.00	22.00

Setup of the Algorithms. We compared the versions of DL-Focl against DL-Foil and Celoe [12], based on a similar sequential covering algorithm available from the latest release of DL-Learner. In the experiments with DL-Focl I, II and III and DL-Foil, the maximum number of specializations to be evaluated per turn is a required parameter. This value was empirically set to 20. In the case of DL-Focl I, the maximum number of runs of the DL-Foil was required. For the sake of the efficiency, the value was set to 3. As a stop condition, we used the omission rate (see below) estimated over the training set. The value was set to $5/|\text{Tr}|$. In the experiments with DL-Focl II, the value of the parameter l used to control the lookahead employed by the algorithm was set to 2 in order to obtain a trade-off between the efficiency and the effectiveness of the algorithm. Finally, in the experiments with Celoe, a proper tuning of the refinement operator was required: the operator was configured so that it could return concept descriptions obtained through all the available concept constructors (possibly also using the datatype properties available in the ontologies). Another required parameter is the time-out used to stop the training phase. This value was set to 10 s (larger values were also preliminarily tested but the decreased efficiency of the process led to no significant improvement).

Evaluation Indices. We adopted a .632 bootstrap as the design of the replications in order to estimate the following indices:

- *match rate* (M%), i.e. cases of test individuals that got exactly the same classification w.r.t. the target and the induced concept descriptions;
- *commission error rate* (C%), i.e. cases of test individuals that received opposite classifications when checked against the target and the induced definition;
- *omission error rate* (O%): i.e. cases of test individuals with a definite membership w.r.t. the target concept that could not be assessed checking the induced definition;
- *induction rate* (I%): i.e. cases of test individuals of whose membership w.r.t. the target concept cannot be determined, that a reasoner could classify given the induced definition.

5.2   Results

The experiments showed promising results that are reported in Table 3.

Table 3. Outcomes of the comparative experiments in terms of: (1) match and induction rate (the higher the better); (2) commission and omission rate (the lower the better)

Dataset	Index	DL-Foil	DL-Focl			Celoe
			I	II	III	
Biopax	M%	95.73 ± 03.74	**96.64 ± 02.80**	95.11 ± 04.77	95.52 ± 04.09	94.53 ± 01.17
	C%	00.13 ± 00.20	00.12 ± 00.27	**00.11 ± 00.19**	00.13 ± 00.16	03.24 ± 00.85
	O%	01.90 ± 03.31	**00.80 ± 02.33**	02.65 ± 04.48	02.20 ± 03.37	01.62 ± 00.38
	I%	02.23 ± 00.40	**02.43 ± 00.35**	02.14 ± 00.72	02.15 ± 00.33	00.61 ± 00.18
NTN	M%	97.78 ± 05.05	99.28 ± 00.91	**99.79 ± 00.21**	97.86 ± 04.85	97.41 ± 00.15
	C%	00.05 ± 00.07	00.05 ± 00.07	00.01 ± 00.19	00.04 ± 00.08	**00.00 ± 00.00**
	O%	02.17 ± 05.00	00.67 ± 00.91	00.19 ± 00.01	02.10 ± 04.85	**00.00 ± 00.00**
	I%	00.01 ± 00.01	00.00 ± 00.01	00.01 ± 00.00	00.00 ± 00.00	**02.59 ± 00.15**
Hdisease	M%	88.75 ± 01.09	**94.26 ± 04.99**	92.26 ± 03.99	95.71 ± 01.11	88.89 ± 01.09
	C%	00.04 ± 00.10	**00.00 ± 00.01**	00.04 ± 00.10	00.01 ± 00.01	**00.00 ± 00.00**
	O%	03.64 ± 01.30	**03.33 ± 01.42**	**03.33 ± 01.42**	04.16 ± 01.11	07.69 ± 00.90
	I%	**07.57 ± 01.42**	02.41 ± 04.89	04.41 ± 04.09	00.12 ± 00.11	04.23 ± 00.24
Financial	M%	**93.52 ± 01.02**	**93.52 ± 01.02**	92.46 ± 01.22	93.49 ± 00.68	87.40 ± 04.74
	C%	**00.22 ± 00.21**	**00.22 ± 00.21**	00.56 ± 00.30	00.27 ± 00.24	06.33 ± 04.33
	O%	**00.00 ± 00.00**	**00.00 ± 00.00**	00.74 ± 00.44	00.19 ± 00.36	00.00 ± 00.01
	I%	**06.26 ± 00.88**	**06.26 ± 00.88**	06.24 ± 00.87	06.05 ± 00.31	**06.26 ± 00.52**
Geoskills	M%	82.60 ± 04.69	**86.60 ± 04.25**	80.20 ± 05.15	**86.60 ± 02.15**	50.20 ± 02.31
	C%	**00.00 ± 00.00**	**00.00 ± 00.00**	**00.00 ± 00.00**	**00.00 ± 00.00**	23.66 ± 02.61
	O%	13.33 ± 04.43	09.33 ± 04.25	15.33 ± 04.43	09.33 ± 04.25	**01.34 ± 00.12**
	I%	04.07 ± 04.09	04.07 ± 04.10	04.07 ± 04.11	04.07 ± 04.11	**24.80 ± 00.89**

In the experiments with the datasets extracted from Biopax, NTN, and Financial, the match rate obtained through the three versions of DL-Focl and DL-Foil exceeded 90%. While the latter allowed us to observe a substantially lower match rate for the datasets extracted from Hdisease and Geoskills, the former had a rate exceeding 90% even in the case of HDISEASE. In both cases, the match rate was yet larger than the one obtained in the experiments with CELOE.

Concerning the experiments with DL-FOIL, the performance of the algorithm was affected by the large number of concepts that can be found in those knowledge bases (almost 1500 and 600 concepts in the problems on HDISEASE and GEOSKILLS, respectively), resulting in a very large search space to traverse via refinement operator. This might imply that sub-optimal solutions were obtained through simplest covering methods such as DL-FOIL algorithm due to the myopic search of such methods and the incompleteness of the refinement operator plugged in the algorithm.

The myopia of DL-FOIL was mitigated by DL-FOCL: the match rate obtained learning concepts via DL-FOIL on the datasets extracted from those ontologies was about 88.75% (HDISEASE) and about 80% (GEOSKILLS), whereas the match rate increased up to 96% and 84% adopting DL-FOCL. In particular, DL-FOCL I showed to be the most promising approach among those proposed in this paper. Despite its simplicity, the repeated-hill climbing optimization strategy showed to be more effective than the others at reducing the problem search myopia. The stop condition based on the omission cases allowed DL-FOCL I to induce more general concept descriptions that led to improve the match rate and decreasing the omission cases and induction rate. This suggests that:

1. DL-FOCL I was able to perform its search through different subspaces than those explored by DL-FOIL;
2. the concepts induced by DL-FOCL I were more cautious than the ones induced via DL-FOIL.

Instead, the performance of DL-FOCL II in most experiments except for those carried out on NTN were even lower than the one obtained through DL-FOIL. In particular, using lookahead to prevent sub-optimal solutions lead to induce overfitting concept descriptions obtained as a disjunction of very complex concepts. Finally, the tabu search employed by DL-FOCL III did not allow us to further improve the match rate. However, the benefit deriving from the integration of tabu search in the learning algorithm was the limited use the instance check service required to evaluate the specializations (that was one of the most time-consuming activity).

Compared to DL-FOIL, CELOE showed a similar trend, although the match rate was generally lower (in the problems related to GEOSKILLS, the rate decreased to 30%). Such a worse performance was likely due to the simplicity of the concepts induced by CELOE. Indeed, its algorithm is biased towards shorter concept descriptions to provide a good generalization and improve the readability of the induced concepts. But, as observed in the experiments, this led to induce poorly predictive concepts, often composed by a (negated) concept name. Conversely, in most cases the algorithms in DL-FOCL and DL-FOIL managed to find a definitions whose sets of retrieved instances tended to overlap with the analogous sets for the target concepts: in its algorithm, after having

Table 4. Average training times (in seconds) for the algorithms considered in the evaluation

Dataset	DL-Foil	DL-Focl			Celoe
		I	II	III	
BioPax	22.74	68.42	18.43	20.43	12.13
NTN	17.41	52.46	12.11	12.20	11.71
Financial	43.75	134.43	89.46	41.24	11.54
HDisease	109.21	345.15	668.21	98.42	12.41
GeoSkills	669.35	1981.36	24587.56	645.21	12.98

found a good disjunct, the search is started over to cover the remaining positive examples, whereas the search performed by Celoe is sometimes stopped prematurely (because a good solution according to the heuristic was found).

The commission error rate of the concepts induced by DL-Focl I, II and III was almost null and significantly lower than the ones produced by Celoe and similar to the one of DL-Foil. In the experiments with all the algorithms, cases of commission were due to the misclassification of test examples whose membership was under-represented in the datasets: there were cases of negative examples were classified as positive in the experiments with BioPax, NTN, GeoSkills, while in the experiments with Financial and HDisease, there were cases of positive examples were misclassified as negative. Similarly to commission errors, omission error cases occurred in the experiments due to the (large) presence of uncertain-membership instances (also considering the availability and the number of disjointness axioms in the ontologies).

As regards the efficiency of the approach[4], the average training times were quite limited. The overall training time (for all the problems and datasets) elapsed in the experiments with DL-Focl I are reported in Table 4 The runtimes were influenced by various aspects: the number of training individuals and the employment of instance checking service to evaluate their membership and determine the score, the number of concepts of the knowledge base needed to generate the candidates. In particular, the longer times of DL-Focl II w.r.t. those observed with DL-Foil were likely due to the exploration of a larger search space by using the lookahead. Instead, the shorter time taken by DL-Focl III was due to the use of the tabu list, that allows to avoid re-computing the score via costly instance checks.

---

[4] The experiments were carried out on a 8-core Ubuntu server with 16 GB RAM.

6 Conclusions and Outlook

In this work, we have proposed DL-FOCL, a family of algorithms designed for limiting the myopia of sequential covering methods employed for solving the concept learning with knowledge bases modeled through standard representations for the Web of Data, and compared it against other algorithms based on a covering approach. In particular, the comparison involved CELOE, currently implemented in a reference framework like DL-LEARNER, and DL-FOIL. The experiments showed that the methods from the DL-FOCL framework are able to find better approximations of a target concept than basic covering methods, even if some of the proposed approach tend to overfit easily.

Various extensions can be investigated. For example, new experiments with further larger knowledge bases and learning problems can be considered. Also, the framework can be enriched integrating further strategies aimed at avoiding local solutions, and designing more *informed* refinement operators, coupled with new heuristics that can help speed up the search of solutions. Approximated inference mechanisms [3] and the use of frameworks for distributed data processing, such as *Apache Spark*[5] and *Flink*[6] may represent interesting additional features for improving the efficiency of the methods.

References

1. Baader, F., Calvanese, D., McGuinness, D.L., Nardi, D., Patel-Schneider, P.F.: The Description Logic Handbook: Theory, Implementation and Applications, 2nd edn. Cambridge University Press, New York (2010)
2. Badea, L., Nienhuys-Cheng, S.-H.: A refinement operator for description logics. In: Cussens, J., Frisch, A. (eds.) ILP 2000. LNCS, vol. 1866, pp. 40–59. Springer, Heidelberg (2000). https://doi.org/10.1007/3-540-44960-4_3
3. Bühmann, L., Lehmann, J., Westphal, P.: DL-Learner - a framework for inductive learning on the Semantic Web. J. Web Sem. **39**, 15–24 (2016)
4. De Raedt, L.: Logical and Relational Learning. Springer, Heidelberg (2008). https://doi.org/10.1007/978-3-540-68856-3
5. Fanizzi, N., d'Amato, C., Esposito, F.: DL-FOIL concept learning in description logics. In: Železný, F., Lavrač, N. (eds.) ILP 2008. LNCS (LNAI), vol. 5194, pp. 107–121. Springer, Heidelberg (2008). https://doi.org/10.1007/978-3-540-85928-4_12
6. Fanizzi, N., d'Amato, C., Esposito, F.: Induction of concepts in web ontologies through terminological decision trees. In: Balcázar, J.L., Bonchi, F., Gionis, A., Sebag, M. (eds.) ECML PKDD 2010. LNCS, vol. 6321, pp. 442–457. Springer, Heidelberg (2010). https://doi.org/10.1007/978-3-642-15880-3_34
7. Gendreau, M., Potvin, J.Y.: Handbook of Metaheuristics, 2nd edn. Springer, New York (2010). https://doi.org/10.1007/978-1-4419-1665-5
8. Heath, T., Bizer, C.: Linked Data: Evolving the Web into a Global Data Space. Synthesis Lectures on the Semantic Web. Morgan & Claypool Publishers, Sebastopol (2011)

---

[5] spark.apache.org.
[6] flink.apache.org.

9. Iannone, L., Palmisano, I., Fanizzi, N.: An algorithm based on counterfactuals for concept learning in the Semantic Web. Appl. Intell. **26**(2), 139–159 (2007)
10. Lehmann, J., Fanizzi, N., Bühmann, L., d'Amato, C.: Concept learning. In: Lehmann, J., Voelker, J. (eds.) Perspectives on Ontology Learning, chap. 2, pp. 71–91. AKA/IOS Press (2014)
11. Lehmann, J., Hitzler, P.: Concept learning in description logics using refinement operators. Mach. Learn. **78**(1–2), 203–250 (2010)
12. Lehmann, J., Auer, S., Bühmann, L., Tramp, S.: Class expression learning for ontology engineering. J. Web Semant. **9**, 71–81 (2011)
13. Lehmann, J., Haase, C.: Ideal downward refinement in the $\mathcal{EL}$ description logic. In: De Raedt, L. (ed.) ILP 2009. LNCS, vol. 5989, pp. 73–87. Springer, Heidelberg (2010). https://doi.org/10.1007/978-3-642-13840-9_8
14. Lehmann, J., Hitzler, P.: A refinement operator based learning algorithm for the $\mathcal{ALC}$ description logic. In: Blockeel, H., Ramon, J., Shavlik, J., Tadepalli, P. (eds.) ILP 2007. LNCS, vol. 4894, pp. 147–160. Springer, Heidelberg (2008). https://doi.org/10.1007/978-3-540-78469-2_17
15. Pazzani, M., Kibler, D.: The utility of knowledge in inductive learning. Mach. Learn. **9**(1), 57–94 (1992)
16. Rizzo, G., d'Amato, C., Fanizzi, N., Esposito, F.: Tree-based models for inductive classification on the Web Of Data. J. Web Sem. **45**, 1–22 (2017)
17. Tran, A.C., Dietrich, J., Guesgen, H.W., Marsland, S.: An approach to parallel class expression learning. In: Bikakis, A., Giurca, A. (eds.) RuleML 2012. LNCS, vol. 7438, pp. 302–316. Springer, Heidelberg (2012). https://doi.org/10.1007/978-3-642-32689-9_25
18. Tran, A.C., Dietrich, J., Guesgen, H.W., Marsland, S.: Parallel symmetric class expression learning. J. Mach. Learn. Res. **18**, 64:1–64:34 (2017)
19. Tran, T., Ha, Q., Hoang, T., Nguyen, L.A., Nguyen, H.S.: Bisimulation-based concept learning in description logics. Fundam. Inform. **133**(2–3), 287–303 (2014)

Boosting Holistic Ontology Matching: Generating Graph Clique-Based Relaxed Reference Alignments for Holistic Evaluation

Philippe Roussille[(✉)], Imen Megdiche, Olivier Teste, and Cassia Trojahn

Institut de Recherche en Informatique de Toulouse, Toulouse, France
{philippe.roussille,imen.megdiche,olivier.teste,cassia.trojahn}@irit.fr

Abstract. Ontology matching is the process of finding correspondences between entities from different ontologies. Whereas the field has fully developed in the last decades, most existing approaches are still limited to *pairwise matching*. However, in complex domains where several ontologies describing different but related aspects of the domain have to be linked together, matching multiple ontologies simultaneously, known as *holistic matching*, is required. In the absence of benchmarks dedicated to holistic matching evaluation, this paper presents a methodology for constructing *pseudo*-holistic reference alignments from available pairwise ones. We discuss the problem of relaxing graph cliques representing these alignments involving a different number of ontologies. We argue that fostering the development of holistic matching approaches depends on the availability of such data sets. We run our experiments on the OAEI Conference data set.

1 Introduction

Ontology matching is an essential task for the management of the semantic heterogeneity problem in diverse environments. It aims at finding correspondences between entities from different ontologies. Diverse approaches have been proposed in the literature [3] and systematic evaluation of them has been carried out over the last fifteen years in the context of the Ontology Alignment Evaluation Initiative (OAEI) [2] campaigns. Despite the progress in the field, most efforts are still dedicated to *pairwise ontology matching* (i.e., matching a pair of ontologies). However, with the increasing amount of knowledge bases being published on the Linked Open Data, covering different aspects of overlapping domains, the ability of simultaneously matching different ontologies, a task so-called *holistic ontology matching* [12,17], is more than ever required. It is typically the case in complex domains, such as bio-medicine, where several ontologies describing different but related phenomena have to be linked together [14]. As stated in [15], the increase in the matching space and the inherently higher difficulty to compute alignments pose interesting challenges to this task.

© Springer Nature Switzerland AG 2018
C. Faron Zucker et al. (Eds.): EKAW 2018, LNAI 11313, pp. 355–369, 2018.
https://doi.org/10.1007/978-3-030-03667-6_23

Early works on the field have addressed the problem of holistic schema matching, in particular the works on attribute matching [6,7,18,19]. In [6], a probabilistic framework determines an underlying model capturing the correspondences between attributes in different schemes. For dealing with complex attribute correspondences, the approach in [7] exploits co-occurrence information across schemes and a correlation mining method. This approach has been extended in [19] improving accuracy and efficiency, by reducing the number of synonymous candidates. In [18], the approach aims at incrementally merging 2-way schemes by clustering the nodes based on linguistic similarity and a tree mining technique. Emerging works have addressed the problem of holistic matching of more expressive structures. In [5], the proposal relies on a cross-domain holistic matching approach for aligning large ontologies by grouping concepts in topics that are aligned locally. More recently, a cluster-based distributed holistic approach for data linking has been proposed in [13]. Although novel approaches dedicated to holistic ontology matching have emerged in the literature in the last years, there is however a lack of reference alignments on which these approaches can be systematically evaluated. According to [14], producing such kind of alignments could be potentially useful to support a next generation of semantic technologies. We argue that fostering the development of these approaches depends on the availability of reference alignments.

This paper addresses the problem of holistic ontology matching and the lack of benchmarks in the field. As such, we attempt to study the problem through these main goals, following a methodology we built in different steps:

- we first designed an algorithm as a mean to allow us to build automatically from existing (and depending on) pairwise alignments a way to test and approach what could be considered as holistic (hence we use the term *pseudo-holistic approach*); mainly by our analysis of the concept of "alignment" through the lens of topological graphs, and our work around the concept to produce nuanced views through different levels of relaxation;
- we then applied our algorithm on the OAEI Conference data set, aiming to produce a baseline for our works in order to produce a similar matching task, as there is no current track providing holistic alignment challenges;
- finally, we chose to check the pertinence of the *pseudo-holistic* concept and produced alignments by evaluating the runners-up state-of-the-art tools of the OAEI track on this new task; so that we can discuss the pertinence of having a tool which can evaluate the point of being *holistic*.

For our experiments, we chose to have our evaluation done both ways: by assessing the generated alignments with the existing tools, we want to show that the holistic dimension is not something that can be reduced to a grouping of pairwise matching; and that some tools already using holistic matching, like LPHOM, outperform traditional tools for such a task. This is, for us, a necessary step so we can proceed further towards a full evaluation of the holistic task, by providing competitors that would help to better asses the performance of LPHOM and other holistic matching techniques, while assessing them on peer-reviewed specific alignments.

We organised our work as follows. Section 2 introduces the problem of holistic matching. Section 3 presents our methodology for creating holistic alignments from existing pairwise alignments. In Sect. 4, we discuss the experiments and results. Section 5 presents related works. Finally, Sect. 6 concludes the paper and gives future directions.

2   Problem Statement

Broadly speaking, the matching process takes as input a set of ontologies, denoted Ω, and determines as output a set of correspondences, called *alignment*. The *pairwise ontology matching* process takes as input two ontologies, $\Omega = \{O_1, O_2\}$, and determines as output a set of correspondences denoted as $A_{12} = \{c_1, c_2, ..., c_M\}$. A correspondence c_i can be defined as $<\{e_1, e_2\}, r, n>$, such that: e_1 and e_2 are ontology entities (e.g. properties, classes, instances) of O_1 and O_2, respectively; r is a relation holding between e_1 and e_2 (usually, $\equiv$, $\sqsupseteq$, $\perp$, $\sqcap$); and n is a confidence measure in the $[0, 1]$ range assigning a degree of trust on the correspondence. The higher the confidence value, the higher the likelihood that the relation holds.

We can see the pairwise matching as a special case of holistic ontology matching. The *holistic ontology matching* takes a set $\Omega = \{O_1, ..., O_N\}$ of ontologies with $N \geq 2$. It consists in determining a set of correspondences as $A_{1...N} = \{c_1, c_2, ..., c_M\}$. Each correspondence c_i is defined as $<\{e_1, ..., e_N\}, r, n>$ such as $\forall j \in [1..N], e_j \in O_j$. For our problem statement, we restrict r to the equivalence relationship between entities.

In case of $N = 3$, each correspondence c_i is defined as a triple correspondence $<\{e_1, e_2, e_3\}, \equiv, n>$ where $e_1 \in O_1$, $e_2 \in O_2$ and $e_3 \in O_3$. Triple correspondences correspond to *cliques* (i.e., a subset of vertices of an undirected graph such that every two distinct vertices in the clique are adjacent) or *Clique-relaxed graphs* as shown in Fig. 1. The main difference between both cases is the value of the confidence value, calculated taking into account the cardinality of the clique (as detailed in Sect. 3.2):

- clique correspondence is $<\{e_1, e_2, e_3\}, \equiv, 1>$
- clique-relaxed correspondence is $<\{e_1, e_2, e_3\}, \equiv, \frac{2}{3}>$.

Fig. 1. Clique-based holistic correspondence (a, left) and clique-relaxed holistic correspondence (b, right).

3   Building Holistic Alignments

In this section, we present a methodology for automatically constructing holistic alignments from available pairwise alignments. This requirement lets us to denote a *pseudo-holistic* approach. This methodology methodology is composed of two main steps:

1. building a graph of all combinations of correspondences in existing pairwise alignments;
2. building the holistic alignments according to different levels of relaxation with respect to complete graphs (cliques): clique-strict method (level 1) and clique-relaxed subgraph method (level 2). In case of level 2, we propose two sub-methods: the first method is a systematic relaxation of cliques, and the second one handles the intra-ontology choice of entities based on ontology relations.

The use of our relaxed methods is to add a complementary idea to the strict clique-approach. While consensus and alignment, on a pairwise basis, can be stated through binary acceptance (this corresponds vs. this does not correspond), we build the relaxed methods on the need to add some blurriness to account for the multiple agreements between ontologies. By using a relaxed consensus, we take into account how holistic agreements can be reached within the group; which is accounted by the first method; and by using a third ontology (WordNet), we find a method to solve consensus from within a group that would appear "natural" from an external onlooker which is here represented by WordNet, acting as a reference and external ambiguity resolver.

3.1   Step 1: Building the Graph of N Pairwise Alignments

This step aims at building a holistic graph $G_H = (V_H, E_H)$ where nodes are entities from the ontologies to be aligned, and edges are correspondences from pairwise alignments, such as:

- $V_H = \{e_{i_k} | e_{i_k} \in \cup_{i=1}^{N} O_i\}$,
- $E_H = \{(e_i, e_j) | \exists <\{e_i, e_j\}, r, n> \in A_{1..N}\}$, with $A_{1..N} = \cup_{k=1, l=k+1}^{N-1} A_{kl}$.

Remark. If we consider $N = 4$, this leads us to the group of $A_{12} \cup A_{13} \cup A_{14} \cup A_{23} \cup A_{24} \cup A_{34}$.

3.2   Step 2: Building Holistic Alignments

This section details the two methods for building the holistic alignments $A_{1...N} = \{c_1, c_2, .., c_i, ..| i \in \mathbb{N}\}$.

Each correspondence should cover the N input ontologies and should be $1:1$ holistic alignment to conserve the $1:1$ requirements of the pairwise alignments. In the following, we explain both levels of methods and the algorithms that we propose to generate the holistic alignments.

Clique-Strict Method (Level 1). The first method concerns the generation of holistic alignments composed of cliques. The cliques are complete graphs
extracted from the holistic graph G_H. The algorithm we developed consists in
searching complete subgraphs composed of N nodes belonging to the N input
ontologies. A clique is considered as the most strongest holistic correspondence,
hence it has the confidence value 1.

Remark. To find a clique in the graph G_H, we use the method *find_cliques*
from the networkx Python module[1]. The structure of the graph G_H built upon
1:1 pairwise alignments guarantees that each ontology is present only once in
the cliques. However, the networkx module can not guarantee the $1 : 1$ holistic
alignments which means that all the N input ontologies are present on the clique
results. That's why we check-up if the final selected cliques covers the N input
ontologies.

Clique-Relaxed Subgraph Method (Level 2). The clique-strict method is
too strict because we are faced most commonly to incomplete graphs that should
be part of the solutions of holistic alignments. To concretely expose the idea, we
notice that the left subgraph in Fig. 2(b) is part of the solution of the complete
graph of Fig. 2(a). Hence, we can infer from the subgraph of Fig. 2(b) a holistic
alignment with a lower level of confidence corresponding to its incompleteness
with respect to the clique.

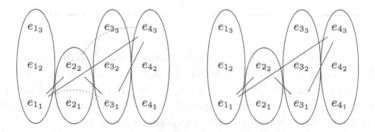

Fig. 2. (a) Example of a clique subgraph; (b) The clique-relaxed subgraph.

In order to compute the confidence of the clique-relaxed subgraph, we define
the notion of *clique-likeness*, which is the geometric distance of a subgraph compared to a clique; for instance, the level of confidence of the graph of Fig. 2(a)
is $\frac{2}{3}$. The formula is as the following for a subgraph denoted $G_i = (V_i, E_i)$:

$$clique\_likeness(G_i) = \frac{2 * |E_i|}{|V_i| * (|V_i| - 1)}$$

---

[1] https://networkx.github.io/documentation/networkx 1.0.1/reference/generated/
networkx.algorithms.clique.find_cliques.html#networkx.algorithms.clique.find_
cliques.

We rely on the *connected_component_subgraphs* method from the networkx Python module[2] to search all the subgraphs of G_H with respect to two conditions, namely that all ontologies should be represented by at least one node, and that each subgraph G_i is maximal. Based on the content of these subgraphs, we provide two methods to generate the holistic alignments.

Method 1: Clique-Relaxed Holistic Alignment Algorithm. This method is a systematic relaxation of cliques, which means that the subgraphs are incomplete cliques composed exactly of one node from the N input ontologies. This method is explained in Algorithm 1.

Algorithm 1. Clique-relaxed holistic alignment algorithm: Method 1

    Data: G_H
    Result: $A_{1..N}$
1 $A_{1..N} \leftarrow \emptyset$;
2 **foreach** $G_i \in$ *connected_component_subgraphs*(G_H) **do**
3       $//G_i = (V_i, E_i)$ is a subgraph of G_H
4       $onto \leftarrow \emptyset$;
5   **foreach** $e_{j_k} \in V_i$ **do**
6 | $onto \leftarrow onto \cup \{j\}$;
7   **end**
8   **if** $|onto| = N$ *and* $|V_i| = N$ **then**
9 | $A_{1..N} \leftarrow A_{1..N} \cup \{< V_i, \equiv, clique\_likeness(G_i) >\}$;
10   **end**
11 **end**

Method 2: Clique-Relaxed Subgraphs Based on Intra-ontology Relations. This method handles the case when the subgraphs are composed of one or several nodes from ontologies O_i, for some or all $i \in [1, N]$. The proposed method will then select only one tuple of nodes based on the intra-ontology relations and the best confidence value of *clique_likeness*.

By taking the example of Fig. 3, we notice that the subgraph have two nodes from O_1, noted e_{1_1} and e_{1_2}, so we have to choose either the solution 1, composed of the clique-relaxed $= \{e_{1_1}, e_{2_1}, e_{3_2}, e_{4_3}\}$ or solution2, composed of the clique-relaxed $= \{e_{1_2}, e_{2_1}, e_{3_2}, e_{4_3}\}$.

- For solution 1 (a), the *clique_likeness*$(G_i) = \frac{1}{3}$.
- For solution 2 (b), we propose that we can use the relationship between e_{1_1} and e_{1_2} to infer new mappings for e_{1_2}. As the $e_{1_2} \subseteq e_{1_1}$ (subclassof relation) and $<\{e_{1_1}, e_{2_1}\}, \equiv, 1>$ thus we can infer the pairwise mapping $<\{e_{1_2}, e_{2_1}\}, \equiv, 1>$. Therefore, the *clique_likeness*$(G_i) = \frac{1}{2}$.

Based on the *clique_likeness* score, we choose the solution 2 because of its higher confidence value (Fig. 4).

---

[2] https://networkx.github.io/documentation/networkx-1.9.1/.

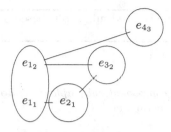

Fig. 3. Example of intra-ontology multiple choice. The circled elements belongs to the same ontologies, the black vertices shows the extra-ontological links while the blue dotted vertices shows intra-ontological links. (Color figure online)

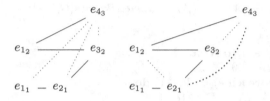

Fig. 4. (a) Solution 1 and (b) solution 2 from Fig. 6.

Algorithm 2 implements *method 2* and complements *method 1*. It can be used by pairwise tools for constructing their holistic alignments, based on the generated pairwise alignments. In this algorithm, the function named *score* calculates a score from a set of entities. For each entity, we normalize its name (lowering case, removing camel case and snake case) so that it can be seen as a sentence (or a word). Through POS, we find the most important word in such sentence, removing duplicates if any ("Conference Paper" and "Paper" are both seen as "Paper" duplicates). We then compute all the hypernyms of all the synonyms of this word, using WordNet. Then, we compute the intersection of the hypernyms of the entities of one candidate; the score being its cardinality.

In the example of Fig. 5, we illustrate the case of $N = 4$ ontologies from the OAEI Conference Track (cmt, conference, iasted and edas). We notice two possible solutions that can be proposed for the subgraph composed of the entities "Submission" (iasted), "Submitted_contribution" and "Paper" (conference), "Paper" (edas), and "Paper" (cmt). In order to find the alignment, we compute the score of the two potential clique-relaxed subgraphs which contains either the entity "Paper" or "Submitted_contribution" (conference). The retained holistic alignment is solution 1, which has the highest score; its confidence value is $\frac{3}{6} = 50\%$.

Algorithm 2. Select clique-relaxed subgraphs based on intra-ontology relations: Method 2

Data: G_H

Result: $A_{1..N}$

```
 1  A₁..ₙ ← ∅ ;
 2  foreach Gᵢ ∈ connected_component_subgraphs(Gₕ) do
 3  │   //Gᵢ = (Vᵢ, Eᵢ) is a subgraph of Gₕ
 4  │   onto ← ∅ ;
 5  │   foreach e_{jₖ} ∈ Vᵢ do
 6  │   │   onto ← onto ∪ {j} ;
 7  │   end
 8  │   if |onto| = N then
 9  │   │   if |Vᵢ| = N then
10  │   │   │   A₁..ₙ ← A₁..ₙ ∪ {¡Vᵢ, ≡, clique_likeness(Gᵢ) >};
11  │   │   end
12  │   │   else
13  │   │   │   for j ← 1 to N do
14  │   │   │   │   Eⱼ ← ∅ ;
15  │   │   │   │   foreach e_{jₖ} ∈ Vⱼ ∩ Vᵢ do
16  │   │   │   │   │   Eⱼ ← Eⱼ ∪ {e_{jₖ}}
17  │   │   │   │   end
18  │   │   │   end
19  │   │   │   s_{max} ← 0 ;
20  │   │   │   c_{max} ← ∅ ;
21  │   │   │   foreach clique ∈ ∏_{j=0}^{N} Eⱼ do
22  │   │   │   │   if score(clique) ≥ s_{max} then
23  │   │   │   │   │   s_{max} ← score(clique) ;
24  │   │   │   │   │   c_{max} ← clique ;
25  │   │   │   │   end
26  │   │   │   end
27  │   │   │   G_{max} ← (c_{max}, {(eⱼ, eₖ)|∃eⱼ ∈ c_{max}, ∃eₖ ∈ c_{max}, ∃(eⱼ, eₖ) ∈ Eᵢ}) ;
28  │   │   │   A₁..ₙ ← A₁..ₙ ∪ {< c_{max}, ≡, clique_likeness(G_{max}) >};
29  │   │   end
30  │   end
31  end
```

---

4 Experiments

4.1 Materials and Methods

Data Set. Our holistic reference data set has been constructed from the OAEI Conference data set[3], which provides real-world and expressive ontologies covering the conference organisation domain [22]. This data set is composed of 16 ontologies and a subset of 21 pairwise reference alignments involving 7 ontologies (ra1). We have applied the 3 methods described above for generating the

---

[3] http://oaei.ontologymatching.org/2017/conference/.

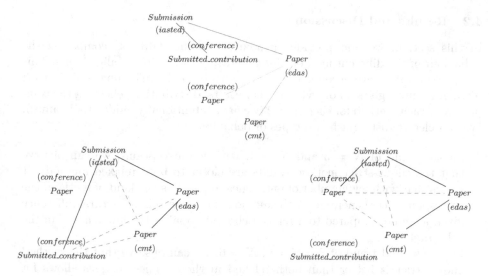

Fig. 5. (a) Original extracted subgraph, (b) method 1, (c) method 2

holistic reference alignments on the basis of ra1. Although transitive closure computed alignments for this track have been constructed and manually checked by evaluators (ra2), they are not available. The version of our holistic data set is hence based on the publicly available original alignments (ra1). All the generated alignments and the code for generating them are available online[4].

Tools. We have applied our methodology to generate holistic alignments from the available results of OAEI 2017 participating tools[5] and compared their results with the LPHOM holistic approach [12]. The available results for the following tools were considered: ALIN, AML, KEPLER, LogMap, LogMapLt, ONTMAT, POMap, SANOM, WikiV3 and XMap. Even though these tools were not developed for that purpose, their results were the only available for a baseline comparison. To the best of our knowledge very few holistic systems are available. We have run the AML-Compound tool[6], but it was not able to generate any alignment for this data set.

Evaluation Metrics. The results are discussed in terms of precision, recall and F-measure. We compare the correspondences from the reference alignment to the correspondences generated by the matchers considering an exact match. For all evaluated alignments we do not take into account their confidence.

Execution Environment. All the experiments have been run on a 32 GB RAM available, 7CPU x64 @3.6 Ghz machine. While LPHOM takes some seconds for generating the alignments, we could not compare its runtime performance with the OAEI tools (only alignments are available).

---

[4] https://github.com/PhilippeRousailleIRIT/EKAW-2018-holistic.
[5] http://oaei.ontologymatching.org/2017/conference/eval.html.
[6] https://github.com/AgreementMakerLight/AML-Compound.

4.2   Results and Discussion

In this section, we first provide an analysis of the data set, comparing the behaviour of the different methods for generating the reference alignments. This comparison takes into account the overall results of the matching tools in each setting. Figure 6 gives an overview of the results' distribution reflecting the complexity of each method for each $N > 2$ (we have intentionally hidden tool names). We can clearly distinguish two types of behaviours:

- for the trend of $N = 3$ and $N = 4$, with few exceptions, we can observe that the clique-strict method results are closer to both relaxed methods. It shows that with few number of ontologies, regardless the kind of method, the correspondences generated by the methods are close. The structural difference given a clique compared to a relaxed clique is smaller the fewer nodes in the sub-graph.
- for the second trend of $N = 5$ and $N = 6$, we can observe that the method clique-strict is better than both relaxed methods. These cliques allows for identifying the common entities shared across the ontologies. In the case of the Conference data set, by manually examining the outputs, the clique-strict alignments are composed of exact matches. It corroborates the intuition that increasing the number of nodes in a subgraph, increases the differences between their structures (cliques and relaxed cliques structures).

Second, we compare the performance of the holistic alignments generated from the pairwise ones coming from the OAEI tools, with respect to the generated holistic reference one. Although this evaluation setting may introduce a bias in the evaluation, in the lack of available fully holistic tools, it is the material

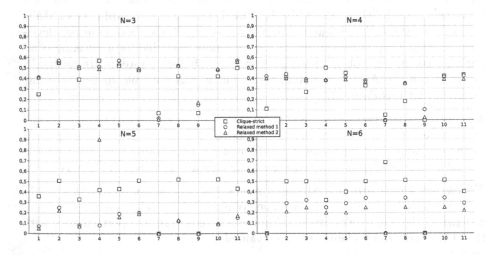

Fig. 6. Comparison of methods according to the number of input ontologies, with the number of ontologies (in abscissa) and the f-measure (in ordinate).

we have for comparison. Table 1 shows the results applying the different proposed methods for generating holistic reference alignments, varying the number of input ontologies (N). Looking at first to the holistic tool, we can observe that, although the LPHOM holistic approach does not perform very well for a small number of ontologies, it is in the top-3 (f-measure) for $N = 6$ ontologies (for all methods). As expected, the tools specifically designed for the pairwise task better perform for $N = 2$. Their performance however mostly decreases with the increasing of N (some are not able to generated alignments for $N = 6$), while LPHOM relatively maintains its performance.

Overall, as Fig. 7 shows, in terms of precision, LPHOM (.56) is of the top-4 systems (AML and ALIN .59, XMap .58 and PopMap .57). The holistic approach privileges precision in detriment of recall (.35), with coherent generated alignments. In terms of F-measure, the given results are intermediate, about .10 points (.42) compared to the best system, which is AML (.52). However, we have to keep in mind that our approach here is *pseudo*-holistic, and thus heavily influenced by the number of ontologies. As the number of ontologies increases, reaching up to 6, the F-measure decreases, showing that there are room for improvements. This can be explained due to the structures of the tasks and the way the tools work: as the matching structures differ from a strict clique approach (which, in a pairwise context, is kept all the time as pairwise alignments are cliques), the limits between matches become blurrier. Most tools will easily find a similarity between two entities, and two groups of entities, but the transient aspect of the pseudo-holistic relaxation cannot be easily translated in terms of strictness. As such, when trying to assess all ontologies at once, only the main and nearly exact matches remain; while when computed pairwise, this information cannot be extrapolated as the similarity matrix does not incorporate the new similarities. Finally, we are ware that the performance of the different matchers compared to LPHOM are not as significant as if our experiments were ran using specifically holistic matchers. However, they are significant enough to show that the holistic matching task has inherent properties.

Table 1. Evaluation results on F-measure. N indicates the number of input ontologies. Higher is better.

Method	Clique-strict					Clique-relaxed: method 1					Clique-relaxed: method 2				
N	*2*	*3*	*4*	*5*	*6*	*2*	*3*	*4*	*5*	*6*	*2*	*3*	*4*	*5*	*6*
ALIN	.30	.24	.11	.36	.00	.42	.42	**.43**	.06	.00	.41	.42	**.41**	.05	.00
AML	**.62**	**.55**	.43	**.52**	.50	**.71**	**.56**	.44	.25	.29	**.71**	**.54**	.41	**.23**	.22
LPHOM	.47	.38	.17	.34	**.50**	.58	.50	.40	.10	**.33**	.58	.49	.38	.09	**.25**
KEPLER	.54	**.56**	**.49**	.43	.33	.59	.50	.39	.10	.25	.59	.48	.37	.10	.20
LogMap	**.61**	**.53**	**.44**	.44	.40	**.67**	**.56**	.41	.19	.29	**.67**	**.54**	.38	**.16**	.20
LogMapLt	.54	.47	.35	.52	.50	.59	.49	.38	.19	**.33**	.58	.48	.36	**.18**	**.25**
OntoMap	.22	.06	.03	.00	**.67**	.03	.00	.00	.00	.00	.03	.00	.00	.00	.00
PopMap	.50	.42	.15	**.53**	.50	.62	.52	.36	.13	**.33**	.62	.50	.34	.12	**.25**
Sanom	.28	.06	.00	.00	.00	.37	.14	.03	.00	.00	.37	.13	.03	.00	.00
Wikiv3	.49	.44	**.43**	**.53**	**.50**	.57	.48	.41	.09	.33	.57	.47	**.39**	.09	.25
XMap	**.59**	.50	.43	.45	.40	**.69**	**.56**	.42	.15	.29	**.69**	**.54**	.39	.14	.22

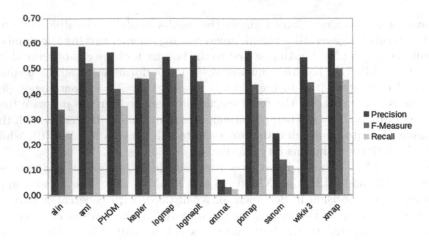

Fig. 7. Average results (precision, recall and f-measure)

5 Related Work

In this section we describe the main related work on (i) holistic approaches and
(ii) holistic ontology reference alignments.

Holistic Approaches. As stated in Sect. 1, most works on holistic matching
give special attention to attribute matching [6,7,19]. These approaches handle simple attributes compared to the more structured schemes of ontologies.
Under a different perspective, a cross-domain holistic approach for matching
large ontologies has been proposed in [5]. In [15], the holistic AML-Compound
system extends the pairwise AML system adapting WordNet similarities and
Jaccard indexes. Recently, an instance-based distributed holistic approach is
presented in [13], which is based on a clustering of entities representing the
same real-world object. Differently from [5–7,19], LPHOM is not restricted to
attributes, while we do not perform cross-domain holistic matching as [5]. Compared to [7], LPHOM can also return simple and multiple correspondences and it
is extensible to new constraints, differently from [15]. As some pairwise matchers
[10,11], we adopt constraints that reduce the possibility of generating incoherent
alignments. With respect to the matching strategies we apply, while the selection strategy in [21] is based on paths in the graph, we reduce the selection to
the maximum-weighted bipartite graph matching (MWGM) problem like OLA
[4] and we adopt a different structural similarity strategy from [8]. Compared
to OLA we do not compute structural similarities but encode structural properties as linear constraints. As CODI [9], we perform both structural matching
(without additional structural similarity computation) and alignment extraction
phases. Unlike CODI whose pairwise approach is reduced to a NP-Hard problem, our solution extends a polynomial problem in both pairwise and holistic
versions [12]. In a holistic and monolingual setting, we apply a combinatorial
optimisation problem using linear programming, as done in [16] in pairwise. The

constraints proposed by [16] for multiple correspondences, can be simply added to our model to enhance the matching of multiple correspondences in the relaxed version of our model.

Holistic Reference Alignments. While systematic evaluation of matching approaches has been dedicated to pairwise systems[7], there is a lack of reference alignments on which these approaches can be systematically evaluated. We argue that fostering the development of these approaches depends on the availability of such data sets. Current holistic approaches are (manually) evaluated on data sets used in the context of the tool development. The closer approach to ours is from [15]. The authors propose to exploit OBO cross-products to create ternary compound alignments between ontologies, in order to create a benchmark. They have created a set of seven cross-products collections each with at least 100 definitions corresponding to ternary compound correspondences. Differently from [15], our correspondences do not involve any logical construction and are not limited to ternary composition of ontologies. This could be rather seeing as generating complex correspondences [20]. Finally, in [13], a reference alignment for multi-source clustering of large data sets from the geographic and music domains has been proposed. They evaluate the efficiency and scalability of the distributed holistic clustering for large data sets with millions of entities from the two domains. While they handle larger data sets focusing on linking discovery, our approach is limited to schema matching [1].

6 Concluding Remarks and Future Work

This paper has proposed a methodology for constructing holistic alignments from existing pairwise alignments. The approach relies on graph cliques involving a different number of ontologies. We applied our approach for generating holistic reference alignments from the original Conference reference alignments. These alignments have been the basis for evaluating alignments from a specific designed matcher and from OAEI matchers, in a holistic setting. Although we propose a pseudo-holistic approach, it is a first step towards the holistic ontology matching evaluation, open new challenges in the field.

As future work, we plan to extend the evaluation of this data set with a manual verification as well as to work on the transitive closure computed alignments. We intend as well to work on other kind of relation than equivalences. This work also opens additional perspectives in the field, once current solutions to manage and evaluate ontology matching (i.e., Alignment API) and weighted and semantic precision and recall measures are limited to deal with pairwise matching.

Acknowledgement. This research received financial support by the SmartOccitania project from the France's Strategic Investment Program (Programme d'investissements d'avenir - PIA) and the French Environment & Energy Management Agency (ADEME).

---

[7] http://oaei.ontologymatching.org/.

References

1. Berro, A., Megdiche, I., Teste, O.: A linear program for holistic matching: assessment on schema matching benchmark. In: Chen, Q., Hameurlain, A., Toumani, F., Wagner, R., Decker, H. (eds.) DEXA 2015. LNCS, vol. 9262, pp. 383–398. Springer, Cham (2015). https://doi.org/10.1007/978-3-319-22852-5_33
2. Euzenat, J., Meilicke, C., Stuckenschmidt, H., Shvaiko, P., Trojahn, C.: Ontology alignment evaluation initiative: six years of experience. J. Data Semant. **15**, 158–192 (2011)
3. Euzenat, J., Shvaiko, P.: Ontology Matching, 2nd edn. Springer, Heidelberg (2013). https://doi.org/10.1007/978-3-642-38721-0
4. Euzenat, J., Valtchev, P.: Similarity-based ontology alignment in OWL-Lite. In: Proceedings of the 16th European Conference on Artificial Intelligence, pp. 333–337 (2004)
5. Gruetze, T., Böhm, C., Naumann, F.: Holistic and scalable ontology alignment for linked open data. In: Proceedings of the 5th Linked Data on the Web Workshop at the 21th WWW (2012)
6. He, B., Chang, K.C.-C.: Statistical schema matching across web query interfaces. In: Proceedings of the 2003 ACM SIGMOD International Conference on Management of Data, SIGMOD 2003, pp. 217–228. ACM 92003)
7. He, B., Chang, K.C.-C., Han, J.: Discovering complex matchings across web query interfaces: a correlation mining approach. In: Proceedings of the 20th International Conference on Knowledge Discovery and Data Mining, pp. 148–157 (2004)
8. Hu, W., Jian, N., Qu, Y., Wang, Y.: GMO: a graph matching for ontologies. In: K-Cap 2005 Workshop on Integrating Ontologies 2005, pp. 43–50 (2005)
9. Huber, J., Sztyler, T., Nößner, J., Meilicke, C.: CODI: combinatorial optimization for data integration: results for OAEI 2011. In: Proceedings of the 6th International Workshop on Ontology Matching (2011)
10. Jean-Mary, Y., Shironoshita, E., Kabuka, M.: Ontology matching with semantic verification. Web Semant. Sci. Serv. Agents World Wide Web **7**(3), 235–251 (2009)
11. Jiménez-Ruiz, E., Cuenca Grau, B.: LogMap: logic-based and scalable ontology matching. ISWC 2011. LNCS, vol. 7031, pp. 273–288. Springer, Heidelberg (2011). https://doi.org/10.1007/978-3-642-25073-6_18
12. Megdiche, I., Teste, O., Trojahn, C.: An extensible linear approach for holistic ontology matching. In: Groth, P. (ed.) ISWC 2016. LNCS, vol. 9981, pp. 393–410. Springer, Cham (2016). https://doi.org/10.1007/978-3-319-46523-4_24
13. Nentwig, M., Groß, A., Möller, M., Rahm, E.: Distributed holistic clustering on linked data. In: Panetto, H., et al. (eds.) On the Move to Meaningful Internet Systems. OTM 2017 Conferences. OTM 2017. Lecture Notes in Computer Science, vol 10574, pp. 371–382. Springer, Cham (2017). https://doi.org/10.1007/978-3-319-69459-7_25
14. Oliveira, D., Pesquita, C.: Compound matching of biomedical ontologies. In: Proceedings of the International Conference on Biomedical Ontology, ICBO 2015, Lisbon, Portugal, 27–30 July 2015 (2015)
15. Pesquita, C., Cheatham, M., Faria, D., Barros, J., Santos, E., Couto, F.M.: Building reference alignments for compound matching of multiple ontologies using obo cross-products. In: Proceedings of the 9th International Workshop on Ontology Matching, pp. 172–173 (2014)
16. Prytkova, N., Weikum, G., Spaniol, M.: Aligning multi-cultural knowledge taxonomies by combinatorial optimization. In: Proceedings of the 24th International Conference on World Wide Web, pp. 93–94. ACM (2015)

17. Rahm, E.: Towards large-scale schema and ontology matching. In: Bellahsene Z., Bonifati A., Rahm E. (eds.) Schema Matching and Mapping. Data-Centric Systems and Applications. Springer, Heidelberg (2011). https://doi.org/10.1007/978-3-642-16518-4_1

18. Saleem, K., Bellahsene, Z., Hunt, E.: PORSCHE: Performance ORiented SCHEma mediation. Inf. Syst. **33**(7–8), 637–657 (2008)

19. Su, W., Wang, J., Lochovsky, F.: Holistic schema matching for web query interfaces. In: Ioannidis, Y., et al. (eds.) EDBT 2006. LNCS, vol. 3896, pp. 77–94. Springer, Heidelberg (2006). https://doi.org/10.1007/11687238_8

20. Thiéblin, É., Haemmerlé, O., Hernandez, N., Trojahn, C.: Towards a complex alignment evaluation dataset. In: OM Workshop at ISWC, pp. 217–218 (2017)

21. Xiang, C., Chang, B., Sui, Z.: An ontology matching approach based on affinity-preserving random walks. In: Proceedings of the 24th International Conference on Artificial Intelligence, pp. 1471–1477 (2015)

22. Zamazal, O., Svtek,V.: The ten-year ontofarm and its fertilization within the onto-sphere. Web Semant. **43**(C), 46–53 (2017)

Prominence and Dominance in Networks

Andreas Schmidt$^{(\boxtimes)}$ and Gerd Stumme

Knowledge and Data Engineering Group, University of Kassel,
Wilhelmshöher Allee 73, 34121 Kassel, Germany
{schmidt,stumme}@cs.uni-kassel.de

Abstract. Topographic prominence and dominance were recently developed to quantify the relative importance of mountain peaks. Instead of simply using the height to characterize a mountain, they provide a more meaningful description based on vertical and horizontal distances in the neighborhood. In this paper, we propose structural prominence and dominance for networks, an adaptation of the topographic measures, for the detection of nodes with strong local importance. We create a network "landscape" which is generated by a node's height and distance to other nodes in the network. We ground our proposed measures on the task of predicting award winners with high and sustainable impact in a co-authorship network. Our experiments show that our measures provide information about a graph, that is not provided by other graph measures.

Keywords: Network analysis · Knowledge discovery · Author impact

1 Introduction

The height of a mountain is a fundamental attribute, that was used for ages by mountaineers to characterize the mountain peaks all around the world. Recently, topographic prominence and dominance have been proposed to get a more accurate description of a mountain's characteristic. In this paper, we transfer the idea of mountain measurement to network analysis. We adapt topographic prominence and dominance, by presuming, that each node is already associated with a height and a distance to other nodes in the network. In contrast to centrality [7–9], our measures are designed to find nodes with strong *local* importance, which we refer to as structural prominence and dominance.

Recently, there has been a controversy about the appropriateness of using only mountain height, as measured by the elevation above the sea level, for comparison with other mountains, because there are regions that are inherently higher than others. For instance, Cho Oyu is among the top ten highest mountains of the world, but much less prominent than Mont Blanc. Based on this observation, two new topographic measures were proposed: prominence, which expresses the relative height of a peak compared to the neighborhood, and dominance, which measures the minimum distance to the next geographic position with at least the same height [11, 17, 18, 21].

© Springer Nature Switzerland AG 2018
C. Faron Zucker et al. (Eds.): EKAW 2018, LNAI 11313, pp. 370–385, 2018.
https://doi.org/10.1007/978-3-030-03667-6_24

Topographic prominence and dominance are illustrated in Fig. 1. Imagine the sea level raised to the height of the greatest peak. Then, by lowering the sea level, further peaks appear and get connected to each other at a certain sea level. The topographic prominence is then the height difference between the peak and the sea level that reveals the connection to a terrain of equal height. In the same way, topographic dominance is measured by shortest horizontal distance to a terrain with at least the same height.

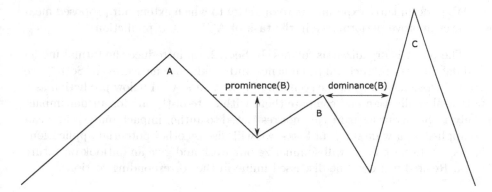

Fig. 1. Illustration of topographic prominence and dominance with three peaks A, B and C. The dominance of B is measured by the vertical distance to the closest point of any peak C, which has at least the same height as B. Prominence is the maximum height difference on a path to a point with at least the same height. If multiple paths exist, the path with the minimum descent is selected. Therefore, prominence of B is defined by the path to A in favor of C.

In this paper, we transfer the idea of topographic prominence and dominance to network analysis and propose measures for finding *outstanding* nodes, i. e., nodes with strong local performance. To assess our measures, we deploy them in Sect. 3, on a scientometrics task: Our aim is to show that our measures provide information about a graph, that is not provided by other graph measures. Therefore, we will set up the classification task of predicting the next year's award winners in an academic co-authorship network. We will use the ACM fellowship award[1] [20] as a ground truth, which is a prize for major and sustainable contributions of an academic author in a research field within Computer Science. By performing an evaluation on different subsets of factors we verify that our measures contribute to the prediction of ACM fellows: First, we investigate the individual performance of our structural prominence and dominance measures compared to established measures for author impact. In a second experiment, we show that our measures contain information that is not provided by other measures and therefore boost performance when they are paired with other factor groups. Finally, we will perform a correlation analysis of structural prominence

---

[1] https://awards.acm.org/fellows.

and dominance compared to established measures, to show that these measures provide indeed different information.

The contribution of this paper is three-fold:

- We adapt topographic prominence and dominance to network analysis and present a formalization that is capable of a generic height and distance function.
- We ground the measures on the problem of ACM fellow prediction in a large scale, real world dataset.
- We perform three experiments to quantify to which extent our proposed measures improve performance in the task of ACM fellow prediction.

The paper is organized as follows. In Sect. 2, we introduce the formal model and definitions of structural prominence and dominance measures. In Sect. 3, we ground these measures in the scenario of next year's ACM fellow prediction as a potential application and compare them with state-of-the-art for author impact analysis. Since our measures are not restricted to author impact analysis and can be applied on a wide range of tasks, we will discuss other potential applications in Sect. 4. In Sect. 5, we will summarize our work and give an outlook on future work. Related work will be discussed inline in the corresponding sections.

2   Definitions

In this section, we present the formal setting and a generic definition for the structural prominence and dominance measures. Different aspects of prominence have been addressed before: For instance, Wasserman and Faust [26] consider an actor to be prominent if the ties of the actor make him particularly visible to the other actors in the network. Knoke and Burt [14] coined the term "prominence" index for a function $p\colon V \to \mathbb{R}_{\geq 0}$, which ranks nodes in a network (V, E) according to their structural properties. According to Brandes et al. [2] "prominence" indices can be divided into two groups, based on status and centrality. To make a distinction from these measures, we suggest to refer to *topographic* prominence and dominance in the context of mountains and *structural* prominence and dominance in the context of networks. Whenever we talk about prominence and dominance without qualifying adjective in the sequel, we refer to the latter.

2.1   Height and Distance

We start with the introduction of a height and a distance function for graphs. Let $G := (V, E)$ be a finite, undirected connected (but not necessarily weighted) graph with vertices V and edges $E \subseteq \{\{u, v\}\colon u, v \in V\}$. In the case of an unconnected graph, we will study each connected component separately.

Let $h\colon V \to \mathbb{R}_0^+$ be a function; we call $h(v)$ the height of node v. Furthermore, let $\mathrm{dist}\colon V \times V \to \mathbb{R}_0^+$ be a semimetric, i.e. $\mathrm{dist}(u, v)$ is positive definite $(\mathrm{dist}(u, v) \geq 0, \mathrm{dist}(u, v) = 0 \Leftrightarrow u = v)$, symmetric $(\mathrm{dist}(u, v) = \mathrm{dist}(v, u))$, but the triangle inequality does not necessarily hold. We call $\mathrm{dist}(u, v)$ the distance between two nodes u and $v \in V$.

For convenience, we also define a neighborhood function $N(v) := \{w \in V : \{v, w\} \in E\}$. Let $S(u, v)$ be the set of all shortest paths (with respect to dist) between nodes $u, v \in V$ and let $S(u)$ be the set of all shortest paths from u to any node v with $h(v) \geq h(u)$, i. e., $S(u) := \cup_{v \in G\{u\}, h(v) \geq h(u)} S(u, v)$.

Our formal model is able to handle different height and distance functions. The distance between two nodes can be measured in the (weighted) graph, e.g. by shortest path distance, or an external data source which provides attributes to measure distance or similarity, e.g. bag of words on documents, content of tweets, web pages, hash tags, amount of third-party funds or the income of an actor. Furthermore, the geographic coordinates and timezone information can be used to compute a distance between entities based on their geo-location. In our application, the distance between two nodes is given by the shortest path length in the graph.

Depending on the type of analysis, one can also choose different height functions based on (weighted) graph properties, e.g. centrality or the (in-/out-)degree of vertices, or using external data sources as a height function, e.g. the number of followers of a user on Twitter. In our application, we consider different author impact measures as height functions, which will be introduced in Sect. 3.1.

Next, we define structural prominence and dominance measures for a node in a graph based on a height and a distance function. Note, that we will use the terms graph and network interchangeable and refer to network whenever it is more appropriate, especially in the context of social network analysis.

2.2 Structural Prominence and Dominance

Structural Prominence. With prominence we measure the height difference on a specific shortest path to a node with at least the same height. This is inspired by topographic prominence, which is defined as the minimum number of meters a mountaineer has to descend when going to a terrain of at least the same height. Formally, we define the prominence of a node $u \in V$ as

$$\mathrm{prominence}(u) := \begin{cases} \min_{P \in S(u)} \max_{w \in P} (h(u) - h(w)) & \text{if } \exists v \in G \backslash \{u\} : h(v) \geq h(u) \\ h(u) & \text{else} \end{cases}$$

Note that dominance accounts only for nodes with lower height than u and can not be lower than 0, because of the maximum along the path P with $u \in P$. Furthermore, there can exist multiple shortest paths between u and v. In this case, we choose the path where the maximum height difference on the path is minimal. This is inspired by a mountaineer who wants to find a way from one peak to another with the least amount of effort, e.g. by choosing the path with the least descent. Similar to topographic prominence, the structural prominence describes the elevation of a node relative to its neighborhood.

There are two special cases for prominence: If a node has the maximum height in the graph, i. e. there exists no other node with at least the same height, the prominence simply becomes the height of the node. This is motivated by a convention of topographic prominence, where the prominence of the highest peak is defined as the difference to sea level. Furthermore, we set prominence to 0, if a direct neighbor of u is higher, which equals to a point the slope of a mountain.

Structural Dominance. With dominance we measure the shortest distance to other nodes of at least the same height. This is inspired by topographic dominance which expresses in which vertical range a peak outperforms its neighborhood. We define the dominance of a node $u \in V$ formally as follows

$$\text{dominance}(u) := \begin{cases} \min\limits_{v \in G \backslash \{u\}:\, h(v) \geq h(u)} \text{dist}(u, v) & \text{if } \exists v \in G \backslash \{u\}:\, h(v) \geq h(u) \\ \max\limits_{v \in G} \text{dist}(u, v) & \text{else} \end{cases}$$

Intuitively, a node is more dominant if nodes with equal or higher height are "far away" from it. So if a node has the greatest height of all nodes in the graph component, its dominance becomes equal to the maximum distance to any other node in the graph. In our application, the distance between two nodes is given by the shortest path length in the graph.

2.3 Further Measures Inspired by Prominence and Dominance

The following measures were inspired by topographic prominence and dominance, but not previously used for the measurement of mountains. With these measures we express the relative position of a node in the height hierarchy. So we developed three measures to quantify the position of a node, relative to its direct neighborhood by counting the number of higher and lower neighbors.

Higher Neighbors. Measures the ordinal position of a node's height compared to the height of its neighbors. For a node $u \in V$ it is defined as

$$N_{\text{higher}}(u) := |\{v \in N(u):\, h(v) \geq h(u)\}|$$

The idea behind the measure is that a node is locally important if the number of higher neighbors is low. We use $h(v) \geq h(u)$ instead of $h(v) > h(u)$, because dominance is also restricted by nodes with at least the same height.

Lower Neighbors. Measures the opposite of higher neighbors, i. e. we count the number of neighbors with lower height:

$$N_{\text{lower}}(u) := |\{v \in N(u):\, h(v) < h(u)\}|$$

The measure is motivated by the idea that a node has local importance if the number of lower neighbors is high. Conceptually, the higher and lower neighbors measures are related to degree centrality [8] - which is the sum of both -, but provide more information by dividing the neighborhood into two distinct groups.

Neighbors Ratio. The idea behind neighbors ratio is, that a node is important if the number of lower neighbors is high and the number of higher neighbors is low. We define neighbors ratio as follows:

$$N_{\text{ratio}}(u) := \frac{N_{\text{lower}}(u)}{N_{\text{higher}}(u) + 1}$$

We add 1 in the denominator to account for the node u, which is at least as high as itself and not included in the set of neighbors. This measure is in particular able to differentiate between nodes that are "on a slope".

3   Grounding of Prominence and Dominance

In this Section we will perform a formal validation of our structural prominence and dominance measures on a co-authorship graph, as an instance of a potential application. Our aim is to show that our measures provide information about a graph, that is not provided by other graph measures. To verify that our proposed measures are in line with our intended modeling, we ground them on the ACM fellowship award [20].

The ACM fellowship is an award that yearly honors researchers for outstanding and sustainable accomplishments in computer science and information technology. A candidate is considered for fellowship if he/she is nominated by an ACM professional member. The nomination has to be accompanied by five endorsers which are also ACM professional members and familiar with the candidate's work. Furthermore, the nominator has to be "senior enough ... to make a credible case ... of the candidates work"[2]. The formal requirement for the candidate is a continuous ACM professional membership for five years and "a sustained level of contribution over time, with clear impact that extends well beyond his/her own organization" (see footnote 2). Candidates are reviewed by the fellow committee and selected according to standards of accomplishments and leadership.

Our evaluation is based on the assumption that the fellows should also be outstanding according to our measures. We know that global factors like the publication and citation count play an important role in the nomination of ACM fellows, but nevertheless we argue, that an author is more likely to be considered for fellowship, if he/she outperforms also locally other (co-)authors in a research area. Having a high publication/citation count is not sufficient when there is a higher-rated author nearby - just like Mount Everest's south summit is not considered being outstanding or prominent. To investigate the importance and predictive power of the structural prominence and dominance measures, we set up a classification task, where we want to predict the fellowship of authors in a co-authorship network, based on a model created on data of the previous year. We compare our structural prominence and dominance measures with state-of-the-art measures for network analysis and author impact. We will recap author

---

[2] https://awards.acm.org/fellows/nominations.

impact measures in the next Section and assume that the reader is familiar with centrality-based measures for network analysis.

3.1   Author Impact Measures

Many measures have been proposed to capture the notion of author impact. One of the key aspects of a scientist's work life is the reputation that is accumulated by writing publications that frequently get cited [19]. Therefore, most measures have focused either on the number of publications, the number of citations or a combination of both. In this section, we will briefly recap the most popular measures for author impact analysis.

Formally, we have a set A of authors, a set P of publications and a binary authorship relation $R_{\text{author}} \subseteq A \times P$. Furthermore, the binary citation relation $R_{\text{cite}} \subseteq P \times P$ captures that p got cited by q iff $(p,q) \in R_{\text{cite}}$. For convenience, we define a function that counts the number of tuples in a generic binary relation R which contains an element e:

$$\text{count}(R, e) := |\{(x, y) \in R \colon x = e\}|$$

Publications. The number of publications is a simple indicator for the author's productivity. For a given authorship relation R_{author} and an author $a \in A$, the publication count refers to the total number of publications related to a, i.e.

$$\text{publications}(a) := \text{count}(R_{\text{author}}, a)$$

Citations. Another simple indicator for the reputation of an author is the number of citations that refer to the author's publication. The citation count for a given authorship relation R_{author}, citation relation R_{cite} and author $a \in A$ is the total number of all publications that reference the publications of a, i.e.

$$\text{citations}(a) := \sum_{(a,p) \in R_{\text{author}}} \text{count}(R_{\text{cite}}, p)$$

h-index. The h-index was proposed by Hirsch [12] as a measure to quantify the productivity of a researcher by the citation performance of the n most cited papers of an author. It is defined as the largest number n such that there exist at least n publications of an author $a \in A$ that have at least been cited n times each, i.e.

$$\text{h-index}(a) := \max_{n \in \mathbb{N}_0}(\{n \colon |\{(a,p) \in R_{\text{author}} \colon \text{citations}(p) \geq n\}| \geq n\})$$

g-index. The g-index was introduced by Egghe [5] to improve the h-index by aggregating the citations of the g most cited papers. Egghe argued that the h-index is insensitive to one or several outstandingly highly cited papers and suggested to accumulate the number of citations. The g-index is defined as the largest number g such that there exist at least g publications of an author that have been cited all together at least g^2 times: Let $P_g \subseteq \{p: (a,p) \in R_{\text{author}}\}$ be the set of g most cited papers from author a. Then the g-index is defined as

$$\text{g-index}(a) := \max_{g \in \mathbb{N}_0}(\{g: g^2 \leq \sum_{p \in P_g} \text{citations}(p)\})$$

Years. The number of active years of a researcher is not directly related to the impact of an author. However, it can be a proxy for the experience and endurance of a researcher, and therefore a meaningful factor for author impact analysis. Formally, we define a function year: $P \to \mathbb{N}$ which maps each publication to the year when it has been published. Then the number of active years of an author is defined as

$$\text{years}(a) := max(\{\text{year}(p): (a,p) \in R_{\text{author}}\}) - min(\{\text{year}(p): (a,p) \in R_{\text{author}}\})$$

3.2   Experiments

Dataset. In our experiments we used publication datasets from DBLP[3] created on 2018-05-01 and Microsoft Academic Graph[4] (MAG) created on 2017-06-09. We selected authors as provided by DBLP and joined their publications in DBLP with the citation information in MAG. As join attribute we used DOI when it was available and used the publication title as a fallback. With this approach we could match 87% of the publication data in DBLP. The characteristics of the joined dataset are given in Table 1.

Table 1. Characteristics of the dataset up to year 2016

	$|A|$	$|R_{\text{author}}|$	$|P|$	$|R_{\text{cite}}|$	$|\{p : (p,q) \in R_{\text{cite}}\}|$
DBLP	2.080.857	12.054.258	2.969.723		
DBLP ⋈ MAG	1.592.565	7.765.656	2.595.221	42.155.445	2.056.242

Next, we matched the official list of ACM fellows[5] to our dataset and identified 893 fellowship authors from the beginning of 1995 to the end of 2016 in our dataset. We created a dataset for each year and labeled authors as a fellow, if they received the fellowship in the corresponding year.

To compute the measures described in Sects. 2 and 3.1, we extracted the authorship and citation relation for the years 1995 to 2016 and constructed the co-authorship graph of all authors, which had at least one publication until the

---

[3] http://dblp.org/xml/release/.
[4] https://www.openacademic.ai/oag/.
[5] https://awards.acm.org/fellows/award-winners.

corresponding year. We verified the quality of the dataset, e.g. by comparing top ranked authors for h-index to the manually created list of Jens Palsberg[6].

In our experiments, we considered all measures from Sect. 3.1 as a height function, and shortest path length in the graph for distance computation. We also computed further factors based on centrality, publication years and shortest path distances to previous fellows in the graph. Since we could not approximate betweenness and closeness centrality [3] due to high computational complexity for such a large network size, we used only degree and eigenvector centrality in our experiments to compare against. The factors used in our experiment are listed in Table 2.

Table 2. Factors for ACM fellow prediction with corresponding groups

Group	Factor	Description
Prominence	Prominence	Adapted topographic prominence and dominance
	Dominance	
	Higher neighbors	Inspired by topographic prominence and dominance
	Lower neighbors	
	Neighbors ratio	
Impact	#publications	Number of publications
	#citations	Total number of citations
	h-index	As proposed by [12]
	g-index	As proposed by [5]
	$i10$-index	Number of publications with at least 10 citations
Years	Min year	Number of years since first publication
	Max year	Number of years since last publication
	Years	Number of years between first and last publication
Centrality	Degree centrality	As proposed by [8]
	Eigenvector centrality	As proposed by [9]
Fellow	Fellow distance	Shortest path distance to previous fellows

Classification Setting. We formulate the task of predicting the next year's ACM fellows as a binary classification problem. In average only 39 authors receive the ACM fellowship per year. So proportionally, the classification task is highly imbalanced, which can lead to reduced performance. We tried to tackle the problem with oversampling, undersampling and cost-sensitive methods [10]. We found that informed undersampling in conjunction with an ensemble of estimators as proposed by [15] worked best: The BalanceCascade algorithm is an approach that systematically selects samples from the majority class to undersample. The idea behind the algorithm is that a training instance is redundant, if a classifier trained on a different subset of instances correctly classifies the

---

[6] http://web.cs.ucla.edu/~palsberg/h-number.html (accessed on 2018-05-09).

training instance. The algorithm iteratively creates models with undersampled training sets and combines the vote of all models to predict the final class. The final prediction will only be positive, if the prediction of each individual models is positive. For estimators in the ensemble, we tried different types of classification models. We experimented with logistic regression with L2 regularization, k nearest neighbors (knn) with 5 nearest neighbors, svm with radial kernel and random forest with 24 estimators. Note that our aim is not to find the best classifier, but to show that a classifier improves when making use of our new measures.

We created an artificial scenario with the task to predict fellows in a set of 1000 nominations. With artificial we mean that this scenario is not real, but since it is not our task to predict nominations we used this approach, because nomination data of fellows is not freely available. For each of the years 1996 to 2016, we created 1000 nominations, included all fellows of year t and sampled non-fellow authors for the rest of the nominations. Then, the task is to predict all fellows in the nominations for year t given a classification model trained on data up to year $t - 1$.

Evaluation Metrics. In the evaluation, we wanted to answer the question: *How meaningful are the structural prominence and dominance measures for the identification of ACM Fellows?* Therefore, we selected average precision [1] as a metric, to account for the fraction of correct predicted fellows at different classifier probability levels. First, we compute the set of distinct probabilities of our classifier model and sort them in descending order to obtain a sequence of n probabilities $P = (p_1, ..., p_n)$. Let A_i be the set of predicted authors with classifier probability $p \geq p_i$ and F the set of true fellows. We compute average precision as:

$$\text{AP} := \sum_{i=2}^{n} \left(\text{recall}_i - \text{recall}_{i-1}\right) \text{precision}_i = \sum_{i=2}^{n} \left(\frac{|A_i \cap F|}{|F|} - \frac{|A_{i-1} \cap F|}{|F|}\right) \frac{|A_i \cap F|}{|A_i|}$$

Note that only classifier probabilities with changes in recall contribute to the average precision. Average precision summarizes the performance as given by a precision-recall curve by approximating the area under the curve. We also experimented with other metrics like roc auc, which shows the ability of the classifier to rank the positive instances relative to the negative instances [6], but found that they were not adequate for our classification problem, because the number of positive class samples is very low compared to the negative class (in average 39 fellows per year). So our problem is more like finding the needle in a haystack, where average precision is more appropriate.

In our experiments, we calculated the average precision for each year and computed the overall average precision by taking the arithmetic mean, which is equal to mean average precision. Following best practices for machine learning evaluation [13], we repeated our experiments and performed a one-sided pairwise t-test with $p < 0.001$ for significance. We will give further details in the following sections.

3.3   Analysis of Single Factor Contribution

First, we were interested in the predictive power of each individual factor for next year's fellows. Therefore, we wanted to answer the question to which extent our structural prominence and dominance measures contribute to the prediction task. In this experiment, we selected logistic regression as a model type, because logistic regression is capable to produce meaningful results with single factors, in contrast to other model types like random forest.

For each factor in Table 2, we created an individual model for the years 1995 to 2015 and measured the model's performance on the nominations in the next year. The results are shown in Table 3. We considered all the factors from Sect. 3.1 as possible height functions. Furthermore, we repeated our experiments 50 times with different subsets used for informed undersampling and averaged the performance over all years and repetitions.

Table 3. Average precision of individual factors with Logistic Regression. The first column shows individual performance, while the other columns show the performance of structural prominence and dominance measures when using the corresponding factor as a height function. We considered all the factors from Sect. 3.1 as possible height functions. The best performing height function for each measure is labeled in bold.

		Prominence	Dominance	Higher neighbors	Lower neighbors	Neighbors ratio
g-index	0.772	**0.088**	0.078	0.236	0.679	**0.545**
h-index	0.766	**0.088**	0.077	0.237	0.679	0.543
#publications	0.684	0.080	0.077	0.316	0.665	0.473
Years	0.559	0.072	0.084	0.291	**0.687**	0.497
#citations	0.143	0.081	**0.086**	**0.562**	0.513	0.162

The results in the first column confirm that h- and g-index capture the notion of author impact very well, because both factors had the highest average precision in our experiment and similar performance, when they were used as a height function for structural prominence and dominance measures. To our surprise, #citations performed poor on its own, but increased performance when it was used as a height function for higher neighbors. This indicates that local measures - like the number of neighbors with more citations - can indeed outperform global factors.

Altogether, our structural prominence and dominance measures achieved low performance as a single factor. We assume that the local properties of these measures are too strict to identify fellows on their own. Nevertheless, we argue that an author is more likely to be considered for fellowship, if he/she locally outperforms other (co-)authors in a research area. Therefore, we investigated the performance of structural prominence and dominance measures in combination with other factors in the next section.

3.4   Analysis of Group Performance

In the second analysis, we adapted the approach of Dong et al. [4], who analyzed the contribution of factors on a group level by using a "jackknife" approach [22]. The rationale for this experiment is that a group of factors is considered important, if the performance drops significantly without the corresponding group. In our experiment, we used a dual formulation: By adding the group of structural prominence measures to any of the other groups, we measure the increase in average precision and therefore the contribution of our measures to the classification task.

First, we defined groups of factors which share the same type of information, e.g. we created a group for author impact measures including h-index, #publications and #citations, because they are all based on the assumption that author impact is captured by number of publications/citations.The groups are listed in Table 2.

In our experiments, we measured the increase in average precision when prominence measures are added to any of the other groups. We considered all the factors from Sect. 3.1 as a height function for prominence measures, but will only report results for g-index, because we found that differences to other height functions were only marginal. To rule out effects of randomness, we repeated our experiments 25 times and performed a one-sided pairwise t-test with $p < 0.001$ to check for significance. The results are listed in Table 4.

Table 4. Average precision of factor groups. For structural prominence and dominance measures we used g-index as a height function. Numbers in bold show significant changes in classification performance according to one-sided pairwise t-test with $p < 0.001$.

	Logistic regression	knn	svm	Random forest
Prominence	0.674	0.561	0.657	0.610
Impact	0.752	0.615	0.766	0.704
Impact + Prominence	0.725	**0.638**	0.760	**0.716**
Years	0.582	0.440	0.566	0.577
Years + Prominence	**0.688**	**0.546**	**0.630**	**0.697**
Centrality	0.666	0.483	0.677	0.591
Centrality + Prominence	**0.674**	**0.557**	0.670	**0.625**
Fellow	0.546	0.300	0.547	0.545
Fellow + Prominence	**0.706**	**0.572**	**0.713**	**0.732**

We observe that average precision increases for almost all groups when they are combined with the group of structural prominence and dominance measures. This indicates that structural prominence and dominance measures provide information about the graph, that is not provided by other graph measures. For knn and random forest algorithm, we notice an significant increase for all groups, while logistic regression and svm algorithm show only significant improvements for the groups *years* and *fellows*. For logistic regression also the increase in performance for *centrality* is significant, when structural prominence and dominance measures are added. We assume that the results for different classification algorithms vary due to the collinearity of factors in the dataset, which are not handled equally by different model types. Therefore, we performed a correlation analysis that will be discussed in the next section.

3.5 Analysis of Factor Correlations

We further examined the relation between the factors by performing a correlation analysis. Our goal is to show that structural prominence and dominance provide different information than the other factors used in our experiments. We selected spearman correlation as a measure (instead of, for instance, pearson correlation), because we were interested in monotonic relationships between our factors and linearity cannot hold for all of our factors. We computed correlations between all pairs of factors for each of the years 1995 to 2016 and averaged the correlation values. The correlation matrix is shown in Table 5.

We can see, that prominence and dominance have very low correlation (≤ 0.4) to any of the other factors. This confirms our hypothesis that our proposed measures indeed provide an individual contribution to the measurement of networks. Furthermore, we observe medium correlation between *higher/lower neighbors* and *degree centrality*, which is not a surprise, because they are conceptually related. The very high correlation between *h-* and *g-index* indicates, that both measures have marginal differences when used for ranking. It is also clear, that *years* and *#publications* have a tendency towards a monotonous relationship and therefore high correlation, because both values can only increase during the career of a scientific author. *Lower neighbors* and *neighbors ratio* are also highly correlated, because *lower neighbors* is used in the *neighbors ratio* measure.

4 Other Potential Applications

We have used the task of predicting next year's ACM fellows as an instance for potential applications for structural prominence and dominance measures. Nevertheless, our measures are not restricted to author impact analysis and can be applied to a wide range of different tasks. In this Section, we will give further ideas for potential applications.

Diversification and Topic-Based Rankings. Structural prominence and dominance put constraints on the distance of nodes in a graph. So by selecting nodes with high prominence and dominance one can get a small subset of nodes with a wide coverage of the graph. This can be exploited to create more diverse rankings which include components of different topics. Applications can be found in information retrieval, e.g. ranking of prominent articles in Wikipedia [24] as well as recommender systems [23].

Table 5. Correlations of individual factors. All correlations ≥0.7 and ≤-0.7 are labeled bold and italic, while all correlations ≥0.9 and ≤-0.9 are labeled bold only.

	dominance g-index	higher neighbors g-index	lower neighbors g-index	neighbors ratio g-index	#publications	#citations	h-index	g-index	i10-index	min year	max year	years	degree centrality	eigenvector centrality	fellow distance
prominence g-index	0.34	-0.32	0.27	0.37	0.07	-0.02	0.03	0.04	-0.02	-0.00	-0.05	0.08	-0.03	-0.19	0.08
dominance g-index		0.19	0.27	0.30	0.17	0.04	0.14	0.15	0.02	-0.09	-0.19	0.15	0.40	0.26	0.11
higher neighbors g-index			0.28	0.18	0.36	0.10	0.33	0.34	0.07	-0.04	-0.28	0.32	*0.73*	0.67	-0.32
lower neighbors g-index				**0.98**	*0.70*	0.02	0.54	0.58	-0.00	0.16	-0.38	0.67	0.66	0.35	-0.21
neighbors ratio g-index					0.67	0.01	0.51	0.54	-0.01	0.14	-0.36	0.64	0.60	0.28	-0.16
#publications						0.04	*0.72*	*0.77*	0.00	0.28	-0.36	**0.92**	0.55	0.43	-0.29
#citations							0.53	0.47	0.64	0.33	0.32	0.07	0.07	0.10	-0.09
h-index								**0.97**	0.22	0.43	-0.06	0.69	0.46	0.38	-0.29
g-index									0.19	0.42	-0.10	*0.75*	0.48	0.40	-0.29
i10-index										0.23	0.23	0.02	0.05	0.07	-0.08
min year											0.65	0.39	0.04	0.04	-0.17
max year												-0.31	-0.37	-0.26	0.08
years													0.50	0.39	-0.27
degree centrality														0.56	-0.26
eigenvector centrality															-0.66

Detection of Local Excellence. The detection of nodes in a network with strong local performance, can be facilitated by structural prominence and dominance measures. Nodes with high prominence and dominance perform locally better than their neighborhood, but don't necessarily have to be top performers according to a global ranking. This can be exploited to find globally unknown entities with local excellence, e.g. for ranking actors/musicians. Advanced applications can be the identification of roles, e.g. in a contact network of a computer science conference [16], or even the inference of relations, e.g. the advisor-advisee relation [25] in an academic network.

5   Conclusions and Future Work

In this paper, we motivated and introduced structural prominence and dominance as new measures for network analysis. We showed that our measures provide information about a graph that is not provided by other graph measures. Furthermore, we grounded these measures on the task of ACM fellow prediction and demonstrated that they provide an individual contribution.

There are different aspects that we want to investigate further in future research: For example, we want to look into the temporal dynamics of structural prominence and dominance. The paradigm for the definition of our measures was a mountain landscape, but - in contrast to mountains - social networks are characterized by high dynamics and structural changes over time. Therefore, we want to further explore the influence of temporal changes on the stability of structural prominence and dominance measures.

Furthermore, we want to combine structural prominence and dominance measures into a single index, which describes the local importance of a node in a network. We believe that such an index can provide valuable information for network analysis, the same way the h-index has provided a clever way to account for multiple aspects in a single scientometrics ranking.

References

1. Baeza-Yates, R.A., Ribeiro-Neto, B.: Modern Information Retrieval. Addison-Wesley Longman Publishing Co. Inc., Boston (1999)
2. Brandes, U., Freeman, L.C., Wagner, D.: Social networks. In: Tamassia, R. (ed.) Handbook of Graph Drawing and Visualization, pp. 805–840. CRC Press, Boca Raton (2014)
3. Brandes, U., Pich, C.: Centrality estimation in large networks. Int. J. Bifurc. Chaos **17**(07), 2303–2318 (2007)
4. Dong, Y., Johnson, R.A., Chawla, N.V.: Can scientific impact be predicted? IEEE Trans. Big Data **2**(1), 18–30 (2016)
5. Egghe, L.: Theory and practise of the g-index. Scientometrics **69**(1), 131–152 (2006)
6. Fawcett, T.: ROC graphs: notes and practical considerations for researchers. Mach. Learn. **31**(1), 1–38 (2004)
7. Freeman, L.C.: A set of measures of centrality based on betweenness. Sociometry **40**(1), 35–41 (1977)
8. Freeman, L.C.: Centrality in social networks conceptual clarification. Soc. Netw. **1**(3), 215–239 (1978)
9. Gould, P.R.: On the geographical interpretation of eigenvalues. Trans. Inst. Br. Geogr. **42**, 53–86 (1967)
10. He, H., Garcia, E.: Learning from imbalanced data. IEEE Trans. Knowl. Data Eng. **21**(9), 1263–1284 (2009). https://doi.org/10.1109/TKDE.2008.239
11. Helman, A.: The Finest Peaks - Prominence and Other Mountain Measures. Trafford Publishing, Victoria (2005)
12. Hirsch, J.E.: An index to quantify an individual's scientific research output. Proc. Natl. Acad. Sci. U.S.A. **102**(46), 16569 (2005)
13. Japkowicz, N., Shah, M.: Evaluating Learning Algorithms: A Classification Perspective. Cambridge University Press, New York (2011)
14. Knoke, D., Burt, R.S.: Prominence. In: Applied Network Analysis, pp. 195–222 (1983)
15. Liu, X.Y., Wu, J., Zhou, Z.H.: Exploratory undersampling for class-imbalance learning. IEEE Trans. Syst. Man Cybern. Part B (Cybern.) **39**(2), 539–550 (2009)
16. Macek, B.E., Scholz, C., Atzmueller, M., Stumme, G.: Anatomy of a conference. In: Proceedings of the 23rd ACM Conference on Hypertext and Social Media, pp. 245–254. ACM (2012)

17. Maizlish, A.: Prominence and orometrics: a study of the measurement of mountains. WWW document (2003). http://www.peaklist.org/theory/theory.html
18. Mattmüller, C.R.: Zur orographischen gliederung von gebirgen. Zeitschrift für Geomorphologie **55**(1), 109–140 (2011)
19. Rawat, S., Meena, S.: Publish or perish: where are we heading? J. Res. Med. Sci.: Off. J. Isfahan Univ. Med. Sci. **19**(2), 87 (2014)
20. Staff, C.: Acm fellows inducted. Commun. ACM **57**(2), 22–22 (2014)
21. Thöni, C.: Wie viele berge gibt es in den schweizer alpen? - von schartenhöhe und dominanz. wissenschaft und bergwelt. Die Alpen, pp. 26–28 (2003)
22. Tukey, J.W.: Bias and confidence in not-quite large samples. Ann. Math. Statist. **29**, 614 (1958)
23. Vargas, S., Castells, P.: Rank and relevance in novelty and diversity metrics for recommender systems. In: Proceedings of the Fifth ACM Conference on Recommender Systems, pp. 109–116. ACM (2011)
24. Vercoustre, A.M., Thom, J.A., Pehcevski, J.: Entity ranking in wikipedia. In: Proceedings of the 2008 ACM Symposium on Applied Computing, pp. 1101–1106. ACM (2008)
25. Wang, C., Han, J., Jia, Y., Tang, J., Zhang, D., Yu, Y., Guo, J.: Mining advisor-advisee relationships from research publication networks. In: Proceedings of the 16th ACM SIGKDD International Conference on Knowledge Discovery and Data Mining, pp. 203–212. ACM (2010)
26. Wasserman, S., Faust, K.: Social Network Analysis: Methods and Applications, vol. 8. Cambridge University Press, New York (1994)

Deploying Spatial-Stream Query Answering in C-ITS Scenarios

Thomas Eiter[1], Ryutaro Ichise[2,3], Josiane Parreira Xavier[4],
Patrik Schneider[1,4(✉)], and Lihua Zhao[3]

[1] Vienna University of Technology, Vienna, Austria
patrik@kr.tuwien.ac.at
[2] National Institute of Informatics, Tokyo, Japan
[3] National Institute of Advanced Industrial Science and Technology, Tokyo, Japan
[4] Siemens AG Österreich, Vienna, Austria

Abstract. Cooperative Intelligent Transport Systems (C-ITS) play an important role for providing the means to collect and exchange spatio-temporal data via V2X between vehicles and the infrastructure, which will be used for the deployment of (semi)-autonomous vehicles. The Local Dynamic Map (LDM) is a key concept for integrating static and streamed data in a spatial context. The LDM has been semantically enhanced to allow for an elaborate domain model that is captured by a mobility ontology, and for queries over data streams that cater for semantic concepts and spatial relationships. We show how this approach can be extended to address a wider range of use cases in the three C-ITS scenarios *traffic statistics*, *events detection*, and *advanced driving assistance systems*. We define for them requirements derived from necessary domain-specific features and report, based on them, on the extension of our query language with temporal relations, delaying, numeric predictions and trajectory predictions. An experimental evaluation of queries that reflect the requirements, using the real-world traffic simulation tool provides evidence for the feasibility/efficiency of our approach in the new scenarios.

1 Introduction

The development of (semi)-autonomous vehicles involves extensive communication between vehicles and the infrastructure, which is covered by Cooperative Intelligent Transport Systems (C-ITS). These systems collect temporal data (e.g., traffic light signal phases) and geospatial data (e.g., GPS positions), which are exchanged in vehicle-to-vehicle, vehicle-to-infrastructure, and combined communications (V2X). This aids (a) to improve road safety by analyzing traffic scenes that could lead to accidents (e.g., red light violations), and (b) to reduce emissions by optimizing traffic flow (e.g., dissolve traffic jams). A key technology for this is the Local Dynamic Map (LDM) [2] as an integration platform for static, semi-static, and dynamic information in a spatial context.

In previous work, we have semantically enhanced the LDM to allow for an elaborate domain model that is captured by a mobility ontology, and for queries

© Springer Nature Switzerland AG 2018
C. Faron Zucker et al. (Eds.): EKAW 2018, LNAI 11313, pp. 386–406, 2018.
https://doi.org/10.1007/978-3-030-03667-6_25

over data streams that cater for semantic concepts and spatial relationships [14]. Our approach is based on ontology-mediated query answering (OQA) and features conjunctive queries (CQs) over DL-Lite$_A$ [10] ontologies that support window operators over streams and spatial relations between objects. We believe that OQA is well suited for C-ITS applications, as an ontology can be used to model vehicles, traffic, and infrastructure details, and map to scalable stream database technology adding dynamicity to the model. For example, the definition of a hazardous situation is complex, ranging from bad road conditions to traffic jams [2]. Therefore, an expressive query language is crucial to fulfill C-ITS specific requirements needed for retrieving dynamic data and expressing complex patterns regarding, e.g., event detection. Furthermore, scalability and swift response time are crucial since fast changing traffic demands a quick response time to avoid accidents [2].

In this paper, we continue the work in [13,14] with the goal of showing how spatial-stream OQA can be used to address a wider set of C-ITS scenarios. For achieving this, the approach in [14] is extended with new domain-specific features beyond "generic" spatial-stream OQA. In cooperation with ITS domain experts from Siemens and the National Institute of Advanced Industrial Science and Technology (AIST), the C-ITS scenarios – *traffic statistics, events detection,* and *advanced driving assistance systems* (ADAS) – were defined and used to single out requirements derived from a domain-specific list of features. We then formulate for each use case, requirements that should be covered by our approach. The focus of the new, more specific features will be on *temporal relations*, e.g., *during*, as well as numerical and trajectory *predictions*. For the assessment, we provide a detailed report on the extension of the implementation with the new features such as the temporal relations. The implementation is evaluated in an experimental setting using queries matching to features, where a real-world traffic simulation is used to generate the data. The results provide evidence for the feasibility and efficiency of our approach in these scenarios. Our contributions are briefly summarized as follows:[1]

- we outline the field of V2X integration using LDMs and provide details on our ontology-based LDM (Sect. 2);
- we define three scenarios, use cases, desired features, and requirements (Sect. 3);
- we present our current approach including data model, query language, and outline the implemented features (Sects. 4 and 5);
- we evaluate our platform regarding the set of features/requirements based on a traffic simulation and assess the results (Sect. 6).

In Sect. 7, we discuss related work, and conclude with ongoing and future work.

---

[1] As to [14], Sects. 3, 5, 6 are entirely new content, and 4 changed with the focus on new features.

2   C-ITS Data Integration and Query Answering

Our setting is the ongoing efforts in data integration and querying in the C-ITS domain. The base technologies for C-ITS are already available and experimentally deployed in infrastructure projects as in [2]. The communication technology is based on the IEEE 802.11p standard, and the data integration effort is the *Local Dynamic Map* (LDM), which are starting points for our work. IEEE 802.11p allows wireless access in vehicular environments, called V2X communications, which enables messaging between vehicles and the infrastructure. The messages are broadcast every 100 ms by traffic participants, i.e., vehicles and roadside ITS stations, to update other participants about their current states [2]. The main standardized message types are *CAMs* (Cooperative Awareness Messages) for frequency status updates of participants, *MAPs* (Map Data Messages) for detailed intersection topologies, *SPATs* (Signal Phase and Timing Messages) for traffic light signal phases, and *DENMs* (Decentralized Environmental Notification Messages).

Local Dynamic Map. The V2X technology does not yet consider the integration of the different types of messages. As a comprehensive integration effort, the EU SAFESPOT project [2] introduced the concept of an LDM, which acts as an integration platform to combine static geographic information system (GIS) maps, with dynamic environmental objects (e.g., vehicles or pedestrians). The integration is motivated by advanced safety applications, which need an "overall" understanding of a traffic environment. The LDM consists of the four layers (see Fig. 1a): *permanent static, transient static, transient dynamic,* and *highly dynamic,* ranging from dynamic (as V2X messages) to permanent static (as GIS maps) information. Recent research by Netten et al. [18], and Shimada et al. [21] suggested that an LDM can be built on top of a spatial relational RDBMS enhanced with streaming capabilities. Netten et al. recognize that an

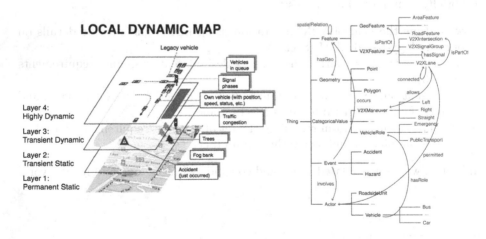

Fig. 1. (a) The four layers of a LDM [2] and (b) LDM ontology

LDM should be represented by a world model, world objects, and data sinks on the streamed input [18]. However, an elaborate domain model captured by an LDM ontology, and extended query processing or rule evaluation methods over spatial data streams, were still missing in the current approaches. An ontology-based LDM has advantages regarding the maintainability and understandability of the model, since dependencies between the concepts are clearly defined and easy extendable without altering the underlying database (DB) schema.

Ontology-Based LDM. With the support of Siemens and AIST domain experts, we have worked on our LDM ontology (shown partially in Fig. 1b, available at http://www.kr.tuwien.ac.at/research/projects/loctrafflog/ LocalDynamicMapITS-v0.4-Lite.owl) to capture the four levels of the LDM, as well as V2X-specific elements such as maneuvers. The LDM ontology is represented in DL-Lite$_A$ [10], which is the logical underpinning for the W3C standard OWL 2 QL. Apart from the restriction to DL-Lite$_A$, our methods are ontology-agnostic; hence other mobility ontologies could be used. We follow a layered approach starting with a simple separation between the top concepts of $V2XFeature$ that is the representation of V2X objects, such as details of an intersection topology including lanes ($V2XLane$) and traffic lights ($V2XSignalGroup$). $GeoFeature$ represents the GIS aspects of the LDM including POIs, areas like parks, and road networks with $Geometry$ as the geometrical representation of them. $Actor$ is the concept that includes persons, vehicles, as well as roadside ITS stations, which are autonomous and are the main generator of streamed data. $CategoricalValues$ specify the different categories such as signal phases, or vehicle roles used in the emergency domain. Besides "domain specific" roles and attributes like $speedLimit$, $hasRole$, $speed$, or $position$, we also introduced generic roles that have an inherent meaning, e.g., $isPartOf$.

Spatial-Stream Query Answering. The OQA component is central to the usage of a semantically enhanced LDM, since it allows us to access the streamed data in the LDM.

Example 1. The following query detects red-light violations on intersections by searching for vehicles (in y) with an *aggregated* trajectory and speed above 30 km/h in a 8s window, projecting 3s into the future (represented as a negative time point), which move on lanes (in x) *during* these lanes signals will turn to "Stop", i.e., red, in a 10s window:

$$q_1(x,y) : LaneIn(x) \land hasLoc(x,u) \land intersects(u,v) \land Vehicle(y)$$
$$\land\ pos(y,v)[\textbf{\textit{traject\_line}},\ 5s,\ -3s] \land speed(y,r)[\textbf{\textit{mov\_avg}},\ 5s,\ -3s]$$
$$\land\ (r > 30) \land \textbf{\textit{during}}(v,s) \land isManaged(x,z)$$
$$\land\ SignalGroup(z) \land hasState(z,s)[last,\ 5s,\ -5s] \land (s = {}'Stop')$$

Query q_1 exhibits the different dimensions that need to be combined: (a) $LaneIn(x)$, $Vehicle(y)$ and $isManaged(x,z)$ (assigning traffic lights z to lanes x) are ontology atoms, which have to be unfolded in respect to the concept/role hierarchies of the LDM ontology; (b) $intersects(u,v)$ and $hasLoc(x,u)$ are spatial atoms, where the first checks spatial intersection and the second returns the object geometries; (c) $speed(y,r)[mov\_avg, 5s, -3s]$ and

$pos(y, v)[traject\_line, 5s, -3s]$ define window operators that aggregate and *predict* the moving average of speed and positions of the vehicles over *speed* and *pos*, respectively, and $hasState(z, s)[last, 5s, -5s]$ returns the traffic lights that have their last phase on "Stop"; (d) the relation $during(v, s)$ checks if "v happens during s", where v is all the occurrences of trajectories on the set of time intervals $t1$, and s are the traffic light phases that are on "Stop" in the set of time intervals $t2$, were $t1$ and $t2$ are derived from the trajectory aggregations and the phase duration of the traffic lights.

3   Development of C-ITS Scenarios

In this section, we present three application scenarios that are used to define requirements and features split into three complexity levels. On the infrastructure side, we have C-ITS (roadside) stations that receive nearby V2X messages and send messages to inform other participants on their current state, i.e., the traffic light phases. Other participants such as vehicles share their states such as their current speed, acceleration, and position. On the vehicle side, ADAS perceive driving environments and make safe driving decisions to improve safety of autonomous vehicles. The ADAS use sensors such as Lidar/Radar or cameras, and process the sensor data to avoid accidents by detecting pedestrians, vehicles, or other obstacles [23]. The sensor data can be linked to our ontology-based LDM and enables the system to represent the driving environments.

S1: Traffic Statistics. The focus of this scenario is on the collection of statistical data that concerns stops, throughput, traffic distribution, or types of participants by aggregating the streaming data on specific intersections. Regarding this scenario, we have identified the following use cases and related challenges:

1. *Object level*: for a single vehicle or station, the average speed, acceleration, number of stops, or on a sensor data such as the temperature could be collected;
2. *Road/Intersection level*: on this level, besides calculating a summary of road/lane level indicators such as average throughput, waiting time, the amount of stops, also matrices regarding transfers (e.g. how many cars head straight on), modality, and type mix, (e.g. which vehicle classes are present) could be determined;
3. *Network level*: on the network level, intersections are represented by nodes connected by roads. We could collect statistical summaries of indicators on intersections. For instance, estimating the transfer times and traffic flow between intersections.

S2: Hazardous Events Detection. An important C-ITS application is *road safety* [2], where a reliable event detection is central to find unexpected, hazardous events. This is a more challenging case, since it requires the combination of the topology, vehicle maneuvers, and temporal relations that might be evaluated over longer and shorter periods. We identified the following events as possibly hazardous:

1. *Simple vehicle maneuvers*: the following maneuvers are relevant for this case and are directly extractable from trajectories: (1) quick slow down/speed up; (2) drive straight on, turn left, turn right; (3) stop, unload, park;
2. *Complex vehicle maneuvers*: the aim is to detect lane changes, overtakes, u-turn as complex maneuvers, which are a composite of simple maneuvers;
3. *Red-light violation*: as shown in Ex. 1, red-light violations can be detected by checking the spatial intersection of lanes that change to "Stop" and vehicles current trajectory taking their speed into account. This could be enhanced by trajectory predictions;
4. *Vehicle breakdown/accident*: this event is based on the stop maneuver, where we identify vehicles that are not moving and are inside a dangerous area of an intersection. This case can be extended to several vehicles;
5. *Traffic congestions*: this is a more complex event, where short and long term observations must be combined. Queuing cars could indicate a congestion and be detected by checking the stop maneuvers of several vehicles that are behind each other, but not stopped by a longer red light phase.

S3: ADAS and Autonomous Driving. ADAS are an important step towards autonomous driving by enabling the vehicle to take control of speed or breaking, where drivers still have the "full" control over the vehicle. The following challenges come for ADAS:

1. *Self monitoring*: Self-monitoring is a central requirement of ADAS, where intelligent speed adaptation is an important feature to improve roadway safety;
2. *Obstructed view*: It concerns dangerous situations where a vehicle might collide with another vehicle, since they have no visual contact due to an obscured view (e.g., buildings). The overlap of predicted trajectories of two vehicles should be checked.
3. *Traffic rules*: The embedding of traffic rules like checking of traffic rules such as right-of-way rules could become an important requirement for autonomous driving.

Features for Spatial-Stream QA. The eight "standard" requirements: volume, velocity, variety, incompleteness, complex domain models, etc., as well as the three entailment levels for stream reasoning systems: stream-, window-, and graph-level entailment identified by [12] are not discussed here, but should hold for mobility stream systems as well. Besides the generic features *F1*, *F2*, *F3*, and *F9*, we also focus on domain specific features that are mapped to requirements crucial for enabling the above scenarios. For this, we distinguish for each feature the levels of fulfillment *basic* (L1), *enhanced* (L2), and *advanced* (L3). We have identified the following feature sets:

- *F1 - Time model*: possible time models are *point-based* (L1), and *interval-based* (L2), where L1 is the "simplest" representation. On point-based data, applying aggregations can be represented by intervals based on point-based data items. If we apply an interval-based model, temporal relations (L3) such as Allen's Time Interval Algebra [1] with operators like *before* can be used for querying and inference.

– *F2 - Process paradigm*: queries that are processed in a pull-based (L1) manner should be the baseline. Push-based processing (L2) in particular with sliding windows is already more challenging. If we allow a combined (L3) processing, we could treat high velocity (resp. low velocity) atoms as push-based (resp. as pull-based).

– *F3 - Query features*: these "basic" features include nesting of queries (L1), or unions of CQs (L2). Other feature relate to the computation of spatial relations using a simple point-set model (L1) or the more detailed *9-Intersection model* (L2).

– *F4 - Numerical aggregations*: aggregations can be "simple" functions such as *sum* or *average* on either a set or multiset (bag) of data items (L1). These could be extended by basic statistical function such as *median* (L2). Aggregation over multisets is important, since we often have data items of different objects in a single stream.

– *F5 - Spatial aggregations*: a wide range of spatial aggregations can be applied to geometric objects like points and lines (L1) and the aggregation functions need to take the peculiarities of geometries into account, e.g., convex vs. concave objects. Smoothing and simplification of complex objects could also be included (L2).

– *F6 - Numerical predictions*: predictions allow the generation of unknown data items projecting from the past into the future. Several prediction functions such as moving average (L1) or exponential smoothing (L2) regression should be available. Depending on the task, also more complex machine learning methods could be envisioned (L3).

– *F7 - Trajectory predictions*: we predict a vehicle's movement, by linearly projecting the trajectory into the future (L1). More accurate results could be achieved by (1) a "point-to-curve" aggregation, and (2) calculating possible paths using a road graph (L2), and the usage of machine learning for trajectory predictions (L3).

– *F8 - Spatial matching*: basic spatial matching is the extraction of specific features such as angles from the objects (L1). Advanced features include the matching of complex geometries such as road graphs (L2).

– *F9 - Rules*: rules will reach beyond the expressivity of query answering and can include "simple" implications as $b(x, y) \land c(y, z) \rightarrow a(x, z)$ (L1), but also more advanced features such as aggregation, negation as failure (L2), and recursion (L3).

Requirements. In Table 1, we show the requirements that are derived by analyzing each scenario and use case regarding the necessary features. The requirements build the base line for the implementation and a later experimental assessment. In case of single features, we only distinguish between L1 to L3 for required, blank for not required, and "P" for possibly required. For instance, in *S2.2* for F1, a point-based time model (L1) suffices for detecting left/right turns, however,

Table 1. Requirement Matrix (L1/L2/L3 is required, blank is not required, P is possibly)

Use case	F1	F2	F3	F4	F5	F6	F7	F8	F9
S1.1 (Object statistics)	L1	L1		L2	P				
S1.2 (Road/Intersection statistics)	L2	L1	L2	L2	L1	L1	L1	P	
S1.3 (Network statistics)	L2	L1	L2	L2	L1	L2	L1	P	P
S2.1 (Simple maneuvers)	L1	L1	L1	L1	L1	P	P	P	
S2.2 (Complex maneuvers)	L2	L2	L2	L1	L1	L1	L1	L1	P
S2.3 (Red-light violation)	L2	L2	L2	L1	L1	L1	L1	L1	P
S2.4 (Vehicle breakdown)	L2	L1	L2	L1	L1	L1		P	P
S2.5 (Traffic congestion)	L2	L3	L2	L2	L1	L2		P	P
S3.1 (Self monitoring)	L1	L2	L1	L1	P	P	P		
S3.2 (Obstructed view)	L1	L2	L2	L1	L1	L1	L1	L1	P
S3.3 (Traffic rules)	L2	L2	L2	L2	L2	L1	L1	L1	L1

if we want to detect u-turns, interval-based model in combination with temporal relations (L2) might be needed. Furthermore, push-based queries are desired for swift reaction on changes. In [14], we partially support L1 for *F1* to *F5*, but we aim to push the level beyond that and need new features such as time intervals, temporal relations, and unions of CQs. *F6*, *F7*, and *F8* are entirely new features.

4   Approach for Spatial-Stream Query Answering

We start from previous work in [14], which introduced spatial ontology-mediated query answering over Mobility Streams using DL-Lite$_A$ [10]. We focus on pull-based queries that are evaluated at one single time point called the *query time* $\mathbb{T}_i$.

Data Model and Knowledge Base. Our data model is *point-based* and captures the *valid time*, extracted from the V2X messages, saying that some *data item* is valid at that time point. Importantly, while evaluating a query, the model can change (temporary) to an *interval-based* model that results from the window and aggregation functions. To capture streaming data, we introduce the *timeline* $\mathbb{T}$, which is a *closed* interval of $(\mathbb{N}, \leq)$. A data *stream* is a triple $D=(\mathbb{T}, v, P)$, where $\mathbb{T}$ is a timeline, $v : \mathbb{T} \to \langle \mathcal{F}, \mathcal{S}_{\mathcal{F}} \rangle$ is a function that assigns to each element of $\mathbb{T}$ data items of $\langle \mathcal{F}, \mathcal{S}_{\mathcal{F}} \rangle$, where $\mathcal{F}$ (resp. $\mathcal{S}_{\mathcal{F}}$) is a *stream (resp. spatial-stream)* *DB*, and the integer P is called *pulse* defining the general interval of consecutive data items on the timeline (cf. [8]); this naturally induces a stream of data items. We always have a *main pulse* with a fixed interval length that defines the highest granularity of the validity of data points, and *larger pulses* for streams with lower frequency can be defined. The pulse also aligns the data items that arrive asynchronously in the DB to the timeline.

Example 2. For the timeline $\mathbb{T} = [0, 100]$, we have the stream $F_{CAM} = (\mathbb{T}, v, 1)$ of vehicle positions and speed at the assigned time points for the individuals c_1, c_2 and b_1: $v(0) = \{speed(c_1, 30), pos(c_1, (5, 5)), speed(c_2, 10), pos(c_2, (4, 4)), speed(b_1, 10), ...\}$ $v(1) = \{speed(c_1, 29), pos(c_1, (6, 5)), speed(c_2, 0), pos(c_2, (5, 4)), speed(b_1, 5), ...\}, ...$ A "slower" stream $F_{SPaT} = (\mathbb{T}, v, 5)$ captures the next signal state of a traffic light: $v(0) = \{hasState(t_1, Stop)\}$ and $v(5) = \{hasState(t_1, Go)\}$. The static ABox contains assertions $Car(c_1)$, $Car(c_2)$, $Bike(b_1)$, and $SignalGroup(t_1)$. A different "annotated" representation by applying the function v on F_{CAM} yields $\{speed(c_1, 30) @t0, ..., speed(c_1, 29)@t1\}$, which is better suited for an interval-based time model.

We consider a vocabulary of individual names Γ_I, domain values Γ_V (e.g., $\mathbb{N}$), and spatial objects Γ_S. A *spatial-stream knowledge base* is a tuple

$$\mathcal{K} = \langle \mathcal{T}, \mathcal{A}, \mathcal{S_A}, \langle \mathcal{F}, \mathcal{S_F} \rangle, \mathcal{B} \rangle,$$

where $\mathcal{T}$ ($\mathcal{A}$, resp.) is a DL-Lite$_A$ TBox (ABox, resp.), $\mathcal{S_A}$ is a spatial DB, and $\langle \mathcal{F}, \mathcal{S_F} \rangle$ is a stream DB with spatial data support. Furthermore, $\mathcal{B} \subseteq \Gamma_I \times \Gamma_S$ is a partial function called the *spatial binding* from $\mathcal{A}$ to $\mathcal{S_A}$ and $\mathcal{F}$ to $\mathcal{S_F}$. The TBox $\mathcal{T}$ and the ABox $\mathcal{A}$ consist of finite sets of *inclusion assertions*, *functionality assertions*, and *membership assertions*. To specify the *localization* of atomic concepts and roles. We extended standard DL-Lite$_A$ (see [10]) with axioms ($loc\ A$), ($loc_s\ A$), and ($loc_s\ Q$) that assign an unspecific or particular location to instances of atomic concepts A or basic roles Q. The extension with streaming consists of the axiom schemes

$$(stream_D\ C) \quad \text{and} \quad (stream_D\ R),$$

where D is a particular stream over either complex concepts C or roles R in $\langle \mathcal{F}, \mathcal{S_F} \rangle$. More details are given in [14].

Example 3. A TBox may contain ($stream_{CAM}$ $speed$), ($stream_{CAM}$ ($loc\ pos$)), ($stream_{CAM}$ $Vehicle$), and ($stream_{SPaT}$ $hasState$), and we have further axioms $Car \sqsubseteq Vehicle$, $Bike \sqsubseteq Vehicle$, and $Ambulance \sqsubseteq \exists hasRole.Emergency$.

Query Language. Our query language is based on conjunctive queries (CQs) and adds spatial-stream capabilities (see Example 1). A spatial-stream CQ $q(\mathbf{x})$ is a formula:

$$\bigwedge_{i=1}^{m} Q_{O_i}(\mathbf{x}, \mathbf{y}) \wedge \bigwedge_{j=1}^{n} Q_{S_j}(\mathbf{x}, \mathbf{y}) \wedge \bigwedge_{k=1}^{o} Q_{D_k}(\mathbf{x}, \mathbf{y}) \wedge \bigwedge_{l=1}^{p} Q_{T_i}(\mathbf{x}, \mathbf{y}) \qquad (1)$$

where $\mathbf{x}$ are the *distinguished* (*answer*) variables, $\mathbf{y}$ consists of *non-distinguished* (*existentially quantified*) variables, objects, and constant values:

- each atom $Q_{O_i}(\mathbf{x}, \mathbf{y})$ has the form $A(z)$ or $P(z, z')$, where A is a class name, P is a property name of the LDM ontology, and z, z' are from $\mathbf{x}$ or $\mathbf{y}$;
- each atom $Q_{S_j}(\mathbf{x}, \mathbf{y})$ is from the vocabulary of *spatial* relations and of the form $S(z, z')$, where z, z' represent geometries matched by S, where S is one of the following relations: $S = \{intersects, contains, next, equals, within, disjoint, outside\}$;

- each atom $Q_{D_k}(\mathbf{x}, \mathbf{y})$ is similar to $Q_{O_i}(\mathbf{x}, \mathbf{y})$ but adds stream operators that relate to Continuous Query Language operators. We have a window $[agr, b, e]$ over a stream D_k, where b and e are the bounds of the window in time units (positive for past, negative for future) and an *aggregate function agr* applied to the data items in the window:
  - $[agr, b]$ represents the aggregate of last or next b time units of stream D_k;
  - $[b]$ represents the single tuple of F_j at index b with $b = 0$ if it is the current tuple;
  - $[agr, b, e]$: represents the aggregate of a window $[b, e]$ in the past/future of D_k.
- each atom $Q_{T_l}(\mathbf{x}, \mathbf{y}) = (T_1(z_1, z_1'), \ldots, T_q(z_q, z_q'))$ represents a disjunction of *temporal* relations, where the variables z_i, z_i' represent matches, i.e., individuals annotated with time points/intervals, which are filtered by the temporal relation T_i. For points, $T_i = T_i^P$ is from $\{<, \leq, =, \geq, >\}$; for intervals, we choose the relations of Allen's Time Interval Algebra [1], i.e., $T_i = T_i^I$ is from $\{before, equal, meets, overlaps, during, starts, finishes\}$ and the set of inverses, e.g., $during^-$, which filter variable matches according to the start/end points of the intervals.

The "historic" window operator $[agr, b, e]$ is derived from Brandt et al. [8] and allows us to query logs represented by data streams. Details on handling the temporal relations and aggregate functions are given below. We also have added a limited form of disjunction in our temporal relations; in general this would move the language beyond CQs.

Query Rewriting with Spatio-Temporal Relations. We consider answering pull-based queries at *a single* time point $\mathbb{T}_i$ with stream atoms that define *aggregate functions* on different window sizes relative to $\mathbb{T}_i$. For this, we consider a semantics based on *epistemic aggregate queries* (EAQ) over ontologies [11] by dropping the order of time for the data and handling the streamed data items as *bags* (multi-sets). Roughly, we perform two steps: (1) calculate only "known" solutions, and (2) evaluate the rewritten query, which includes the TBox axioms as well, over them. Each EAQ is evaluated over *filtered and merged temporary* ABoxes. The filtering and merging, relative to the window size and $\mathbb{T}_i$, creates for each EAQ a temporary ABox $A_{\boxplus_\phi}$, which is the union of the static ABox A and the filtered streaming data items from the stream DB. The EAQs are then applied on $A_{\boxplus_\phi}$ by grouping and aggregating the normal objects, constant values, and spatial objects. We use a *bag-based epistemic semantics* for the queries, in which we locally close our world for the specific window and avoid "wrong" aggregations due to the open world semantics of DL-Lite$_A$. For details see [14].

At first sight, spatial and temporal relations could be treated similarly. As shown in [14], we evaluate spatial relations regarding their *Point-Set Topological Relations*. It amounts to pure set theoretic operations on point sets using the function $points(p)$, which defines the (infinite) set of points of a geometry p that is a sequence $p = (p_1, \ldots, p_n)$ of (defined) points. For instance, the relation $inside(x, y)$ between geometries is defined as $\{(x, y) : points(y) \subseteq points(x)\}$. However, for temporal relations, we distinguish point-based relations that can be encoded as simple arithmetic filters, from interval-based relations, where in Allen's Time Interval Algebra (IA) [1] 13 relations can hold between two intervals. The domain of IA relations is the set of intervals $\{[p_1], \ldots, [p_k]\}$ over the linear order of $\mathbb{T}$ defined as $[p_i] = [\underline{p_i}, \overline{p_i}]$ with $\underline{p_i} < \overline{p_i}$. The binary *basic IA* relations are defined according to their start/end points as follows [1]:

$before(x,y){=}\{(x,y) : \underline{x} < \overline{x} < \underline{y} < \overline{y}\}; \quad meets(x,y){=}\{(x,y) : \underline{x} < \overline{x} = \underline{y} < \overline{y}\};$
$overlaps(x,y){=}\{(x,y) : \underline{x} < \underline{y} < \overline{x} < \overline{y}\}; \; starts(x,y){=}\{(x,y) : \underline{x} = \underline{y} < \overline{x} < \overline{y}\};$
$finishes(x,y){=}\{(x,y) : \underline{y} < \underline{x} < \overline{x} = \overline{y}\}; \; during(x,y){=}\{(x,y) : \underline{y} < \underline{x} < \overline{x} < \overline{y}\};$
$equal(x,y){=}\{(x,y) : \underline{y} = \underline{x} < \overline{x} = \overline{y}\}.$

IA relations can be interpreted over the sets of intervals $\mathbb{I}_A$ and $\mathbb{I}_B$ in two ways: (a) *IA filtering*, where each relation is treated as a single binary constraint. In that sense, the temporal relation acts as a filter on all intervals in $\mathbb{I}_A \times \mathbb{I}_B$ that match the relations regarding their start/end points; (b) *IA reasoning*, which requires the computation of the path consistency of all temporal relations over the intervals in $\mathbb{I}_A \cup \mathbb{I}_B$ using the predefined composition table of [1]. The composition table is defined as a set of transitive rules on basic relations, which are applied until no new *general* relations can be inferred. For instance, if we have the edges $during(I_1, I_2)$ and $during(I_2, I_3)$, we can infer a new relation $during(I_1, I_3)$. Note that only with approach (b) all possible (chained) relations between intervals are derivable. A well-known representation for IA relations are IA graphs (also called IA networks), which are directed graphs, where the vertices are the intervals of $\mathbb{I}_A$ and $\mathbb{I}_B$ and the edges represent the IA relations that hold between two intervals. Hence, an IA graph (closed by transitive rules) is a materialization of all relations that can hold between intervals, and can be used to check the relations if a directed edge exists.

Our intervals are an intermediate product of the EAQ evaluation and annotate the resulting objects. As mentioned, for each stream atom we have a temporary ABox derived from $\mathbb{T}_i$ and the window $[agr, b, e]$. In a first approach, we directly use $\mathbb{T}_i$ and the window size for the interval generation. For instance, having $\mathbb{T}_5$ and $speed[avg, 3, -1]$, we would annotate each grouped/aggregated match with the interval $[2, 6]$. In a second, approach, we extract for each grouped/aggregated match of an EAQ the upper and lower bounds of the time points annotated to the data items in that window, where the window size is the outer bound. More sophisticated approaches might include the segmentation of the data items, thus creating different fragmented subintervals.

Query Evaluation. The four types of query atoms need different evaluation techniques over separate DB entities. Ontology atoms are evaluated over the static ABox A using a "standard" DL-Lite$_A$ query rewriting, i.e., PerfectRef [10]. For spatial atoms, we need to dereference the bindings to the spatial ABox S_A and evaluate the spatial relations to filter spatial objects. Stream atoms are computed as EAQ to group and summarize over the temporary ABoxes of the different streams. For temporal atoms, we consider three techniques. For time points, we simply add the filter conditions to the rewritten query. For intervals, two techniques are suitable: (a) IA filtering, hence we can rewrite each IA relation of Q_{T_l} into a filter that encodes the equation with the start/end points (as defined before); (b) IA reasoning, where the closed IA graph is constructed applying the transitive rules on all intervals derived from an EAQ. We then extract all derived intervals with the annotated objects from the IA graph that hold according to the queried relations in Q_{T_l}.

In [14], we introduced two spatial query evaluation strategies assuming that *no bounded variables* occur in spatial atoms and the CQ is *acyclic* (roughly has no proper cycle between join variables). One strategy is based on the query hypergraph and the derived join plan and is well-suited for implementing spatial-stream CQs, as it gives us fine-grained caching, full control over the evaluation, and possibly handling different DB entities. Details are given in standard DB literature such as [17].

Example 4. The following example of a simplified q_1, where the layers distinguish between ontology (first), stream/temporal (second), and spatial (third line) atoms:

$$q_2(x, y) : LaneIn(x) \land isManaged(x, z) \land SignalGroup(z) \land Vehicle(y)$$
$$\land\ pos(y, v)[line,\ 10s] \land during(v, s) \land hasState(z, s)[last,\ 5s, -5s]$$
$$\land\ hasLoc(x, u) \land intersects(u, v) \land (s = 'Stop')$$

Based on the hypergraph decomposition, we have the following evaluation order:

(1) $q_{2_{F1}}(y, v@i_v) : Vehicle(y) \land pos(y, v@i_v)[line, 10s]$;
(2) $q_{2_{N1}}(x, u) : LaneIn(x) \land hasLoc(x, u)$;
(3) $q_{2_{F2}}(z, s@i_s) : SignalGroup(z) \land hasState(z, s@i_s)[last, 5s, -5s] \land (s = 'Stop')$;
(4) $q_{2_{T1}}(y, v) : q_{2_{F1}}(y, v@i_v) \land during(v@i_v, s@i_s) \land q_{2_{F2}}(z, s@i_s)$;
(5) $q_2(x, y) : q_{2_{T1}}(y, v) \land intersects(u, v) \land q_{2_{N1}}(x, u)$.

Stream Aggregation and Predictions. For *normal objects* and *constant values*, we allow the aggregate functions $count, first$, and $last$ on the stream data items. For *last* and *first*, we need to search the bag of data items, as the sequence of time is lost. This is achieved by iteratively checking if we have a match at one of the points in time. In the implementation, the first and last match can be simply cached while processing the stream. For *individuals* and *constant (numerical) values*, we allow a range of aggregation and prediction functions on the streamed data items:

- *order*: $first$, $last$, where they give the first or last element in the stream, respectively;
- *simple*: $count$, min, max, sum, and avg;
- *descriptive statistics* (DS): $mean$, sd, var, $median$, where each function calculates the mean, standard deviation, variance, and median as expected;
- *predictions*: We apply predefined regression methods to predict values from existing (time-series) data items inside a window. Model building (i.e., the training) and prediction should be fast, hence we support the following lightweight methods: (a) mov_avg calculates the moving average of the past values; (b) exp_smooth applies simple exponential smoothing; and (c) $grad\_boost$ uses gradient boosting with regression trees.

Note, since the order of items is lost due to the bag semantics, the temporal annotation (e.g., $speed(c_1, 50)@10$) are needed in the prediction functions as the second dimension. We allow different regression methods with increasing complex models. On small windows with a required fast response time, mov_avg and exp_smooth is preferable, while on larger windows, e.g., for traffic predictions, $grad\_boost$ could be applied.

For *spatial objects*, geometric aggregate functions are applied to the bag of data items that represent geometries, i.e., the sequence of points $p = (p_1, \ldots, p_n)$. We allow these functions to derive new geometries (among others):

- *point*: we evaluate the function *last* to get the last data item p_n on the stream;
- *line*: we create a sequence of points representing a path by calculating a total order on the bag of points, such that we have a starting point using *last* and iterate backwards finding the next point by *Euclidean distance*;
- *line_angle*: the angle (in degrees) of *line* regarding a reference system is calculated;
- *traject_line* and *traject_heading* are simple techniques to project possible trajectories from past points. The former is linearly projecting the trajectory based on the previous points and the current speed. The later calculates the trajectory based on the last point and the last heading of the vehicle.

For the trajectory computation, besides a simple linear also a curvature-based models could be applied. To improve the accuracy of the model, we could use the speed of the last data points, so a speed-up or slow down would be taken into account.

5   Implementation

We have implemented a prototype of our spatial-stream OQA approach in JAVA 1.8 using the stream RDBMS PIPELINEDB 9.8.1 (https://www.pipelinedb.com/). The system architecture is shown in Fig. 2a. We chose PIPELINEDB, as it is built on top of PostgreSQL (https://www.postgresql.org/) and PostGIS (http://postgis. net/) and thus supporting stream and spatial data. It distinguishes between *streams* and *continuous views*, where streams are write-only, so the query evaluator has to access the read-only continuous views. We created 1-to-1 mappings from streams to continuous views, and further to the TBox concepts and roles; e.g., vehicle positions are fed into the stream $stream\_pos(id, pos, tp)$, where id is the vehicle id, pos its position, and tp the time point of adding; $stream\_pos$ is accessed via the continuous view $view\_pos$, which is mapped to the property pos. We also provide an integration framework that constantly receives V2X messages and adds the raw message data either to normal tables of the static DB, spatial tables of the GIS DB, or the *streams* of the stream DB.

Implementation Details. The parser/decomposer component is used for parsing the input spatial-stream CQ, and then decomposing the query hypertree using Gottlob et al.'s (https://www.dbai.tuwien.ac.at/proj/hypertree/) implementation. Depending on the size of the CQ, the decomposition can be expensive,

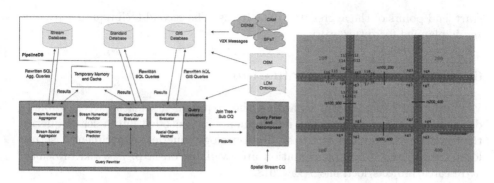

Fig. 2. (a) System architecture and (b) Four intersection scenario

hence it is performed as a preprocessing step, whereas the decompositions are cached in-memory. The decomposer gives us the join tree J_q and the sub CQs assigned to each tree node. For each node, we also keep the label that includes the subquery type, window size, and aggregation/prediction function. The query evaluator traverses J_q bottom up, left-to-right, and (1) checks if the result of a sub CQ are cached; (2) if not, instantiates one of the evaluators according to the sub CQ type.

Ontology evaluator: this evaluator uses the DL-Lite$_A$ query rewriter OWLGRES 0.1 [22], but a more efficient implementation as in ONTOP [20] is planned.

Stream evaluator: for each stream sub CQ q_i, it detemporalizes the streams by grouping/aggregating the data items by performing the following steps:

(1) extract the data items according to the defined window size;
(2) evaluate q_i (no rewriting) and store the "known solutions" in memory as $R_{i,1}$;
(3) evaluate q_i' (with rewriting) over $R_{i,1}$ and store it in memory as $R_{i,2}$;
(4) apply the prediction function on $R_{i,2}$ and add the predicted data items;
(5) apply the grouping/aggregation function on $R_{i,2}$, and produce the outcome $R_{i,3}$.

Predictors: the prediction function is an integrated part of the stream evaluator, where we apply the predictions on the aggregated data items. We provide a standard implementation for the functions *mov_avg* and *exp_smooth*. For *grad_boost*, we use the state-of-art library XGBOOST (https://xgboost.readthedocs.io/en/latest/).

Spatial evaluator: it handles the different spatial relations. For performance reasons, we do not compile them to SQL, but evaluate the spatial relations in-memory using the functions of the JTS TOPOLOGY SUITE (https://github.com/locationtech/jts).

Temporal evaluator: this evaluator supports the mentioned *IA filtering* technique, since temporal relations can be directly rewritten into SQL by encoding the relations as joins, where each relations is encoded as a filter on the start/end points of the aggregated data items. The second technique *IA reasoning* is planned for future work.

6   Experiments and Evaluation

We evaluated our platform regarding the requirements/features (cf. Table 1) derived from the use cases. The requirements are encoded into a set of queries that include the desired features. The ontology, queries, experimental setup, logs, results, and the implementation are available on http://www.kr.tuwien.ac.at/research/projects/loctrafflog/ekaw2018.

Scenario Data. For having realistic traffic data, we generated our streaming data with the microscopic traffic simulation tool PTV VISSIM (http://vision-traffic.ptvgroup.com/en-us/products/ptv-vissim/), which allows us to simulate realistic driving and traffic light behavior, as well as the possibility to create unexpected events like accidents. We extract the actual state of each Vissim simulation step, and store the result as JSON in a log, and provide a log player that replays the simulation by feeding the data to PIPELINEDB. For varying the data throughput, we adjust the following parameters: (a) replay with 5 ms, 10 ms, 50 ms, 100 ms delay, where 5 ms are the fastest updates (i.e., simulating sensors) and 100 ms is the real-time speed of the Vissim simulation; (b) we simulate light, medium, and heavy traffic in our scenario, where we have approx. 20, 50, and 150 vehicles respectively. We modeled a real-world scenario shown in Fig. 2b, which is based on a grid layout with four intersections of four roads crossing, and two incoming and outgoing lanes per street. The two incoming lanes of each side have traffic light controllers assigned; all maneuvers (turn left/right, straight on) to outgoing lanes are allowed. The main traffic flow is from north to south and west to east. We encode the structure of the full intersections into static ABox instances as follows: (a) intersections, roads, lanes, signal groups, and vehicles as concept assertions; (b) geometries for each lane, road, etc. as attribute assertions; and (c) lane connectivity, signal group assignments, etc. as role assertions.

Queries for Experiments. Based on the requirements, we derived a set of queries to assess each scenario. Each query aims at answering a specific problem of the use case taking the set of features into account. Note that commas between atoms are conjunctions, disjunctions are explicitly stated using *or*. For the use case *S1.1* (object statistics), query $q_{1.1}$ determines the average and max speed of BMWs and VWs in the last 10 s.

$$q_{1.1}(x, u, v) : Vehicle(x), vehicleMaker(x, z), (z='BMW' \text{ or } z='VW'),$$
$$speed(x, u)[avg, 10s], speed(x, v)[max, 10s]$$

For the use case *S1.2* (intersection statistics), we count vehicles according to their engine type. Sub-queries $q_{1.2a}$ and $q_{1.2b}$ select cars with either diesel or petrol engine that pass intersection $i100$. Query $q_{1.2}$ aggregates the sub-queries and returns the count of diesel in y and petrol vehicles in z, respectively:

$q_{1.2a}(x, y)$: $Vehicle(y), pos(y, z)[line, 10s], vehicleEngine(y, m), (m = 'Petrol'),$
        $intersects(z, u), hasLoc(x, u), Intersection(x), x = 'i100'$

$q_{1.2b}(x, y)$: $Vehicle(y), pos(y, z)[line, 10s], vehicleEngine(y, m), (m = 'Diesel'),$
        $intersects(z, u), hasLoc(x, u), Intersection(x), x = 'i100'$

$q_{1.2}(x, y, z)$: $q_{1.2a}(x, y)[count, 10s], q_{1.2b}(x, z)[count, 10s]$

For the use case *S1.3* (network statistics), we have two linked intersections $i100$ and $i200$. Query $q_{1.3}$ traces the vehicles that start at $i100$ and counts those passing through $i200$. A delay of 7s allows to check the vehicle's position 7s later, and the temporal relation *before* ensures that a vehicle first passes $i100$ and then $i200$.

$q_{1.3a}(x, v)$: $Vehicle(x), pos(x, v)[line, 6s], intersects(v, u), Intersection(r),$
        $hasLoc(r, u), (r = 'i100')$

$delay(7s)$

$q_{1.3b}(x, z)$: $Vehicle(x), pos(x, z)[line, 6s], intersects(z, w), Intersection(r),$
        $hasLoc(r, w), (r = 'i200')$

$q_{1.3c}(x)$: $q_{1.3a}(x, v), before(v, z), q_{1.3b}(x, z)$

For the use case *S2.1* (simple maneuvers), query $q_{2.1}$ returns all vehicles x and y that turned left or right in the last 6s. Then both results are combined by unions of CQs resulting in all vehicles performing the two maneuvers.

$q_{2.1l}(x, z)$: $Vehicle(x), pos(x, y)[line, 6s], match(y, z)[angle, -175, -15],$
        $intersects(y, u), hasLoc(r, u), Intersection(r), (r = 'i100')$

$q_{2.1r}(x, z)$: $Vehicle(x), pos(x, y)[line, 6s], match(y, z)[angle, 15, 175],$
        $intersects(y, u), hasLoc(r, u), Intersection(r), (r = 'i100')$

$q_{2.1}(x, z)$: $q_{2.1l}(x, z)$ or $q_{2.1r}(x, z)$

In use case *S2.2* (complex maneuvers), query $q_{2.2}$ detects illicit lane changes in terms of crossing the middle marker (i.e., a white line). This is detected by evaluating whether a vehicle has moved from in-lane, temporally to an out-lane or vice versa.

$q_{2.2}(x, y)$: $LaneIn(z), hasLoc(z, u), intersects(u, v), pos(x, v)[line, 6s, 3s],$
        $Vehicle(x), pos(x, w)[line, 3s, 0s], intersects(t, w), hasLoc(y, t), LaneOut(y)$

For the use case *S2.3* (red-light violation), we modified Ex. 1 by taking trajectory and speed prediction into account, which allows us a more precise detection of violations, since we can rule out vehicles that are slowing down or are about to change lanes.

$q_{2.3}(x, y)$: $LaneIn(x), hasLoc(x, u), intersects(u, v), pos(y, v)[traject\_line, 5s, -3s],$
        $Vehicle(y), speed(y, r)[mov\_avg, 5s, -3s], (r > 10), hasSignalGroup(x, z),$
        $SignalGroup(z), hasState(z, Stop)[last, 5, -5]$

For the use case *S2.4* (vehicle breakdown), we check with $q_{2.4}$, if a car has stopped for longer than 30s, while (using the *during* relation) it is located inside our intersections, but not on one of the park lanes (using the *disjoint* relation).

$q_{2.4}(x, y)$: $Vehicle(x), speed(x, r)[avg, 30s], (r < 1), pos(x, v)[line, 15s], inside(v, u),$
        $hasLoc(y, u), Intersection(y), during(v, r), disjoint(v, z), hasLoc(p, z), ParkLane(p)$

The use case *S2.5* (traffic congestion) can be evaluated by a query similar to *S2.4*, but with the extension that stop-and-go traffic can be excluded by checking if there is no movement while the traffic light phases are on "Go".

$q_{2.5}(x, y)$: $Vehicle(x), speed(x, r)[avg, 30s], (r < 1), pos(x, v)[line, 30s], intersects(v, u),$
$hasLoc(y, u), LaneIn(y), hasSignalGroup(y, z), SignalGroup(z),$
$hasState(z, s)[last, 30s], (s = 'Go'), during(s, r)$

For the use case *S3.1* (self monitoring), we aim to detect with $q_{3.1}$, if our ego vehicle is exceeding the speed limit that is assigned to the lane our car is driving on.

$q_{3.1}(x, y)$: $LaneIn(y), hasLocation(y, u), intersects(u, v), pos(x, v)[line, 5s],$
$Vehicle(x), isEgo(x), speed(x, r)[max, 5s], speedLimit(y, s), (r > s)$

In use case *S3.2* (obstructed view) we compute query $q_{3.2}$, where our system (as part of the ego vehicle) aims to detect cars that very likely will collide in 2s on a busy intersection by checking if our predicted trajectories will cross another car.

$q_{3.2}(x, y)$: $Vehicle(y), isEgo(y), pos(y, v)[traject\_line, 2s, -1s], intersects(v, w), (r > 10),$
$Vehicle(x), speed(x, r)[mov\_avg, 5s, -2s], pos(x, w)[traject\_line, 2s, -1s]$

In *S3.3* (traffic rules), our ego vehicle approaches an uncontrolled intersection at the same time with other vehicles. According to traffic rules in Austria, preference is given to the vehicles on the main road. We can express these traffic rules in positive Datalog rules as:

$willCross(x, y) \land straightOn(x) \land turnLeft(y) \rightarrow giveWay(y, x)$
$willCross(x, y) \land turnRight(x) \land turnLeft(y) \land crossOpposLane(y) \rightarrow giveWay(y, x)$
$vehicle(x) \land vehicle(y) \land giveWay(y, x) \rightarrow stop(y)$

The atom $willCross(x, y)$ matches all vehicles that might collide and can be evaluated by $q_{3.2}(x, y)$ (modified without $isEgo(x)$). The atoms $turnLeft(x), turnRight(x)$, and $straightOn(x)$ can be evaluated by the queries $q_{2.1l}(x), q_{2.1r}(x)$, assuming the queries are atomic rules with $q(x)$ as the head. Then, the rules of *S3.3* can be expressed as unions of CQs, but this approach is not feasible if we need rule chaining and transitive rules.

Results. We conducted our experiments on a Mac OS X 10.13.3 system with an Intel Core i7 2.9 GHz, 8 GB of RAM, and a 250 GB SSD. The average of 21 runs for query rewriting time and evaluation time was calculated. The results are in Table 2 presenting the number of subqueries $\#Q$ with stream queries in brackets, the size of rewritten atoms $\#A$, and t as the average evaluation time (AET) in seconds for different traffic densities and update delay in ms. The new experiments confirm results of [14] with closer to "real-world" queries and simulation data. The AET ranges between 0.86s and 2.06s with the exception of use case *S3.3*, which emulates rules using unions of CQs. Query $q_{3.1}$ shows the highest delay of 2.06s, since the join condition of $(r > s)$ is evaluated inline and not on the DB, which adds a delay of 0.4s with larger windows. Our baseline query is $q_{1.1}$ tested with 100 ms delay and low traffic. It has an AET of 0.86s, where 0.23s is the time-to-load (TOL), 0.63s is needed for query evaluation of two stream atoms, where we added an artificial delay of 0.18s before each stream atom evaluation. The artificial delay is empirically determined and needed for PIPELINEDB to set up the *continuous views* (CVs); ignoring this would lead to missing results. Note that the baseline time still could be reduced by (a) precompiling the program, which shortens evaluation by 0.2s, and (b) parallelization of stream atom evaluation that improves performance by approx. 20%; details are available on the results website. The added functions for statistics, matching, and predictions, i.e., *mov_avg* and *traject_line* do not affect performance, since they are applied on small windows with few data items. However, if we would apply *gradboost* for predictions on larger windows, our query time could rise considerably, since prediction time (without a preprocessed training step) can be above 20s.

Table 2. Results (t in secs) for scenario with (l)ow, (m)edium, and (h)eavy traffic

	$\#Q$	$\#A$	(l) with ms delay				(m) with ms delay				(h) with ms delay			
			5	10	50	100	5	10	50	100	5	10	50	100
$q_{1.1}$	3(2)	42	1.35	1.18	0.95	0.86	1.45	1.30	0.99	0.88	1.46	1.35	1.14	0.99
$q_{1.2}$	6(2)	43	1.30	1.20	1.01	0.96	1.33	1.24	1.04	1.00	1.41	1.38	1.07	1.01
$q_{1.3}$	8(2)	44	1.44	1.35	1.15	1.08	1.47	1.37	1.23	1.09	1.45	1.44	1.30	1.20
$q_{2.1}$	6(2)	43	1.31	1.20	1.01	0.98	1.43	1.29	1.09	0.99	1.48	1.40	1.13	1.02
$q_{2.2}$	7(2)	45	1.36	1.26	1.05	1.00	1.47	1.29	1.08	1.03	1.51	1.43	1.13	1.06
$q_{2.3}$	7(3)	50	1.57	1.50	1.27	1.21	1.63	1.53	1.30	1.22	1.72	1.65	1.37	1.27
$q_{2.4}$	5(2)	46	1.24	1.21	0.98	0.92	1.28	1.24	1.06	0.97	1.28	1.29	1.13	0.99
$q_{2.5}$	7(3)	43	1.44	1.38	1.16	1.08	1.50	1.41	1.20	1.11	1.55	1.47	1.26	1.17
$q_{3.1}$	5(2)	43	1.85	1.72	1.40	1.32	1.89	1.79	1.48	1.35	2.06	2.04	1.57	1.38
$q_{3.2}$	5(3)	63	1.41	1.34	1.23	1.17	1.48	1.43	1.27	1.20	1.56	1.51	1.31	1.21
$q_{3.3}$	12(5)	43	3.02	2.80	2.42	2.39	3.26	2.98	2.58	2.38	3.36	3.20	2.66	2.44

Feature Coverage. As shown with the queries, we covered in the implementation all initial levels (L1) of features that are defined in the scenarios/uses cases. We support temporal relations and a (partial) interval-based data model (*F1*) evaluated by pull-based queries (*F2*). Then, we allow temporal relations and nested queries that include unions of CQs (*F3*). But, we have not yet implemented the *IA reasoning* for temporal relations, since an in-memory evaluation of the transitive rules completing the IA graph needs further investigation. Regarding *F4* and *F5*, we have implemented the initial set of numerical, descriptive statistical, and spatial aggregation functions. For *F6*, we covered *mov_avg* and *exp_smooth* for fast, simple predictions, and support *grad_boost* for long-term traffic forecasting. For trajectory prediction (*F7*), we have implemented a method based on a simple linear path calculation. But, more accurate trajectory predictions would be desired. Feature *F8* is covered by the atom *match*(*y*, *z*)[*angle*, 0, 15], and *F9* is partially covered by unions of CQs, but transitive rules are out of scope for this work.

7 Related Work and Conclusions

RDF stream processing engines, such as C-SPARQL [5], SPARQLstream [9], and CQELS [15], were proposed for processing RDF streams integrated with linked data sources. EP-SPARQL [3] and LARS [6] introduce languages that extend SPARQL respectively CQs with stream reasoning, but translate KBs into more expressive, less efficient logic programs. Closest to our spatial-stream QA approach is the work of (i) [19] that supports spatial operators as well as aggregate functions over temporal features, (ii) [9] that allows evaluating OQA queries over stream RDBMS, and (iii) [8] that extends SPARQL with aggregate functions and statistic methods and is evaluated over streamed and ordered ABoxes. Temporal QA is also investigated in [4,7], both are on the theoretical side and provide no implementation yet. The work of Netten et al. [18] and Lécué et al. [16] focus on longer-term diagnosis, but neglect the streaming nature of C-ITS data.

This work is sparked by applying spatial-stream QA as an integration and QA effort for streamed mobility data, e.g., vehicle movements, in a spatial context over the complex mobility domain. In [14], we have introduced simple aggregate queries over streams, which often do not suffice to capture more complex use cases. We present an extension with temporal relations, and numerical/trajectory predictions, which allows us to query complex mobility patterns such as traffic statistics or complex events such as (potential) accidents. Based on the newly developed scenarios of *traffic statistics*, *event detection*, and *ADAS*, we have defined a set of domain-specific features such as trajectory computation, which are matched with the scenarios/use cases to define the requirements. Given the new features, we adjusted our LDM ontology, our spatial-stream query language, and extended our methods accordingly. We also redesigned our system architecture and give insights on the new components for temporal relations, prediction and trajectory calculation. The experimental evaluation provides evidence for the feasibility and efficiency of our approach in the mentioned scenarios.

As discussed in feature coverage, ongoing and future research should be directed to extend the languages, methods, and the platform to fulfill the defined requirements, which will allow us to apply them to more scenarios such as logistics.

Acknowledgements. This work has been supported by the Austrian Research Promotion Agency project LocTraffLog (FFG 5886550) and DynaCon (FFG 861263).

References

1. Allen, J.F.: Maintaining knowledge about temporal intervals. Com. ACM **26**(11), 832–843 (1983)
2. Andreone, L., Brignolo, R., Damiani, S., Sommariva, F., Vivo, G., Marco, S.: Safespot final report. Technical report D8.1.1 (2010). Available online
3. Anicic, D., Fodor, P., Rudolph, S., Stojanovic, N.: EP-SPARQL: a unified language for event processing and stream reasoning. Proc. WWW 2011, 635–644 (2011)
4. Artale, A., Kontchakov, R., Kovtunova, A., Ryzhikov, V., Wolter, F., Zakharyaschev, M.: First-order rewritability of temporal ontology-mediated queries. Proc. IJCAI 2015, 2706–2712 (2015)
5. Barbieri, D.F., Braga, D., Ceri, S., Valle, E.D., Grossniklaus, M.: C-SPARQL: a continuous query language for RDF data streams. Int. J. Semant. Comput. **4**(1), 3–25 (2010)
6. Beck, H., Dao-Tran, M., Eiter, T., Fink, M.: LARS: a logic-based framework for analyzing reasoning over streams. Proceedings of AAAI 2015, pp. 1431–1438 (2015)
7. Borgwardt, S., Lippmann, M., Thost, V.: Temporalizing rewritable query languages over knowledge bases. J. Web Sem. **33**, 50–70 (2015)
8. Brandt, S., Kalayci, E.G., Kontchakov, R., Ryzhikov, V., Xiao, G., Zakharyaschev, M.: Ontology-based data access with a horn fragment of metric temporal logic. In: Proceedings of AAAI 2017, pp. 1070–1076 (2017)
9. Calbimonte, J.-P., Mora, J., Corcho, O.: Query Rewriting in RDF Stream Processing. In: Sack, H., Blomqvist, E., d'Aquin, M., Ghidini, C., Ponzetto, S.P., Lange, C. (eds.) ESWC 2016. LNCS, vol. 9678, pp. 486–502. Springer, Cham (2016). https://doi.org/10.1007/978-3-319-34129-3_30
10. Calvanese, D., Giacomo, G.D., Lembo, D., Lenzerini, M., Rosati, R.: Tractable reasoning and efficient query answering in description logics: The DL-Lite family. J. Autom. Reasoning **39**(3), 385–429 (2007)
11. Calvanese, D., Kharlamov, E., Nutt, W., Thorne, C.: Aggregate queries over ontologies. In: Proceedings of ONISW 2008, pp. 97–104 (2008)
12. Dell'Aglio, D., Valle, E.D., van Harmelen, F., Bernstein, A.: Stream reasoning: a survey and outlook. Data Sci. **1**(1–2), 59–83 (2017). IOS Press
13. Eiter, T., Parreira, J.X., Schneider, P.: Detecting mobility patterns using spatial query answering over streams. In: Proceedings of Stream Reasoning Workshop (2017)
14. Eiter, T., Parreira, J.X., Schneider, P.: Spatial ontology-mediated query answering over mobility streams. In: Blomqvist, E., Maynard, D., Gangemi, A., Hoekstra, R., Hitzler, P., Hartig, O. (eds.) ESWC 2017. LNCS, vol. 10249, pp. 219–237. Springer, Cham (2017). https://doi.org/10.1007/978-3-319-58068-5_14
15. Le-Phuoc, D., Dao-Tran, M., Xavier Parreira, J., Hauswirth, M.: A native and adaptive approach for unified processing of linked streams and linked data. In: Aroyo, L., Welty, C., Alani, H., Taylor, J., Bernstein, A., Kagal, L., Noy, N., Blomqvist, E. (eds.) ISWC 2011. LNCS, vol. 7031, pp. 370–388. Springer, Heidelberg (2011). https://doi.org/10.1007/978-3-642-25073-6_24
16. Lécué, F., Tallevi-Diotallevi, S., Hayes, J., Tucker, R., Bicer, V., Sbodio, M.L., Tommasi, P.: Smart traffic analytics in the semantic web with STAR-CITY: scenarios, system and lessons learned in Dublin city. J. Web Sem. **27**, 26–33 (2014)
17. Maier, D.: The Theory of Relational Databases. Computer Science Press, Rockville (1983)

18. Netten, B., Kester, L., Wedemeijer, H., Passchier, I., Driessen, B.: Dynamap: A dynamic map for road side its stations. In: Proceedings of ITS World Congress (2013)

19. Quoc, H.N.M., Le Phuoc, D.: An elastic and scalable spatiotemporal query processing for linked sensor data. In: Proceedings of SEMANTICS 2015, pp. 17–24. ACM (2015)

20. Rodríguez-Muro, M., Kontchakov, R., Zakharyaschev, M.: Ontology-based data access: *Ontop* of databases. In: Alani, H., Kagal, L., Fokoue, A., Groth, P., Biemann, C., Parreira, J.X., Aroyo, L., Noy, N., Welty, C., Janowicz, K. (eds.) ISWC 2013. LNCS, vol. 8218, pp. 558–573. Springer, Heidelberg (2013). https://doi.org/10.1007/978-3-642-41335-3_35

21. Shimada, H., Yamaguchi, A., Takada, H., Sato, K.: Implementation and evaluation of local dynamic map in safety driving systems. J. Transp. Technol. **5**(2), 102–112 (2015)

22. Stocker, M., Smith, M.: Owlgres: a scalable OWL reasoner. In: Proceedings of OWLED 2008 (2008)

23. Zhao, L., Ichise, R., Liu, Z., Mita, S., Sasaki, Y.: Ontology-based driving decision making: a feasibility study at uncontrolled intersections. IEICE Trans. Inf. Syst. **100**(D(7)), 1425–1439 (2017)

Metaproperty-Guided Deletion from the Instance-Level of a Knowledge Base

Claudia Schon[1(✉)], Steffen Staab[1,2], Patricia Kügler[3], Philipp Kestel[3],
Benjamin Schleich[3], and Sandro Wartzack[3]

[1] Institute for Web Science and Technologies, University of Koblenz-Landau,
Koblenz, Germany
{schon,staab}@uni-koblenz.de
[2] Web and Internet Science Research Group, University of Southampton,
Southampton, UK
[3] Engineering Design, Friedrich-Alexander-Universität Erlangen-Nürnberg (FAU),
Erlangen, Germany

Abstract. The ontology modeling practice of engineering metaproperties of concepts is a well-known technique. Some metaproperties of concepts describe the dynamics of concept instances, i.e. how instances can and cannot be altered. We investigate how deletions in an ontology-based knowledge base interact with the metaproperties *rigidity* and *dependence*. A particularly useful effect are *delete cascades*. We evaluate how rigidity and dependence may guide delete cascades in an engineering application. A case study in the area of product development shows that beyond explicitly defined deletions, our approach achieves *further* automated and desirable deletions of facts with high precision and good recall.

1 Introduction

Ontological metamodeling is a well-known technique which is used in various areas [8,10]. Intuitively, metaproperties allow concepts and roles to be addressed like domain elements and to be assigned to metaclasses or to be linked via meta roles.

In this paper we consider the metaproperties *rigidity* and *dependence* and their interaction with deletions. A property is rigid, if it is essential to all its instances. For example in most scenarios the property of *being a petrol* usually represented as the concept *Petrol* is rigid, since nothing can stop being a petrol. For the sake of simplicity, we will avoid the term *property* in the following and say that the corresponding *concept Petrol* is rigid. In contrast to this, the concept *SubsidisedFuel* is usually not rigid, since such a fuel can start or stop being subsidised at any time.

A concept depends on another concept, if for each instance of the first concept there is necessarily an individual of the second concept. For example, concept

C. Schon and P. Kügler—Work supported by DFG EVOWIPE

C. Faron Zucker et al. (Eds.): EKAW 2018, LNAI 11313, pp. 407–423, 2018.
https://doi.org/10.1007/978-3-030-03667-6_26

PetrolEngine depends on concept *Petrol*. In other words: something cannot be a petrol engine without being fueled by some kind of petrol.

Metaproperties not only provide information about concepts or their relationship to one another, but also about dynamic aspects of the instances of a concept and describe if and how they can be changed. For example the rigidity of concept *Petrol* indicates that in general, it is not desirable to delete the fact that superplus is a petrol from the knowledge base while maintaining all other facts about superplus. Moreover, deleting the fact that superplus is a petrol removes an essential property of superplus such that one could conclude that superplus no longer exists and should therefore be completely removed from the knowledge base. The dependence metaproperty describes dynamic aspects as well. For example, the fact that a petrol engine depends on the existence of at least one petrol it can be fueled by indicates that in general, deleting these petrols should result in the deletion of the fact that the engine in question is a petrol engine. In accordance with delete cascades in relational databases, we call additional deletions performed because of dependencies *cascading deletions*.

In general, metaproperties in a knowledge base (KB) depend on the conceptualization of the domain. We suggest to account for the variability of conceptualizations by explicitly modeling the context in which the KB is used. We use context-sensitive metaproperties to model this aspect and to take the context into account when determining cascading deletions.

In many domains, cascading deletions are desired by the user. For example, in product development, where the KB representation of a new product model is derived from existing ones, it is necessary to modify the existing model representation to accomodate the requirements of the new product. The reuse of existing models makes it necessary to delete aspects from the KB which are not applicable anymore. The EVOWIPE[1] project is situated in the domain of product development and aims at developing methods to support the product developer in the process of deleting aspects from KBs. In the domain of product development, the KB may harbor many dependencies that can be exploited to maintain the model validity by providing cascading deletions to the product developer freeing him from error-prone manual work [13].

Related work in knowledge representation refers to the deletion of a symbol from a knowledge base as a *forgetting* operation that affects the signature and the formula set of a knowledge base [17], while the notion of *contraction* is used to refer to the consistency-preserving deletion of facts from the knowledge base, which need not necessarily affect the signature [9]. These contraction operators however do not support cascading deletions.

Thus, we assume that when a product developer — or another knowledge representation-lay user — formulates a *delete* operation, intelligent assistance may and should use the ontology and its metamodel in order to guide the deletion process such that a new valid product model is represented in the ensued knowledge base.

---

[1] https://west.uni-koblenz.de/en/research/evowipe.

In our example, deleting *Petrol*(*superplus*) has the following effect: the rigidity of *Petrol* first leads to the forgetting of individual *superplus* (by deleting several facts around *superplus*), as well as the cascading deletion of all assertions *PetrolEngine*(*e*) for which superplus was the only petrol engine *e* could be fueled by.

Thus, the main contributions of this paper are:

- The modeling of knowledge about dynamics of concept instances through context-sensitive metaproperties and the use of these metaproperties to obtain operators for additional and cascading deletions. Section 3 formalizes several alternative operators to accomplish additional and cascading deletions of instance-level assertions based on metaproperties.
- An implementation of our approach for OWL [18] KBs with metaproperties stored in annotations and SPARQL update queries to specify the deletions.
- A quantitative evaluation of our approach with a real KB from product development. This evaluation presented in Sect. 4 confirms that the cascading deletions performed by our operators are desired by the engineers working with the KB.

1.1 A Modeling Example from Product Development

Consider a KB $\mathcal{K} = (\mathcal{T}, \mathcal{A})$ that will serve as a running example throughout the paper:

$$\mathcal{T} = \{PetrolEngine \equiv \exists canBeFueledBy.Petrol, \qquad (1)$$
$$Manifold \sqsubseteq \exists isConnectedTo.PetrolEngine, \qquad (2)$$
$$CatalyticConverter \sqsubseteq \exists isWeldedTo.Manifold, \qquad (3)$$
$$ExhaustPipe \sqsubseteq \exists isConnectedTo.Manifold, \qquad (4)$$
$$PassengerSeat \sqsubseteq \exists isSecuredBy.SeatBelt\} \qquad (5)$$

$$
\begin{aligned}
\mathcal{A} = \{ &PetrolEngine(pte), & &isConnectedTo(mf, pte), \\
&Petrol(superplus), & &ExhaustPipe(ep), \\
&Petrol(v\text{-}power), & &isConnectedTo(ep, mf), \\
&canBeFueledBy(pte, superplus), & &CatalyticConverter(cc), \\
&Manifold(mf), & &isWeldedTo(cc, mf) \}
\end{aligned}
$$

Suppose the KB is used in product development where it is reasonable to assume that the manifold of a car depends on the petrol engine and the exhaust pipe depends on the manifold implying that each individual of concept *Manifold* is related via role *isConnectedTo* to an individual of concept *PetrolEngine*. The same applies to individuals of concept *ExhaustPipe* regarding concept *Manifold*. These dependencies can be modeled by manually adding the *dependence* metaproperty to the concepts *ExhaustPipe* and *Manifold*. Please note that the dependency cannot be read from the structure of the axioms. For example, although axiom (5) has the same structure as axiom (2), the *PassengerSeat* is not dependent on *SeatBelt*.

Assume that petrol engine *pte* is supposed to be replaced by an electric engine. It is reasonable to assume that deleting the petrol engine should result in the deletion of the manifold *mf* since it depends on the petrol engine which then should result in the deletion of the exhaust pipe *ep* since it depends on the manifold *mf*. In accordance with delete cascades in relational databases, we call these additional deletions of *manifold(mf)* and *exhaustpipe(ep)* *cascading deletions*. In Sect. 3 we show how to accomplish these cascading deletions with the help of metaproperties.

2   Background and Preliminaries

We introduce syntax and semantics of the description logic (DL) $\mathcal{SHOIN}$ which corresponds to OWL-DL. Given a set of *atomic roles* N_R, the set of *roles* is defined as $N_R \cup \{R^- \mid R \in N_R\}$, where R^- denotes the *inverse role* corresponding to the atomic role R. A *role inclusion axiom* is an expression of the form $R \sqsubseteq S$, where R and S are roles. A *transitivity axiom* is of the form $Trans(S)$ where S is a role. An RBox $\mathcal{R}$ is a finite set of role inclusion axioms and transitivity axioms. $\sqsubseteq^*$ denotes the reflexive, transitive closure of $\sqsubseteq$ over $\{R \sqsubseteq S, Inv(R) \sqsubseteq Inv(S) \mid R \sqsubseteq S \in \mathcal{R}\}$. A role R is *transitive* in $\mathcal{R}$ if there exists a role S such that $S \sqsubseteq^* R$, $R \sqsubseteq^* S$, and either $Trans(S) \in \mathcal{R}$ or $Trans(Inv(S)) \in \mathcal{R}$. If no transitive role S with $S \sqsubseteq^* R$ exists, R is called *simple*. Let N_C be the set of *atomic concepts* and N_I a set of individuals. The set of *concepts* is inductively defined using the following grammar:

$$C \rightarrow \top \mid \bot \mid A \mid \neg C \mid C_1 \sqcap C_2 \mid C_1 \sqcup C_2 \mid \exists R.C \mid \forall R.C \mid \geq nS \mid \leq nS \mid \{a\}$$

where $A \in N_C$, C_i are concepts, $R \in N_R$, $S \in N_R$ a simple role and $a \in N_I$.

A *general concept inclusion* (GCI) is of the form $C \sqsubseteq D$ with C and D concepts. A TBox $\mathcal{T}$ is a finite set of GCIs also called axioms. In our setting, an ABox $\mathcal{A}$ is a finite set of assertions of the form $A(a)$ and $R(a, b)$, with A an atomic concept, R an atomic role and a, b are individuals from N_I. A knowledge base (KB) $\mathcal{K}$ is a triple $(\mathcal{R}, \mathcal{T}, \mathcal{A})$ with signature $\Sigma = (N_C, N_R, N_I)$. The tuple $\mathcal{I} = (\cdot^{\mathcal{I}}, \Delta^{\mathcal{I}})$ is an *interpretation* for $\mathcal{K}$ iff $\Delta^{\mathcal{I}} \neq \emptyset$ and $\cdot^{\mathcal{I}}$ assigns an element $a^{\mathcal{I}} \in \Delta^{\mathcal{I}}$ to each individual a, a set $A^{\mathcal{I}} \subseteq \Delta^{\mathcal{I}}$ to each atomic concept A, and a relation $R^{\mathcal{I}} \subseteq \Delta^{\mathcal{I}} \times \Delta^{\mathcal{I}}$ to each atomic role R. $\cdot^{\mathcal{I}}$ then assigns values to more complex concepts and roles as described in Table 1. $\mathcal{I}$ is a *model* of $\mathcal{K}$ ($\mathcal{I} \models \mathcal{K}$) if it satisfies all axioms and assertions in $\mathcal{R}$, $\mathcal{T}$ and $\mathcal{A}$ as shown in Table 1. If there is no model for $\mathcal{K}$, $\mathcal{K}$ is called inconsistent. An assertion A of the form $B(a)$ or $R(a, b)$ is entailed by a KB $\mathcal{K}$, denoted by $\mathcal{K} \models A$, iff $\mathcal{I} \models A$ for all models $\mathcal{I}$ of $\mathcal{K}$.

2.1   Justification-Based Deletion

Since this paper only considers deletions of ABox assertions, we restrict the following definitions to ABox assertions. In the following, $\mathcal{A}_d$ denotes the set of

ABox assertions that are supposed to be deleted. When deleting $\mathcal{A}_d$ from a KB, it is not sufficient to only remove all elements contained in $\mathcal{A}_d$ from the ABox since even after their removal they might still be entailed by the KB.

Definition 1 (Justification [11]). *Let $\mathcal{K} = (\mathcal{R}, \mathcal{T}, \mathcal{A})$ be a KB and α be an ABox assertion. $\mathcal{J} \subseteq \mathcal{A}$ is a justification for α in $\mathcal{K}$ if $(\mathcal{R}, \mathcal{T}, \mathcal{J}) \models \alpha$ and for all $\mathcal{J}' \subset \mathcal{J}$, $(\mathcal{R}, \mathcal{T}, \mathcal{J}') \not\models \alpha$. The set of all justifications for α in $\mathcal{K}$ is denoted by $Just(\alpha, \mathcal{K})$.*

To accomplish the deletion of $\mathcal{A}_d$ from a KB $\mathcal{K}$, we suggest to follow [19] and use root justifications.

Definition 2 (Root Justification [19]). *Let $\mathcal{K} = (\mathcal{R}, \mathcal{T}, \mathcal{A})$ be a KB, $\mathcal{A}_d = \{\alpha_1, \ldots, \alpha_n\}$ a set of ABox assertions and $Just(\alpha_i, \mathcal{K})$ the set of all justifications of α_i in $\mathcal{K}$. A set $J \in \cup_{i=1}^n Just(\alpha_i, \mathcal{K})$ is a root justification for $\mathcal{A}_d$ in $\mathcal{K}$ iff there is no $J' \in \cup_{i=1}^n Just(\alpha_i, \mathcal{K})$ with $J' \subset J$.*

Since the set of all root justifications for $\mathcal{A}_d$ in $\mathcal{K} = (\mathcal{R}, \mathcal{T}, \mathcal{A})$ corresponds to the set of all minimal subsets of $\mathcal{A}$ which together with $\mathcal{R}$ and $\mathcal{T}$ imply an assertion in $\mathcal{A}_d$, it is sufficient to delete exactly one element from each root justification in order to prevent any assertion in $\mathcal{A}_d$ from being entailed. This corresponds to the construction of a minimal hitting set for the set of all root justifications for $\mathcal{A}_d$ in $\mathcal{K}$.

Definition 3 (Hitting Set). *Let $S = \{S_1, \ldots S_n\}$ be a set of sets. A hitting set for S is a set $H \subseteq \cup_{i=1}^n S_i$ with $H \cap S_i \neq \emptyset, \forall 1 \leq i \leq n$. If no proper subset of H is a hitting set for S, H is called a minimal hitting set.*

Definition 4 (Deletion). *Let $\mathcal{K} = (\mathcal{R}, \mathcal{T}, \mathcal{A})$ be a KB and $\mathcal{A}_d$ a set of ABox assertions. Let furthermore J be the set of all root justifications for $\mathcal{A}_d$ in $\mathcal{K}$. A deletion Del of $\mathcal{A}_d$ in $\mathcal{K}$ is a minimal hitting set of J.*

Intuitively, a deletion Del of $\mathcal{A}_d$ in $\mathcal{K}$ is a minimal subset of the ABox $\mathcal{A}$ such that no element in $\mathcal{A}_d$ is entailed by $(\mathcal{R}, \mathcal{T}, \mathcal{A} \setminus Del)$.

In general, there can be several minimal hitting sets for the set of all root justifications for the assertions in $\mathcal{A}_d$. Each of these hitting sets corresponds to a deletion of $\mathcal{A}_d$ in $\mathcal{K}$. Choosing one specific deletion can be done by using various semantics [2].

3   Metaproperty-Guided Deletion

We now address the task to perform cascading deletions of ABox assertions from a KB. We will use the context-sensitive metaproperties rigidity and dependence to guide deletion and to achieve the desired cascading behavior. These metaproperties have to be added manually to the KB.

Table 1. Model-theoretic semantics of $\mathcal{SHOIN}$. R^+ is the transitive closure of R.

Concepts and Roles	
$\top^{\mathcal{I}} = \Delta^{\mathcal{I}}$	$\{a\}^{\mathcal{I}} = \{a^{\mathcal{I}}\}$
$\bot^{\mathcal{I}} = \emptyset$	$(\forall R.C)^{\mathcal{I}} = \{x \mid \forall y : (x,y) \in R^{\mathcal{I}} \Rightarrow y \in C^{\mathcal{I}}\}$
$(\neg C)^{\mathcal{I}} = \Delta^{\mathcal{I}} \backslash C^{\mathcal{I}}$	$(\exists R.C)^{\mathcal{I}} = \{x \mid \exists y : (x,y) \in R^{\mathcal{I}} \wedge y \in C^{\mathcal{I}}\}$
$(C \sqcup D)^{\mathcal{I}} = C^{\mathcal{I}} \cup D^{\mathcal{I}}$	$(\geq n\, S)^{\mathcal{I}} = \{x \mid |\{y \mid (x,y) \in S^{\mathcal{I}}\}| \geq n\}$
$(C \sqcap D)^{\mathcal{I}} = C^{\mathcal{I}} \cap D^{\mathcal{I}}$	$(\leq n\, S)^{\mathcal{I}} = \{x \mid |\{y \mid (x,y) \in S^{\mathcal{I}}\}| \leq n\}$
$(R^-)^{\mathcal{I}} = \{(y,x) \mid (x,y) \in R^{\mathcal{I}}\}$	

TBox & RBox axioms	ABox assertion
$C \sqsubseteq D \Rightarrow C^{\mathcal{I}} \subseteq D^{\mathcal{I}}$	$A(a) \Rightarrow a^{\mathcal{I}} \in A^{\mathcal{I}}$
$R \sqsubseteq S \Rightarrow R^{\mathcal{I}} \subseteq S^{\mathcal{I}}$	$R(a,b) \Rightarrow (a^{\mathcal{I}}, b^{\mathcal{I}}) \in R^{\mathcal{I}}$
$\mathit{Trans}(R) \Rightarrow (R^{\mathcal{I}})^+ \subseteq R^{\mathcal{I}}$	

3.1   Context-Sensitive Metaproperties

A concept is called *rigid*, if it is essential to all its individuals. For instance, in most scenarios the concept *Person* is rigid, since one cannot stop being a person. In contrast to that, the concept *Student* is not rigid, because one can start or stop being a student at any time. We adapt this notion of rigidity to DL KBs and specify this metaproperty such that it has a certain scope of validity which we denote by *context*.

Definition 5 (Set of Rigid Concepts, Rigid Assertions). *For a KB $\mathcal{K} = (\mathcal{R}, \mathcal{T}, \mathcal{A})$ with signature $\Sigma = (N_C, N_R, N_I)$ and a context ct. The set $Rigid(\mathcal{K}, ct) \subseteq N_C$ denotes the set of rigid concepts in context ct. An ABox assertion stating that an individual belongs to a concept that is element of $Rigid(\mathcal{K}, ct)$ is called* rigid assertion *w.r.t. ct.*

If the KB $\mathcal{K}$ is clear, we slightly abuse notation such that for a set of ABox assertions S, $Rigid(S, ct)$ denotes the set of rigid assertions in S w.r.t. context ct.

In the scope of this paper, we consider concept C to be *dependent* on concept D, if for all instances c of C there necessarily exists an instance d of D. As an example, [10] uses the concept of a *Parent* which is dependent on the concept *Child*. In other words: one cannot be a parent without having a child. We adapt this notion of dependency to description logic KBs and specify these dependencies w.r.t. a certain context.

Definition 6 (Set of Dependencies/Violated Dependencies). *Let $\mathcal{K} = (\mathcal{R}, \mathcal{T}, \mathcal{A})$ be a KB and ct a context identifier. In context ct concept C depends on concept D w.r.t. role R in $\mathcal{K}$, if in context ct for every individual c with $\mathcal{K} \models C(c)$ there necessarily exists an individual $d \in Ind(\mathcal{A})$ with $\mathcal{K} \models D(d)$ and $\mathcal{K} \models R(c,d)$. For a context ct, the set of dependencies in $\mathcal{K}$ is given as*

$$Dep(\mathcal{K}, ct) = \{(C, D, R) \mid \text{in context ct concept } C \text{ depends on concept } D$$
$$\text{w.r.t. role } R \text{ in } \mathcal{K}\}.$$

The set of assertions violating a dependency in an KB and a context ct is defined as

$$violatedDep(\mathcal{K}, ct) = \{C(c) \mid (C, D, R) \in Dep(\mathcal{K}, ct) \text{ and } \mathcal{K} \models C(c) \text{ and }$$
$$\neg \exists d \in Ind(\mathcal{A}) \text{ with } \mathcal{K} \models R(c, d) \text{ and } \mathcal{K} \vdash D(d)\}$$

Please note that, one concept may be dependent on another concept in one context and not in another.

3.2   Requirements for Metaproperty-Guided Deletion

Rigidity provides information about the epistemic status of concepts, which can be used to understand the dynamics of instances of this concept. Given a knowledge base $\mathcal{K}$ at time t_1 a deletion transaction initiated by a user will cause a transition that makes $\mathcal{K}$ become $\mathcal{K}'$ at time t_2. Metaproperties indicate what may and what should not be an allowed transition. The rules that guide such transitions vary for rigid and non-rigid assertions. Furthermore, these rules take dependencies into account. Systematic analysis of different examples has led to the following requirements for deletion:

1. The deletion of a rigid assertion $C(a)$ should result in *forgetting* individual a from the signature of the KB. This corresponds to removing all assertions containing individual a from the ABox.
2. The deletion of a non-rigid assertion $D(b)$ should result in the *contraction* of $D(b)$ from the KB. This corresponds to determining a deletion for $D(b)$ in the KB and removing this deletion from the KB. The resulting KB can still contain assertions mentioning individual b.
3. The deletion of an assertion should be performed such that the set of rigid assertions removed by the deletion is minimal w.r.t set inclusion.
4. The deletion should have a cascading behavior: a deletion can lead to the violation of dependencies leading to further deletions, which in turn can violate dependencies, and so on. These deletions caused by dependencies are called *cascading deletions*.

Please note that cascading deletions are fundamentally different from deleting inferred assertions. The assertions that are removed by cascading deletion are not assertions that could be inferred, but assertions that must be deleted due to violated dependencies.

3.3   Rigidity-Guided Deletion

We now introduce rigidity-guided deletion which considers the rigidity metaproperty and fulfills requirements 1, 2 and 3.

Example 1. Consider the KB given in Sect. 1.1. Suppose this KB is used in the context of product development *pd* and assume that *Petrol* is a rigid concept in this context. Hence, $Petrol \in Rigid(\mathcal{K}, pd)$. Assume $PetrolEngine(pte)$ is supposed to be deleted i.e. $\mathcal{A}_d = \{PetrolEngine(pte)\}$. This deletion can be accomplished by deleting one of the two following sets from the ABox, which both constitute a deletion of $\mathcal{A}_d$ from $\mathcal{K}$:

$$Del_1 = \{PetrolEngine(pte), Petrol(superplus)\} \tag{6}$$

$$Del_2 = \{PetrolEngine(pte), canBeFueledBy(pte, superplus)\} \tag{7}$$

The rigidity of *Petrol* indicates that it is preferable not to delete assertions using this concept. Intuitively, it makes sense not to remove the information that *superplus* is a petrol but rather the information that *pte* can be fueled by petrol. Which leads to choosing Del_2 and fulfills requirement 3.

Let us now consider a different scenario, where for some reasons we really want to delete the fact that *superplus* is a petrol, meaning $\mathcal{A}_d = \{Petrol(superplus)\}$. The rigidity of concept *Petrol* indicates that an essential property of individual *superplus* is supposed to be deleted. Therefore, we suggest to entirely remove *superplus* from KB. The result is the deletion of $Petrol(superplus)$ and $canBeFueledBy(pte, superplus)$. Please note that the deletion of $canBeFueledBy(pte, superplus)$ is not necessary to prevent $Petrol(superplus)$ from being entailed but rather constitutes an additional deletion caused by the rigidity metaproperty of *Petrol*. This fulfills requirement 2.

The rigidity-guided deletion puts these ideas into practice by minimizing the set of removed rigid assertions and forgetting individuals occurring in rigid assertions which will be deleted.

Definition 7 (Rigidity-Guided Deletion). *Let $\mathcal{K} = (\mathcal{R}, \mathcal{T}, \mathcal{A})$ be a KB, ct be a context and $\mathcal{A}_d$ the set of ABox assertions supposed to be deleted from $\mathcal{K}$. Let Del be a deletion of $\mathcal{A}_d$ with minimal $Rigid(Del, ct)$ w.r.t. set inclusion. A rigidity-guided deletion of $\mathcal{A}_d$ from $\mathcal{K}$ in context ct is*

$$\mathcal{K}_{\mathcal{A}_d}^{rig} = \big(\mathcal{R}, \mathcal{T}, (\mathcal{A} \setminus Del) \setminus RigidDel(\mathcal{A}, Del, ct)\big)$$

with

$$RigidDel(\mathcal{A}, Del, ct) = \{D(a), R(a, b), R(b, a) \in \mathcal{A} \mid \exists C(a) \in Rigid(Del, ct)\}.$$

Please note that there can be more than one deletion *Del* with minimal $Rigid(Del, ct)$. In this case, the result of the rigidity-guided deletion is not specified and we suggest to let the user decide which of the solutions best implements her intentions.

3.4   Dependency-Guided Deletion

Now we introduce *dependency-guided deletion* which considers the dependency metaproperty and fulfills requirement 4.

Example 2. Consider the KB $\mathcal{K} = (\mathcal{T}, \mathcal{A})$ given in Sect. 1.1 that could be used in two different contexts namely product development (pd) and a car repair shop (crs). In the context of product development, the manifold depends on the petrol engine. Removing a specific motor in this context is usually only done if a different kind of motor is supposed to be used. Therefore, it is desired that the deletion of the engine results in the deletion of the manifold which might result in further deletions. In the context of a car repair shop, it is usually desirable to replace only those parts for which replacement is absolutely necessary. Deleting a motor in this context usually means that a defective motor is to be replaced by a new motor of the same type. Therefore, it is desirable in this context not to remove the manifold. The fact that the catalytic converter is welded to the manifold leads to dependencies in both contexts, meaning that the removal of the manifold results in the removal of the catalytic converter in both contexts. This leads to the following set of dependencies:

$$Dep(\mathcal{K}, pd) = \{(PetrolEngine, Petrol, canBeFueledBy), \tag{8}$$
$$(Manifold, PetrolEngine, isConnectedTo), \tag{9}$$
$$(ExhaustPipe, Manifold, isConnectedTo), \tag{10}$$
$$(CatalyticConverter, Manifold, isWeldedTo)\} \tag{11}$$
$$Dep(\mathcal{K}, crs) = \{(CatalyticConverter, Manifold, isWeldedTo)\} \tag{12}$$

We now consider a product developer who wants to replace the petrol engine by an electric engine. For this, he wants to delete $PetrolEngine(pte)$ leading to $\mathcal{A}_d = \{PetrolEngine(pte)\}$. To prevent $\mathcal{A}_d$ from being entailed, one of the two sets Del_1 given in (6) and Del_2 given in (7) presented in Example 1 have to be deleted from the ABox. Suppose we choose Del_2. Taking a closer look at the ABox reveals that after deleting $PetrolEngine(pte)$ from the ABox, manifold mf is not connected to an individual of concept $PetrolEngine$ anymore. Due to the open world semantics, the fact that there is no petrol engine connected to the manifold mf explicitly mentioned in the ABox does not contradict $Manifold(mf)$, which is still contained in the ABox. We argue that this might not correspond to the product developer's intention. We suggest so called *dependency-guided* deletion which uses the dependence metaproperty specified in the current context in order to determine additional deletions which are likely to be intended by the user. In our case, we delete $Manifold(mf)$ as well, since the deletion of $PetrolEngine(pte)$ violated dependency (9). Furthermore, dependency-guided semantics has a cascading behavior. In our example, this means that the deletion of $Manifold(mf)$ leads to the violation of dependencies (10) and (11) resulting in the deletion of both $ExhaustPipe(ep)$ and $CatalyticConverter(cc)$.

Overall, the deletion of $PetrolEngine(pte)$ in the context of product development leads to the deletion of the following set of assertions:

$$\{PetrolEngine(pte), canBeFueledBy(pte, superplus), Manifold(mf),$$
$$ExhaustPipe(ep), CatalyticConverter(cc)\}$$

Next consider a mechanic in a car repair shop who wants to replace a broken petrol engine by a new petrol engine of the same type leading to deletion of *PetrolEngine(pte)* in the context *crs*. Since the deletion of {*PetrolEngine(pte)*} does not violate any dependencies in this context, no cascading deletions are performed.

Next we define the *Casc*-operator. Given a certain context, a KB $\mathcal{K}$ and a set of assertions $\mathcal{A}_d$ that are supposed to be deleted, the *Casc*-operator computes a set of ABoxes. Each of these ABoxes constitutes a possible result of the cascading deletion for the context under consideration.

Definition 8 (*Casc*-operator). *Let $\mathcal{K} = (\mathcal{R}, \mathcal{T}, \mathcal{A})$ be a KB, ct a context and $\mathcal{A}_d$ a set of assertions that are supposed to be deleted from $\mathcal{K}$. Then*

$$Casc_1(\mathcal{K}, ct, \mathcal{A}_d) = \{\mathcal{A} \setminus Del \mid Del \text{ a deletion for } \mathcal{A}_d \text{ in } \mathcal{K}\}$$

For $n \in \mathbb{N}$, $n \geq 1$

$$Casc_{n+1}(\mathcal{K}, ct, \mathcal{A}_d) = \{S \setminus Del \mid S \in Casc_n(\mathcal{K}, ct, \mathcal{A}_d) \text{ and } Del \text{ a deletion for}$$
$$ViolatedDep((\mathcal{R}, \mathcal{T}, S), ct) \text{ in } (\mathcal{R}, \mathcal{T}, S)\}$$

There is always an $i > 0$ such that $Casc_i(\mathcal{K}, ct, \mathcal{A}_d) = Casc_j(\mathcal{K}, ct, \mathcal{A}_d)$ for all $j \geq i$. For convenience, for this i we set $Casc(\mathcal{K}, ct, \mathcal{A}_d) = Casc_i(\mathcal{K}, ct, \mathcal{A}_d)$.

Definition 9 (Dependency-Guided Deletion). *Let $\mathcal{K} = (\mathcal{R}, \mathcal{T}, \mathcal{A})$ be a KB, ct a context, and $\mathcal{A}_d$ a set of assertions that is supposed to be deleted from $\mathcal{K}$. Then $\mathcal{K}_{\mathcal{A}_d}^{dep} = (\mathcal{R}, \mathcal{T}, \mathcal{A}^{dep})$ with $\mathcal{A}^{dep}$ the largest (w.r.t. set inclusion) set in $Casc(\mathcal{K}, ct, \mathcal{A}_d)$ is a dependence-guided deletion of $\mathcal{A}_d$ from $\mathcal{K}$ in context ct.*

In general there can be more than one element which is maximal w.r.t. set inclusion in $Casc(\mathcal{K}, ct, \mathcal{A}_d)$. In this case, the dependency-guided deletion is not specified and we suggest to let the user decide which of the solutions best implements her intentions.

The combination of the rigidity and dependency metaproperties will be investigated in the next section.

3.5   Cascading Deletions

The operator for *cascading deletion* considers both the rigidity and the dependence metaproperty and fulfills all four requirements given in Sect. 3.2.

Combining the behavior of rigidity- and dependency-guided deletions does not only add the deletions performed by each individual deletion but interactions between rigid concepts and dependencies can lead to further deletions: the cascading deletions caused by the dependency-guided deletion can lead to the deletion of rigid assertions which leads to the deletion of all assertions containing certain individuals. This can result into the violation of dependencies.

Recall that by Definition 7 for a context *ct*, *RigidDel($\mathcal{A}$, Del, ct)* denotes the set of all assertions in the $\mathcal{A}$ containing an individual which occurs in a rigid assertion in *Del*.

Definition 10 ($Casc^{rd}$**-operator**). *Let* $\mathcal{K} = (\mathcal{R}, \mathcal{T}, \mathcal{A})$ *be a KB, ct a context, and* $\mathcal{A}_d$ *a set of assertions that is supposed to be deleted from* $\mathcal{K}$. *Then*

$$Casc_1^{rd}(\mathcal{K}, ct, \mathcal{A}_d) = \{(\mathcal{A} \setminus Del) \setminus RigidDel(\mathcal{A}, Del, ct) \mid Del \text{ a deletion of } \mathcal{A}_d \text{ in } \mathcal{K}\}$$

For $n \in \mathbb{N}, n \geq 1$

$$\begin{aligned}
Casc_{n+1}^{rd}(\mathcal{K}, ct, \mathcal{A}_d) = \{S \setminus Del' \mid &S \in Casc_n^{rd}(\mathcal{K}, ct, \mathcal{A}_d) \text{ and } Del \text{ a deletion of } \\
&ViolatedDep((\mathcal{R}, \mathcal{T}, S), ct) \text{ in } (\mathcal{R}, \mathcal{T}, S) \text{ and } \\
&Del' = Del \cup RigidDel(S, Del, ct)\}
\end{aligned}$$

There is always an $i > 0$ such that $Casc_i^{rd}(\mathcal{K}, ct, \mathcal{A}_d) = Casc_j^{rd}(\mathcal{K}, ct, \mathcal{A}_d)$ for all $j \geq i$. For convenience, for this i we set $Casc^{rd}(\mathcal{K}, ct, \mathcal{A}_d) = Casc_i^{rd}(\mathcal{K}, ct, \mathcal{A}_d)$.

Definition 11 (Cascading Deletion). *Let* $\mathcal{K} = (\mathcal{R}, \mathcal{T}, \mathcal{A})$ *be a KB, ct a context, and* $\mathcal{A}_d$ *a set of assertions that is supposed to be deleted from* $\mathcal{K}$. *Then* $\mathcal{K}_{\mathcal{A}_d}^{rd} = (\mathcal{R}, \mathcal{T}, \mathcal{A}^{rd})$ *with* $\mathcal{A}^{rd}$ *the largest (w.r.t. set inclusion) set in* $Casc^{rd}(\mathcal{K}, ct, \mathcal{A}_d)$ *is a* cascading deletion *of* $\mathcal{A}_d$ *from* $\mathcal{K}$ *in context ct.*

In general there can be more than one element that is maximal w.r.t. set inclusion in $Casc^{rd}(\mathcal{K}, ct, \mathcal{A}_d)$. In this case, the cascading deletion is not specified and we suggest let the user decide which of the solutions best implements her intentions.

Example 3. Consider the KB given in Example 1 together with the dependencies stated in Example 2 and the following set of rigid concepts:

$$\begin{aligned}
Rigid(\mathcal{K}, pd) = \{&Petrol, PetrolEngine, Manifold, ExhaustPipe, \\
&CatalyticConverter\}
\end{aligned}$$

Consider a product developer who is confronted with the political decision that, for environmental reasons, *superplus* is no longer allowed to be used as petrol for newly developed cars. Therefore, he wants to delete *Petrol(superplus)* leading to $\mathcal{A}_d = \{Petrol(superplus)\}$. In the first step, the rigidity of *Petrol* leads to the deletion of both *Petrol(superplus)* and *canBeFueledBy(pte, superplus)*. In the resulting ABox, dependency (8) is violated since there is no petrol left that can be used to fuel petrol engine *pte*. Therefore, in the next step *PetrolEngine(pte)* is deleted. The rigidity of concept *PetrolEngine* causes individual *pte* to be entirely removed from the ABox leading to the deletion of *PetrolEngine(pte)* and *isConnectedTo(mf, pte)*. Again dependencies are violated which leads to further cascading deletions. The overall result of the $Casc^{rd}$-operator is $Casc^{rd}(\mathcal{K}, ct, \mathcal{A}_d) = \{\{Petrol(v\text{-}power)\}\}$. The ABox in $Casc^{rd}(\mathcal{K}, ct, \mathcal{A}_d)$ constitutes the ABox resulting from the cascading deletion.

3.6   Design Decisions

In belief revision, a deletion operator should usually fulfill the so-called success postulate, which states that deletion of a non-tautological statement from a KB results in a KB that does not entail the statement. This is only possible, if consistency is established. This is why we decided to design the metaproperty-guided deletion operators such that they remove all inconsistencies present in a KB even if they have nothing to do with the deletion actually performed. Following this line, we decided to design the operators for both dependency-guided deletion and the cascading deletion such that they delete assertions that have already violated dependencies in the original ABox and even if they have nothing to do with the deletion performed. This behavior of the operators is desired in our project's area of application of product development and is intended to support the product developer. Other areas of application in which this behavior is not desired are conceivable. For this, the deletion operators would have to be adjusted.

3.7   Implementation

We have implemented the three deletion operators as an intelligent assistant[2] which uses SPARQL update queries (with empty insert statement) to specify the deletions. Our implementation uses Pellet [22] for the computation of justifications.

4   Evaluation

To evaluate if the cascading deletions are user-intended, we performed a case study[3]. with a KB $\mathcal{K}$ that formalizes a test rig. Engineers developed the KB [13] in the EVOWIPE project. The KB contains 15 concepts, 17 roles and 26 individuals. After a training on the metaproperties dependence and rigidity provided by us, the engineers decided where to add these metaproperties to their ontology. In the resulting KB, two concepts carry the rigidity metaproperty and 8 dependencies are stored (as annotations of concepts).

To evaluate if the deletions performed by the cascading deletion are desired, a questionnaire consisting of 40 questions of the form presented in Fig. 1 was used. We systematically created the questions for the survey. In general, we observed that:

- If the deletion of $D(b)$ leads to the cascading deletion of $C(a)$, then often exists R such that $\mathcal{K} \models R(a, b)$.
- If the deletion of $R(a, b)$ leads to the cascading deletion of $C(a)$, then often exists D such that $\mathcal{K} \models D(b)$.

---

[2] Implementation available at: https://github.com/Institute-Web-Science-and-Technologies/SparqlUpdater.

[3] The KB and the questionnaire used in the case study are available at: https://west.uni-koblenz.de/sites/default/files/research/datasets/evaluation_testrig.zip.

Of course other cases are conceivable where the cascading deletion performs several cascading steps, but for the systematic creation of the questions in the questionnaire we have restrict ourselves to the two cases mentioned above.

We determined all pairs $(C(a), D(b))$ and $(C(a), R(a, b))$ with $\mathcal{K} \models C(a)$, $\mathcal{K} \models D(b)$ and $\mathcal{K} \models R(a, b)$. This has led to 183 assertion pairs. For 20 of these pairs, the deletion of the second component leads to a cascading deletion of the first component. For all remaining pairs, the deletion of the second component does not affect the first component.

For the questionnaire, we selected 11 pairs where the deletion of the second component leads to the cascading deletion of the first component and randomly selected 29 pairs where the deletion or the second component does not have any effect on the first component. We have intentionally oversampled such that the proportion of cascading deletions in the questionnaire is much higher than in the whole set of pairs to prevent subjects from being inclined to always pick the same negative answer.

Results and Discussion. Seven experts from product development, two of whom are co-authors of this paper, answered the questionnaire consisting of 40 questions, leading to 280 asked questions out of which 277 were answered. When they answered the questions, the engineers used the KB and their background knowledge. For inter-rater agreement, we counted both 'rather yes' and 'yes' answers as 'yes' and both 'rather no' and 'no' answers as 'no' and computed Fleiss' Kappa for the results. The Fleiss' Kappa value indicates by how much the raters agreement exceeds an agreement if the questionnaires are completed randomly. For our questionnaire, the Fleiss' Kappa value is 0.561. For the interpretation of Kappa values, [14] suggest $\kappa < 0$ corresponds to poor agreement, $0 \leq \kappa < 0.2$ to slight agreement, $0.2 \leq \kappa < 0.4$ to fair agreement, $0.4 \leq \kappa < 0.6$ to moderate agreement, $0.6 \leq \kappa < 0.8$ to substantial agreement and $0.8 \leq \kappa \leq 1$ to (almost) perfect agreement.

For evaluation of precision and recall, we created a gold standard answer of either 'yes' or 'no' for each of the 40 questions by majority vote of the responses. We compared the result of the majority vote to the result of the operator for cascading deletions leading to a precision of 1 and recall of 0.48.

The precision of 1 indicates, that the engineers agreed with all 11 cascading deletions. There is no case were the cascading deletion deletes an assertion and the engineers want to keep this assertion. The comparatively lower recall of 0.48 suggests that there are deletions desired by the engineers which are not performed by our approach. Analyzing the questions where most engineers wanted to delete the suggested assertion but our approach did not perform this deletion reveals three causes for the discrepancies:

– For some questions, our approach did not perform the deletion desired by the engineers because the corresponding metaproperties were not set in the ontology. Since the metaproperties for the case study were set manually during the creation of the ontology, they were forgotten in some places. This was only revealed after analyzing the results of the questionnaire. The engineers are currently working on extracting some of these metaproperties automatically with the help of *revers engineering* which supports a systematic analysis of product structures and can be used to extract some of the dependencies.

- In one case, a modeling error in the KB was revealed: The concept *subfunction* was not modeled as a subconcept of the *function* concept. This modeling error prevented the desired deletion from being implemented by our approach.
- In two cases the analysis revealed that the notion of dependency used by our approach is not sufficient. The engineers need counting dependencies in some cases, i.e. something is only a subassembly if it has at least two parts. Our current notion of dependency cannot map such counting dependencies and therefore cannot perform the desired cascading deletions.
- In some cases, the analysis revealed that the engineers expected the dependencies to be symmetric. For example concept *solution_principle* is modeled to be dependent on concept *function* w.r.t. role *fulfils*. Role *fulfils* is symmetric to role *isFulfiledBy*. The engineers expected in this case that the fact that concept *function* depends on concept *solution_principle* w.r.t. role *isFulfiledBy* follows from the KB, which currently is not the case. We think that this can be regarded as a *mutual dependency* which is not yet supported by our current approach.

The engineers added the metaproperties whose absence had been noticed and fixed the modeling error. On the improved KB, the precision of our approach is 1, recall has risen to 0.7.

We want to focus on the observed counting dependencies as well as mutual dependencies in future work in order to be able to cover more of the desired deletions. Furthermore, we will analyze which of the other notions of dependencies mentioned in [21] could be useful in the context of product development.

Assume the fact that
measuring_normal_forces belongs to class *function*
is supposed to be deleted. In your opinion, should the fact that
calculation(low_rpm_no.)via_spring_rate+valve_position belongs to class *solution_principle*
be deleted as well?
☐ yes   ☐ rather yes   ☐ rather no   ☐ no

Fig. 1. Example question from the questionnaire answered by seven experts from the FAU.

5   Related Work

Ontological metamodelling has a long tradition and is used in various areas [8]. We build our approach on two of the metaproperties used in the OntoClean methodology [10]. However in [10], the metaproperties are not used for the task of updating KBs.

The problem of belief revision and updating KBs has received much attention in research [2]. Usually, approaches in this area have the goal to perform the desired changes while maintaining as much of the original KB as possible. In the model-based approach the set of models of the KB resulting from a change operation should be as close as possible to the set of models of the original KB [12,16]. Opposed to the model-based approach, in [4,5,15] the number of axioms and assertions changed by the update are supposed to be minimal. In [4,5,15] instance level deletion, insertion and repair are addressed for DL-Lite KBs. [7] addresses the same tasks for $\mathcal{SHI}$ KBs. In all these approaches, the computed deletions are minimal and a cascading behavior is not considered.

With respect to SPARQL update, [1] addresses the problem of handling inconsistencies introduced by SPARQL updates in $DL\text{-}Lite_{\mathrm{RDFS}_-}$ which covers RDFS and concept disjointness axioms. Different semantics of SPARQL ABox updates are defined and skillful query-rewriting is used to perform the updates. These rewritings exploit the fact that in $DL\text{-}Lite_{\mathrm{RDFS}_-}$ inconsistencies are caused by at most two ABox assertions and furthermore rely on the fact that the ABox is materialized.

The cascading behavior of the dependency-guided deletion introduced in this paper is related to the K-operator used in the autoepistemic description logic $\mathcal{ALCK}$ [6]. Intuitively, the K-operator can be interpreted as 'known to be'. For example the concept K$ExhaustPipe$ is interpreted as the set of all individuals for which it is known that they belong to the concept $ExhaustPipe$ meaning that only individuals whose membership to concept $ExhaustPipe$ is explicitly stated in the ABox are interpreted such that they belong to K$ExhaustPipe$. The K-operator can be used to state dependencies like the fact that the manifold depends on the petrol engine as

$$Manifold \sqsubseteq \exists \mathsf{K}isConnectedTo.\mathsf{K}PetrolEngine$$

intuitively meaning that for every manifold a petrol engine has to be explicitly stated which is known to be connected to the manifold. However it is not possible to state that this dependency is only valid in a certain context. Furthermore, the rigidity metaproperty cannot be stated using the K operator. Up till now only few DL-reasoners support the K-operator and those reasoners only support the K-operator within queries whereas the KB itself is not allowed to use the operator.

In [3] truth maintenance systems are used to track deductive dependencies between statements in an RDF store. In contrast to this, the dependencies used in this paper can change depending on the context and do not necessarily constitute deductive dependencies. In relational databases, certain dependencies can be enforced by adding integrity constraints which are checked during udpates. [20] introduces static integrity constraints to OWL making it possible, for example, to add a constraint stating that "every person must have a social security number" to an OWL KB.

6   Conclusion and Future Work

In this paper, we presented three different deletion operators: The rigidity-guided deletion performs additional deletions by forgetting an individual from the KB's signature. The dependency-guided deletion relies on dependencies present in the KB and shows a cascading behavior by removing assertions violating these dependencies. The third operator, called cascading deletion exploits both rigidity and dependence metaproperties. The interaction of these two metaproperties leads to interesting deletion cascades, which provide intelligent assistants to users, e.g. product developers. In a case study in the area of product development we have shown that the cascading deletions performed by our approach are desired by the product developers. The case study revealed that the product developers would like further deletions, the implementation of which we will tackle in the future. To achieve this, we plan to analyze other types of dependencies in KBs and then exploit them for deletion.

Up till now we only considered deletions. However in practice deletions go hand in hand with insertions. Inserting assertions can easily lead to violated dependencies. We want to use these violated dependencies to make suggestions to the user for further insertions. This cannot be accomplished with a local closed world assumption, since it does not allow to consider transitions between different states of a KB. In contrast to that, dependencies could be checked for each insertion and additional insertions preventing the violation of dependencies could be automatically generated and suggested to the user.

References

1. Ahmeti, A., Calvanese, D., Polleres, A., Savenkov, V.: Handling Inconsistencies Due to Class Disjointness in SPARQL Updates. In: Sack, H., Blomqvist, E., d'Aquin, M., Ghidini, C., Ponzetto, S.P., Lange, C. (eds.) ESWC 2016. LNCS, vol. 9678, pp. 387–404. Springer, Cham (2016). https://doi.org/10.1007/978-3-319-34129-3_24
2. Alchourrón, C.E., Gärdenfors, P., Makinson, D.: On the logic of theory change: partial meet contraction and revision functions. J. Symb. Log. **50**(2), 510–530 (1985)
3. Broekstra, J., Kampman, A.: Inferencing and truth maintenance in RDF schema. In: PSSS, vol. 89, CEUR Workshop Proceedings. CEUR-WS.org (2003)
4. Calvanese, D., Kharlamov, E., Nutt, W., Zheleznyakov, D.: Updating ABoxes in DL-Lite. In: AMW, vol. 619, CEUR Workshop Proceedings (2010). CEUR-WS.org
5. De Giacomo, G., Lenzerini, M., Poggi, A., Rosati, R.: On instance-level update and erasure in description logic ontologies. J. Log. Comput. **19**(5), 745–770 (2009)
6. Donini, F.M., Lenzerini, M., Nardi, D., Nutt, W., Schaerf, A.: An epistemic operator for description logics. Artif. Intell. **100**(1–2), 225–274 (1998)
7. Furbach, U., Schon, C.: Semantically guided evolution of $\mathcal{SHI}$ ABoxes. In: Galmiche, D., Larchey-Wendling, D. (eds.) TABLEAUX 2013. LNCS (LNAI), vol. 8123, pp. 134–148. Springer, Heidelberg (2013). https://doi.org/10.1007/978-3-642-40537-2_13

8. Gasevic, D., Djuric, D., Devedzic, V.: Model Driven Engineering and Ontology Development, 2nd edn. Springer, Heidelberg (2009). https://doi.org/10.1007/978-3-642-00282-3

9. Grau, B.C., Kharlamov, E., Zheleznyakov, D.: Ontology contraction: beyond the propositional paradise. In: AMW, vol. 866, CEUR Workshop Proceedings, pp. 62–74. CEUR-WS.org (2012)

10. Guarino, N., Welty, C.A.: An overview of OntoClean. In: Staab, S., Studer, R. (eds.) Handbook on Ontologies, International Handbooks on Information Systems, pp. 201–220. Springer, Heidleberg (2009). https://doi.org/10.1007/978-3-540-92673-3_9

11. Horridge, M.: Justification based explanation in ontologies. Ph.D. thesis, University of Manchester (2011)

12. Kharlamov, E., Zheleznyakov, D., Calvanese, D.: Capturing model-based ontology evolution at the instance level: the case of dl-lite. J. Comput. Syst. Sci. **79**(6), 835–872 (2013)

13. Kügler, P., et al.: Ontology-based approach for the use of intentional forgetting in product development. In: Marjanovic, D., Storga, M., Pavkovic, N., Bojcetic, N., Skec, S. (eds.) DESIGN 2018 (2018)

14. Landis, J.R., Koch, G.G.: The measurement of observer agreement for categorical data. Biometrics **33**(1), 159–174 (1977)

15. Lenzerini, M., Savo, D.F.: On the evolution of the instance level of DL-Lite knowledge bases. In: Description Logics, vol. 745, CEUR Workshop Proceedings. CEUR-WS.org (2011)

16. Liu, H., Lutz, C., Milicic, M., Wolter, F.: Foundations of instance level updates in expressive description logics. Artif. Intell. **175**(18), 2170–2197 (2011)

17. Lutz, C., Wolter, F.: Foundations for uniform interpolation and forgetting in expressive description logics. In: IJCAI, pp. 989–995. IJCAI/AAAI (2011)

18. McGuinness, D., Kendall, E., Bao, J., Patel-Schneider, P.: OWL 2 web ontology language quick reference guide (second edition). Technical report, W3C, December 2012. http://www.w3.org/TR/2012/REC-owl2-quick-reference-20121211/

19. Moodley, K.: Debugging and repair of description logic ontologies. Master's thesis, University of KwaZulo-Natal, Durban, South Africa (2010)

20. Motik, B., Horrocks, I., Sattler, U.: Adding integrity constraints to OWL. In: OWLED, vol. 258, CEUR Workshop Proceedings. CEUR-WS.org (2007)

21. Simons, P.: Parts: A Study in Ontology. Clarendon Press, Oxford (1987)

22. Sirin, E., Parsia, B., Grau, B.C., Kalyanpur, A., Katz, Y.: Pellet: A practical OWL-DL reasoner. J. Web Sem. **5**(2), 51–53 (2007)

On Extracting Relations Using Distributional Semantics and a Tree Generalization

René Speck[1(✉)] and Axel-Cyrille Ngomo Ngonga[2(✉)]

[1] Leipzig University, AKSW Group, Hainstraße 11, 04109 Leipzig, Germany
speck@informatik.uni-leipzig.de
[2] Paderborn University, DICE Group, Warburger Straße 100, 33098 Paderborn, Germany
axel.ngonga@upb.de

Abstract. Extracting relations out of unstructured text is essential for a wide range of applications. Minimal human effort, scalability and high precision are desirable characteristics. We introduce a distant supervised closed relation extraction approach based on distributional semantics and a tree generalization. Our approach uses training data obtained from a reference knowledge base to derive dependency parse trees that might express a relation. It then uses a novel generalization algorithm to construct dependency tree patterns for the relation. Distributional semantics are used to eliminate false candidate patterns. We evaluate the performance in experiments on a large corpus using ninety target relations. Our evaluation results suggest that our approach achieves a higher precision than two state-of-the-art systems. Moreover, our results also underpin the scalability of our approach. Our open source implementation can be found at https://github.com/dice-group/Ocelot.

Keywords: Distant supervision · Relation extraction
Distributional semantics · Tree generalization

1 Introduction and Motivation

Knowledge extraction is the process of extracting facts in unstructured text automatically by, for instance, extracting relevant elements such as entities and relationships between these entities. Identifying token spans that constitute entity mentions and assigning types (e.g. Person) to these spans as well as relations (e.g. spouse) between entity mentions, is a key step to structuring knowledge from unstructured text for further analysis [10,18]. One application area of increasing importance is Question Answering (QA) with systems built on knowledge graphs like DBpedia. Such QA systems are typically composed of two stages: (1) the query analyzer, and (2) the retrieval stage [9,21]. Common techniques in the first stage are, for instance, named entity recognition and linking as well as relation extraction. Consider the following question from the QALD

© Springer Nature Switzerland AG 2018
C. Faron Zucker et al. (Eds.): EKAW 2018, LNAI 11313, pp. 424–438, 2018.
https://doi.org/10.1007/978-3-030-03667-6_27

dataset [23]: "Is Michelle Obama the wife of Barack Obama?". A common way to answer this question with a QA system is to produce a semantic representation of this question within the first stages (see Listing 1.1). In the second stage, this semantic representation is converted into SPARQL (see Listing 1.2) to query the knowledge base for further analytics and to create an answer to this question.

```
@prefix its: <http://www.w3.org/2005/11/its/rdf#> .
@prefix nif: <http://persistence.uni-leipzig.org/nlp2rdf/ontologies/nif-core#> .
@prefix rdf: <http://www.w3.org/1999/02/22-rdf-syntax-ns#> .
[ a nif:Phrase ;
        nif:anchorOf "Michelle Obama" ;
        nif:beginIndex "3"
        its:taIdentRef <http://dbpedia.org/resource/Michelle_Obama> ] .
[ a rdf:Statement ;
        rdf:subject <http://dbpedia.org/resource/Michelle_Obama> ;
        rdf:predicate <http://dbpedia.org/ontology/spouse> ;
        rdf:object <http://dbpedia.org/resource/Barack_Obama> ] .
[ a nif:Phrase ;
        nif:anchorOf "Barack Obama" ;
        nif:beginIndex "30"
        its:taIdentRef <http://dbpedia.org/resource/Barack_Obama> ].
```

Listing 1.1. Example semantic representation of the question "Is Michelle Obama the wife of Barack Obama?" in an RDF/TURTLE serialization.

```
PREFIX dbo: <http://dbpedia.org/ontology/>
PREFIX dbr: <http://dbpedia.org/resource/>
ASK WHERE { dbr:Michelle_Obama dbo:spouse dbr:Barack_Obama}
```

Listing 1.2. A SPARQL query to ask DBpedia for the trueness of the statement.

Collections of semantically-typed relational patterns as provided by Patty [17] and Boa [8] are often used in the first stage of QA systems to match and link word patterns in questions to a knowledge base. For example, HAWK [22] uses Boa, whereas AskNow [5] uses Boa and Patty to match and link word patterns. QA systems require high precision, minimal human effort and scalability from the relation extraction components they rely on. With our approach, we improve upon the precision achieved by the state of the art while keeping the distant supervision and scalability it abides by.

We propose a closed relation extraction approach based on distant supervision by using distributed semantics and a tree generalization process. It extracts sets of trees from a corpus where each set expresses a target relation from a knowledge base. These trees are then generalized using both a tree generalization approach and distributional semantics. One of the main advantages of this paradigm is that it is less sensitive to semantic drift. In the state-of-the-art systems, Boa and Patty one pattern is often matched to several relations which results in a significant number of false positives [21]. For example the pattern "was born" appears 876 times in Patty and corresponds to six DBpedia predicates. In Boa, this pattern appears three times and corresponds to three DBpedia predicates. Whereas each of the computed generalized tree patterns matches to only one relation in our approach.

The rest of this paper is structured as follows. After reviewing previous work in Sect. 2, we introduce preliminaries in Sect. 3 and our proposed approach in Sect. 4. Subsequently, we present our evaluation in Sect. 5 and the error analyses in Sect. 6. We conclude by discussing our results in Sect. 7.

2   Previous Work

Numerous approaches for extracting relations have been developed in the recent past. Approaches for *closed relation extraction* [8,17] (in contrast to *open relation extraction* [3,4,6,12,24]), are based on vocabularies that define relations a priori, i.e., in a domain ontology or an extraction template. Consequently, such systems require no mapping of the extracted relations to a vocabulary and thus produce less uninformative or incoherent elements from unstructured text [1]. *Supervised learning approaches* are a core component of a vast number of relation extraction tools as they offer high precision and recall. The need for manually labeled training data makes these methods not scalable to thousands of relations found on the Web. More promising approaches are *semi-supervised bootstrapping approaches* [2,8,20] and *distant supervision approaches* [1,16,17], since these do not need a complete manually labeled training corpus. In recent years, distant supervision has become an important technique because of the availability of large knowledge bases. It utilizes facts from a knowledge base for labeling mentions of these facts in an unannotated corpus to create a training set. Thus, it fulfills the needs of large-scale applications with minimal human effort.

Boa [8] is a bootstrapping strategy for extracting RDF from unstructured data. Its idea is to use the Web of Data as background knowledge for the extraction of natural language patterns that represent predicates found on the Web of Data. These patterns are used to extract instance knowledge from natural language text. This knowledge is finally fed back into the Web of Data. Boa provides a repository of natural language representations of predicates found on the Web of Data.

Patty [17] is a large resource for textual patterns that denote binary relations between entities based on distant supervision. Patty uses frequent itemset mining and the patterns are semantically typed as well as organized into a subsumption taxonomy with scores, support and confidence. The taxonomy is available online but not in machine-readable data to use it by the community. We asked the authors to provide the source-code and the database with the results as well as the measures but we could not receive it.

One drawback of both state-of-the-art systems, Boa and Patty, is that one pattern can be matched to several relations which results in a significant number of false positives. Thus, this leads to a noisy behavior in applications such as Question Answering. Another drawback of these two systems is that both extract relations that are enclosed by named entities only. For instance, both systems cannot find the relation in the sentence "Michelle Obama and Barack Obama are married." as the verb which mentions a relation is not enclosed by the named entities. We address these drawbacks by operating on dependency parse trees and using a generalization approach inspired by [11] which tackles the semantic drift issue faced by many current approaches.

3   Preliminaries and Notations

In this section we define the terminology and notation used in this paper.

Corpus. Let $w \in \Sigma^*$ be a word that is a finite sequence over an alphabet Σ and let s be a sentence that is a finite sequence of words $s = (w_i)_{i=1,2,\dots}$. We denote the set of words of a sentence s with $W(s)$. A corpus $\mathcal{C}$ is a set of sentences.

Knowledge Base. Let $\mathcal{K} = (S, R, P, \gamma)$ be a knowledge base with a set of statements $S \subseteq R \times P \times R$ (i.e. facts), a set of resources R (i.e. things of the real world), a set of predicates P (i.e. relationships between things) and a labelling function that maps each resource and predicate to a word $\gamma : R \cup P \to \Sigma^*$.

Tree. Let $T = (V, A, E, \phi_A, \psi)$ be an attributed dependency parse tree (directed and ordered) with a finite set of vertices V, a set of edges $E \subseteq V \times V$, a vertex labelling function family $\phi_A = \{\phi_a | a \in A\}$ where A is a finite set of vertex attributes[1] so that $\phi_a : V \to \Sigma_a^*$ as well as with an edge labelling function $\psi : E \to \Sigma_E^*$.

We refer for a specific tree T with $V(T)$ for vertices, $E(T)$ for edges, $\phi_{T,A}$ for the vertex labelling function family and ψ_T for the edge labelling function. We denote the root vertex with $root_T$ and the root dependency vertex with sn_T.

Subtree. Let T be a tree and $v \in V(T)$. The ordered sequence of child vertices of v in T is denoted by $cn_T(v) = (u_i)_{i=1,2,\dots}$ with $u \in V(T)$. We then denote by $T(v)$ the subtree $T' = (V', A', E', \phi_A', \psi')$ with $root_{T'} = v$, $V' = cn_T(v) \cup \{v\}$, $E' = E \cap V' \times V'$, $\phi_A' = \phi_{A \upharpoonright V'}$ and $\psi' = \psi_{\upharpoonright E'}$.

$\leq$ **Relation.** For trees T_1 and T_2, we have $T_1 \leq T_2$ iff the following holds:

1. if sn_{T_2} exists, then:
   (a) $sn_{T_1} = root_{T_1}$, $sn_{T_2} = root_{T_2}$
   (b) $\phi_{T_1,lemma}(root_{T_1}) = \phi_{T_2,lemma}(root_{T_2})$
   (c) $\phi_{T_1,pos}(root_{T_1}) = \phi_{T_2,pos}(root_{T_2})$
2. if sn_{T_2} does not exist, then:
   (a) $attribute := \phi_{T_2,general}(root_{T_2})$
   (b) if $attribute = label$, then $A^* := \{label, lemma, pos\}$
   (c) if $attribute = lemma$, then $A^* := \{lemma, pos\}$
   (d) for each a in A^*
   $$\phi_{T_1,a}(root_{T_1}) = \phi_{T_2,a}(root_{T_2})$$
   (e) if $attribute \in \{pos, ner, domain, range\}$, then
   $$\phi_{T_1,attribute}(root_{T_1}) = \phi_{T_2,attribute}(root_{T_2})$$
3. for each edge $(root_{T_2}, v_2)$ in $E(T_2)$ there exists an edge $(root_{T_1}, v_1)$ in $E(T_1)$ with $\psi_{T_2}(root_{T_2}, v_2) = \psi_{T_1}(root_{T_1}, v_1)$ such that: $T(v_1) \leq T(v_2)$

We define $T_1 \simeq T_2$ as $T_1 \leq T_2$ and $T_2 \leq T_1$. $T_1 < T_2$ is defined as $T_1 \leq T_2$ and $T_1 \not\simeq T_2$.

---

[1] $A := \{label, lemma, pos, ner, domain, range, general\}$ are the vertex attributes used throughout this paper.

4   Approach

This section initially presents an overview of the data flow and subsequently provides insights into each package of our proposed framework.

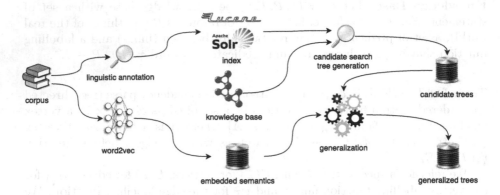

Fig. 1. The data flow of the proposed framework.

4.1   Overview

The data flow of our framework, dubbed Ocelot, is depicted in Fig. 1. The goal is to harvest generalized dependency tree patterns, which are useful for a wide range of applications to extract relations from unstructured text.

Ocelot starts by preprocessing the corpus with natural language processing tools to acquire linguistic annotations. These annotations are stored in an index for a fast search. Thereafter, it queries a knowledge base for predicates which are the target relations, related resources as well as labels of these resources. These labels serve as search keywords to query candidate sentences in the index that might contain target relations. The dependency parse trees on these candidate sentences are created and stored. In the generalization step, the candidate trees are generalized by linguistic annotations as well as are scored and ranked. Ocelot relies on distant supervision and thus introduces errors by semantic drift [2, 20]. To reduce this drift, it filters ambiguous trees. Ocelot utilizes embedded semantics by training word2vec [14] on the corpus. The vector representation of the labels from the knowledge base for the predicates as well as from other sources, for instance Wordnet, are used in the generalization step to filter out ambiguities among trees to reduce semantic drift. In the following, we explain each of these steps in detail.

4.2   Linguistic Annotation

We begin with an input corpus, which is first preprocessed. The core of the preprocessing consists of removing possible markup from the corpus (e.g. HTML tags). We then sample the frequency distribution of the sentences' length (number of tokens in a sentence including the end punctuation). On this distribution, the mean μ and standard deviation σ are calculated to filter out sentences that are very long and thus require long processing time in the framework. Ocelot then selects sentences with a minimum of four[2] and a maximum of $\mu + 2\sigma$ tokens. Linguistic annotations (lemmas, POS-tags, named entities)[3] are computed for the selected sentences (with Stanford Core NLP in our current implementation). Based on the assumption "if two entities participate in a relation, at least one sentence that mentions these two entities might express that relation" stated in [19], we discard sentences which contain less than two named entities. The remaining sentences and annotations are stored in a Solr index for a fast search.

4.3 Candidate Selection

This step's main functions are to find candidate sentences from the index that might express target relations and to parse these candidate sentences to dependency parse trees. We rely on background knowledge from the given knowledge base to search for candidates. In the first step, the predicates with the highest numbers of resource instances are chosen from the knowledge base. These selected predicates serve as target relations in Ocelot. For each target relation p, the candidate selection queries $\mathcal{K}$ for the set

$$S_p = \{(s,p,o) : (s,p^*,o) \in \mathcal{K} \to p = p^*\}. \tag{1}$$

With the labelling function γ, given by the knowledge base, we get the labels for resources that we employ to search in the index. As some extended labeling functions are available for some knowledge bases (e.g. [7] proposes an extension of the method originally proposed in [13] to gather additional labels DBpedia), we assume the existence of a method which can generate extended labels for any resource $r \in R$ and call this method $\pi(r)$. Then, the sets Π_s and Π_o of all labels for all subject resp. object resources of a target relation are given by

$$\Pi_s = \bigcup_{(s,p,o) \in S_p} \pi(s) \cup \gamma(s) \text{ and } \Pi_o = \bigcup_{(s,p,o) \in S_p} \pi(o) \cup \gamma(o). \tag{2}$$

Therewith, the set Ω contains candidate sentences with tokens that mention subject and object resources of a target relation

$$\Omega = I(\mathcal{C}, \Pi_s) \cap I(\mathcal{C}, \Pi_o), \text{ with } I(A,B) = \{a|a \in A \wedge \exists b \in (B \cap W(a))\} . \tag{3}$$

To reduce semantic drift, only candidate sentences with tokens which mention subject and object resources and which are tagged as named entities by the linguistic annotation package are collected. These candidate sentences are parsed to candidate dependency parse trees.

---

[2] The shortest sentence with a relation has at least two tokens for the named entity arguments, one token for the relation mention and one for the end punctuation.

[3] Seven types are applied (`Place`, `Person`, `Organization`, `Money`, `Percent`, `Date`, `Time`).

4.4   Embedded Semantics

This step serves as preprocessing for the subsequent generalization step. We create word-level embeddings on the corpus and use predicate labels from the knowledge base to find semantically similar words in several sources. We trained the continuous skip-gram model [15] implemented in the open-source software word2vec[4] on the corpus. This model is based on the idea that similar words are more likely to be neighbours if their word level embeddings represent lexical and semantic regularities. Thus, this model predicts words within a certain range to either side of a current word and captures syntactic and semantic regularities of words. We retrieve labels from the knowledge base for each of our target relations as well as from Wikidata[5] and merge them for each relation. We call these labels "seed labels". Then, we sum up the vector representation of each of the seed labels to one vector, the seed vector. Thereafter, for each seed label we query OxfordDictionary,[6] Wordnik[7] and Wordnet[8] to find similar words. To reduce semantic drift in this step, we rearrange these similar words to the seed labels with the help of the vector representations. Hence, for each similar word we choose its vector representation and calculate the cosine similarity between this vector and all the seed vectors to measure the similarity. We rearrange all similar words to the relation where the cosine similarity between the seed vector of a relation and the vector of the similar word has the highest value.

4.5   Generalization

The input of the generalization steps are the candidate trees as well as the results of the embedded semantics module. The goal is to generalize, filter, score and rank the candidate trees. Function 1 together with Function 2 define the algorithm to generalize the extracted dependency parse trees.

Function 1 takes two input parameters, i.e., two trees T_1 and T_2, and returns a generalized or an empty tree T. In the first line, T is initialized with an empty tree. In the next two lines, the root vertices of both trees are preserved and Function 2 is called to generalize the vertices of the trees. The generalized tree is stored in T. In line 4, a set is generated containing all edge labels from outgoing edges of the root vertices that have the same edge labels in both trees. In lines 5 to 7, we iterate over all outgoing edges of the root vertices in the trees that have the same labels. For each combination, Function 1 is recursively computed. Lines 10 to 13 show that only edges which do not subsume another edge are preserved. Finally, line 14 adds the edge to tree T.

Function 2 defines the part of the algorithm to generalize vertices of two trees, T_1 and T_2. This function takes an empty or partly generalized tree T together with the trees T_1 and T_2 as well as the root vertices of these trees $v_1 = root_{T_1}$

[4] https://code.google.com/archive/p/word2vec.
[5] https://www.wikidata.org.
[6] https://www.oxforddictionaries.com.
[7] https://www.wordnik.com.
[8] https://wordnet.princeton.edu.

Function 1. $generalize(T_1, T_2)$

---

1   initialize T with $V(T) = \varnothing$ and $E(T) = \varnothing$;
2   $v_1 = root_{T_1}$; $v_2 = root_{T_2}$;
3   $generalizeVertices(T, T_1, v_1, T_2, v_2)$;
4   $L = \{\psi_{T_1}(v_1, v_1')|(v_1, v_1') \in E(T_1), (v_2, v_2') \in E(T_2), \psi_{T_1}(v_1, v_1') = \psi_{T_2}(v_2, v_2')\}$;
5   **foreach** l in L **do**
6   **foreach** v_1' with $(v_1, v_1') \in E(T_1)$ and $\psi_{T_1}(v_1, v_1') = l$ **do**
7   **foreach** v_2' with $(v_2, v_2') \in E(T_2)$ and $\psi_{T_2}(v_2, v_2') = l$ **do**
8                $v' = root(generalize(T(v_1'), T(v_2')))$;
9                $add = true$;
10   **foreach** v_p with $(v, v_p) \in E(T)$ **do**
11   **if** $add = true$ **then**
12   **if** $T(v_p) \leq T(v')$ **then** $add = false$;
13   **if** $T(v') < T(v_p)$ **then** remove (v, v_p) from $E(T)$;
14   **if** $add = true$ **then** add edge (v, v') to $E(T)$;
15 **return** T;

---

and $v_2 = root_{T_2}$. The generalized tree is stored in T. In the first line, the function compares the root vertices with the root dependency vertices of the trees. If the vertices have the same labels, a new vertex is created with this label and is set as root along with the root dependency vertex. In case the given vertices differ from the root dependency vertices but have the same label, lemma or POS-tag, a new vertex is created and is set with common attributes in lines 9 to 16. In lines 18 to 22, vertices without the same lemma and POS-tags are compared and added to the generalized tree in cases where their other attributes are equal.

After the tree generalization steps, Ocelot filters false candidate tree patterns with the embedded semantics package. It retains tree patterns that contain one of the labels that occur in the label set of the corresponding target relation.

Through the generalization process, the number of trees that a tree generalizes is observed. The trees are ranked by this number and by the number of vertices. Thus, a generalized tree that generalizes the most trees and has the fewest number of vertices has the highest rank.

Figure 2 illustrates a generalized tree pattern on two example sentences. The red edges in the dependency parse trees mark deleted edges, the remaining edges together with the linguistic annotations in bold font symbolize the resulting generalized dependency parse tree. Named entity arguments are illustrated in curly brackets and POS-tags in square brackets.

5   Evaluation

In this section, we present our experimental setup as well as the quantitative and qualitative evaluations we carried out.

Function 2. $generalizeVertices(T, T_1, v_1, T_2, v_2)$

---

1   **if** $sn_{T_1} = v_1$ and $sn_{T_2} = v_2$ **then**

2   **if** $\phi_{T_1, label}(v_1) = \phi_{T_2, label}(v_2)$ **then**

3   initialize a new vertex v ;

4        $sn_T := v; \; root(T) := v$;

5        $\phi_{T, label}(v) := \phi_{T_1, label}(v_1)$;

6        $V(T) := V(T) \cup v$;

7   **else**

8   **if** $\phi_{T_1, lemma}(v_1) = \phi_{T_2, lemma}(v_2)$ and $\phi_{T_1, pos}(v_1) = \phi_{T_2, pos}(v_2)$ **then**

9   initialize a new vertex v ;

10        $\phi_{T, lemma}(v) := \phi_{T_1, lemma}(v_1)$;

11        $\phi_{T, pos}(v) := \phi_{T_1, pos}(v_1)$;

12        $V(T) := V(T) \cup v$;

13   **if** $\phi_{T_1, label}(v_1) = \phi_{T_2, label}(v_2)$ **then**

14          $\phi_{T, label}(v) := \phi_{T_1, label}(v_1)$;

15          $\phi_{T, general}(v) := label$;

16   **else** $\phi_{T, general}(v) := lemma$;

17   **else**

18   **foreach** $a \in \{pos, ner, domain, range\}$ **do**

19   **if** $\phi_{T_1, a}(v_1) = \phi_{T_2, a}(v_2)$ **then**

20            $\phi_{T, general}(v) := a$;

21            $\phi_{T, a}(v) := \phi_{T_1, a}(v_1)$;

22            $V(T) := V(T) \cup v$;

5.1   Setup

For the experiments, we used the English Wikipedia as corpus $\mathcal{C}$ and DBpedia as knowledge base $\mathcal{K}$. For the index, we chose the implementation of Apache Solr with Lucene. The index contained 93,499,905 sentences in total with an average of $\mu = 22$ tokens per sentence and with a standard deviation of $\sigma = 15.8$ tokens. Our pipeline processed 88.44% of the sentences in the index. For the target relations queried from the DBpedia knowledge base, we chose the top ten of each combination of resource types[9] we took into account. Thus, we ended up with 90 target relations. Table 1 depicts an excerpt with the top-three target relations of each combination from DBpedia.

5.2   Quantitative Evaluation

In the quantitative evaluation, we first manually evaluated the filter approach to reduce semantic drift based on the embedded semantics package. Then, we compared the F1-Score, Precision and Recall of the results with the embedded semantics filter with the results of two state-of-the-art systems, Patty and Boa.

    The precision (P), i.e., how many of the generalized trees express the correct relation for the top-k ranked generalized trees with and without the filter

---

[9] In our approach we utilize **Organization**, **Person** and **Place**.

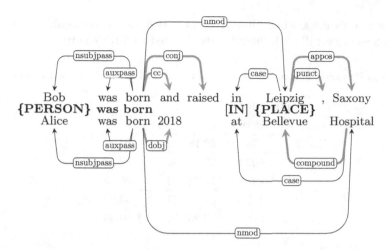

Fig. 2. The generalization process on two example sentences: "Bob was born and raised in Leipzig, Saxony." and "Alice was born 2018 at Bellevue Hospital.". The red edges mark deleted edges, the remaining edges together with the linguistic annotations in bold font symbolize the resulting generalized dependency tree pattern. Named entity arguments are illustrated in curly brackets and POS-tags in square brackets.

Table 1. Excerpt of top-three predicates for each domain/range combination.

rdfs:domain	rdfs:range		
	Organization	Person	Place
Organization	dbo:sisterStation	dbo:bandMember	dbo:hometown
	dbo:affiliation	dbo:formerBandMember	dbo:ground
	dbo:broadcastNetwork	dbo:notableCommander	dbo:headquarter
Person	dbo:almaMater	dbo:parent	dbo:deathPlace
	dbo:formerTeam	dbo:child	dbo:birthPlace
	dbo:debutTeam	dbo:spouse	dbo:nationality
Place	dbo:tenant	dbo:leaderName	dbo:district
	dbo:operator	dbo:architect	dbo:locatedInArea
	dbo:governingBody	dbo:saint	dbo:department

approach through the embedded semantics package, is depicted in Table 2. Each row shows the top-k ranked trees, i.e., sorted by the number of trees a generalized tree generalizes and the number of vertices in a tree. The columns with NF denote the results without the filter and F with the filter. For instance, the top-1 ranked trees without filtering are 55 in total with a precision of 58.18%. With filtering, we obtain 19 top-1 ranked trees with a precision of 94.74%. Our results show that the precision without filtering decreases with higher values of k but that the precision with filtering remains more stable. For example, the precision without filtering for $k = 5$ is 2.93% points lower than for $k = 1$ while it decreases by only 0.3% when filtering is used. Because of the significant increase of the precision overall with filtering, we decided to filter the trees.

Table 2. Precision and number of trees, without filter (NF) and with filter (F).

top k	NF		F	
	# trees	P	# trees	P
1	55	58.18	19	94.74
2	102	57.84	30	93.33
3	143	57.34	40	95.00
4	182	54.95	47	93.62
5	219	55.25	54	94.44

We manually compared the patterns of Boa and Patty with the generalized trees of our approach Ocelot. The results are depicted in Table 3. We manually assessed the patterns for each tool with the measures precision (P), recall (R) and F-Score (F1). To be comparable with the other systems we created a pattern-like representation from our trees. We compared the top 1–5 patterns for the four target relations (spouse, birthPlace, deathPlace and subsidiary) supported by all three systems. Our approach reached higher values on all five k for all three measures.

Table 3. Precision, Recall and F-Score averaged over spouse, birthPlace, deathPlace and subsidiary for the top k patterns. Best results are in bold font.

top k	Boa	Patty	Ocelot
	P/R/F1	P/R/F1	P/R/F1
1	75.00/8.120/14.58	75.00/9.550/16.67	**100.0/13.12/22.92**
2	62.50/12.66/20.94	62.50/15.39/24.24	**87.50/21.23/33.64**
3	58.33/18.51/27.86	66.67/24.94/35.36	**91.67/34.35/48.93**
4	56.25/23.05/32.42	62.50/29.48/38.99	**91.67/40.19/54.73**
5	60.00/32.60/41.46	60.00/34.03/42.29	**86.67/43.77/56.55**

5.3   Qualitative Evaluation

We evaluated the quality of our approach against the state-of-the-art tool Boa. For the relation extraction with Boa, we chose the top-10 patterns from the Boa index as well as the top-10 from Ocelot. We compared the relation extraction results of Boa and Ocelot on the first 100 sentences of the top-three viewed articles about persons in Wikipedia. The results are shown in Table 4. We replaced named entities in sentences with their types as this is the preprocessing step for both tools. The ✗ indicates that the system found no relation in the sentence.

The bold marked relations in the table indicate correct extractions. With Boa, we extracted one correct relation, `birthPlace`, on one sentence, "(Person) was born in (Place)", but also a false positive relation `deathPlace` on the same sentence. With Ocelot, we were able to extract four correct relations.

A benefit of Ocelot is that it finds relations that not only enclosed by the named entities like Boa and Patty. That is the reason why Ocelot extracts the relation in: "(Person) and (Person) were married" but Boa and Patty cannot.

Table 4. Example relation extraction with Boa and Ocelot.

Examples	Boa	Ocelot
(Person) and his wife (Person)	✕	**dbo:spouse**
(Person) and (Person) were married	✕	**dbo:spouse**
(Person) met (Person)	dbo:spouse	dbo:spouse
(Person) was born in (Place)	dbo:deathPlace **dbo:birthPlace**	**dbo:birthPlace**
(Person) was born in 1905 in (Place)	✕	**dbo:birthPlace**
(Person) returned to (Place)	dbo:deathPlace dbo:birthPlace	✕
(Person) moved to (Place)	dbo:deathPlace dbo:birthPlace	✕

6   Error Analysis

Data extracted from semi-structured sources, such as DBpedia, often contains inconsistencies as well as misrepresented and incomplete information [25]. For instance, at the time of writing this paper, the DBpedia resource `dbr:England` is a subtype of `dbo:Person` and a `dbo:MusicalArtist`, instead of being an instance of `dbo:Place` and of `dbo:PopulatedPlace`. Consequently, the data used by our approach for distance supervision was partly erronenous. For example, the labels of `dbr:England` served as labels for target relations with person arguments, e.g. `spouse`, because `dbr:England` is of the wrong type in DBpedia. The integration of multiple knowledge bases and a type check over multiple knowledge bases could potentially solve this type mismatch.

The low recall of Ocelot might be due to the missing coreference resolution system in the proposed approach. We aim to integrate such an approach into our framework in future works. Due to the filtering of trees with the embedded semantics package, it might be the case that trees counting as true positive are filtered out because their semantic is not covered by the embedded semantics package. Increasing the number of external sources may increase the recall of our system.

7   Conclusion

In this paper we presented our approach Ocelot, a distant supervised closed relation extraction approach based on distributional semantics and a tree generalization. In a two-fold evaluation, quantitative and qualitative, we showed that our approach harvests generalized dependency tree patterns of high quality, and that it extracts relations from unstructured text with its generalized trees of higher precision than two state-of-the-art systems.

With our contribution we push forward the quality of relation extraction and thus the quality of applications in areas such as Knowledge Base Population and Semantic Question Answering. Moreover, we provide the source-code of our approach together with the version numbers of all utilized tools and all settings as well as the datasets used in this paper at https://github.com/dice-group/Ocelot. We have now integrated the results of this work, the generalized trees, into the Fox framework, which can be found at http://fox-demo.aksw.de.

The main advantages of this framework are that it is open source, and provides additional features such as named entity recognition and disambiguation, linked data by several RDF serialisations[10] and a freely usable RESTful web service that is ready to use by the community. We have now provided a system for knowledge extraction out of unstructured text that presents the extracted entities and relations in a machine readable format to the community.

Acknowledgement. This work has been supported by the H2020 project HOBBIT (no. 688227), the BMWI projects GEISER (no. 01MD16014E) and OPAL (no. 19F2028A), the EuroStars projects DIESEL (no. 01QE1512C) and QAMEL (no. 01QE1549C).

References

1. Augenstein, I., Maynard, D., Ciravegna, F.: Relation extraction from the web using distant supervision. In: Janowicz, K., Schlobach, S., Lambrix, P., Hyvönen, E. (eds.) EKAW 2014. LNCS (LNAI), vol. 8876, pp. 26–41. Springer, Cham (2014). https://doi.org/10.1007/978-3-319-13704-9_3
2. Curran, J.R., Murphy, T., Scholz, B.: Minimising semantic drift with mutual exclusion bootstrapping. In: Proceedings of the 10th Conference of the Pacific Association for Computational Linguistics, pp. 172–180 (2007)
3. Del Corro, L., Gemulla, R.: Clausie: clause-based open information extraction. In: Proceedings of the 22nd International Conference on World Wide Web, WWW 2013, pp. 355–366. ACM, New York (2013). https://doi.org/10.1145/2488388. 2488420, https://doi.org/10.1145/2488388.2488420
4. Draicchio, F., Gangemi, A., Presutti, V., Nuzzolese, A.G.: FRED: from natural language text to RDF and OWL in one click. In: Cimiano, P., Fernández, M., Lopez, V., Schlobach, S., Völker, J. (eds.) ESWC 2013. LNCS, vol. 7955, pp. 263–267. Springer, Heidelberg (2013). https://doi.org/10.1007/978-3-642-41242-4_36

---

[10] We provided an example of an RDF serialisation of the framework in Listing 1.1.

5. Dubey, M., Dasgupta, S., Sharma, A., Hoffner, K., Lehmann, J.: Asknow: a framework for natural language query formalization in sparql. In: Proceedings of the Extended Semantic Web Conference 2016 (2016). http://jens-lehmann.org/files/2016/eswc_asknow.pdf
6. Fader, A., Soderland, S., Etzioni, O.: Identifying relations for open information extraction, pp. 1535–1545 (2011)
7. Gerber, D., et al.: Defacto - temporal and multilingual deep fact validation. Web Semant. Sci. Serv. Agents World Wide Web (2015). http://svn.aksw.org/papers/2015/JWS_DeFacto/public.pdf
8. Gerber, D., Ngonga Ngomo, A.C.: Bootstrapping the linked data web. In: 1st Workshop on Web Scale Knowledge Extraction @ ISWC 2011 (2011)
9. Höffner, K., Walter, S., Marx, E., Usbeck, R., Lehmann, J., Ngonga Ngomo, A.C.: Survey on challenges of question answering in the semantic web. Semant. Web J. 8(6) (2017). http://www.semantic-web-journal.net/system/files/swj1375.pdf
10. Krause, S., Li, H., Uszkoreit, H., Xu, F.: Large-scale learning of relation-extraction rules with distant supervision from the web. In: Cudré-Mauroux, P., Heflin, J., Sirin, E., Tudorache, T., Euzenat, J., Hauswirth, M., Parreira, J.X., Hendler, J., Schreiber, G., Bernstein, A., Blomqvist, E. (eds.) ISWC 2012. LNCS, vol. 7649, pp. 263–278. Springer, Heidelberg (2012). https://doi.org/10.1007/978-3-642-35176-1_17
11. Lehmann, J., Bühmann, L.: AutoSPARQL: let users query your knowledge base. In: Antoniou, G., Grobelnik, M., Simperl, E., Parsia, B., Plexousakis, D., De Leenheer, P., Pan, J. (eds.) ESWC 2011. LNCS, vol. 6643, pp. 63–79. Springer, Heidelberg (2011). https://doi.org/10.1007/978-3-642-21034-1_5
12. Mausam, Schmitz, M., Bart, R., Soderland, S., Etzioni, O.: Open language learning for information extraction. In: Proceedings of the 2012 Joint Conference on Empirical Methods in Natural Language Processing and Computational Natural Language Learning, EMNLP-CoNLL 2012, Association for Computational Linguistics, Stroudsburg, PA, USA, pp. 523–534 (2012). http://dl.acm.org/citation.cfm?id=2390948.2391009
13. Mendes, P.N., Jakob, M., Garcia-Silva, A., Bizer, C.: Dbpedia spotlight: shedding light on the web of documents. In: Proceedings of the 7th International Conference on Semantic Systems (I-Semantics) (2011)
14. Mikolov, T., Chen, K., Corrado, G., Dean, J.: Efficient estimation of word representations in vector space. CoRR (2013). http://arxiv.org/abs/1301.3781
15. Mikolov, T., Sutskever, I., Chen, K., Corrado, G., Dean, J.: Distributed representations of words and phrases and their compositionality. In: Proceedings of the 26th International Conference on Neural Information Processing Systems, NIPS 2013, vol. 2, pp. 3111–3119. Curran Associates Inc., USA (2013). http://dl.acm.org/citation.cfm?id=2999792.2999959
16. Mintz, M., Bills, S., Snow, R., Jurafsky, D.: Distant supervision for relation extraction without labeled data. In: Proceedings of the Joint Conference of the 47th Annual Meeting of the ACL and the 4th International Joint Conference on Natural Language Processing of the AFNLP, Association for Computational Linguistics, pp. 1003–1011 (2009). http://www.aclweb.org/anthology/P09-1113
17. Nakashole, N., Weikum, G., Suchanek, F.: Patty: a taxonomy of relational patterns with semantic types. In: Proceedings of the 2012 Joint Conference on Empirical Methods in Natural Language Processing and Computational Natural Language Learning, EMNLP-CoNLL 2012, Association for Computational Linguistics, Stroudsburg, PA, USA, pp. 1135–1145 (2012). http://dl.acm.org/citation.cfm?id=2390948.2391076

18. Ren, X., Wu, Z., He, W., Qu, M., Voss, C.R., Ji, H., Abdelzaher, T.F., Han, J.: Cotype: joint extraction of typed entities and relations with knowledge bases. In: Proceedings of the 26th International Conference on World Wide Web, pp. 1015–1024 (2017)
19. Riedel, S., Yao, L., McCallum, A.: Modeling relations and their mentions without labeled text. In: Balcázar, J.L., Bonchi, F., Gionis, A., Sebag, M. (eds.) Machine Learning and Knowledge Discovery in Databases, pp. 148–163. Springer, Heidelberg (2010)
20. Riloff, E., Jones, R.: Learning dictionaries for information extraction by multi-level bootstrapping. In: Proceedings of the Sixteenth National Conference on Artificial Intelligence and the Eleventh Innovative Applications of Artificial Intelligence Conference Innovative Applications of Artificial Intelligence, AAAI 1999/IAAI 1999, American Association for Artificial Intelligence, Menlo Park, CA, USA, pp. 474–479 (1999). http://dl.acm.org/citation.cfm?id=315149.315364
21. Singh, K., Mulang', I.O., Lytra, I., Jaradeh, M.Y., Sakor, A., Vidal, M.E., Lange, C., Auer, S.: Capturing knowledge in semantically-typed relational patterns to enhance relation linking. In: Proceedings of the Knowledge Capture Conference, K-CAP 2017, pp. 31:1–31:8. ACM, New York (2017). https://doi.org/10.1145/3148011.3148031, https://doi.org/10.1145/3148011.3148031
22. Usbeck, R., Ngomo, A.-C.N., Bühmann, L., Unger, C.: HAWK – hybrid question answering using linked data. In: Gandon, F., Sabou, M., Sack, H., d'Amato, C., Cudré-Mauroux, P., Zimmermann, A. (eds.) ESWC 2015. LNCS, vol. 9088, pp. 353–368. Springer, Cham (2015). https://doi.org/10.1007/978-3-319-18818-8_22
23. Usbeck, R., Ngomo, A.-C.N., Haarmann, B., Krithara, A., Röder, M., Napolitano, G.: 7th open challenge on question answering over linked data (QALD-7). In: Dragoni, M., Solanki, M., Blomqvist, E. (eds.) SemWebEval 2017. CCIS, vol. 769, pp. 59–69. Springer, Cham (2017). https://doi.org/10.1007/978-3-319-69146-6_6. https://svn.aksw.org/papers/2017/ESWC_2017_QALD/public.pdf
24. Yates, A., Cafarella, M., Banko, M., Etzioni, O., Broadhead, M., Soderland, S.: Textrunner: Open information extraction on the web. In: Proceedings of Human Language Technologies: The Annual Conference of the North American Chapter of the Association for Computational Linguistics: Demonstrations, NAACL-Demonstrations 2007, Association for Computational Linguistics, Stroudsburg, PA, USA, pp. 25–26 (2007). http://dl.acm.org/citation.cfm?id=1614164.1614177
25. Zaveri, A., Rula, A., Maurino, A., Pietrobon, R., Lehmann, J., Auer, S.: Quality assessment for linked data: a survey. Semantic Web Journal (2015). http://www.semantic-web-journal.net/content/quality-assessment-linked-data-survey

A Query Model for Ontology-Based Event Processing over RDF Streams

Riccardo Tommasini[1,2]([envelope]), Pieter Bonte[1,2], Emanuele Della Valle[1,2], Femke Ongenae[1,2], and Filip De Turck[1,2]

[1] DEIB, Politecnico di Milano, Milan, Italy
{riccardo.tommasini,emanuele.dellavalle}@polimi.it
[2] Ghent University - imec, Ghent, Belgium
{pieters.bonte,femke.ongenae,filip.deturck}@ugent.be

Abstract. Stream Reasoning (SR) envisioned, investigated and proved the possibility to make sense of streaming data in real-time. Now, the community is investigating more powerful solutions, realizing the vision of expressive stream reasoning. Ontology-Based Event Processing (OBEP) is our contribution to this field. OBEP combines Description Logics and Event Recognition Languages. It allows describing events either as logical statements or as complex event patterns, and it captures their occurrences over ontology streams. In this paper, we define OBEP's query model, we present a language to define OBEP queries, and we explain the language semantics.

Keywords: Stream processing · Semantic web · Stream reasoning
Complex event processing

1 Introduction

Stream Reasoning (SR) is evolving fast. Answering information-needs in real-time has a business-critical role for many applications. SR research is pushing the boundaries of the state-of-the-art, addressing three crucial challenges towards real-time decision-making: (1) enabling continuous analytics over heterogeneous data streams, (2) enabling event detection considering both domain knowledge and streams of events, and (3) solving (1) and (2) simultaneously [6,10,17].

The SR solution for continuous data integration is RDF Stream Processing (RSP). RSP engines adopt the Data Stream Management Systems (DSMS) processing model to tame velocity and combine it with semantic technologies, which can tame data variety (e.g., RDF and SPARQL) [10]. Therefore, RSP engines can execute continuous analytical tasks over heterogeneous data streams.

For event detection, there is not a unified SR solution [10]. On the one hand, there is the ETALIS logic-programming framework that offers a time-aware rule-based language for SR and complex event processing (CEP). ETALIS treats event detection as a reasoning task exploiting the relation between event-recognition languages and temporal reasoning [7]. On the other hand, RSP proposals for CEP aim at providing a unified language for event detection and analytics [1,8].

© Springer Nature Switzerland AG 2018
C. Faron Zucker et al. (Eds.): EKAW 2018, LNAI 11313, pp. 439–453, 2018.
https://doi.org/10.1007/978-3-030-03667-6_28

EP-SPARQL [1] and RSEP-QL [8] extend respectively SPARQL 1.0 and an RSP-QL [9] with time-aware operators. Both started from a language for continuous analytics and added operators for event detection, as showed in [19]. To preserve the operational semantics of the base languages, existing constructs are reused to define events and, thus, events are not first-class objects in the resulting language. However, the notion of event is critical for CEP languages as CEP users expect two clear ways to define events, i.e., providing schema or types, or using temporal operators [4,6,7].

In this paper, we investigate the foundations of Ontology-Based Event Processing (OBEP) [18]. OBEP enables event detection over RDF Streams without neglecting events first-class nature. It seamlessly combines temporal operators with a family of knowledge representation languages around the notion of event. OBEP's users can specify and compose events working with high-level abstractions. Moreover, OBEP works with RDF Streams, i.e., it can be combined with RSP analytics solutions.

The remainder of the paper is organized as follow: Sect. 2 introduces the notions relevant to understand the content of the paper. Section 3 explains OBEP data model and query model. Section 4 formalizes the evaluation semantics of the language. Section 5 compares OBEP to existing stream reasoning languages and shows how OBEP simplifies the encoding of SR tasks compared to the state-of-the-art. Finally, Sect. 6 concludes the paper and presents the future work.

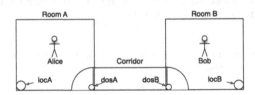

Fig. 1. Running example.

2   Preliminaries

In this section, we detail the required background and preliminary knowledge to introduce our contributions[1]. To this extent, we present a running example also depicted in Fig. 1.

Two rooms, *Room A* and *Room B* are connected through a corridor. Room A is armed with a door sensor *sA* that monitors whether the door is *open* or *closed*. A people sensor *sB*, deployed in *Room B*, tracks the people inside. We also assume that either *Alice* or *Bob* can be in the room at a given time, that nobody else can be in the room and that the people sensor is capable of detecting when *nobody* is in the room.

Description Logics (DLs) are a family of knowledge representation languages with reasoning capabilities [3]. We introduce the syntax of a simplified

---

[1] Due to the lack of space, we focus on the essential definition, and we provide references for the interested reader.

DL^2, explaining the basic notions required to understand the remainder of the paper.

DL defines *concepts* to represent the classes of individuals and *roles* to represent binary relations between the individuals. Basic concepts C can be defined as follows: $C :: = A_i|\top|\bot|\neg C|C_1 \sqcap C_2|C_1 \sqcup C_2|\exists P_1.C_1|\forall P_1.C_1$ where A denotes an atomic concept, P denotes an atomic role or its inverse P^-, $\top$ resembles the top concept, $\bot$ denotes the bottom concept, $\sqcap$ the conjunction of concepts, $\sqcup$ the disjunction of concepts, $\exists P.C$ states that there should exist a role P to an individual of the type C and $\forall P.C$ denotes that all roles P should be linked to an individual of the type C. To model the domain, we can define inclusion axioms of the form

$$C_1 \sqsubseteq C_2 \text{ and } P_1 \sqsubseteq P_2$$

where the equivalence between two concepts (e.g. $C_1 \equiv C_2$) can be interpreted as both C_1 and C_2 include each other (i.e. $C_1 \sqsubseteq C_2$ and $C_2 \sqsubseteq C_1$).

A DL knowledge base consists of a terminological box (TBox) that collects intentional knowledge and an assertion box (ABox) that collects extensional knowledge. Listings 1.1 and 1.2 show a DL TBox and ABox respectively, that model the situations illustrated in Fig. 1.

1	atomic concepts: Room, Person, Sensor
2	deployedIn ≡ armedWith⁻
3	observedBy ≡ observes⁻
4	observesPerson ⊑ observes
5	observesNobody ⊑ observes
6	observesClosedDoor ⊑ observes
7	observesOpenDoor ⊑ observes

Listing 1.1. Intensional knowledge describing Figure 1.

1	Room(RoomA)
2	Room(RoomB)
3	Person(Bob)
4	Person(Alice)
5	Sensor(sA)
6	Sensor(sB)
7	armedWith(RoomA, sA)
8	armedWith(RoomB, sB)

Listing 1.2. Extensional knowledge describing Figure 1.

RDF Statement, RDF Graph and SPARQL Dataset. An *RDF statement* is a triple (subject,predicate,object) $\in (I \cup B) \times (I) \times (I \cup B \cup L)$, where I, B and L are respectively the sets of IRIs, blank nodes, and literals. A finite set of RDF statements is called a *RDF graph* A SPARQL Dataset (DS) is a set of pairs (u,G) where G is an RDF Graph and u is an IRI or a special symbol *def* denoting the default graph. For example, DS = { (def, G_0),(u_1,G_1)..}. A comprehensive discussion on SPARQL semantics can be found in [14].

Continuous Reasoning (CR) identifies those logic frameworks that are able to perform reasoning tasks over time. CR is based on the notion of ontology stream [5,16].

Definition 1. *An Ontology Stream S^T is an unbounded sequence of pairs (A_i, t_i) where A_i is a set of ABox axioms compliant with a static TBox T, and t_i is a non-decreasing timestamp. $S^T (i)$ returns the pair (A_i, t_i).*

Continuous reasoning can be reduced to traditional static DL reasoning if we consider the union of all the ABox axioms in a windowed ontology stream.

---

[2] We refer the reader to Horrocks et. al. [11] for a thorough discussion of a more expressive DL.

```
1  CONSTRUCT  {?person  :isIn ?room }
2  FROM NAMED WINDOW <win> ON <stream> [RANGE 5s STEP 1s]
3  FROM <static_data>
4  WHERE { ?room a :Room ; :armedWith ?locSensor .
5         WINDOW <win> { ?locSensor :observes ?p .
6                       ?p a :Person }}
```

Listing 1.3. An example of RSP-QL query.

Definition 2. *A windowed ontology stream $S^T_{[o,c)}$ is a finite portion of an ontology stream, i.e., all the pairs $(A_i, t_i) \in S^T(i)$ such that $o \le t_i < c$.*

RDF Stream Processing (RSP) identifies a family of SR approaches that aim to answer continuous queries over heterogeneous data streams [10]. To this extent, the fundamental notion is the one of RDF Stream [9]:

Definition 3. *An RDF Stream is a set of pairs (G_i, t_i), where G_i is an RDF Graph, and t_i is a timestamp, e.g., $S = \{(G_1, t_1), (G_2, t_2), (G_3, t_3), (G_4, t_4), ...\}$.*

An example of an RDF Stream is depicted in Table 1. Column names are the timestamps, while each entry is an RDF graph.

Table 1. An example of an RDF Stream. We use the following abbreviations: :ocd=observesClosedDoor, :ood=observesOpenDoor, :obsP=observesPerson, :obsN=observesNobody. Column names are the timestamps, while each entry is an RDF graph.

1	2	3	4	5	6	7	8
	sA :ocd :doorA	sA :ood :doorA	sA :ood :doorA		sA :ood :doorA	sA :ocd :doorA	
	sB :obsP :Bob	sB :obsP :Bob	sB :obsN :empty		sB :obsN :empty	sB :obsP :Alice	

A second important concept is the one of Continuous Queries over RDF Streams. RSP-QL [9] is a reference model that unifies all the existing RSP dialects [10]. Listing 1.3 shows an example of an RSP-QL query that continuously reports who is in the rooms in the example (see Fig. 1). RSP-QL queries can be executed under an entailment regime combining RSP with OWL reasoning [10].

Table 2. Most common event operators ($\mathcal{L}$) and their (informal) semantics.

Operator	Cardinality	Matches
A AND B	Binary	When A and B are detected at the same time.
A OR B	Binary	When A or B or both are detected at a given time.
A SEQ B	Binary	When B is detected after A.
FIRST A	Unary	When the first occurrence of A is detected
LAST A	Unary	When the last occurrence of A is detected
ALLEN's Algebra	Binary	Denoted 12 relations between intervals

Complex Event Processing (CEP) aims at recognizing and combining events over streams of data [1,4,13]. Event recognition relies on the notion of

Event Type that characterizes events conceptual specification, and allows the assertions of Event Expressions w.r.t. a given CEP language [12]. Although many approaches populate CEP state-of-the-art – i.e., from Event-Condition-Action (ECA) [4] to Event Calculus [12] – a standard CEP language is still missing.

Since one of our requirements is considering events as first-class objects, we opted for Chackvrathy et al. [4] event algebra as a solid foundational formalism. Chackvrathy et al. defines events as data occurrences that happen completely or not at all (atomic). They distinguish between physical events, which are known and manipulated by the system, and conceptual events that are abstract specifications functional to the recognition task. Conceptual and physical events are linked via functional mappings that depends on the approach [4].

We consider the most language operators common to existing approaches in the Stream Reasoning state-of-the-art. Table 2 summarizes these operators ($\mathcal{L}$) and reports their semantics informally. Later on in the paper, we will formalize these operators w.r.t. our approach[3].

3 Ontology Based Event Processing

In this section, we present the foundational aspects of OBEP: we discuss its data model, the building block of OBEP queries as well as the semantics of the most relevant operators.

3.1 Data Model

Similar to existing approaches in Stream Reasoning state-of-the-art [1,8], OBEP data model is based on RDF Streams: any RDF Graph in an RDF Stream represents an OBEP physical event. On the other hand, OBEP data model relies on the notion of Ontology Stream to represent conceptual events as logically defined event types. Although these notions are intuitively related, to the best of our knowledge, it is still missing a formal explanation of their relations. Therefore, in the following we provide a few intuitive yet necessary definitions that reconcile the two presented above. Moreover, we introduce the concept of Event Stream, that is required for the definition of OBEP query model. To support our formalization, we exploit the following helper functions: (i) *axioms* :: G → L, and (ii) *triples* :: L → G; where L is a set of logical axioms and G is the corresponding RDF Graph.

Definition 4. *A Well-Grounded RDF Stream S^D is an RDF Stream such that for each pair $(G_k, t_k) \in S^D$, the RDF Graph G_k is expressed according to a static TBox D, and G_i contains only triples of the form <:s rdf:type :C>, where <:C rdf:type owl:Class>, and <:s :p :o>, where <:p rdf:type owl:ObjectProperty>, and :s, :o are individuals. Literals are not considered.*

Example 1. The RDF Stream of Table 1 is a Well-Grounded RDF Stream w.r.t. the ontology of Listing 1.1.

---

[3] Due to the lack of space, we only present SEQ, FIRST, and DURING operators. The remaining ones are available in our extended version at https://github.com/riccardotommasini/obep.

Proposition 1. *For each Well-Grounded RDF Stream an Ontology Stream exists. Given a Well-Grounded RDF Stream $S^D = (G_1, t_1),...(G_k, t_k)$ where G_i are defined according to a static TBox D. We denote with $\mathcal{D} = axioms(D)$ the set of TBox axioms obtained converting triples from D^4, and we denote with $A_k = axioms(G_k)$ the set of ABox axioms obtained converting triples from the RDF Graph G_k. The sequence of pairs $(A_1, t_1),...,(A_k, t_k)$ about $\mathcal{D}$ is an Ontology Stream (denoted with S^D).*

Definition 5. *An Event Stream $S^{\mathcal{E}}$ is an Ontology Stream, where (i) the static TBox $\mathcal{E}$ contains some axioms of the form $E \sqsubseteq B$ where B is a basic concept, and E, which is distinguishable from other atomic classes[5], is a logical event. (ii) for some $(A_i, t_i) \in S^{\mathcal{E}}$ it is true that $A_i \models^{\mathcal{E}} E_i(e)$ with E_i a logical event and e an individual. We call (A_i, t_i) a Physical Event.*

Proposition 2. *For each Well-Grounded RDF Stream an Event Stream exists. Given a Well-Grounded RDF Stream S^D from Proposition 1, we know that there is an Ontology Stream S^D. Let's consider a static sub-set of $\mathcal{D}$, e.g., $\{E_1,...,E_n\}$, denoted as $\mathcal{E}$; $(A_1, t_1)...(A_k, t_k)$ is an Event Stream (denoted as $S^{\mathcal{E}}$), if $A_k \models^{\mathcal{E}} E(e)$ for some k. We call E a logical event and we call (A_k, t_k) a Physical Event.*

3.2   Building Blocks of OBEP Queries

The OBEP query model is based on an abstract event specification, generically called complex events. We distinguish between Logical and Composite Events.

Definition 6. *Logical Events are logic assertions $H \leftarrow B$, where H is an atomic DL concept and B is a DL basic concept as specified in Sect. 2.*
  The abstract syntax[6] of Logical Event is

EVENT H AS B

  The helper function named(B) returns all the concepts and roles used in B.

Example 2. (**cont'd**) In Listing 1.4, we define the Logical Event $BusyRoom \sqsubseteq B$, where B is $Room \sqcap \exists armedWith.(Sensor \sqcap \exists observesPerson)$ where named(B) = {Room, Sensor, Person, armedWith, observesPerson}.

```
1   EVENT BusyRoom AS
2     (Room and armedWith some (Sensor and observesPerson some Thing))
3
4   EVENT FreeRoom AS
5     (Room and armedWith some (Sensor and observesOpenDoor some Thing))
```

Listing 1.4. Examples of Logical Events.

---

[4] We consider only the rules (i) <:s rdf:type :C> → C(s); (ii) <:s :p :o> → P(s,o).

[5] We implemented this mechanism using OWL Annotation Properties since they do not impact the reasoning, but allows distinguishing TBox axioms.

[6] We will use Manchester Syntax to express B https://www.w3.org/TR/owl2-manchester-syntax/.

Definition 7. *A **Composite Event** is an assertion* $H \leftarrow E$ *where:*

- *H is an atomic DL concept denoting a logical event.*
- *E is an event expression.*

The abstract syntax for composite events is

$$EVENT \; H \; MATCH \; E$$

The helper function named(E) returns all the events used in E.

Example 3. (**cont'd**) In Listing 1.5, we define the complex event *Exiting* using OBEP syntax where named(Exiting) = {BusyRoom, FreeRoom}, and *Entering* using OBEP syntax where named(Exiting) = {BusyRoom, FreeRoom},

```
1    EVENT Entering MATCH FreeRoom SEQ BusyRoom
2    EVENT Exiting MATCH BusyRoom SEQ FreeRoom
```

Listing 1.5. A Complex Event without guards.

Logical and Composite Events are **Complex Events**, i.e., assertions H ← L where (i) H is an atomic DL concept, and (ii) L is either (a) a basic DL concept or (b) an event expression.

Last but not least, we have to discuss which results a query generates. OBEP consumes streaming data and it produces streams as output. Inspired by SPARQL query forms[7], we introduce a return clause that allows alternative output stream formats.

Definition 8. *A **Return Clause** is a function that determines the type of stream to output from an OBEP query, i.e.,*

$$\mathcal{R} :: \mathcal{LE} \to S$$

where $\mathcal{LE}$ is a list of logical events and S is either an Event Stream, i.e., $(At_1, t_1)...(A, t_n)$ or a Well Grounded RDF Stream, i.e., $(triples(At_1), t_1)... (triples(At_n), t_n)$.

the abstract syntax of the return clause is

$$RETURN \; LE \; AS \; [EVENT|RDF] \; STREAM$$

where L is a list logical events $[E_1,...,E_n]$ defined in a OBEP query.

3.3   Query Definition

Building on the previous definitions, we can finally define an OBEP query.

Definition 9. *An OBEP query is a tuple* $< S^D, K, \mathcal{E}, \mathcal{CE}, \mathcal{R}, ET >$ *where:*

- *S^D is a Well Grounded RDF Stream as defined in Definition 4.*
- *K is a static ABox.*
- *$\mathcal{E}$ is a set of Logical Events axioms defined as in Definition 6.*
- *$\mathcal{CE}$ is a set of Composite Events defined as in Definition 7.*

---

[7] https://www.w3.org/TR/rdf-sparql-query/#QueryForms.

- *$\mathcal{R}$ is a return clause.*
- *ET is the set of evaluation time instants.*

We can now define an evaluation function considering the query definition.

Definition 10. *Given an OBEP query $Q = <S^D, K, \mathcal{E}, \mathcal{CE}, \mathcal{R}, ET>$ we define the evaluation of $\mathcal{E}$ and $\mathcal{CE}$ over S^D and K, at time $t \in ET$, with the return clause $\mathcal{R}$ as:*

$$eval(S^D, \mathcal{E}, \mathcal{CE}, \mathcal{R}, t)$$

Applying the evaluation semantics of the Return Clause we obtain

$$eval(S^D, \mathcal{E}, \mathcal{CE}, \mathcal{R}, t) = \mathcal{R}(eval(S^D, \mathcal{E}, \mathcal{CE}, t))$$

According with Proposition 2, given that $\mathcal{E}$ is a static set of TBox axioms based on D, we can assert the following equivalence:

$$eval(S^D, \mathcal{E}, \mathcal{CE}, t) = eval(S^{\mathcal{E}}, \mathcal{CE}, t)$$

Last but not least, we pose two conditions that allow to evaluate independently each composite event definition [7], i.e.,

$$eval(S^{\mathcal{E}}, \mathcal{CE}, t) = \bigcup_{\pi \in \mathcal{CE}} eval(S^{\mathcal{E}}, \pi, t)$$

1. Composite Events must not have circular-dependencies, i.e., given $H_1 \leftarrow L_1 \in \mathcal{CE}$, $\nexists\ H_2 \leftarrow L_2 \in \mathcal{CE}$, such that $H_1 \in named(L_2)$ and $H_2 \in named(L_1)$;
2. the Composite Event assertions set $\mathcal{CE}$ can be stratified to ensure a loop-free evaluation across partitions.

4   OBEP Semantics

In this section, we present the evaluation semantics of logical and composite event expressions. To this extent, we will exploit the following helper function:

- *explain* :: $\mathcal{T} \times A \times C \rightarrow \mathcal{G}$, where $\mathcal{T}$ is a set of TBox axioms, A is a set of ABox axioms w.r.t. $\mathcal{T}$ and C is a class concept. *explain* returns the set of RDF Graphs $\mathcal{G}$ with $G_i \in \mathcal{G}$ and axioms(G_i) a minimal subset of A such that axioms$(G_i) \models^{\mathcal{T}} C(c)$, where c is a an individual.

4.1   Complex Event Evaluation Semantics

Definition 11. *Evaluation Semantics of Complex Event Expressions. Given an event stream $S^{\mathcal{E}}$, a time instant t, and a Logical Event E we define*

$$[\![E]\!]_{S^{\mathcal{E}}}^t$$

as the evaluation of E at t over $S^{\mathcal{E}}$.

Although Event streams are defined with one timestamp for each pair (A,t), we adopted a two-point time semantics for the evaluation. This approach, introduced in [1,2], allows formulating interval-based temporal operators.

Logical Events are the first building block. Their evaluation aims at asserting the logical equivalence between an atomic concept H denoting a logical event and a basic concept B defined in the TBox $\mathcal{E}$. We define K as the static, time independent, ABox describing background information.

$$[E]_{S^\mathcal{E}}^t = \{(A, t_k, t_k) \mid (A_k, t_k) \in S^\mathcal{E} \wedge t_k < t \wedge \exists c \in A \wedge A_k \cup K \models^\mathcal{E} E(c)$$
$$\wedge A \in \text{explain}(\mathcal{E}, A_k \cup K, E)\}$$

Example 4. Let's consider the event stream $S^\mathcal{E}$ obtained from the Well-Grounded RDF Stream from Fig. 1 w.r.t. the TBox of Listing 1.1, and the logical event expression of Listing 1.4. Let's also consider the static knowledge base K of Listing 1.2. We want to evaluate if the logical event BusyRoom occurs in $S^\mathcal{E}$ at t = 8 considering the static knowledge base K.

$[BusyRoom]_{S^\mathcal{E}}^8 = \{$
({Room(rb) Person(Bob) Sensor(sb) armedWith(rb,sb) obsP[8](sb,Bob) },2,2),
({Room(ra) Sensor(sa) armedWith(ra,sa) ocd[9](sa,doorA) },2,2),
({Room(rb) Person(Bob) Sensor(sb) armedWith(rb,sb) obsP(sb,Bob) },3,3),
({Room(rb) Person(Alice) Sensor(sb) armedWith(rb,sb) obsP(sb,Alice) },7,7),
({Room(ra) Sensor(sa) armedWith(ra,sa) ocd(sa,doorA) },7,7)}

Composite Events are the second building block of the OBEP semantics. Their evaluation aims at asserting the logical equivalence between an atomic concept H denoting a logical event and a complex event expression E.

$$[H \textbf{ MATCH } E]_{S^\mathcal{E}}^t = \{ (A \cup H(c), t_1, t_2) \mid (A, t_1, t_2) \in [E]_{S^\mathcal{E}}^t, c \text{ is a named}$$
$$\text{individual.} \}$$

Composite Event Expressions combine logical events according to the $\mathcal{L}$ operators. Their evaluation aims to check when a specific temporal relation occurs between two or more logical events.

$[\textbf{FIRST } E]_{S^\mathcal{E}}^t = \{ (A, t_1, t_2) \mid (A, t_1, t_2) \in [E]_{S^\mathcal{E}}^t \wedge \nexists (A', t_3, t_4) \in [E]_{S^\mathcal{E}}^t$ such that $t_3 \leq t_4 < t_1 \leq t_2 \}$.

Example 5. (**cont'd**) [FIRST $BusyRoom]_{S^\mathcal{E}}^t = \{(\text{Room(rb) Person(Bob) Sensor(sb) armedWith(rb,sb) obsP(sb,Bob) },2,2)\}$

$[E_1 \textbf{ SEQ } E_2]_{S^\mathcal{E}}^t = \{ (A_2, t_1, t_4) \mid (A_1, t_1, t_2) \in [E_1]_{S^\mathcal{E}}^t \wedge (A_2, t_3, t_4) \in [E_2]_{S^\mathcal{E}}^t$ $\wedge t_1 \leq t_2 < t_3 \leq t_4 \}$.

Example 6. (**cont'd**) [BusyRoom SEQ FreeRoom $]_{S^\mathcal{E}}^t =$
{ (Room(rb) Person(Bob) Sensor(sb) armedWith(rb, sb) obsN(sb, nobody) },3,4), ({Room(rb) Person(Alice) Sensor(sb) armedWith(rb, sb) obsP(sb, Alice) },6,7), ({Room(ra) Sensor(sa) armedWith(ra, sa) ocd(sa, doorA) },6,7) }

---

[8] ObservesPerson.
[9] ObservesClosedDoor.

$[\textbf{LAST } E]_{S\mathcal{E}}^t = \{ (A,t_1,t_2) \mid (A,t_1,t_2) \in [E]_{S\mathcal{E}}^t \wedge \nexists (A',t_3,t_4) \in [E]_{S\mathcal{E}}^t$ such that $t_1 \leq t_2 < t_3 \leq t_4 \}.$

Example 7. (**cont'd**) $[$ LAST BusyRoom $]_{S\mathcal{E}}^t =$
$\{ (\{Room(ra)\ Sensor(sa)\ armedWith(ra,sa)\ ocd(sa,doorA) \},7,7) \}$

$[E_1 \textbf{ AND } E_2]_{S\mathcal{E}}^t = \{ (A,t_1,t_2) \mid A = A_1 \cup A_2 \wedge (A_1,t_1,t_2) \in [E_1]_{S\mathcal{E}}^t \wedge (A_2,t_1,t_2) \in [E_2]_{S\mathcal{E}}^t \}$

Example 8. (**cont'd**) $[$ BusyRoom AND FreeRoom $]_{S\mathcal{E}}^t =$
$\{ (\{ Room(ra)\ Sensor(sa)\ armedWith(ra, sa)\ observesClosedDoor(sa, doorA)$
$Room(rb)\ Sensor(sb)\ Person(Bob)\ armedWith(rb, sb)\ observesPerson(sb, Bob)$
$\},3,3) \}$

$[E_1 \textbf{ DURING } E_2]_{S\mathcal{E}}^t = \{ (A_1, t_1, t_2) \mid (A_1, t_1, t_2) \in [E_1]_{S\mathcal{E}}^t \wedge (A_2, t_3, t_4) \in [E_2]_{S\mathcal{E}}^t \wedge t_3 < t_1 \wedge t_2 < t_4 \}.$

Example 9. (**cont'd**) $[$ OpenDoor DURING Exiting $]_{S\mathcal{E}}^t =$
$\{ (\{observesOpenDoor(sa,doorA) \},3,3)\}$

4.2 Matching Negative Patterns

A common feature in Event Processing Languages [1,4] is the detection of negative patterns, i.e., the negation of the detection at a given time instant. We define the **Negative Event Evaluation Semantics** as

$$[NOT\ E]_{S\mathcal{E}}^t = \{ (A, t_k, t_k) \mid A = \bigcup A_k \setminus A_k^U \wedge A \neq \emptyset \text{ where}$$
$$(A_k, t_k, t_k) \in S^{\mathcal{E}} \wedge t_k < t \wedge A_k^U = \bigcup A'_k \text{ for each } (A'_k, t_k, t_h) \in [E]_{S\mathcal{E}}^t \}$$

4.3 Guarded Complex Event Patterns

The assertion of a Complex Event H depends on the truth value of the logical expression L that characterizes it. In the following, we explain how to the truth value of L can be modified using Guards.

Definition 12. *A **Guard** is a boolean function that poses a condition to the evaluation of a complex event expression [4]. OBEP provides two types of guards: Data Guards and Time Guards.*

Data Guards or Filters are conditions to a composite event, within an event expression, evaluated w.r.t. the related physical event.

Since (Well-Grounded) RDF Streams are OBEP's underlying data model, we opted for SPARQL syntax and semantics to express data guards. Listings 1.6 shows an example of an OBEP query with filters.

```
1    EVENT Entering MATCH FreeRoom SEQ BusyRoom WITHIN (5 min)
2        IF { EVENT BusyRoom { ?room :armedWith ?sensor . }
3             EVENT FreeRoom { ?room :armedWith ?sensor . } }
```

Listing 1.6. OBEP query With Frame and Filters.

Given a Complex Event H $\leftarrow^G$ CExp, a filter is a SPARQL ASK query q, where restriction w.r.t. a logical event E ∈ named(CExp), denotes (i) a *Triples-Block* if E is used in any unary sub-expression; (ii) an *OptionalGraphPattern* if E is used in a Disjunction sub-expression; (iii) a *GraphGraphPattern* if E is used in any remaining sub-expression.

```
ASK
FROM NAMED  :BusyRoom
FROM NAMED  :FreeRoom
WHERE {   GRAPH :BusyRoom { ?room  :armedWith ?sensor }
          GRAPH :FreeRoom { ?room  :armedWith ?sensor } }
```

Listing 1.7. SPARQL ASK query equivalent to Listing 1.6 conditions.

Listing 1.7 shows the SPARQL query equivalent to the filter at Lines 2–3 in Listing 1.6. Having chosen SPARQL to specify filters, the evaluation scope of a filter is a SPARQL dataset that we name the Event Dataset (EDS).

Considering a H $\leftarrow^G$ CExp, the EDS, to evaluate the filter against, is built as follow: EDS = {(def, ∅), (E_i, triples(A_k))...} where E_i ∈ named(CExp) and (A_k, t_k) ∈ $[\![E_i]\!]^t_{S\mathcal{E}}$.

The EDS is populated with RDF graphs subsuming a logical event E_i ∈ named(CExp). It is worth to note that, since the evaluation semantics is defined using sets, a combinatorial blow-up w.r.t. the cardinality of named(CExp) is possible[10]. Nevertheless, we are using this representation only to explain the semantics of OBEP data guards. The most common implementation [4,7] push the evaluation of data guards close to the related patterns, reducing drastically the number of combinations to evaluate.

Example 10. (**cont'd**) The data guards for the logical events detecting, respectively, *BusyRoom* at 8, i.e., (G_1={ :ra a :Room ; :ew :sa . :sa a :DoorSensor ; :obs [:closed a :Status] . },2,2), and *FreeRoom* at 8, i.e., (G_2={ :ra a :Room ; :ew :sa . :sa a :DoorSensor ; :obs [:open a :Status] . },3,3). are evaluated over the EDS that contains {(def,∅), (BusyRoom, G_1), (FreeRoom, G_2)}.

We define the complex event patterns clause evaluation in presence of data guards as follow:

$$[\![\text{H MATCH E IF F}]\!]^t_{S\mathcal{T}} = \{ (A \cup H(c), t_1, t_2) \mid (A, t_1, t_2) \in [\![\text{H MATCH E}]\!]^t_{S\mathcal{T}} \wedge [\![F]\!]_{EDS} \neq \emptyset \}$$

To avoid meaningless filters, we must define the vocabulary that can be used in their formulation. We chose to consider all those classes and properties used in Logical Events, which is determined by the following function.

Given a complex event H $\leftarrow^G$ CExp, ∀ E_i ∈ named(CExp),

$$allowed(E_i) = \begin{cases} named(E_i) & if\ logical\ E_i \\ \bigcup_{E_j \in named(E_i)} named(E_j) & if\ composite\ E \end{cases}$$

Time Guards or Frames are functions that determine a portion of an ontology stream, restricting the scope of an evaluation, e.g., consider the windowed stream $S^{\mathcal{E}}_{[5,15)}$.

---

[10] Virtually, the EDS is populated by all the combination of events instances.

Complex event expressions are evaluated over a whole event stream $S^{\mathcal{E}}$. However, most of the use-cases pose strict requirements on responsiveness. Therefore, we define the following function, which restricts the evaluation to a finite portion of $S^{\mathcal{E}}$.

$$\text{WITHIN} :: \text{D} \times S^{\mathcal{E}} \to S_D^{\mathcal{E}}$$

where D indicates a Duration, $S^{\mathcal{E}}$ is an event stream and $S_D^{\mathcal{E}}$ is a windowed event stream. We define the complex event patterns clause evaluation in presence of guards as follow:

$$[\![\text{H } \mathbf{MATCH} \text{ E } \mathbf{WITHIN} \, \imath]\!]_{S^{\mathcal{E}}}^t = [\![\text{ H } \mathbf{MATCH} \text{ E}]\!]_{S_{[t-\imath,t)}^{\mathcal{E}}}^t$$

Definition 13. *A **Guarded Complex Event** is an assertion* $H \leftarrow^G E$ *with H* $\leftarrow E$ *a Complex Event as in Definition 7 and G an optional guard as defined above.*

Notably, the semantics of the negation is not compatible with the one of data guards due to the impossibility of determining a vocabulary that is consistent with the incoming data.

5   Comparison with Existing Languages

In this section, we compare EP-SPARQL and RSEP-QL with OBEP. Table 3 summarizes the comparison, listing each language operators, reasoning support and first-class objects. Listings 1.8, 1.9, and 1.10 show the same query written with each language respectively.

Table 3. OBEP vs EP-SPARQL vs RSEP-QL. **Legend**: O-* = Optional, r = recent, n = naive, c = chronological, u = unrestricted; FCO: first-class objects.

	Operators	Allen's Algebra	Reasoning	Policies	FCO
EP-SPARQL	SEQ, O-SEQ, EQUALS, O-EQUALS, AND	Yes	RDFS	r, c, u	triples
RSEP-QL	FIRST, LAST, SEQ	No		n, r, c, u	BGP
OBEP	SEQ, FIRST, LAST, OR, AND, NOT	Yes	DL	u	Events

EP-SPARQL [1] is a SPARQL 1.0 extension for complex event processing over RDF Streams. It supports the temporal operators listed in Table 3 and Allen's algebra relations. EP-SPARQL can answer queries over RDF streams in combination with a RDFS background knowledge. Its syntax extends SPARQL 1.0 (see Listings 1.8), while the execution model is based on ETALIS [2]. EP-SPARQL queries are translated into ETALIS rules, flattening events and Basic Graph Pattern (BGP) patterns to the same structure, i.e., predicates of the form $triple(s,p,o)$. Consequently, pattern-maching is forced to happen at attribute level, and EP-SPARQL can handle seamlessly BGP evaluation and event detection. However, this approach drastically reduces ETALIS expressiveness since EP-SPARQL events are not first-class objects but triple predicates [15].

```
SELECT  ?comp ?r2
WHERE  {{{
        {?comp  :rank ?r1 } SEQ {?comp  :rank ?r2 }
        FILTER  (?r1 < r2) }
        SEQ
        {{ ?comp  :price ?p1 . } SEQ { ?comp  :price ?p2 . }
        FILTER  (?p1 < ?p2*0.5) } }
 UNION
      {{ {?comp  :rank ?r1 } SEQ {?c  :rank ?r2 }
           FILTER  (?r1 > r2) }
      SEQ  { { ?comp  :price ?p1 . } SEQ { ?comp  :price ?p2 . }
          FILTER  (?p1 > ?p2 *0.5) }}
 FILTER  ( getDURATION() < "P1H"^^xsd:duration )
```

Listing 1.8. EP-SPARQL.

```
REGISTER  <StockChange> CONSTRUCT { ?company :price1 ?p1 ; price2 ?p2. }
FROM NAMED :S WIN [LND 1H] AS :w1
EVENT ON :w1 { ?company  :price ?p1 . } AS Price1
EVENT ON :w1 { ?company  :price ?p2 . } AS Price2
WHERE   {  MATCH { Price1 SEQ Price2} }

CONSTRUCT { ?company :price ?p1 . }
FROM NAMED :S WIN [LND 1H] AS :w1
FROM NAMED :StockRaise WIN [LND 1H] AS :w2
EVENT ON :w1 { ?company  :rank ?r . } AS RankChange
EVENT ON :w2 { ?company  :price1 ?p1 ; :price2 ?p2 . } AS PriceFall
WHERE   {  MATCH { RankChange SEQ PriceFall}
            FILTER (?p1 < ?p2 * 0.5)}
```

Listing 1.9. RSEP-QL (Partial)

```
1    EVENT RankChange AS rank some .
2    EVENT StockPrice AS price some .
3
4    EVENT UpRank MATCH RankChange AS R1 SEQ RankChange AS R2 WITHIN 1H
5    IF { EVENT R1 { ?company :rank ?r1 . }
6          EVENT R2 { ?company :rank ?r2 . }
7          FILTER  ( ?r1 < ?r2 ) }
8
9    EVENT DownRank MATCH RankChange AS R1 SEQ RankChange AS R2 WITHIN 1H
10   IF { EVENT R1 { ?company :rank ?r1 . }
11         EVENT R2 { ?company :rank ?r2 . }
12         FILTER  ( ?r1 > ?r2 ) }
13
14   EVENT UpPrice MATCH StockPrice AS S1 SEQ StockPrice AS S2 WITHIN 1H
15   IF { EVENT S1 { ?company :price ?p1 . }
16         EVENT S2 { ?company :price ?p2 . }
17         FILTER  ( ?p2 < ?p1 * 0.5) }
18
19   EVENT DownPrice MATCH StockPrice AS S1 SEQ StockPrice AS S2 WITHIN 1H
20   IF { EVENT S1 { ?company :price ?p1 . }
21         EVENT S2 { ?company :price ?p2 . }
22         FILTER  ( ?p2 > ?p1 * 0.5) }
23
24   EVENT Alert MATCH
25      (UpRank SEQ UpPrice) OR (DownRank SEQ DownPrice) WITHIN 1H
26   RETURN Alert AS RDF STREAM
```

Listing 1.10. OBEP.

RSEP-QL [8] extends RSP-QL [9] with event detection operators (see Table 3). RSEP-QL pattern matching is based on basic event patterns (BEP), which are defined extending BGP contextually to a time-preserving window operator, named window function. BEP are labeled to allow their reuse, but labels do not have a well-defined semantics. Event-pattern operators in RSEP-QL work according to SPARQL operators and, thus, we can conclude that events are not first-class object, but an abstraction build on top existing RSP-QL features (BGP and Windows Operators).

Operators. OBEP, EP-SPARQL and RSEP-QL employ the same temporal model based on two timestamps. Although EP-SPARQL operational semantics is based on ETALIS, RSEP-QL showed we could redesign it using RSP-QL primitives. Therefore, the languages are substantially similar in terms of operators.

Selection or Consumption policies. RSEP-QL is the most expressive and fully captures EP-SPARQL behaviors. OBEP does not specify any policy, and it adopts an unrestricted selection which is the default for EP-SPARQL.

Syntax. As shown in the following examples, the OBEP approach results in better organized queries than existing ones. Let's consider the following query, a simple extension of an example from [2]: *Provide all the ranking augments that are followed by a stock price increase, and all the ranking decrements that are followed by a stock price decrease.*

EP-SPARQL query, in Listing 1.8, requires the use of a UNION pattern, to represent the alternatives cases. The query is not unmanageable, but it is easy to show that it becomes too complicated when event definitions become more complicated than one triple. Listing 1.9 reports only a sub-example of the same query translated in RSEP-QL. Indeed, RSP-QL does not support UNION patterns, and we are forced to create a query-network that produces the results. Finally, Listings 1.10 shows how OBEP handles the use-case. Although OBEP is as succinct as EP-SPARQL, the query shows a more organized structure, providing a clear separation between event definitions and processing. Moreover, it allows sharing, and even extending event definitions across queries, which was not possible in EP-SPARQL and only partially in RSEP-QL.

6   Conclusion and Future Work

In this paper, we studied the foundation of Ontology-Based Event Processing (OBEP) [18]: an approach for event definition and detection on RDF Streams.

In this paper, (i) we defined OBEP's data and query models, and (ii) we explained the evaluation semantics of OBEP's operators[11]. Moreover, (iii) we showed why OBEP is alternative to existing RSP approaches for event detection, i.e., EP-SPARQL, and RSEP-QL.

Future work for OBEP comprises the introduction of synthesized events, enabling simple analytical queries. Moreover, we aim at studying OBEP performance systematically, investigating how different DL impact the performance. Last but not least, we aim at combining OBEP and existing RSP approaches towards a unified language that tames variety and velocity as well as reconciles analytics and event detection rules [6].

---

[11] An extended version of this paper, with more examples and all the operators semantics is at https://github.com/riccardotommasini/obep.

References

1. Anicic, D., Fodor, P., Rudolph, S., Stojanovic, N.: EP-SPARQL: a unified language for event processing and stream reasoning, pp. 635–644 (2011)
2. Anicic, D., Rudolph, S., Fodor, P., Stojanovic, N.: Stream reasoning and complex event processing in ETALIS. Semant. Web **3**(4), 397–407 (2012)
3. Baader, F.: The Description Logic Handbook: Theory, Implementation and Applications. Cambridge University Press, New York (2003)
4. Chakravarthy, S., Mishra, D.: Snoop: an expressive event specification language for active databases. Data Knowl. Eng. **14**(1), 1–26 (1994)
5. Chen, J., Lécué, F., Pan, J.Z., Chen, H.: Learning from ontology streams with semantic concept drift. In: Proceedings of the Twenty-Sixth International Joint Conference on Artificial Intelligence, IJCAI 2017, Melbourne, Australia, 19–25 August 2017, pp. 957–963 (2017). https://doi.org/10.24963/ijcai.2017/133
6. Cugola, G.: Processing flows of information: from data stream to complex event processing. ACM Comput. Surv. **44**(3), 15 (2012)
7. Cugola, G., Margara, A.: TESLA: a formally defined event specification language. In: Proceedings of the Fourth ACM International Conference on Distributed Event-Based Systems, DEBS, Cambridge, United Kingdom (2010)
8. Dell'Aglio, D., Dao-Tran, M., Calbimonte, J., Phuoc, D.L., Della Valle, E.: A query model to capture event pattern matching in RDF stream processing query languages. In: Knowledge Engineering and Knowledge Management - 20th International Conference, EKAW, Bologna, Italy (2016)
9. Dell'Aglio, D., Della Valle, E., Calbimonte, J., Corcho, Ó.: RSP-QL semantics: a unifying query model to explain heterogeneity of RDF stream processing systems. Int. J. Semantic Web Inf. Syst. **10**(4), 17–44 (2014)
10. Dell'Aglio, D., Della Valle, E., van Harmelen, F., Bernstein, A.: Stream reasoning: a survey and outlook **1**(1–2), 59–83 (2017)
11. Horrocks, I., Kutz, O., Sattler, U.: The even more irresistible SROIQ. In: KR, vol. 6, pp. 57–67 (2006)
12. Luckham, D.C.: The Power of Events: An Introduction to Complex Event Processing in Distributed Enterprise Systems. Addison-Wesley Longman Publishing Co., Inc., Boston (2001)
13. Paschke, A.: ECA-RuleML: an approach combining ECA rules with temporal interval-based KR event/action logics and transactional update logics. CoRR abs/cs/0610167 (2006)
14. Pérez, J., Arenas, M., Gutiérrez, C.: Semantics and complexity of SPARQL. ACM Trans. Database Syst. **34**(3), 16:1–16:45 (2009)
15. Le-Phuoc, D., Dao-Tran, M., Pham, M.-D., Boncz, P., Eiter, T., Fink, M.: Linked stream data processing engines: facts and figures. In: Cudré-Mauroux, P., et al. (eds.) ISWC 2012. LNCS, vol. 7650, pp. 300–312. Springer, Heidelberg (2012). https://doi.org/10.1007/978-3-642-35173-0_20
16. Ren, Y., Pan, J.Z.: Optimising ontology stream reasoning with truth maintenance system. In: Proceedings of the 20th ACM Conference on Information and Knowledge Management, CIKM 2011, Glasgow, United Kingdom, 24–28 October 2011, pp. 831–836 (2011). https://doi.org/10.1145/2063576.2063696
17. Stuckenschmidt, H., et al.: Towards expressive stream reasoning. In: Semantic Challenges in Sensor Networks, 24–29 January 2010
18. Tommasini, R., Bonte, P., Della Valle, E., Mannens, E., De Turck, F., Ongenae, F.: Towards ontology based event processing. In: OWLED2016, the International Experiences and Directions Workshop on OWL (2016)
19. Zemke, F., Witkowski, A., Cherniack, M., Colby, L.: Pattern matching in sequences of rows. Technical report, Technical Report ANSI Standard Proposal (2007)

A Random Walk Model for Entity Relatedness

Pablo Torres-Tramón[(✉)] and Conor Hayes

Insight Centre for Data Analytics, NUI Galway, Galway, Ireland
{pablo.torres,conor.hayes}@insight-centre.org

Abstract. Semantic relatedness is a critical measure for a wide variety of applications nowadays. Numerous models, including path-based, have been proposed for this task with great success in many applications during the last few years. Among these applications, many of them require computing semantic relatedness between hundreds of pairs of items as part of their regular input. This scenario demands a computationally efficient model to process hundreds of queries in short time spans. Unfortunately, Path-based models are computationally challenging, creating large bottlenecks when facing these circumstances. Current approaches for reducing this computation have focused on limiting the number of paths to consider between entities.

Contrariwise, we claim that a semantic relatedness model based on random walks is a better alternative for handling the computational cost. To this end, we developed a model based on the well-studied Katz score. Our model addresses the scalability issues of Path-based models by pre-computing relatedness for all pair of vertices in the knowledge graph beforehand and later providing them when needed in querying time. Our current findings demonstrate that our model has a competitive performance in comparison to Path-based models while being computationally efficient for high-demanding applications.

Keywords: Entity relatedness · Path-based semantics · Random walks

1 Motivation

Graph-based semantic relatedness assessment between two entities has been applied to a wide verity of applications such as Word Sense Disambiguation (WSD) [3,16], Entity Search [9,22], Named Entity Disambiguation (NED) [16, 20] and, more recently, the *cold start* problem found in recommender systems [21]. In all these cases, semantic relatedness serves two purposes: (*i*) as a pre-processing step for regular input [3,16,20] or (*ii*) as intermediary step in their processing pipeline [9,21,22]. For instance, entity search requires to identify a set of named entities that are semantically close to an original entity under certain user requirements. In this case, semantic relatedness is regarded as a proximity measure between pairs of entities that are under exploration. A similar situation occurs in NED as well. Here semantic relatedness is used to quantify

© Springer Nature Switzerland AG 2018
C. Faron Zucker et al. (Eds.): EKAW 2018, LNAI 11313, pp. 454–469, 2018.
https://doi.org/10.1007/978-3-030-03667-6_29

the solution space such that the instance whose entities have the highest pairwise semantic relatedness is the solution to the disambiguation problem. The number of queries required by these applications in their normal activity can easily reach the thousands in short time spans. Therefore, these applications configure a scenario where the computational performance of semantic relatedness becomes critical.

Unfortunately, graph-based semantic relatedness models are computationally costly. The reason for this cost is rooted in the formalisation of these models. Most of them were designed as a ranking of aggregating path-based scores [12,16,20,22]. Thus, they require to enumerate a large number of paths between the input entities. Finding these paths is the cause of the high cost as this task is very expensive for even slightly dense graphs. Although knowledge graphs are far from being dense, the execution time of this model can be high in practice. Current attempts to improve the runtime performance of these models are focused on limiting the number of paths to enumerate [16,20,22] by setting an upper bound on the number of paths to find. However, this strategy fails to reduce the complexity as it does not set a bound on the plausible number of paths to check. Hence keeping the same complexity in the worst case.

Rather than enumerating paths, a more scalable alternative can be achieved by using random walks. A walk is a generalisation of paths such that cycles (or edge repetitions) are permitted. Such freedom is exploited extensively as certain linear algebra properties allow us to represent the walk finding problem as a linear equation system [17]. Surprisingly, walks are normally overlooked as a source of semantics. In this paper, we propose an algorithm for semantic relatedness using a random walk model based on the well-known Katz centrality [17]. We argue that random walks, in general, have been underestimated as a source of relatedness. Our work demonstrates that random walks can have a performance as good as direct paths while being substantially more efficient. We found that the relatedness scores generated by our model are ranking-equivalent to a well-known path-based model. Our model reduces dramatically the time required for processing a single query, being ideal for high-demanding applications.

The rest of this paper is structured in the following way: In the next section, we introduce our method, detailing its mathematical foundations as well as its properties. In the third section, a detailed description of the implementation is given. Later, in the fourth section, we evaluate our algorithm, comparing its performance against the state-of-the-art methods as well as their runtimes. Next, we give an account of the related work in section five. Finally, our conclusions and future work.

2   Method

Before presenting the proposed method, it is necessary to introduce a series of mathematical concepts required for the formalisation of our method.

2.1   Preliminaries

A knowledge base is a set of facts coded in the form of triples, which in turn are formed by a subject, an object, and a predicate. The intersection of subjects (or objects) between different triples allows us to chain triples around a common subject (or object). Naturally, this leads to viewing a knowledge base as a graph-like structure.

Definition 1 (Knowledge Graph). *Given a set of triples* $T \in \mathbb{S} \times \Sigma \times \mathbb{O}$ *such that* $\mathbb{S} \cap \mathbb{O} \neq \emptyset$. *A knowledge graph is a tuple* $G = (\mathcal{V}, \mathcal{E}, \sigma)$ *such that its vertices are defined by* $\mathcal{V} = \mathbb{S} \cap \mathbb{O}$, *its edges as* $\mathcal{E} = \{(i, j) : (i, p, j) \in T\} \subseteq \mathcal{V}^2$, *and* $\sigma : \mathcal{E} \longrightarrow \Sigma$ *is a map for an edge to the set of predicate labels* Σ. *For each triple* $(i, p, j) \in T$ *there is an equivalent inverse edge* $\hat{e} = (j, i) \in \mathcal{E}$ *such that its type is given by the type of the original edge* $(\sigma(e) = \sigma(\hat{e}))$. *The resulting graph* G *is strongly connected, i.e. any vertex* i *is reachable from any other vertex* j *and the adjacency matrix of the graph is symmetrical.*

The imposition of symmetry is a common practice in the field [7,16,22]. By setting it, we can traverse the graph in both directions having the same relationships defined in the original triple set. Semantically speaking, this implies that for every subject-object relationship, there is an equivalent-opposite relationship connecting the entities. The same situation occurs when considering a sequence of edges. If there is a sequence of edges connecting two entities, then there is an equivalent-opposite sequence of edges that connects the same pair of entities in the opposite direction. Therefore, it is easy to visualise that, for any two entities pairs, the number of sequences connecting them is the same. This assumption is crucial to the formalisation of the proposed method as it makes the adjacency matrix symmetrical.

Definition 2 (Walk). *Let* $G = (\mathcal{V}, \mathcal{E}, \sigma)$ *be a knowledge graph. A walk* W *in* G *is a finite, non-empty sequence of edges* $e_1, e_2, \ldots, e_k \in \mathcal{E}$ *connecting* v_1 *and* v_{k+1}. *The vertices* $v_1 \in e_1$ *and* $v_{k+1} \in e_k$ *are normally called as the initial and final vertices of the sequence respectively. The length of a walk (denoted as* $|W|$) *is indicated by the cardinality of the sequence.*

Basically, a walk starts at some given vertex and follows a certain sequence of edges until reaching the final vertex. In semantic terms, the length of a walk reflects the effort of moving along the graph from one entity to another. As the length increases, less pertinent become the sequence. In order to compare walk-based methods against paths-based ones, it is then necessary to formalise the latter as well.

Definition 3 (Path). *Let* $G = (\mathcal{V}, \mathcal{E}, \sigma)$ *be a knowledge graph. A path* P *in* G *is a walk connecting* v_1 *and* v_{k+1} *such that there is no repetition of vertices in the sequence.*

Katz centrality [17] is a classical score from social network analysis that measures the overall influence for each vertex in the graph. The original formalisation was based on the geometric progression $(\beta A)^0 + (\beta A)^1 + (\beta A)^2 + \ldots$ for an adjacency matrix A and real, positive value β which converges under certain conditions. In this work, however, a formalisation based on random walks is used instead. A random walk model is a Markov chain such that the next vertex in the chain will be selected independently at any given time (or step) k, regardless of previously visited vertices. Katz centrality can also be formalised in this way.

Definition 4 (Katz). *Let G be a knowledge graph and A its adjacency matrix. Let $\beta \in (0,1] \subset \mathbb{R}$ be a given parameter. Let D be a diagonal matrix such that $D_{(i,i)} = \sum_i(A_{:,i})$. The transition matrix T is given by $T = D^{-1}A$. A Katz random walk process over G is a Markov chain M such that:*

$$M_{k+1} = \beta T M_k \tag{1}$$

Where k is the number of steps or time. The initial value of Katz $M_0 = I$, which is the identity matrix.

Each pair (i,j) of the resulting matrix M_k is the probability of reaching vertex j by randomly walking k steps from vertex i. For each step taken, β is a penalty value that reduces the influence of the walks in the final probability.

Knowing that $M_0 = I$, let us consider the following operator for this random walk process whenever a given value $t \in \mathbb{Z}_{>0}$ is given.

$$\Delta_0^t = \sum_{k=0}^{t} M_k = \sum_{k=0}^{t} (\beta T)^k \tag{2}$$

Here, only the probabilities of the walks formed for a certain time range are considered. Thus, for any t, $\Delta_0^t(i,j)$ is the probability of reaching vertex j from vertex i by randomly walking t or less steps. It has been a well-extended practice in the field to only consider sequences up to a certain length, normally 4 [16,20] or 5 [22]. Therefore, this operator will be used to control the length of the walks. When $t \to \infty$, then Δ_0^t converges exactly to the Katz centrality. The convergence exists whenever β is less than the reciprocal of the spectral radius ρ of the transition matrix T, i.e. $\beta < 1/\rho(T)$.

2.2 Queries

Given a knowledge graph G and certain input vertex j, the probability of randomly walking from any other vertex in the graph until reaching j in t or fewer steps can be written as it follows:

$$Pr(X_{\leq t} = j|X_0) = \sum_{k=1}^{t} Pr(X_k = j|X_0)Pr(S = 0)^k \tag{3}$$

where S is a uniform random variable and it represents the probability of a walk to finish at any vertex at random. The probability $Pr(X_k = j|X_0)$ is the combined probability of any random walks starting at any vertex at time 0 and reaching vertex j at time k. Now, it is evident that if a walk reaches j, it must have a sequence of edges $(X_0, X_1), (X_1, X_2), \ldots, (X_{k-1}, X_k)$ such that $X_k = j$. Each unique vertex X_l in this sequence is an independent random variable. Thus, the probability of a walk is given by the joint probability of its vertices in the sequence of edges. Therefore, the expression $Pr(X_0|X_k = j)$ can be written as follows:

$$Pr(X_0|X_k = j) = \left(\prod_{l=0}^{k-2} Pr(X_l|X_{l+1}) \right) Pr(X_{k-1}|X_k = j) \qquad (4)$$

The expression $Pr(X_l|X_{l+1})$ (as well as $Pr(X_{k-1}|X_k = j)$) is the probability of randomly walk from X_l to X_{l+1} for any $l < k$. In the absence of data, we need to resort to heuristics in order to estimate $Pr(X_l|X_{l+1})$ for any pair $(l, l+1) \in \mathcal{E}$ assumming that this probabilities do not change for any pair $(l, l+1)$.

1. EQV: Each edge has the same probability.
2. PFITF [22]: The probability of a single edge is proportional to the amount of information contained by this edge at the local context and the frequency of the edge type across the entire graph. The local context for an edge is the set of edges incoming or outgoing to any of its two vertices.
3. EXCL [16]: Each edge probability is proportional to the level of the rareness of its type, considering only the local context.

These three heuristics defined the three different transition matrices that were used in the evaluation section. Once these probabilities are estimated, a ranking-preserving solution for $Pr(X_{<t} = j|X_0)$ can be computed directly using the Katz operator over the transition matrix.

$$Pr(X_{\leq t} = j|X_0) \propto \Delta_0^t(., j) \qquad (5)$$

where $(., j)$ means to select the column j of the resulting matrix. This column contains the probability of randomly walking from any vertex to vertex j.

Now, if a sample set of pairs of entities is given, then a solution can be generated by the same principle. Suppose that τ is the set of target vertices and be ι the set of initial vertices defined by the sample set of pairs. The probability to estimate in this case is given by $Pr(X_{\leq t} \in \tau|X_0 \in \iota)$

$$Pr(X_{\leq t} \in \tau|X_0 \in \iota) \propto \Delta_0^t(i, j) \quad \forall i \in \iota, \, j \in \tau \qquad (6)$$

2.3   Properties

Δ_0^t is the basic operation for solving $Pr(X_{\leq t} \in \tau|X_0 \in \iota)$. Here a comparison between the ranking produced by this operator and a previous path-based relatedness called *Katz Relatedness* [16,20] is conducted since both are based on a similar principle. Before proceeding to compare their rankings, both scores will be re-defined in terms of a path and walk contribution respectively and presented as similarity (resemblance) measures.

Definition 5 (Walk-based Relatedness). *Let G be a knowledge graph and $t \in \mathbb{Z}_{>0}$ the step parameter. Let $\hat{\Delta}_0^t$ be a normalisation operator $\hat{\Delta}$ such that $\hat{\Delta}_0^t$ is symmetric. The function $\phi : (i,j) \in \mathcal{E} \longrightarrow \mathbb{R}$ is called Walk Relatedness at t such that:*

$$\phi(i,j) = \begin{cases} \hat{\Delta}_0^t(i,j) & \text{if } i \neq j \\ 1 & \text{otherwise} \end{cases} \tag{7}$$

Proposition 1. *Function ϕ is a similarity measure.*

Proof. It is necessary to prove that ϕ is symmetric and $\forall i, j \in \mathcal{E}, \quad \phi(i,i) \geq \phi(i,j)$. The first condition is trivial since $\hat{\Delta}_0^t$ is symmetric. For the second case, $\hat{\Delta}_0^t(i,j) \leq 1$ for every pair (i,j) $i \neq j$. Since $\phi(i,i) = 1$, then it is evident that the second condition holds.

As this definition required, it is necessary to introduce a normalisation for the resulting matrix of Katz operator (Eq. 2). To this end, the following normalisation is applied to the result of the Katz operator.

$$\hat{\Delta}_0^t = norm(\Delta_0^t + {\Delta_0^t}^T) \tag{8}$$

where *norm* is the max-min normalisation. Notice that adding Δ_0^t with its transpose generates a symmetric matrix. This addition has also a semantic implication for our model. It reflects the probability of reaching j from i in both directions.

Katz Relatedness cannot be expressed as a geometric series of the transition matrix. Instead, it must be defined in terms of the paths connecting each pair (i,j).

Definition 6 (Path-based Relatedness). *Let G be a knowledge graph. Let $\mathcal{P}_{(i,j)} = \bigcup_{k=1}^{t} \mathcal{P}_{(i,j)}^k$ be the union of the set of paths connecting vertices (i,j) in G with length k. The function $\psi : \mathcal{V}^2 \longrightarrow [0,1] \subset \mathbb{R}$ is called Path-based Relatedness such that:*

$$\psi(i,j) = \begin{cases} \frac{1}{|\mathcal{P}(i,j)^t|}\sum_{k=1}^{t}\sum_{P \in \mathcal{P}_{(i,j)}^k} Pr(P)\beta^k & \text{if } i \neq j \\ 1 & \text{otherwise} \end{cases} \tag{9}$$

Notice that the operator Δ_0^t can also be written in terms of individual contributions of its constituents, similar to Eq. 3.

Proposition 2. *Function ψ is a similarity measure.*

Proof. Each path connecting (i,j) have a reciprocal path in the opposite direction, thus $\psi(i,j) = \psi(j,i)$. By definition, the relatedness between an entity and itself is $\psi(i,i) = 1$. It is evident then that $\psi(i,i) \geq \psi(i,j) \; \forall i, j \in \mathcal{E}$.

Naturally, both relatedness functions, ϕ and ψ, induce a partial order over the set of unordered pairs of vertices. Thus, the subsequent binary relationships are defined for any $i, j, k, l \in \mathcal{V}$:

$$\begin{aligned} (i,j) \preceq_\phi (k,l) &\iff \phi(i,j) \leq \phi(k,l) \\ (i,j) \preceq_\psi (k,l) &\iff \psi(i,j) \leq \psi(k,l) \end{aligned} \tag{10}$$

3 Implementation

So far, knowledge graphs have been formalised as a conventional graph with the particularity of having many relationship types. However, it is this very same particularity that makes knowledge graph a multi-graph. A multi-graph (or multi-dimensional graph) is a generalisation of a graph where each edge has a type associated. A single adjacency matrix cannot represent this type of graph. Instead, a collection of adjacency matrices, one for each relationship, is required. Thus, the adjacency matrix is indeed a tensor. A tensor is a generalisation of a matrix such that there is a third additional coordinate. For multi-graphs, this new coordinate represents the type of the relationship for a given pair of vertices (i, j).

Evidently, tensors are more memory-consuming than matrices for storing data. Notice that, for each relationship, there is a $m \times m$ matrix to fill, requiring in total $m \times m \times k$ storage space. This situation makes it difficult to employ tensor models for implementing knowledge graphs in practice. One well-extended alternative to tensors is collapsing the data into a single adjacency matrix. Here, each element (i, j) for each relationship k is summed across the entire set of relationships. The following equation show the resulting adjacency matrix:

$$A(i,j) = \sum_{k=0}^{|k|} T(i, j, k) \tag{11}$$

where $T(i, j, k)$ represents the adjacency for vertices (i, j) and the type k. The resulting adjacency matrix only requires $m \times m$ storage space and it can be used safely to compute a geometric progression, producing the exact result. A more detailed proof of this technique can be consulted here [1].

Although this compression significantly reduces the overall memory consumption, it still requires $m \times m$ space in memory. For a large knowledge graph, this amount of space is still unfeasible. We observed, however, that the knowledge graph (and therefore the adjacency matrix) is quite sparse. Indeed, it was observed in the experiments that the sparsity level is about 99.9% for the knowledge graph employed. The level of the sparsity of a graph is intrinsically connected to its completeness. In general, knowledge graphs suffer a lack of completeness [13]. Thus, the number of relationships is often low. The implementation of our method takes advantage of this issue by storing the adjacency matrix as a sparse matrix. In sparse matrices, only non-zero values are stored, alleviating significantly the requirements of memory. Using sparse matrices makes the storage space needed by the adjacency matrix linear to the number of triples of the knowledge graph. We used the well-known Numpy[1] framework and its sparse package to implement our method.

Once the adjacency matrices are collapsed and stored as one matrix, the Katz operato (Eq. 2) can be computed directly from it. The high sparsity of the matrix is critical in this step to reduce the computation of the geometric

---

[1] http://www.numpy.org.

Algorithm 1. Computing Δ_0^t

Data: A: collapsed adjacency matrix, t: number of steps, β
Result: Δ_0^t
1 m = size(A), D = eye(m), M = eye(m);
2 **for** $i < t$ **do**
3 | M = M*(β*A);
4 | D = D + M;
5 **end**

---

progression. Since there is a high number of zeros in the matrix, the resulting matrices of the successive multiplications are also sparse. Therefore, the computation is dramatically reduced. As depicted in Algorithm 1, the final number of multiplications is given by the length of the progression. In each iteration, the adjacency matrix is multiplied by itself and the parameter β and stored for the next iteration. At the same time, the resulting multiplication is accumulated.

4 Evaluation

At the beginning of this paper, we argued that some real-world applications such as WSD [16] or recommender systems [21] require relatedness functions in order to rank a set of pairs. Hence, such ability will be tested using pairs of words as input in this evaluation. There are a few ground truth datasets that can be useful in this setting. Before going into their details, it is necessary first to describe the knowledge graph used in this evaluation. Later, we will compare human-produced rankings with the ones generated by our method and other state-of-the-art methods. Finally, a detailed account of the computational performance of the method will be provided.

4.1 WordNet

Since we are basing our evaluation in rankings of pairs of words, it is then necessary to select a Knowledge Graph according to these requirements. Among the available alternatives, we found that WORDNET[2] presented two important features for our evaluation: (*i*) it is relatively small in comparison to general purposes knowledge databases and (*ii*) it is a good fit when analysing of pairs of words. Due to the cost of multiplying large matrices, we opted for selecting a relatively small knowledge graph. We left for the future the exploration of alternatives methods to reduce the amount of computation.

WORDNET was introduced as a general purpose lexical database in the beginnings of the 90s [18]. In WORDNET, words (referred as lemmas) are linked to abstract entities, known as concepts or *synsets*, which in turn are inter-linked among themselves with certain semantic relationships. Each relationship has a

---

[2] https://wordnet.princeton.edu.

type associated that represent the semantic associations between both concepts. A concept might have several lemmas linked to it and vice-versa. Concepts are abstract ideas/objects that are evoked by a word when is used in a certain context or predicate. For example, lemmas: *car* and *automobile* normally refer to self-propelling objects that generally use a combustion engine to self-propel. However, other uses of the word *car* are valid as well in different contexts. For instance, a *car* might refer to a train wagon. As we mentioned, concepts are inter-linked according to some semantic relationships. For example, one concept might be part of a more general concepts (e.g. *car* $\longrightarrow$ *vehicle*) or they can refer to opposite ideas (e.g. *good* $\longrightarrow$ *bad*). WORDNET represents these semantic associations using a fixed set of relationship types. The latest version of WORDNET, (WN31), contains 26 relationship types.

The resulting graph generated from these concepts and its relationships was used for computing the Katz operator. During this process, it was found that some few concepts do not have any edge to other concepts in the graph. Therefore, these were removed from the graph as we assumed that this must be strongly connected. In summary, the resulting graph was composed by 116,787 vertices and 378,203 relationships, with an average degree of 6.476.

4.2   Ground Truth Datasets

Ground Truth datasets are composed by a list of pairs of words, where each pair have a real, positive score associated. These scores were granted by a set of human assessors, who evaluated the degree of semantic association between the words. The scores determine the position of the pair in the ranking. It is assumed that in the input list, the pairs of words do not necessarily must have words in common. Instead, we assumed that each pair was generated independently of the others, discarding any relationship among themselves.

In the literature, there are several ground truth datasets that fit this purpose. Among these, the following three were selected:

1. MC [19] (28 pairs of words): This dataset was designed to investigate the semantic and the contextual similarity for words.
2. RG [23] (65 pairs of words): In this classical dataset, the authors explored the strength of synonymy between pairs of words. The list of pairs was composed by 65 pairs, including highly related and unrelated pairs.
3. WS-SIM [2] (97 pairs of words): This dataset is a subset of the original dataset proposed here [11]. Agirre *et al.* claimed that the original dataset contained pairs of words for similarity and relatedness, and thus they divided the pairs in two groups: similarity and relatedness pairs. In this evaluation, only similarity pairs were used.

The words in these datasets are presented in plain text format. There is no information about the context in which they were present originally to the human assessors, or any other information that can help us to determine the sense of the word. Therefore, it is necessary to disambiguate these words to determine their senses. Fortunately, Schwartz *et al.* [24] already completed this step. In their work, they labelled the input words using WORDNET concepts, obtaining a *synset* label for each word. It was necessary to drop some pairs of words from the datasets to produce a consistent label assignment as there were some cases where it was not possible to determine the WORDNET concept suggested by the words.

4.3 Evaluation Metrics

In order to evaluate our rankings with respect to the one produced by human assessors, we used Spearman correlation. This metric measures the correlation between two random variables, generating an output value that ranges in the interval $[-1, 1]$. When there is a positive correlation then the output value would be close to 1. Instead, if there is a negative correlation then the output would be near to -1. When there is no correlation, the output is close to 0.

Before comparing the outputs, the scores produced by our algorithm as well as the scores assessed by human assessors were transformed into positions. If two pairs or more had an equal score, the same position number was assigned to all of them. In order to decide whether two scores were equal, we defined a value $\epsilon > 0$ such that if $|\phi(i, j) - \phi(l, k)| < \epsilon$ then the scores in question were considered to be equal. Since equal pairs have the same position in the ranking, the next pair started at the position indicated by the last position assigned plus the number of pairs holding that position. This transformation was done for any ranking evaluated. The evaluation metrics were then computed using these lists of positions as the input.

4.4 Discussion

We proceeded to compute the Katz operator for the following values: $t \in [2, 3, 4]$ using WN31 as the knowledge graph and applying the 3 different weighting schemes. The Spearman correlation between the rankings generated for the ground truth datasets and the human-produced rankings are shown in Table 1.

We observed that none of the weighting schemes is superior to any other for every dataset. Instead, each dataset has a scheme whose performance is better than the rest. For instance, EXCL weighting scheme has the best performance for WS-SIM dataset. However, it performs relatively poor in the others. EQV and PTITF have a similar performance for RG, but EQV is significantly better than PTIFT when ranking MC.

We noted as well that the best results were achieved whenever $\beta \in [0.5, 1]$ for every datasets MC and RG. Only dataset WS-SIM showed a more balanced distribution when using exclusivity scheme, being $\beta = 0.5$ the setting with the best performance. This is consistent with *de facto* value in random processes for this parameter ($\beta = 0.85$) [2]. As $\beta \longrightarrow 1$, the contributions of larger paths become more relevant in the final score. Therefore, we can deduce that the inclusion of these paths significantly increases the performance of the relatedness. For instance, the best result for MC was obtained when $\beta = 1.0$.

In the case of the number of steps (t), we observed that the best performances are well distributed across the range examined in this evaluation. We also considered the case of $t = 1$ (not displayed for the sake of space), finding the performance substantially poorer than any other case. Evidently, the inclusion of larger paths can dramatically increase the performance, particularly $t = 2$ for datasets MC and RG. However, after reaching a peak, the inclusion of larger paths did not increase necessarily the correlation. It is interesting to note that in every scheme examined, the performance was slightly similar when $t \in [2,3]$ for MC and RG, being $t = 2$ marginally better. In contrast, the difference between the results obtained for WS-SIM using the same range of t were significantly larger, obtaining better performance when $t = 3$.

The correlations for ϕ and ψ were very similar for the analysed datasets as we expected. It was necessary to set β in the range of $[0.05, 0.2]$ as larger values performed poorly in this case. This situation was also observed before [16].

4.5   Runtime

We evaluated the execution runtime for: (i) generating Δ_0^t (Fig. 1) and (ii) solving queries using ϕ and ψ (Fig. 2). The measurements were conducted in a 24 core machine with 100 GB of RAM on Ubuntu 12.10. The query runtimes were obtained by measuring the wall time needed to solve each query in our datasets using different configurations. In total we executed $3,800$ instances for each function.

As we expected, the cost of computing Δ_0^t increased quickly as the number of steps did. However, the average of runtime for the maximum t tested was less than 100s. Thus, commodity hardware is more than enough for computing this operator for the range examined. The cause of these low runtimes is due to the high sparsity of the transition matrix. This dramatically reduces the number of operations needed when computing the geometric progression.

For the case of query evaluation, the results show that the average time required for solving a single query using ψ increased exponentially as the steps did. The runtimes show that some of these queries were very costly to handle using this model. For instance, there were cases that required more than 10^t ms to complete a single query. The function ψ was implemented using a simple BFS algorithm with some minor optimisations. Although optimising BFS is out of the scope of this paper, it is worth to mention that there are many optimisations for BFS that can be used to improve the performance of ψ [10].

In contrast, the computational cost was close to constant for single queries using ϕ. A relevant proportion of the queries required less than 1ms in order to get completed.

Table 1. Spearman Correlation of our method with different parameters (β, t, weighting scheme) for each dataset

Method	Weight	β	MC			RG			WS-SIM		
			$t=2$	$t=3$	$t=4$	$t=2$	$t=3$	$t=4$	$t=2$	$t=3$	$t=4$
$\phi(i,j)$	EQV	0.25	0.788	0.788	0.788	0.780	0.785	0.785	0.568	0.626	0.625
		0.50	0.788	0.788	0.763	0.780	0.785	0.779	0.570	0.632	0.613
		0.75	0.788	0.788	0.774	0.780	0.785	0.782	0.571	0.635	0.621
		1.00	0.788	0.790	0.801	0.780	0.786	0.794	0.570	0.640	0.620
	PFITF	0.25	0.796	0.795	0.795	0.782	0.785	0.788	0.552	0.598	0.591
		0.50	0.796	0.795	0.795	0.782	0.785	0.792	0.553	0.614	0.596
		0.75	0.796	0.796	0.772	0.782	0.785	0.780	0.551	0.614	0.589
		1.00	0.796	0.796	0.767	0.782	0.785	0.775	0.550	0.615	0.590
	EXCL	0.25	0.785	0.764	0.764	0.780	0.786	0.786	0.578	0.627	0.629
		0.50	0.785	0.785	0.785	0.780	0.784	0.787	0.580	0.645	0.630
		0.75	0.785	0.785	0.785	0.780	0.784	0.790	0.578	0.644	0.621
		1.00	0.785	0.779	0.755	0.780	0.782	0.778	0.577	0.644	0.616
$\psi(i,j)$	EQV	0.05	0.782	0.795	0.784	0.781	0.781	0.786	0.552	0.598	0.577
		0.10	0.782	0.795	0.785	0.781	0.781	0.787	0.542	0.587	0.552
		0.15	0.782	0.795	0.765	0.781	0.781	0.779	0.528	0.575	0.521
		0.20	0.782	0.795	0.710	0.781	0.781	0.747	0.520	0.538	0.407
	PFITF	0.05	0.787	0.787	0.769	0.779	0.779	0.785	0.524	0.575	0.536
		0.10	0.787	0.794	0.782	0.779	0.779	0.785	0.508	0.555	0.498
		0.15	0.787	0.799	0.781	0.779	0.776	0.777	0.496	0.539	0.451
		0.20	0.787	0.788	0.735	0.779	0.763	0.750	0.478	0.497	0.376
	EXCL	0.05	0.782	0.778	0.787	0.780	0.781	0.789	0.576	0.625	0.621
		0.10	0.782	0.752	0.765	0.780	0.773	0.784	0.575	0.622	0.613
		0.15	0.782	0.753	0.769	0.780	0.767	0.773	0.570	0.614	0.602
		0.20	0.782	0.747	0.753	0.780	0.759	0.758	0.569	0.606	0.576

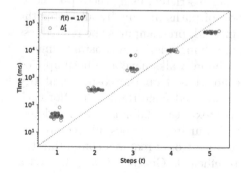

Fig. 1. Execution runtime for Δ_0^t using a range of t.

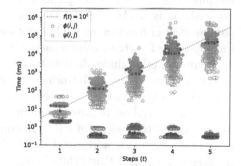

Fig. 2. Execution runtime for ϕ and ψ using a range of t

5   Related Work

Entity relatedness is a well-studied problem [4–6,8,9,16,20,22]. The origins of the field are rooted in computational linguistics [6], where for many years functions for assessing semantic relatedness have been developed. The emergence of large knowledge graph during the 90s and earlier 2000s triggered the development of graph-based models [5,9,16,20,22]. Here, the semantics between entities is determined according to sequences connecting the entities. Other forms of semantics under this approach included isomorphism of sequences and join operations between them.

Depending on the application, graph-based models can be classified into two broad categories. On the one hand, semantic relatedness is used as a tool for conducting an exploratory search over a knowledge graph. In this scenario, a single user wants to find hidden connections that are neither obvious nor intuitive from the relationships themselves. Thus, the main objective of semantic relatedness here is to generate a minimum, connected subgraph that explains why two (or more) entities are related [9,22]. Different techniques have been employed to this end, including path covering in graphs [9] and SPARQL query listing [22] Optionally, paths composing the resulting subgraph can be ranked individually when the subgraph is large. These rankings of paths aim to display to the user the most relevant paths that integrate the subgraph [22]. An important number of applications have been developed for this use-case [8,15].

On the other hand, semantic relatedness is regarded as a ranking function. Here, the need is centred on the partial order generated by the semantic relatedness function [4,16,20,21]. The resulting ranking is then used as the input for another problem (e.g. WSD [16] or recommender systems [21]). Nunes et al. [20] proposed a ranking function that employed a mixture of textual and graph-based scores. Their graph score quantified the walks connecting a pair of entities in a similar fashion as Katz measure does. However, they restricted the type of walks considered in their score, allowing only paths. This idea was taken by Hulpuş et al. [16] where the paths were further restricted, using the top-k shortest paths only. In both cases, the restriction of paths marginally alleviates the computational requirements. Our method instead, pre-computes the relatedness for any pair of vertices using random walks, solving queries in constant time.

Semantic relatedness models based on random walks have also been applied before. Agirre et al. [3] introduced a method based on the cosine similarity between two vectors that represent the Personalised Page Rank (PPR)for each word. Their method required to define a context, that later is used for determining the initial weight of PPR. In contrast, our method does not require any context or any other additional data. Moreover, it only requires computing the progression a single time, thus being more efficient. Gentile et al. [14] used a random walk model inspired in eigencentrality to derive a semantic relatedness score for concepts. They employed a parameter t to control the length of the walks in a similar fashion as our approach. However, they set this parameter to a fixed value ($t = 2$) as opposite to our method in which it is variable.

6 Conclusions

In this work, a method for entity relatedness based on the Katz centrality has been introduced. The proposed method is significantly more efficient than state-of-the-art methods based on graph properties for the same use-case scenario. While being more efficient, the proposed method has a similar performance than state-of-the-art methods, being an effective solution when a large number of entity rankings is demanded. As a drawback, our method requires theoretically $O(m^2)$ space in order to store the relatedness scores. However, the high sparsity of Δ_0^t suggests that this setback is much smaller in practice.

If the technique is to prove useful, a more efficient storage solution needs to be designed. Based on the experiments outlined here, approximated distances matrix appeared to be a reliable option for this end. Our evaluation only incorportated a relatively small knowledge graph (WORDNET), therefore it is espically relevant to evaluate the peformance on larger knowledge graphs, such as BABEL-NET[3] or DBPEDIA[4]. Additionally, we hope to conduct a more robust evaluation to validate the rankings produced by this method and those generated by human assessors. Finally, alternative random walk models present a good opportunity for exploring alternatives to Katz centrality, for instance pagerank.

Acknowledgements. This publication has emanated from research conducted with the financial support of Science Foundation Ireland (SFI) under Grant No. SFI/12/RC/2289, co-funded by the European Regional Development Fund

References

1. Acar, E., Dunlavy, D.M., Kolda, T.G.: Link prediction on evolving data using matrix and tensor factorizations. In: IEEE International Conference on Data Mining Workshops, ICDMW 2009, pp. 262–269. IEEE (2009)
2. Agirre, E., Alfonseca, E., Hall, K., Kravalova, J., Paşca, M., Soroa, A.: A study on similarity and relatedness using distributional and wordnet-based approaches. In: Proceedings of Human Language Technologies: The 2009 Annual Conference of the North American Chapter of the Association for Computational Linguistics, pp. 19–27. Association for Computational Linguistics (2009)
3. Agirre, E., Soroa, A.: Personalizing PageRank for word sense disambiguation. In: Proceedings of the 12th Conference of the European Chapter of the Association for Computational Linguistics, pp. 33–41. Association for Computational Linguistics (2009)
4. Aleman-Meza, B., Halaschek, C., Arpinar, I.B., Sheth, A.P.: Context-aware semantic association ranking (2003)
5. Anyanwu, K., Sheth, A.: ρ-queries: enabling querying for semantic associations on the semantic web. In: Proceedings of the 12th international conference on World Wide Web, pp. 690–699. ACM (2003)
6. Budanitsky, A., Hirst, G.: Evaluating wordnet-based measures of lexical semantic relatedness. Comput. Linguist. **32**(1), 13–47 (2006)

---

[3] https://babelnet.org.
[4] https://wiki.dbpedia.org.

7. Cheng, G., Shao, F., Qu, Y.: An empirical evaluation of techniques for ranking semantic associations. IEEE Trans. Knowl. Data Eng. **29**(11), 2388–2401 (2017)
8. Cheng, G., Zhang, Y., Qu, Y.: Explass: exploring associations between entities via top-K ontological patterns and facets. In: Mika, P., et al. (eds.) ISWC 2014. LNCS, vol. 8797, pp. 422–437. Springer, Cham (2014). https://doi.org/10.1007/978-3-319-11915-1_27
9. Fang, L., Sarma, A.D., Yu, C., Bohannon, P.: REX: explaining relationships between entity pairs. Proc. VLDB Endow. **5**(3), 241–252 (2011)
10. Filtz, E., Savenkov, V., Umbrich, J.: On finding the K shortest paths in RDF data. In: Proceedings of the 5th International Workshop on Intelligent Exploration of Semantic Data (IESD 2016) Co-located with the 15th International Semantic Web Conference (ISWC 2016), vol. 18 (2016)
11. Finkelstein, L., et al.: Placing search in context: the concept revisited. In: Proceedings of the 10th International Conference on World Wide Web, pp. 406–414. ACM (2001)
12. Fionda, V., Pirrò, G.: Meta structures in knowledge graphs. In: d'Amato, C., et al. (eds.) ISWC 2017. LNCS, vol. 10587, pp. 296–312. Springer, Cham (2017). https://doi.org/10.1007/978-3-319-68288-4_18
13. Galárraga, L., Razniewski, S., Amarilli, A., Suchanek, F.M.: Predicting completeness in knowledge bases. In: Proceedings of the Tenth ACM International Conference on Web Search and Data Mining, pp. 375–383. ACM (2017)
14. Gentile, A.L., Zhang, Z., Xia, L., Iria, J.: Semantic relatedness approach for named entity disambiguation. In: Agosti, M., Esposito, F., Thanos, C. (eds.) IRCDL 2010. CCIS, vol. 91, pp. 137–148. Springer, Heidelberg (2010). https://doi.org/10.1007/978-3-642-15850-6_14
15. Heim, P., Lohmann, S., Stegemann, T.: Interactive relationship discovery via the semantic web. In: Aroyo, L., et al. (eds.) ESWC 2010. LNCS, vol. 6088, pp. 303–317. Springer, Heidelberg (2010). https://doi.org/10.1007/978-3-642-13486-9_21
16. Hulpuş, I., Prangnawarat, N., Hayes, C.: Path-based semantic relatedness on linked data and its use to word and entity disambiguation. In: Arenas, M., et al. (eds.) ISWC 2015. LNCS, vol. 9366, pp. 442–457. Springer, Cham (2015). https://doi.org/10.1007/978-3-319-25007-6_26
17. Katz, L.: A new status index derived from sociometric analysis. Psychometrika **18**(1), 39–43 (1953)
18. Miller, G.A., Beckwith, R., Fellbaum, C., Gross, D., Miller, K.J.: Introduction to wordnet: an on-line lexical database. Int. J. Lexicogr. **3**(4), 235–244 (1990)
19. Miller, G.A., Charles, W.G.: Contextual correlates of semantic similarity. Lang. Cogn. Process. **6**(1), 1–28 (1991)
20. Pereira Nunes, B., Dietze, S., Casanova, M.A., Kawase, R., Fetahu, B., Nejdl, W.: Combining a co-occurrence-based and a semantic measure for entity linking. In: Cimiano, P., Corcho, O., Presutti, V., Hollink, L., Rudolph, S. (eds.) ESWC 2013. LNCS, vol. 7882, pp. 548–562. Springer, Heidelberg (2013). https://doi.org/10.1007/978-3-642-38288-8_37
21. Piao, G., Breslin, J.G.: Measuring semantic distance for linked open data-enabled recommender systems. In: Proceedings of the 31st Annual ACM Symposium on Applied Computing, pp. 315–320. ACM (2016)
22. Pirrò, G.: Explaining and suggesting relatedness in knowledge graphs. In: Arenas, M., et al. (eds.) ISWC 2015. LNCS, vol. 9366, pp. 622–639. Springer, Cham (2015). https://doi.org/10.1007/978-3-319-25007-6_36

23. Rubenstein, H., Goodenough, J.B.: Contextual correlates of synonymy. Commun. ACM **8**(10), 627–633 (1965)
24. Schwartz, H.A., Gomez, F.: Evaluating semantic metrics on tasks of concept similarity. In: Cross-Disciplinary Advances in Applied Natural Language Processing: Issues and Approaches, pp. 324–340. IGI Global (2012)

Slicing and Dicing a Newspaper Corpus for Historical Ecology Research

Marieke van Erp[1(✉)], Jesse de Does[2], Katrien Depuydt[2], Rob Lenders[3],
and Thomas van Goethem[3]

[1] DHLab, KNAW Humanities Cluster, Amsterdam, Netherlands
marieke.van.erp@dh.huc.knaw.nl
[2] Instituut voor de Nederlandse Taal, Leiden, Netherlands
{jesse.dedoes,katrien.depuydt}@ivdnt.org
[3] Radboud University Nijmegen, Nijmegen, Netherlands
{r.lenders,tgoethem}@science.ru.nl

Abstract. Historical newspapers are a novel source of information for historical ecologists to study the interactions between humans and animals through time and space. Newspaper archives are particularly interesting to analyse because of their breadth and depth. However, the size and the occasional noisiness of such archives also brings difficulties, as manual analysis is impossible. In this paper, we present experiments and results on automatic query expansion and categorisation for the perception of animal species between 1800 and 1940. For query expansion and to the manual annotation process, we used lexicons. For the categorisation we trained a Support Vector Machine model. Our results indicate that we can distinguish newspaper articles that are about animal species from those that are not with an F_1 of 0.92 and the subcategorisation of the different types of newspapers on animals up to 0.84 F_1.

Keywords: Natural language processing · Lexicology · Humanities
Historical ecology · Digital libraries

1 Introduction

Digital newspaper archives are becoming a widely used resource for humanities and social sciences researchers [5,18,23]. However, making sense of the large amounts of data that these archives contain requires computational methods, which are often not (yet) part of the standard toolkit of humanities and social sciences researchers. In this work, we present an interdisciplinary collaboration between language technologists and historical ecologists to slice and dice part of the Dutch National Library's newspaper corpus for the study of interactions between humans and animals. For historical ecology, this approach is challenging: not only because the data is quite unknown territory, but also because studying this material calls for an interdisciplinary approach. The latter is not always straightforward to accomplish. In this project, we have designed a strategy that enables more researchers to make use of the full potential of digital newspapers.

© Springer Nature Switzerland AG 2018
C. Faron Zucker et al. (Eds.): EKAW 2018, LNAI 11313, pp. 470–484, 2018.
https://doi.org/10.1007/978-3-030-03667-6_30

Recent reintroduction and recolonisation of large mammals and increased competition for space in a multi-use landscape has resulted in higher probabilities of human-animal conflicts. However, where we used to regularly encounter predatory species in the Netherlands (e.g. wolves) or venomous species (e.g. vipers), now encounters with these species are quite rare. Understanding past human-animal conflicts can shed light on the type of conflicts to be expected and how to resolve or even prevent them. It is therefore important to characterise these past relations. How were these animals perceived and why? Were the perceived threats justified? How did people and animals cope with these (adverse) interactions? Answers to these and other questions can help current and future management and policy with regards to human-animal interactions [12].

Digital newspapers archives form an excellent basis to start a comprehensive study on pest and nuisance species. Currently, the majority of such newspaper analyses are done manually, but with the growing size of these collections (the current Dutch National Library's corpus contains 60 million digitised pages), it is increasingly necessary to develop automatic techniques to tackle the time-consuming task of data collection and filtering according to their relevance to historical ecology research, allowing the researcher to focus on in-depth analyses.

In this paper, we investigate how language technology tools and resources can be ported to the historical ecology domain, which presents interesting challenges: off the shelf state-of-the-art topic classification turned out to be not very suitable for the historical ecology domain and part-of-speech taggers choke on OCR errors. Therefore, the choice was made to focus on investigating a custom, but efficient approach to article classification. The goal of this research is not to develop a new algorithm or system. Instead, our contribution lies in the development of a strategy for the application of state-of-the-art language technology to new domains and in closing the gap between the digital and the humanities.

The contributions of this work are threefold: (1) an annotated research dataset for Dutch historical ecology research, (2) enriched dialect lexicon, (3) a workflow and software for humanities and social sciences researchers to port newspaper classification to their domain.

The remainder of this paper is organised as follows. Background and related work are described in Sect. 2, followed by a description of our data in Sect. 3. Our experimental setup and experiments are presented in Sects. 4 and 5 respectively. We discuss a deep reading case using our data, as well as the strengths and weaknesses of our approach in Sect. 6 and end with conclusions and pointers for future work in Sect. 7. Our code and experiments are available at https://github.com/clariah/serpens.[1]

2   Background and Related Work

The field of historical ecology studies the interactions between humans and their environment over long-term periods of time. Research programs in this field share

---

[1] Due to copyright restrictions it is not possible to include the article texts, but the articles are freely accessible through the Dutch National Library newspaper portal.

the belief that understanding present ecological conditions requires knowledge on past interactions with human societies [2]. Topics range from documenting changes in population abundances and ecosystem functioning to studying human perception of animals [16]. Historical ecologists commonly rely on a diverse set of sources, including physical evidence (e.g. archaeological remains, pollen records and genetic analyses), but also on more typical humanities and social sciences sources (e.g. maps, written anecdotes, oral histories, photographs, newspapers and restaurant menus) [11]. Digital newspapers collections are a relatively new source in historical ecology and can be used to document the decline of burbot [4], study narratives on the wolf [7] and badger [19], analyse viper bites in a socio-economic perspective [12], and record catch rates of the Australian snapper [21].

In the past, newspaper analyses were hampered by limited accessibility to newspapers collections. Major digitisation projects have made many collections available to researchers, but the breadth and depth of these digital collections are both a blessing and a curse. For example, searching for vernacular names of animals typically leads to an overwhelming number of results, which are not always relevant to the research question because animal names are used in proverbs and sayings or as surnames. Search interfaces for these collections do not offer solutions for these problems, preventing researchers from focusing on a deeper analysis of the relevant articles. This results in the majority of newspaper analyses currently being done manually which is extremely time consuming.

Apart from dealing with a considerable amount of irrelevant results, the historical language barrier further challenges to retrieval of correct results. Dealing with historical Dutch means dealing with a great variety in spelling and with animal names changing over time. Query expansion based on spelling and dialect variations can mitigate some of these problems [9].

Classification of newspaper articles is a core task in information retrieval, benefiting a wide range of stakeholders such as news aggregators [10] and investment intelligence [20]. Many approaches use some variant of document classification as described in [15, Chap. 13]. Walma [22] presents manual classification of the different meanings of 'morphine' in the Dutch National Library's newspaper collection, and highlights the problems which are similar to our use case. She argues that crowdsourcing and further specification of the article category in the corpus (for example to feuilleton, letters and news) would be helpful. While this may help with some of the filtering, it cannot be used to classify an article topic, or mitigate the recall issue. The Dutch National Library is continually improving its collection, but there are many dimensions to article classification (cf. [13]) such that efficient domain adaptations such as the one described in this paper will remain necessary in the near future.

3   Data

In our work, we rely on both structured and unstructured resources. Structured resources include lexicons and thesauri containing domain knowledge. In this section, we further describe the resources that we use.

3.1   Unstructured Data: National Library Newspaper Corpus

The original texts from 1.3 million newspapers, 1.5 million magazine pages and 320,000 books from the 15th to the 21st century have been made available by the Dutch National Library through the Delpher portal.[2]

For two reasons, the data used in this research is scoped to newspaper articles published between 1800 and 1940. This scoping is motivated by (1) The OCR quality on these is most likely better than on the older material and (2) this period also saw the "biological reveil", a reawakening of interest in biological, in the Netherlands, which also may be reflected in mentions of animals in newspapers [3].

3.2   Structured Data: Taxonomic Resources and Lexicons

From the ATHENA project,[3] we use a list of pest and nuisance species. For each species, this list provides its Latin name and its common vernacular name. Due to the local and temporal variance in animal names we also employ diachronic lexicons that each contain Dutch language variations across time and dialects[4,5] [14].

The main source of information is the DIAMANT lexicon [6], which contains both spelling variations (e.g. *bonsinc, buntsems, bunzing, bunsing, bonsingen, bunsingen, bonksems, bonghsen, bonsens, bontsinck, bonzing* for *bunzing* and (near-)synonyms (*ulk, ulling*), both obtained by semi-automatic analysis and manual correction of information from the *Dictionary of Middle Dutch (MNW)* and the *Dictionary of the Dutch Language (WNT)*[6]. In the work done for this paper, the lexicon was expanded with links between the historical dictionary entries and the Dutch Species Register,[7] thus enabling the expansion of variant forms from a canonical designation of a species. The Dutch historical word form lexicons for OCR and OCR postcorrection[8] have been used to estimate OCR quality.

3.3   OCR Quality

While the Delpher newspaper data was digitised and OCR'ed relatively recently, the OCR quality is not consistent and of perfect quality. Most OCR software will give an indication of the certainty of its decisions by attaching a score to a document or batch of documents. However, these scores often give an indication of the errors at the character level, while for our purpose, it is more useful to know how many words (or tokens) are correct in a text, as information extraction techniques do not read as easily over character errors as humans do. Moreover,

---

[2] http://www.delpher.nl.
[3] http://www.athena-research.org/.
[4] http://ivdnt.org/onderzoek-a-onderwijs/projecten/gigant.
[5] http://ivdnt.org/onderzoek-a-onderwijs/projecten/diamant.
[6] http://gtb.ivdnt.org.
[7] https://www.nederlandsesoorten.nl/.
[8] https://ivdnt.org/downloads/taalmaterialen/tstc-int-historische-woordenlijst.

this information was not accessible in the downloaded articles. To get an indication of the OCR quality, we developed a lexicon-based OCR quality check. This method checks what proportion of tokens present in an article occurs in the Dutch historical lexicons developed by INT.

Figure 1 shows the results of this measure per 10-year interval. Fortunately, the majority of the texts scores about 70%, although there is some difference between the different time periods. The scores are also provided with our annotated dataset, such that researchers can choose to exclude articles with a lower OCR score.

The OCR quality measure was not always helpful. We calculated the OCR quality for the entire article but noticed that a high scoring article does not always mean that the quality of the context (snippets) of our search term is equally high. Hence the annotation 'Bad OCR' is still possible for an occurrence in an article deemed of good OCR quality according to the lexicon coverage.

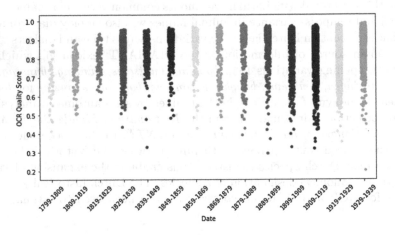

Fig. 1. Lexicon-based OCR check on annotated data

3.4 Data Categories

In [8], we developed nine document categories for the natural history domain. These categories are based on analysis of 8,045 manually annotated articles from the Dutch National Library's newspaper corpus in which the term 'bunzing' (European polecat) or 'lynx' occurred. The categories were chosen based on a combination of practicality and research interests. The most important categorization is the distinction between 'animal' and 'no beast'. The 'animal' category is subdivided in finer categories more driven by the research questions. First, there is the distinction of 'figurative' use of the word, such use may provide a general sense of perception. Then there are the categories reporting on real life human-animal interaction. These categories can be typed by sentiment, i.e.

positive ('natural history'), neutral ('hunt for economic reasons', 'accidents' and 'other') and negative ('nuisance material', 'nuisance immaterial' and 'pest control'). The categories will, in first place, be used as filters for more detailed qualitative analysis. A secondary use case is quantitative, for example, for analysing the number of mentions of organised hunting parties through time. Furthermore, an additional category 'bad OCR' was added. This category is not specific to the ecology domain, but an artifact of the newspaper digitisation process where the article was illegible and the annotator could not decide to which category to assign the article. This results in the following categories:

Natural history. General articles about the animal, e.g. it subsists on birds or x number were stuffed and became part of a museum collection

Nuisance, material damages. The article mentions the animal as causing material damages, e.g. beetles damaging crops or lynxes killing chickens

Nuisance, immaterial damages. The article mentions the animal as a nuisance without material damages e.g. polecats found to walk over someone's face whilst they were in bed, or (possibly irrational) fear for a certain animal

Pest control. Organised hunt to bring down the number of pest species, e.g. ad for hunting dogs

Hunt for economic reasons. Hunting to use the fur, meat or other parts of the animal e.g. an article mentioning that the hunting season has started again

Prevention. Non-lethal actions against pest species, e.g. advice in the newspaper on which plants keep away pest species. As there was only one article annotated in this category, it was excluded from the classification experiments.

Accidents. Mention of an unintentional encounter with the animal, e.g. roadkill

Figurative. Figurative language featuring the animal e.g. eyes like a lynx

Other beast. Mentions of animals in other settings e.g. drawings or religion

No beast. Articles not pertaining to the animal, e.g. a ship named 'Lynx' or a person whose last name is 'Bunzing'

Bad OCR Illegible text due to an abundance of OCR errors e.g. "illlllllliiiiliilitlll" instead of "Best Broadcast Seeder in the World".

4   Experimental Setup

We carried out a series of experiments to investigate an optimal balance between annotation effort and performance. The motivation for this is to investigate the minimal annotation effort needed across different animal species in order to automate as much of the data preparation for historical ecologists. Additionally, our findings may be ported to other domains where there is a clear information need and little training data available (e.g. medicine [22] or criminal acts [1]). Our workflow is presented in Fig. 2.

1. **Query construction:** Queries are based on the animal taxonomy lists containing known pest and nuisance species compiled by the ATHENA project.[9]

---

[9] http://www.athena-research.org/.

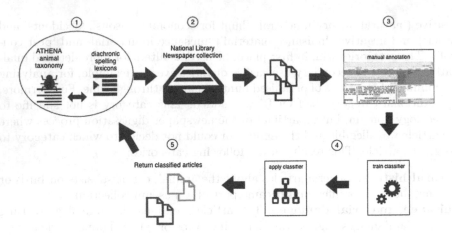

Fig. 2. Experimental setup

These lists contain the species' scientific name as well as the vernacular. From this list, we decided to focus on the mammals that are known pest and nuisance species. We complement this list with spelling variations of the vernacular name from the DIAMANT lexicon (cf. above). As the synonym detection was still partly work in progress when we collected the research data, we focused on spelling variation and inflection. For one species, we also included a synonym and its spelling variations, namely for muskrat / Ondatra zibethicus. We queried for both 'muskusrat' and 'bisamrat' as these are both very common. Upon inspection of the newspaper corpus, we find that 'bisamrat' is only used after 1910 in our corpus, and 'muskusrat' occurs throughout.[10]

2. **Article retrieval:** The National Library's API was used to retrieve the OCR'ed text for each newspaper article matching the query as well as the article's metadata. This resulted in a total of 25,400 articles for the 8 performed queries.

3. **Manual annotation:** 9,931 Articles were annotated manually by a historical ecologist and a lexicologist through the annotation environment shown in Fig. 3. In this environment, the annotator is shown a snippet of the article around the query match. If necessary s/he can choose to see the full text of the article or the scanned image of the article. Annotation is done by selecting a category from a fixed list. In this environment, annotating 1,000 articles took 4 to 5 hrs. on average. Statistics on the annotated articles are presented in Table 1.

4. **Train and test classifier:** We train and test various classifiers on the dataset, as well as with varying amounts of training data to find a sweet spot of good results with a low annotation load. The test scenarios are further detailed in Sect. 5

---

[10] https://www.delpher.nl/nl/kranten/ngram.

5. Return documents: The classified documents are returned to the user and the enrichments are fed back to the ATHENA Research portal as well as the CLARIAH Timbuctoo research data portal.[11] Furthermore, information from the classified documents is fed back to the DIAMANT lexicon. Currently, we do not detect new variants or species names, but we to provide additional word senses and attestations of the already known species names, thus enriching semantic information in the lexicon and the information on the diachronic distribution of terms. The combination of the time stamp of the article and the classification were used to select either quotations with a more recent date than present in the entry describing an animal, or to track potential meanings not yet described. For the latter, *bunzing* (polecat) is a good example, since it lacked the meaning "fur" and "piece of cloathing made of polecat fur."

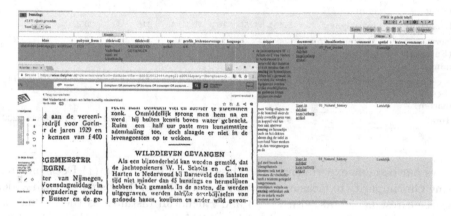

Fig. 3. Screen shot of the SERPENS annotation environment

5   Experiments and Results

In our experiments, all texts are preprocessed as following: the mentions of the animal name are substituted by the value $=ANIMAL=$. This is to prevent the classifier from classifying based on the species name, rather than the context in which it occurs. There are for example class imbalances as we saw that the retrieved articles for 'bunzing' (European polecat) are more often about the animal than for example the articles retrieved for 'lynx'. The texts are then transformed into a bag of words representation and normalised using tf.idf [15, Chap. 6].

We first perform an exploratory 10-fold cross validation experiment on the entire dataset to gain insights into which classifier is most promising. Table 2

---
[11] https://timbuctoo.huygens.knaw.nl/.

Table 1. Dataset statistics with NH (natural history), NM (nuisance material), NI (nuisance immaterial), PC (pest control), H (hunt), A (accidents), F (figurative), O (other), and BO (bad OCR)

Vernacular	Taxonomic name	Total	NH	NM	NI	PC	H	A	F	O	NB	BO
Beverrat (coypu)	Myocastor coypus	51	31	-	-	14	6	-	-	-	-	-
Bisamrat (muskrat)	Ondatra zibethicus	238	42	6	10	109	61	-	2	8	-	-
Boommarter (European pine marten)	Martes martes	135	45	3	-	47	37	1	2	-	-	-
bunzing (European polecat)	Mustela putorius	2833	636	356	95	472	734	229	119	14	166	12
Hermelijn (stoat)	Mustela erminea	395	10	1	-	11	364	-	5	-	3	1
lynx (lynx)	Lynx lynx	5,491	325	16	5	4	316	-	205	-	4620	-
Nerts (European mink)	Mustela lutreola	296	-	1	-	-	34	-	1	-	46	214
Steenmarter (beech marten)	Martes foina	501	56	5	-	16	397	-	-	-	13	14
Total		9,940	1,144	388	110	669	1,947	230	334	22	4,848	239

shows our baseline experiments. The classifiers we tested are: (1) Decision Tree using Gini impurity to measure the quality of a split and 'best split' at each node. (2) K-nearest neighbors with k = 3 and Euclidean distance as the evaluation metric, and brute force search algorithm. (3) A linear Support Vector Machine using Stochastic Gradient Descent training using libsvm (4) Multinomial Naive Bayes and (5) Linear Support Vector Classification using liblinear using the default settings in scikit learn.[12] The reported metrics are macro averages.

The top half of the table shows the results on the entire newspaper article, the bottom half on only the snippet surrounding the species name that matched the query. As the results indicate, the results on the snippets are slightly better than those on the full texts. We suspect that this is due to the fact that newspaper articles are not always about only one topic. In particular longer articles sometimes discuss animals as well as other issues.[13]

We see here that the Linear Support Vector outperforms the other classifiers. Instead of focusing on further parameter tuning, we delve into the analysis of the text snippets classification and various training/test setups using this classifier.

---

[12] http://scikit-learn.org/stable/index.html.

[13] For example https://www.delpher.nl/nl/kranten/view?coll=ddd&identifier=KBN RC01:000057072:mpeg21:a0081 which is an installment of a translation an Edison Marshall story discussing the trials and tribulations of several travellers, which includes a passage on hunting a muskrat.

Table 2. Results of 10-fold cross-validation experiments using different algorithms

Class	Precision	Recall	F_1-score	Correct
Classification on full article text				
Decision Tree	0.648	0.646	0.647	6,413
K-Nearest Neighbours	0.769	0.655	0.690	6,500
Support Vector Machine	0.692	0.730	0.685	7,245
Naive Bayes	0.553	0.546	0.422	5,421
Linear Support Vector Classification	0.774	0.769	0.770	7,640
Classification on text snippets				
Decision Tree	0.640	0.644	0.642	6,386
K-Nearest Neighbours	0.794	0.694	0.720	6,876
Support Vector Machine	0.749	0.752	0.717	7,453
Naive Bayes	0.743	0.754	0.711	7,472
Linear Support Vector	0.797	0.796	0.796	7,884

When taking a closer look at the per-class performance of the Linear Support Vector in Table 3, we see that the large classes perform best, which is to be expected. As the 'Bad OCR' category can contain articles that could potentially fall in any of the content categories, it is no surprise that the classifier has difficulties predicting this class. The same holds for 'Other beast', which, on top of its diversity, is also very small (only 22 examples).

The confusion matrix in Fig. 4 provides some more information on which classes the classifier had difficulties with. For example, the classifier has some trouble distinguishing between 'Pest control' and 'Hunt for economic reasons'. This is no surprise, as certain species were both seen as a pest but their fur could still be sold, so the distinction between the classes is not always easy to make. Furthermore, 'Figurative' and 'No beast' also get confused regularly, which can be explained by figurative language use indeed often being about something other than an animal.

As it is most important for researchers to not have to spend time on irrelevant documents, we also ran a series of experiments in which we reduced the categorisation problem to two classes: beast vs no beast. In the 'beast' category, we lumped together the categories 'Natural history', 'Nuisance material', 'Nuisance immaterial', 'Pest control', 'Hunt economical', 'Accidents', and 'Figurative'. Potentially, this could also speed up the initial manual annotation as the annotator would only need to distinguish between two classes.

This results in scores that are going into the 90% range, as presented in Table 4. For these experiments, we also include the Naive Bayes results, as the performance here is approaching that of the Linear Support Vector classifier. The class balance (nearly 50–50) is probably also helping the classifiers here.

For these experiments, we annotated nearly 10,000 examples. Whilst this is a useful exercise to get to know the data, this is not desirable to repeat for every

Table 3. Per-class results of 10-fold cross validation experiments using a linear support vector model

Class	Precision	Recall	F_1-score	Correct
Natural history	0.644	0.725	0.682	829
Nuisance material	0.599	0.639	0.618	248
Nuisance immaterial	0.500	0.464	0.481	51
Pest control	0.471	0.462	0.466	309
Hunt economical	0.866	0.831	0.848	1618
Accidents	0.602	0.552	0.576	127
Figurative	0.581	0.656	0.616	219
Other beast	0.143	0.045	0.069	1
Nobeast	0.923	0.913	0.918	4426
Bad OCR	0.293	0.256	0.273	56
Avg/Total	0.797	0.796	0.796	7,884

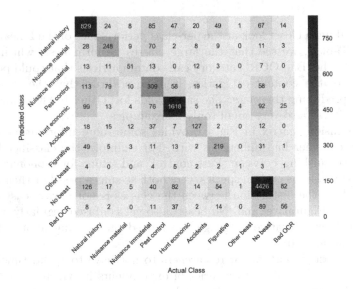

Fig. 4. Confusion matrix 10-fold cross-validation linear support vector

Table 4. Results of 10-fold cross validation experiments two classes

Class	Linear support vector				Naive Bayes			
	Precision	Recall	F_1-score	Correct	Precision	Recall	F_1-score	Correct
Beast	0.919	0.928	0.924	4,453	0.880	0.974	0.925	4,719
No beast	0.928	0.919	0.923	4,497	0.971	0.867	0.916	4,202
Avg/Total	0.924	0.924	0.924	8,950	0.925	0.921	0.920	8,921

domain. We therefore investigate the bias and variance via the learning curves presented in Fig. 5. On the left-hand side, we have plotted the learning curves for the all classes experiments using the snippets and the Linear Support Vector classifier and Naive Bayes, on the right-hand side, for the two-class classification setup as described in Table 4.

As Fig. 5b and d illustrate, for the two-class setup, an increase in training data quickly leads to very little improvement of the results. Even only ∼1,000 annotated examples show a potential to obtain a good classification.

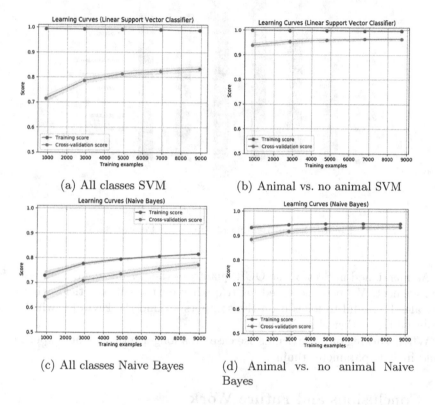

(a) All classes SVM

(b) Animal vs. no animal SVM

(c) All classes Naive Bayes

(d) Animal vs. no animal Naive Bayes

Fig. 5. Learning curves for all classes and animal vs no animal classification

6   Discussion

We have started using the created dataset to study the impact of different pest and nuisance species on human practices and how the public perception of these animals has changed. We show an example in Fig. 6. In this figure, an example of distant reading [17], the class distribution of the data for European polecats (bunzing) is plotted per 10-year interval. This can be used to identify interesting periods to investigate when the researcher is for example looking for mentions of animals in the context of hunt for economic reasons (1910–1919 would be a good candidatem 1880–1889 less so). It should be noted that there are gaps in the digitisation of the newspapers and some articles may be published by several newspapers, therefore such analyses should also be seen in the context of the total corpus distribution and combined with close reading analyses.

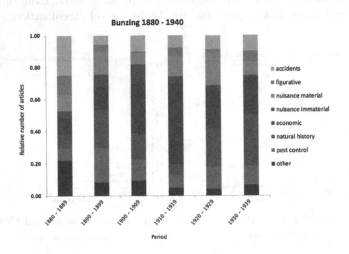

Fig. 6. Distant reading of European Polecat data

As mentioned in Sect. 3, the OCR quality of the corpus remains an issue for improvement. We now measured OCR quality on the entire article, whereas it may also be useful to focus it on the snippets around the keyword, which were also used for further classification.

When working on a particular use case on a longer term, further experiments could include parameter tuning.

7   Conclusions and Future Work

We have presented a case study on porting language technology to the historical ecology domain. Our experiments show that even ~1,000 examples can yield a good basis for distinguishing relevant from irrelevant newspaper articles, automating a major data filtering task that had impeded large scale historical ecology studies thus far.

With nearly 10,000 examples F_1 of up to 0.92 are obtained. The annotated dataset that we have created in the course of this research is available for researchers, and it has already been used by the lexicologists on this project to extend their lexicons, indicating that interdisciplinary research is a mutually beneficial undertaking.

Furthermore, our workflow can be adopted by other domains to bootstrap their data filtering problem, although we recommend performing such experiments in an interdisciplinary setting as different domains and datasets may still need some adaptations. We are working with a team of social economic historians to adopt this workflow in a project on diamonds as commodities.[14]

We will further expand the lexicons with "folk names", using dialect dictionaries and popular books on animals to increase the coverage of the lexicons, in particular for regional newspapers.

Our presented classification may also be complemented by an unsupervised method, such as unsupervised topic modelling or clustering. This may help us identify more articles concerning 'Pest control' regardless of the species name. This is something to be investigated in future work as well as multilabel classification. The National Library's newspaper corpus is already annotated with broad article categories such as 'advertisement', 'article' and 'family announcement' but a further classification such as 'news', 'feuilleton' and 'letter' (as also suggested by [22]) may help improve filtering.

As some of the relevant classes are difficult to predict using only the text, we are investigating further analysis of the articles and their text features. Some of the animal names are quite polysemous (e.g. 'das', which can mean 'badger', 'scarf' or 'tie', it's the name of a beer brand as well as of an insurance company and has several figurative uses) therefore additional information from for example word sense disambiguation may be helpful.

Our use case presents one step into the direction of closing the gap between the digital and the humanities.

Acknowledgments. The research for this paper was made possible by the CLARIAH-CORE project financed by NWO: http://www.clariah.nl. We thank the Dutch National Library for providing access to their newspaper corpus.

References

1. Arulanandam, R., Savarimuthu, B.T.R., Purvis, M.A.: Extracting crime information from online newspaper articles. In: Proceedings of the Second Australasian Web Conference-Volume 155, pp. 31–38. Australian Computer Society, Inc. (2014)
2. Balée, W.: The research program of historical ecology. Annu. Rev. Anthropol. **35**, 75–98 (2006)
3. van Berkel, K.: Vóór Heimans en Thijsse: Frederik van Eeden sr. en de natuurbeleving in negentiende-eeuws Nederland, vol. 63. Koninklijke Nederlandse Akademie van Wetenschappen (2006)
4. Bosveld, J., Kranenbarg, J., Lenders, H., Hendriks, J.: Historic decline and recent increase of burbot, in the Netherlands. Hydrobiologia 757
5. Brukner, P., Gara, T.J., Fortington, L.V.: Traumatic cricket-related fatalities in australia: a historical review of media reports. Med. J. Aust. **208**(6), 261–264 (2018)

---

[14] https://www.clariah.nl/projecten/research-pilots/db-ccc.

6. Depuydt, K., de Does, J.: The diachronic semantic lexicon of dutch as linked open data. In: Proceedings of the Eleventh International Conference on Language Resources and Evaluation (LREC 2018). European Language Resources Association (ELRA), Paris, France, May 2018
7. Dirke, K.: Where is the big bad wolf? Notes and narratives on wolves in swedish newspapers during the eighteenth and nineteenth centuries. In: Masius, P., Sprenger, J. (eds.) A Fairy Tale in Question. Historical Interactions Between Humans and Wolves, pp. 101–118. The White Horse Press, Cambridge (2015)
8. van Erp, M., van Goethem, T., Depuydt, K., de Does, J.: Towards semantic enrichment of newspapers: a historical ecology use case. In: Proceedings of the Second Workshop on Humanities in the Semantic Web (WHiSe II) Co-located with 16th International Semantic Web Conference (ISWC 2017), Vienna, Austria, 22 October 2017. http://ceur-ws.org/Vol-2014/paper-05.pdf
9. Gotscharek, A., Reffle, U., Ringlstetter, C., Schulz, K.U., Neumann, A.: Towards information retrieval on historical document collections: the role of matching procedures and special lexica. IJDAR **14**(2), 159–171 (2011)
10. Koperski, K., Bhatti, S., Liang, J., Klein, A.: Cluster-based identification of news stories, August 25 2015, uS Patent 9,116,995
11. Kwok, R.: Historical data: hidden in the past. Nature **549**, 419–421 (2017)
12. Lenders, H.J.R.: Ten a penny? Deadly viper bites in the netherlands in a socio-economic perspective. Litteratura Serpentium **34**, 290–316 (2014)
13. Lonij, J., Harbers, F.: Genre classifier (2016). http://lab.kb.nl/tool/genre-classifier
14. Maks, I., van Erp, M., Vossen, P., Hoekstra, R., van der Sijs, N.: Integrating diachronous conceptual lexicons through linked open data. Presented at DHBenelux 2016, 9–10 June 2016
15. Manning, C.D., Raghavan, P., Schütze, H.: Introduction to Information Retrieval. Cambridge University Press, Cambridge (2008)
16. Mcclenachan, L., Cooper, A., McKenzie, M., Drew, J.: The importance of surprising results and best practices in historical ecology. BioScience **65** (2015). https://doi.org/10.1093/biosci/biv100
17. Moretti, F.: Distant Reading. Verso Books (2013)
18. Nerghes, A., Hellsten, I., Groenewegen, P.: A toxic crisis: metaphorizing the financial crisis. Int. J. Commun. **9**, 27 (2015)
19. Runhaar, H., Runhaar, M., Vink, H.: Reports on badgers meles meles in Dutch newspapers 1900–2013: same animals, different framings? Mammal Rev. **45**(3), 133–145 (2015)
20. Seo, Y.W., Giampapa, J.A., Sycara, K.: Financial news analysis for intelligent portfolio management. Technical report. CMU-RI-TR-04-04, Carnegie Mellon University (2004)
21. Thurstan, R., Campbell, A., Pandolfi, J.: Nineteenth century narratives reveal historic catch rates for australian snapper (pagrus auratus). Fish Fish. **17**, 210–225 (2016)
22. Walma, L.: Filtering the 'news': uncovering Morphine's multiple meanings on Delpher's Dutch newspapers and the need to distinguish more article types. TS: Tijdschrift voor Tijdschriftstudies **38**, 61–78 (2015)
23. Yzaguirre, A., Smit, M., Warren, R.: Newspaper archives + text mining = rich sources of historical geo-spatial data. IOP Conf. Ser. Earth Environ. Sci. **34**(1), 012043 (2016)

Using SPARQL – The Practitioners' Viewpoint

Paul Warren[✉] and Paul Mulholland

Knowledge Media Institute, The Open University, Milton Keynes, UK
{paul.warren,paul.mulholland}@open.ac.uk

Abstract. A number of studies have analyzed SPARQL log data to draw conclusions about how SPARQL is being used. To complement this work, a survey of SPARQL users has been undertaken. Whilst confirming some of the conclusions of the previous studies, the current work is able to provide additional insight into how users create SPARQL queries, the difficulties they encounter, and the features they would like to see included in the language. Based on this insight, a number of recommendations are presented to the community. These relate to predicting and avoiding computationally expensive queries; extensions to the language; and extending the search paradigm.

Keywords: SPARQL · User survey · Query construction · User difficulties

1 Introduction

Understanding how SPARQL is being used is beneficial for query optimization, for the evolution of the language, and to provide insight into how the language should be taught. The availability of log data from SPARQL endpoints has enabled a number of usage studies. This paper reports on a survey of SPARQL users which complements these previous studies by providing some insight into the user experience. Apart from providing the users' own reported usage of language features, we also report on the users' perceived difficulties, their modes of thinking about queries, and their suggestions for additional features.

Section 2 provides a brief overview of previous related work. Section 3 then provides information on the survey respondents, their tools and the data they query. Section 4 reports on usage patterns, and compares these results to those found from log data analysis. Section 5 reports on the difficulties which people experience, and how that might inhibit the creation of queries. Section 6 reports on the query construction process. Section 7 then reports on two general questions; one relating to additional requirements for the language; the other being an opportunity for respondents to make any final comments. Finally, Sect. 8 makes some recommendations, specifically for those developing tools and for those thinking about extending the SPARQL language. Note that, in Sects. 3–7, the various survey questions have been grouped together by themes; the order of presentation here is not exactly as in the survey.

© Springer Nature Switzerland AG 2018
C. Faron Zucker et al. (Eds.): EKAW 2018, LNAI 11313, pp. 485–500, 2018.
https://doi.org/10.1007/978-3-030-03667-6_31

2   Previous Work

Gallego et al. (2011) analyzed logs from the USEWOD2011 challenge, specifically from DBpedia and Semantic Web Dog Food (SWDF). They concluded that most queries were relatively simple. The majority contained a single triple pattern (66.5% for DBpedia and 97.5% for SWDF), with an exponential decline in number of queries with increasing number of triples. 4.25% of DBpedia queries and 2.19% of SWDF queries used joins. The most common join type was subject-to-subject (SS), at 59.2% of all DBpedia joins and 60.5% of SWDF; subject-to-object (SO), at 35.9% of DBpedia joins and 32.7% of SWDF; and object-to-object (OO), at 4.7% of DBpedia joins and 4.5% of SWDF. They noted that chains in 98% of the queries had length one, with the longest chain of subject-to-object triples being of length five.

An emphasis on simplicity, complemented by a long tail of complex queries was also found by Buil-Aranda et al. (2015), who noted that "around 50% of the queries contain just a single triple pattern", and also by Rietveld and Hoekstra (2014). The latter compared an analysis of DBpedia logs with DBpedia queries created using a SPARQL editor, YASGUI. The assumption, based on the work of, e.g. Raghuveer (2012), is that the majority of the former came from applications. Thus, it is possible to compare queries generated by applications with those generated manually. This indicates that the manual queries are more complex, having on average more triple patterns and more joins. Moreover, the manual queries tended to use more SPARQL features, e.g. the LIMIT feature was used by 42% of the manually-generated queries, but only 12% of the DBpedia queries overall. This suggests that the use of SPARQL queries within an application should be seen as somewhat different from the use of SPARQL in interactive mode.

3   The Respondents and Their Environment

Potential respondents were contacted by email, using a variety of mailing lists[1]. There were 53 respondents. The survey used a web survey tool, *Online surveys*[2], and contained 20 questions covering a wide range of the aspects of working with SPARQL. Although respondents were not obliged to answer all questions, almost all the questions were answered by the majority of the respondents, with many questions achieving around 50 responses. When asked for their primary application area, the majority (58%) of the respondents selected 'computer science and information technology' from the list of application areas. 13% indicated 'social sciences and the humanities', whilst 4% indicated each of 'biomedical', 'business and economics', 'engineering' and 'physical sciences. Finally, 15% allocated themselves to the 'other' category. This included three (6%) who specifically referred to activities related to Wikidata software.

---

[1] semantic-web@w3.org;   https://www.w3.org/community/geosemweb;   https://www.link-edin.com/groups/{86246, 2002133, 60636, 129217, 38506, 138726, 3063585}; https://groups.google.com/forum/#!forum/semantic_web.

[2] https://www.onlinesurveys.ac.uk/;   survey   at   https://openuniversity.onlinesurveys.ac.uk/sparql-survey-3.

Table 1 illustrates how respondents replied to the question: 'How would you best describe your role?'. The table also gives the percentage breakdown for those respondents who had described their application area as 'computer science and information technology', showing that respondents in this category were under-represented as end-users but over-represented as developers and researchers.

Table 1. Response to question: *how would you best describe your role?*

	%age overall N = 53	%age CS & IT N = 30
end-user using SPARQL to query linked data	32%	23%
developer using SPARQL to create end-user applications	30%	37%
researcher into RDF, SPARQL, Linked Data etc.	30%	37%
other	8%	3%

Respondents were then asked whether they used a software client to assist in query building, e.g. to provide auto-completion or enable natural language queries. The question was specifically directed at those who identified themselves as end-users. However, there was no restriction on answering the question, and there were 45 respondents to this question, far more than had identified themselves as end-users. Of these 45, 29% used a software client; 9 respondents used the Wikidata query service.

The majority of respondents had been using SPARQL for some time. Of the 52 responses to the question on how many years they had been working with SPARQL, 44% were in the 'more than 5' category; 13% '4 to 5'; 10% '3 to 4'; 15% in each of the categories '2 to 3' and '1 to 2'; and only 2% responded with 'less than 1'.

Table 2 gives the responses to a question about typical number of triples in the databases being queried. Here, there seems to be a polarization. 50% were divided equally between the highest and lowest categories, with the other 50% divided amongst the remaining categories.

Table 2. Typical number of triples in database being queried (millions) - %age of respondents.

<1	1 to 3	3 to 10	10 to 30	30 to 100	100 to 300	300 to 1,000	>1,000
25%	8%	10%	8%	12%	2%	12%	25%

In summary, the respondents were relatively experienced in using SPARQL; were end-users, developers and researchers, with a number playing multiple roles; were chiefly users of SPARQL directly, although with some using software clients; and worked with knowledgebases ranging from the quite small to the very large. Although the question was not asked directly, it appears that an appreciable number work with Wikidata.

4   Usage Patterns

There were eight questions concerned with the kinds of queries which users create. Some questions asked about frequency of use; these were required to be answered as 'frequently', 'occasionally', or 'never'. In these cases, 0 was assigned to 'never', 0.5 to 'occasionally', 1 to 'frequently', and a composite index was calculated by taking the mean of these data. Where appropriate, the tables show this index, and also the standard deviation calculated from the data.

4.1   Triple Patterns

Table 3 shows the response to a question about frequency of use of the eight triple patterns. These are the patterns created by the use of either a constant or variable in each of the subject, predicate and object positions, e.g. VCC represents a variable as subject, a URI as predicate and URI or literal as object. In addition, the table shows the results of the analysis which Gallego et al. (2011) conducted with DBpedia and SWDF and the analysis which Rietveld and Hoekstra (2014) conducted with DBpedia logs and YASGUI queries to DBpedia. As pointed out in Sect. 2, the last of these comes from queries generated manually, whilst the other log data is assumed to be dominated by queries from applications.

Table 3. Frequency of use of triple patterns.

	VCC	VCV	CCV	CVV	VVC	CVC	VVV	CCC
Survey responses (N = 50)								
Index, s.d.	0.84, 0.3	0.80, 0.3	0.77, 0.3	0.74, 0.4	0.62, 0.4	0.51, 0.4	0.44, 0.4	0.41, 0.4
Query log analysis from Gallego et al. (2011) - %age of queries using triple pattern								
DBpedia	7.00%	3.45%	66.35%	21.56%	0.37%	0.20%	0.04%	1.01%
SWDF	46.08%	4.21%	47.79%	0.52%	0.19%	0.006%	1.18%	0.001%
Query log analysis from Rietveld and Hoekstra (2014) - %age of queries using triple pattern								
DBpedia	19.92%	19.06%	42.71%	6.10%	3.92%	0.06%	1.88%	0.17%
YASGUI	45.91%	36.22%	7.10%	2.95%	2.88%	0.12%	1.61%	0.28%

The triples are ordered from left to right in decreasing size of the composite index. Whilst the ranking from the various analyses is not identical, there is clearly some correlation. In particular, there is general agreement on the division between the most used four triples and the least used four. The only exception to this is Gallego et al.'s (2011) SWDF analysis, which gives less prominence to CVV and more to VVV. The 'top' four include only one triple with a variable in the predicate position (CVV).

A Spearman's rank correlation between the survey responses for the top four triples, revealed that there are three significantly correlated pairs[3] (CCV/VCC, CVV/CCV, VCC/VCV) and three pairs which are not significantly correlated (VCV/CVV, VCV/

---

[3]   At the p < 0.5 level; note that, because of the ties, the p-values are not exact. Statistical analysis was undertaken using the R statistical package (R Core Team 2014).

CCV, VCC/CVV). Moreover, there is a significant gap between these two groups. The least significant correlation of the first group (VCC/VCV) has p = 0.028, whereas the highest correlation of the second group (VCV/CVV) has p = 0.192. High correlation between triple pairs could indicate that the two triples are frequently used together in a query. However, it might be that people who use one triple of a pair, also tend to use the other, albeit in different queries. It may be relevant to note that the most correlated pair (VCC and CCV) are triples with only one variable; in one case as subject, in the other case as object.

A k-means cluster analysis of the users, based on their response to this question, with k = 2, gave a breakdown into two approximately equal clusters. In one cluster (which we call *light users*), the triples most used were VCC, VCV and CCV. The other cluster (which we call *power users*) used these triples, but also made considerable use of CVV, VVC, and CVC. Thus, the differentiating factor between the two clusters was the use of a variable as predicate. The majority (59%) of the end-users were in the light user category; the majority (75%) of the developers were in the power user category. Setting k = 3 gave a breakdown into those who used chiefly VCC and VCV; a group who used these two triples, but also made considerable use of CVV, CCV, and to a lesser-extent VVC; and a group who made considerable use of all eight triples. The first group can be characterised by not using a variable in the predicate position. The second group make some use of variable predicates, chiefly CVV and VVC. The third group uses all the triples. Thus, the three groups can be largely characterised by their use of variable predicates. Setting k = 4 leaves the first and last of these three groups little changed, but redistributes the other group into one which extends the repertoire of the first group by the use of CCV and another which extends further by making greater use of CVV and VVC. Once again, the differentiating factor is the use of a variable predicate.

4.2 Number of triple Patterns Per Query

Figure 1 shows the responses to a question about how many triple patterns the respondents typically use in a query, and the maximum number of triples they use.

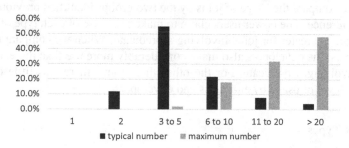

Fig. 1. Typical (N = 51) and maximum (N = 50) number of triple patterns per query - %age respondents by category

This data differs from the log analysis of Gallego et al. (2011) and Rietveld and Hoekstra (2014), which found a large number of queries with only one triple. However, a person who 'typically' uses two or three triples, may still make appreciable use of one triple queries. Moreover, a study by Bielefeldt et al. (2018) revealed that, of queries generated manually (i.e. not by script), 17.3% contained at most one triple.

4.3   The Joins

Table 4 shows the response to a question about the kinds of joins respondents use. The joins are ordered by the composite index. The responses indicate a clear distinction between the three most popular and the three least popular. The table also shows log data analyses. That from Gallego et al. (2011) is more indicative of a split into three groups, with OO occupying an intermediate position. That from Rietveld and Hoekstra (2014) gives more prominence to SS and less to SO. In any case, there is clear agreement that joins involving a predicate are not often used. Of this latter category, the most used is SP. This might indicate the use, for example, of a triple with a variable as predicate, and then that same variable occurring as the subject of rdfs:subPropertyOf in another triple.

Table 4. Frequency of use of joins.

	SS	SO	OO	SP	OP	PP
Survey responses (N = 48)						
Index, s.d.	0.85, 0.3	0.81, 0.3	0.75, 0.4	0.46, 0.4	0.40, 0.4	0.34, 0.3
Query log analysis from Gallego et al. (2011) - %age of queries						
DBpedia	59.23%	35.88%	4.66%	0.19%	0.00%	0.04%
SWDF	60.50%	32.74%	4.46%	2.13%	0.03%	0.13%
Query log analysis from Rietveld and Hoekstra (2014)[a] - %age of queries						
DBpedia	74%	19%	2%	5%	<1%	<1%
YASGUI	84%	15%	<1%	<1%	<1%	<1%

[a]These data are approximate, having been interpreted from a bar chart.

When we compare the usage of joins by the two groups identified previously, there is a clear difference. The power users claim to make more use of each type of join, and this difference is greater for joins involving a predicate. When we compare end-users and developers, the developers also make considerably more use than the end-users of the joins involving a predicate. For the other three joins, there was little difference between the level of usage by end-users and developers.

4.4   Query Types

Table 5 shows the response to a question about the form of query result respondents use, along with related analysis of log data from Gallego et al. (2011) and from Rietveld and Hoekstra (2014). The data illustrate the complete dominance of SELECT, which is confirmed by the more recent study of Bielefeldt et al. (2018). The survey respondents put more emphasis on CONSTRUCT than is apparent from the log analysis; this might be a consequence of the respondents being self-selecting. On the other hand, the YASGUI data puts greater emphasis on DESCRIBE and ASK.

Table 5. Query types.

	SELECT	CONSTRUCT	DESCRIBE	ASK
Survey responses (N = 50)				
Index, s.d.	0.95, 0.2	0.49, 0.4	0.30, 0.3	0.28, 0.3
Query log analysis from Gallego et al. (2011) - %age of queries				
DBpedia	96.9%	1.5%	0.002%	1.6%
SWDF	99.7%	0.01%	0.002%	0.2%
Query log analysis from Rietveld and Hoekstra (2014) - %age of queries				
DBpedia	96.17%	3.00%	0.56%	0.26%
YASGUI	93.91%	0.72%	1.49%	3.87%

When we compare the usage of the query types by the light and power users, for three of the query types there is little difference between the two groups. The exception is CONSTRUCT, which is much more used by the power users than the light users. Comparing end-users and developers, there was little difference in the use of SELECT and ASK; the former because it was heavily used by both sets of users; the latter because it was little used. There was a very big difference in the use of CONSTRUCT; 76% of the end-users claimed never to use it, whilst for developers this figure was 20%[4]. For DESCRIBE, there was a similar but less exaggerated difference; 59% of the end-users and 27% (see Footnote 6) of the developers never used this query type.

4.5 Query Features

Respondents were asked which features they used, from the list shown in Table 6. The table also provides data from Gallego et al. (2011) and Rietveld and Hoekstra (2014), showing the percentage of queries containing each of the features. The log analyses did not include all the features covered by the survey; conversely the log analyses included features not covered by the survey. The survey data shows an extensive use of FILTER and OPTIONAL, with some use of the other four features. Whilst MINUS has the lowest index, this was the result of having a far greater proportion of 'never' responses than the other five features; the proportion of 'frequently' responses was slightly greater than for UNION.

When we compare the usage profiles for the light and power users, there is no appreciable difference. BIND and FILTER have very similar indices for both groups; FILTER NOT EXISTS, MINUS and OPTIONAL are slightly less used by the power users than the light users; whilst UNION is more used by the power users. The pattern is quite similar when we compare end-users with developers; the latter make less use of all the features except UNION. However, in this case MINUS is appreciably less used by the

---

[4] This percentage was calculated out of a total of 15; one of the developers did not respond to the question about query types.

developers. Only 12% of the end-users claimed never to use MINUS, compared with 38% of the developers.

Table 6. Query features.

	FILTER	OPTIONAL	BIND	FILTER NOT EXISTS	UNION	MINUS
Survey responses (N = 51)						
Index, s.d.	0.90, 0.2	0.86, 0.3	0.76, 0.3	0.71,0.3	0.61, 0.3	0.51, 0.4
Query log analysis from Gallego et al. (2011) - %age of queries						
DBpedia	49.19%	16.61%			11.84%	
SWDF	47.28%	0.41%			0.46%	
Query log analysis from Rietveld and Hoekstra (2014) - %age of queries						
DBpedia	15.11%	3.14%			4.46%	
YASGUI	30.35%	1.71%			24.04%	

4.6 Property Paths

Of the 52 respondents who replied to the question whether they used property paths, 37 (71%) answered that they did. There was no appreciable difference between the light users and the power users nor between end-users and developers. Of the 37 who use property paths, 34 answered each of a subsequent ten questions about frequency of use of the syntax forms described in the SPARQL1.1 standard[5]. The responses to these questions are shown in Table 7. Note that four of the syntax forms are little used: brackets to deviate from the natural order of precedence as specified in the standard; and the three forms of negated predicate sets.

Table 7. Property path syntax forms; survey responses (N = 34)

Syntax form	Index, s.d.	Syntax form	Index, s.d.
Sequence path: elt1/ elt2	0.80, 0.3	Negated predicate set with forward predicates: !iri or !(iri_1| ... | iri_n)	0.16, 0.3
Zero or more uses of elt: elt*	0.80, 0.3		
One or more uses of elt: elt+	0.66, 0.3	Negated predicate set with reverse predicates: ! ^iri or !($^iri_1$| ... |^iri_n)	0.07, 0.2
Alternative paths: elt1| elt2	0.56, 0.3		
Inverse path: ^elt	0.40, 0.4	Negated predicate set with forward and reverse predicates: !(iri_1| ... | iri_1|iri_m| ... | iri_n)	0.07, 0.2
Zero or one uses of elt: elt?	0.37, 0.4		
Brackets used for precedence	0.18, 0.3		

---

[5] https://www.w3.org/TR/sparql11-query/; see Sect. 9.1 of the standard.

The Gallego et al. (2011) study did not consider property paths, having been undertaken before their introduction in SPARQL 1.1. The Rietveld and Hoekstra (2014) study did not consider the individual property path constructs but did include the four patterns using property paths[6] in their analysis. It is for this reason that their data in Table 3 do not sum to 100%. They found that 6.19% of the DBpedia triple patterns used a property path, whilst for the YASGUI data this figure was 2.94%. In both cases, the dominant property path pattern was V*C (i.e. beginning with a variable and terminating with a URI or literal). Bonifati et al. (2017) provide information on property path usage and also indicate very limited use of negated property paths.

A number of syntax forms were originally proposed which were not included in the final SPARQL1.1 recommendation[7]. Respondents who use property paths were asked about their usage of these forms, were they to be available in the SPARQL standard. Of the 37 who previously indicated that they used property paths, 30 responded to this set of questions. The results are shown in Table 8. Whilst care is always required in interpreting the answers to hypothetical questions, the data does suggest some support for these features. Indeed all the features in Table 8 are appreciably more popular than the four least popular syntax forms of Table 7.

Table 8. Property path syntax forms not in SPARQL1.1; survey responses (N = 30)

Syntax form	Index, s.d.	Syntax form	Index, s.d.
Fixed number of occurrences of a subpath	0.45, 0.4	Between m and n occurrences of a subpath	0.38, 0.3
Between 0 and m occurrences of a subpath	0.45, 0.3	n or more occurrences of a subpath	0.37, 0.3

A final question about property paths asked whether respondents were likely to use complex property paths requiring nesting or recursion. To illustrate, two examples were given and represented diagrammatically, as shown in Figs. 2 and 3. Both examples were taken from the online appendix to Angles et al. (2017). The query represented by Fig. 2 is for pairs of individuals who have co-starred together, or are linked by a train of co-stars (i.e. forming transitive closure of 'co-star'), but such that at least one of the pair, and all intermediate individuals have also directed a movie. This query can be achieved using a nested regular expression. The query represented by Fig. 3 is for pairs of individuals who have co-starred in a movie and co-directed a (possibly different) movie, or linked by a train of such co-stars/co-directors. This query can be achieved using recursion, e.g. as with a Datalog program.

---

[6] I.e., the four possibilities generated by beginning the path with either a variable or a constant (URI or literal) and terminating with a variable or constant: V*C, V*V, C*V, and C*C.

[7] See https://www.w3.org/TR/sparql11-property-paths/.

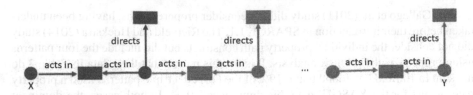

Fig. 2. Query pattern formed with a nested regular expression; the query represents the transitive closure of the subpattern in red (on far left).

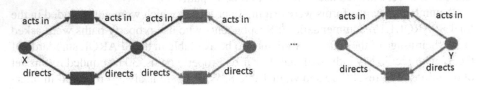

Fig. 3. Query pattern formed using recursion; the query represents the recursive application of the subpattern in red (on far left).

Of the 47 who responded to this question, the majority (70%) were in the 'occasionally' category. 13% responded with 'frequently' and 17% with 'never'. The index, calculated on the same basis as for previous questions, was 0.48. This suggests that, were such syntactic forms to be available, they would enjoy some usage.

5   Difficulties

There were three questions which related to the difficulties people experience in creating queries. The questions were similar, but had slightly different emphases.

5.1   Difficulties Preventing Query Creation

Respondents were asked whether there were any queries which they would like to use, but do not, for particular reasons. Table 9 shows the responses to this question.

Table 9. Difficulties preventing query creation - %age of responses

Difficulty	%age	N	Difficulty	%age	N
Hard to write or understand	26%	42	Not available	30%	37
Speed or other aspect of performance not acceptable	56%	39	Other	7%	29

Associated with the first of these response options, a number of respondents commented on the complexity of queries, including nested queries. The second generated a number of comments about timeouts, e.g. the Wikidata Query Service 60 s timeout. A respondent commented that "there are probably ways to optimize" but "that gets into the 'hard to write or understand'". Amongst the requirements for additional features, there were four which extended the functionality of property paths, e.g. finding a path between two individuals and returning a traversed path. Another requirement was to use CONSTRUCT to create a temporary graph over which queries could be run. This approach has, in fact, been suggested by Reutter et al. (2015). A few comments were concerned with grouping and aggregation. Finally, associated with the 'other' category, there was a request for recursive queries.

5.2 Difficulties with SPARQL

Respondents were asked to describe any particular difficulties they had with SPARQL. This elicited 28 responses. Eight respondents' comments related to query efficiency, e.g. the occurrence of timeouts; four of these described difficulties in understanding or predicting what causes inefficiency. Three respondents had concerns relating to documentation. Three were concerned about variability, e.g. between SPARQL endpoints. Three mentioned the need for additional features. One of these cited the need to return paths from a graph, and the need for recursion; the other two were more detailed additional language features. Three referred to complexity or difficulties of understanding, although one of these suggested that "the problem is usually not SPARQL but the source model". Two referred to SPARQL endpoints; one to the difficulty of maintaining resilient and responsive endpoints, the other concerned about their availability. One thought procedurally and therefore had difficulties with SPARQL's declarative approach; the respondent wanted "an alternative syntax that better mirrors the underlying structure of the query".

5.3 Query Inhibitors

The final question in this category asked if respondents were prevented from creating the kind of queries they wanted, either by the limitations of the tools available, by the difficulty of conceiving queries, or for some other reason. Table 10 shows the percentage experiencing difficulties in each of the non-exclusive categories.

Table 10. Difficulties inhibiting query creation - %age of responses

Inhibitor	%age	N
Limitations of tools available	49%	39
Difficulties of conceiving queries	32%	41
Other	20%	30

There were 14 comments associated with the limitations of tools. Five of these were concerned with execution time, four complaining about timeouts, and another commenting that triplestore query engines are sometimes not fast enough. The remainder covered a disparate range of topics, many specific to implementations. The most general comments referred to the difficulty of debugging SPARQL queries and to the need for property paths. Regarding the former, the respondent sometimes had "to remove elements and gradually add back pieces". Regarding the latter, the respondent wanted "to run queries about chains of indefinite length with particular conditions at each link".

There were eight comments associated with the second category of response. One respondent commented on the difficulty of complex property paths and wanted "a good graph visualisation tool highlighting specified paths in real-time". Another commented that some queries required much testing and re-reading of the SPARQL manual. A third respondent admitted to sometimes abandoning a complex query and creating "multiple simple queries instead". The remaining comments were not related to the conception of queries; three were concerned with aspects of documentation.

Finally, there were seven comments associated with the 'other' category. One comment referred to the problem of timeouts, which made it necessary to reduce the query or "slice the data". One respondent noted the "lack of recursion, iteration, and results formatting" and another wanted "better standard function libraries". Another commented that the limitations of SPARQL were not intuitive; so that this led to a realisation "oh, I cannot do what I want".

6 Query Construction

There were three questions which asked about the process of query construction, with different emphases and response options.

6.1 Approach to Query Design

Respondents were asked which of four non-exclusive options, plus 'other', described their approach to designing a query; with the choice of specifying 'frequently', 'occasionally' or 'never'. Table 11 shows the responses to these options. The use of previous queries was universal[8]; one respondent commented on having "quite a large collection". Similarly, all but one respondent sometimes worked directly in the query language. On the other hand, a first impression is that respondents made little use of their own representations. However, closer examination of the data revealed that 38% of the 53 respondents made some use of either an internal or an external representation, or both. Comments included a number of references to graphical representations, one use of pseudocode, and use of Anzo[9], which generates queries from a model. Associated with the 'other' response were four references to use of Wikidata facilities, e.g. the query builder and query helper, plus a reference to Anzo.

Table 11. Approach to designing a query

Approach	Index, s.d.	N	Approach	Index, s.d.	N
Refer to a previous similar query	0.81, 0.2	51	Use own internal representation	0.21, 0.4	48
Work directly in query language	0.86, 0.2	52	Use own external representation	0.18, 0.3	49
			Other	0.13, 0.3	38

---

[8] I.e. all responses were either 'frequently' or 'occasionally'.
[9] From Cambridge Semantics: https://www.cambridgesemantics.com/.

6.2   Mental Processes

Respondents were asked about their mental processes when creating a model. Table 12 shows the responses to the non-exclusive options. The motivation for this question is the view that some people prefer to reason graphically, and others verbally (Ford 1995). The majority (53%) of respondents to the question used both forms of reasoning. An appreciable number (41%) never used a graphical approach, whereas only a small number (14%) never used a verbal approach; 7% claimed not to use either approach. One respondent admitted to having a desk "messy with circle-and-arrow sketches". Another respondent thought in sentences "subject predicate object". There was also a respondent who, "on rare occasions ... used features such as Jena's[10] ability to expose the algebra".

Table 12.   Mental processes when designing a query

Mental process	Index, s.d.	N	Mental process	Index, s.d.	N
Graphical, e.g. visualization	0.41, 0.4	51	Words and symbols	0.74, 0.4	51

6.3   Procedural Versus Declarative Approaches to Query Construction

The final question in this category asked whether, when creating a query, respondents thought in terms of how the solution is arrived at (procedural) or what the solution should look like (declarative). Table 13 shows the two non-exclusive responses. Most people use both approaches. Two respondents commented on the need to think procedurally to create efficient queries. On the other hand, one respondent left the creation of an efficient query to the optimizer. Another respondent resorted to procedural thinking when a timeout occurred.

Table 13.   Procedural and declarative approaches to query design

Approach	Index, s.d.	N	Approach	Index, s.d.	N
How solution arrived at	0.66, 0.3	47	What solution should look like	0.77, 0.3	49

7   General Questions

There were two questions which were very general, one about additional features users would like to see, and another giving an opportunity to make final comments.

---

[10] Jena is an open-source framework providing Semantic Web tools, see https://jena.apache.org/.

7.1   Additional Features

This question asked explicitly what additional features or differences of approach, e.g. alternative syntaxes, respondents would like to see introduced into SPARQL. The question elicited a wide range of responses, a few of which were repetitions of points made earlier.

Six respondents raised issues which related to standardization, in various guises. One respondent wanted to see the Blazegraph[11] extensions incorporated into the SPARQL standard. Other suggestions included the definition of simple subsets of SPARQL; more standardized functions; and standardized support for text indexes.

Five respondents referred, directly or indirectly, to property path features. One of these confirmed a requirement for 'between m and n occurrences of a subpath', as discussed in Sect. 4. Another wanted path finding between two resources, and another to count the edges between subject and object.

Concerns about efficiency were also present. One respondent noted that query optimizers usually did not interpret the query but rather an underlying language, and that this affected the efficiency of filters. Another wanted "benchmarks about the expensiveness of a query"; although admitting that this might be more an issue for the endpoint software than for SPARQL itself. A third suggested "control structures for conditional execution to avoid timeouts".

Other features sought included recursion, which was mentioned by three respondents, and aggregation, mentioned by two; one of these wanted more aggregation operators, the other wanted the ability to order by arbitrary expressions. One respondent reiterated a requirement, previously noted in Sect. 5, to use CONSTRUCT to create temporary graphs. Another respondent found CONSTRUCT "painful and verbose and hard to post process client side", comparing SPARQL unfavourably with GraphQL[12]. Related to this, although not mentioning CONSTRUCT explicitly, another respondent wanted 'to randomly subsample a set of results before passing it on to the next step in the query'. Other requirements included: better search facilities, based on keyword search, the use of a distance metric, and approximate results; improvements to federated queries, e.g. resilience to component failure and transparency in authentication; and an improved and standardised feature for obtaining the full context of a node.

7.2   Final Comments

16 respondents took the opportunity to make final comments. Eight were in praise of the language. Of the more critical comments, there was one reference to the timeout problem; the respondent wanted a warning when a complex query had been created. Another was concerned about the cumbersome syntax, making "a scratch pad of copy-paste snippets … essential". One respondent raised the issues of infrastructural performance, stability and resiliency; this respondent suggested the use of Linked Data Fragments and hybrid approaches involving SPARQL.

---

[11] Blazegraph's uses include the Wikidata Query Service: https://www.blazegraph.com.

[12] GraphQL allows the structure of the required data to be defined: https://graphql.org/.

8 Recommendations

In this section we make some recommendations to those developing tools and to those concerned with the further development of the SPARQL standard.

8.1 Recommendations for Tool Developers

Section 4 suggested a division into *light users* and *power users*. Although, in reality, these are extreme points of a range, it would be useful for tool developers to bear in mind the different needs of these users.

The survey identified a concern with timeouts. It was not that respondents disputed the need for the latter, rather that they wanted to better understand when their queries would be computationally expensive. It would be useful to warn users when a query is likely to be computationally expensive. This certainly does not need to be precise; a statistical approach which gave a reasonable indication in the great majority of cases would be valuable. Additionally, users need a simple, clear model of query execution to help them assess the likely cost of a query. Again, this does not have to be precise; it would be sufficient to have an approximation which, on most occasions, gives users a rough idea of the cost of their query.

Also relevant here, there were suggestions about extending the search paradigm, e.g. through standardized text indexes, distance metrics, and approximation.

8.2 Recommendations for Those Developing the SPARQL Standard

Users made a wide range of suggestions for enhancements to the language. Many of these related to property paths, where some users are looking for more sophisticated features, e.g. finding the path between two resources, returning the path length, and creating path queries with particular conditions at each link. More generally, some users wanted the inclusion of recursion. Other comments related to aggregation, e.g. more aggregation operators and the ability to order by arbitrary expressions.

Finally, related to the subject of timeouts considered previously, it would be useful to define subsets of the language e.g. for particular kinds of applications, such that when users stayed within those subsets they could be reasonably confident of avoiding very expensive queries. This would be analogous to the profiles of OWL.

References

Angles, R., Arenas, M., Barceló, P., Hogan, A., Reutter, J., Vrgoč, D.: Foundations of modern query languages for graph databases1. ACM Comput. Surv. (CSUR) **50**(5), 68 (2017)

Bielefeldt, A., Gonsior, J., Krötzsch, M.: Practical linked data access via SPARQL: the case of wikidata. In: Proceedings of the WWW 2018 Workshop on Linked Data on the Web (LDOW 2018). CEUR Workshop Proceedings. CEUR-WS. org (2018)

Bonifati, A., Martens, W., Timm, T.: An analytical study of large SPARQL query logs. Proc. VLDB Endowment **11**(2), 149–161 (2017)

Buil-Aranda, C., Ugarte, M., Arenas, M., Dumontier, M.: A preliminary investigation into SPARQL query complexity and federation in Bio2RDF. In: Alberto Mendelzon International Workshop on Foundations of Data Management, p. 196 (2015)

Ford, M.: Two modes of mental representation and problem solution in syllogistic reasoning. Cognition **54**(1), 1–71 (1995)

Gallego, M.A., Fernández, J.D., Martínez-Prieto, M.A., de la Fuente, P.: An empirical study of real-world SPARQL queries. In: 1st International Workshop on Usage Analysis and the Web of Data (USEWOD2011) at the 20th International World Wide Web Conference (WWW 2011), Hyderabad, India (2011)

R Core Team. (2014): R: A language and environment for statistical computing. R Foundation for Statistical Computing, Vienna, Austria (2013). ISBN 3-900051-07-0

Raghuveer, A.: Characterizing machine agent behavior through SPARQL query mining. In: Proceedings of the International Workshop on Usage Analysis and the Web of Data, Lyon, France (2012)

Reutter, J.L., Soto, A., Vrgoč, D.: Recursion in SPARQL. In: International Semantic Web Conference, pp. 19–35. Springer (2015)

Rietveld, L., Hoekstra, R.: Man vs. machine: Differences in SPARQL queries. In: Proceedings of the 4th USEWOD Workshop on Usage Analysis and the Web of Data, ESWC (2014)

In-Use Papers

Combining Machine Learning and Semantics for Anomaly Detection

Badre Belabbess[1,2](✉), Musab Bairat[1], Jeremy Lhez[2], and Olivier Curé[2]

[1] ATOS, 95870 Bezons, France
{badre.belabbess,musab.bairat}@atos.net
[2] LIGM (UMR 8049), CNRS, ENPC, ESIEE, UPEM, 77454 Marne-la-Vallée, France
{jeremy.lhez,olivier.cure}@u-pem.fr

Abstract. The emergence of the Internet of Things and stream processing forces large scale organizations to consider anomaly detection as a key component of their business. Using machine learning to solve such complex use cases is generally a cumbersome, costly, time-consuming and error-prone process. It involves many tasks from data cleansing, to dimension reduction, algorithm selection and fine tuning. It also requires the involvement of various experts such as statisticians, programmers and testers. With RAMSSES, we remove the burden of this pipeline and demonstrate that these tasks can be automated. Our system leverages on a Lambda architecture based on Apache Spark to analyze historical data, perform cleansing and deal with the curse of dimensionality. Then, it identifies the most interesting attributes and uses a continuous semantic query generator executed over streams. The sampled data are processed by self-selected machine learning methods to detect anomalies, an iterative process using end user annotations improves significantly the accuracy of the system. After a description of RAMSSES's main components, the performance and relevancy of the system are demonstrated via a thorough evaluation over real-world and synthetic datasets.

Keywords: Real time · Streaming · Machine learning
Knowledge extraction · Anomaly detection · Smart water management

1 Introduction

In a global context of smart cities and highly efficient business systems for large companies, identifying potentially harmful singularities that could lead to environmental or economic risks opened a new world of possibilities. Therefore, the growing research domain of anomaly detection [1] reached multiple fields from medicine (*e.g.*, to identify malignant tumors in MRI images) to finance (*e.g.*, to discover cases of credit card transaction frauds) or information technology (*e.g.*, to detect hacking situations in computer networks). Machine learning proposes a powerful set of approaches that can help solving such use cases in an efficient way. However, it represents a heavy process with strict rules that assumes an extensive time-consuming list of tasks such as data analysis, data cleansing, dimension

© Springer Nature Switzerland AG 2018
C. Faron Zucker et al. (Eds.): EKAW 2018, LNAI 11313, pp. 503–518, 2018.
https://doi.org/10.1007/978-3-030-03667-6_32

reduction, sampling, proper algorithms selection, hyper-parameters fine-tuning and so on. It also involves several experts that will work collectively to find the right approaches. Therefore, any attempt to solve a use case with machine learning methods rapidly becomes an important team effort that requires great resources and top-notch skills. RAMSSES was specifically designed to remove the burden of machine learning heavy process and ease the deployment of an efficient solution for use cases related to detecting singularities related to Internet of Things (IoT).

Within the scope of the Waves project[1], RAMSSES aims at identifying irregularities in large potable water networks overseen by a worldwide company. The actual volume of lost water in the world has peaked to 32 billions m^3/year corresponding to a loss of US\$ 14 billion/year with 90% of them being invisible due to the underground nature of the network. Our project partner's French water network counts around 100.000 Km of pipelines outfitted with more than 3.000 sensors and delivers potable water to roughly 12 million customers. The premise of this paper is to show that one can draw new knowledge and find hidden patterns by mixing quantitative and semantic approaches leading to a powerful system for supporting strategic business decisions. In summary, the main contributions of the RAMSSES platform are: (i) An automatic method to realize data pre-processing such as dimension reduction handled by a continuous query generator that leverages on semantic web technologies; (ii) An automatic approach to select attributes in a multidimensional large dump by analyzing the data profile; (iii) A complex set of rules to automatically select the proper machine learning algorithm by carefully analyzing the profile of the data ingested such as variables dependency or distribution type; and (iv) An extensive evaluation on both real and synthetic datasets to assess the overall performance of the platform.

2   Architecture

RAMSSESS was designed to process both massive dynamic and static data using a fault-tolerant distributed architecture that can easily scale. Figure 1 gives a general overview of the system's architecture. The main goal is to face real-time heavy throughputs of data as well as to compute intensive models for machine learning purposes. To meet the needs of a robust, fault-tolerant system, able to serve a wide range of workloads and use cases, and in which a low latency of reads and writes is required, we adopted a Lambda architecture [2]. This type of big data architecture solves the problem of heavily calculating functions on real-time data by decomposing the problem into three layers: *a batch layer* that manages an immutable append-only master dataset and pre-computes query functions called batch views; *a serving layer* which indexes the batch views for ad hoc low latency querying; and *a speed layer* that uses fast and incremental algorithms over recent data only.

---

[1] https://www.waves-rsp.org/.

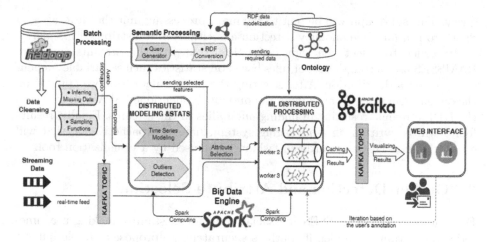

Fig. 1. RAMSSES architecture

A general end to end scenario for RAMSSES starts with storing historical time-series data of a use case for pre-analysis purpose. Caching heavy loads of data needs a robust distributed file system for storing and retrieving files in record time. Due to its massive capacity and reliability, Hadoop Distributed File System (HDFS) [3] is a storage system well suited to Big Data requirements. In combination with YARN [4], this system increases the data management capabilities of the Hadoop cluster and therefore allows petabytes of data to be processed efficiently. RAMSSES leverages on a distributed Spark cluster to take care of the batch processing part during the first stage. However, in most cases, raw data contains dirty records that need to be cleansed to increase the accuracy of the main processing modules. Two steps occur here, the system will infer missing data based on interpolation and expectation-maximization techniques. Moreover, dimension reduction techniques such as graph-based kernel PCA [5] will be attempted on the dataset to ease in decreasing the complexity of the dataset. Due to space constraints, the data cleansing stage will not be detailed in this paper.

Next, a distributed modelization unit will apply several time-series models on the cleansed/sampled data to put it in the right structure. This unit aims at finding specific outliers based on mathematical and statistical techniques that will leverage on the generated time-series structure. The outliers found will be used in ranking the features so that the system applies machine learning models only on the required attributes, thus significantly reducing the processing time. This method enforces a dynamic data allocation by optimizing the size in each packet of transferred data between HDFS and the Apache Spark engine. The extraction of the minimum required data for machine learning processing is handled by the semantic unit. After converting the reduced data into RDF, based on an ontology carefully designed to fit the use case, a query generator will select the minimum size graph using top ranked features based on a SPARQL query. This sub-graph will be sent to the main processing unit that leverages on Spark to run multiple anomaly detection algorithms in a distributed manner.

In order to select the right algorithm that fits the streams signature RAMSSES uses a complex set of rules based on statistics such as variables dependency or data distribution. After selecting the proper algorithm, we apply it on the output generated from running the previously mentioned SPARQL query on the RDF streams, resulting in finding anomalies in the streams. Finally, results found will be written on a messaging system, namely Apache Kafka, that will queue the messages in an ordered fashion to be used by a visualization tool.

3   Outlier Detection and Attribute Selection

Data processed by RAMSSES is associated with timestamps, making it a time-series set of values. To identify outliers accurately, we propose a simple but yet powerful pipeline based on a combination of time-series modelization and outliers detection models selected from established research papers [6,7]. RAMSSES builds a specific model used in computing an expected value at time T, then a number of errors E are computed by comparing the expected value with the actual value at time T. The system will automatically determine thresholds on E and outputs the most probable anomalies (Fig. 2).

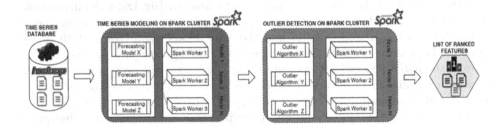

Fig. 2. Outlier detection process

First, our system needs to model received data into a proper time series shape based on a set of models such as the *Simple Exponential Smoothing Model* or the *Multiple Linear Regression Model*. Then, RAMSSES should detect outliers automatically using a set of algorithms selected amongst various libraries such as Yahoo's EGADS framework [8] such as the *Adaptive Kernel Density Change Point Detector* or the *K-Sigma Model*. The complete list of models used for time series modelization and outlier detection is available on github. The main criteria used to select these algorithms are:

1. *Genericity:* Since we aim at solving different use cases, the applied models should be able to adapt to various data shapes. Therefore, all selected models have been able to generate a proper time series and detect outliers against models that have been tested against 8 use cases (see datasets in Evaluation

Section). All the other models outputting errors or simply unable to produce clean results were discarded.

2. *Accuracy:* The results computed by all the models for each evaluation dataset were assessed using well know statistical functions [9] such as cross-amplitude function (CAF), cross-correlation function (CCF) and coherency function (COF). We discarded the models that showed abnormal or biased results for the 3 functions.
3. *Complexity:* Our system targets low latency and high speed performance by distributing the operations in a cluster of machines. Hence, for each model applied to every dataset in the evaluation, we assessed the average running time and selected the ones that produced the fastest results under 10 s (a constraint set with the partner for his dashboards that can be changed as a parameter).

Algorithm 1 Feature Ranking

Input: Tabular dataset D
Output: HashMap ranked features

1: Initialize HashMap out.
2: Let COL be a column from the dataset D
3: for all COL do
4:     let $anomsMap$ be a HashMap to hold anomalies index and count
5:     let TSM be one of the time series building models.
6:     for all TSM do
7:         build COL time series using TSM
8:         let AD be one of the outliers detection models.
9:         for all AD do
10:             List $<$ anomalies $>$list= AD.run(TSM) { run AD against TSM}
11:             let $anomaly$ be anomaly in $list$
12:             for all $anomaly$ do
13:                 anomsMap.put(anomaly.getIndex(),
                    anomsMap.get(anomaly.getIndex())+1)
14:             end for
15:         end for
16:     end for
17:     $maxCount$ = anomsMap.getCommonAnomaliesMaxCount()
18:     $out.put$(COL.getName, maxCount)
19: end for
20: order out ASCENDING based on count value
21: Export out to CSV

Algorithm 1 illustrates the overall process of feature selection. After building the new time-series structure based on the models available in our system, all algorithms from the outlier detection module are run in order to obtain a list of ranked features, *i.e.*, the columns with the highest proportion of outliers. Therefore, we generate a new abstract outlier object including its index, value, and time-stamp. Finally, we count the number of common outliers obtained from running all algorithm combinations on every time-series model. The result of this process is a number of outliers for each of the features. The features are ranked depending on these count values. Results are then aggregated in a file and forwarded to the semantic query generator component that will use it as a base in the WHERE clause of the SPARQL query.

4 Query Generator

The query generation process creates relevant, precise SPARQL queries without any end-user intervention. These queries are executed continuously on the speed layer of our lambda architecture to detect anomalies automatically. The inputs of this generator are: **(i)** A text file containing ranked features. **(ii)** data streams which correspond to RDF graphs. It will be on such elements that the query will be executed. **(iii)** The static knowledge base of the project, *i.e.*, domain knowledge. Since streams are generally very compact, redundant knowledge (*e.g.*, geographical coordinates) are stored in a static way. **(iv)** The terminology (Tbox) used by the static and dynamic graphs (*i.e.*, concept and property hierarchies used in the domain vocabulary).

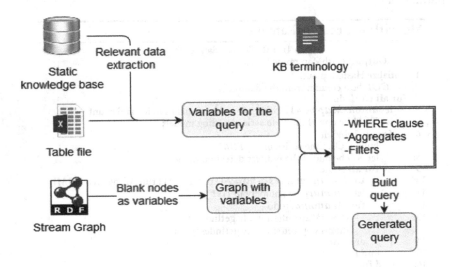

Fig. 3. Continuous query generation process

Figure 3 presents an overview of the query generation system. The main part of the query, the most difficult to build, is the WHERE clause. We initialize it using the dynamic graph coming from the stream, and we replace all blank nodes by variables. It is an easy operations, which gives us a valid clause, but way too imprecise; we need to specify it much more. Our next step is to identify what are the variables of the query SELECT clause. For this purpose, we parse the ranked features file and identify the information that can be associated to our graph URI. The matching looks for both properties and objects: the former represents relevant links between concepts, the latter gives the variables to be fetched by the SELECT part of the query. For the objects identified, we replace the literal in the graph by a variable, and add it to the SELECT clause (it is always a literal, since it is stored in a column of the input file).

At this stage we know there is a subgraph of our actual WHERE clause, composed of the interlinked triples containing the URI of the elements matched from the ranked features file, which is relevant. However, we still have to decide which ones of the remaining triples are irrelevant. For each one linked to the subgraph, we identify three possibilities: (i) the triple's object is a leaf and has a data type property, (ii) the triple's object is a leaf and has an object property and (iii) the triple's object is not a leaf (it leads to a graph, and has an object property).

a. Input Stream (extract)
_:1 type ssn:Sensor
_:1 measures _:2
_:2 hasFlow _:3
_:2 hasUnit qudt.cubicMeterPerHour
_:3 hasValue "4.4"
_:3 timestamp "07:15:00"

b. Generated Query
SELECT ?value ?timestamp
WHERE {
?x1 hasFlow ?x2
?x2 hasValue ?value
?x2 timestamp ?timestamp
}

Fig. 4. Query generation based on a stream

In the first two cases, we have to identify if the triple's object is static or dynamic, by querying the static database. If the object is stored in the static base, we have a redundant information, and it is not required in the query. If not, it is relevant for the query. When the triple leads to another graph, we need to know if it is relevant for the query, or independent. Using the Tbox of the project, we can verify if the initial properties (at the root of the subgraph) are *disjoint* or *inverse*. In such cases, the whole subgraph can be discarded since it is not relevant for the query. In case the Tbox is incomplete (*i.e.*, missing concepts, properties or individuals), such method can be problematic. Also, if the properties are not disjoint, we have to deal with the whole subgraph, and check every triple which is a costly operation. To specify the query even more, it is possible to use mathematical methods to identify eventual schemes in the ranked features file. A simple example is presented in Fig. 4, but the query can be more complex.

5   Machine Learning

5.1   Clustering Algorithms and Configuration

RAMSSES aims at identifying unusual behaviors through monitoring sensor data streams. Abnormal events refer to events which deviate from those considered normal based on historical patterns. In this unsupervised context, i.e. data with no predefined categories, RAMSSES has to detect anomalies which have not been previously encountered. The process is based on estimating a model of typical behaviors from past observations and comparing current observations against this model. The system is meant to provide a list of efficient and generic algorithms that can adapt to various use cases.

K-means: This algorithm is used to find groups in data based on a variable k. It iteratively assigns data points to one of the k groups based on the features provided, and data points are clustered based on the features similarities. The result is a list of centroids which can be used to categorize new data and label it. Each centroid of a cluster is a collection of feature values which define the resulting groups. In anomaly detection use cases, the model is used to cluster new data based on euclidean distance between new data point and centroids of the model clusters. If this distance is further than a certain threshold for all of the available clusters, we consider this value to be an anomaly.

Bisecting K-means: It is a combination of k-means clustering and hierarchical clustering. It splits one cluster into two sub-clusters at each step by using K-means, instead of partitioning the data into clusters in each iteration, until k clusters are obtained. This algorithm is based on K-means but has the main advantage of being more efficient when k is large. Moreover, Bisecting K-means produce clusters of similar sizes, while K-means is known to produce clusters of widely different sizes. To detect an anomaly, the distance of incoming data points from centroids is calculated, and a data point is considered an anomaly if this distance was further than a certain threshold.

Gaussian Mixture Model (GMM): It is a probabilistic model that assumes all the data points are generated from a mixture of a finite number of Gaussian distributions with unknown parameters. One can think of mixture models as generalizing K-means clustering to incorporate information about the covariance structure of the data as well as the centers of the latent Gaussian. In anomaly detection use cases, this algorithm is used to find the probability of an incoming data point to belong to one of the model clusters, where the model was built using clean data with no anomalies or labeled anomaly data. If the resulting probability is less than 0.05% for all of the clusters of the model, the data point is considered an anomaly, since there is not enough confidence that this data point will be following one of the clusters.

5.2 Selecting Algorithms and Automation

We rely on historical batch data to select one of the aforementioned algorithms and apply it to the streaming data for anomalies retrieval. To achieve this result, multiple statistical data analysis are needed to choose automatically the proper algorithm without human intervention. The process is organized into 4 main steps:

Data Standardization: This concept arise when continuous independent variables are measured at different scales, which means that these variables do not contribute equally to the analysis. The idea is to rescale the original variable to have an equal range and/or variance. It is important to standardize variables before running machine learning algorithms because cluster analysis techniques depend on the concept of measuring the distance between the different observations we're trying to cluster. There are different techniques for standardizing data [10], our system uses Z-Score method since it is one of the most popular methods among data scientists. In this case, we rescale an original variable to have a mean of zero and standard deviation of one.

Distribution Type: Data distribution is a very important factor to decide which clustering algorithm should be used. For example, there are some clustering algorithms that works very well with a normal distribution (*e.g.*, Gaussian Mixture Model) where other performs very well for multinomial distributed data (*e.g.*, Latent Dirichlet allocation). To decide which algorithm to use, a distribution test is done on the historical dataset to check if the data is following a normal distribution or not. There are many methods to perform this test [11], the one chosen was the D'Agostino's K-squared test for its popular goodness-of-fit measure. It is based on transformations of the sample kurtosis and skewness, and has power only against the alternatives that the distribution is skewed and/or kurtic.

Variables Dependency: Finding the correlation is another important step when deciding which clustering algorithm should be used on certain data. Some models work well with dependent variables where other performs better with independent variables. Several methods can be used to determine variables dependency in a dataset, if it is a categorical variable, then Chi-Square test can be used, if it's a quantitative value, then the Simple Pearson Correlation can be used. As this work is focusing on quantitative anomaly detection, we'll only focus on Pearson Correlation method. Pearson correlation is a linear measure between two variables X and Y. It results in a value between $+1$ and -1, where 1 is a total positive linear correlation, 0 is no linear correlation, and -1 is a total negative linear correlation.

Dataset Complexity: A very useful statistic in deciding which clustering algorithm to choose is having a sense of the complexity of the data that includes data size and features space count. Some algorithms are really time-consuming due to the complex mathematics used and don't perform well with very large datasets. To select the proper algorithm, we are following a straight forward approach. Taking into consideration that Gaussian Mixture model will fail for high-dimensionality data, if the dataset has high dimensions (*i.e.*, larger than 50 dimensions) and larger than 50,000 records in terms of size, K-means based algorithms will be suggested.

6 Evaluation

6.1 Methodology and Datasets

All of the datasets used in the evaluation are real datasets except one that is generated. All of them are labeled and can be found in well-known benchmarks [12] except the auto-generated synthetic dataset and Yahoo production traffic dataset that can be found in specific research papers [13]. In order to evaluate our system, a cleaning process was performed by removing records that are labeled as anomalies, the resulting dataset was used to estimate the number of clusters. Then the model is built using the cleaned data with the following parameters: k as being the estimated number of clusters, *1000* as being the maximum number of iterations, and *1e−9* the distance threshold above which clusters centroids converge. Other parameters are default parameters of the Spark Machine Learning Library (Table 1).

Table 1. Evaluation datasets details [14]

Name	Description	Size	Dimensions	Anomalies
ALOI	Color image collection	50,000	27	3.02%
Shuttle	Space shuttle radiator positions	46,464	9	1.89%
Speech	Recorded English language	3,686	400	1.65%
Pen	45 writers handwritten digits	809	16	11.1%
KDD	Simulated IP attack traffic	620,089	38	0.17%
Thyroid	UCI medical ML repo	6,916	21	3.61%
YahooS5	Yahoo services metrics	1,441	1	7.49%
Synthetic	Artificially generated	4,000	2	3%

Finally, the original dataset that includes anomalies were run against the model, and the number of detected anomalies are recorded. This approach for evaluation was applied on a local machine and on a cluster for the sake of evaluating if the system is scalable and performs faster when it's distributed.

6.2   Clustering Evaluation

In this evaluation, all datasets are real world measures from different sources, each one is labeled to indicate clustering quality. Before discussing the results, we will explain the key metrics. We assume the standards semantics for True Positive, False Negative, True Negative and False Positive, resp. TP, FN, TN and FP. We evaluated RAMSSES against all the datasets. For each one, the system suggested an algorithm to use, but for the sake of critical comparison of the results, we included the results when using other algorithms to see if the suggested algorithm was the best choice or not. Table 2 lists the results obtained, within each group. The bold Entries represents results with suggested algorithm by the system.

As we can see in Table 2, some of the datasets had excellent results in terms or both accuracy and precision by using the algorithm suggested by RAMSSES. *Shuttle, Yahoo S5, and Pen* datasets recorded very good results for the clustering task and most of the real anomalies were detected. We can note as well that in datasets where the suggested algorithm is *Gaussian Mixture*, such as *Thyroid dataset*, the results were reasonably good when we consider both accuracy and precision, while in fact when using other algorithms, *i.e.*, K-Means, we have excellent accuracy result but very poor precision. Therefore, we can conclude that for many datasets, the system achieved an optimum for both accuracy and precision whenever an algorithm was suggested. The table highlights also the

Table 2. Clustering Results

Dataset	Est K	Algorithm	Accuracy	Precision	Error	Recall	F-Measure
ALOI	10	**K-Means**	**0.961**	**0.043**	**0.039**	**0.117**	**0.063**
	10	**Bi.K-Means**	**0.961**	**0.032**	**0.039**	**0.093**	**0.047**
	10	Gaussian Mixture	0.969	0.003	0.030	0.285	0.008
YahooS5	15	**K-Means**	**0.990**	**0.990**	**0.009**	**0.892**	**0.939**
	15	**Bi.K-Means**	**0.965**	**0.660**	**0.034**	**0.847**	**0.742**
	15	Gaussian Mixture	0.212	0.990	0.782	0.087	0.160
Thyroid	5	**Gaussian Mixture**	**0.605**	**0.632**	**0.394**	**0.056**	**0.104**
	5	K-Means	0.954	0.008	0.045	0.029	0.012
	5	Bi.K-Means	0.955	0.004	0.044	0.016	0.006
Shuttle	5	**K-Means**	**0.989**	**0.980**	**0.011**	**0.654**	**0.784**
	5	**Bi.K-Means**	**0.989**	**0.981**	**0.010**	**0.655**	**0.786**
	5	Gaussian Mixture	0.981	0.019	0.782	0.5	0.013
Speech	3	**K-Means**	**0.973**	**0.016**	**0.026**	**0.027**	**0.020**
	3	**Bi.K-Means**	**0.974**	**0.016**	**0.026**	**0.027**	**0.020**
	NA	NA	NA	NA	NA	NA	NA
Synthetic	3	**Gaussian Mixture**	**0.504**	**0.650**	**0.496**	**0.038**	**0.073**
	3	K-Means	0.982	0.725	0.018	0.696	0.710
	3	Bi.K-Means	0.975	0.5	0.024	0.612	0.550
Pen	5	**K-Means**	**0.954**	**0.667**	**0.045**	**0.895**	**0.764**
	5	**Bi.K-Means**	**0.961**	**0.733**	**0.038**	**0.904**	**0.810**
	5	Gaussian Mixture	0.111	0.99	0.888	0.111	0.200
KDD	10	**K-Means**	**0.989**	**0.476**	**0.011**	**0.075**	**0.129**
	10	**Bi.K-Means**	**0.989**	**0.476**	**0.011**	**0.075**	**0.129**
	10	Gaussian Mixture	0.957	0.99	0.043	0.038	0.074

fact that RAMSSES adjusted remarkably well with the *Synthetic datasets*, even though with less clustering quality. Finally, for *ALOI and Speech datasets*, we had very poor results in terms of precision for all used algorithms. Spark failed when trying to run the *Speech* dataset, explaining the absence of results on the Gaussian Mixture algorithm.

6.3   Performance Evaluation

In this section, we will show and discuss the running time for using Spark MLLib clustering algorithms. We first run on a local machine with maximum parallelism. Then we move to an Amazon Web Services (AWS) cluster to observe if RAMSSES can truly scale and perform better in a real distributed mode.

Local Evaluation: All of the clustering tasks using the three clustering algorithms were first run on a local machine whose specifications are: (a) MacBook Pro running macOS Sierra; (b) Intel Core i7 CPU 2,5 GHz with 4 cores; (c) 16 GB DDR3 RAM, (d) L2 Cache (per Core): 256 KB, L3 Cache: 6 MB; (e) 500 GB SSD; (f) Spark 2.0.0 with Java 8. Figure 5 shows the running time for different datasets using different algorithms. Please note that for the *KDD* dataset, when running *Gaussian Mixture* algorithm, the running time was *13146.025* s, which is approximately *3.65* h. So it was excluded from the graph because it will make other values unreadable due to graph scale.

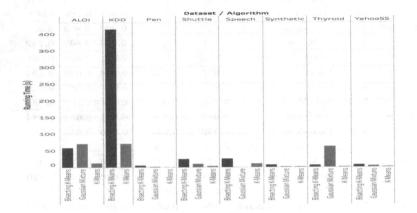

Fig. 5. Running time for datasets using different algorithms

Generally speaking, *Bisecting K-means* takes more time than *K-means*. Nonetheless, when the number of dimensions of the dataset gets higher, *Gaussian Mixture* gets a lower running time performance, thus becoming the slowest algorithm among the three for large datasets.

Cluster Evaluation: In this part, we will evaluate if RAMSSES truly performs better in terms of running time due to it's distributed nature. We used *KDD* dataset as it's the largest dataset we have, and we can notice running time difference when distributing the clustering process. We will compare it with local performance using the previously mentioned MacBook Pro with full utilization of its 4 cores. Amazon AWS service was used to create a cluster with one master node and four workers (machines), all of them of type EMR m3.xlarge, with the following specifications: **(a)** Intel Xeon E5-2670 2.6 GHz Processors, 4 cores;

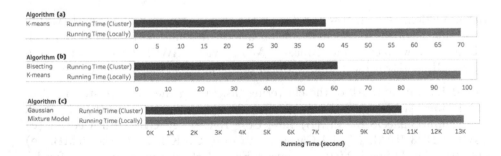

Fig. 6. Local vs cluster running time for ML algorithm

(b) 15 GB of RAM; (c) 2 × 40 GB SSD; (d) Spark 2.0.0 with Java 8. As shown by Fig. 6, we had 41.4%, 37.75% and 19.76% performance enhancements for K-Means, Bisecting K-Means and Gaussian Mixture algorithms respectively. These tests demonstrate that RAMSSES is able to scale and perform better when distributed.

6.4   Continuous Query Generator Evaluation

We based our evaluation on two parameters: the relevance of the continuous queries, and their impact on the processed streams. The tests have been realized on sensor measures archived by our partner; due to their proprietary nature, the dataset are not made public. They represent a year of measures over 3 different geographical zones (2 French ones and one international). For each zone, we have records for 15 different measure types, stored in RDF files and organized by year of emission. In total, one million of each type of measure is archived per year, for a size on disk of 3.4Go.

The validation of the query generator has been performed using panels of 5 domain experts from the partner company. Intuitively, we presented them a set of about ten queries over the 3 zones, concerning different types of measures, and asked them if the queries would retrieve information that could help in detecting anomalies. For the simplest queries, the output was judged extremely satisfying (95% of the queries were judged as relevant). With queries implying more parameters, some imprecisions may occur, but after discussion we found out that adjusting the relevant parameters in the input file solves most of the problems. The general method consists in changing the labels of the columns, so they can be identified as ontological concepts more easily. The main issue remains with more complex queries, where some specifications such as aggregates and additional parameters need to be added to the query.

We consider now a real-world Waves stream example. The inputs coming from the stream (for example in Fig. 4a) are composed of RDF triples coming from each sensor. We also have a file listing the relevant elements that need to be conserved to build the query. We use this file to identify the triples that are essential for the query building, generating a WHERE clause with a subgraph including all of them (Fig. 4b). This list of elements can be built using tabular files in our use case. We can associate the label of the columns to some of the properties in our ontology (in red in the figure), and associate the values in the columns to objects (in blue). These values will represent the variables in our query, and the labels will only be triples to specify the WHERE clause. In our example, we have three triples extracted that arc linkcd, and thus we have reduced the graph by half its original size. In this example it only represents three triples, but with the number of sensors, the different measures types, and the frequency of the measures, it can make a significant improvement. Other use cases can get different gains depending on the stream triples and the list of relevant elements.

Table 3. Query generator performance improvement

Zones	Measure	Triples	Size
Geographical zone 1 (France)	75%	50%	29%
Geographical zone 2 (France)	66%	52%	32%
Geographical zone 3 (Asia)	72%	46%	27%

Table 3 presents the gains for each zone with queries generated on the archives: the first column gives the percentage of removed measure types, the 'Triples' column provides the number of triples from the stream retained for the query processing. Finally, the last column represents the gain in size of retrieved streams from our query (*e.g.*, in zone 1, 29% of the 1 million triples streamed were processed by our query). The validation of the generated query has been performed with the help of domain experts for our use case. We generated and executed our query using the data they gave us, and presented our results to their appreciation. The results are presented in Table 4, for different queries.

Table 4. Domain experts evaluation

Evaluator	Queries						
	1	2	3	4	5	6	7
1	✓	✓	✓	✓	✓	×	✓
2	✓	✓	✓	✓	×	✓	×
3	✓	✓	✓	×	✓	×	×
4	✓	✓	✓	✓	✓	×	×
5	✓	✓	✓	✓	✓	✓	×

The three first ones are variations of the example presented previously, adapted to different kinds of measures, and were very satisfying. The two next one were more specific queries, which is also very satisfying: one expert complained about some missing parameter, but it could be added to the result by adapting the input data to the tabular file. The last queries were the most tricky, and aimed at obtaining a very specific result using some values from a specific cell (thus needing some filtering). About half of the evaluators judged the precision satisfying, the other half evaluated it insufficient. As we mentioned, the main difficulty for our query generation system is to build aggregates using the input data, and this is our main focus for now.

7   Conclusion

In this paper, we presented RAMSSES, a scalable system enabling the detection of anomalies on real time streams using a mix of machine learning techniques and a semantic web approach. Leveraging on the statistical characteristics of historical data, the system relies on a complex set of rules to select the best algorithm that can be applied to find data singularities. The features identified as potential support for anomaly detection then need to be retrieved from data streams. The queries that are retrieving these information are automatically generated in the form of SPARQL queries since streams are modeled as RDF graphs. The answer sets of these are then processed by machine learning methods to detect anomalies in close to real time.

To the best of our knowledge, RAMSSES is the first system aiming to automatize the complete process of dimension reduction, feature selection, query generation and anomaly detection. A task that is generally performed manually by end-users needing some expertise in both the domain of application and machine learning. Computing on a distributed environment to handle massive data, RAMSSES proposes the algorithm that could yield the best results, therefore we also evaluated its performance and scalability both locally and on a real cluster. RAMSSES is being used in production at one of the Waves's partner. Some of our future works concern the integration of third party libraries to support clustering algorithms that are not yet supported by Spark, support for textual data (currently, RAMSSES only deals with numerical data), tackling expressive ontologies (up to the OWLQL and OWLRL profiles) in our query generator component.

References

1. Chandola, V., Banerjee, A., Kumar, V.: Anomaly detection: a survey. ACM Comput. Surv. **41**, 15:1–15:58 (2009)
2. Nathan Marz, J.W.: Big Data Principles and best practices of scalable realtime data systems. Manning, 1st edn. (2015)
3. Shvachko, K., Kuang, H., Radia, S., Chansler, R.: The hadoop distributed file system. In: Proceedings of the 2010 IEEE 26th Symposium on Mass Storage Systems and Technologies (MSST), MSST 2010, Washington, DC, USA, pp. 1–10. IEEE Computer Society (2010)
4. Vavilapalli, V.K.: Apache hadoop yarn: Yet another resource negotiator. In: Proceedings of the 4th Annual Symposium on Cloud Computing, SOCC 2013, New York, NY, USA, pp. 5:1–5:16. ACM (2013)
5. Boutsidis, C., Mahoney, M.W., Drineas, P.: Unsupervised feature selection for principal components analysis. In: Proceedings of the 14th ACM SIGKDD International Conference on Knowledge Discovery and Data Mining, KDD 2008, pp. 61–69. ACM (2008)
6. S. C. from the ITISE Conference, Time Series Analysis and Forecasting. Springer (2016)
7. Aggarwal, C.C., Reddy, C.K.: Data Clustering: Algorithms and Applications. Chapman & Hall/CRC, 1st edn. (2013)

8. Laptev, N., Amizadeh, S., Flint, I.: Generic and scalable framework for automated time-series anomaly detection. In: Proceedings of the 21st ACM SIGKDD International Conference on Knowledge Discovery and Data Mining, pp. 1939–1947. ACM (2015)
9. Box, G.E.P., Jenkins, G.: Time Series Analysis. Forecasting and Control. Holden-Day, Incorporated (1990)
10. Trebuna, J.P., Fil'o, M.: The importance of normalization and standardization in the process of clustering. In: Proceedings of IEEE 12th International Symposium on Applied Machine Intelligence and Informatics, SAMI (2014)
11. Yazici, B., Asma, S.: A comparison of various tests of normality, vol. 77, pp. 175–183, February 2007
12. Goldstein, M.: Unsupervised anomaly detection benchmark (2015)
13. YAHOO, S5 - a labeled anomaly detection dataset (2015)

EROSO: Semantic Technologies Towards Thermal Comfort in Workplaces

Iker Esnaola-Gonzalez[1,2]([⊠]), Jesús Bermúdez[2], Izaskun Fernández[1],
and Aitor Arnaiz[1]

[1] IK4-TEKNIKER, Iñaki Goenaga 5, 20600 Eibar, Spain
{iker.esnaola,izaskun.fernandez,aitor.arnaiz}@tekniker.es
[2] University of the Basque Country (UPV/EHU), Paseo Manuel Lardizabal 1,
20018 Donostia-San Sebastián, Spain
jesus.bermudez@ehu.eus

Abstract. Thermal comfort in workplaces not only has a direct impact on occupants working efficiency, but also on their morale and health. Therefore, there is a need to establish HVAC (Heating, Ventilation and Air Conditioning) control strategies that ensure comfortable thermal situations in these environments. KDD (Knowledge Discovery in Databases) processes may be used to calculate optimal HVAC control strategies that could ensure thermal comfort within a workplace. This paper presents EROSO (thERmal cOmfort SOlution), a framework that combines KDD processes and Semantic Technologies for ensuring thermal comfort in workplaces. Specifically, this paper focuses on EROSO's approach for supporting the KDD's Interpretation phase where Semantic Technologies are used to obtain an explanation of predictive model's temperature predictions with regards to the thermal comfort regulations they satisfy. Furthermore, this result interpretation supports facility managers in the task of selecting the optimal HVAC control strategies. The EROSO framework is implemented in a real workplace and it is compared with an already existing solution implemented in the same physical scenario. Results show that Semantic Technologies make the proposed solution more usable and extensible, as well as ensuring a thermal comfort situation throughout the working day.

1 Introduction

Approximately 90% of people spend most of their time in buildings, so feeling comfortable while staying indoors is a must. According to the ANSI/ASHRAE Standard 55-2017, thermal comfort is defined as follows: "that condition of mind that expresses satisfaction with the thermal environment and is assessed by subjective evaluation". Being a subjective sense, under the same conditions a person may be shivering while another one may break a sweat.

Although many times being an overlooked factor, extensive research has been conducted proving the impact of thermal comfort on humans. Some studies such as [7,8] show the relation between indoor environment conditions and working

© Springer Nature Switzerland AG 2018
C. Faron Zucker et al. (Eds.): EKAW 2018, LNAI 11313, pp. 519–533, 2018.
https://doi.org/10.1007/978-3-030-03667-6_33

efficiency or productivity, which have a direct effect on company revenues. There is also work like [10] demonstrating that indoor environment conditions can have a significant impact on occupants comfort, morale, health and wellbeing in commercial office buildings. [11] shows that having an uncomfortable thermal situation involves many risks including clinical diseases, health impairments, and reduced human performance and work capacity. Therefore, all these evidences reinforce the need of comfortable thermal conditions in workplaces.

However, since thermal comfort sensation may vary greatly from one person to another, it is difficult to establish the delimitations of thermal comfort zones in workplaces. This is why these conditions are dependent on each country or region's legislation. There is no EU law outlining a minimum and maximum temperature permitted in workplaces. The Directive 89/654/EEC - workplace requirements[1] states: "during working hours, the temperature in rooms containing workstations must be adequate for human beings, having regard to the working methods being used and the physical demands placed on the workers". Some EU countries do have some more specific guidelines though. According to UK's HSE (Health and Safety Executive)[2], "the law does not state a minimum or maximum temperature, but the temperature in workrooms should normally be at least 16 °C or 13 °C if much of the work involves rigorous physical effort". In Spain there are more strict guidelines. The Ministry of Employment and Social Security, and INSHT (National Institute of Security, Health and Wellbeing at Work) by means of the Real Decreto 486/1997[3] establishes comfort temperatures between 17 °C and 27 °C where sedentary work takes place, and between 14 °C and 25 °C for light work places. In addition, the RITE (Thermal Facility Regulation in Buildings) approved by the Real Decreto 1027/2007[4] establishes indoor conditions between 23 °C and 25 °C in summer, and between 21 °C and 23 °C in winter. The previous paragraphs are evidences of the significance of the case study.

Facility managers and people in charge of workplaces' thermal conditions need to set up an HVAC (Heating, Ventilation and Air Conditioning) control strategy that sustains a comfortable environment and avoids the aforementioned working efficiency loss and health risks[5]. For that purpose, a predictive model that forecasts the behaviour of the building ambient conditions could be helpful. This predictive model can be built based on the KDD (Knowledge Discovery in Databases), a five steps process leading to the extraction of useful knowledge from raw data [6], and which may be applicable for instance in decision support systems. The five steps can be summarized as follows: (i) Selection of Data samples and subset of variables on which knowledge extraction will be performed; (ii) Preprocessing tasks to ensure quality of data and its preparation

---

[1] https://osha.europa.eu/en/legislation/directives/2.

[2] http://www.hse.gov.uk.

[3] http://www.boe.es/buscar/pdf/1997/BOE-A-1997-8669-consolidado.pdf.

[4] https://www.boe.es/boe/dias/2007/08/29/pdfs/A35931-35984.pdf.

[5] Most times, workplaces are complex buildings which cannot be climatized with rather simple systems like a thermostat-based reactive system.

for a subsequent analysis; (iii) Transformation or production of a projection of the data to a form in which data mining algorithms can work and improve their performance; (iv) Data Mining by selecting the algorithm that best matches the user's objectives and applications to search for hidden patterns and models; and (v) Interpretation and evaluation of the results, patterns and models derived, in support of decision making processes. The KDD process may involve significant iteration and may contain loops between any two of the mentioned steps.

The Interpretation phase comes right after the Data Mining phase and aims at discovering hidden patterns from results. Usually, any result of a Data Mining phase is interpreted by human experts who use their expertise in possibly different domains. However, nowadays there is a shortage of people with analytical skills to interpret data [14] and even for expert data analysts without such domain knowledge it may not be straightforward to understand and interpret those results [2]. Furthermore, even for a domain expert, obtaining a complete and satisfactory explanation may end up becoming a laborious and time-consuming process, and part of the knowledge can still remain unrevealed or unexplained. This could lead to making decisions that may not be optimal, with all the associated risks it entails. Those data analysts could benefit from a framework supported by technologies that enable domain knowledge representation, management of data semantics, and data interrrelationships in order to aid them at interpreting those results. This paper presents EROSO[6] (thERmal cOmfort SOlution), a framework that combines KDD processes and Semantic Technologies for ensuring thermal comfort in workplaces. Specifically, this paper focuses on EROSO's approach for supporting the Interpretation phase where Semantic Technologies are used to obtain an explanation of predictive models' temperature predictions with regards to the thermal comfort regulations they satisfy. Furthermore, this results interpretation supports facility managers in the task of selecting the optimal HVAC control strategies.

The feasibility of EROSO has been tested in a real workplace in Spain. Specifically it has been tested in IK4-TEKNIKER building's "Open Space", an office where over 250 people work. The implementation of EROSO in the Open Space has been tested by the facility manager and two workers, and it has been compared with an already existing solution implemented in the same physical scenario.

Summarizing, the main contribution of this paper is the support of the KDD Interpretation phase with Semantic Technologies to obtain an explanation of predictive models' (in particular regression models[7]) temperature predictions with regards to the thermal comfort regulations they satisfy. This study is interesting and novel not only because predictive models' results interpretation is an untapped field, but also because it shows that Semantic Technologies have a potential to bridge the gap between Predictive Analytics results and data analysts, helping them obtaining an explanation of these results towards an optimal decision making for specific business goals.

---

[6] "Eroso" means comfortable in Basque language.

[7] Regression is a technique used to predict a range of numeric values.

The rest of this paper is structured as follows. Section 2 introduces the related work. Section 3 presents the EROSO framework. Section 4 shows EROSO's implementation on a real workplace and compares it against an already existing solution. Finally, the conclusions of this work are presented in Sect. 5.

2   Related Work

In the last years, Semantic Technologies have been proposed to enhance different phases of the KDD process. According to [3], the advent of Internet of Things (IoT) and (Linked) Open Data are particularly promising in real time predictive data analytics for effective decision support. A detailed and extended survey on Semantic Web Technologies within the KDD process can be found in [12]. The survey claims that, while many impressive results can be achieved already today, the full potential of Semantic Web Technologies for KDD is still to be unlocked.

As regards to the Interpretation phase within the KDD process, some research efforts have been dedicated to bridge the semantic gap between data mining results and users. According to [4], data mining results and discovered patterns should be presented in a formal and structured format, so that they are capable to be interpreted as domain knowledge. Encoding these results in the formal structure of resources like ontologies could in turn enable other processes (e.g. decision making) to take leverage of current results. In [13] LOD (Linked Open Data) is used as background knowledge to generate hypothesis for explaining statistics data. In [2] LOD is exploited for interpreting results obtained with a specific data mining technique called sequential pattern extraction. In this case, LOD is used to provide additional dimensions and build a navigation exploration structure of the results, easing their interpretation. In [15], given the data-to-ontology mappings, some discovered associations can be matched to their corresponding semantic relations from the ontology, which represents a potential explanation for the discovered associations. Regarding the clustering data mining methods, in [17] subgroups obtained after applying Subgroup discovery methods are explained through ontologies. It is claimed that while subgroup describing rules are themselves good explanations of the subgroups, domain ontologies can provide additional descriptions to data and alternative explanations of the constructed rules. In [16] Dedalo, a framework which is able to exploit Linked Data to generate explanations for clusters is presented. The framework traverses Linked Data with different strategies such as heuristic scoring measures of the properties to inspect, in order to find the best explanation for each cluster. So far, most research conducted on Semantic Technologies for KDD's Interpretation phase focused on the one hand, on describing the found subgroups or clusters by explaining typical features in them, and on the other, on using background knowledge to provide explanation of datasets. However, to the extent of our knowledge, no relevant work has been conducted to obtain an explanation of predictive models' results. Predictive models are part of Predictive Analytics, which combine statistics and current and historical facts to predict unknown events, to identify future trends and allows organizations to act upon them. Namely, within the Predictive Analytics field, the work in this paper pursues obtaining an explanation of regression models' results, where a collection of numeric values is predicted.

3   The EROSO Framework

EROSO is a framework that combines KDD processes and Semantic Technologies for ensuring thermal comfort in workplaces. For that purpose, it obtains an explanation of predictive model's temperature predictions with regards to the thermal comfort regulations they satisfy. Furthermore, this results interpretation supports facility managers in the task of selecting the optimal HVAC control strategies. Figure 1 shows an overview of the EROSO framework.

Fig. 1. EROSO framework's overview.

EROSO uses (see (1) in Fig. 1) a predictive model to forecast the temperatures for the upcoming hours within a workplace, according to different HVAC control strategies (e.g. activate the HVAC system at 6:00 at 23 °C until 14:00) used as input. That is, for each HVAC control strategy used as input for the predictive model, a temperature prediction for the upcoming hours is obtained. Once these predictions are obtained, a script developed in Apache JENA for Java[8] is triggered (see (2) in Fig. 1). This script annotates predictions data according to a domain ontology (the EEPSA ontology) and stores annotated data in an RDF Store[9]. It also executes a set of predefined SPARQL Construct rules to classify predictions according to the thermal comfort regulations they are forecasted to satisfy. Facility managers use a graphic interface to select the thermal comfort regulation they want at their workplace (see (3) in Fig. 1). This triggers the generation and execution of a SPARQL query against the RDF Store, thus showing the HVAC control strategies forecasted to satisfy the selected thermal regulation. Finally, facility managers select and implement the optimal HVAC control strategy in their workplace's BMS (Building Management System)[10] (see (4) in Fig. 1).

---

[8] https://jena.apache.org.

[9] An excerpt of the RDF model generated for the Open Space implementation is available at https://raw.githubusercontent.com/iesnaola/eepsa/master/EKAW2018/model.owl.

[10] A BMS (Building Management System) is the system in charge of setting HVAC control strategies in buildings.

3.1   The EEPSA Ontology

In the predictive models result interpretation task for thermal comfort in workplaces tackled in this study, four areas of knowledge are identified: (i) the predictive models, (ii) the HVAC systems, (iii) the thermal comfort regulations, and (iv) workplaces themselves. The EEPSA (Energy Efficiency Prediction Semantic Assistant) ontology[11] developed in a previous research work [5] for energy efficiency in tertiary buildings covers concepts that overlap with the ones required by the EROSO framework. Namely, the EEPSA ontology covers three main areas of discourse: (i) buildings and spaces (e.g. workplaces), (ii) the devices deployed in them (e.g. HVAC systems), and (iii) the data gathered and actuations made by those devices (e.g. HVAC control strategies). Thanks to its modular design, the EEPSA ontology facilitates its adaptation to new requirements by adding new modules or extending existing ones. This led to the EEPSA ontology's version 1.3, which meets EROSO framework's requirements.

One of the main contributions of this new EEPSA ontology version is the addition of the forecasting4eepsa (Forecasting for EEPSA) module[12]. This module comprises the necessary terms to represent the predictive models, the procedures they implement, and the results obtained, by reusing and extending the SEAS Forecasting ontology[13] (which is a module of the SEAS Ontology [9] that extends the Procedure Execution ontology (PEP)[14]). The SEAS Forecasting ontology defines the class *seas:Forecaster* whose individuals implement *seas:Forecasting* processes and make individuals of class *seas:Forecast*. This ontology has been extended with class *f4eepsa:ForecastResult* in order represent forecast results as well as with class *f4eepsa:ForecastingInput* to represent inputs of forecasting processes. Furthermore, a prediction may contain many prediction results (one for each predicted instant); therefore, property *f4eepsa:hasForecastResult* has been defined. Figure 2 shows an overview of the forecasting4eepsa module.

Listing 1.1 shows an illustrative example of the statements involving the concepts introduced by the forecasting4eepsa module. *:predictiveProc20180215* represents the temperature forecasting procedure for date 2018-02-15 that has been implemented by the *:vectorLinearRegrModel* predictive model, and individual *:prediction20180214_2300* represents the prediction made. This prediction, which has been generated on 2018-02-14 at 23:00 and forecasts temperature inside the *:openSpace*, is related to three individuals of class *f4eepsa:ForecastResult* through *f4eepsa:hasForecastResult* property, representing the prediction results for three specific time instants. The temperature prediction for *:openSpace* on 2018-02-15 at 15:00 is 22.5 °C.

---

[11] https://w3id.org/eepsa.

[12] https://w3id.org/forecasting4eepsa.

[13] https://w3id.org/seas/ForecastingOntology.

[14] https://w3id.org/pep/.

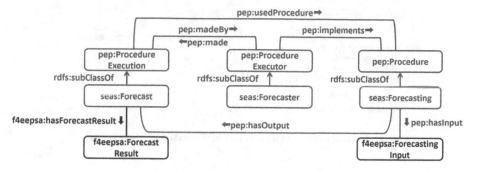

Fig. 2. Forecasting4eepsa module overview.

```
:predictiveProc20180215  rdf:type  seas:Forecasting.
:vectorLinearRegrModel  rdf:type  seas:Forecaster;
        pep:implements  :predictiveProc20180215.
:prediction20180214_2300  rdf:type  seas:Forecast;
        pep:madeBy  :vectorLinearRegrModel;
        seas:forecastsProperty  m3-lite:Temperature;
        seas:forecasts  :openSpace;
        prov:generatedAtTime  "2018-02-14T23:00:00";
        f4eepsa:hasForecastResult  :tempPredAt01pm;
        f4eepsa:hasForecastResult  :tempPredAt02pm;
        f4eepsa:hasForecastResult  :tempPredAt03pm.
:tempPredAt03pm  rdf:type  f4eepsa:ForecastResult;
        owl-time:inXSDDateTimeStamp  "2018-02-15T15:00:00";
        qudt:numericValue  "22.5";
        qudt:unit  m3-lite:DegreeCelsius.
```

Listing 1.1. Statements representing a Predictive Model and its predictions.

Since HVAC systems and their control strategies represent another main area of discourse addressed in this study, the measurements4eepsa module[15] imported by the EEPSA ontology has been extended with knowledge representing HVAC systems and HVAC control strategies among others. Class *m4eepsa:HVAC*, which is a subclass of *seas:Actuator*, is a simplified representation of a real-world HVAC system, and *m4eepsa:HVACControlStrategy* has been defined as subclass of *seas:Actuation* to represent HVAC control strategies made by HVAC systems. Furthermore, an HVAC control strategy makes different actuations (with property *m4eepsa:hasActuation*) over time. Each actuation's result (represented with an individual of class *sosa:Result*) is characterized mainly by a date time when the actuation takes place (with property *sosa:resultTime*), a temperature that the space is aimed to have (with property *m4eepsa:temperatureSetpoint*), and the number of AHUs[16] activated (with property *m4eepsa:numberOfActiveAHUs*). Figure 3 shows an overview of measurements4eepsa module's extension.

---

[15] https://w3id.org/measurements4eepsa.

[16] AHU (Air Handling Unit) is an HVAC system component used to regulate and circulate air. There may be more than one AHUs associated to a single HVAC system, usually in charge of conditioning a specific space or zone.

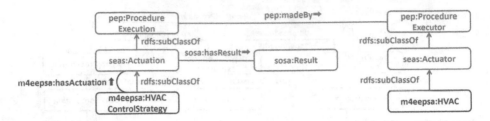

Fig. 3. Measurements4eepsa module's extension overview.

Listing 1.2 shows an illustrative example with the statements concerning the mentioned concepts. *:hvac_Z013* represents an HVAC system acting on *:openSpace* space. This HVAC makes an HVAC control strategy which is composed of three actuations. One of those actuations (*:actuation_20180215_2300*) activates 6 AHUs with a flow temperature of 30 °C on 2015-12-15 at 15:00.

```
: hvac_Z013  rdf:type  m4eepsa:HVAC;
        seas:actsOn  :openSpace;
        pep:made  :actuation_strat20180215.
: actuation_strat20180215  rdf:type  m4eepsa:HVACControlStrategy;
        m4eepsa:hasActuation  :actuation_20180215_2100;
        m4eepsa:hasActuation  :actuation_20180215_2200;
        m4eepsa:hasActuation  :actuation_20180215_2300.
: actuation_20180215_2300  rdf:type  seas:Actuation;
        sosa:hasResult  :actuation_20180215_2300_res.
: actuation_20180215_2300_res  rdf:type  sosa:Result;
        sosa:resultTime  "2018-02-15T23:00:00";
        m4eepsa:numberOfActiveAHUs  "6";
        m4eepsa:temperatureSetPoint  :setPoint0084.
: setPoint0084  rdf:type  sosa:Result;
        qudt:numericValue  "30";
        qudt:unit  m3-lite:DegreeCelsius.
```

Listing 1.2. Statements representing an HVAC system and its control strategy.

Last but not least, the EEPSA ontology has been extended with terms describing thermal comfort regulations. A class *eepsa:ThermalComfortRegulation* has been defined representing HVAC control strategies that fulfill a set of regulations and guidelines that ensure occupants' comfort with the thermal environment. This class has subclasses such as *eepsa:INSHTForSedentarySituation* and *eepsa:HSESituation*, which describe HVAC control strategies fulfilling thermal comfort regulations for workplaces defined by different entities. These are expected to be completed with more comfort regulations. Furthermore, as a future work, the EEPSA ontology should not only contain temperature regulations, but also other factors like humidity or air flow, which have been demonstrated to have a direct impact on occupants comfort [8].

In EROSO, data is annotated with the EEPSA ontology terms thus providing them with semantics. In this paper's context, semantic annotation of data means to build an RDF data representation, giving identifiable URIs to resources and inter-relating them with appropriate terms from other ontologies. When linking or mapping predictive models' results, data is better represented by setting structures, formal types and relations among them, so that new knowledge exploitation capabilities are at hand. For example, full fledged data querying which may lead to further fine-grained data retrieval for analytic purposes.

3.2 Semantic Technologies in Use

In the following section, focus is placed on Semantic Technologies used by the EROSO framework to obtain an explanation of predictive model's temperature predictions with regards to the thermal comfort regulations they satisfy. Furthermore, the support in the task of selecting the optimal HVAC control strategies for a workplace is also covered in this section.

The Ontology-Driven Rules. The EROSO framework contains a set of rules that classify semantically annotated predictions. These rules have been designed by domain experts and they represent knowledge regarding the thermal comfort domain. Namely, these rules classify HVAC control strategies, used as inputs for the predictive model, in the thermal comfort regulation classes they are forecasted to satisfy. One of the defined rules (shown in Listing 1.3) classifies HVAC control strategies forecasted to satisfy a thermal comfort regulation defined by INSHT during the working hours. This regulation determines that temperatures within a workplace where sedentary works are carried out, have to be maintained between 17 °C and 27 °C during the working hours.

```
CONSTRUCT {?hvacControlStrategy
  rdf:type eepsa:INSHTForSedentarySituation}
FROM <myGraph>
WHERE
{ ?prediction rdf:type seas:Forecast;
     pep:usedProcedure ?predictiveProcedure.
 ?predictiveProcedure pep:hasInput ?input.
 ?input f4eepsa:hasParameter ?hvacControlStrategy.
  { SELECT (COUNT(?predResult) AS ?count), ?prediction
   FROM <myGraph>
   WHERE{ ?prediction f4eepsa:hasForecastResult ?predResult.
    ?predResult qudt:numericValue ?temperatureVal.
    ?predResult owl−time:inXSDDateTimeStamp ?dateTime.
   BIND(xsd:time(?dateTime) AS ?time).
   FILTER(
    xsd:double(?temperatureVal) >= 17 &&
    xsd:double(?temperatureVal) <= 27 &&
    ?temperatureUnit = m3−lite:DegreeCelsius &&
    xsd:time(?time) >= xsd:time(08:00) &&
    xsd:time(?time) <= xsd:time(17:00) ) }
   GROUP BY ?prediction }
 FILTER (?count= 10) }
```

Listing 1.3. SPARQL Construct rule classifying HVAC control strategies forecasted to satisfy the thermal comfort regulation defined by INSHT. This rule is for a workplace where the working day starts at 8:00 and ends by 17:00.

The EROSO framework contains rule-based knowledge instead of using ontology class definitions because OWL2-DL expressivity is not enough to achieve the desired inferences. SPARQL Construct rules have been used to describe this knowledge and every rule is parametrizable so that it can be applied to different workplaces. These parameters are filled with the workplace's working periods. This information is retrieved from the corresponding workplace's "workplace profile", where this information is previously saved. All ontology-driven rules are automatically filled once, and they are automatically executed every time new predictions are stored in the RDF Store.

The Ontology-Driven Queries. Once the ontology-driven rules are executed, the HVAC control strategies are classified in the RDF Store and they remain ready to be retrieved. EROSO has a single parametrizable SPARQL query to retrieve the HVAC control strategies according to the thermal comfort regulation aimed by the user. Listing 1.4 shows this parametrizable SPARQL query. The execution of this SPARQL query is managed by a graphic interface that isolates facility managers from the underlying SPARQL query language in which they might not be experts, easing the interaction with the framework.

```
SELECT ?hvacControlStrategy
FROM <myGraph>
WHERE {
?hvacControlStrategy rdf:type $REGULATION
?predictiveProcedure pep:hasInput ?hvacControlStrategy .
?prediction pep:usedProcedure ?predictiveProcedure;
        seas:forecasts $LOCATION;
        f4eepsa:hasForecastResult ?predResult .
?predResult owl-time:inXSDDateTimeStamp ?dateTime .
FILTER ( ?dateTime = xsd:dateTime($DATE)) }
```

Listing 1.4. SPARQL parametrizable query that retrieves HVAC control strategies forecasted to satisfy a specific thermal comfort regulation inside a location and on a date. $REGULATION, $LOCATION, and $DATE are parameters.

The graphic interface shows two dropdown lists: one with the thermal comfort regulations defined in EROSO, and the other with the locations managed by EROSO. When the facility manager chooses a thermal comfort regulation from the list and clicks on the "Info" button, a text description of the regulation is shown. When both the thermal regulation sought and the location where this regulation is sought are selected, after clicking the "Retrieve" button, the filling of the SPARQL query is triggered. On the one hand, the formal parameters $REGULATION and $LOCATION are replaced by the chosen regulation's and location's corresponding URIs. On the other, the $DATE is replaced by the next day's date. Once the SPARQL query is complete, it is automatically executed.

The HVAC control strategies forecasted to produce conditions that meet the thermal comfort selected in the dropdown list, are shown in the results section. Furthermore, for each HVAC control strategy, the user will visualize its temperature prediction both in a table (with numeric values) and plotted in a line chart (graphically). Afterwards, the facility manager chooses the optimal HVAC control strategy from the results section and implements it in the BMS.

4   Experiment Results and Analysis

The EROSO framework has been implemented and tested in the Open Space, a large office located in Spain where over 250 people work on a daily basis. The implementation makes use of a predictive model generated as part of a previous research work to predict Open Space's temperature for the upcoming 24 hours. 20 different HVAC control strategies are used as inputs of the predictive model, so 20 different temperature predictions are obtained. This forecasting process is automatically executed daily at 17:00, so that the facility manager can make a decision on which HVAC control strategy to implement, in order to ensure next day's thermal comfort. In this section, this EROSO implementation is compared with an already existing solution implemented in the Open Space, known as OSCS (Open Space Comfort Solution).

4.1   OSCS: The Existing Solution in the Open Space

The OSCS makes use of the same predictive model used by EROSO's implementation in the Open Space and it also uses the same 20 HVAC control strategies as inputs to make temperature predictions. Currently, the OSCS seeks to comply with just one thermal comfort regulation, which consists in having a temperature over a predefined threshold of 21 °C when the working day starts at 8:00[17]. Furthermore, the OSCS automatically selects the first HVAC control strategy found predicting the predefined comfort regulation. That is, even though 20 HVAC strategies are available to make forecasts, when a prediction fulfils the defined thermal comfort requirement, the forecasting process stops. The found strategy is then stored on a PostgreSQL database, alongside with the temperatures forecasted to produce during the next 24 hours. The OSCS offers a graphic interface where these stored temperatures are graphically shown in a line chart. Nevertheless, many times facility managers have expressed their difficulties at trying to figure out in the line chart which temperature corresponds to a given instant.

---

[17] Due to the characteristics of the Open Space, it was assumed that once this temperature was achieved at the beginning of the working day, a comfortable thermal situation would be maintained throughout the working day. However, it has been proved that when certain outdoor conditions are given, this is not true.

4.2   Results Analysis and Discussion

In order to compare the EROSO implementation in the Open Space with the OSCS, the following criteria were evaluated:

- Usability: The quality of the interaction and facility managers' overall satisfaction with the system. It is measured via a survey and interviews.
- Extensibility: The ability of the system to be extended with additional functionalities or modifying existing ones (e.g. adding new thermal comfort regulations).
- Thermal comfort: The duration of periods when comfortable thermal situations occur during the working day.

Usability. IK4-TEKNIKER's facility manager and two workers were surveyed with the SUS (System Usability Scale) scale [1] after testing the EROSO framework. The average score obtained was 77.5 out of 100, so it can be concluded that overall interaction with EROSO framework is good. The feedback received in the interviews indicated that having different thermal comfort regulations available in the system, provides users with a bigger flexibility to choose the adequate HVAC control strategy for each situation. This aspect was highlighted by three interviewees, who foresee it very important when managing a workplace that may host different events (e.g. IK4-TEKNIKER building's Auditorium where currently EROSO is being implemented) or a space with changing requirements. The possibility of selecting different thermal comfort regulations in EROSO is enabled by Semantic Technologies.

Extensibility. Being based on Semantic Technologies, the EROSO framework is easier to extend or modify compared with the OSCS. For example, if a new predictive model is added to the system to make predictions, the OSCS needs to modify, compile and deploy the solution, as well as performing some tasks in the database to register the new predictive model. By contrast, EROSO just needs to add a new instance of the already existing class *seas:Forecaster* in its RDF Store. Furthermore, if the facility manager has other comfort needs or criteria, it would be enough to define a SPARQL construct rule and a class representing that regulation as a subclass of *eepsa:ThermalComfortRegulation*. On the contrary, OSCS has just one comfort criterion (exceeding a threshold temperature at 8:00) and adding more comfort criteria would mean a modification of the source code, its recompilation and deployment.

Thermal Comfort. The overall thermal comfort achieved by the HVAC control strategies proposed by EROSO and the OSCS have been compared. For that purpose, for each of the proposed HVAC control strategy, predicted temperatures for the Open Space have been recorded during 15 working days (from 5th to 25th February 2018). For each prediction, it has been calculated the amount of time that would not meet a certain thermal comfort regulation. That is, the amount of time when, if implementing the HVAC control strategies proposed by the different frameworks, the Open Space temperature would not be between the values defined by a certain regulation. For this experiment two thermal comfort regulations have been used: RITE for winter days (between 21 °C and 23 °C during working hours) and INSHIT for sedentary work (between 17 °C and 27 °C during working hours). Results show that EROSO does not propose any HVAC control strategy that does not predict a temperature fulfilling the aimed regulation's temperature requirements. Although the HVAC control strategies proposed by OSCS fulfil INSHT regulation, there is a mean duration of 2 h and 48 min when they do not ensure a temperature that fulfils RITE's regulation. Table 1 summarizes this experiment's results. Thanks to the aforementioned flexibility enabled by the Semantic Technologies, EROSO users can seek different thermal regulations and the system recommends different HVAC control strategies accordingly. This flexibility is valuable because different thermal comfort regulations may be necessary even for the same space. For example when committing to RITE regulation, which defines different thermal requirements depending on the season of the year.

Table 1. Comparison of mean discomfort duration per day (according to RITE regulation for winter days and INSHT regulation) suffered if HVAC control strategies proposed by EROSO and the OSCS were applied.

Framework	RITE Winter regulation	INSHT regulation
EROSO	0 h 00 min	0 h 00 min
OSCS	2 h 48 min	0 h 00 min

5 Conclusions and Future Work

This paper tackles an important field that may affect workers' health and working efficiency, which may as well have consequences on the economic success of a company. EROSO is a framework that combines KDD processes and Semantic Technologies for ensuring thermal comfort in workplaces. Specifically, this paper focuses on EROSO's approach for supporting the Interpretation phase where Semantic Technologies are used to obtain an explanation of predictive model's temperature predictions with regards to the thermal comfort regulations they satisfy. Furthermore, this results interpretation supports facility managers in the task of selecting the optimal HVAC control strategies.

EROSO has been implemented in the Open Space. This implementation is compared with an already existing solution implemented in the Open Space: the OSCS. It has been proved that EROSO exploits Semantic Technologies' potential to support the KDD Interpretation phase, as well as tackling OSCS's weaknesses. Results show that usability of the EROSO framework is overall good. Being based on Semantic Technologies, the EROSO framework is more flexible and easier to extend or modify compared with the OSCS. Furthermore, this flexibility enables facility managers selecting the adequate HVAC control strategy if workplace's requirements vary. Finally, the EROSO framework recommends HVAC control strategies that may ensure a satisfactory thermal comfort in the Open Space throughout the working day, while OSCS may have periods when thermal comfort may not be achieved.

5.1   Future Work

There are some aspects of the EROSO framework that are going to be addressed and improved in the future.

So far, EROSO tackles comfort in workplaces from a thermal (temperature) point of view. However, it has been proved that other factors such as humidity or air flow also affect the indoor comfort [8], so that the solution should be extended to take this factors into account.

With regards to the SPARQL rules and parametrizable SPARQL query presented, Custom Datatypes for Quantity Values[18] should be considered in order to complete and simplify them.

Furthermore, existing thermal comfort regulations defined in EROSO should be complemented with more regulations and with criteria such as the user preferences, the energy consumption or the cost of the selected HVAC control strategies. This could provide facility managers with an even higher flexibility when deciding which HVAC control strategies to set up as well as enabling a ranking of the results according to different criteria.

Currently the EROSO framework is not integrated with BMSs, so that the HVAC control strategy has to be implemented manually. The future development of a connector for BMSs is expected to automatize the HVAC control strategy selection process. With this improvement, the facility manager would set a thermal comfort regulation for the upcoming week, and the EROSO framework would set up the optimal HVAC control strategy. In the first test version of this implementation, the facility manager would be asked to confirm EROSO's decision. In the final version, the facility manager would receive a notification of the HVAC control strategy selected by EROSO for the upcoming working day.

The EROSO framework addresses workplaces. However, thermal comfort has a relevant impact in other type of buildings as well. As future use cases, it is foreseen its implementation in farms and dwellings. In the former case, EROSO is expected to be implemented in a poultry farm where thermal comfort is a critical aspect due to its impact on animals' welfare. In the latter, EROSO would consider Demand Response programmes that encourage users to shift their energy consumption either in response to price signals caused by peak demands or in exchange for an agreed-upon incentive.

Acknowledgement. Part of this work received funding from FEDER/TIN2016-78011-C4-2-R.

---

[18] http://ci.emse.fr/lindt/v1/custom_datatypes.

References

1. Brooke, J.: SUS-A quick and dirty usability scale. Usability evaluation in industry, pp. 189–194 (1996)
2. d'Aquin, M., Jay, N.: Interpreting data mining results with linked data for learning analytics: motivation, case study and directions. In: Proceedings of the Third International Conference on Learning Analytics and Knowledge, pp. 155–164 (2013)
3. Derguech, W., Bruke, E., Curry, E.: An autonomic approach to real-time predictive analytics using open data and internet of things. In: Ubiquitous Intelligence and Computing, 2014 IEEE 11th International Conference on and IEEE 11th International Conference on and Autonomic and Trusted Computing, and IEEE 14th International Conference on Scalable Computing and Communications and Its Associated Workshops, pp. 204–211 (2014)
4. Dou, D., Wang, H., Liu, H.: Semantic data mining: a survey of ontology-based approaches. In: 2015 IEEE International Conference on Semantic Computing (ICSC), pp. 244–251 (2015)
5. Esnaola-Gonzalez, I., Bermúdez, J., Fernandez, I., Arnaiz, A.: Semantic Prediction Assistant Approach applied to Energy Efficiency in Tertiary Buildings. Semantic Web journal, to appear. http://www.semantic-web-journal.net/
6. Fayyad, U., Piatetsky-Shapiro, G., Smyth, P.: From data mining to knowledge discovery in databases. AI Mag. **17**(3), 37 (1996)
7. Haynes, B.P.: The impact of office comfort on productivity. J. Facil. Manag. **6**(1), 37–51 (2008)
8. Hedge, A., Gaygen, D.E.: Indoor environment conditions and computer work in an office. HVAC&R Res. **16**(2), 123–138 (2010)
9. Lefrançois, M.: Planned ETSI SAREF extensions based on the W3C&OGC SOSA/SSN-compatible SEAS ontology patterns. In: Workshop on Semantic Interoperability and Standardization in the IoT, SIS-IoT, 11 p. (2017)
10. Mulville, M., Callaghan, N., Isaac, D.: The impact of the ambient environment and building configuration on occupant productivity in open-plan commercial offices. J. Corp. R. Estate **18**(3), 180–193 (2016)
11. Parsons, K.: Human thermal environments: the effects of hot, moderate, and cold environments on human health, comfort, and performance. CRC Press (2014)
12. Ristoski, P., Paulheim, H.: Semantic web in data mining and knowledge discovery: a comprehensive survey. In: Web Semantics: Science, Services and Agents on the World Wide Web (2016)
13. Ristoski, P., Paulheim, H.: Analyzing statistics with background knowledge from linked open data. In: Workshop on Semantic Statistics (2013)
14. Sivarajah, U., et al.: Critical analysis of Big Data challenges and analytical methods. J. Bus. Res. **70**, 263–286 (2017)
15. Svátek, V., Rauch, J., Ralbovský, M.: Ontology-enhanced association mining. In: Ackermann, M., et al. (eds.) EWMF/KDO -2005. LNCS (LNAI), vol. 4289, pp. 163–179. Springer, Heidelberg (2006). https://doi.org/10.1007/11908678_11
16. Tiddi, I., d'Aquin, M., Motta, E.: Dedalo: looking for clusters explanations in a labyrinth of linked data. In: Presutti, V., d'Amato, C., Gandon, F., d'Aquin, M., Staab, S., Tordai, A. (eds.) ESWC 2014. LNCS, vol. 8465, pp. 333–348. Springer, Cham (2014). https://doi.org/10.1007/978-3-319-07443-6_23
17. Vavpetič, A., Podpečan, V., Lavrač, N.: Semantic subgroup explanations. J. Intell. Inform. Syst. **42**, 233 254 (2014)

Divided We Stand Out! Forging Cohorts fOr Numeric Outlier Detection in Large Scale Knowledge Graphs (CONOD)

Hajira Jabeen[1(✉)], Rajjat Dadwal[2(✉)], Gezim Sejdiu[1(✉)],
and Jens Lehmann[1,2(✉)]

[1] University of Bonn, Bonn, Germany
{jabeen,sejdiu,lehmann}@cs.uni-bonn.de
[2] Fraunhofer IAIS, Sankt Augustin, Germany
{rajjat.dadwal,jens.lehmann}@iais.fraunhofer.de
https://www.uni-bonn.de/

Abstract. With the recent advances in data integration and the concept of data lakes, massive pools of heterogeneous data are being curated as Knowledge Graphs (KGs). In addition to data collection, it is of utmost importance to gain meaningful insights from this composite data. However, given the graph-like representation, the multimodal nature, and large size of data, most of the traditional analytic approaches are no longer directly applicable. The traditional approaches could collect all values of a particular attribute, e.g. height, and try to perform anomaly detection for this attribute. However, it is conceptually inaccurate to compare one attribute representing different entities, e.g. the height of buildings against the height of animals. Therefore, there is a strong need to develop fundamentally new approaches for the outlier detection in KGs. In this paper, we present a scalable approach, dubbed CONOD, that can deal with multimodal data and performs adaptive outlier detection against the cohorts of classes they represent, where a cohort is a set of classes that are similar based on a set of selected properties. We have tested the scalability of CONOD on KGs of different sizes, assessed the outliers using different inspection methods and achieved promising results.

Keywords: Knowledge graph · Cluster · Outlier · Blocking · Cohort
RDF · DBpedia

1 Introduction

Numeric outlier detection has been of interest for the database and data mining community for efficient and automatic detection of errors, frauds, and abnormal patterns. A range of algorithms have been devised for outlier detection of homogeneous set of features like in traditional Databases or tabular data. However, with the current influx of large-scale heterogeneous data in the form of

© Springer Nature Switzerland AG 2018
C. Faron Zucker et al. (Eds.): EKAW 2018, LNAI 11313, pp. 534–548, 2018.
https://doi.org/10.1007/978-3-030-03667-6_34

knowledge graphs (KGs), most of the traditional algorithms are no longer directly (out-of-box) applicable and there is a strong need to develop fundamentally new approaches to deal with the volume and variety of large-scale KGs.

A KG defines classes and relations among these classes in a schema, allows linking of arbitrary entities (instances of classes) with defined relationships and covers a variety of domains. A multitude of approaches are being used to populate and curate KGs. These range from crowdsourcing (DBpedia, Freebase), application of natural language processing techniques (NELL) to automatic extraction of knowledge (YAGO, DBpedia). The liberal nature of these curation methods – the knowledge being entered is neither restricted nor cross-validated – makes them prone to various kinds of errors that can get camouflaged in different dimensions. These errors can be extraction errors like parsing errors, e.g. "3–4" can be interpreted as "3", and "–4", representation errors and conversion errors, e.g. the units of measurements cm, inches, feet are mixed, or data entry errors.

Numeric data can be associated with entities belonging to numerous classes and one property can be associated with several different types, e.g. the property "height" can be associated to a building, an animal, or a person. It is of utmost importance to treat a particular property in correspondence with the type of entities it represents when performing outlier detection. In this paper, we have focused on outlier detection on numeric literals within a KG.

Anomaly or outlier detection is mostly regarded as an unsupervised learning task dealing with identifying unlikely and rare events. Outliers are usually the extreme values that deviate from the remaining observations. It is challenging to devise a scalable yet generic method that can detect outliers across different dimensions automatically without manual intervention. In this paper, we have targeted the above challenges of detection of outliers in multimodal and multivariate data with different distributions coming from disparate sources curated as a large KG. We propose an unsupervised numeric outlier detection method that is generic and yet scales to large KGs. Our approach 'Forging Cohorts for Numeric Outlier Detection in large scale KGs (CONOD)' proceeds in two stages. In the first stage, the data is linearly cohorted using the type information of the entities. In the second stage, the outlier detection is performed on common numerical literal properties within each cohort. The major contributions of CONOD are (1) Scalability, (2) Genericness (3) Linear time cohorting, (4) Applicability to multimodal data. We have tested the scalability of CONOD on DBpedia and its scaled-out versions. To the best of our knowledge, CONOD is the first open source, generic method for unsupervised numeric outlier detection on KGs.

The rest of the paper is structured as follows: Sect. 2 discusses the preliminaries, Sect. 3 reviews the related work and identifies the existing research gaps, followed by the proposed approach, Experiments and evaluation, and Conclusions and future work in Sects. 4, 5, and 6 respectively.

2   Preliminaries

2.1   Semantic Web and DBpedia

The rationale behind the semantic web is to represent information by providing machine and human understandable descriptions of real world things (resources). The Resource Description Framework (RDF) is a W3C standard model for representing semantic relationships between data items. The RDF data is represented as a set of triples containing a subject, a predicate, and an object. Subjects are the resources represented by unique URIs, objects can either be a resource or a literal. The predicate is the relationship between the subject and the object. The membership of a resource to its classes is defined by the *rdf:type* property and each resource can belong to many classes.

DBpedia [7] is a community effort to extract structured information from Wikipedia and to make this information available on the Web in the form of linked data[1]. DBpedia released its first dataset in 2007 by the developers of University of Mannheim and University of Leipzig. Wikipedia consists of information like images, numerical attributes, e.g. population or height, links to external web pages and structural information. In its current version, DBpedia contains information about 4.58 million things, including 1,445,000 persons, 735,000 places (including 478,000 populated places), 87,000 movies among many others.

2.2   Anomaly Detection

Outlier or anomaly detection is a technique for "finding patterns in data that do not conform to the expected normal behavior" [1]. A broad range of outlier detection methods have been proposed in the literature and they can be roughly categorized as being based on nearest neighbors, clusters, or metrics like density, distance, depth, and statistics for outlier detection. In this work, the focus is to apply a simple outlier detection method for univariate numerical outliers. Therefore, we discuss a few prominent, univariate, statistical methods for outlier detection.

Grubbs' Method. The Grubbs' method [5] also known as the maximum normed residual test is used to detect a single outlier in a univariate data set that follows an approximately normal distribution. The Grubbs' test is defined as: $G = \frac{\max|Y_i - \bar{Y}|}{s}$, with $\bar{Y}$ and s denoting the sample mean and standard deviation, respectively. The Grubbs' test statistic is the largest absolute deviation from the sample mean in units of the sample standard deviation. The Grubbs' procedure tests the hypothesis whether the value that is the furthest from the uniform sample mean is an outlier. Therefore, it is not suited for data that is non uniformly distributed or contains blocks of outliers.

Inter Quartile Range. The Inter Quartile Range IQR method [10] is the amount of spread in the middle 50% of a dataset. It is the distance between the

---

[1] https://en.wikipedia.org/wiki/DBpedia.

first quartile $Q1$, Median M (or $Q2$) and third quartile $Q3$ of the given numerical dataset. Quartiles divide a rank-ordered data set into four equal parts. The values that separate parts are called the first, second, and third quartiles; and they are denoted by $Q1$, $Q2$, and $Q3$, respectively.

$Q1$ is the median of all the values smaller than the median M whereas the $Q3$ is the median of all the values higher than the median M. IQR is the measure of variability defined by the difference between $Q3$ and $Q1$. The data points which are smaller than $Q1 - 1.5 * IQR$ and greater than $Q3 + 1.5 * IQR$ are considered as outliers. The constant value 1.5 depends upon the distribution of the data and can be adjusted accordingly.

Median Absolute Deviation. Median Absolute Deviation (MAD) [9] measures the variability of a univariate sample of quantitative data in statistics. It is more resilient to outliers in a data set than the standard deviation method. MAD is defined as the median of the absolute deviations from the data's median for univariate data. The median absolute deviation is defined as:

$$MAD = b * median\left(|X_i - median(X)|\right)$$

Outlier detection using MAD can be performed by calculating $A = Median + 2.5 * MAD$, and $B = Median - 2.5 * MAD$. Any value in the input set X which is greater than A and less than B is considered an outlier.

Leys et al. [9] have surveyed different methods of outlier detection. They argue that the 'mean' of any data have zero breakdown point(One infinite value in data shifts the mean to infinite) that makes it unsuitable for the calculation of outliers. Whereas Median breakdown value is about 50%, meaning that the median can resist up to 50% of outliers. MAD also has the same breaking point, whereas IQR has a breakdown point of 25%. Based on the resilience, we have chosen MAD and IQR to find the outliers in RDF data.

2.3 Apache Spark for Big Data Processing

Apache Spark is a scalable, in-memory, general-purpose cluster computing framework with APIs available in Java, Python, and Scala[2]. Apache Spark, consolidated under one stack, consists of several independent special purpose libraries.

1. **Spark Core** includes basic functionalities of spark like task scheduling, memory management, fault recovery and interaction with the storage system. It is also home to the Resilient Distributed Dataset (RDD) API.
2. **Spark SQL** is the component of the Spark stack that deals with structured data by providing the DataFrames API. The basic SQL operations can be performed on DataFrames.
3. The **Cluster Manager** is designed for distributed computing where parallel operations run on various computer nodes. Spark can use its inbuilt standalone scheduler or can use other cluster managers like Apache Mesos or Hadoop yarn.

---

[2] https://spark.apache.org/docs/latest/.

Resilient Distributed Dataset (RDD). RDD [15] is an immutable and distributed scala collection. In Spark, everything is expressed as RDD. An RDD can be created by:

1. Loading an external dataset in Spark,
2. Parallelizing an existing collection of objects,
3. Manipulating existing RDDs.

Two types of operations can be performed on RDDs:

1. Transformation: Return another RDD after applying a function on existing RDDs This is done via a lazy execution, i.e. the result is not immediately computed.
2. Action: Compute a result based on an RDD and either return or save it to an external storage system. Here, the computation is eager, i.e. the result is immediately computed.

The lazy evaluation of Spark helps in achieving fault tolerance and optimizing performance. Spark creates a lineage graph for all transformations and executes it optimally when an action is triggered. This lineage graph is used to recover lost computing information upon a node failure. Spark offers a range of inbuilt functions for RDD operations executing in parallel with little to no programming overhead.

3   Related Work

The literature on outlier detection in KGs is relatively scarce because KGs had mainly been considered for data consolidation or curation and their potential for analytics has gained momentum in the recent years only. Below, we discuss a few existing outlier detection methods for KGs.

Weinand et al. [14] presented an experimental approach for the detection of numeric outliers from DBpedia. The authors argued that the traditional outlier detection approaches are limited by the existence of natural outliers. Therefore, they group similar objects together and then apply outlier detection exclusively on these grouped objects to overcome this problem. The grouping incurs high complexity as it uses the type information, which is not always present or is either too generic (e.g. owl:Thing as only type) or is inaccurate. Due to being computationally expensive, the proposed method was tested on only part of DBpedia using the SPARQL endpoint for three numerical properties (*DBpedia-owl:populationTotal, DBpedia-owl:height*, and *DBpedia-owl:elevation*). Additionally, the authors have compared different outlier detection techniques, i.e., Inter Quartile Range (IQR), Kernel Density Estimators (KDE) [12] and dispersion estimators and reported that the IQR performs better than other methods tested. In a similar approach [13] Paulheim used hot encoding for type vectors of entities and clustered them into groups before performing anomaly detection on numerical features for identification of wrong links in the data.

Fleischhacker et al. [4] presented an outlier detection method that crosschecks the results of outliers by exploiting the *"sameAs"* properties in the knowledge base and also makes an effort towards differentiating between natural outliers and actual outliers in the data. The outlier detection method is carried out by dataset inspection through specialized SPARQL queries against the knowledge base. In the first step the authors select the interesting properties for outlier detection. In the second step, the subpopulation is sought by using specialized operators for developing a set of constraints (top-down ILP algorithms for discovery of datalog rules) against classes, properties, and property values. This exploration is organized as a lattice where the root node consists of a property and the corresponding number of instances. After the lattice has been determined, the next step is to find the outliers on all unpruned nodes of the lattice. The results of the outlier score are stored as a set of constraints which returns the corresponding instance set. The classification of outliers into natural or real is done with the help of data interlinking property by comparing with different datasets. This procedure helps in better handling natural outliers and thus reducing the false positive rate. However, building the lattice for the subpopulation discovery requires substantial memory and computation [11]. In addition, the method requires manual querying of data in order to extract the required information. Therefore, the method is unsuitable for very large scale knowledge bases.

Debattista et al. [3] have presented a preliminary approach for distance-based outlier detection for linked data quality improvement. They detect incorrect RDF statements by applying a distance-based clustering method for pointing out the outliers in linked data.

In summary, the outlier detection methods discussed above have the limitations of:

(a) Accessing the data through a SPARQL endpoint(slow, unreliable),
(b) Using Clustering(mostly with quadratic complexity),
(c) Using Sub-latex search(complex).

and therefore are not scalable to large-scale knowledge graphs, which is the main contribution of this work.

4 Approach

In this section, we detail **CONOD**, a scalable and generic algorithm for numeric outlier detection in KGs. In order to deal with the multimodality of the data, we have used a cohort-based approach. A cohort can be defined as the set of classes that share some similarities based on their selected features. CONOD can be divided into following steps (1) data cleaning, (2) cohort creation, (3) property selection, (4) outlier detection(IQR) and (5) output, as shown in Fig. 1. Algorithm 1 describes the working of CONOD that takes RDF triples as input, creates RDD, applies a series of transformations and actions, and returns a list of outliers as output.

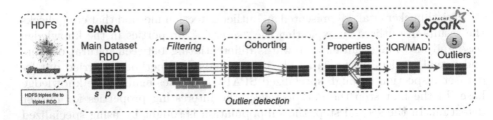

Fig. 1. CONOD execution pipeline

Algorithm 1. CONOD

    Result: Outliers list
    input : *RDF*: an RDF dataset
1 *RDD mainDataset = RDF.toRDD < Triple > ()*
2 *mainDataset.cache()*
3 *Numerics ← filter(mainDataset)*
4 *Subjects ← filter(mainDataset)*
5 *FilteredData ← Numerics ∪ Subjects*
6 *PairedRDD ← FilteredData.GroupBy(Subjects)*
7 *VectorizedData ← Vectorize(PairedRDD)*
8 *Hashes ← LSHASH(VectorizedData)*
9 *Cohorts ← similarityByJoin(Hashes, Hashes, threshold)*
10 *Properties ← Cohorts.getPProperties()*
11 *Outliers ← IQROutlier(Properties)*

4.1 Data Cleaning and Filtering

KGs are created by collecting data from different sources represented in the form of triples. These triples can contain relationships of numerous types. As we are interested in numerical values for the outlier detection, we use a data filtering step to extract the data of interest. Here, we also assume that the data contains a schema and has the information about the rdf:type for most of the resources and is possibly enriched with Linked data Hypernyms [6].

The Linked Hypernyms Dataset (LHD) provides types in DBpedia namespace. These types are extracted from the first sentences of Wikipedia articles from different languages using Hearst pattern matching over part-of-speech annotated text and disambiguated to DBpedia concepts. The cleaning step selects the triples with objects having literals of type "xsd:integer, xsd:nonNegativeInteger and xsd:double". At a later stage, for cohorting, we use the information about type and LHD of the subjects of filtered triples. Therefore, we also filter the type information at this stage. This filtering is done in step 1–5 of Algorithm 1.

4.2 Creation of Cohorts

In this step, the filtered data is used for creation of cohorts by using Locality Sensitive Hashing (LSH) [2]. LSH is an important class of hashing techniques. LSH uses a family of functions ("LSH families") to hash data points into buckets, so that the data points which are close to each other are in the same buckets with high probability, while data points that are far away from each other are likely in different buckets. As discussed in the previous sections most of the outlier detection methods use some sort of clustering to find the outliers in the data which are quadratic in nature. The proposed LSH based cohorting achieves scalable performance using linear complexity. The process of cohorting can be described as:

1. Select the type information and LHD types of each subject and represent them as a key-value pair, with subject as the key and type-and-LHD information as the values.
2. Convert this type information into vectors named featureVectors.
3. Create hashes of the featureVectors using LSH hashing.
4. Find similarity between hash-vectors and create cohorts.
5. Output cohorts.

We have experimented with two different vectorizing models CountVectorizer and HashingTF. We have used similarity join method for measuring the similarity among different values. This can be seen in step 6–9 of Algorithm 1.

4.3   Properties in Cohorts

Once the cohorts of subjects are created, we group the numerical properties of these subjects within each cohort and perform outlier detection for each property in parallel. This is step 10 in Algorithm 1.

4.4   Outlier Detection, and Output

Algorithm 1 uses the IQR method to find outliers from the group of properties in Step 11. The implementation of IQR is described in Algorithm 2. The IQR algorithm takes numeric properties as input, prepares a list of numbers corresponding to each property, applies the IQR method on this list and returns the list of outliers. The list of outliers is saved in HDFS for analysis purposes, e.g. classification of outliers, outlier analysis etc.

Algorithm 2. IQROutlier

Result: Outliers list

input : numericProperties: Group of properties from each cohort

1 $RDD\ numericRDD = numericProperties.toRDD < Triple > ()$

2 $listNumerics \leftarrow filter(numericRDD)$

3 $sortedList \leftarrow sort(listNumerics)$

4 $Q_1 \leftarrow firstQuartile(sortedList)$

5 $Q_3 \leftarrow thirdQuartile(sortedList)$

6 $IQR \leftarrow Q_3 - Q_1$

7 $lowerRange \leftarrow Q_1 - 1.5 * IQR$

8 $upperRange \leftarrow Q_3 + 1.5 * IQR$

9 $outliersList \leftarrow$
   $filter(listNumerics < lowerRange\ or\ listNumerics > upperRange)$

4.5 Implementation

We have used the distributed in-memory computing framework *Apache Spark* to support horizontal scalability. CONOD has been implemented as a module in SANSA [8], an open source[3] *data flow processing engine* for performing distributed computation over large-scale RDF datasets. It provides data distribution, communication, and fault tolerance for manipulating massive RDF graphs and applying machine learning algorithms on the data at scale. We have used the SANSA-RDF layer for the ingestion of RDF data and its representation as RDDs. The algorithm is provided as an API in the machine learning layer of SANSA.

5 Experiment and Evaluation

We have tested the performance of CONOD on a cluster with 4 servers having a total of 256 cores, and each server has Xeon Intel CPUs at 2.3 GHz, 256 GB of RAM and 400 GB of disk space, running Ubuntu 16.04.3 LTS (Xenial) and connected via a Gigabit Ethernet2 network.

We have used Spark Standalone mode with Spark version 2.2.1 and Scala with version 2.11.11. Each Spark executor is assigned a memory of 250 GB.

Table 1 provides an overview of the results generated by CONOD. Out of 117544372 triples, 22375991 numeric literals were selected for anomaly detection after the filtering process. These triples belong to 1567 distinct properties. From these properties only 408 were found to have outliers and the total number of outliers found in DBpedia are 24015, which is approximately 0.1% of numeric literals present in the data.

Table 1. Statistics for DBpedia large file (16.6 GB)

Statistics	Value
Distinct Properties	2863
Triples (including duplicates)	117,544,372
Numeric literals after filtering process (including duplicates)	22,375,991
Filtered distinct numerical properties	1,567
The number of properties with outliers	408
Total number of outliers	24,015
– Runtime TV series has total number of outliers	482
– Built-year property of buildings has total number of outliers	86
– PostalCode of area has total number of outliers	176

---

[3] https://github.com/SANSA-Stack.

5.1   Execution Time

In this section, we discuss the scalability and runtime performance of CONOD. The runtime does not include the time for data ingestion from Hadoop file system.

Datasets and Execution Time. In order to test the scalability, applicability, and efficiency of CONOD in terms of execution time, we have tested the approach on different sizes of DBpedia as shown in Table 2.

Table 2. Dataset description

Dataset categorization	Dataset size
DBpedia-Small	110 MB
DBpedia-Medium	3.7 GB
DBpedia	16.6 GB
DBpedia * 2	32 GB
DBpedia * 4	64 GB
DBpedia * 8	128 GB

The execution times of CONOD on different datasets are shown in Fig. 2. We can see the run time increased with the increase of data. For DBpedia-Small it took only 2 min while for DBpedia * 8, it took approximately 5.9 h. This can be noted that the time taken by CONOD increases by a factor of 1.5 when we double the size of data depicting the linear increase in runtime corresponding to the data size.

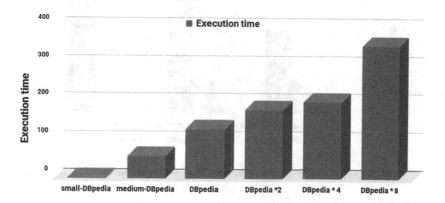

Fig. 2. CONOD: Execution time of different datasets

Comparison with Other Approaches. In order to show the scalability and comparison with traditional methods, we have implemented a Cartesian product based similarity method for cohorting similar subjects (by using DataFrame's crossJoin function in Spark). This has also helped us to evaluate the speedup gained with CONOD. Here, we compare the runtime for both approaches, i.e., cohorting of classes by using the Cartesian product and CONOD (using two different vectorizing methods namely, CountVectorizerModel and HashingTF). In Fig. 3, it can be noted that the execution time of the small dataset is almost equal for all the three methods because the small dataset does not require more resources like memory or execution cores.

For the medium-DBpedia, the DataFrame crossJoin function takes less time compared to other approaches. The other two approaches take more time due to approximate similarity join function that calculates the approximate similarity for finding the similar items in our algorithm and also the process of computing the vector from strings and creation of vocabulary for the vectorizing is noticeable for the medium sized data. Due to this reason, the execution time of HahingTF and CountVectorizerModel model is more as compared to crossJoin on medium datasets However, on DBpedia dataset, The DataFrame crossJoin approach fails on the cluster being tested due to its $O(n^2)$ complexity and we have represented this with three dots in Fig. 3. The CountVectorizerModel approach takes more time than the HashingTF on the large dataset as it scans the data twice, first time for building the model, and second time for the transformation. CountVectorizerModel needs extra memory equal to the number of unique features whereas HashingTF does not require additional space. By examining the results shown in the figure, it can be inferred that CONOD (HashingTF) performs better than the other approaches explored in this paper for larger datasets.

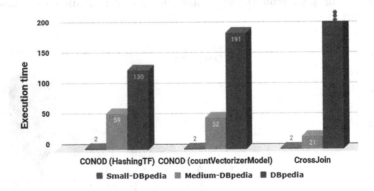

Fig. 3. Execution time comparison of different approaches

5.2   Visualization of Outliers

Given a large number of outliers detected against a number of different properties, it is not straightforward to assess the quality of outliers. Therefore, we have created two dimensional scatter plots of the numerical values of a few randomly selected properties in order to visualize the outliers and analyze them.

We have used python matplotlib[4] library for creating the graphs. The red color in the graph corresponds to the outliers, whereas green represents the normal data values.

Built (Year) Property of Buildings. Built property represents the year when a building is built. Listing 1.1 shows that Foolad Shahr Stadium was built in 1988.

dbr:Foolad_Shahr_Stadium	dbo:built	1998^^xsd:integer.
dbr:Ivaylo_Stadium	dbo:built	1958^^xsd:integer.

Listing 1.1. Built property in DBpedia

The Fig. 4 shows the scatter plot of built property. The x-axis represents the years and the y-axis represents the frequency of occurrence of each year. Since built property signifies the past events, any value greater than the current year can be considered as a real outlier. e.g. a value in the x-axis shows that year has value around $0.9 \times 1e^{19}$ and this is a outlier. The graph also shows an erroneous value that Metropolitan Life Insurance Company Hall of Records building was built in the year 9223372036854775807. One can observe in the zoomed-in graph, that the values near zero are shown as outliers in the plot.

Width Property of Cars. We have plotted the outlier graph for the width of automobiles in Fig. 5. The width property of cars has range xsd:double and xsd:integer. The Listing 1.2 shows that the automobile named as Toyota Avalon has width 1997 in DBpedia.

dbr:Jaguar_S−Type	dbo:width	"2007"^^xsd:integer.
dbr:Toyota_Avalon	dbo:width	"1997"^^xsd:integer.

Listing 1.2. RDF data of width property of cars present in DBpedia

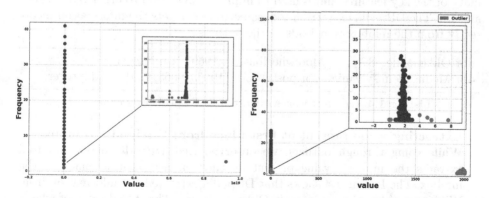

Fig. 4. Outliers 'Built-year'   **Fig. 5.** Outliers 'Width of cars'

---

[4] https://matplotlib.org/.

The value around 2000 in the graph is an outlier because DBpedia extraction tool has extracted year in place of width.

The zoomed-in graph in Fig. 5 shows that most of the cars have width range from 0.627 to 3.011 and the values out of this range are outliers.

5.3   Manual Inspection of Outliers

In the manual inspection of outliers, we have compared the outliers with the corresponding Wikipedia pages to observe the reason. Given the large size of the knowledge base and a large number of outliers detected, the manual inspection of outliers of all the values is not feasible.

---

dbr:GS&WR_Class_201   dbo:builddate   188718951901^^xsd:integer.
dbr:GE_UM12C   dbo:builddate   19631966^^xsd:integer.

Listing 1.3. Example of real outliers in DBpedia

Therefore, we randomly sampled some values for inspection. We have found some unusual patterns in the output as shown in the Listing 1.3 and classified them as real outliers.

The inspection also enabled us to figure-out the reasons behind these outliers in DBpedia.

Erroneous Information in Wikipedia. Given that Wikipedia is being maintained and updated by the community, and input to the pages is not strictly validated, Wikipedia is prone to containing erroneous information. This incorrect information results in the outliers in DBpedia. The correctness of these outliers is difficult to assess as it needs to be confirmed from the external sources or to be validated by experts.

DBpedia Extraction Tool. The infobox section of Wikipedia presents a summary of the key features and is used to improve navigation to other interrelated articles. The DBpedia extraction tool sometimes extracts the information incorrectly from the infobox that leads to the outliers.

---

dbr:Oldsmobile_88   dbo:wheelbase   1969^^xsd:integer.
dbr:Media,_Pennsylvania   dbr:postalCode   190631906519091^^xsd:integer.

Listing 1.4. Incorrect values extracted by DBpedia extraction tool

1. **Extracting value present at first place from Wikipedia Infobox**
   While going through outliers, we observed that DBpedia extraction tool extracts the numeric value present at the starting position place in the infobox. The Listing 1.4 shows that DBpedia extracted the information from Wikipedia about the car, namely Oldsmobile 88[5]. The actual value of wheelbase of Oldsmobile 88 is 124 in. whereas DBpedia extracted year 1969 present at the starting position.

---

[5] https://en.wikipedia.org/wiki/Oldsmobile_88.

2. **Concatenation of numbers**
   Sometimes DBpedia extraction tool removes the hyphens, comma or other separators between the values and merges them into one number. e.g. The maximum length of the postal code is ten digits worldwide[6]. However, in the Listing 1.4, it is shown that Media Pennsylvania has postal code '190631906519091'.

3. **Problems Interpreting and Converting Units**
   There are some properties in DBpedia dataset which use different units of measurement. While converting these values, it can do some incorrect calculation. For example, it has extracted hyphen as a negative sign appended to the value. e.g. If a TV show duration is 11–12 and 24–26 min. The DBpedia extraction tool extracts values for runtime property in minutes i.e., -12 min from the infobox of Arthur TV series and the resulting runtime is $(-12 * 60 = -720\,s)$.

4. **Infobox properties without starting year**
   Some events on Wikipedia have no starting date, and the value for those events is empty and is written like - 1998 DBpedia extracts this value as a negative year.

5. **Removing characters from alphanumeric value[7]**
   In some observations DBpedia extraction tool removes the letters from alphanumeric values e.g. idoxifene with property unii has value 456UXE9867, and in DBpedia, it is stored as 456 only. Also IUPAC name is alphanumeric, but DBpedia extracted it as -88.

6   Conclusions and Future Work

In this paper, we have presented CONOD a simple, generic and scalable method to discover numeric outliers from KGs. CONOD is the first open source and distributed outlier detection algorithm for knowledge graphs. It makes use of Local similarity hashing to achieve faster cohorting. We have analyzed the results of CONOD for scalability and it has been found scalable up to a dataset of 128 GB size on the available cluster. We have analyzed the resulting outliers both manually and graphically. The analysis shows the validity of the resulted outliers and also helped us in pointing out a few limitations of DBpedia extraction framework. CONOD can be extended by addition of more features prior to cohorting to obtain more meaningful cohorts. We can also choose from a range of different vectorization methods. An important branch to explore would to include other data types at literal positions for outlier detection. We can also explore the fact that the outliers can be present at the subject and predicate position of the triples by making use of semantic relationships to detect these outlier values.

Acknowledgment. This work was partly supported by the EU Horizon2020 projects WDAqua (GA no. 642795), Boost4.0 (GA no. 780732) and BigDataOcean (GA no. 732310).

---

[6] https://en.wikipedia.org/wiki/Postal_code.
[7] https://en.wikipedia.org/wiki/Idoxifene.

References

1. Chandola, V., Banerjee, A., Kumar, V.: Anomaly detection: a survey. ACM Comput. Surv. (CSUR) **41**(3), 15 (2009)
2. Datar, M., Immorlica, N., Indyk, P., Mirrokni, V.S.: Locality-sensitive hashing scheme based on p-stable distributions. In: Proceedings of the Twentieth Annual Symposium on Computational Geometry, pp. 253–262. ACM (2004)
3. Debattista, J., Lange, C., Auer, S.: A preliminary investigation towards improving linked data quality using distance-based outlier detection. In: Li, Y.F., et al. (eds.) JIST 2016. LNCS, vol. 10055, pp. 116–124. Springer, Cham (2016). https://doi.org/10.1007/978-3-319-50112-3_9
4. Fleischhacker, D., Paulheim, H., Bryl, V., Völker, J., Bizer, C.: Detecting errors in numerical linked data using cross-checked outlier detection. In: Mika, P., et al. (eds.) ISWC 2014. LNCS, vol. 8796, pp. 357–372. Springer, Cham (2014). https://doi.org/10.1007/978-3-319-11964-9_23
5. Grubbs, F.E.: Procedures for detecting outlying observations in samples. Technometrics **11**(1), 1–21 (1969)
6. Kliegr, T.: Linked hypernyms: enriching DBpedia with targeted hypernym discovery. Web Semant. Sci. Serv. Agents World Wide Web **31**, 59–69 (2015)
7. Lehmann, J., et al.: DBpedia-a large-scale, multilingual knowledge base extracted from Wikipedia. Semant. Web **6**(2), 167–195 (2015)
8. Lehmann, J., et al.: Distributed semantic analytics using the SANSA stack. In: d'Amato, C., et al. (eds.) ISWC 2017. LNCS, vol. 10588, pp. 147–155. Springer, Cham (2017). https://doi.org/10.1007/978-3-319-68204-4_15
9. Leys, C., Ley, C., Klein, O., Bernard, P., Licata, L.: Detecting outliers: do not use standard deviation around the mean, use absolute deviation around the median. J. Exp. Soc. Psychol. **49**(4), 764–766 (2013)
10. McGill, R., Tukey, J.W., Larsen, W.A.: Variations of box plots. Am. Stat. **32**(1), 12–16 (1978)
11. Melo, A., Theobald, M., Völker, J.: Correlation-based refinement of rules with numerical attributes. In: FLAIRS Conference (2014)
12. Parzen, E.: On estimation of a probability density function and mode. Ann. Math. Stat. **33**(3), 1065–1076 (1962)
13. Paulheim, H.: Identifying wrong links between datasets by multi-dimensional outlier detection. In: WoDOOM, pp. 27–38 (2014)
14. Wienand, D., Paulheim, H.: Detecting incorrect numerical data in DBpedia. In: Presutti, V., d'Amato, C., Gandon, F., d'Aquin, M., Staab, S., Tordai, A. (eds.) ESWC 2014. LNCS, vol. 8465, pp. 504–518. Springer, Cham (2014). https://doi.org/10.1007/978-3-319-07443-6_34
15. Zaharia, M., et al.: Resilient distributed datasets: a fault-tolerant abstraction for in-memory cluster computing. In: Proceedings of the 9th USENIX Conference on Networked Systems Design and Implementation (2012)

Decision Support Models to Assist in the Diagnosis of Meningitis

Viviane M. Lelis[1], María-Victoria Belmonte[2],
and Eduardo Guzmán[2(✉)]

[1] Instituto Federal de Educao, Ciencia e Tecnología da Bahia,
Campus Vitória da Conquista, Bahia, Brazil
[2] Dpto. Lenguajes y Ciencias de la Computación,
Universidad de Málaga, 29071 Málaga, Spain
guzman@lcc.uma.es

Abstract. Meningitis diagnostic is a challenge especially in less developed countries where medical resources are limited, and the cost of treatments are not always affordable. For this reason, it would be desirable to have available any solution that could perform early diagnostics on meningitis to find the suitable treatment, at least for the more severe types of this disease (bacterial, meningococcal, ...). In this paper, we present a set of clinical decision support models to assist physicians in the meningitis diagnostics. These models try to answer to the following two research questions: *Can it be diagnosed reliably if a patient has meningitis? Can it be determined whether it is a bacterial or aseptic case?* To explore the performance of our models, we have conducted validation experiments with a dataset of patients. For this purpose, we have counted with data of patient meningitis diagnostics in Brazil. The database was provided by the Directorate of Health Information of the Secretary of Health of the Brazilian State of Bahia and contained over 16,000 records. Several indexes have been computed to show the model accuracy, but the best corresponds to the ADTree classifier with a precision of 0.859 and a ROC area over 0.86. Validation results show a good performance of the models, suggesting, therefore, that our proposal can effectively support physicians' decisions on meningitis management and treatment.

Keywords: Decision support models · Diagnostic models · Data mining

1 Introduction

Meningitis is an inflammation of the membranes that cover the brain and spinal cord, i.e. dura mater, arachnoid, and pia mater. Aseptic Meningitis (AM), caused by a virus, is relatively light and is cured in one or two weeks without any specific treatment. Bacterial Meningitis (BM) is, however, much more severe and can cause brain damage, hearing or learning loss and, in some cases, even results in death. Particularly, this situation is especially dramatic in less developed countries and regions, where the lack of resources often leads to delays in making immediate Laboratory Cerebrospinal Fluid (CSF) tests that prevent a diagnosis on time. According to World Health Organization, in western countries, BM occurs annually in a rate of about 3 people per 100,000.

© Springer Nature Switzerland AG 2018
C. Faron Zucker et al. (Eds.): EKAW 2018, LNAI 11313, pp. 549–564, 2018.
https://doi.org/10.1007/978-3-030-03667-6_35

In Brazil, however, this rate is higher: 45.8 per 100,000 individuals and the mortality rate in cases of meningococcal meningitis is 20%, even with proper diagnosis and treatment. Consequently, BM represents a major challenge in public health due to its significant morbidity, mortality and sequelae. There are different bacteria causing BM, but Neisseria meningitides (meningococcus) has a significant epidemic potential and may cause causes Meningococcal Disease (MD), which can lead to bloodstream infections (bacteremia or septicemia). Several international Clinical Practice Guidelines (CPGs) and local bulletins issued by public health authorities contain recommendations for the meningitis diagnosis and management. All of them agree in demanding immediate medical attention for BM cases, since delays in the initiation of proper therapy clearly increase the morbidity and mortality risks. The initial treatment approach to the patient with suspected acute BM depends on early recognition of the meningitis syndrome, rapid diagnostic evaluation and emergent antimicrobial and adjunctive therapy [1–3].

The problem, in less developed countries regarding the meningitis diagnostic and treatment, is that rural areas often do not have the required resources to make early test laboratories. For this reason, they have to recommend immediate hospitalization of patients who exhibit some symptoms of meningitis. This, in turn, leads to further problems: First, in many cases patients are immediately exposed to aggressive treatments before confirming the meningitis diagnostic, and independently of its etiology, viral or bacterial. Second, the cost of this default treatment is not affordable for those less developed countries. Moreover, many patients with few financial resources and severe cases of meningitis are diagnosed late and, therefore, the treatment does not avoid their decease. Consequently, in this paper we have tried to provide with a pair of clinical decision support models able to assist physicians in the diagnostic of having meningitis and the type of this disease, in terms of observable symptoms. In our previous research [4], we focused on building a decision model, DM2, to help diagnose meningococcal meningitis by applying data mining techniques. In this work, we complemented DM2 with two further decision models: Meningitis Classification Decision Model (DM1) and Etiology Identification Decision Model (DM3). In both of them, we have explored different classification techniques. Through these models, we have tried to answer to the following research questions: *(RQ1) Can it be diagnosed reliably if a patient has meningitis? (RQ2) Can it be determined the etiological origin, bacterial or aseptic, of the disease?*

The responses to these questions have been developed through 10 cross-fold validation procedures of the two decision models presented in this paper. These validation procedures have been tested with a dataset of real patients. For this purpose, we have counted with data of patient meningitis diagnostics in Brazil. The database was provided by the Directorate of Health Information (DIS) of the Secretary of Health of the Brazilian State of Bahia (SESAB) and contained 16,205 records. Results show that the techniques applied are suitable for diagnosing the meningitis. Several indexes, such as precision, recall or ROC area, have been computed to show the model accuracy, but the best corresponds to the ADTree classifier with a precision of 0.859 and a ROC area over 0.86. These results indicate that our model can indeed help lead to a non-invasive and early diagnosis of this pathology.

In healthcare, a Clinical Decision Support System (CDSS) acquires patient data as the input and provides back patient-specific assessment and recommendations by using healthcare process or knowledge-based models, such us diagnosis or treatments. Most of the early proposals of CDSS [5], as MYCIN [6], used rule-based expert systems. These systems required a vast amount of prior knowledge on the part of decision making, in order to provide the right answers to well-formed questions. Nowadays, most of the CDSS employ data mining tools. These systems do not require a prior knowledge on the part of the decision-making components. Instead, they are designed to find new and unsuspected patterns and relationships in a given set of data; then they apply this newly discovered knowledge to a new set of data [7].

Data mining techniques such as clustering, classification, logical and association rule-based reasoning, and other methods has been widely used. It has found its way into a large number of applications that uses data mining tools in healthcare settings to support the diagnosis of different pathologies. Diabetes [8], asthma [9], arrhythmia [10], glaucoma [11], sleep apnea [12], cancer [13], liver [14] or cerebrovascular diseases [15] are just some examples. Regarding meningitis diagnosis, we have found some decision support systems but they do not use data mining techniques. Fuzzy Cognitive Maps [16], Case Base Reasoning [17], Rough Sets [18, 19] or Neural Networks [20] are some of the techniques used. In general, those approaches have used smaller datasets than ours, and even some of them are not obtained from real data [17]. In addition, most of them use symptoms obtained from invasive medical tests [17, 20], which invalidates them for the early detection of meningitis in rural areas; and some of them are intended only for children [16, 20]. In relation to the results, all of them do not present better results than ours, e.g., [16] has a sensitivity of 83.3% and a specificity of 80% with a validation set of 16 cases [20] has a predicting accuracy of 59% for meningococcal meningitis with 114 cases, or [17] has an accuracy about 90% but with a small and virtual validation base case (30 cases).

2 Methods

2.1 Meningitis Management in Brazil

The Brazilian guide to Epidemiological Surveillance [3] describes recommendations for meningitis diagnosis and management. Moreover, meningitis is part of the National List of Compulsory Notification Diseases (Ministerial Order GM/MS n° 2472, August 31th, 2010). For this, all suspected cases are compulsory reportable regardless of the etiologic agent, that is, they must be notified to health authorities, so they can provide an immediate and appropriate epidemiological research and assess the need to adopt control measures relevant. All suspect cases must also be registered in the SINAN, the Notifiable Diseases Information System of the Brazilian government.

According to [3], in Brazil all meningitis cases are a medical emergence and require immediate hospitalization, i.e., even in those cases where there only mere suspicion the patient should be admitted, receive medication and support measures (serum, ventilation etc.). The reason, in Brazil meningitis has great epidemic potential and high mortality, due to socio-economic and climatic conditions of the majority of the population.

Figure 1, briefly, illustrates this process. It is considered as *meningitis suspected* case those of children over one year old and adults with fever, severe headache, vomiting in jet, stiff neck, signs of meningeal irritation (Kernig, Brudzinski), seizures, and/or red spots on the body. In children under one year of age, the classic symptoms listed above may not be so evident. In these cases, it is important to consider for the suspected diagnosis, signs of irritability, as persistent crying, and checking for bulging fontanelle. A *case definition* is a specific set of criteria that an individual must meet to be considered a case of the disease under investigation [21]. For meningitis case definition, it is essential the collection of patient samples (blood, feces, urine and liquor), preferably before using the first dose of antibiotic. Consequently, it is considered a meningitis case when the patient presents the typical clinical symptoms cited above and alterations in the CSF cytological test, which can be checked at a local lab. Such alterations in CSF can increase cellularity and biochemistry (Table 3). Furthermore, there are some criteria to confirm a meningitis diagnosis and to determine its etiology. However, culture of CSF and/or blood in a specialized laboratory is considered the gold standard, i.e., is the only test that currently confirms the diagnosis, though in Brazil the result of CSF analysis could take even 30 days to be ready. The *closure of the case* should be performed after checking all the information necessary for its completion and reporting it to the SINAN database

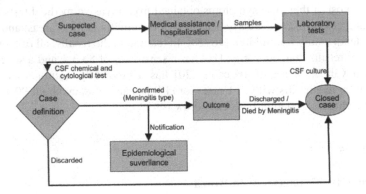

Fig. 1. Meningitis management process in Brazil extracted from [3]. (Color figure online)

The goal of the models we have developed is not to replace human expert, but to offer them data-driven diagnostics that could help by providing additional evidence in the task of making a diagnosis. If Fig. 1 shows the real meningitis management process in Brazil; Fig. 2 adapts that behavior according to our proposal, showing the interdependence among models. Once a patient arrives to a health center with meningitis suspected symptoms, DM1 is in charge of deciding whether s/he has meningitis. If it suggests that the patient has meningitis, the physician can submit the patient information to DM2 [4], in order to determine the potential severity of that pathology. It will determine the probability of having MD. In this way, when the patient is in the initial evaluation, and before being hospitalized and start laboratory tests, our system could predict, practically at the same time, if the patient has meningitis and if it is MD.

If s/he is positive for DM1, or DM1 and DM2, and according to the Brazilian guide, the patient should immediately receive the first dose of an empirical antibiotic (in the health center of the municipality or in the rural area). Then, the patient would be derived to a hospital to start the conventional invasive tests to confirm the diagnosis and to determine the concrete type of meningitis.

Once all the required tests have been performed at the hospital, this information is used as input of DM3, to determine the meningitis etiology, bacterial or aseptic, and depending of it continue with the most appropriate treatment (to continue the antimicrobial therapy in the bacterial case or interrupt it in the viral one). In this way, DM3 could help to diagnose the meningitis etiology in a short period of time (only some hours are needed to obtain the chemical and cytological results of the blood sample). The culture of CSF and/or blood in a specialized laboratory can takes 30 days to be ready.

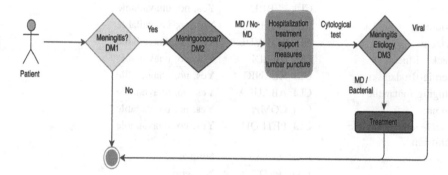

Fig. 2. Flowchart of meningitis diagnostic procedure of our models.

2.2 Meningitis Database

Meningitis database used in this work was obtained from SINAN. As we mentioned above, the database and its data dictionary were provided by the DIS of the SESAB. This database referred to 16,205 public and no identified records of suspected and confirmed meningitis cases occurred in Bahia, in the period from 2007 to 2013. SINAN meningitis database is designed using the criteria employed to meningitis management above mentioned (Fig. 1), i.e., suspected cases are also registered even if the final diagnosis (classification and meningitis type) does not confirm the suspicion.

The complete database is composed of 69 attributes related to: patient profile, date of the case, case classification, vaccination, contacts before and after manifestation of the disease, signs and symptoms, hospitalization, procedures realized and chemical and cytological analysis. Table 1 illustrates the selection of attributes that have been used in the studies performed in this paper. Note that the patient age is not included in the database. It however contained the birthdate and the date in which the patient was first attended by a physician. Using the difference between these two values, the age of each individual was obtained. The selected attributes met the data requirements of the decision models developed in this work, and they will be better detailed in the following sections. The remaining discarded attributes contained information concerning to some personal data, vaccinations, contacts of patients with suspected cases, hospitalization and others clinical tests performed, not interesting for the goals of this work.

Table 1. Selected attributes from SINAN meningitis database.

Attribute	Name in database	Possible values
Age		=<5, >5, missing
Living zone	CS_ZONA	Urban and peri-urban, rural, unavailable
Sex	CS_SEXO	M, F, unavailable
Headache	CLI_CEFALE	Yes, no, unavailable
Fever	CLI_FEBRE	Yes, no, unavailable
Vomiting	CLI_VOMITO	Yes, no, unavailable
Seizures	CLI_CONVUL	Yes, no, unavailable
Neck stiffness	CLI_RIGIDE	Yes, no, unavailable
Kernig/Brudzinski	CLI_KERNIG	Yes, no, unavailable
Bulging fontanelle	CLI_ABAULA	Yes, no, unavailable
Coma	CLI_COMA	Yes, no, unavailable
Petechiae/hemorrhagic suffusion	CLI_PETEQU	Yes, no, unavailable
Leucocytes	LAB_LEUCO	Numeric
Protein	LAB_PROT	Numeric
Glycorrhachia	LAB_GLICO	Numeric
Neutrophils	LAB_NEUTRO	Numeric
Lymphocytes	LAB_LINFO	Numeric
CSF aspect	LAB_ASPECT	(1) Cleared (2) Purulent (3) Hemorrhagic (4) Murky (5) Xanthochromic (6) Other (7) Ignored (8) Unavailable
Case classification	CLASSI_FIN	Confirmed, Discarded, Unavailable
Type of causative agent	CON_DIAGES	(1) Meningococcemia (2) Meningococcal meningitis (3) Meningococcal meningitis with meningococcemia (4) Tuberculous meningitis (5) Meningitis by other bacteria (6) Unspecified meningitis (7) Aseptic meningitis (8) Meningitis due to other etiology (9) Meningitis by haemophilus (10) Pneumococcal meningitis

Aiming to delimit the scope of this study, we grouped the 10 types of causative agents (Table 1) into 4 groups, taking into account the probable etiological origin of the disease: (1) Meningococcal Disease (types 1, 2, 3), (2) BM (types 5, 9, 10), (3) AM (type 7) and, (4) tuberculous meningitis, meningitis due to other etiology and unspecified meningitis (types 4, 6, 8). The percentages of incidence in SINAN database for each group were: 7.9%, 15.9%, 34.6% and 11.1% respectively. Due to the lower incidence and severity of its cases, the group 4 was not considered in the studies performed in this paper.

2.3 Data Preparation

As explained in above section, we had available patient database of over 16,000 registers with 69 attributes. Consequently, a previous stage of preprocessing was required to obtain the datasets needed to infer our data-driven classification models. Firstly, a previous stage of dimensionality reduction was performed. The goal was to reduce the number of features under consideration [12] to strictly those required to construct the models. Even though, in literature there are several techniques for this purpose, in our studies, feature selection has been done according to the requirement of our work, i.e. only to take symptoms or data that are directly observable or easy to be obtained (Table 1).

For the task of dimension reduction, we took into account the expertise of a physician, specialist in epidemiological diseases such as meningitis, who suggested us which symptomatic evidences could be obtained as soon as possible from a patient that is suspect of having meningitis. Accordingly, we selected nine symptoms available in the SINAN database, which can be observed directly and without requiring invasive tests. Headache, fever, vomiting, seizures, neck stiffness, Kernig/Brudzinski, bulging fontanelle, coma and petechiae were used. Furthermore, other three attributes were suggested by the medical doctor, that is, the living area (i.e. rural, urban or peri-urban), the patient gender and the patient age. In addition, the case classification and type of causative agent were also used, since it was necessary confirm or discard the diagnostics results inferred by the classification model. Finally, for DM3, it was employed some chemical and cytological analysis data (leucocytes, protein, glycorrhachia, neutrophils, lymphocytes and CSF aspect). These attributes are easily obtained by means of a chemical and cytological analysis of a blood sample.

2.4 Performance Evaluation Indicators

As will be explained in the next subsections, we have conducted several studies to determine the classification models, which best fits our dataset. Several statistical measures have been employed to evaluate the diagnostic ability of the binary classifiers. Usually, in order to discover the accuracy of a prediction, the confusion matrix (or contingency table) is built first. It is a two-by-two matrix representing the dispositions of the set of instances, which relates the predictive power of the model with the real data, and it also forms the basis for many common metrics [22]. For example, in the BM diagnosis (Table 4), TP cases are those where the model predicts that the patient has BM

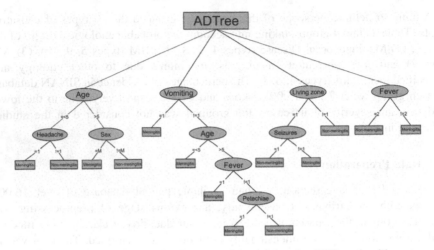

Fig. 3. DM1. Resulting decision tree after applying the ADTree algorithm.

and s/he does actually has it. Otherwise, it would be a FN. If the patient was diagnosed with BM by the model, but however s/he actually does not have it, we get a FP. Otherwise a TN is returned. Additionally, some evaluation parameters were used to measure the accuracy of the prediction models. TP-Rate (TP/TP+FN), FN-Rate (FN/TP +FN), FP-Rate (FP/FP+TN), TN-Rate (TN/FP+FN), precision, recall, specificity, F-measure, accuracy and ROC area were the parameters selected. Statistical analyses to obtain the data-driven decision models have been performed using the Waikato Environment for Knowledge Analysis tool (WEKA).

Table 2. Performance of Decision Models on 10-fold cross-validation.

Model	DM1				DM3 (Bacterial)	DM3 (Aseptic)
	J48	Random Forest	Naive Bayes	ADTree		
TP-Rate	0.860	0.846	0.858	0.859	0.797	0.848
FN-Rate	0.140	0.154	0.142	0.142	0.203	0.152
TN-Rate	0,744	0.748	0.746	0.768	0.847	0.713
FP-Rate	0.256	0.252	0.254	0.237	0.153	0.287
Precision	0.809	0.803	0.809	0.821	0.611	0.907
Recall	0.810	0.803	0.809	0.859	0.797	0.848
F-Measure	0.809	0.803	0.808	0.839	0.692	0.877
ROC	0.826	0.847	0.854	0.869		
Specificity	0.804	0.790	0.802	0.762	0.847	0.712

A validation process is required to determine whether the constructed model is able to provide accurate estimates of having meningitis or on determining the type of meningitis. Cross-validation is one of the most accepted validation techniques and is used to estimate the accuracy of a model that will be implemented in practice. Its goal is to ensure that the results of a prediction model are independent from the data used to construct it. For this purpose, datasets are split into two parts several times and the algorithm for generating the prediction model is applied each time changing the part used for generation and, consequently, the part used for model validation. Finally, average of the measurements obtained from evaluating different partitions is used as a model performance indicator. When a K-fold cross-validation is performed, sample data are divided into K subsets. One of the subsets is used for the test data and the remaining (K-1) as training data. The cross-validation process is repeated for K iterations, with each one of the possible subsets of test data. In this paper, we used 10-fold cross-validation, which is probably the most extended value.

3 Results

3.1 Meningitis Classification Decision Model (DM1)

Objective: The goal of this model is to assist in the classification of a symptomatic patient, i.e., to help with discarding or prioritizing of the attendance of a suspicious case of meningitis, without specifying its etiology. It is based only on non-invasive aspects of a patient that is, taking into account only the symptoms presented by the patient when he/she arrives at the health facility, before performing any laboratory tests.

Data Preprocessing: We selected nine symptoms directly observed above mentioned, living area, sex, age and case classification. Medical guidelines used in this work [1–3] indicate that meningitis symptoms in children could not be as evident as in adults. These documents clearly highlight that the most vulnerable group are children under (or equal to) 5 years old. Even children younger than 9 months may not have the classical signs of meningeal irritation. In this group, other signs may be present: bulging fontanelle, irritability, persistent crying, problems of suckling, etc., but except for bulging fontanelle, the SINAN dataset has not specific fields for children younger than 9 months old. For this reason, regard the patient age, and taking into account the advises of medical expert, we have set the age threshold in 5 years old, having as a result, two categories in the age attribute. In addition, we removed all records with missing or unknown values for the selected attributes, since to infer our model using supervised techniques these values were required. After it, 4,512 instances remained on training dataset. Then, we explored different classification algorithms (J48, ADTree, Random Forest, Naive Bayes ...) to see which one showed the best performance results. Alternating Decision Tree (ADTree) was the classifier that exhibited the best results. Figure 3 shows the decision tree obtained after applying the ADTree algorithm. The following attributes were selected by this algorithm to generate the model: age, living zone, sex, headache, fever, vomiting, seizures and petechiae.

Validation: DM1 10-fold cross-validation performance indicators are presented in the first four columns of Table 2, where those techniques showing best performance were included. In addition, Table 4 contains the confusion matrix, the first one, corresponding to DM1 performance evaluation.

3.2   Etiology Identification Decision Model (DM3)

Objective: This model was built to identify the probable etiological origin of the disease among the most frequent causative agents: bacterium or virus. Unlike the previous one, it is based on data obtained from the CSF chemical and cytological analysis (blood sample). In addition, this decision rule-based model has not been learnt from data but from the human expert knowledge, taking into account the CPGs suggestions. Table 3 summarizes the characteristics of the clinical analysis that determine the type of etiology (bacterial or aseptic) for this model [3]. Trying to find the best one, several decision rules were tested using data stored in our dataset, such us: leucocytes, protein, chlorides, glycorrhachia, neutrophils, lymphocytes and CSF aspect. However, the rules that exhibited the best result did not use all these attributes.

Following the medical expert's recommendations, we grouped the six possible types of CSF aspect that can be found in dataset only in two groups, i.e., clear and turbid. This last group involves the following values: purulent, hemorrhagic, murky, xanthochromic or other. In addition, we did not use the attribute *microscopy* (row 2) because these data are better specified in the attribute *leucocytes* (row 7), which takes only two values: lymphocytes or neutrophils. Table 3 suggests that CSF findings in cases of bacterial meningitis are: turbid aspect, predominance of polymorph nuclear cells, leucocytes greater than 500 per mm^3 being, among them, neutrophils from 200 to thousands, reduced chlorides, increased protein and reduced glycorrhachia.

Table 3. CSF chemical and cytological analysis interpretation (GES 2009)

Laboratorial diagnosis	Normal	Bacterial	Aseptic
Aspect	Clear	Turbid	Clear
Microscopy	Lymph mononuclear	Predominance of polymorph nuclear	Mononuclear (lymphocyte & monocytes)
Chlorides	Normal	Reduced	Normal
Leucocytes mm^3	<5	>500	<500
Protein mg/dl	Adults: 15 to 40 Newborns: <120	>100 Increased	15 to 40 Slightly increased
Glycorrhachia mg/dl	2/3 of the blood glucose value	Reduced	Normal
Leucocytes		200 to Thousands (neutrophils)	5 to 500 (lymphocytes)

Some values of the CSF attribute were not explicit in Table 3; instead we use categories following the medical literature recommendations. For instance, chloride is labelled as "reduced" if its value is lower than 120 [23]. We have conducted several experiments to determine the rule that leads to the most accurate diagnostics of bacterial meningitis. When we added chloride in the rule the hits increase a lot, reaching 115 of 117 tested cases, that is, 92.7% of accuracy. However, many cases of aseptic meningitis also were diagnosed as being bacterial, increasing the errors of diagnosis of this second type. This means that many cases of aseptic can also present reduction of chlorides, leading DM3 to a worse performance. For this reason, we chose not to use chloride values in the decision rule.

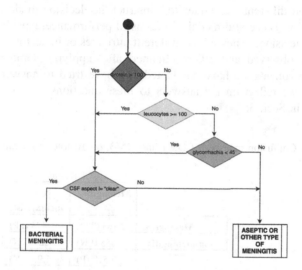

Fig. 4. Etiology Decision Model, DM3: Bacterial Meningitis

Furthermore, decreased glucose levels in CSF are important data for the bacterial meningitis diagnosis. For reduced glycorrhachia we found in the literature the threshold value of 40 [23]. However, in our tests we found slightly better results (two percentage points) when we changed that threshold to 45. Accordingly, for bacterial meningitis (including MD cases), we achieved the best results, that is, the greatest number of correct diagnoses, employing the decision model on the Fig. 4. Decision rule coded in that model, states that: if any of the conditions for protein or leucocytes or glycorrhachia are met and, at the same time, the CSF aspect is not "clear", DM3 will consider it a BM case. On the other hand, for AM (viral), Table 3 suggests that CFS findings are the following: clear aspect, predominance of mononuclear cells, leucocytes less than 500 per mm^3 being, among them, lymphocytes from 5 to 500, protein slightly increased, i.e., from 15 to 40 and normal glycorrhachia. The best rule we found is coded in the decision model on the Fig. 5. This rule states that, if the patient was not previously identified as a bacterial case and meets any of the conditions of that rule, is considered an aseptic case. **Validation:** To perform the validation of these DMs, the records set were grouped according to the valued stored in meningitis type attribute

(CON_DIAGES, Table 1). Moreover, the records with missing data of the attributes employed in the rules were deleted. These actions reduced the number of records to 6,350 cases. Last two columns of Table 2 show the performance of this model when a 10-fold cross-validation has been performed. Note that in these cases, ROC value does not make sense, since there is no a probability value generated after applying the rules unlike the other model evaluation. Table 4 contains the confusion matrices, the last two, corresponding to DM3 performance evaluation.

4   Discussion

We have explored different techniques to construct the decision models described in this paper. The most successful models, in terms of performance, have been chosen to support medical decisions. They all use different attributes or indicators as input; some of them directly observed and others obtained after applying some medical tests. Through the experiments we have conducted, we have tried to answer our research questions. Next, we reflect on the answers to these questions in terms of statistical evidence shown in Sect. 3:

Table 4. Confusion matrices of DM1 and DM3, on 10-fold cross-validation

		Reality	
		Meningitis	**Non-meningitis**
Prediction	**Meningitis**	2,163 (TP)	473 (FP)
	Non-meningitis	355 (FN)	1,521 (TN)
		2,518 (P)	1,994 (N)

		Reality	
		Bacterial	**Non-bacterial**
Prediction	**Bacterial**	1,169 (TP)	745 (FP)
	Non-bacterial	297 (FN)	4,139 (TN)
		1,466 (P)	4,884 (N)

		Reality	
		Aseptic	**Non-aseptic**
Prediction	**Aseptic**	4,139 (TP)	421 (FP)
	Non- aseptic	745 (FN)	1,045 (TN)
		4,884 (P)	1,466 (N)

(RQ1) Can a patient be reliably diagnosed as having meningitis? One of the main goals here was to give physicians data-driven diagnostic evidence to confirm having or not having meningitis. The evolution of this disease strongly depends on the timeliness of the treatment. Delays in proper medication or in carrying out invasive medical tests could lead in many cases to death. As mentioned, less-developed countries or some areas of the

world are often unable to provide adequate care due to a lack of resources. For this reason, it is essential to have at least some kind of well-founded evidence that can help physicians perform early diagnostics to find the suitable treatment of a patient. Our proposal uses patient information that can be obtained quickly and easily to determine if a patient has meningitis or not, even before he/she is hospitalized and the laboratory tests started. The ADTree algorithm exhibited the best performance for this purpose with a precision of over 80%. Furthermore, the F-measure which is a performance indicator relating precision and recall also provides a value of over 0.8. Finally, the model's performance was measured by area under the ROC curve. An area value of almost 0.87 was achieved; a value of over 0.80 is traditionally considered to be good. ROC is commonly used in medical decision making, and in recent years has been increasingly adopted by the machine learning and data mining research communities [22].

(RQ2) Can it be determined the etiological origin of the disease? To answer this question, we have counted with specialized documentation on this topic, i.e. CPGs and other documents from Brazilian Ministry of Health, and mainly with the expert knowledge of physicians. Unfortunately, to confirm a diagnosis of this type, where the disease's etiological origin needs to be determined, medical tests are needed. Although, unlike the CSF culture, only a few hours are needed to obtain the chemical and cytological results of the blood sample. In terms of the attributes measured in those tests and following both the recommendations found in literature and the advice of physicians, several models were defined and tested in order to find those that demonstrated the best performance for the more common etiological cases of meningitis, i.e. bacterial and aseptic. To build the model we only took into account those attributes about which we had information in the dataset provided by SINAN, and that were originally obtained from the chemical and cytological analyses. Several combinations of those attributes were tested, tuning them with different parameter values. The best decision rules were coded in the decision models, DM3, represented in Figs. 4 and 5. Attributes such as CSF aspect, leucocytes and proteins are significant for both models. A BM diagnosis also requires information about glycorrhachia, whereas the AM model includes an attribute on lymphocytes values. The DM3 results from the experiments conducted with the AM cases show similar results regarding DM1, i.e. values in general greater than 0.8. In the case of BM, DM3 results show a worse performance where the lowest indicator value is precision with 0.61 and the greatest is specificity with 0.85.

An average of 20% FN rate can be found in our three models. We have studied and analyzed the input data in order to find the reason of that results. We have concluded that most of these cases could correspond to erroneous input data. Note that the original dataset contained many errors since this information was collected manually by medical staff of health centers. At the beginning of this research we filtered and fixed most of them attending to criteria of coherence and consistency suggested by the experts. We suspect however that most of those FN cases correspond to incorrect information since other similar cases (with the same values in predictors) led to correct diagnostics.

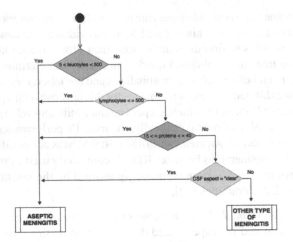

Fig. 5. Etiology Decision Model, DM3: Aseptic Meningitis.

5 Conclusions and Further Work

In this paper, we have presented two knowledge-based decision support models, whose goal is to help physicians in the diagnostic of meningitis. Meningitis is one of the pandemic diseases that many less developed countries suffer especially due to the lack of economic resources to face it. More severe type of meningitis demand immediate medical attention, since delays increase the mortality risks. The main goal of this work has been, therefore, provide tools to accomplish an early meningitis diagnostic, mainly through observable symptoms, and to give support to physicians to avoid the mandatory treatments for those cases where they are un-useful. Our models can predict if a patient has meningitis before being hospitalized and starting laboratory invasive tests; and it also can help to perform an early diagnostic on meningitis etiology. The nature and peculiarities of experimental data and expert knowledge used in the models proposed have been discussed. For this purpose, we used the dataset provided by the DIS of the SESAB, with over 16,000 meningitis patients' records from 2007 to 2013.

With respect to the near future work, we are currently working on the development of an agent-based architecture, which integrates our set of clinical decision support models in the meningitis diagnostics, into an environment to help physicians on decision support on meningitis. The goal is to provide them with a tool with an easy and usable interface, which should be also able to detect potential epidemics and notify them to the suitable medical authorities. The results provided by these three models can provide useful information to medical services to early diagnose meningitis. However, their diagnostics should be only taken as an evidence to support the medical decisions, since the percentage of FN is around 20%. In this sense, we are collecting new patient data to explore the validity of our models.

References

1. Tunkel, A.R., et al.: Practice guidelines for the management of bacterial meningitis. Clin. Infect. Dis. **39**(9), 1267–1284 (2004). https://doi.org/10.1086/425368
2. WHO: World Health Organization: Meningococcal meningitis. Fact sheet N°141 (2015)
3. GES: Brasil, Ministéio da Saùde, Secretaria de Vigilância em Saùde. Guide to Epidemiological Surveillance. 7th edn. Chapter 12, pp. 21–47 (2009). http://bvsms.saude.gov.br/bvs/publicacoes/guia_vigilancia_epidemiologica_7ed.pdf
4. Lelis, V.M., Guzmán, E., Belmonte, M.V.: A Statistical Classifier to Support Diagnose Meningitis in Less Developed Areas of Brazil. J. Med. Systems **41**, 145 (2017)
5. Ozaydin, B., Hardin, J.M., Chhieng, D.C.: Data mining and clinical decision support systems. In: Berner, E. (ed.) Clinical Decision Support Systems. Health Informatics. Springer, Cham (2016). https://doi.org/10.1007/978-3-319-31913-1_3
6. Shortliffe, E.H., Davis, R., Axline, S.G., Buchanan, B.G., Green, C.C., Cohen, S.N.: Computer-based consultations in clinical therapeutics: explanation and rule acquisition capabilities of the MYCIN system. Comput. Biomed. Res. **1975**(8), 303–320 (1975)
7. Shirabad, J.S., Wilk, S., Michalowski, W., Farion, K.: Implementing an integrative multi-agent clinical decision support system with open source software. J. Med. Syst. **36**(1), 123–137 (2012)
8. Han, J., Rodriguez, J.C., Beheshti, M.: Discovering decision tree based diabetes prediction model. In: Kim, T., Fang, W.C., Lee, C., Arnett, K.P. (eds.) ASEA 2008. Communications in Computer and Information Science, vol. 30. Springer, Heidelberg (2009). https://doi.org/10.1007/978-3-642-10242-4_9
9. Farion, K., Michalowski, W., Wilk, S., O'Sullivan, D., Matwin, S.: A tree-based decision model to support prediction of the severity of asthma exacerbations in children. J. Med. Syst. **34**(4), 551–562 (2010)
10. Alickovic, E., Subasi, A.: Medical decision support system for diagnosis of heart arrhythmia using DWT and random forests classifier. J. Med. Syst. **40**(4), 108 (2016)
11. Huang, M.L., Chen, H.Y.: Glaucoma classification model based on GDx VCC measured parameters by decision tree. J. Med. Syst. **34**(6), 1141–1147 (2010)
12. Ting, H., Mai, Y.T., Hsu, H.C., Wu, H.C., Tseng, M.H.: Decision tree based diagnostic system for moderate to severe obstructive sleep apnea. J. Med. Syst. **38**(9), 94 (2014)
13. Chao, C.M., Yu, Y.W., Cheng, B.W., Kuo, Y.L.: Construction the model on the breast cancer survival analysis use support vector machine, logistic regression and decision tree. J. Med. Syst. **38**(10), 106 (2014)
14. Abdar, M., Zomorodi-Moghadam, M., Das, R., Ting, I.H.: Performance analysis of classification algorithms on early detection of liver disease. Expert Syst. Appl. **67**, 239–251 (2017)
15. Yeh, D.Y., Cheng, C.H., Chen, Y.W.: A predictive model for cerebrovascular disease using data mining. Expert Syst. Appl. **38**(7), 8970–8977 (2011)
16. Mago, V.K., Mehta, R., Woolrych, R., Papageorgiou, E.: Supporting meningitis diagnosis amongst infants and children through the use of fuzzy cognitive maps. BMC Med. Inform. Decis. Mak. **12**, 98 (2012)
17. Ocampo, E., Maceiras, M., Herrera, S., Maurente, C., Rodríguez, D., Sicilia, M.A.: Comparing Bayesian inference case-based reasoning as support techniques in the diagnosis of Acute Bacterial Meningitis. Expert Syst. Appl. **38**, 10343–10354 (2011)
18. Revett, K., Gorunescu, F., Goronesu, M., Ene, M.: A machine learning approach to differentiating bacterial from viral meningitis. In: IEEE International Symposium on Modern Computing (2006)

19. Gowin, E., Januszkliewicz-Lewandowska, D., Slowinski, R., Blaszczynski, J., Michalak, M., Wysocki, J.: With a little help from a computer: discriminating between bacterial and viral meningitis based on dominance-based rough set approach analysis. Medicine **96**, 32 (2017)
20. Weitzel, L., Teixeira de Assis, J., Soares, A.: Medical training simulation system to assist novice physicians in diagnostics problem solving. In: Proceedings of the 6th WSEAS International Conference on Neural Networks, Lisbon, pp. 239–243 (2005)
21. TNS: Technical note SUS: Case definition and epidemiological surveillance, Josué Laguardia and Maria Lúcia Penna. Inf. Epidemiol. SUS v.8 n.4, Brasília, December 1999
22. Fawcett, T.: ROC graphs: notes and practical considerations for researchers. Mach. Learn. **31** (1), 1–38 (2004)
23. Mejía, G., Ramelli, M.: Interpretación clínica del laboratorio. Ed. Médica Panam (2006)

Position Papers

A Framework to Conduct and Report on Empirical User Studies in Semantic Web Contexts

Catia Pesquita[1]([⊠]), Valentina Ivanova[2], Steffen Lohmann[3],
and Patrick Lambrix[2]

[1] LASIGE, Faculdade de Ciências da Universidade de Lisboa, Lisbon, Portugal
`clpesquita@fc.ul.pt`
[2] Linköping University, Linköping, Sweden
`patrick.lambrix@liu.se`
[3] Fraunhofer IAIS, Sankt Augustin, Germany
`steffen.lohmann@iais.fraunhofer.de`

Abstract. Semantic Web technologies are being applied to increasingly diverse areas where user involvement is crucial. While a number of user interfaces for Semantic Web systems have become available in the past years, their evaluation and reporting often still suffer from weaknesses. Empirical evaluations are essential to compare different approaches, demonstrate their benefits and reveal their drawbacks, and thus to facilitate further adoption of Semantic Web technologies. In this paper, we review empirical user studies of user interfaces, visualizations and interaction techniques recently published at relevant Semantic Web venues, assessing both the user studies themselves and their reporting. We then chart the design space of available methods for user studies in Semantic Web contexts. Finally, we propose a framework for their comprehensive reporting, taking into consideration user expertise, experimental setup, task design, experimental procedures and results analysis.

Keywords: Semantic Web · Empirical evaluation · User study
User interface · Literature review · Design space · Protocol · Reporting

1 Motivation

The Semantic Web enables intelligent agents to create knowledge by interpreting, integrating and drawing inferences from the abundance of data at their disposal. It encompasses approaches and techniques for expressing and processing data in machine-readable formats. Semantic Web technologies are being applied to increasingly diverse areas where user involvement is crucial. Providing carefully designed user interfaces, visual representations and interaction techniques has the potential to foster a wider adoption of Semantic Web technologies and to lead to higher quality results in different application contexts where ontologies and Linked Data are employed.

© Springer Nature Switzerland AG 2018
C. Faron Zucker et al. (Eds.): EKAW 2018, LNAI 11313, pp. 567–583, 2018.
https://doi.org/10.1007/978-3-030-03667-6_36

As the number of user interfaces for Semantic Web systems is growing, one important step is to evaluate their capabilities and features in order to reveal their usefulness together with their advantages and disadvantages. As organizers of the VOILA workshop series[1], we noticed that both the assessment of interactive Semantic Web approaches as well as the reporting on conducted user studies still suffer from weaknesses.

We can basically distinguish at least three evaluation approaches: (i) *formal evaluation*, based on defined models, for instance, a cost-based model where costs are assigned to different user actions executed in order to achieve a certain goal; (ii) *automated evaluation*, aiming to reveal computational—as opposed to visual—scalability and efficiency of approaches and algorithms, and (iii) *empirical evaluation*, based on the observation of users who interact with a system. In this paper, we focus on this latter category—empirical evaluation.

In short, empirical evaluation refers to the testing of user interfaces by real users. The various methods are usually categorized into quantitative methods (e.g., controlled experiments) and qualitative methods (e.g., inspection methods). Drawing from relevant literature [1], all common evaluation methods exhibit to a different extent the following factors: (i) *generalizability* (or external validity, i.e., the extent to which the results apply beyond the immediate setting, time and participants), (ii) *precision* (or internal validity, i.e., the degree to which one can be definite about the measurements that were taken and about the control of the factors that were not intended to be studied) and (iii) *realism* (or ecological validity, i.e., the degree to which the experimental situation reflects the type of environment in which the approach will be applied); they serve different purposes and are eventually conducted during different stages of user interface development (e.g., formative vs. summative evaluations).

Regarding external validity, one differentiating aspect in conducting empirical evaluations for the Semantic Web versus other fields of study is that users of Semantic Web tools can typically not be categorized along a single axis of expertise. Considering that Semantic Web tools are often used in domains where information complexity is an issue (e.g., life sciences, governance, health care), it becomes essential to be able to understand user expertise both with the domain that underlies the data being used and explored by the tool, but also with knowledge modeling and representation concepts. This poses challenges in assessing population validity, since both expertise axes need to be considered.

Another issue is the generalizability to other situations, for instance, when applying an approach to different datasets, especially those with varying degrees of semantic complexity. Ecological validity (i.e., the degree to which the experimental situation reflects the type of environment in which the approach will be applied) is also of particular concern in Semantic Web contexts, since both population and dataset characteristics need to be accounted for.

In this paper, we present a review of empirical evaluations published in the Semantic Web community in recent years (Sect. 2). We then discuss the design

---

[1] VOILA: International workshop series on "Visualization and Interaction for Ontologies and Linked Data", see http://voila.visualdataweb.org.

space of evaluation methods for interactive Semantic Web systems (Sect. 3), and use this as a springboard to outline a protocol for reporting on user studies in Semantic Web contexts (Sect. 4). The design space and protocol together constitute a framework for conducting and reporting on empirical user studies in Semantic Web contexts. In Sects. 5 and 6, we summarize related work and provide a discussion, before we conclude the paper in Sect. 7.

2 Literature Review of User Studies in Semantic Web Contexts

We define a user study in the context of the Semantic Web (SW) as any user-based empirical evaluation of a system, tool or method that employs SW technologies. The purpose of the evaluation may span different aspects, such as the assessment of graphical user interfaces, ontology and Linked Data visualizations or user interaction techniques.

2.1 Methodology

We conducted a literature review covering the following four conference and workshop series dedicated to the SW, in their 2015, 2016 and 2017 editions: (i) ISWC (International Semantic Web Conference), (ii) ESWC (Extended Semantic Web Conference), (iii) VOILA (International Workshop on Visualization and Interaction for Ontologies and Linked Data) and (iv) IESD (International Workshop on Intelligent Exploration of Semantic Data). The first two venues were selected given their primacy in SW-dedicated conferences, whereas the latter two for their specific targeting of user interaction and visualization in SW contexts.

We restricted the review to papers where the expressions "user study", "user evaluation", "empirical evaluation", "interaction" and/or "visualization" appeared in the abstract—also taking into account spelling differences (e.g., "Visualization" and "visualisation") and word form variations (e.g., plural forms). This resulted in a total of 87 papers. All papers were analyzed in their entirety and split into three groups: (i) papers that include a report of a user study (46 papers); (ii) papers that do not report on a user study but present a SW approach addressing user interactions (35 papers); (iii) papers that do not report on a user study and do not present an interactive approach, such as position papers (six papers).

This distribution can already be seen as an indicator of the lack of user studies in SW publications that report on a system, tool or method concerned with user interaction.

Each paper of the first group was further categorized within three aspects: (i) *purpose*, (ii) *users* and iii) *evaluation methods*. We followed an inductive analysis approach to identify the major categories or themes within each aspect [2]. Each paper was assigned a category and code to reflect a relevant characteristic. For instance, Mitschick et al. [3] write that their "[...] interface provides an expressive but still approachable way of querying for specific entities and their accompanied information" and thus was assigned the code *querying* under the *purpose* category.

A running list of codes was shared between all four coders (all researchers, namely the authors of this paper) to ensure code reuse when possible. After each paper was coded by one researcher, the full list of codes was edited to ensure coherence and remove any remaining duplicates, and codes were organized in a hierarchy. For *purpose*, we defined two broad categories: *learning & understanding* and *creating & managing*; for *users*, we defined *participant number, participant expertise* and *participant recruitment*; and for *evaluation method*, we defined *quantitative* and *qualitative*. Finally, the code assignment for each paper was revised by at least two of the other researchers.

The classification resulting from the literature review and coding is available as a table on the Web, published under a Creative Commons license.[2]

2.2 Purpose

Purpose describes the general intent of the operations[3] supported by the evaluated approach. We induced a list of operations from the reviewed papers, which fit into two broad categories: *learning & understanding* and *creating & managing*. *Learning & understanding* is concerned with information and knowledge acquisition needs, whereas the purpose of *creating & managing* operations is the creation of new content, its manipulation and lifecycle support. These categories are further discussed in Sect. 3. The results of the classification are listed in Table 1. Note that several of the users studies reported in the 46 papers looked at more than one operation type and purpose.

Table 1. Purposes and operations reported in papers that included user studies

Purpose	Operation	N. of user studies
Learning & understanding	Exploration	17
	Navigation	1
	Search	8
	Querying	10
	Question answering	1
	Explanation	2
Creating & managing	Modeling	10
	Editing	9
	Validation	1
	Mapping	1
	Annotation	5

---

[2] The classified papers can be accessed at: http://survey.visualdataweb.org.

[3] We use the term *operation* instead of *task* here to differentiate it from *evaluation tasks*.

Our systematic literature review revealed that the majority of works aim to support information exploration and seeking behaviors. These behaviors differ from navigation and information retrieval where users' information needs and questions of interest can be specified and expressed in advance before an interaction with a SW approach. Information exploration activities are usually more open-ended with evolving (on the basis of current observations) information needs, personal experience, motivation and context. These are high-level complex activities characterized by uncertainty and acquiring unexpected findings as the exploration progresses. Users may lack knowledge in the area of interest (often referred to as *exploratory search* [4]) or may possess domain expertise, without being familiar with a particular multi-dimensional dataset (and employing an exploratory environment to understand and use it).

2.3   Users

Regarding users, we classified the papers according to three aspects: (i) *participant number*, (ii) *participant expertise* and (iii) *participant recruitment*. Table 2 shows the result of this classification. The categories are non-exclusive, i.e., in several studies, users with diverse areas and levels of expertise are recruited. Further, a couple of papers included more than one user study with different numbers of participants.

Table 2. Distribution of the reviewed papers according to user aspects

User aspect	Category	N. of user studies
Participant number	Not reported	3
	1–9	9
	10–19	16
	20–29	18
	30+	8
Participant expertise	Not reported	4
	SW	14
	IT	10
	Domain	8
	Non-expert	12
	Diverse	14
Participant recruitment	Not reported	25
	Researchers	4
	Students	11
	Clients/users	4
	Crowdsourcing	1

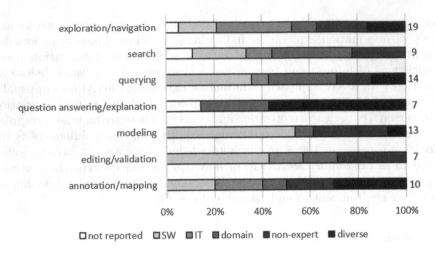

Fig. 1. User expertise by type of purpose and operation. The numbers on the right indicate the total numbers of user studies within each operation.

The majority of user studies were conducted with sample sizes between ten and 29 participants. Of the 46 reported studies, 14 employ a diverse mixture of participants, while only four do not mention any user area and/or level of expertise. The situation is less encouraging with regards to the used recruitment method. Nearly none of the papers explicitly reports the method used to recruit the study participants. Some do (more or less detailed) indicate the population to which the participants belong (e.g., students, researchers, etc.), so we took those as our (broad) recruitment categories. Still, more than half of the study reports do not include a description of the recruitment method they employed. Further, students were recruited as participants in eleven studies, which can be critical, as this may result in a sampling bias and can negatively affect the population validity when the participating students do not match well the needs and characteristics of the target population (i.e., the actual users of a SW tool, method or system).

To further understand the impact of participant expertise across user studies in SW contexts, we looked into each *purpose* category and determined the area of *participant expertise* within it (cf. Fig. 1). This revealed that the participant expertise is not uniformly distributed across purposes. One interesting finding is that domain expertise is more frequent in querying, search and question answering/explanation, and SW expertise clearly dominates in modeling, but also has a high prevalence in editing/validation and querying.

2.4   Evaluation Methods

Regarding the evaluation methods, ten studies report using qualitative strategies, while 39 employ quantitative approaches (cf. Table 3; note that the categories are non-exclusive again, i.e., a number of user studies applies more than one quantitative method). The most popular evaluation approach is the use of questionnaires. Surprisingly, standard questionnaires are only used in eight studies, whereas the authors of 20 studies apply their own custom questionnaires. More than half of the studies report using tasks in some fashion to support the evaluation. Of these, the majority records time to complete a task and uses success metrics or both (i.e., classical time and error measures). Few of the studies include comparative evaluations (eight in total), of which six use within-subjects designs and two use between-subjects designs. Although some study reports include detailed descriptions of the used evaluation methods and tasks (e.g., [5,6]), in most cases, only little space is dedicated to describing the design and procedure of the user evaluation (these descriptions often take up less than a page of the papers).

3 Design Space

The literature review we conducted revealed several limitations of empirical user studies in SW contexts that are shared by a majority of works. In the following, we chart the design space of such studies with the aim of giving SW researchers a guide to help them design and successfully conduct user studies. We have structured the design space into six dimensions: (i) purpose, (ii) users, (iii) tasks, (iv) setup, (v) procedure and (vi) analysis and presentation of data. For each dimension, we identify the main concerns to be taken into consideration, define categories to systematize procedures and techniques, and offer guidelines to support the design of adequate user studies. Based on these six dimensions, we then define the minimum information required to report on a user study in SW contexts.

Table 3. Distribution of reviewed papers according to evaluation method aspects

Type of evaluation	Category	N. of studies
Qualitative	Unspecified	7
	Observation	1
	Open interview	2
	Total number of studies	10
Quantitative	Standard questionnaire	8
	Custom questionnaire	20
	Task success	13
	Task time	2
	Task success and time	9
	Non-tracked task	3
	Comparative within subjects	6
	Comparative between subjects	2
	Total number of studies	39

3.1 Purpose

As already introduced, interactive SW approaches can typically be classified in two general categories based on their purpose: *learning & understanding* and *creating & managing*. Both categories include several high-level operations, which could also be present in the other category as supporting operations:

1. *Learning & understanding:* The main purpose of these approaches is to provide means for satisfying information needs and acquiring knowledge. This might be done due to different reasons, such as generating or validating a hypothesis, using a dataset or ontology in application development, looking up particular information or exploring a topic of personal interest due to curiosity. This category encompasses high-level tasks, such as exploration, navigation, search, querying and question answering (cf. Table 1). All of them aim at satisfying information needs, however, they differ in the extent the information need is defined at the beginning. Exploration is usually a more open-ended activity with vague initial goals which are evolving as it progresses (cf. Sect. 2.2). In comparison, direct search (as opposed to "exploratory search" [4] often mentioned in information retrieval) and querying have more clearly specified initial goals which might change as results are retrieved.
2. *Creating & managing:* the main purpose of these approaches is to provide means for creating and editing content. This might be authoring an ontology or creating a dataset by, for instance, creating mappings to publish content in various formats in RDF (high-level operations: modeling, editing and publishing data). Other operations might include linking datasets or ontologies, and discovering and resolving quality issues. This category also covers high-level tasks, such as documentation and annotation which create meta-data.

3.2 Users

More than half of the reviewed user studies have a reported *number of participants* too low to support quantitative analysis for user testing [7]. In fact, this may be one of the reasons why user studies are not common even in publications presenting systems for end-users. However, 10 ± 2 users have been reported to be often enough to detect 80% of the issues at least in qualitative usability studies [8]. Using crowdsourcing platforms may alleviate this issue, but it limits the type of evaluations that can be conducted [9].

Beyond concerns about the number of participants, SW researchers also need to take into consideration the skills and experiences of participants, since they can have an impact on the performance when using a SW approach to solve problems. Assessing user competence is a general concern in information systems research [10,11], and its importance is magnified in SW contexts [12,13], given that both *expertise of the participants* with SW concepts and with the domain at hand can impact user performance and experience. Due to the specificity and complexity of some of the domains where SW applications are applied (e.g., biomedicine, earth sciences), understanding the level of domain expertise required of target users and mapping it to the study participants should be a major focus of SW researchers designing user studies, since more significant conclusions can be drawn when there is a more significant overlap between the characteristics of study participants and target users, thus ensuring *population validity*. This is an increased concern in crowdsourced studies, where finding the 'right crowd' is still a challenge [14]. Also, recruitment strategies can have an impact on the results, due to bias (e.g., *selection bias* and *sampling bias*) as well as researchers who are testing their own tools (*experimenter bias*).

3.3   Tasks

Most of the reviewed SW user studies employ tasks as the basis for empirical evaluations. Defining tasks is typically an integral part of designing a user-based evaluation, more so in SW user studies where task complexity should be aligned with the different aspects of user expertise. To ensure *ecological validity*, the evaluation tasks should mirror typical tasks target users are expected to perform using the system, and their definition needs to be articulated with care, taking into account the user characterization as well as experimental setup and procedure. In SW user studies, it is particularly important when considering task performance to be able to discern if failure was due to the user's unfamiliarity with the domain of the SW resources being used, i.e., to ensure *construct validity* or, in other words, that the evaluation is measuring what it is supposed to measure. It is also crucial to take into consideration the characteristics of the datasets used in the evaluation, including their domain and semantic complexity. Understanding how these articulate with user expertise is necessary for an adequate interpretation of results.

A task needs also to coordinate with the evaluation method employed in the study, e.g., open-ended tasks may be best employed with *think-aloud* techniques, case studies or observation techniques, whereas specific action-based tasks will allow quantitative measures, such as time to complete and accuracy. The majority of the studies we reviewed report on approaches that have exploration as their main target purpose. Designing such environments involves computational and algorithmic approaches entangled with visualization and interaction techniques to foster information seeking behaviors. Due to the nature of exploratory behavior, designing tasks to support the evaluation of such environments presents a particular challenge [15].

3.4   Setup

Two aspects should be addressed regarding experimental setup: setting conditions and study design. Setting conditions can influence the result of a test, thus special attention should be devoted to minimizing the variance of non-tested conditions (room, lighting, display size, etc.), i.e., maximizing *internal validity*.

It is often advisable to perform a comparative study when there are similar approaches available that can be compared to. Such comparisons against a baseline are often well suited to show the benefits and limitations of a new piece of work. Only eight of the reviewed SW user studies used a comparative approach, with different designs. Most popular is a within-subjects design where the study participants are exposed to both approaches, i.e., they first interact with one approach and then with the other. In this setting, it is important to control for *order effects* (e.g., by *counter-balancing*).

An alternative is a between-subjects design, where the study participants are split into two groups and each group sees and evaluates only one of the approaches. However, a main drawback of the between-subjects design is that it usually requires a much larger number of study participants to get useful and reliable data. This might be the main reason why it was applied in only two of the reviewed studies.

If more than two approaches (or conditions) are compared, counterbalancing quickly multiplies and study designs using Latin Squares and other incomplete counterbalanced measures need to be applied. One paper in our study used a Latin Square design to compare different visual querying interfaces [5]. Naturally, the more complex the study design gets, the more complex the analysis and the higher the probability that errors are made in the analysis of the results. Thus, keeping the study design as simple as possible is usually advisable.

3.5   Procedure

Many of the reviewed user studies evaluate the usability of the proposed tool or system, and while most do so using custom questionnaires, eight studies use standard questionnaires, such as the popular System Usability Scale (SUS) or the Post-Study System Usability Questionnaire (PSSUQ). Usability commonly comprises of effectiveness, efficiency, and satisfaction, which can be evaluated in different ways: effectiveness is typically measured through task success, efficiency is measured through task speed, and satisfaction is measured through user feedback, as discussed in [16].

However, we observe that several of the reviewed user studies are limited to the evaluation of the usability of a tool or system, which is an important aspect but often not sufficient to fully evaluate an interactive system or tool and answer the research questions addressed in the work. In particular for exploratory tasks, which were very common in the reviewed user studies (cf. Table 1), cognitive measures are often required [17], such as looking at insights obtained while using an exploration tool [18] or associated metrics based on engagement, novelty, task success and time as well as learning [19].

Other ways to study exploratory behavior and cognitive processes is via eyetracking and the aforementioned think-aloud method. For instance, Fu et al. use eyetracking to compare indented lists and graphs as two different types of ontology visualizations [20]. Mitschick et al. applied a think-aloud method to learn about the cognitive model of the study participants [3].

3.6   Analysis and Presentation of Data

In a first step, data analysis concerns the collection and organization of data. There are several methods to compile and analyze both qualitative [21] and quantitative data [22].

When participants have diverse backgrounds and expertise levels and areas, it is useful to report separately on results for each group. In fact, comparative studies (either of several systems or of several user groups) pose additional challenges for experimental design and data analysis, especially when obtaining statistically significant results is a goal of the study. This requires a rigorous experimental design, in a much more controlled setting and with a larger sample of participants.

4   Reporting on Semantic Web User Studies

Our guidelines take inspiration from the molecular biology field where 'minimum information' guidelines to describe experiments were proposed quite early [23]. Our goal with defining the minimum information required to describe user studies in SW contexts is to ensure that the recorded information is sufficient to: (i) support the *interpretation* of the conducted user study; (ii) enable the *comparison* to similar evaluations; and (iii) permit the *replication* of the user study. These requirements imply that a detailed description of several aspects of the user study needs to be produced, and that the description should be as unambiguous as possible.

According to our guidelines, the minimum information about a user study in a SW context includes a description of the following six aspects:

1. **Purpose:** This aspect describes the general types of operations that are supported by the interactive approach under evaluation. We propose to categorize purposes into four non-exclusive types (the first two fall into the *learning & understanding* category and the last two in the *creating & modifying* category):
   - *exploration:* includes operations such as exploratory search, browsing and navigation; it can be applied to operations where the information need is not clearly defined or the goal is general discovery and insight generation;
   - *search:* includes search, querying and question answering; it applies to the more focused examination of SW content with a clear information need or specific target in mind;
   - *creation:* includes operations such as modeling ontologies or RDF content, and creating mappings between SW resources; it applies to tasks where SW content is created;
   - *management:* includes assessment, validation, annotation and editing of SW resources; it applies to operations where existing SW content is manipulated;

2. **Users:** This aspect contains information about the intended users of an approach, the participants of the user study and how well the two groups overlap. Many of the reviewed works do not describe their *target users*, which makes assessing the population validity nearly impossible.
   A proper description of target users should include expected demographics but also *expertise levels in both SW and the domain* covered by the approach. Likewise, the demographics together with the SW and domain expertise of the study participants should also be reported, as well as information on the *participant recruitment*, i.e., which type of participants were recruited (e.g., domain experts recruited from a company, students of a university course, etc.) and how they were recruited.

3. **Tasks:** This aspect describes the tasks required of the participants. We separate tasks from the experimental procedure, because the same tasks can be utilized with different procedures and systems (and vice-versa). To support interpretation and reproducibility as well as allow for comparison, the report should include the exact task descriptions (e.g., the task form) given to the participants. For multi-purpose systems, tasks should further be categorized according to their purpose. Furthermore, the data used in each task should also be reported on and made available when possible. Exact descriptions of tasks and data are essential to support the assessment of ecological validity.

4. **Setup:** The setup should clearly describe the *type of evaluation* (controlled experiment, field study, etc.) and the *setting and interaction context* of the study participants. Further information of relevance is the exact *experimental design of the study*, such as the independent and dependent variables measured. Descriptions of design types and assignment procedures are, for instance, described by Field and Hole [24].

5. **Procedure:** The different *phases* of the evaluation should be described in chronological order to provide the reader with a clear picture of the procedure from the moment the participants arrived to the moment they left. Common phases to cover are: introduction, briefing of users (ethical issues), form filling and questionnaire (demographic information, etc.), instruction material, training (if any) and the actual testing session, post-test interview, and debriefing. Examples of *issues* to report on are: whether any assistance was given; how the tasks were presented to the participants (on paper/on screen, etc.) and how they were executed; how responses were given (clicking on a button, using the keyboard, etc.), and the overall participation time.

6. **Analysis:** This aspect should report on the selected *data analysis method* and show awareness of potential biases. For quantitative analyses, it must also be clarified which *response measures* (dependent variables) were used for analysis, which type of statistical test was used and how this relates to the study design. Findings should be reported, together with the *test statistics* and any other descriptive measures. Also, the results from any standardized or custom questionnaires as well as observations made and relevant responses to any interview questions should be reported as part of this aspect.

5   Related Work

This work intersects with both usability testing and information visualization evaluation. In both domains there is a considerable body of literature concerning best practices and challenges in the design of experimental evaluations [22,25]. However, user studies in SW contexts have specific characteristics that require tailored approaches for their evaluation.

Some recent works by the SW community have focused on building resources to foster the evaluation of user interfaces and interactive Semantic Web tools. A catalog of aggregated statistics on user interactions with over 200 BioPortal ontologies was recently released, containing information of user clicks, queries and reuse counts for over half a million users in a 3-year period [26]. Dragisic et al. [12] have created benchmarks that simulate different levels of user expertise to evaluate robustness of interactive ontology alignment systems. In [27], Ivanova et al. provide a set of requirements that foster the user involvement for large-scale ontology alignment tasks. Gonzalez et al. [28] developed a quality in use model for Semantic Web Exploration Tools (SWETs). A framework of exploration operations was proposed by Nunes and Schwabe [29]. Combining these operations would result in more complex exploration tasks. A follow-up work [30] then describes an analytical evaluation framework based on it. In [31], Garcia et al. present a benchmark for SW user interface evaluation that provides data, tasks and an environment to measure low-level performance metrics (keystrokes and clicks). All twelve tasks fall under the exploration and search categories, and are focused on the evaluation of SW browsers. This interest in supporting the evaluation of exploratory interactions matches the results of our literature review where the most popular operation supported by the systems was exploration.

6   Discussion

Nearly half of the papers we reviewed did not present a user study despite presenting a system or tool with support for user interaction and graphical user interface. Few of the works that did conduct a user study reported enough detail to allow an adequate interpretation or even the reproducibility of the experiments.

One challenge for experimental design for SW interactive evaluation is that many times tools need to support diverse users. A classical dichotomy is the Knowledge Engineer vs. the Domain Expert. Another dimension opposes SW novices/laymen to SW experts. Of the 46 papers with user study reports we reviewed, only four conducted studies for SW experts and domain experts, and three for SW experts vs. novices. Designing experiments that take into account different areas and levels of expertise is necessary to support these types of tools. Determining expertise is another challenge, and only one study conducted a pre-assessment to stratify participants.

While ensuring both ecological and population validity is a concern in any user empirical evaluation, it is of particular importance in SW studies, where the impact of both user expertise and dataset characteristics can jeopardize the generalizability of conclusions.

One of the areas lacking detail was target user and participant description. Although demographical data was nearly always reported, recruitment strategies were generally not described. Getting students to evaluate systems is a common strategy, with well-known limitations [7]. Beyond bias issues, they represent a fairly homogeneous population that may not align well with the target users. We hypothesize that finding the right participants for the study may be one of the reasons behind the lack of user studies.

Another possible cause is lack of space in a publication. The thorough description of empirical evaluations requires a considerable amount of space, which can be difficult when faced with a page limit. When space is an issue, one might be forced to focus on the details most important to the outcome of the evaluation, and to those needed to enable the correct interpretation, replication, and comparison. However, the aim should always be to describe the conducted user evaluation as completely as possible, supporting the assessment and interpretation of the results. Although true reproducibility of user studies can be difficult—it is difficult enough to conduct a rigorous controlled experiment in one setting—providing a detailed description of the user study may allow for insightful comparisons between studies. This could, for instance, foster the evaluation of systems that have similar purposes and support similar operations, or the evaluation of the same system with different groups of users by a different research team. We would like to encourage SW researchers to make use of the publication of supplementary materials and other persistent data sharing options to provide detailed descriptions of their empirical evaluations if space does become an issue.

7   Conclusions

We have conducted a literature review of 87 papers published in Semantic Web venues between 2015 and 2017 that mention user interaction or visualization. Nearly half of these did not report on a user study, despite presenting approaches that supported user interaction. We classified the remainder according to the information they contained about the purpose and operations supported by the approaches under evaluation, study participants (number, expertise, recruitment) and evaluation methods employed.

The literature review served as the basis for charting the design space along six dimensions: (i) purpose, (ii) users, (iii) tasks, (iv) setup, (v) procedure and (vi) analysis and presentation of data. Based on these six dimensions, we proposed a protocol representing the minimum information required to report on a user study to ensure that it can be interpreted, compared and at best even replicated.

Our findings support our impression as VOILA organizers that comparatively few user studies are being conducted in SW contexts and that even fewer are reported adequately. However, the SW community seems to increasingly recognize the importance of evaluating interactive SW approaches, as indicated by the recent release of corresponding benchmarks and data collections. We hope that our discussion of the design space, and the framework composed by the guidelines, recommendations and reporting protocol we presented provides guidance and can foster the realization of more user studies for SW approaches with higher quality both in experimental design and in reporting. We aim as future work to validate the protocol by promoting its adoption within the VOILA community, a natural step in furthering the consolidation of user studies in SW contexts.

Acknowledgements. Catia Pesquita is funded by the Portuguese FCT through the LASIGE Strategic Project (UID/CEC/00408/2013), and also by FCT grant PTDC/EEI-ESS/4633/2014. Patrick Lambrix is funded by the Swedish e-Science Society (SeRC). Steffen Lohmann is partly funded by the Fraunhofer Cluster of Excellence Cognitive Internet Technologies (CIT).

References

1. McGrath, J.E.: Human-Computer Interaction, pp. 152–169. Morgan Kaufmann Publishers Inc., San Francisco (1995)
2. Thomas, D.R.: A general inductive approach for analyzing qualitative evaluation data. Am. J. Eval. **27**(2), 237–246 (2006)
3. Mitschick, A., Nieschalk, F., Voigt, M., Dachselt, R.: IcicleQuery: a web search interface for fluid semantic query construction. In: 3rd International Workshop on Visualization and Interaction for Ontologies and Linked Data. CEUR Workshop Proceedings, vol. 1947, pp. 99–110. CEUR-WS.org (2017)
4. Marchionini, G.: Exploratory search: from finding to understanding. Commun. ACM **49**(4), 41–46 (2006)
5. Vega-Gorgojo, G., Slaughter, L., Giese, M., Heggestøyl, S., Soylu, A., Waaler, A.: Visual query interfaces for semantic datasets: an evaluation study. J. Web Semant. **39**, 81–96 (2016)
6. Nuzzolese, A.G., Presutti, V., Gangemi, A., Peroni, S., Ciancarini, P.: Aemoo: linked data exploration based on knowledge patterns. Semant. Web **8**(1), 87–112 (2017)
7. Lazar, J., Feng, J.H., Hochheiser, H.: Research Methods in Human-Computer Interaction. Morgan Kaufmann, San Francisco (2017)
8. Hwang, W., Salvendy, G.: Number of people required for usability evaluation: the 10 ± 2 rule. Commun. ACM **53**(5), 130–133 (2010)
9. Kittur, A., Chi, E.H., Suh, B.: Crowdsourcing user studies with mechanical Turk. In: SIGCHI Conference on Human Factors in Computing Systems, pp. 453–456. ACM (2008)
10. Marcolin, B.L., Compeau, D.R., Munro, M.C., Huff, S.L.: Assessing user competence: conceptualization and measurement. Inf. Syst. Res. **11**(1), 37–60 (2000)
11. Ziemkiewicz, C., Ottley, A., Crouser, R.J., Chauncey, K., Su, S.L., Chang, R.: Understanding visualization by understanding individual users. IEEE Comput. Graph. Appl. **32**(6), 88–94 (2012)
12. Dragisic, Z., Ivanova, V., Lambrix, P., Faria, D., Jiménez-Ruiz, E., Pesquita, C.: User validation in ontology alignment. In: Groth, P., et al. (eds.) ISWC 2016. LNCS, vol. 9981, pp. 200–217. Springer, Cham (2016). https://doi.org/10.1007/978-3-319-46523-4_13

13. Dadzie, A.S., Pietriga, E.: Visualisation of linked data - reprise. Semant. Web **8**(1), 1–21 (2017)
14. Sarasua, C., Simperl, E., Noy, N., Bernstein, A., Leimeister, J.M.: Crowdsourcing and the Semantic Web: a research manifesto. Hum. Comput. (HCOMP) **2**(1), 3–17 (2015)
15. White, R.W., Roth, R.A.: Exploratory search: beyond the query-response paradigm. Synth. Lect. Inf. Concepts, Retr. Serv. **1**(1), 1–98 (2009)
16. Frøkjær, E., Hertzum, M., Hornbæk, K.: Measuring usability: are effectiveness, efficiency, and satisfaction really correlated? In: SIGCHI Conference on Human Factors in Computing Systems, pp. 345–352. ACM (2000)
17. Huang, W., Eades, P., Hong, S.H.: Beyond time and error: a cognitive approach to the evaluation of graph drawings. In: 2008 Workshop on BEyond Time and Errors: Novel EvaLuation Methods for Information Visualization - BELIV, pp. 3:1–3:8. ACM (2008)
18. Saraiya, P., North, C., Duca, K.: An insight-based methodology for evaluating bioinformatics visualizations. IEEE Trans. Vis. Comput. Graph. **11**(4), 443–456 (2005)
19. White, R.W., Drucker, S.M., Marchionini, G., Hearst, M., Schraefel, M.C.: Exploratory search and HCI: designing and evaluating interfaces to support exploratory search interaction. In: CHI 2007 Extended Abstracts on Human Factors in Computing Systems, pp. 2877–2880. ACM (2007)
20. Fu, B., Noy, N.F., Storey, M.A.: Eye tracking the user experience-an evaluation of ontology visualization techniques. Semant. Web **8**(1), 23–41 (2017)
21. Miles, M.B., Huberman, A.M., Saldana, J.: Qualitative Data Analysis. Sage, Los London (2013)
22. Rubin, J., Chisnell, D.: Handbook of Usability Testing: How to Plan, Design, and Conduct Effective Tests. Wiley, Hoboken (2008)
23. Brazma, A., et al.: Minimum information about a microarray experiment (MIAME) - toward standards for microarray data. Nat. Genet. **29**(4), 365–371 (2001)
24. Field, A., Hole, G.: How to Design and Report Experiments. Sage, London (2003)
25. Plaisant, C.: The challenge of information visualization evaluation. In: Working conference on Advanced visual interfaces, pp. 109–116. ACM (2004)
26. Kamdar, M.R., Walk, S., Tudorache, T., Musen, M.A.: BiOnIC: a catalog of user interactions with biomedical ontologies. In: d'Amato, C., et al. (eds.) ISWC 2017. LNCS, vol. 10588, pp. 130–138. Springer, Cham (2017). https://doi.org/10.1007/978-3-319-68204-4_13
27. Ivanova, V., Lambrix, P., Åberg, J.: Requirements for and evaluation of user support for large-scale ontology alignment. In: Gandon, F., Sabou, M., Sack, H., d'Amato, C., Cudré-Mauroux, P., Zimmermann, A. (eds.) ESWC 2015. LNCS, vol. 9088, pp. 3–20. Springer, Cham (2015). https://doi.org/10.1007/978-3-319-18818-8_1
28. González Sánchez, J.L., García González, R., Brunetti Fernández, J.M., Gil Iranzo, R.M., Gimeno Illa, J.M.: Using SWET-QUM to compare the quality in use of Semantic Web exploration tools. J. Univers. Comput. Sci. **19**, 1025–1045 (2013)
29. Nunes, T., Schwabe, D.: Frameworks for information exploration-a case study. In: 4th International Workshop on Intelligent Exploration of Semantic Data - IESD (2015)

30. Nunes, T., Schwabe, D.: Frameworks of information exploration-towards the evaluation of exploration systems. In: 5th International Workshop on Intelligent Exploration of Semantic Data - IESD (2016)
31. García, R., Gil, R., Gimeno, J.M., Bakke, E., Karger, D.R.: BESDUI: a benchmark for end-user structured data user interfaces. In: Groth, P., et al. (eds.) ISWC 2016. LNCS, vol. 9982, pp. 65–79. Springer, Cham (2016). https://doi.org/10.1007/978-3-319-46547-0_8

Author Index

Printed in the United States
By Bookmasters